THE NATIONAL UNDERWRITER COMPANY

2011 FIELD GUIDE TO ESTATE PLANNING, BUSINESS PLANNING & EMPLOYEE BENEFITS
Donald F. Cady, J.D., LL.M., CLU

Authoritative and easy to use, *2011 Field Guide to Estate Planning, Business Planning & Employee Benefits* provides you with the concepts, techniques, analysis, illustrations and authoritative guidance used in estate, business and employee benefits planning. Over 200 presentation tools and illustrations will enable you to present the concepts simply and clearly to your clients.

This is the first book out in the market that covers the estate planning implications of the Tax Relief Act of 2010 for advisors and their clients.

2011 Field Guide to Estate Planning, Business Planning & Employee Benefits delivers up-to-date information on:

- Estate Planning

- Life Insurance

- Business Valuation

- Cross Purchase Agreements

- Split-Dollar Insurance

- Disability Income

- And much more!

Highlights of the 2011 Edition

2011 Field Guide to Estate Planning, Business Planning & Employee Benefits has been completely updated to include:

- The 2010 Tax Relief Act's impact upon estate planning techniques, to include the increased and indexed exemption

- New terms and concepts: "Portability" and "SIMPLE Cafeteria Plans"

- Updated qualified plan contribution limitations, college costs, facts about the costs of raising a child, the cost of child care, the value of a homemaker, the value of an education, and tax tables

- The Patient Protection and Affordable Care Act's impact on self-insured health reimbursement arrangements

- Free supplements – available only to current customers – will keep you updated on the implications of all the important new changes and developments as they occur

Also Available

To ensure you have reliable sales tools and guidance on the financial planning side, order *2011 Field Guide to Financial Planning,* which covers stocks, bonds, mutual funds, property & liability insurance, health insurance, and much more. *2011 Field Guide to Financial Planning* is completely updated to include the requirements of the reintroduced IRA charitable rollover, Social Security calculations, reintroduced IRA charitable rollover, and much more.

To place orders for *Field Guide* or any of our products, or for additional information, contact Customer Service at **1-800-543-0874.**

2011
FIELD GUIDE

TO ESTATE PLANNING, BUSINESS PLANNING & EMPLOYEE BENEFITS

Illustrated Sales Tools & Concepts
Planning Pointers and Charts • Terms & Concepts
Checklists • Statistics • Tables

Donald F. Cady, J.D., LL.M., CLU

This publication is designed to provide accurate and authoritative information in regard to the subject matter covered. It is sold with the understanding that the publisher is not engaged in rendering legal, accounting or other professional service. If legal advice or other expert assistance is required, the services of a competent professional should be sought. **– From a Declaration of Principles jointly adopted by a Committee of the American Bar Association and a Committee of Publishers and Associations.**

Circular 230 – The content in this publication is not intended or written to be used, and it cannot be used, for the purposes of avoiding U.S. tax penalties.

ISBN: 978-1-936362-16-5
ISSN: 1053-4407

The National Underwriter Company
P.O. Box 14367, Cincinnati, Ohio 45250-0367

Printed in U. S. A.

ABOUT SUMMIT BUSINESS MEDIA

Summit Business Media (SBM) is the leading B2B media and information company serving the insurance, investment advisory, professional services, and mining investment markets through a variety of channels, including print, online, and live events. Through its Media and Reference Divisions, the company publishes 18 magazines and 150 reference titles. The Event Division hosts a dozen conferences in support of Summit's magazine brands. SBM's Data Division, comprised of Highline Data, Judy Diamond Associates, Agent Media, and Kirschner's, is the leading data provider of financial and marketing information on insurance companies, life and property-casualty agents, and investment advisors.

Summit, a Wind Point company, employs nearly 400 employees in a dozen offices across the United States. For more information, please visit summitbusinessmedia.com.

ABOUT THE NATIONAL UNDERWRITER COMPANY

For over 110 years, The National Underwriter Company has been the first in line with the targeted tax, insurance, and financial planning information you need to make critical business decisions. Boasting nearly a century of expert experience, our reputable Editors are dedicated to putting accurate and relevant information right at your fingertips. With Tax Facts, Tools & Techniques, Advanced Markets AdvisorFX, Field Guide, FC&S®, and other resources available in print, on CD, and online, you can be assured that as the industry evolves National Underwriter will be at the forefront with the thorough and easy-to-use resources you rely on for success.

The National Underwriter Company
Update Service Notification

This National Underwriter Company publication is regularly updated to include coverage of developments and changes that affect the content. If you did not purchase this publication directly from The National Underwriter Company and you want to receive these important updates sent on a 30-day review basis and billed separately, please contact us at (800) 543-0874. Or you can mail your request with your name, company, address, and the title of the book to:

The National Underwriter Company
5081 Olympic Boulevard
Erlanger, KY 41018

If you purchased this publication from The National Underwriter Company directly, you have already been registered for the update service.

National Underwriter Company Contact Information

To order any National Underwriter Company title, please

- call 1-800-543-0874, 8-6 ET Monday – Thursday and 8 to 5 ET Friday
- fax 1-800-874-1916 anytime, or
- mail to The National Underwriter Company, Orders Department, 5081 Olympic Blvd, Erlanger, KY 41018

ACKNOWLEDGMENTS

I am most grateful to the many individuals – financial services professionals, clients, students, and allied professionals – who have both knowingly and unknowingly contributed to this book. It is the product of their many insights, tough questions, sales and planning ideas.

I also wish to express my sincere appreciation to Richard Niles, J.D., the staff editor of The National Underwriter Company, for his shared tax expertise, and to Connie L. Jump for her research contributions.

Over the years it has been my privilege to work with many talented editors at the National Underwriter Company. Listed by years contributed, this book has greatly benefited from the efforts of: William J. Wagner, J.D., LL.M., CLU (1989-2010), Deborah A. Miner, J.D., CLU, ChFC (1991-2010), April K. Caudill, J.D., CLU, ChFC (1990-2007), Sonya E. King, J.D. (1999-2010), Joseph F. Stenken, J.D., CLU, ChFC (1998-2009), Darlene K. Chandler, J.D., CLU, ChFC (1990-2000), William W. Thomas, III, J.D., CLU (1991-1999), John H. Fenton, J.D., M.S.B.A. (2003-2008), Peter A. Fossett, J.D. (1992-1996), Deborah Price Rambo, J.D. (1999-2002), Kimberely J. Adams, J.D. (1995-1997), Scott W. Baker, J.D. (1995-1997), Frank J. Bitzer, J.D., CEBS (1999-2001), Edward A. Lyon, J.D. (1992-1993), Dennis A. Repenning, J.D. (1989-1990), Mary E. Bell, J.D. (1998), and Janine G. Cochran, J.D. (1997).

And finally, a special word of thanks to my wife, Joan, for her love and understanding in providing me the time and environment for writing, and for those long walks together on the beach.

Donald F. Cady, February 1, 2011
Fort Myers Beach, Florida

ABOUT THE AUTHOR

 Donald F. Cady is an attorney and a Chartered Life Underwriter. He is a graduate of St. Lawrence University with a B.A. in Economics, where he received the Wall Street Journal Award for excellence in that subject. He received his J.D. degree from Columbia University School of Law, holds the degree of LL.M. (Taxation) from Emory University School of Law, and is a member of the New York Bar.

Don is an independent consultant working with The National Underwriter Company in providing support materials and services to the financial planning industry. In addition to this publication, he is the author of *Field Guide Online*[1], the web version of this book. He is also the author of *Field Guide To Financial Planning*, published annually by The National Underwriter Company (call 1-800-543-0874, or go to http://www.nationalunderwriter.com/servlet/the-Financial-Planning/Categories).

For 20 years Don was with the Aetna Life Insurance & Annuity Company in various advanced underwriting positions. Prior to this, Don was a member of the U.S. Army Judge Advocate Generals Corps, with tours of duty in both Vietnam and Europe. He and his wife live in Fort Myers Beach, Florida.

Don has been a frequent speaker on the subjects of estate planning, business planning, and employee benefits, before business and professional organizations, estate planning associations, life underwriter's meetings and various civic groups. Through these appearances, together with his work with agents, their clients and advisers, Don has shared the frustrations of trying to effectively explain and communicate planning concepts and techniques to both student and laymen. This edition of *Field Guide* represents his response to that challenge.

Don can be reached by e-mail at donaldfcady@gmail.com.

---

[1] *Field Guide Online* is a trademark of The National Underwriter Company.

ABOUT THE EDITOR

Richard Niles, J.D., Richard Niles is a senior developmental editor for taxation and financial planning with Summit Business Media. He has been involved in legal, financial, and tax publishing for over thirty years. He began his career with Prentice-Hall, where he developed and revised federal and state taxation publications. While with the American Institute of CPAs, Richard initiated many continuing education tax and financial planning courses, as both self-study and seminars.

EDITORIAL DIRECTOR

Diana B. Reitz, CPCU, AAI, is the editorial director of the Reference Division of The National Underwriter Company. As such she is responsible for the overall integrity of all division publications. She previously was the Director of the Property & Casualty Publishing Department of the Reference Division.

Ms. Reitz has been with The National Underwriter Company since 1998, when she was named editor of the Risk Financing and Self-Insurance manuals and associate editor of the *FC&S Bulletins*®. She also is co-author of the National Underwriter publication, *Workers Compensation Coverage Guide,* and has edited and contributed to numerous other books and publications, including *The Tools & Techniques of Risk Management and Insurance, Claims* magazine, ProducersWEB, and *National Underwriter Property & Casualty* newsweekly.

Prior to joining The National Underwriter she was with a regional insurance broker, concentrating on commercial insurance. She is a graduate of the University of Maryland and St. Francis College.

TABLE OF CONTENTS

Page

APPENDIX

INTRODUCTION

The Purpose Of This Book

This book is intended to provide you with a ready means of identifying and understanding the concepts and techniques used in estate, business, and employee benefit planning. Recognizing that we live in a world of visual communication, numerous drawings and charts have been included to assist you in identifying and understanding many of the concepts which are most frequently encountered when working with clients and other professionals. It can serve as a desktop reference source, a classroom training aid, or, carried in your briefcase, as a resource to be shared with your client or his advisors. However, it is not intended to be a replacement for competent legal or tax counsel; only qualified professionals can provide such advice.

Organization

The Field Guide has been organized into three sections, dealing with the subjects of estate planning, business planning, and employee benefits. Each section is in turn divided into units typically consisting of a chart and accompanying text. Following most of the charts you will find a section entitled "Information Required For Analysis & Proposal." This is the minimum information you must obtain in order to prepare an analysis and proposal for your client. Also included are cross references to *Tax Facts on Insurance & Employee Benefits*, and the footnotes. Following the charts, you will find references that support the subjects of estate planning, business planning, and employee benefits. Terms & Concepts contains expanded discussions of the materials previously referred to in the text and footnotes.

In using this book, first refer to the chart and read the accompanying text. Also, be sure to read the footnotes; they will provide you with a better understanding of the subject matter and references to additional materials.

Cross References To Tax Facts On Insurance & Employee Benefits

No attempt is made to provide either an exhaustive technical analysis or extensive citations to legal authority (Internal Revenue Code sections, regulations, case law, revenue rulings, and private letter rulings). For these purposes, you are encouraged to refer to the appropriate questions in the 2011 edition of *Tax Facts on Insurance & Employee Benefits*, published by The National Underwriter Company in two volumns. The cross references contain the question number followed by a brief description of the material covered (e.g., "**Q 243**. Valuation of closely held business interest for federal estate tax purposes").

Where appropriate, there are also cross references to the 2011 edition of *Tax Facts on Investments*, published by The National Underwriter Company.

Tax Facts News, published monthly by The National Underwriter Company, keeps the reader informed on current developments, major changes, and ongoing revisions to our tax laws.

All of these publications are updated online as needed and are available for purchase at www.NUCOstore.com.

TABLE OF CONTENTS

Page

POINTERS

The Tax Relief, Unemployment Insurance Reauthorization, and Job Creation Act of 2010.

The 2011 edition of this book is going to press shortly after passage of The Tax Relief, Unemployment Insurance Reauthorization, and Job Creation Act of 2010 (hereafter referred to as The 2010 Tax Act). Despite its title, the impact of this legislation on the practice and art of estate planning will be immediate and far reaching. Unfortunately, because this law sunsets on January 1, 2013, it continues much of the uncertainty regarding the estate tax laws created by EGTRRA for the past ten years.

In a nutshell. Referred to as the "applicable exclusion amount," The 2010 Tax Act provides an estate tax exemption of $5,000,000 per person (by providing a credit of $1,730,800), transfers above this amount are taxed at a rate of 35 percent, and the estate taxes and gift taxes are reunified (in contrast to 2009 when estates up to $3,500,000 were exempt from taxation but gifts in excess of $1,000,000 were taxed). Beginning in 2012, the $5,000,000 applicable exclusion amount will be indexed for inflation. Most importantly, any unused applicable exclusion amount may be carried over to a surviving spouse (see the portability discussion below). The 2010 Tax Act exempts estates up to $5,000,000 from federal estate taxes *whether or not* the estate is properly planned (up to $10,000,000 for a husband and wife). For all but the very wealthy, *this law has effectively repealed the federal estate tax*, albeit for only two years. See also, footnote 6 on page 21.

Portability. The 2010 Tax Relief Act allows any unused exemption to be passed to a surviving spouse without the need to re-title assets and establish complex wills and trusts (e.g., by the use of QTIP, credit shelter, by-pass, or family trusts). If no applicable exclusion amount had been used by the deceased who dies in 2011, $5,000,000 could be carried over to the surviving spouse. However, the surviving spouse can only claim this unused exclusion if the executor of the deceased spouse's estate had previously filed an estate tax return electing to take advantage of any unused applicable exclusion amount. To fully benefit from this portability, under current law both spouses must die within the two-year period 2011-2012. Portability does not apply to generation-skipping transfers. Despite the advent of portability, there remain many non-tax reasons to use trust wills in estate plans. See the further discussion of portability on page 475.

Indexing. Should it remain a permanent part of the estate tax law, indexing would protect the exemption from being eroded over time. To appreciate the value of such projection, refer to the consumer price index table on page 314.

2012 And Beyond. By its very nature, estate planning is intended to provide some degree of predictability over the long-term. Unfortunately, because the provisions of The 2010 Tax Act expire at the end of 2012, the sunset provisions of EGTRRA 2001 will continue to create a degree of uncertainty and confusion. Making predictions about the future of the estate tax is risky business. [Who could have predicted as recently as 2008 that in 2010 the executors of billionaires dying in that year would have the option of opting out of the federal estate tax, or that there would be no generation skipping tax in 2010?] Nevertheless, there are indicators that should not be ignored. Leading up to enactment of The 2010 Tax Relief Act there was little, if any, serious debate about retaining the $1,000,000 exemption; the controversy centered upon whether the exemption should be either $3,500,000 or $5,000,000. More importantly, there was virtually no objection to either indexing or portability. Unlike an increase in the exemption to $5,000,000, the portability and indexing provisions of The 2010 Tax Act appeared to have had widespread bipartisan support. Given this environment, it is most likely that these features will become a permanent part of the estate tax laws. With indexing, portability, and a generous exemption, the vast majority of individuals *can no longer be motivated to do estate planning to save federal estate taxes*. But federal taxes are not the only game in town.

State death taxes. The phase-out of the state death tax credit, and its replacement with a deduction, has resulted in a substantial loss of revenue in many states. The 2010 Tax Act has extended that deduction to the end of 2012. Individual states have not suffered this revenue loss at the hands of Congress, and no matter what happens to the federal estate tax many of your client's estates will continue to be subject to state death taxes that are independent of the federal estate tax (see the discussion of decoupling of state death taxes on page 381).

Gifts. Each and every year, your high net worth clients should continue to take full advantage of the opportunity to make $13,000 "present interest" gifts (chart on page 47).

Grantor Retained Annuity Trusts (GRATs). The 2010 Tax Act did not contain the anticipated restrictions on GRATs as wealth transferring devices (chart, page 59). Relatively low values and low interest rates make this an attractive planning technique for high net worth clients.

Flexibility. In order to adjust to future changes in the uncertain world of estate taxes, increased flexibility should be built into your client's estate plans. Disclaimers offer a surviving spouse the opportunity to adjust to changing circumstances by controlling the amount of property going into the nonmarital trust after your client's death (pages 25 and 389). See also, the discussion of post mortem planning, on page 476.

Estate Planning Is More Than Tax Planning.

Estate planning is primarily about people and their desire to provide for their loved ones! Given proper motivation, most clients will devote the time and energy that is necessary to develop and adopt an effective estate plan.

The Nontax Reasons For Estate Planning. The primary objectives of most estate plans involve estate creation, support and care of a surviving family and the orderly transfer of property during lifetime or at death. This often involves providing for the care of minor children, support for disabled children and elderly parents, and protection of loved ones from creditors. For some individuals the motivation to plan their estates is found in a strong desire to assure the survival of a business, or to provide for their church or a charity.

Life insurance. Are there enough life insurance proceeds, liquid assets, and other sources of income to maintain the current living standards of your client's surviving family? Unfortunately, all too many individuals remain underinsured. In this regard, see Facts About Human Life Value in the Courtroom, on page 96. For those clients needing insurance to pay taxes, delaying the purchase of currently needed life insurance could be disastrous, particularly if your client becomes uninsurable while waiting for Congress to end the uncertainty and confusion of sun-setting tax laws. Where appropriate, convertible term insurance should be used. Some companies are offering permanent policies that give the policyowner the option of surrendering the policy without penalty if the federal estate tax is repealed.

Trusts. In moderate sized estates, QTIP, credit shelter, by-pass, and family trusts *will no longer be used to save taxes*. But with substantial estates a trust will can freeze the value of property during the surviving spouse's lifetime so that future appreciation will not be subject to federal estate taxes upon the surviving spouse's death. However, there remain many convincing nontax reasons to fund a bypass trust at the first death. See the chart on page 25. For many of your clients, the life insurance trust will continue to be an effective means of accomplishing multiple objectives. See the chart on page 51.

Coordination With Business Plans And Employee Benefits.

It is often difficult, if not impossible, to design an effective estate plan without considering your client's business disposition plans and employee benefit programs. Effective planning cannot be achieved unless there is an awareness of the interplay between the various strategies and techniques of estate planning, business planning, and employee benefits. For example, the liquidity needs of a business owner's estate plan are directly influenced by whether the business is to be sold, continued, or liquidated (chart, page 118). If the business is to be *sold*, then a funded purchase agreement may well provide all of the dollars needed for estate liquidity and family income. If the business is to be *continued*, then an employee benefit, such as split-dollar, could provide the necessary funds.

ESTATE PLANNING MATRIX

In the traditional sense, estate planning means preparing for the orderly and efficient transfer of assets at death. Within this definition, the basic objectives of estate planning are set forth in the discussion of the Estate Funnel on page 10.

However, estate planning has also come to involve planning for the accumulation and distribution of an estate during lifetime as well as at death. It must also be recognized that comprehensive estate planning will often involve the concepts and techniques contained in the business planning and employee benefits chapters of this guide. For example, although additional estate liquidity would be provided from the sale of a business interest, estate taxes will be increased through inclusion of the proceeds of the sale in the taxable estate. Likewise, an effective estate plan should maximize employee benefits, while at the same time taking into consideration their impact upon the estate.

The following matrix should provide a better understanding of how the concepts and techniques, represented in the charts, can be used to solve estate planning problems.

PROBLEM	SOLUTION(S)	PAGE
Loss of Estate Value Through Estate Tax	TRUST WILL provides the opportunity to reduce estate taxes.	24
	QTIP TRUST provides opportunity to reduce taxes while controlling disposition of estate.	34
	GIFTS & SPLIT-GIFTS remove property from the estate.	46
	LIFE INSURANCE AS PROPERTY shows how life insurance can be excluded from the gross estate for federal tax purposes.	70
	LIFE INSURANCE TRUST can remove life insurance death proceeds from the estate.	50
	CHARITABLE REMAINDER TRUST can remove from estate taxable property that can be replaced by life insurance in a Wealth Replacement Trust.	54
	GRANTOR RETAINED ANNUITY TRUST allows a grantor to retain an annuity interest while at the same time reducing estate taxes.	58

Loss of Estate Value Through Estate Tax (continued)	GENERATION-SKIPPING TRANSFERS shows use of exemption in 2011 to transfer $5,000,000 to grandchildren.	38
Estimating the Estate Tax	FEDERAL ESTATE TAX explains the calculations.	18
Payment of Estate Costs	LIFE INSURANCE PRODUCTS can be used to provide funds to pay these costs. Chart compares alternative plans and explains their basic characteristics and essential differences.	74
Distribution of Estate	SIMPLE WILL can provide for the distribution of estate assets, including specific bequests.	22
	TRUST WILL offers added tax savings and the post death management of assets.	24
	REVOCABLE LIVING TRUST (RLT) is a will substitute offering many advantages during lifetime and at death.	28
	POUR-OVER WILL functions as a "fail safe" device to transfer property at death into the RLT.	32
Replacement of Income: Upon Death	LIFE INSURANCE PRODUCTS can provide funds to replace lost income in case of death (one approach to determining the necessary funds is contained in the discussion of HUMAN LIFE VALUE on page 14).	74
Upon Disability	DIABILITY – THE LIVING DEATH demonstrates the need for proper planning before disability occurs.	238
Upon Retirement	DEFERRED ANNUITY can be used to accumulate funds on a tax-favored funds.	282
Insufficient Income or Assets for Custodial Care In Retirement	LONG-TERM CARE planning provides an understanding of the risk and cost of long-term care and how the risk can be managed.	254
Management of Assets and Orderly Payment of Income to Spouse and Children	LIFE INSURANCE TRUST provides for both asset management and ongoing payments.	50
	TRUST WILL with provisions for both asset management and payment of continuing income to beneficiaries.	24
	REVOCABLE LIVING TRUST can provide for management of assets both before and after death.	28
Guardianship of Children	SIMPLE WILL with provisions for appointment of guardian (TRUST WILL can also contain these same provisions).	22

THE ESTATE FUNNEL

The estate funnel helps to explain the types of property found in most estates, the problems often encountered in settling an estate, and the objectives of estate planning.

All property is created in one of two ways, either people at work or capital at work. Wages are the product of **people at work**, while interest, dividends, and capital appreciation are the products of **capital at work**.

The property found in most estates generally falls into one of five categories:

Personal property, such as furniture, cars, jewelry, cash, bonds, savings, and other personal effects.

Real estate, such as a home, a vacation house, land, and rental property such as apartments or office buildings.[1]

Business interests, in the form of closely held corporations, partnerships, or sole proprietorships.

Life insurance, either group insurance or individual policies.

Government benefits, such as social security, disability, retirement, and survivor income benefits.

Unfortunately, at death there is often a great deal of **CONFLICT**. This occurs due to the differing and conflicting ways in which many of these assets pass to the family or other heirs. For example, personal property can pass by will, by state law if there is no will, by title, or by trust.[2] Real estate and business interests may also pass by all of these means, as well as by agreement. Generally life insurance passes by beneficiary designation, and government benefits by federal statute.

These conflicts, together with the generally slow probate process, can easily result in a **DELAY** of *1 to 2 years or more*.[3]

Considerable **EXPENSE** may also be incurred during the estate settlement process. For example, existing debts must be paid. There are also medical expenses, funeral expenses, attorney fees, income taxes, and estate taxes. The final result is often a *shrinkage of 30% or more* by the time an estate is passed to the surviving family.[4]

The basic objectives of estate planning are to provide for the orderly and efficient accumulation, conservation, and distribution of an estate, while **avoiding conflict**, **shortening delays,** and **reducing expenses**.[5]

Footnotes on page 13

PEOPLE AT WORK - CAPITAL AT WORK

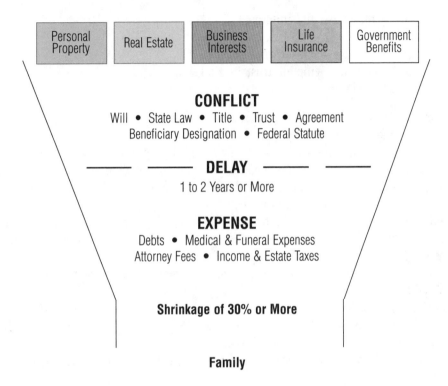

Personal Property | Real Estate | Business Interests | Life Insurance | Government Benefits

CONFLICT
Will • State Law • Title • Trust • Agreement
Beneficiary Designation • Federal Statute

DELAY
1 to 2 Years or More

EXPENSE
Debts • Medical & Funeral Expenses
Attorney Fees • Income & Estate Taxes

Shrinkage of 30% or More

Family

OBJECTIVES OF ESTATE PLANNING

Avoid Conflict • Shorten Delays • Reduce Expenses

INFORMATION REQUIRED FOR ANALYSIS & PROPOSAL

1. Names of client, spouse, and children.
2. Dates of birth.
3. For client and spouse – smoker/nonsmoker.
4. Type of wills (simple, exemption trust, marital share, etc.).
5. Trusts established.

Assets (determine how titled – individual, joint, etc.)

6. Personal and intangible property:

    liquid – cash, checking accounts, certificates of deposit, money market funds, mutual funds, municipal bonds, corporate bonds, annuities, options, etc.

    illiquid – contents of home, personal effects, jewelry, collections, cars, notes, leases, royalties, and tax sheltered investments.

    employee benefits – individual retirement accounts, HR-10 plans, tax deferred annuities, 401(k) plans, and vested deferred compensation and pension plan benefits (including beneficiary designations).

7. Real estate: home, vacation home, land, lots, commercial property, and investment property.
8. Business interests: corporations, partnerships, sole proprietorships, and farming operations.
9. Insurance: group and individual life insurance, disability and health coverage (including ownership and beneficiary designations).
10. Government benefits: social security disability payments, survivor benefits, and retirement payments.

Liabilities

11. Short-term debt: bills payable, loans, notes, consumer debt.
12. Long-term debt: home mortgage and home equity loans.

Obligations and Objectives

13. Debt to be paid at death (including final expenses).
14. Charitable bequests.
15. Monthly income required by surviving family.
16. Monthly income required by spouse after children are grown.
17. Cost for children's education (per year).
18. Monthly income in case of long-term disability or retirement.

Special Circumstances

19. Support for ex-spouse or children from prior marriage.
20. Support for other dependents.

Footnotes

[1] Where more than one person owns real estate or certain types of personal property, the **form** of ownership determines how the property is passed upon death. The form of ownership also determines the extent to which the property is includable in the gross estate for federal estate tax purposes:

    a. Where the property is owned in a **tenancy in common**, each tenant – or co-owner – has a fractional, divisible interest in the property. Upon the death of a co-owner, his fractional interest is probate property and passes by will or by state intestacy laws. Each surviving co-tenant retains his proportionate interest in the property. The fair market value of the decedent's fractional interest is includable in the federal gross estate.

    b. Where the property is owned in **joint tenancy with right of survivorship**, each joint tenant has an undivided interest in the entire property. The survivorship right is the key characteristic: upon the death of a joint tenant, the decedent's interest passes by operation of law to the surviving tenant or tenants. The decedent's interest is not a probate asset and therefore cannot be disposed of by will or intestacy law. For federal estate tax purposes, joint tenancy with right of survivorship does not necessarily prevent all or any of the property from inclusion in the federal gross estate upon the death of a joint owner. However, a joint-and-survivorship property interest created *between spouses* after 1976 is considered to be a "qualified joint interest." As such, only *one-half* of the value is included in the gross estate for federal tax purposes. All other joint-and-survivorship property is *fully* includable in the gross estate of the first owner to die, except to the extent that the decedent's estate can demonstrate that the survivor contributed to the purchase price. However, jointly owned property obtained through gift or inheritance is included in proportion to the decedent's ownership interest.

    c. Some states recognize a **tenancy by the entirety**. Generally, this form of ownership parallels joint-and-survivorship property except that it may be created by husband and wife only.

    d. In **community property** states each spouse is considered to own an undivided one-half interest in such property during the marriage, and each spouse is free to dispose of his or her share of community property upon death. One-half of the fair market value of community property is includable in the decedent spouse's estate. See the expanded discussion of community property on pages 365-366.

[2] The unlimited marital deduction allows jointly owned property to pass to a surviving spouse free of the federal estate tax. However, having virtually all property in joint title with right of survivorship can defeat the potential estate tax advantages of the Trust Will (chart, page 25). When property is jointly owned, it passes by law directly to the surviving spouse and therefore cannot pass into the non-marital, or "B" trust. Such over qualification of the unlimited marital deduction means that the property may be subject to taxation upon the subsequent death of the surviving spouse. Furthermore, there may be certain *income tax* disadvantages to having property jointly owned if and when the surviving spouse sells the property. See page 530 for an expanded discussion of stepped-up basis.

[3] For specific examples of the time delays that can occur when the valuation of closely held stock is left to chance, refer to the materials on pages 185-191. See also page 482 for a discussion of the probate process.

[4] Typical estate debts, costs, and taxes for various size estates are set forth on page 85. See also page 348 for a discussion of asset protection techniques.

[5] During the fact finding phase of estate planning it is important to obtain for review numerous client documents (see page 82). See also, Survivor Checklist on page 90. However, a nonattorney should not provide specific advice regarding the modification or drafting of legal documents, since this activity could be construed as the unauthorized practice of law.

HUMAN LIFE VALUE

In determining how much life insurance should be carried for family income purposes, two basic methods are used. The **needs approach** involves a determination of the family's income requirements. The **human life value approach** involves a capitalization of that part of the breadearner's income devoted to the support of his family.[1]

Calculating an individual's human life value involves first determining the amount of his income allocated to family support. This is done by deducting income taxes, personal life and health insurance premiums, and the cost of self-maintenance from the breadearner's annual income from personal efforts. Assume that the result is $10,000 per year.[2]

The next step involves determining the number of working years to retirement. Our example assumes the figure of 5 years.[3] A reasonable discount rate is then applied to arrive at the present value of these anticipated future earnings. For example, 5 percent might be used as representing a conservative after-tax rate of return for the surviving family.

NO GROWTH. The present value of future earnings after the first year can then be calculated by multiplying them by the appropriate discount factors (e.g., multiplying the $10,000 expected to be earned for the family in the second year by a factor of .9524, we find that its present value is $9,524). When this amount is added to the present values of anticipated earnings in the other years, we determine a human life value of $45,459 (for the limited five-year period).[4]

8% GROWTH. However, it is important to anticipate that in future years the income devoted to the breadearner's family will likely *increase*. If we assume an annual increase of 8 percent, earnings are projected to be $10,800 in the second year. The present value of these earnings is $10,286 ($10,800 x .9524). Adding this amount to the present values of the anticipated earnings in the other years, we determine a human life value of $52,941, *16 percent more* than if "no growth" had been projected.

The more years to retirement, the greater is the contrast between "no growth" and "growth." An accurate estimate of human life values requires not only projections of anticipated growth but periodic reviews and updates of insurance needs.[5]

Footnotes on page 17

NO GROWTH

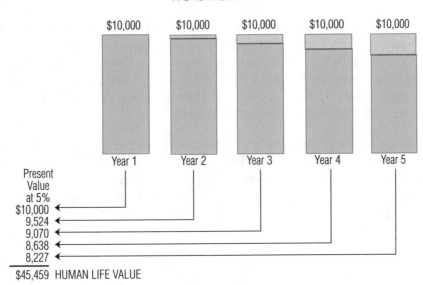

$10,000 $10,000 $10,000 $10,000 $10,000

Year 1   Year 2   Year 3   Year 4   Year 5

Present
Value
at 5%
$10,000
9,524
9,070
8,638
8,227

$45,459   HUMAN LIFE VALUE

8% GROWTH

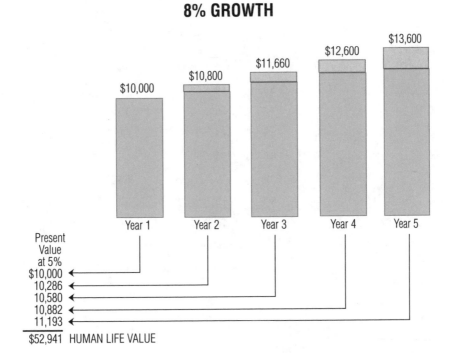

$13,600

$12,600

$11,660

$10,800

$10,000

Year 1   Year 2   Year 3   Year 4   Year 5

Present
Value
at 5%
$10,000
10,286
10,580
10,882
11,193

$52,941   HUMAN LIFE VALUE

INSURANCE NEEDS AS A PERCENTAGE OF EARNINGS

A simplified **needs approach** to determining how much life insurance should be carried for family income purposes is contained in the following table. Developed by First National Bank of New York City (Citibank), it is based upon the assumption that a typical family can maintain its standard of living if they are provided with a continuing income equal to 75 percent of their after-tax income before the death of the breadearner. If income drops below 60 percent, the family's living standard would be substantially lowered.

The following factors assume that the breadearner is covered by social security and that insurance proceeds will be invested to yield a net of 5 percent per year, after taxes and inflation. To use the table, multiply "your client's present gross earnings" by the factor under "present age of your client's spouse." For example, if your client has present gross earnings of $40,000, and the age of the spouse is 45 years, it would take $320,000 of life insurance to provide a 75 percent net-income replacement (8.0 x $40,000 = $320,000).

These results are only approximations of the amount of life insurance needed. It is generally a good practice to confirm the results with a more detailed needs analysis comparing specific family income objectives to available resources.

Your Client's Present Gross Earnings	Present Age of Your Client's Spouse							
	25 Years		35 Years		45 Years		55 Years	
	75%	60%	75%	60%	75%	60%	75%	60%
$ 7,500	4.0	3.0	5.5	4.0	7.5	5.5	6.5	4.5
9,000	4.0	3.0	5.5	4.0	7.5	5.5	6.5	4.5
15,000	4.5	3.0	6.5	4.5	8.0	6.0	7.0	5.5
23,500	6.5	4.5	8.0	5.5	8.5	6.5	7.5	5.5
30,000	7.5	5.0	8.0	6.0	8.5	6.5	7.0	5.5
40,000	7.5	5.0	8.0	6.0	8.0	6.0	7.0	5.5
65,000	7.5	5.5	7.5	6.0	7.5	6.0	6.5	5.0

Footnotes

[1] In the discussion of the Estate Funnel on page 10, it was recognized that there are essentially two ways to earn money. One is by "capital at work," that is, income from savings, stocks, bonds, and real estate holdings. The other is by "people at work," that is, income from individual work and effort. Human life value is a measure of "people at work." The concept is of particular importance to the client who has little capital, or relatively high earnings as compared to capital assets. Many highly compensated professionals, such as physicians, attorneys, and accountants, have estates that are relatively modest in comparison to their incomes. Because of this, their families become highly dependent upon "people at work," with little "capital at work" in reserve.

[2] The $10,000 figure was chosen for illustration because it is an easy number from which to make further determinations of human life value. If the actual amount were $20,000, the human life value figures would be twice those illustrated; and if the actual amount were $50,000, the human life value figures would be five times those illustrated.

[3] Although five years have been selected for purposes of demonstrating the concept of human life value, most individuals who are concerned about family income requirements have far more than five working years until retirement (e.g., a 35-year-old breadearner anticipating retirement at age 65 would have thirty years to retirement).

[4] A table of human life values at varying growth rates appears on page 98. Factors for calculating human life value can be obtained from the Future Value Table, on page 562, and the Present Value Table, on page 564. The following is an example of how to use this table to calculate the human life value assuming: (1) a 41-year-old breadearner; (2) age 65 retirement; (3) earnings of $55,000 per year, of which $45,000 is devoted to family maintenance; and (4) a projected 4 percent rate of earnings growth.

Working Years to Retirement:	24
Projected Growth in Earnings:	4%
Factor From Table (page 98)	215,465
Number of $10,000s	x 4.5
	$969,593

Note that in calculating human life value the first year earnings are not discounted in the chart on page 15 and in the table on page 98. This recognizes that the surviving family needs funds immediately upon the breadearner's death, not one year after his death.

[5] Life insurance offers a replacement for human life value by providing "capital at work" to replace "people at work." But what type of life insurance should be used? Obviously, insurance providing a *decreasing* death benefit appears inappropriate for the client whose human life value may increase in the future (e.g., upon periodic review the growth rate is found to be greater than initially projected). At the very least, insurance providing a *level* death benefit is necessary. It might even be advisable for the younger client to "take an option on tomorrow," by purchasing coverage which will provide *additional* insurance in later years through increasing term riders, paid-up additions, guaranteed purchase options, or an increasing death benefit equal to the annual increase of universal life cash values (sometimes referred to as either Option 2 or Option B). With two wage-earner families the use of a first-to-die life insurance product may be appropriate (page 415). When applying for insurance to cover an increasing human life value it is important to be familiar with any financial underwriting requirements (see expanded discussion on page 414).

FEDERAL ESTATE TAX

One of the potential expenses of settling larger estates is the federal estate tax.[1] It is a continuous lien on your client's property, but its foreclosure date is yet to be determined. Proper planning involves anticipating and reducing the estate tax liability wherever possible as well as providing for payment of the tax. Unlike other expenses of settling an estate, it can be particularly burdensome in that it is generally due and payable *in cash* 9 months after death.[2]

The estate tax computation is not difficult, and in many ways resembles the calculations involved in determining income tax. When we file our income tax return each year, the calculations involve terms such as gross income, taxable income, deductions, and credits.

When an *estate* tax return is filed, we are likewise dealing with terms such as gross estate, adjusted gross estate, taxable estate, deductions, and credits.[3]

Generally, the **gross estate** includes *all* property of any description and wherever located, to the extent the decedent had any interest in the property at the time of death.[4] It may even include property previously given away or over which the decedent had no control at the time of his death.

To illustrate, assume that in 2011 we have an unmarried individual with an estate totaling $8,000,000. In determining the adjusted gross estate, we can subtract the decedent's debts, such as loans, notes, and mortgages, plus the debts of the estate, such as funeral and administrative expenses. If these debts totaled $500,000, then the **adjusted gross estate** would be $7,500,000. For this discussion, assume that the taxable estate is also $7,500,000.[5] With a taxable estate of $7,500,000 the **tentative tax** would be $2,780,800.

However, in 2011 there is an **estate tax unified credit** available which can offset up to $1,730,800 of the tentative tax. Generally, the unified credit allows an individual to pass $5,000,000 of property free of federal estate taxes upon death.[6]

After taking advantage of the credit, the estate will still owe a tax of $1,050,000, which means that the amount of the original estate remaining for the children or other heirs has been reduced to $6,450,000. This represents shrinkage of 14 percent.[7]

Footnotes on page 21

GROSS ESTATE
$8,000,000

$500,000

ADJUSTED GROSS ESTATE
(Taxable Estate)

$7,500,000

$2,780,800

BENEFIT OF UNIFIED CREDIT

$1,730,800

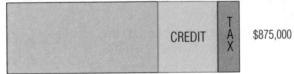

$875,000

REMAINING

$6,625,000

INFORMATION REQUIRED FOR ANALYSIS & PROPOSAL

Current listing and values of all property to include:

1. Cash.
2. Liquid assets (stocks, bonds).
3. Real estate (home, land, rental property).
4. Personal property (household goods, collections, and jewelry).
5. Business interests (closely held stock, partnership interests, and sole proprietorships).
6. Life insurance owned or insurance payable to estate (group insurance and individual policies).
7. Employee benefits (IRA, HR-10, 403(b) plan, pension/profit sharing, and 401(k) plan).
8. Current debts (short-term and long-term).

Note: A copy of the client's latest personal financial statement should disclose most of this information. Be sure to determine how the assets are titled (i.e., separate, joint ownership with spouse, community property, etc.). A copy of wills and trusts should also be obtained. See also pages 12 and 82.

CROSS REFERENCES TO TAX FACTS ON INVESTMENTS (2011)

Footnotes

[1] This chart illustrates the federal estate tax as modified by The 2010 Tax Relief Act for the years 2011 and 2012. Unless Congress changes the law, in 2013 and thereafter estates over $1,000,000 will be subject to the estate tax, the unified credit will be $345,800, and this estate would be subject to a top rate of 55% (under the sunset provisions of EGTRRA 2001). See Estate Tax Pointers on page 5.

[2] If certain strict conditions are met, payment of the *federal* estate tax can be deferred (see page 383). However, this does not mean that payment of applicable state inheritance and estate taxes can be similarly postponed (see page 87). A federal estate tax return (Form 706), if required, must be filed, and the tax paid, by the executor within nine months after death. The *penalty* for failure to file a timely return is 5 percent of the tax for each month the return is past due, up to a maximum of 25 percent. A detailed listing of these penalties is on page 468.

[3] The instructions to the United States Estate Tax Return (Form 706) are 33 pages in length. The actual estate tax return (Form 706) is 40 pages in length.

[4] The gross estate also includes "income in respect of a decedent" (IRD), which refers to those amounts to which a decedent was entitled as gross income, but which were not includable in his taxable income for the year of death. IRD is subject to income taxation in the hands of the person who receives it. For an expanded discussion see page 425.

[5] For purposes of illustration, this chart assumes there is no surviving spouse and that the adjusted gross estate is equal to the taxable estate. In the usual calculation sequence, debts (including funeral expenses), administrative expenses, and losses during administration are subtracted from the gross estate (as reduced by exclusions) to arrive at the adjusted gross estate. Charitable and marital deductions are then subtracted from the adjusted gross estate to determine the taxable estate. The principal deduction in this latter step has always been the marital deduction. Since it has been assumed that there is no surviving spouse, there can be no marital deduction, and therefore the adjusted gross estate is equal to the taxable estate. In community property states, the assumption of "no surviving spouse" means that all property is assumed to be separately owned.

[6] Under The 2010 Tax Relief Act this $5,000,000 is known either as the "applicable exclusion amount" or the "basic exclusion amount." The $5,000,000 indexed for inflation is referred to as the "basic exclusion amount." When there is a surviving spouse, the "applicable exclusion amount" includes the $5,000,000 basic exclusion amount, plus the deceased spousal unused exclusion amount (i.e., the unused exclusion of the last deceased spouse). In 2012 the basic exclusion amount of $5,000,000 is subject to indexing for post 2010 inflation. In the past this exemption has been variously referred to as the "exemption equivalent," "estate tax exemption equivalent," "unified credit equivalent," and "unified credit exemption equivalent."

[7] Because of the "unified" gift and estate tax rates, prior taxable gifts made during his lifetime would, in effect, reduce the amount of credit available at death. Upon death all adjusted taxable gifts made since 1976 are added to the estate when calculating the estate tax. However, this is not as bad as it might first appear, since the estate is, in effect, given a credit for prior gift taxes actually paid, or payable. The impact of this system generally is to push later transfers made during lifetime or at death into higher and higher tax brackets (due to the progressive estate and gift tax rates).

SIMPLE WILL

A will is the single most basic and necessary tool in estate planning. By having a will, we can be sure that property goes to *whom* we want, and in the *amounts* we want, rather than as provided under a state's intestacy laws.

Although there are various types of wills, the most common is often called the *simple* will.[1] The majority of simple wills provide for: (1) payment of just debts and expenses; (2) appointment of an executor or executrix; (3) specific bequests; (4) transfer of the entire estate to the surviving spouse; (5) if there is no surviving spouse, then transfer of the estate to children or other heirs; and (6) appointment of a guardian or guardians for minor children and their property.

UPON THE FIRST DEATH, the simple will generally passes *all* property to the surviving spouse. No matter how large the estate, *no taxes* will be paid on this transfer. This is possible because of the unlimited marital deduction.

UPON THE SECOND DEATH, provided the estate does not exceed $10,000,000, the estate will not be subject to federal estate taxes.[2]

For the individual who has a relatively small estate, the simple will is usually adequate. However, this most basic of wills does not take advantage of the opportunity to place assets in trust and provide for the continued management of estate assets for a surviving spouse and assure that the estate will eventually pass to children upon the death of the surviving spouse.

---

[1] Some commentators have suggested that, because it passes all property to the surviving spouse, the simple will should be called the "I love you" will. Without a will, property passes according to state law (see Degrees Of Kindred, page 100, Intestate's Will, page 101, and State Laws On Intestate Succession, pages 102-109).

[2] The 2010 Tax Relief Act provides each spouse with an estate tax exemption of $5,000,000 (called the "basic exclusion amount"). When there is a surviving spouse, the deceased spouse's unused basic exclusion may be added to the surviving spouse's basic exclusion (called the "applicable exclusion amount"). Without prior planning this enables a married couple to pass to their children up to $10,000,000 free of federal estate taxes (2 × $5,000,000 = $10,000,000). However, the surviving spouse can only claim this unused exclusion if the executor of the deceased spouse's estate files an estate tax return making a deceased spousal unused exclusion amount (DSUEA) election. With portability of the exclusion between spouses, it is no longer necessary to establish an exemption trust or by-pass will in order to realize federal estate tax savings (see discussion on page 475). This law is effective for the years 2011 and 2012, after which the exemption is scheduled to return to $1,000,000, unless there is further Congressional action. See also, footnote 6 on page 21.

ESTATE

UPON THE FIRST DEATH

All Property To Spouse

↓

No Taxes

UPON THE SECOND DEATH

To Children

↓

TRUST WILL

A will creating a trust can provide for the continued management of estate assets for a surviving spouse and assure that the estate will eventually pass to children upon the death of the surviving spouse. With large estates a trust can freeze the value of property during the surviving spouse's lifetime so that future appreciation will not be subject to federal estate taxes upon the surviving spouse's death.[1]

UPON THE FIRST DEATH, with the typical trust will, the estate is divided into *two* parts, with one part placed in a family or nonmarital trust ("B" trust in the chart).[2] No taxes are paid on this since the amount is equal to or less than the applicable exclusion amount (i.e., the amount in 2011 that each individual can pass tax-free to the next generation).[3]

Unless there is a disclaimer, the remaining estate is passed to the surviving spouse.[4] This qualifies for the unlimited marital deduction and can be passed free of federal estate taxes.[5] Although it is sometimes given outright, this portion of the estate is often placed in trust, which is referred to as either the "A" trust or the "marital deduction" trust.[6] If the property is placed in trust, the spouse should be given a life estate with a power of appointment or a QTIP interest.[7]

The surviving spouse can also be given a right to *all income* from the "B" trust, as well as the right to demand, each year, either $5,000 or 5 percent of the trust corpus, whichever amount is larger. Property subject to a $5,000 or 5 percent demand right held at death is subject to taxation in the surviving spouse's estate only to the extent of the demand right.

UPON THE SECOND DEATH in 2011, unless the surviving spouse's estate exceeds $5,000,000, the estate will not be subject to federal estate taxation.[8] The amount previously placed in the "B" trust passes tax-free to the children under the terms previously established in that trust. Since the surviving spouse has no power to control the disposition of property placed in this trust, it is not included in her estate.

Footnotes on page 27

ESTATE

UPON THE FIRST DEATH

To Spouse   To Trust

UPON THE SECOND DEATH

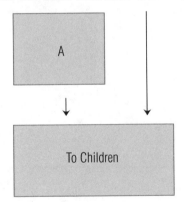

INFORMATION REQUIRED FOR ANALYSIS & PROPOSAL

Attorney Drafting Will Must Know

1. Spouse's name.
2. Children's names.
3. Name of executor/executrix.
4. Ages of minor children.
5. Names and ages of other beneficiaries.
6. Trustee after testator's death.
7. To whom, in what amounts, and when trust *income* is to be paid.
8. To whom, in what amounts, and when trust *corpus* is to be paid.

CROSS REFERENCES TO TAX FACTS ON INVESTMENTS (2011)

Q 7572. Description of the estate tax marital deduction.

Q 7573. Credits which may be taken against the estate tax.

Footnotes

[1] See footnote 6 on page 21 for an explanation of terms "applicable exclusion amount" and "basic exclusion amount" and page 475 for a discussion of the portability of the unused exclusion between spouses.

[2] This is often referred to as a *limited* trust will, in that the amount placed in the "B" trust is limited to the applicable exclusion amount, $5,000,000 in 2011 if no lifetime taxable gifts were made (see footnote 6, page 21). This trust is also referred to as a exemption, bypass, unified credit, credit shelter, credit amount, or credit equivalent bypass trust. If most property is held by a husband and wife in joint title with right of survivorship, the "A" trust could be *overqualified* and there may not be $5,000,000 of other property available to place in the "B" trust. In contrast, when a tax-driven formula is used to determine the amount going to the "B" trust, it may become overfunded (e.g., when a will directs that the amount to the "B" trust shall be the maximum amount that can be passed without paying an estate tax). In contrast to the Trust Will, see the Marital Plan Will, page 515.

[3] In large estates in 2011 the $5,000,000 generation skipping transfer tax (GSTT) exemption can be used when there is a desire to pass property to grandchildren while avoiding estate or gift taxation at the children's generation (see chart, page 39).

[4] There may be occasions when it is desired to give the surviving spouse the opportunity to take more, or less, property than would be received under the typical trust will. This can be accomplished with the use of disclaimers, which are more fully explained on page 389.

[5] There may be circumstances in which the testator will *not* wish to take advantage of the unlimited marital deduction. For example, by taking full advantage of the marital deduction, the business asset will continue to appreciate in the estate of the surviving spouse. This potential appreciation would be eliminated by passing the business to the children or other heirs upon the first death. However, the cost to do this is the early payment of estate taxes on business values in excess of $5,000,000. Of course, considerations other than financial ones may influence the ultimate decision (e.g., adult children working in the family business have a strong desire to take over operation and full ownership of the business, rather than to receive the business upon the ultimate death of the surviving parent). Generally, the marital deduction is unavailable when the surviving spouse is not a United States citizen unless the transfer is to a qualified domestic trust (see expanded discussions, pages 463 and 487). For an expanded discussion of the marital deduction, see page 450.

[6] One type of marital deduction trust is also referred to as a "power of appointment" trust, in that the surviving spouse is given a general power of appointment over the trust during lifetime or at death. For a discussion of the power of appointment trust, see page 450.

[7] Refer to page 35 for a chart illustrating the use of a qualified terminable interest property trust. Also, see page 481 for a discussion of powers of appointment.

[8] In 2011 the combined estates of husband and wife would have to exceed $10,000,000 before they would be subject to the federal estate tax. However, the estates could be subject to state death taxes (see page 87).

REVOCABLE LIVING TRUST

The revocable living trust (RLT) is a *will substitute* that can accomplish many estate planning objectives. It is an agreement that is established during lifetime and it may be amended or revoked at any time prior to the grantor's disability or death. The primary advantages of the RLT allow a grantor to: (1) provide for the management of assets upon his mental or physical disability and avoid conservatorship proceeding; (2) reduce costs and time delays by avoiding probate; (3) lessen the chances of a successful challenge or election against a will; (4) maintain confidentiality by not having to file a public will; and (5) avoid ancillary administration of out-of-state assets.[1]

Two additional documents are typically executed together with the RLT:[2]

- The **durable power of attorney** authorizes the power-holder to act for the grantor when the grantor is disabled.[3]
- The **pour-over will** functions as a "fail safe" device to transfer at death any remaining assets into the RLT, to undergo minimal probate as a means of clearing the estate of creditor claims, and to appoint guardians of any minor children.[4]

DURING LIFETIME. The grantor establishes the RLT and typically names himself as the sole trustee. This is accompanied by a retitling and transfer of property to the trust.[5] Because the grantor maintains full control over trust assets there are no income, gift, or estate tax consequences.[6]

UPON DISABILITY. If the grantor becomes disabled due to legal incompetency or physical incapacity, a designated successor trustee steps in to manage the grantor's financial affairs.[7] Disability is determined under trust provisions providing a standard of incapacity (e.g., certification by two physicians that the grantor is unable to manage his financial affairs). Also, during the grantor's disability, the holder of the durable power of attorney is authorized to transfer additional grantor-owned assets to the trust.

UPON DEATH. The RLT becomes irrevocable when the grantor dies. Under the grantor's pour-over will, any probate assets not previously placed in the RLT during lifetime are transferred to the RLT as part of the grantor's residuary estate. Assets held in trust are then disposed of according to the terms of the trust. This can include an outright distribution to the trust beneficiaries, or the trust may contain provisions establishing separate tax-savings subtrusts similar to the marital and family trusts under the exemption trust will.[8]

Although the RLT is not a panacea, it clearly offers substantial benefits for many individuals. The utility of a funded revocable trust increases with the grantor's age, when there is an increased likelihood of incompetency or incapacity and the need for asset management.[9]

Footnotes on page 31

DURING LIFETIME

Grantor Establishes Trust
&
Transfers Assets

↓

Revocable Living Trust

Managed By Grantor As Trustee

UPON DISABILITY

| Revocable Living Trust | ← Assets Can Be Transferred | Durable Power Of Attorney |

Managed By Successor Trustee
For Grantor's Benefit

UPON DEATH

| Trust Becomes Irrevocable (not subject to probate) | ← Remaining Assets Transferred | Pour-Over Will (subject to probate) |

Trust Assets Distributed To Beneficiaries
Or Transferred To Subtrusts

Beneficiaries ← → Subtrusts

Marital Trust   Family Trust

INFORMATION REQUIRED FOR ANALYSIS & PROPOSAL

Attorney Drafting Trust Instrument Must Know
1. Name of trust grantor.
2. Name of trust grantor's spouse.
3. Name of individual who will be successor trustee.
4. Name of institution that will be alternate successor trustee.
5. Name of beneficiaries other than grantor.
6. Ages of minor beneficiaries.
7. Approximate size of grantor's gross estate (i.e., will estate be subject to federal estate taxes or state death taxes).
8. To who, in what amounts, and when trust *income* is to be paid.
9. To who, in what amounts, and when trust *corpus* is to be paid.

Attorney Drafting Pour-Over Will Must Know
1. Name of testator.
2. Name of testator's spouse.
3. Name of individual who will be personal representative or executor.
4. Name of individual or institution who will be successor personal representative or alternate executor.

Attorney Drafting Durable Power Of Attorney Must Know
1. Name of grantor.
2. Name of individual to be given the power.
3. Type of power to be given (e.g., *general* durable power of attorney or *special* durable power of attorney).

CROSS REFERENCES TO TAX FACTS ON INSURANCE & EMPLOYEE BENEFITS (2011)

Q 95. When income of funded life insurance trust is taxed to grantor.
Q 96. When income is taxable to trust or to trust beneficiaries.

CROSS REFERENCES TO TAX FACTS ON INVESTMENTS (2011)

Q 7557. Computation of federal income tax for trusts and estates.
Q 7558. Description of the grantor trust and how it is taxed.
Q 7565. Items that are included in a decedent's gross estate.
Q 7584. Types of transfers that are subject to taxation.

Footnotes

[1] There is disagreement among commentators regarding the contestability of the RLT. Clearly, wills are subject to being challenged (see pages 327 and 334). Likewise, a trust can be attacked under contract law based on fraud, forgery, lack of mental capacity, and duress. However, it seems reasonable that once a RLT has been in existence and administered by the grantor for a number of years, it would be less vulnerable to a *successful* attack than a will that comes into being upon the testator's death. It has also been suggested that the perceived privacy or confidentiality advantage is largely illusory, since most individuals are not all that concerned that their probate records will be available for public scrutiny. It has also been observed that it is wise to evaluate the actual costs being avoided, since establishing and maintaining a RLT involves both time and expense; and in most states and locations attorneys' fees and probate costs are quite reasonable (most estates never actually pay executor fees, since the typical will provides for a waiver of fees and commissions if a family member is appointed to act as executor). It is true that with both RLTs and wills: assets must be collected and distributed, bills must be paid, and tax returns must be filed. In the final analysis, the undoubted benefit of having professionals who enthusiastically advocate the use of RLTs is that it motivates their clients to do sorely needed planning. The merits of the RLT should be carefully evaluated in light of individual circumstances and needs.

[2] Other documents that should be considered as part of a comprehensive estate plan include: (1) **revocable assignments** transferring property to the RLT that is not subject to precise titling (e.g., jewelry); (2) the **appointment of a health care representative** to act for the grantor in health care matters (e.g., to sign insurance forms); and (3) a **living will** stating that in case of a terminal illness or condition the grantor does not wish to be subject to procedures that serve only to prolong the dying process (see page 446).

[3] The durable power of attorney is discussed on page 394.

[4] The RLT cannot be used to designate the guardian of a minor child. This must be done under a will that is subject to court approval. See Pour-Over Will chart on page 33.

[5] Although there is a fair amount of paperwork involved in transferring title to existing property, or putting new acquisitions in the name of a trust, it is likely that the grantor is better prepared to accomplish this task while alive and competent, than a conservator in case of disability or an executor in case of death. When done by the grantor, it facilitates management or transfer of assets upon the grantor's incompetency or death (and likely saves time and money). Even a partial transfer of assets to a RLT can reduce the size of an estate to the point where it qualifies for a summary probate and unsupervised administration. Before *real property* is transferred, it should be ascertained that the transfer would not cause acceleration of a note or mortgage, reassessment of the property for tax purposes, or loss of a real estate homestead exemption.

[6] Because the trust is revocable the assets are not removed from the grantor's estate, and since the grantor is considered the owner of the trust corpus, there are no income tax advantages (i.e., as a "grantor trust" all trust income is taxed to the grantor, see page 418). A transfer of property from the trust to someone other than the grantor would be subject to gift taxes (see chart, page 47). As long as the grantor is the trustee there is no requirement that a separate income tax return be filed. However, once a successor trustee takes over during disability a separate informational return must be filed. After title is transferred, the grantor would receive account statements reading: "John Q. Jones, as Trustee of the John Q. Jones Revocable Trust dated January 7, 2010."

[7] In those states (such as Florida) requiring executors or personal representatives to be state residents, the RLT can be used to facilitate the use of an out-of-state trustee.

[8] In and of itself, the RLT is not a tax-saving device. But the trust can offer estate tax benefits if it contains provisions similar to the Trust Will (see chart, page 25).

[9] With a young entrepreneur who is actively investing, buying and selling property, as a matter of convenience, property is often not transferred to the RLT. In these situations, the necessary transfers are made using the power of attorney and pour-over will.

POUR-OVER WILL

The "pour-over will" is typically executed at the same time as the revocable living trust (RLT).[1] As a last will and testament, the essential functions of this document include:

- Providing for payment of obligations, expenses, and taxes not paid by the RLT (i.e., to clear the estate of creditor claims).
- Transferring tangible personal property.[2]
- Naming guardians of minor children.
- Functioning as a "fail-safe" device.

Generally the most important function of the pour-over will is in providing a fail-safe device. Assets not transferred (either intentionally or unintentionally) to the RLT prior to death will not be governed by the provisions of the RLT.[3] After death this clean-up feature sweeps these assets into the trust, thereby carrying out the grantor's intentions. Should the trust itself become invalid, or otherwise unavailable, the pour-over will can also direct distribution of all assets as would have been made under the trust.[4]

DURING LIFETIME. The grantor establishes a RLT and thereafter transfers property to the trust.[5] At the same time the grantor executes a pour-over will, the primary beneficiary of which is the RLT.

UPON DEATH. Any assets not transferred prior to death will become part of the grantor's estate. Since these assets are now part of the estate, they must *pass thru probate* before they can be transferred ("poured over") to the trust.[6] The assets are then distributed as provided for in the trust. However, provided the RLT has been diligently funded during the grantor's lifetime, it is possible that few, if any, assets will actually have to be transferred under the pour-over will (i.e., there will be a minimal probate for purpose of clearing the estate of the claims of creditors and the naming of guardians of minor children when both parents have died).

---

[1] The term "pour-over will" is not used in the legal document, but rather is merely used as an apt means of describing the process of transferring assets from the probate estate to the trust.

[2] The will may pass tangible personal property to a surviving spouse, make specific bequests to children and others, or make reference to distribution according to separate written and signed lists making gifts to named individuals.

[3] Unless passed by joint tenancy with rights of survivorship or beneficiary designation, these assets will likely be distributed through the probate process under the state intestacy statutes. See State Laws On Intestate Succession on pages 102-109.

[4] In the absence of both a trust and a pour-over will, the *entire* estate will be distributed through the probate process under the state intestacy statutes (e.g., in North Carolina with only one child, real property goes ½ to spouse and balance to child, with respect to personal property, spouse gets first $30,000 plus ½ of balance, with remainder to child, see page 107).

[5] See the Revocable Living Trust chart on page 29.

[6] Passing assets through probate can be both time-consuming and costly. See the discussion on page 482.

DURING LIFETIME

Will Executed

Pour-Over Will

Trust Established
&
Assets Transferred

Revocable Living Trust

UPON DEATH

Assets Must Passs Thru PROBATE

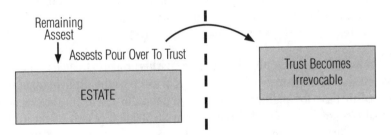

Remaining
Assest

Assests Pour Over To Trust

ESTATE

Trust Becomes
Irrevocable

QTIP TRUST

With large estates the QTIP trust provides a way to defer estate taxes by taking advantage of the marital deduction, yet "control from the grave" by directing who will eventually receive the property upon the death of the surviving spouse.[1]

Under such a trust all income must be paid at least annually to the surviving spouse.[2] The trust can be invaded only for the benefit of the surviving spouse, and no conditions can be placed upon the surviving spouse's right to the income (e.g., it is not permitted to terminate payments of income should the spouse remarry). However, in order to qualify the executor must make an irrevocable election to have the marital deduction apply to property placed in the trust.[3] This requirement not only gives the executor the power to determine how much, if any, of the estate will be taxed at the first death, it also provides great flexibility for post death planning based upon changing circumstances.[4]

Our example assumes that in 2011 we have an estate of $11,500,000.[5]

UPON THE FIRST DEATH, the estate is divided into *two* parts, with one part equal to $5,000,000 placed in a family or nonmarital trust ("B" trust in the chart).[6] No taxes are paid on this amount since the trust takes full advantage of the $1,730,800 unified credit (i.e., the amount of credit in 2011 that allows each individual to pass $5,000,000 tax-free to the next generation). The remaining $6,500,000 is placed in the QTIP trust.[7]

The executor may elect to have all, some, or none of this property treated as marital deduction property. Assume that in order to avoid appreciation of assets in the surviving spouse's estate and obtain a stepped-up basis for additional assets taxed upon the first death the executor decides to make a partial election of $5,750,000 (i.e., of the $6,500,000 placed in the QTIP trust only $5,750,000 will be sheltered from estate taxes at the first death).[8] This means that $750,000, the "nonelected" property, will be taxed at the first death. Although $262,500 of estate taxes must be paid, the remaining $487,500 will now be excluded from the taxable estate of the surviving spouse (any appreciation of this property after the first death will also be excluded).[9] If authorized under the trust document or by state law, the executor can sever the QTIP trust into separate trusts.[10]

UPON THE SECOND DEATH, the estate subject to taxation is limited to $5,750,000 (the amount remaining in the trust for which estate taxes were deferred). After paying taxes of $262,500, there remains $5,487,500.[11] This amount, together with the $487,500 from the severed trust and the $5,000,000 from the "B" trust, are passed to the beneficiaries under the terms previously established in these trusts.[12]

Footnotes on page 37

ESTATE

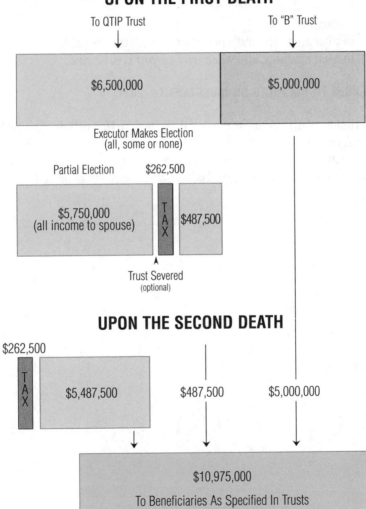

$11,500,000

UPON THE FIRST DEATH

To QTIP Trust

To "B" Trust

$6,500,000

$5,000,000

Executor Makes Election
(all, some or none)

Partial Election $262,500

$5,750,000
(all income to spouse)

T
A
X

$487,500

Trust Severed
(optional)

UPON THE SECOND DEATH

$262,500

T
A
X

$5,487,500

$487,500

$5,000,000

$10,975,000

To Beneficiaries As Specified In Trusts

INFORMATION REQUIRED FOR ANALYSIS & PROPOSAL

Attorney Drafting Will And Trust Must Know
1. Spouse's name.
2. Children's names.
3. Name of executor/executrix.
4. Ages of minor children.
5. Information regarding children of prior marriages.
6. Names and ages of other beneficiaries.
7. Trustee after testator's death.
8. To whom, in what amounts, and when trust *income* is to be paid.
9. To whom, in what amounts, and when trust *corpus* is to be paid.

CROSS REFERENCES TO TAX FACTS ON INVESTMENTS (2011)

Q 7572. Description of the estate tax marital deduction (to include qualified terminable interest property).

Q 7573. Credits which may be taken against the estate tax.

Q 7597. Description of the gift tax marital deduction (to include qualified terminable interest property).

Footnotes

[1] QTIP stands for "qualified terminable interest property." Assets placed in a QTIP trust are referred to as qualified terminable interest property. Under the Trust Will, to take advantage of the unlimited marital deduction the traditional "A" trust (marital trust) must give the surviving spouse the power to appoint, during lifetime or at death, all property placed in this trust in favor of the surviving spouse or the surviving spouse's estate (see chart, page 25). However, this arrangement is objectionable to some individuals, since control is lost over the eventual disposition of the property (e.g., a surviving widow could pass the property to her new husband or to her children by a prior marriage).

[2] Property placed in a QTIP trust must be income producing and the surviving spouse is typically given the power to force the trustee to make trust property productive. The spouse's *income* interest may be contingent upon the executor's election. Also, limited powers given to the spouse to invade the *corpus* of the QTIP trust may be contingent (e.g., upon the executor's election or upon the spouse not remarrying).

[3] This election by the executor *cannot* be mandated by the deceased prior to his death. It must be done on the estate tax return and cannot be revoked after the date for filing the return.

[4] For a discussion of the nontax reasons why a testator may *not* wish to take advantage of the marital deduction, see footnote 5, page 27.

[5] To simplify the example, the taxes are calculated assuming no debts, expenses, deductions, or prior taxable gifts, and no prior use of the unified credit.

[6] Funding of the "B" trust is limited to the applicable exclusion amount, $5,000,000 in 2011 (see footnote 6, page 21, and footnote 2, page 27). For example, rather than using a tax-driven formula to allocate property to the "B" trust, a single QTIP type trust is established. This allows the surviving spouse to disclaim assets that then pass into either the marital trust or the "B" trust.

[7] This example shows the QTIP trust being used only with the "B" trust (family trust). When the "A" trust (marital trust) is also used, it provides the executor even greater flexibility in allocating assets between the QTIP trust and "A" trust (see chart, page 25).

[8] The taxpayer has made a decision that it is worth paying $262,500 of estate taxes in order to shift subsequent appreciation on the remaining $487,500 out of the surviving spouse's estate and obtain a stepped-up basis at the prior spouse's death.

[9] Liquidity for paying estate taxes at the first death might come from the tax-free death proceeds paid to an irrevocable Life Insurance Trust (see chart, page 51).

[10] The division of the QTIP trust must be done on a fractional or percentage basis to reflect the partial election. It is not necessary that each asset be divided pro rata between the severed trusts; so long as it is based upon the fair market value of all trust assets at the time of the division.

[11] The estate has a right of recovery for any taxes paid, unless waived by the deceased spouse (if there is no waiver, then the failure to recover is subject to gift taxes).

[12] Lifetime QTIP trusts can be used as an alternative to outright gifts.

GENERATION-SKIPPING TRANSFERS

The basic intent of the federal estate tax system is to tax property as it is passed from one generation to the next. The generation-skipping transfer (GST) tax is intended to prevent wealthy families from reducing estate taxes by skipping one or more generations (e.g., grandparents pass their estate to grandchildren in order to reduce or avoid estate taxes in their children's estates).

The GST tax is in *addition* to the normal estate or gift tax and is applied to the transfer of property to a person two or more generations younger than the transferor (e.g., from grandparent to grandchild).[1] The *maximum* estate tax rate, 35 percent in 2011, is used in calculating the GST tax.[2] However, there is an exemption which allows aggregate transfers of $5,000,000, during lifetime or at death, to be exempt from the GST tax ($10,000,000 total for both husband and wife).[3]

To illustrate, assume that Grandparents have an estate totaling $16,000,000. Assume also that their Children have substantial estates in their own right and the Grandparents desire to fully use their GST tax exemptions.

UPON THE FIRST GRANDPARENT'S DEATH. In order to take maximum advantage of the GST tax exemption in 2011, $5,000,000 must be passed to the Grandchildren. This $5,000,000 could be placed in a family or nonmarital trust (the "B" trust) that would provide income to the surviving Grandparent.[4]

UPON THE SECOND GRANDPARENT'S DEATH. Again, in order to take maximum advantage of the GST tax exemption, an additional $5,000,000 must now be passed to the Grandchildren. After payment of $2,100,000 in federal estate taxes on a taxable estate of $6,000,000, $5,000,000 is passed to the Grandchildren. In order to avoid any GST taxes, the remaining $3,900,000 is passed to the Children.[5] The $5,000,000 originally placed in the "B" trust is also distributed to the Grandchildren. Of the original $16,000,000 estate, estate taxes totaling $2,100,000 have been paid at the second death. Full use of the Grandparent's GSTT exemptions has the potential of producing estate tax savings of $3,500,000 at the Children's generation.[6]

Application of the GST tax can be quite complicated and its impact is substantial in larger estates. Careful analysis by qualified counsel is essential if unexpected tax consequences are to be avoided.[7]

Footnotes on page 41

GRANDPARENT'S ESTATE

$16,000,000

UPON THE FIRST GRANDPARENT'S DEATH

To Spouse   To Trust
                                (GSTT Exemption)

$11,000,000 $5,000,000
"A"   "B"
Trust   Trust

UPON THE SECOND GRANDPARENT'S DEATH

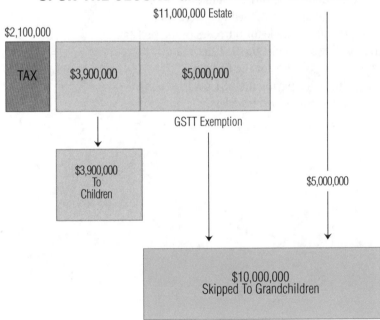

$11,000,000 Estate

$2,100,000

TAX $3,900,000 $5,000,000

GSTT Exemption

$3,900,000
To
Children

$5,000,000

$10,000,000
Skipped To Grandchildren

INFORMATION REQUIRED FOR ANALYSIS & PROPOSAL

1. Size of grandparent's estate.
2. Nature of prior gifts, if any, made by grandparents.
3. Numbers and ages of children and grandchildren.
4. Size of children's estates and ability of children to support themselves without inherited assets.

See also information required for exemption trust wills on page 26.

CROSS REFERENCES TO TAX FACTS ON INSURANCE & EMPLOYEE BENEFITS (2011)

Q 56. Life insurance proceeds and annuities are subject to GST tax.
Q 57. Gifts to life insurance trust and the GST tax.
Q 58. Leveraging the exemption with a life insurance trust.

CROSS REFERENCES TO TAX FACTS ON INVESTMENTS (2011)

Q 7575. Overview of the generation-skipping transfer tax.
Q 7576. What is a generation-skipping transfer (GST).
Q 7577. Determination of the GST tax and exemption.
Q 7578. How individuals are assigned to generations.
Q 7579. Split gifts can be made for purposes of the GST tax.
Q 7580. Credits allowed against the GST tax.
Q 7581. Return requirements for the GST tax.
Q 7582. Who is liable for paying the GST tax.
Q 7596. Discussion of "qualified transfers."

Footnotes

[1] Because grandchildren are two or more generations below the grandparent (transferor), they are known as *skip persons*, whereas children are known as *nonskip persons* (the transferor's spouse is also a nonskip person, since she is of the same generation as the transferor). When the transfer is directly from one generation to a person two or more generations younger than the transferor it is referred to as a "direct skip" (e.g., in his will grandfather leaves property to grandchild). In the case of a direct skip, the GST tax is payable at the time of the transfer, not upon the death of the person in the skipped generation (e.g., the GST tax is payable upon the grandfather's death, not when the child dies). Any transfer is generally not subject to the GST tax if the person in the intervening generation (the child) is not alive at the time of the transfer to the skip person (the grandchild).

[2] The amount of tax is calculated by multiplying the "taxable amount" by the "applicable rate." In fact, the applicable rate is itself a product of the maximum federal estate tax rate times the "inclusion ratio." The inclusion ratio, in turn, depends on allocations of the "GST exemption." For example, assume G transfers irrevocably in trust for his grandchildren $7,200,000 in 2011 and allocates all his $5,000,000 GST exemption to the transfer. The applicable fraction is 5,000,000 ÷ 7,200,000, or .6944. The inclusion ratio is 1 minus .6944, or .3056. The maximum estate tax rate, 35 percent, is applied against the inclusion ratio of .3056. The resulting applicable rate, 10.6944 percent, is applied against the value of the property transferred, $7,200,000, to produce a GST tax of $770,000. Under The 2010 Tax Relief Act the applicable rate in determining GST taxes for 2010 transfers was zero, meaning that in 2010 there was no GST tax.

[3] In 2011, the generation-skipping exemption is $5,000,000 (this is the same as the estate tax applicable exclusion amount). Unless there is further Congressional action the exemption is scheduled to revert to $1,000,000 in 2013 (subject to indexing for inflation). This exemption can be elected on the gift tax return of the transferor, or on the estate tax return if claimed on a bequest. There is no GST tax imposed on direct skip gifts that come within the gift tax annual exclusion (see chart on page 47) or that are "qualified transfers." In general, qualified transfers are payments for the education or medical care of a skip person. Special rules apply to transfers in trusts such as the irrevocable life insurance trust (see footnote 7 below).

[4] Since it also applies to taxable distributions and terminations, it is not possible to use a trust to avoid application of the GST tax. A taxable *distribution* may occur with a distribution from a trust to the grandchild of the grantor. A taxable *termination* occurs upon the death of the child where a trust provides for a life income to the child with remainder to the grandchild. But, in this example, allocation of the full $5,000,000 GST tax exemption eliminates the GST tax because the inclusion ratio is zero (1 - (5,000,000 ÷ 5,000,000) = 0). For further discussion, see footnote 2 above.

[5] Upon the second death the entire estate could be passed to the Grandchildren, but that would require payment of a GST tax in addition to the federal estate tax.

[6] This assumes that the Child's estate, often referred to as the "intervening generation's estate," would be subject to a maximum federal estate tax rate of 35 percent in 2011 (.35 × $10,000,000 = $3,500,000).

[7] Although a life insurance trust can be very effective in leveraging the GST tax exemption, application of the GST tax can be complicated. The GST tax generally applies to an irrevocable life insurance trust whenever grandchildren are trust beneficiaries. It is essential to maintain a zero inclusion ratio (see footnotes 2 and 4 above). To shelter such a trust from the GST tax, the exemption must be allocated by filing a timely gift tax return *after each gift* to the trust.

INSTALLMENT SALE & PRIVATE ANNUITY

Both the installment sale and the private annuity are used to transfer future appreciation through sale of property (e.g., a business interest) from one individual to another, in our example, from parent to child. There are, however, substantial differences in both the tax implications and resulting rights and obligations.[1]

INSTALLMENT SALE. The primary distinguishing characteristic of the installment sale, as compared to the private annuity, is the *fixed schedule* of payments made by the buyer. The parent (as seller) can spread a large gain and the resulting income tax liability over a number of years, while at the same time transferring future appreciation to the child (as purchaser).

The child's obligation to the parent may be *secured*, which also distinguishes the installment sale from the private annuity. With respect to the parent, each payment is divided into gain, interest income, and a nontaxable recovery of basis. If the parent dies, payments continue to the parent's estate.[2] Although the child's obligation could be cancelled by the parent's executor, or passed by will to the child, previously unreported gain would still be taxable to the estate.[3]

PRIVATE ANNUITY. The private annuity obligates the child to make payments for the *lifetime* of the parent, and the obligation may not be secured in any way. Unlike the installment sale, the parent must recognize the entire amount of the gain or loss at the time of the transaction, and the child cannot deduct any part of the payments.[4] Each payment is divided into interest income and a nontaxable recovery of basis. Because payments terminate at the parent's death, the annuity is considered to have no value and should escape taxation in the parent's estate.

In considering a private annuity, both parties must recognize that if the parent lives for many years, the child could end up paying more for the asset then would have been paid with an installment sale. The parent must also recognize that the expected income could be in jeopardy if the child were to die. However, providing for insurance on the child's life sufficient to meet the annuity obligation can usually eliminate this risk.

Footnotes on page 45

INSTALLMENT SALE

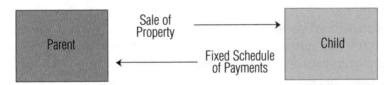

- May be secured

- Each payment is divided into gain, interest income, and a nontaxable recovery of basis

- Child deducts interest portion

- If parent dies, payments continue until obligation satisfied

PRIVATE ANNUITY

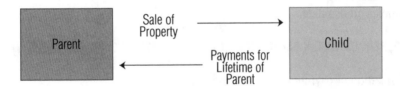

- May not be secured

- Each payment is divided into interest income and a nontaxable recovery of basis

- Child cannot deduct any part of payments

- When parent dies, payments terminate

INFORMATION REQUIRED FOR ANALYSIS & PROPOSAL

Installment Sale
1. Value of property to be sold.
2. Seller's cost basis in property.
3. Number of years payments are to be made.
4. Interest rate to be used.
5. Purchaser:
   a. Sex.
   b. Date of birth.
   c. Smoker/nonsmoker.

Private Annuity
1. Value of property.
2. Seller's cost basis in property.
3. Seller's date of birth.
4. Purchaser:
   a. Sex.
   b. Date of birth.
   c. Smoker/nonsmoker.

CROSS REFERENCES TO TAX FACTS ON INSURANCE & EMPLOYEE BENEFITS (2011)

Q 3551. Taxation of payments received under private annuity.

Q 3552. Tax consequences to obligor under private annuity.

Q 3570. Usual private annuity results in nothing to be included in estate of annuitant (unless benefits payable to survivor).

CROSS REFERENCES TO TAX FACTS ON INVESTMENTS (2011)

Q 7512. Nature and taxation of installment sale.

Footnotes

[1] The selection of either the installment sale or the private annuity depends upon a consideration of many factors, which include: the relative income and anticipated marginal tax brackets of the parties; the age of the seller; the need for flexibility in determining payments and tax consequences; the degree of trust between the parties; and the relationship between the parties (i.e., family members or disinterested third persons).

The tax implications can be compared by summarizing the breakdown of payments and tax allocations. The following calculations assume that real estate valued at $250,000 is transferred, with a cost basis to the seller of $100,000. The installment sale calculation assumes payments are made over a period of years approximating the seller's life expectancy under the Section 7520 mortality table (21.5 years) and uses 3.35 percent interest (the November 2010 long-term applicable federal rate). The private annuity calculation uses 2.0 percent interest (the November 2010 Section 7520 applicable federal rate).

	21-Year Installment Sale	Private Annuity To Male, Age 60
Annual Payment	$16,770	$14,941
Taxation To Seller:		
Gain	7,143	n/a
Interest Income	4,865	4,610
Nontaxable Recovery Of Basis	4,762	10,331
Taxation To Purchaser:		
Interest Expense	4,865	-0-
Nondeductible Capital Expenditure	11,905	14,941

Note that such comparisons are heavily influenced by the assumed interest rate and the duration of the installment sale, as well as the age of the seller, who is also the annuitant in the private annuity arrangement. See also, footnote 4 below regarding proposed regulations.

[2] Use of an installment sale to purchase part or all of a business, or other property interest, after the owner's death offers little or no tax advantage to the estate. Because of the stepped-up basis, the estate will usually have no taxable gain, and thus no tax reason to spread gain over a period of years. In fact, reliance on the installment sale could be to the detriment of the estate and the heirs if the purchaser fails to make the agreed payments. Provided the business owner is insurable, funding a buyout agreement with life insurance is generally far better than an installment sale. If an installment sale is used, life insurance on the purchaser's life will assure that, if the purchaser dies, funds are available to make the required payments.

[3] The cancellation of an obligation between "related" parties (i.e., parent and child) will result in the seller, or his estate, having to recognize gain in an amount equal to the difference between the fair market value of the obligation on the date of cancellation and the seller's basis in the obligation. Passing a note by will to the purchaser is treated as a cancellation. There is no stepped-up basis, since this is "income in respect of a decedent," or IRD (see footnote 4 on page 21, and page 425). See also the expanded discussion of Self-Cancelling Installment Notes (SCINs) on page 520.

[4] In October of 2006, the IRS issued proposed regulations that require the entire amount of the gain, or loss, to be recognized at the time of the sale (i.e., the parents would be in the same position as if they had sold the property for cash and then purchased the annuity). The regulations are effective for exchanges made after October 18, 2006 (except the effective date is delayed until April 18, 2007, for exchanges involving an unsecured annuity contract issued by an individual, provided the property that is exchanged is not sold or disposed of for a two year period). Any gain to the parent will be a capital gain if the asset qualifies for capital gain treatment. In this regard, see the discussion of the Capital Gains on page 353. Recovery of basis is spread equally over a period of years measured by the parent's life expectancy. After this period, each annuity payment will be entirely interest income.

GIFTS & SPLIT-GIFTS

Making gifts on a regular basis is an estate planning tool which can be used to pass property to family and friends without the need to file any gift tax return.[1]

INDIVIDUAL GIFTS. To illustrate, assume that a donor has money that is not needed for his own support. Under the federal gift tax provisions, an individual may give – under most circumstances – up to $13,000 per person, as indexed in 2011 for inflation, annually free of gift tax.[2] Thus, with three children the donor could give each of them $13,000 per year.[3] This per-donee exclusion is allowed each and every year, but it is *not cumulative* (i.e., an exclusion unused in any year may not be "carried over" to the following year).

In order for the gift to be one that qualifies for the annual exclusion, it must be a *present interest gift*: the donee must be entitled to its immediate use and enjoyment.[4] If within the year the donor makes only present-interest gifts, and gifts do not exceed a total of $13,000 per donee, the donor will *not* be required to file a gift tax return for that year and – under most circumstances – have no further income, gift, or estate tax consequences from the gift.[5] Likewise, the gift is not included in the donee's taxable income.

SPLIT-GIFTS. With split-gifts the spouse joins in making the gift, and this allows a married couple to increase their gifts to $26,000 per year to each donee. This can be done without tax consequences, provided it is a present interest gift. The funds could still be entirely either the husband's or the wife's, but by having a spouse join in making each gift, they are able to double the amount of their tax-free gifts. However, in order to claim the benefits of these provisions of the law, they must file a gift tax return.[6] Gift taxes, if any, are normally paid by the donor.[7]

Present interest gifts that qualify for the annual exclusion are particularly attractive in reducing the donor's estate, since they will: (1) avoid the gift tax; and (2) likely be excluded from his estate for federal estate tax purposes no matter how soon death occurs after making the gift (e.g., the day after or even the moment after the gift is made).[8]

Footnotes on page 49

INDIVIDUAL GIFTS

SPLIT-GIFTS

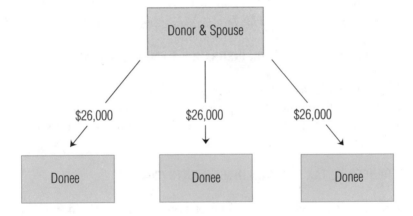

INFORMATION REQUIRED FOR ANALYSIS & PROPOSAL

To Determine Attitude Toward Making Gifts
1. Have prior gifts been made? If so, to whom and in what amounts?
2. Has client ever filed a gift tax return? If so, obtain copies.
3. Has client established trusts? If so, obtain copies.
4. Client's attitude regarding making cash gifts to children or others.
5. Would client consider making gifts in trust?

To Determine Ability To Make Gifts
6. Amount of cash available for gifts.
7. Other property available for gifts.
8. Inventory of life insurance policies owned by client or spouse.
9. Is client married (split-gifts)?

To Determine Benefits From Making Gifts
10. Numbers and ages of children and grandchildren.
11. Size of estate (i.e., to determine if currently subject to estate taxes).
12. Anticipated rate of estate growth.
13. Are client and spouse insurable?

See also information required for life insurance trusts on page 52.

CROSS REFERENCES TO TAX FACTS ON INSURANCE & EMPLOYEE BENEFITS (2011)

Q 67. Valuation of life insurance for gift tax purposes.
Q 160. Use of annual exclusion to make gifts of policies and premiums.
Q 164. Gift of life insurance policy to minor qualifies for annual gift tax exclusion.
Q 166. Gift of policy within 3 years of death.

CROSS REFERENCES TO TAX FACTS ON INVESTMENTS (2011)

Q 7570. Circumstances under which value of property given within 3 years of death is included in estate.
Q 7583. General discussion of federal gift tax.
Q 7584. Types of transfers subject to gift tax.
Q 7591. Valuation of net gifts (donee pays tax).
Q 7592. Gift to minor generally qualifies for annual exclusion.
Q 7595. "Split-gift" provisions.
Q 7596. Gift tax exclusions.
Q 7597. Gift tax marital deduction.
Q 7599. Unified credit and how it is applied against gift tax.
Q 7600. Filing of return and payment of tax.

Footnotes

[1] The return is 4 pages in length (Form 709) and the accompanying instructions are 12 pages in length.

[2] The $10,000 annual exclusion for gifts is indexed for inflation and was increased to $13,000 for the years 2009, 2010 and 2011. This cost-of-living adjustment is the percentage, if any, by which the Consumer Price Index (CPI) for the preceding calendar year exceeds the CPI for the base calendar year (for these purposes a CPI calendar year ends August 31). However, any increases are rounded down to the next lowest multiple of $1,000.

[3] While gifts are generally discussed in a family setting, anyone can make gifts under these rules, whether the donor is a father, mother, child, distant relative, or even a benevolent stranger. In most states a gift to a minor under either the Uniform Transfers to Minors Act or the Uniform Gift to Minors Act will qualify as a present interest gift, even though the minor does not have legal capacity to make demands upon the custodian (see Minors And Life Insurance on page 459). The irrevocable life insurance trust offers an excellent means of taking advantage of the yearly opportunity to make present interest gifts through annual gifts to the trust for premium payments (see chart, page 51).

[4] When a gift is made late in the year in the form of a check it should be deposited in time to clear the donor's bank by the end of the year, otherwise the gift might not be considered complete until the following year. Payments made directly for medical or educational bills are not considered gifts for gift tax purposes, and therefore are not subject to gift taxes (the funds should be paid to the provider of medical services or the educational institution, not to the donee). Gifts to a charity can qualify for the gift tax charitable deduction (see discussion regarding charitable gifts of life insurance, page 356, and charitable remainder trust chart, page 55).

[5] Although the donee is not liable for income taxes upon receiving the gift, if the property is subsequently sold the donee would be liable for reporting and paying taxes on any gain realized from the sale. For the purpose of calculating gain, the donee's income tax basis is generally the same as the donor's basis in the property, often referred to as a "substituted" basis.

[6] The gift tax return, Form 709, must be filed by the donor on or before April 15 following the close of the calendar year in which the donor makes the gift, except that an extension of time granted for filing the income tax return serves also as an extension of time for filing the gift tax return. In order to avoid having to file a gift tax return, one spouse could transfer funds to the other spouse, and thereafter each spouse could then make separate gifts to the trust. Only a husband and wife can take advantage of split-gifts; unmarried individuals may not.

[7] Although the donor is the party having primary liability for payment of the gift tax, a gift can be made subject to a condition that the gift tax is paid by the donee (or by the trustee if the gift is in trust). The value of the gift is reduced by the amount of the tax. In effect, the amount of the gift tax paid by the donee reduces the value of the gift and the gift tax liability. This net gift technique can be useful when the donor desires to transfer large amounts of property, but does not have cash to pay the gift tax. However, the donor ends up in the same position whether she transfers $1,350,000 to a donee and the donee pays $350,000 in gift tax, or she transfers $1,000,000 to a donee and pays the $350,000 gift tax herself. If the donor gives property, the donor will have to recognize income to the extent any gift tax paid by the donee exceeds the donor's basis in the property.

[8] One important exception is that proceeds of a life insurance policy *transferred* by gift from the insured within three years of the insured's death are brought back into the insured's estate.

LIFE INSURANCE TRUST

The trust is one of the most basic tools of estate planning. When made irrevocable and funded with life insurance, it accomplishes multiple objectives. For example, it can:

- Provide Income for a Family
- Provide Funds for Estate Settlement Costs
- Avoid Increasing Estate Taxes
- Avoid Probate Costs
- Provide for Management of Assets
- Maintain Confidentiality
- Take Advantage of Gift Tax Laws
- Help Create a Minimal Drain on Present Funds

DURING LIFETIME, it is possible for a grantor to establish a trust that will eventually accomplish all of these objectives. The beneficiaries of such a trust are normally members of the grantor's family and likely to be estate beneficiaries.[1]

Once the trust is created, policies on the life of the grantor can be given to the trust. If no such policies are available, then the trustee would obtain the needed life insurance.[2] In either case, funds are given to the trust, which, in turn, pays the premiums to the insurance company.

In order to take full advantage of the gift tax laws, the beneficiaries must have a limited right to demand the value of any gifts made to the trust each year.[3] However, in order not to defeat the purpose of the trust, the beneficiaries should not exercise this right to demand. In this way, each year up to $13,000 per beneficiary, as indexed for inflation in 2011, can be given tax-free to the trust.[4]

UPON DEATH, the grantor's property passes to his estate. At the same time, the insurance company also pays a death benefit to the trust. If the policies have been purchased by the trustee, or if the grantor has lived for over 3 years after having given the insurance to the trust, the death benefit will be received free of federal estate taxes.[5]

There are basically two ways the trustee can make these funds available for payment of estate settlement costs. The trust either **makes loans** to the estate, or the estate **sells assets** to the trust. In any event, guided by specific will and trust provisions the beneficiaries can receive distributions of **income** and **property**.[6]

Footnotes on page 53

DURING LIFETIME

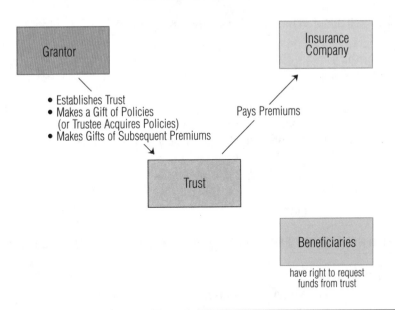

Grantor

- Establishes Trust
- Makes a Gift of Policies
  (or Trustee Acquires Policies)
- Makes Gifts of Subsequent Premiums

Insurance
Company

Pays Premiums

Trust

Beneficiaries

have right to request
funds from trust

UPON DEATH

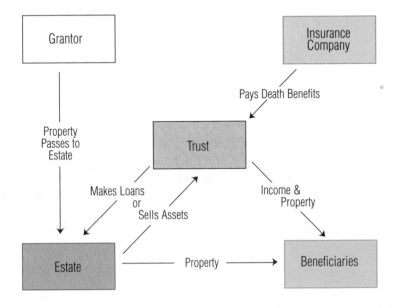

Grantor

Insurance
Company

Pays Death Benefits

Property
Passes to
Estate

Trust

Makes Loans
or
Sells Assets

Income &
Property

Estate

Property

Beneficiaries

INFORMATION REQUIRED FOR ANALYSIS & PROPOSAL

1. Name of individual to be insured (usually trust grantor).
2. Sex.
3. Date of birth.
4. Smoker/nonsmoker.

Attorney Drafting Trust Instrument Must Also Know

5. To whom, in what amounts, and when trust *income* is to be paid.
6. To whom, in what amounts, and when trust *corpus* is to be paid.
7. Trustee during insured's lifetime.
8. Trustee after insured's death.
9. Names of beneficiaries.
10. Ages of minor beneficiaries.

CROSS REFERENCES TO TAX FACTS ON INSURANCE & EMPLOYEE BENEFITS (2011)

Income Tax

Q 93.   When income of funded trust taxed to grantor.

Q 96.   When income taxable to trust or to trust beneficiaries.

Q 98.   Death proceeds received by trust free of income taxes.

Estate Tax

Q 121. When proceeds either included or excluded from insured's estate.

Q 123. When value of trust assets included in estate of income beneficiary.

Q 124. Insurance proceeds included in insured's estate when trustee *required* to pay estate debts and taxes.

Q 125. Transfer of income-producing property to trust.

Gift Tax

Q 99.   Value of gift when policy transferred to trust.

Q 104. Qualification for gift tax annual exclusion.

Q 105. Annual exclusion and irrevocable trust for minor beneficiary (Sec. 2503(c)).

Q 106. Qualification for annual exclusion of gifts to trust to pay premiums (Crummey rules).

Q 107. When lapse of withdrawal right can result in gift from one beneficiary to another beneficiary.

Footnotes

[1] Just as the surviving spouse is often made a beneficiary of the family trust under the Trust Will ("B" trust on page 25), the surviving spouse can also be made a beneficiary and given "present interest" demand powers under the irrevocable life insurance trust (see footnote 4 below).

[2] During the insured's lifetime the trustee is typically an individual other than the grantor who: (1) takes possession of the life insurance policies; (2) applies for a taxpayer identification number using IRS form SS-4, Application for Employer Identification Number; (3) opens a checking account; (4) receives funds placed in the trust; (5) notifies beneficiaries of their right to make demands of these funds; and (6) pays premiums as they come due. It is usually advisable for a corporate trustee to be named at the insured's death. The new trustee then administers the life insurance proceeds according to the trust provisions.

[3] With respect to a demand power, the IRS has taken the position that the annual exclusion is available only when the powerholder is a *primary* trust beneficiary who has a substantial economic interest in the trust (e.g., child of the insured who stands to receive distributions from the trust). However, a Tax Court case has held that a powerholder who is a beneficiary with only a *contingent remainder interest* would also qualify for the annual exclusion (e.g., grandchild would only take under the trust if his parent, who is the primary beneficiary, were deceased).

[4] The *right* to demand qualifies gifts for the annual exclusion as "present interest" gifts. Where there is more than one trust beneficiary this power is often limited to the greater of $5,000 or 5 percent of the trust corpus (often referred to as a "5-or-5" power). This right is considered a general power of appointment. When the beneficiary fails to exercise a general power of appointment, the "lapse" is deemed a non present interest gift from that beneficiary to the other trust beneficiaries to the extent that the property with respect to which the power lapsed exceeds the greater of $5,000 or 5 percent of the trust corpus. Such "gifts" *between beneficiaries* will result in an unnecessary utilization by the beneficiaries of their unified credit, or even payment of gift taxes. When premiums exceed $5,000 times the number of trust beneficiaries, one means of avoiding a lapse of the beneficiary's power of withdrawal is to use a *"hanging" Crummey power*. With this provision the beneficiary's entire power of withdrawal does not terminate within a specified period of time, but rather the beneficiary retains and accumulates his rights to demand gifts to the trust in excess of the "5-or-5" limit ($5,000, or 5 percent of the trust corpus, whichever is greater). Such accumulations of future rights of withdrawal (i.e., the hanging powers) give beneficiaries the right to demand distribution of prior gifts which exceeded the "5-or-5" limits. If in a future year the grantor makes no gifts to the trust, these accumulated powers lapse within the limits of the "5-or-5" power. The building up of substantial cash values would accelerate the lapse of these accumulated powers, since each beneficiary would have the right to demand the *greater of* $5,000, or 5 percent of the trust corpus (e.g., 5 percent of $150,000 in cash values is $7,500, and this is substantially more than $5,000). The *testamentary power of appointment* provides another means of avoiding the lapse of amounts in excess of $5,000 or 5 percent. Under such an arrangement, amounts exceeding $5,000 or 5 percent "partially lapse" to a limited testamentary power of appointment in favor of a designated class of beneficiaries (typically, the power holder's heirs). If the power is not exercised in the holder's will, then the amounts subject to the power vest in the trust. However, the amounts subject to this power are likely to be included in the holder's estate. The *cumulative power of appointment* is another technique used to avoid this problem (see page 379 for an additional discussion of present interest gifts).

[5] Provided the policy is purchased by another person, including a trustee, it now appears certain that, provided the proceeds are payable outside the estate, the death benefits of a life insurance contract will be excluded from the insured's estate no matter when death occurs (see the discussion on pages 409-410).

[6] There may also be provisions in both the trust and the grantor's will which provide for a merging of the trust and estate assets, with subsequent management of the combined assets for the beneficiaries. These are often referred to as "pour-over" provisions.

CHARITABLE REMAINDER TRUST

The charitable remainder trust enables an individual to make a substantial deferred gift to a favored charity while retaining a right to payments from the trust. Under the right circumstances use of such a trust offers multiple tax and nontax advantages, particularly to the individual who owns substantially appreciated property. These advantages include a charitable deduction resulting in reduced taxes, an increase in current cash flow, avoidance of capital gains upon a sale of the appreciated property, the eventual reduction or elimination of estate taxes, and the satisfaction of knowing that property placed in the trust will eventually pass to charity. When combined with a wealth replacement trust, the full value of the estate can still be preserved for heirs.

DURING LIFETIME the grantor, after establishing a charitable remainder trust, gives property to the trust while retaining a right to payments from the trust.[1] A **unitrust** provides for the grantor to receive annually a fixed *percentage* of the trust value (valued annually), whereas an **annuity trust** provides for the grantor to receive annually a fixed *amount*.[2] Either type of trust could require that payments be made for the joint lives of the grantor and another person, such as the grantor's spouse.

At the time the property is given to the trust, the grantor can claim a current income tax deduction equal to the present value of the charity's remainder interest.[3] Upon receipt of the gift, the trustee will often sell the appreciated property and reinvest the proceeds in order to better provide the cash flow required to make the payments to the grantor. This sale by the trust is usually free of any capital gains tax.[4]

The tax savings and increased cash flow offered by the use of a charitable remainder trust will often enable the grantor to use some or all of these savings to fund a **wealth replacement trust** for the benefit of his heirs, thereby providing for the tax effective replacement of property which had been transferred to the charitable remainder trust. If the wealth replacement trust is established as an irrevocable life insurance trust it is often possible to gain gift tax advantages during the grantor's lifetime, while at death entirely avoiding inclusion of the life insurance proceeds in the estates of the grantor and his spouse.[5]

UPON DEATH the property placed in the charitable remainder trust passes to the designated charity. At the same time a tax-free death benefit is paid to the wealth replacement trust, which funds can then be paid as income or corpus to the grantor's heirs pursuant to the terms of this trust.

Footnotes on page 57

DURING LIFETIME

UPON DEATH

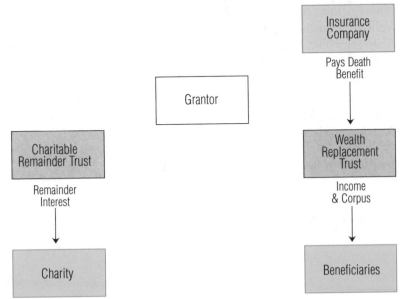

INFORMATION REQUIRED FOR ANALYSIS & PROPOSAL

1. Fair market value of property transferred to trust.
2. Date of transfer to trust.
3. Payout rate (if unitrust) or amount (if annuity trust).
4. Payment frequency (annually, semiannually, quarterly, or monthly).
5. Age of person whose life determines length of payments.
6. Age of joint annuitant (if payout for two lives).
7. Discount rate (as published monthly by IRS).

See also information required for life insurance trusts on page 52.

CROSS REFERENCES TO TAX FACTS ON INSURANCE & EMPLOYEE BENEFITS (2011)

Q 68. Charitable contribution deductions may be taken for the gift of a life insurance policy, life insurance premiums, maturing annuity, and endowment contract.

CROSS REFERENCES TO TAX FACTS ON INVESTMENTS (2011)

Q 7534. Maximum annual limits on income tax deductions allowed for charitable contributions.

Q 7572. Value of spouse's interest in a charitable remainder trust will generally qualify for the estate tax marital deduction.

Q 7606. How remainder interests are valued.

Q 7598. A gift tax deduction is generally allowed for gifts to charitable organizations.

Q 7950. When charitable deduction allowed for contributions to a charitable remainder trust.

Q 7951. Charitable remainder annuity trust defined.

Q 7952. Charitable remainder unitrust defined.

Q 7953. Pooled income fund defined.

Q 7955. Deduction for gift to charitable remainder annuity trust or unitrust.

Q 7956. Beneficiary subject to four-tier income tax treatment.

See also cross references to life insurance trusts on page 52.

Footnotes

[1] The term "grantor" is used to describe a person who establishes a trust, whereas the term "donor" is used to describe a person who makes a gift. For simplicity, only the term "grantor" has been used in describing the charitable remainder trust.

[2] Characteristics common to both unitrusts and annuity trusts are: (1) payments must be made at least annually and may not be less than 5 percent, nor more than 50 percent, of the net fair market value of the trust assets (determined when trust is created with an annuity; determined annually with a unitrust); (2) value of charity's remainder must be at least 10 percent of trust assets; (3) the trustee cannot be required to invest in specific assets (e.g., stock in a corporation or life insurance); and (4) payments may be for a term not greater than 20 years, or for the life or lives of the beneficiary(ies). Any individual beneficiary must be living when the trust is created.

[3] Selection of a payout rate can have a substantial impact upon the current income tax deduction (i.e., the present value of the charitable remainder interest). If the deduction is to be meaningful, the payout rate is usually limited to 7 percent or less. For example, assuming a $100,000 gift to a charitable remainder unitrust to be paid for the beneficiary's life, the following table illustrates the interrelationship of the beneficiary's age and the selected payment percentage:

Age of Beneficiary	Payout	Deduction
50	5%	25,943
	10%	9,413
60	5%	37,656
	10%	17,530
70	5%	51,905
	10%	30,197

[4] With gifts of long-term capital gain property, the full present value of the remainder interest is deductible if the property is intangibles or real estate. Tangible personal property is not appropriate.

Whether the deduction can be taken in a particular year depends upon the application of three percentage limitations that relate to the taxpayer's "contribution base" (i.e., adjusted gross income computed without regard to net operating loss carryback). These limits depend upon whether the gift is to a public charity or a private foundation (see page 480); and whether the gift is one of either cash or ordinary income property, or a gift of long-term capital gain property. The deduction cannot usually exceed the following percentages of the taxpayer's contribution base:

	Cash or Ordinary Income Property	Long-Term Capital Gain Property
Public Charities	50%	30%
Private Foundations	30%	20%

If the gift is made to a public charity there is a five-year carryover of any unused deduction.

A charitable remainder trust (CRT) that has unrelated business income (UBI) is subject to income taxation on all of its income. Generally, UBI is the net income from the conduct of a trade or business that is not substantially related to the exempt purpose of the CRT. Income from property that is debt-financed and not related to the exempt function of the CRT is generally considered UBI. However, debt-financed income is excluded from UBI for the first ten years following transfer to the CRT if the debt had been placed on the property more than five years prior to the transfer.

[5] The "wealth replacement trust" is another name for an irrevocable life insurance trust (see chart on page 51). For an expanded discussion of the gift and estate tax ramifications of an irrevocable life insurance trust, see the discussion on page 50. Funding with survivorship life insurance can be particularly attractive (see page 535).

GRANTOR RETAINED ANNUITY TRUST (GRAT)

The Grantor Retained Annuity Trust (GRAT) is an estate planning technique that can be used to transfer *future* appreciation to family members, or others, free of gift and estate taxes provided the grantor survives the trust term.[1]

TRUST ESTABLISHED. In order to implement a GRAT, the grantor creates an irrevocable trust for a specified number of years, names his children as trust beneficiaries, and transfers to the trust property that has a potential for substantial appreciation.[2] The grantor retains the right to receive, for the term of the GRAT, a "qualified annuity interest" based on either a specified sum or fixed percentage of the initial value of the property transferred to the trust. This annuity is mandatory and must be paid at least annually. The annual payment may be increased, provided the increase is not greater than 120 percent of the prior year's payment. Additional contributions to the GRAT are not permitted.

Only the value of the remainder interest payable to the trust beneficiaries is subject to the gift tax. This value is determined by subtracting from the fair market value of the property transferred to the trust the present value of the annuity retained by the grantor.[3] The value of this annuity is increased by a longer-term trust, larger annuity payments, and lower assumed interest rate used to make the present value calculation. To summarize, gift tax exposure is *reduced* if the present value of the retained annuity is increased and the value of the remainder interest is decreased:[4]

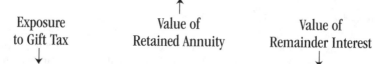

| Exposure
to Gift Tax | Value of
Retained Annuity | Value of
Remainder Interest |

DURING TRUST TERM. Tax-free annuity payments are made to the grantor. Trust assets may be used to make these payments. For federal tax purposes the GRAT is considered a grantor trust, meaning that the grantor pays taxes on all trust income.[5] Should the grantor die before the end of the trust term, the annuity payments continue to be made to the Grantor's Estate and the property is subject to estate taxes.[6]

AT END OF TRUST TERM. Any property remaining in the trust, including appreciation and earnings, is paid to the trust beneficiaries (i.e., the remainder interest). Provided the grantor lives to the end of the trust term (and does not die within 3 years of the transfer), this property is not subject to estate taxes.[7]

Footnotes on page 61

TRUST ESTABLISHED

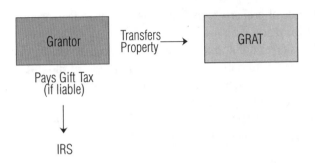

| Grantor | Transfers Property → | GRAT |

Pays Gift Tax
(if liable)

↓

IRS

DURING TRUST TERM

| Grantor (pays taxes on trust income) | ← Pays Annuity (tax-free) | GRAT |

IF GRANTOR DIES BEFORE END OF TRUST TERM

| Grantor's Estate | ← Continues Annuity Payments | GRAT (property subject to estate taxes) |

AT END OF TRUST TERM

If Grantor lives to end
of trust term, property
in GRAT is not subject
to estate taxes.

GRAT

Remainder
Paid to

↓

Trust
Beneficiaries

INFORMATION REQUIRED FOR ANALYSIS & PROPOSAL

1. Fair market value of property transferred to trust (provide appropriate appraisals).
2. Term of trust (in years).
3. Annuity to be paid (as dollar amount or percent of initial trust value).
4. Payment frequency (annually, semiannually, quarterly, or monthly).
5. Increase in annuity as a percent, if any (not to exceed 120 percent of prior year).
6. Age of grantor (if grantor retains reversion).
7. Date of transfer to trust (needed to set payment dates and determine Section 7520 interest rate as published monthly by IRS).

CROSS REFERENCES TO TAX FACTS ON INVESTMENTS (2011)

Q 7558. Grantor trust and how it is taxed.

Q 7584. Types of gifts subject to gift tax.

Q 7596. Gift tax exclusions.

Q 7599. Unified credit and how it is applied against gift tax.

Q 7601. Valuation of property for gift tax purposes.

Q 7617. General discussion of the Chapter 14 valuation rules.

Q 7619. Special valuation rules under Chapter 14 that apply to transfer of an interest in trust, to include grantor retained annuity trusts.

Footnotes

[1] Section 2702 of the Internal Revenue Code provides the basic rule that if a transferor makes a gift in trust for the benefit of the *transferor's family,* for purposes of gift taxation any interest retained by the transferor (grantor) will be valued at zero (the so-called "zero-value rule"). If the retained interest has no value, then the gift tax value of the remainder interest is equal to the full fair market value of the property transferred to the trust (not a good gift-tax result for the transferor). But this zero-value rule does not apply when the retained interest is a "qualified annuity interest" meeting requirements set forth under Treasury Regulations (e.g., trust must be irrevocable, mandatory payments must be made at least annually, no payments may be made to anyone other than the grantor, and increases in annuity payments may not be greater than 120 percent of the prior year's payment). A "qualified annuity interest" is valued using the valuation tables provided by Code Section 7520 and a "Section 7520" interest rate in effect for the month in which the valuation date occurs (i.e., when the property is transferred to the GRAT). This chart describes a GRAT meeting the requirements for a qualified annuity interest (i.e., grantor's children are trust beneficiaries).

[2] The effectiveness of the GRAT can be further enhanced by selecting assets that offer discounts for lack of control and marketability (e.g., a family limited partnership, page 163).

[3] A "zeroed out" GRAT occurs when the value of the grantor-retained annuity is essentially equal to the value of the asset transferred to the trust, resulting in a nominal gift or no gift because the remainder interest has virtually no value for gift tax purposes.

[4] Conversely, exposure to the gift tax is increased when the value of the retained annuity is decreased and the value of the remainder interest is increased. It is important to keep the value of the gift low, as the transfer to the trust is considered a gift of a future interest and the $13,000 gift tax annual exclusion is not available (see chart on page 47). To the extent there is available unified credit, it is allocated to the gift; otherwise, the grantor pays a gift tax on the transfer.

[5] The grantor trust rules are discussed on page 418.

[6] The effectiveness of the GRAT as a wealth transferring device is dependent upon: (1) the grantor surviving the trust term (i.e., not dying until the remainder interest passes to the trust beneficiaries); and (2) the property held in the trust appreciating at a rate that is higher than the Section 7520 interest rate used to determine the present value of the annuity paid to the grantor (i.e., the more the appreciation, the more that will pass to the trust beneficiaries free of both gift and estate taxes). Should the grantor die before the end of the trust term, any unified credit utilized when making the gift would be restored to the estate (i.e., the tax effect is the same as if the GRAT had never existed).

[7] Lower Section 7520 interest rates make GRATs particularly attractive, since the effect is to allow more assets to be placed in trust with less exposure to the gift tax (see footnote 1 above). For example, assume that a grantor transfers an asset with a fair market value of $100,000 into either: (1) a 5-year GRAT paying the grantor a fixed annuity of $20,000 per year; or (2) a 10-year GRAT paying the grantor a fixed annuity of $10,000 per year; with the remainder interest passing to the grantor's children. The following table compares the results of varying Section 7520 interest rates and GRAT durations.

		GRAT Funded With $100,000			
		$20,000/year for 5-years		$10,000/year for 10-years	
Date	Section 7520 Interest Rate	Retained Annuity	Gift of Remainder	Retained Annuity	Gift of Remainder
Dec - 2009	3.2%	$91,074	$8,926	$84,438	$15,562
Dec - 2006	5.8%	$84,708	$15,292	$74,303	$25,697
Dec - 2000	7.0%	$82,004	$17,996	$70,236	$29,764

PRIVATE SPLIT-DOLLAR

Whereas a traditional split-dollar plan involves an employer and an employee, a private split-dollar plan is an agreement between individuals, or between an individual and a trust.[1] A private split-dollar plan enables an insured to *both* have the policy cash values available for emergency and retirement purposes and exclude life insurance proceeds from his estate. For example, assume that a married couple wishes to establish a private split-dollar plan.[2]

DURING LIFETIME. The individual who will become the insured establishes an irrevocable life insurance trust with his spouse and children as trust beneficiaries.[3] The trustee then applies for a life insurance policy on his life and enters into a collateral assignment split-dollar agreement with the spouse. This agreement provides for the sharing of both premiums and death benefits between the spouse and the trust. However, the spouse owns all cash values and retains the sole right to borrow against or withdraw policy cash valves.[4]

The trust's share of the premium is equal to the "economic benefit" of the death benefit payable to the trust.[5] To fund the trust's portion of the premium, the insured makes annual gifts to the trust. These will qualify as "present interest" gifts provided the trust beneficiaries have Crummey withdrawal powers.[6]

The spouse pays the balance of the premium. These funds either come from the spouse's separate property or are given by the grantor (insured) to his spouse free of any gift tax liability (i.e., the marital deduction enables married persons to pass unlimited amounts of property to each other during lifetime or upon death free of gift or estate taxes).[7]

Prior to or during retirement the spouse can access policy cash values free of income taxes through withdrawals or loans against the policy. By this means the insured has indirect access to the cash values.[8]

UPON DEATH. The death benefit payable to the spouse is the greater of the total premiums paid by the spouse or the policy cash values (less any outstanding loans). The trust receives the balance of the death benefit. Since the insured had no incidents of ownership in the policy, none of the death benefit is included in his estate.[9] Guided by the specific provisions of the trust, these estate tax-free proceeds are used to pay trust income and principal to the trust beneficiaries.

Footnotes on page 65

DURING LIFETIME

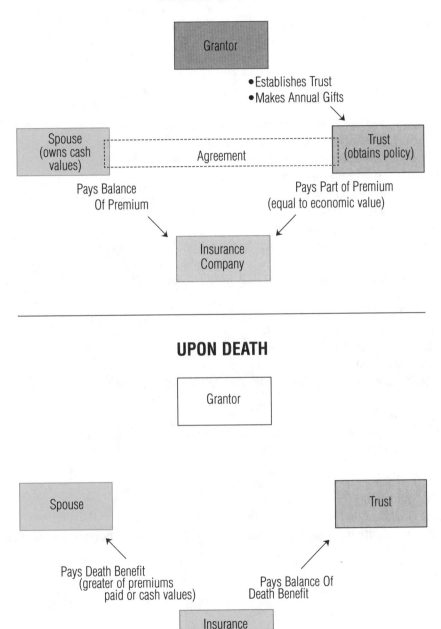

Grantor

- Establishes Trust
- Makes Annual Gifts

Spouse
(owns cash
values)

Agreement

Trust
(obtains policy)

Pays Balance
Of Premium

Pays Part of Premium
(equal to economic value)

Insurance
Company

UPON DEATH

Grantor

Spouse

Trust

Pays Death Benefit
(greater of premiums
paid or cash values)

Pays Balance Of
Death Benefit

Insurance
Company

INFORMATION REQUIRED FOR ANALYSIS & PROPOSAL

1. Name of individual to be insured.
2. Sex.
3. Date of birth.
4. Smoker/nonsmoker.
5. Amount of desired death benefit.

Attorney Drafting Trust Instrument And Split-Dollar Agreement Must Also Know
6. To whom, in what amounts, and when trust *income* is to be paid.
7. To whom, in what amounts, and when trust *corpus* is to be paid.
8. Trustee during insured's lifetime.
9. Trustee after insured's death.
10. Names of beneficiaries.
11. Ages of minor beneficiaries.
12. Name of spouse who will be a party to the split-dollar agreement.

CROSS REFERENCES TO TAX FACTS ON INSURANCE & EMPLOYEE BENEFITS (2011)

Split-Dollar
Q 98.   Death proceeds received by trust free of income taxes.
Q 122.   Description of private split-dollar and how it is taxed.
Q 3789. Description of split-dollar.
Q 3792. Income tax consequences of transfer or "rollout" of split-dollar policy.

Estate Tax
Q 121.   When proceeds either included or excluded from insured's estate.
Q 245.   Estate taxation of split-dollar.

Gift Tax
Q 64.   Gift taxation of split-dollar.
Q 104.   Qualification for annual gift tax exclusion.
Q 106.   Qualification for annual exclusion of gifts to trust to pay premiums (Crummey rules).

Footnotes

[1] Prior to 2002 there was little authority for private split-dollar plans. In Notice 2002-8 the IRS acknowledged the existence of private split-dollar plans without actually sanctioning them. The final split-dollar regulations issued in 2003 specifically state that they apply "for gift tax purposes, including private split-dollar life insurance arrangements." Such affirmative guidance on how to structure private split-dollar plans may encourage more of these plans to be established for wealth transfer purposes.

[2] When involving family members, such an arrangement is also referred to as "family split-dollar."

[3] This trust would be similar to that shown in the Life Insurance Trust chart on page 51. Private split-dollar involving both an irrevocable life insurance trust and a split-dollar plan requires a great deal of planning, implementation, and ongoing administration. If estate tax-free death benefits are important, but access to cash values is unimportant, then third party ownership or an irrevocable life insurance trust should be considered. On the other hand, if access to cash values is important, but estate tax-free death benefits are unimportant, then the insured might better own the policy (see the discussion of life insurance as property on page 70).

[4] This is a "nonequity collateral assignment plan" intended to be taxed under the economic benefit regime set forth in the split-dollar regulations (compare with other designs discussed on page 226). As the insured ages, a plan subject to gift taxation under the economic benefit regime can become difficult to maintain. This is due to the substantial gifts that must be made to the trust to cover the increasing value of the insurance coverage (see footnote 3, page 229). When there is a need for permanent life insurance, such as to pay estate taxes, it is important to establish an "exit strategy" for maintaining the policy (see Split-Dollar Rollout, page 528).

[5] Under the regulations, this "economic benefit" is measured by "life insurance premium factors" to be published by the IRS. Until these factors become available, the Table 2001 rates on page 552 should be permissible.

[6] For an expanded discussion of Crummey withdrawal powers, see page 379. As the insured gets older the trust's portion of the premium will increase substantially, particularly if the insured lives past age 80 (see footnote 3, page 229). If the spouse is also a trust beneficiary, failure of the trust to pay its portion of the premium could be considered a gift by the spouse to the trust with a retained life interest. This would cause a portion of death proceeds to be included in the *spouse's* estate (see discussion of retained life estate on page 410). To avoid imputed gifts from the spouse to the trust, the trust must continue paying for any death benefits it receives (even if premiums are not currently being paid). If the trust's portion of the premium exceeds the amount that can be qualified as a present interest gift to the trust, then a portion of the gift becomes taxable and the insured must either use some of his unified credit or pay gift taxes. Attempts to avoid these problems have involved: (1) establishing a trust-owned premium prepayment account; and (2) reducing in later years the death benefit paid to the trust.

[7] The marital deduction is more fully discussed on page 450.

[8] A stable marriage and confidence in the noninsured spouse is essential. To avoid income taxation, withdrawals are made up to the spouse's income tax basis in the policy. Thereafter, loans could be taken against the policy (see page 458). Other less attractive alternatives involve having the cash values owned by a QTIP trust, adult child, S corporation, or limited partnership.

[9] However, if the spouse dies *before* the insured, and the spouse's interests in the policy cash values pass in any way that cause the insured to have an incident of ownership in the policy, upon his subsequent death the death proceeds will be included in his estate. This means that the insured cannot be a trustee of a trust holding the policy, nor can he act as executor of the deceased spouse's estate if the policy is part of the estate. See discussion of incidents of ownership on page 409.

INTENTIONALLY DEFECTIVE TRUST

The intentionally defective trust is a wealth-transferring device used by larger estates. It is an irrevocable trust that has been carefully drafted to cause the grantor to be taxed on trust income, yet have trust assets excluded from the grantor's estate.[1] Once established, it can offer multiple planning opportunities and benefits, particularly when combined with both gifts and installment sales.[2]

TRUST ESTABLISHED. When establishing the trust, the grantor will typically retain a right to substitute assets of equivalent value. Retention of this right in a nonfiduciary capacity violates one of the grantor trust rules.[3] The grantor is then considered the "owner" of the trust for income tax purposes, but not for estate, gift, and generation-skipping tax purposes. As to income taxes, the grantor and the trust are considered one and the same; trust income, deductions, and credits are passed through to the grantor.

Once established, the grantor then makes a gift of cash or other liquid assets to the trust, equal in value to 10 percent or more of the value of the property that will be sold to the trust in the subsequent installment sale.[4]

INSTALLMENT SALE. Thereafter, the grantor and the trustee enter into a sales agreement providing for the purchase of additional assets from the grantor at fair market value. Under this agreement the trustee gives the grantor an installment note providing for payment of interest only for a number of years, followed by a balloon payment of principal at the end of the term.[5] The assets sold will typically consist of property subject to a valuation discount (e.g., a non-controlling interest in a limited partnership, a limited liability company, or an S corporation).[6] The amount of this valuation discount is immediately removed from the grantor's estate.[7]

SUBSEQUENT ADVANTAGES. Payment of taxes by the grantor upon the trust income enables the trust to grow income tax-free, and is a tax-free gift from the grantor to the trust beneficiaries. The interest and principal payments by the trust are "tax neutral," meaning that they have no income tax consequences for either the grantor or the trust. Any growth of invested trust assets is excluded from the grantor's estate.[8]

If appropriate, the trustee could also use cash flow in excess of required interest payments to purchase life insurance on the grantor. Since the grantor/insured is not the "owner" of the trust for estate tax purposes, the death proceeds would be excluded from the grantor's estate.

Footnotes on page 69

TRUST ESTABLISHED

INSTALLMENT SALE

SUBSEQUENT ADVANTAGES

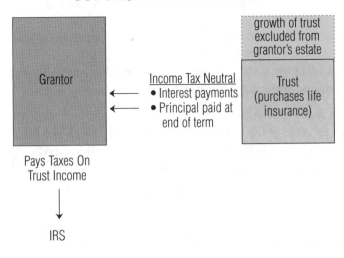

INFORMATION REQUIRED FOR ANALYSIS & PROPOSAL

1. Names and ages of trust beneficiaries.
2. To who, in what amounts, and when trust income is to be paid?
3. To who, in what amounts, and when trust corpus is to be paid?
4. Trustee(s) of trust (both before and after grantor's death).
5. Client's: (a) Date of birth; (b) Sex; (c) Smoker/nonsmoker.
6. Client's annual taxable income (to determine marginal tax bracket).
7. Approximate size of estates of both client and spouse (generally, gross estates less outstanding debts and liabilities).
8. Extent to which client and spouse have used their annual gift exclusion ($13,000 each in 2010 and 2011).
9. Extent to which client and spouse have each used their available gift tax unified credit ($1,730,800 each in 2011, allowing them to each give $5,000,000 of property).
10. Property available for the initial gift.
11. Nature of income-property available for installment sale (preferably, an asset subject to valuation discount).
12. Client's cost basis in income-property.
13. Anticipated annual income from income-property.
14. Length (term) of the installment note.
15. Minimum interest rate to be paid on installment note (applicable federal rate).

CROSS REFERENCES TO TAX FACTS ON INSURANCE & EMPLOYEE BENEFITS (2011)

Income Tax

Q 92. When life insurance trust will provide income tax savings for grantor.

Q 93. Income of trust used to pay premiums on life insurance policy insuring grantor is taxed to grantor.

Q 94. Income of trust used to pay premiums on life insurance policy insuring grantor's spouse is taxed to grantor.

Q 97. With a "defective trust," grantor is allowed to take income tax deduction for interest paid on loan against trust-owned policy.

Estate Tax

Q 121. When proceeds of life insurance either included or excluded from insured's estate.

Q 125. Transfer of income-producing property to trust. When proceeds of life insurance either included or excluded from insured's estate.

CROSS REFERENCES TO TAX FACTS ON INVESTMENTS (2011)

Q 7512. Installment sale and how it is taxed.

Q 7558. Grantor trust and how it is taxed.

Q 7599. Gift tax unified credit.

Footnotes

[1] This trust is also referred to as a "grantor trust," or an "intentionally defective irrevocable trust (IDIT)." Historically, the inadvertent inclusion of these powers in a trust resulted in the grantor being taxed on the trust income. Since the grantor was usually in a *higher* tax bracket than the trust, the results were undesirable, and the trust was considered defective. Today, the grantor will likely be in a *lower* tax bracket than the trust (compare the federal income tax tables on page 549).

[2] The intentionally defective trust is most often merely funded with a large gift of income-producing property. The additional installment sale funding is typically used when the grantor has no available gift tax exemption, or when the needs of the trust are very large (e.g., to pay premiums on a very large life insurance policy).

[3] See page 418 for a more complete explanation of the grantor trust rules, and other applications of the defective trust.

[4] In order to keep the trust free of any generation-skipping transfer taxes (GSTT), the grantor should file a gift tax return allocating GST exemption to the trust in the amount of the gift. However, provided it falls within the grantor's available annual exclusion and/or gift tax exemption, the gift can be made without paying gift taxes (see chart, Gifts & Split-Gifts on page 47). The primary reason for making this initial gift is to establish that the trust has a degree of independence from the grantor. The concern here is that the IRS might challenge the installment sale as a sham, by arguing that it is unlikely a valuable asset would be sold to someone who has no ability to pay. Funding of the trust prior to the installment sale will also help defend against a challenge by the IRS that the asset should be brought back into the grantor's estate under the Section 2036(a)(1) theory that the sale was actually a transfer with a retained interest. See also, the discussion on page 410.

[5] Unlike the assets sold, the note will not appreciate in the grantor's estate. However, upon the grantor's death the assets will not receive a stepped-up basis. Although the term of the note could be 20 years or more, to avoid any suggestion that the transaction creates an income interest for the grantor's lifetime, the term should be less than the grantor's life expectancy. The federal mid-term rate is used for installment notes of more than three years, and not more than nine years; whereas, the higher federal long-term rate is used for notes of more than nine years. Choice of a shorter deferral period takes advantage of lower interest rates, reduces the amount paid to the grantor, and improves the chances that the loan will be paid off prior to the grantor's death. See footnote 7, below.

[6] Such discounts can range from 35 percent to as much as 65 percent. Rather than selling assets directly to the trust, the grantor will often place the assets in a family limited partnership, which is then sold at a discount to the trust.

[7] If the grantor dies prior to final payment, the estate includes the promissory note. There is disagreement among commentators, as to whether gain on the outstanding note must be recognized upon the grantor's death (i.e., at death the defective trust becomes non-defective, and the estate becomes a separate tax-paying entity).

[8] The installment sale to a defective grantor trust resembles a grantor retained annuity trust (GRAT). See page 419. Both are intended to remove an asset from the grantor's estate and affect a tax-free transfer of assets to heirs. Although many features of the defective grantor trust are superior to a GRAT, unlike the GRAT there is no specific statutory authority for a defective trust (the IRS will not issue a ruling on them). The defective trust is a sophisticated estate planning technique that should only be undertaken with the advice of competent tax counsel.

LIFE INSURANCE AS PROPERTY

Life insurance differs from most other kinds of contracts because life insurance can potentially place specific rights in three types of persons: the *insured*, the *owner*, and the *beneficiary*. These characteristics make life insurance unique when compared to other types of property. In fact, their arrangement will determine whether or not the death benefit will be subject to estate or even gift taxes.[1]

A Death proceeds *Will* **be included in the gross estate** if the insured possesses any incidents of ownership in the contract at the time of his death, or within three years of his death, no matter who might be the beneficiary.[2]

B Likewise, when the insured's estate is named beneficiary, the death proceeds will be included in the gross estate, even though the insured may have possessed no incidents of ownership.

C Death proceeds *Will Not* **be included in the gross estate** of the insured if he possesses no incidents of ownership in the policy at death or within three years before death and proceeds are not payable to his estate. However, there may be gift tax problems where the insured, the owner, and the beneficiary are all different persons. This arises, for example, where one spouse is the insured, the other spouse the owner (with a right to change beneficiaries), and a child the beneficiary. When the insured dies, the surviving spouse will be considered as having made a gift of the death proceeds to the child. For purposes of the gift tax, property owned by one person (the surviving spouse) is transferred upon the insured's death to another (the child). This deemed transfer from owner to beneficiary is a gift and could result in the surviving spouse having to pay a *gift tax*, or in having to use up some or all of the available unified credit.[3]

D To avoid these estate and gift tax problems, all incidents of ownership should be held by the beneficiary from the issuance of the policy.[4] For example, one individual would be the insured and the policy would be owned by and payable to either his spouse, a child, or an irrevocable life insurance trust.[5] This arrangement will assure that the proceeds from the life insurance contract are received untouched, untaxed, and on time: **untouched** in that they would be payable directly to the heirs; **untaxed** in that they would be free of income and estate taxes; and **on time** in that they would be paid when needed at death, whether death occurs immediately or at some indefinite time in the future.[6]

Footnotes on page 73

Death Proceeds WILL Be Included In Estate

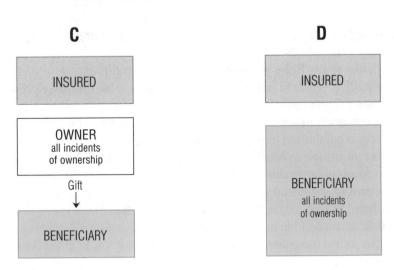

A

INSURED
any incident
of ownership

BENEFICIARY

B

INSURED

OWNER
all incidents
of ownership

BENEFICIARY
(estate of insured)

Death Proceeds WILL NOT Be Included In Estate

C

INSURED

OWNER
all incidents
of ownership

Gift
↓

BENEFICIARY

D

INSURED

BENEFICIARY
all incidents
of ownership

INFORMATION REQUIRED FOR ANALYSIS & PROPOSAL

1. Obtain copies of all insurance policies.
2. Determine original applicant, owner and beneficiary from photostat copy of application contained in policy.
3. Review endorsements that may reveal a subsequent change of owner or beneficiary.
4. Ascertain premium payor.

TRANSFER FOR VALUE

The following transfers of ownership will not violate the transfer for value rules:

1. A bona fide gift (as to another family member) – is not considered to be a transfer for value.
2. Transfers for value to:
   a. the insured.
   b. a partner of the insured.
   c. a partnership in which the insured is a partner.
   d. a corporation in which the insured is a stockholder or an officer.
   e. a corporation from another corporation in a tax-free reorganization.

Note: An expanded discussion of these rules is contained on pages 541-542.

CROSS REFERENCES TO TAX FACTS ON INSURANCE & EMPLOYEE BENEFITS (2011)

Q 7.   Rules for taxing living proceeds of life insurance contracts.
Q 32.   For death proceeds to be excludable from income, a life insurance policy must meet certain requirements.
Q 40.   Circumstances under which death proceeds are included in insured's gross estate.
Q 41.   Proceeds payable to estate are included in gross estate.
Q 44.   Proceeds payable to beneficiary other than estate yet included in gross estate.
Q 45.   "Incidents of ownership" which cause death proceeds to be included in estate.
Q 46.   Incident of ownership as fiduciary will generally not cause death proceeds to be included in gross estate (but see Fifth Circuit position in text).
Q 52.   Estate taxation of life insurance policy given away within 3 years of death.
Q 156. Policy owned by someone other than insured can result in gift if beneficiary is not also owner.
Q 206. Sale or other transfer for value will cause loss of income tax exemption for death proceeds.
Q 207. Transactions that constitute a "transfer for value."
Q 3644. Basic discussion of the life insurance contract.

Footnotes

[1] As property, the cash values of a life insurance policy are potentially subject to income taxes when there is a *withdrawal* from or *surrender* of the policy. However, when received, the cash values are taxed under the "cost recovery rules," meaning that such amounts are included in gross income only to the extent they exceed the investment in the policy (e.g., cash surrender values of $21,000 and total premiums of $15,000 would result in a $6,000 taxable gain, assuming no dividends and no prior distributions from the policy). A *loan* is not includable in income provided the policy is not a modified endowment contract. Distributions and loans from a modified endowment contract are taxed under different rules (see expanded discussion on pages 441-442).

[2] Thus, if the insured owns a contract of insurance on his own life and then makes a gift of the policy to another, he would have to live *more than* 3 years before the proceeds would be excluded from his estate. An incident of ownership includes the right to:

     a. change the beneficiary.
     b. surrender or cancel the policy.
     c. assign the policy.
     d. revoke an assignment.
     e. pledge the policy for a loan.
     f. obtain a policy loan.

[3] As shown in Diagram "C" of the chart, *gift* tax consequences may result when owner and beneficiary are not the same (i.e., "non-parallel" owner and beneficiary). However, when the deemed transfer of death proceeds occurs in a corporate setting, it can cause serious *income* tax problems when a contract owned by a corporation pays a death benefit to the widow of a stockholder. Payment of the death benefit will likely be non-deductible to the corporation and taxable as a *dividend* to the widow – despite the fact that under a different arrangement the payment could have qualified as a tax-free receipt of death proceeds. At best, the corporation could deduct the payment as a salary continuation expense, but the payment would be includable in the gross income of the estate or beneficiary as "income in respect of a decedent." See discussion on page 425.

[4] After numerous losses, including the *Leder, Headrick,* and *Perry* cases, the Internal Revenue Service issued an action on decision announcing it would no longer litigate the issue of whether life insurance proceeds are includable in the insured's estate, where the life insurance policy is procured by a third party at the instance of the insured, the insured pays the insurance premiums, and the insured dies within three years of procurement of the policy by the third person (i.e., the "beamed transfer" theory). For an expanded discussion, see Estate Taxation of Life Insurance, pages 409-410. Also see ownership and beneficiary arrangements on page 89.

[5] With the unlimited marital deduction the decedent spouse's estate may well be free of federal estate taxes, but substantial taxes may be levied at the surviving spouse's death. For this reason, if it is desired to reduce exposure to estate taxes, the spouse of the insured should *not* be owner and beneficiary of the policy. Where the spouse is both owner and beneficiary, the arrangement is often referred to as a "cross-owned policy" and the death benefit received upon the insured's death will *increase* the surviving spouse's estate. In order to shift these death benefits from one generation to another free of estate taxes, it may be advisable to have the policy owned by an adult child, or placed in a Life Insurance Trust, as described in the chart on page 51. See also the discussion of minors and life insurance on page 459.

[6] The underlying principles discussed in this chart are as applicable to the analysis of existing policies as they are to proposed new insurance coverage. With many new clients, some of the easiest, yet most effective, estate planning recommendations will come from a policy audit involving an analysis and restructuring of the ownership and beneficiary provisions of existing insurance. As to new insurance, it is important to be familiar with the requirement that an applicant have an insurable interest in the life to be insured (see expanded discussion, page 429). Life insurance proceeds payable to a C corporation are not necessarily free of income taxes (see Corporate Alternative Minimum Tax, pages 374-376. Also, for the death benefits to be income tax-free, employer-owned life insurance must meet strict notice and consent requirements (see Company Owned Life Insurance (COLI), pages 367-369).

LIFE INSURANCE PRODUCTS

TERM INSURANCE. If an estate plan is to be built on a solid foundation, life insurance protection is essential. Term insurance provides protection for a *limited* period of time for a younger person whose insurance needs must be met on a modest budget. However, the premium for this protection will usually increase each and every year, until it becomes prohibitively expensive for most people to maintain. While term insurance can provide a lot of protection for a lesser cost, it builds no cash values and has no permanent values. In this sense it has been described as "rented" but not "owned."[1]

PERMANENT INSURANCE, in contrast to term insurance, provides for a tax-deferred build-up of cash values over the life of the contract.[2] This cash value element, combined with level or limited premium increases, means that the death benefit will be available for an *unlimited* period. While the outlay for permanent insurance is usually greater than term insurance in the early years, most plans provide for payment of a level premium. Even if the plan requires an increasing premium, these increases are usually limited in both amount and duration. Typically, both the cash values and the death benefits are guaranteed, unless they are dependent upon payment of projected dividends.[3]

UNIVERSAL LIFE INSURANCE offers flexible premium payments, an adjustable death benefit, and cash values that are sensitive to current interest rates.[4] Most contracts pay a *current interest rate* which is highly competitive with that available in the money market. However, these rates are subject to change and are not guaranteed over the life of the contract. The *guaranteed interest rate* is usually very modest and will likely result in a lapse of the policy if additional premiums are not paid. Likewise, most universal life policies offer lower *current (nonguaranteed) mortality* charges, but provided for higher *guaranteed mortality* charges. Taken together, the lower guaranteed interest rate and higher guaranteed mortality charges represent the "down-side risk" of a universal life contract. The policyholder is asked to accept this risk in return for the opportunity to receive the benefits of higher current interest rates and lower charges for the amount-at-risk element in the contract.[5]

VARIABLE LIFE INSURANCE is similar to universal life insurance, except that the underlying cash values can be invested in an equity portfolio, typically a mutual fund or bonds.[6] The policyowner is usually given the opportunity to redirect his investment to another portfolio although some limitations and restrictions may be imposed.[7]

Footnotes on page 77

TERM LIFE INSURANCE
(increasing premium)

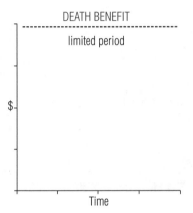

PERMANENT INSURANCE
(fixed premium)

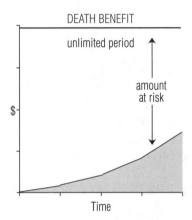

UNIVERSAL LIFE INSURANCE
(flexible premium)

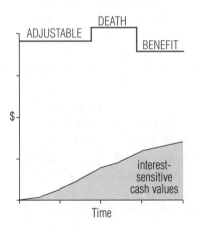

VARIABLE LIFE INSURANCE
(flexible premium)

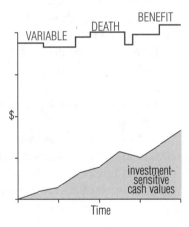

INFORMATION REQUIRED FOR ANALYSIS & PROPOSAL

1. Name of individual to be insured.
2. Sex.
3. Date of birth.
4. Smoker/nonsmoker.

To Determine Type of Contract
5. Reasons for purchase – temporary vs. permanent need.
6. Funds available for purchase – term vs. permanent (cash value).
7. Attitude toward risk – suitability for variable life.
8. Income – suitability for variable life.
9. Net worth – suitability for variable life.

CROSS REFERENCES TO TAX FACTS ON INSURANCE & EMPLOYEE BENEFITS (2011)

Q 2.   Premiums for personal life insurance not deductible.

Q 5.   Annual cash value increases generally not taxable income to policyholder.

Q 8.   Taxation of distributions from policies classified as modified endowment contracts.

Q 20.   Income tax consequences to seller of life insurance or endowment contract.

Q 21.   Income tax consequences to purchaser of life insurance or endowment contract.

Q 22.   When exchange of one contract for another is considered nontaxable.

Q 26.   Income taxation of an "accelerated death benefit."

Q 30.   Death proceeds generally received free of income taxes.

Q 32.   For death proceeds to be excludable from income, a life insurance policy must meet certain requirements.

Q 36.   Income taxation of death proceeds of policy previously transferred for value.

Q 37.   Income taxation of death proceeds of policy previously transferred as a gift.

Q 141.   Estate taxation of life insurance policy that insures more than one life.

Q 153.   Gift taxation of life insurance policy that insures more than one life.

Q 3539. Income tax results when contract surrendered for cash values.

Q 3644. Basic discussion of the life insurance contract.

Q 3771. Income taxation of life insurance policy that insures more than one life.

Footnotes

[1] Term insurance is available in many forms, the most common being annual renewable, five-year renewable (and/or convertible), 10-year renewable and convertible (R&C), 15-year R&C, 20-year R&C, and term to a specific age, such as age 65. A specialized form of term insurance, decreasing term, is also available, and usually purchased to cover a decreasing loan or mortgage obligation. Term insurance can be tailored to fit almost any temporary insurance need – level, decreasing, or even increasing.

[2] Permanent life insurance is often called "whole life." This is because, so long as the policy remains in force, it provides protection for the "whole of life." The whole of life is assumed to be to age 100 under many mortality tables, although in recent years lesser ages have been used (i.e., age 90 or 95). If the insured lives to age 100, the policy endows with the cash values equaling the face amount of the policy.

[3] Both term and permanent insurance are available as *participating* policies, which offer the opportunity for dividends that may be used to: reduce the premium outlay; purchase paid-up additions (which accrue their own cash values); enhance the amount of available death benefit through a combination of one-year term insurance and paid-up additions (the fifth dividend option); or augment the cash values by being left to accumulate at interest.

[4] Universal life insurance has many unique features not found in traditional whole life policies. Most importantly, your client *controls* many aspects of the contract because of the built-in flexibility of the universal life policy. Specific features of universal life include:

    a. An adjustable death benefit that may be increased or decreased to suit the obligations and needs of the insured (often subject to insurability if the death benefit is increased).

    b. Tax-deferred current interest earnings on cash values.

    c. Flexible premiums that allow changes in payments to suit individual needs (but see the discussion regarding life insurance premium limitations, pages 441-442).

[5] Interest-sensitive whole life is a hybrid between permanent (whole life) insurance and universal life insurance. It is also known as excess-interest whole life, current assumption whole life, irreplaceable life, pseudo universal life, fixed premium universal life, and adjustable cash value whole life. The product typically requires a fixed premium, and in return provides a *guaranteed* death benefit and minimum interest rates, and current higher nonguaranteed interest rates. Premiums are usually fixed, although additional funds can be "dumped" into the policy in order to vanish, or short pay, premiums. As with universal life, a surrender charge is often assessed when the contract is surrendered in the early years, although some contracts allow withdrawals of "excess" earnings. A "bailout feature" may be offered, which enables the policyholder to withdraw funds without penalty if the credited interest rate drops below a certain level.

[6] Variable life insurance is considered a fourth type of insurance, in that the death benefit and cash values reflect the performance of an underlying portfolio of equity investments, such as stocks and bonds. While these investments can provide a hedge against inflation, and the possibility for growth in both cash reserves and death benefits, there is also the risk that investment performance will be poor and that the cash reserves will decrease or be lost. Since variable life insurance is a security, the agent must hold a valid federal securities license (and state license where required) in order to sell the product. In addition, *a prospectus must be delivered* with or preceding a specific proposal to a prospect or client.

[7] In recent years, joint life insurance policies insuring multiple-lives have become popular for funding a variety of insurance needs (see First-To-Die Insurance, page 415, and Survivorship Life Insurance, page 535). Company owned life insurance (COLI) is used to fund a number of nonqualified benefits (pages 367-369). A table of comparative Insurance Company Ratings is set forth on page 567. See also, Life Insurance Default Risk, page 438.

DISCOUNTED DOLLARS

The death benefits of a life insurance contract are often referred to as "discounted," in the sense that payment of a relatively small yearly premium, from 1 to 5 percent of the death benefit, depending upon age and rating category, will guarantee that the full face amount will be available when needed.

In this sense, the purchase of life insurance is analogous to the *leverage* obtained by the individual who invests in property with a small down payment and a large mortgage. The investor expects to benefit from the future appreciation of an asset worth many times his cash investment, whereas payment of modest insurance premiums enables the insured to provide a substantial death benefit as security for his family.

WITH INSURANCE, assume that a 35-year-old insured purchases $100,000 of level death protection for his family requiring an annual premium of $1,000 per year.[1] This purchase guarantees $100,000 of discounted dollars payable upon death at any time. The *discount* is represented by the difference between the death benefit and *cumulative premiums* paid.[2] After 20 years the discount would amount to $80,000 ($100,000 - $20,000). If our insured lives for 40 years and pays premiums totaling $40,000 there is still a discount of $60,000.[3]

WITHOUT INSURANCE, a surviving family might be forced to borrow in order to pay estate settlement costs. Repaying a 6 percent loan of $100,000 in 10 equal annual installments requires total payments of $135,870.[4] If the family were able to obtain a 40-year loan under the same terms, its total payments would be $265,880. However, it is unlikely that a surviving family would be able to borrow money at only 6 percent interest. A more realistic rate would probably be 12 percent, in which case the family's total repayments are more likely to be $176,990 over 10 years, or $485,240 over 40 years.

Paying estate settlement costs with the discounted dollars of life insurance is far better than putting a surviving family in the position of having to borrow large sums of money at high rates of interest. Most families would find it far easier to pay premiums totaling $40,000 over a 40-year period than to make loan repayments of $485,240 over a similar period of time.[5] Properly arranged, the discounted dollars provided from a life insurance contract will be received untouched, untaxed, and on time: **untouched** in that they are paid directly to the beneficiary; **untaxed** in that they are free of income and estate taxes; and **on time** in that they are paid when needed, whenever death occurs.[6]

Footnotes on page 81

WITH LIFE INSURANCE

WITHOUT LIFE INSURANCE

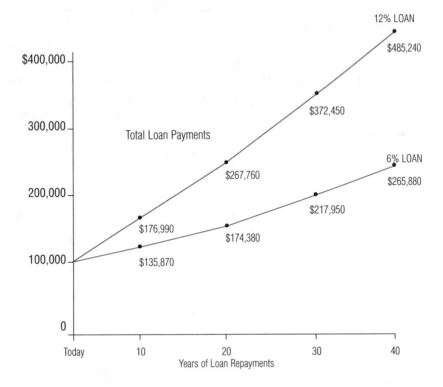

WHY LIFE INSURANCE?

Estate and business continuation plans are only as good as the financial arrangements that support them. The cash for estate settlement costs must come from somewhere. The family must have the cash sooner or later, since everyone is going to die. The only question is when.

There are three ways to pay these estate settlement costs:

(1) *From Estate Resources – the 100% method.* But in most cases the estate will not have sufficient liquid assets. Even when the costs can be paid by selling estate assets, the family pays 100-cent dollars from the decedent's hard-earned and hard-taxed estate. Under the Insurance Plan, the family pays the costs with discounted dollars – discounted to the extent that the cumulative premiums paid will likely be far less than the insurance proceeds received by the family.

(2) *By Borrowing the Money – the 100%+ method.* But the credit standing of the family could be affected by the decedent's death. Changing economic trends also influence a lender's decisions about making loans. By borrowing, the family is obligated to pay interest as well as to pay back the principal. Under the Insurance Plan, the borrower pays the equivalent of 1 to 5 percent interest during his life and his family never has to worry about paying back the principal.

(3) *The Insurance Plan – the discounted dollars method.* This is the only funding device that will guarantee a definite sum of money to be available at an indefinite time in the future. The cost of that money will be only a few cents on the dollar when death occurs in the early years of the contract, and may involve a substantial discount even when death does not come for many years. Furthermore, this money will be income tax-free to the family, since the death proceeds of life insurance are received free of federal income tax.

Footnotes

[1] This example assumes the purchase of a non-participating permanent contract. If participating insurance were illustrated, the premium might be higher, but dividends would likely be available. If the dividends were used to *reduce* premiums, the "cumulative premiums" would increase at a decreasing, or slower, rate. If the dividends were used to buy *paid-up additions* (the fifth dividend option), the "death benefit" would not be level, but would increase from year to year. If the dividends were used to purchase *term insurance*, then the "death benefit" would also increase, but at a much faster rate, until the age at which the term coverage was no longer available. At this point, the coverage in excess of the basic amount initially issued would terminate.

[2] The *cash values* of the contract have intentionally not been mentioned. The concept of discounted dollars involves only the *cumulative* premium payments relative to the death benefit payable. However, under many circumstances, cumulative cash values will exceed total payments in the later years of the contract, depending upon the product, the age of the insured at the time of issue, and the rating. The term "discounted dollars" should *not* be used in discussing the cost of a life insurance policy. In this regard, see the discussion of the interest adjusted net cost method on page 430.

[3] The actual life expectancy for a 35-year-old male is 43.05 years. For other average future life spans, see the Commissioners 2001 Standard Ordinary Mortality Table (page 555).

[4] From the Amortization Table on page 566, it can be seen that a loan of $1,000 for 10 years at 6 percent interest requires annual payments of $135.87. Therefore, annual payments for a $100,000 loan would be $13,587 (100 x $135.87).

[5] This chart also demonstrates the benefits of *insuring existing liquidity* in an estate. For example, if $100,000 of estate liquidity were preserved for the surviving family, and amortized over 10 years at only 6 percent, they would receive $35,870 of interest income over that period. If they were able to amortize this same $100,000 over 10 years at 12 percent, they would receive $76,990 of interest income. Amortizing the $100,000 at 12 percent for longer periods of 20 and 30 years would yield total interest income of $167,760 and $272,450. Actually, these figures would be higher if the family reinvests the original $100,000 as it is repaid to them. The purchase of discounted dollars will assure that this existing liquidity is preserved. Over 20 years, your client would pay cumulative premiums of $20,000. On the other hand, if your client died, the preserved liquidity would provide at least $167,760 of interest income for the family, if amortized at 12 percent over the same 20-year period.

[6] Life insurance proceeds payable to a C corporation are not necessarily free of income taxes. For an expanded discussion, see Corporate Alternative Minimum Tax, pages 374-376. With a living benefits rider it has become possible for the death benefit to be paid prior to death if the insured has a terminal illness that is expected to result in death within twelve months (see page 343).

CHECKLIST OF DOCUMENTS

		Check As Obtained
1.	Wills – client	❏
	– spouse	❏
2.	Trust Agreements	❏
3.	Life Insurance Policies – client	❏
	– spouse	❏
4.	Medical Insurance Policies	❏
5.	Disability Income Policies	❏
6.	Personal Balance Sheet (or similar listing of cash, securities, real estate, personal effects, mortgages and other liabilities)	❏
7.	Business Balance Sheets	❏
8.	Business Profit and Loss Statements	❏
9.	Business Disposition Agreements (buy/sell agreements, partnership agreements, etc.)	❏
10.	Employee Benefits (retirement plans, stock options, deferred compensation, etc.)	❏
11.	Income Tax Return (most recent)	❏
12.	Gift Tax returns	❏
13.	Dates of Birth (of family members)	❏

14. Other: _____

  _____

  _____

  _____

  _____

Date of Meeting: _____
Time: _____
Place: _____

GIFT TAX CALCULATION STEPS

Gross Value of Current Gift(s)	$_____
Less: 50% of Gift if Split-Gift(s)	(_____)
Annual Exclusion[1]	(_____)
Marital Deduction[2]	(_____)
Charitable Deduction[2]	(_____)
Current Taxable Gift(s)	$_____
Plus: Sum of All Prior Taxable Gifts	_____
Total Cumulative Taxable Gifts	$_____
Tax on Total Cumulative Taxable Gifts[3]	$_____
Less: Taxes Paid on Prior Taxable Gifts	(_____)
Tentative Tax	$_____
Less: Unified Credit	(_____)
Gift Tax Payable[4]	$_____

ESTATE TAX CALCULATION STEPS

Gross Estate	$_____
Less: Debts of Decedent	(_____)
Administration Expenses	(_____)
Losses during Administration	(_____)
Adjusted Gross Estate	$_____
Less: Marital Deduction[2]	(_____)
Charitable Deduction[2]	(_____)
State Death Tax Deduction	(_____)
Taxable Estate	$_____
Plus: Adjusted Taxable Gifts	_____
Computation Base	$_____
Tentative Tax[3]	$_____
Less: Post-1976 Gift Taxes Payable	(_____)
Unified Credit	(_____)
Pre-1977 Gift Tax Credit	(_____)
Foreign Death Tax Credit	(_____)
Credit for Tax on Prior Transfers	(_____)
Estate Tax Payable[5]	$_____

---

[1] See page 46 for details regarding the gift tax annual exclusion.

[2] Full value of property passed to spouse or charity may be taken as a deduction.

[3] See page 550 for estate and gift tax rates.

[4] Transfer taxes payable during life may also include the generation-skipping transfer tax.

[5] Transfer taxes payable at death may also include the generation-skipping transfer tax (see chart, page 39).

HISTORY OF THE FEDERAL ESTATE TAX[1]

In view of the following tortured history, it is hard to imagine what will happen to the federal estate tax post 2012.

1797 – The first federal "estate" tax was passed to help fund a naval buildup. This was actually a stamp duty on legacies and intestate shares of personalty, and was not effective until 1798. The tax was 25¢ on a share over $50 and under $100, 75¢ on a share between $100 and $500, plus $1 per additional $500 share, or portion thereof.

1802 – The stamp tax was *repealed*.

1862 – To help fund the Civil War, Congress imposed a *legacy* tax on personalty if personal estate exceeded $1,000 (share of spouse was exempt) and a *stamp* tax on probates of wills and letters of administration (from 50¢ to $20 for estates up to $150,000, with $10 more for each additional $50,000, or fraction thereof).

1864 – The legacy tax was *increased* and a succession tax on realty was added, ranging from 1% to 6% on the basis of relationship to the deceased.

1870 – The legacy succession tax was repealed.

1872 – The stamp tax was *repealed*.

1894 – At the beginning of the Spanish-American War, a 2% "income" tax was imposed upon "money and value of all personal property acquired by gift or inheritance."

1898 – The rates were changed, and ranged from .75% to 2.25%, but estates under $10,000 were exempt (as well as legacies to surviving spouses).

1902 – The "income" tax was repealed.

1916-21 – The modern estate tax was enacted, followed by a succession of changes. Initially, there was an exemption of $*50*,000, and the rates ranged from 1% on the first $50,000, to 10% on estates over $5 *million*. Thereafter, the 1% rate increased to 1.5%, then to 2%; and the 10% rate *increased* to 15%, then to 25% (on estates over $10 million).

1924 – The gift tax was imposed, a state credit was allowed, and the estate tax was increased on all taxable estates over $*100*,000 (estates over $10 million were taxed at 40%).

1926 – The gift tax was repealed, the exemption was raised from $50,000 to $100,000, and the 1924 rates were retroactively removed. As a result, $250 million was refunded to just seven estates, while other estates received lesser refunds.

1931 – The exemption was reduced from $100,000 to $50,000, and rates were more than doubled.

1932 – For estates over $1 million, the maximum rate was increased from 19% to 45%.

1934 – For estates over $10 million, the maximum rate was increased to 60%.

1935 – The exemption was further reduced to $40,000, and the rates were increased to 2% on the first $10,000 bracket, and increased to 70% on amounts over $50 million.

1940 – To help finance World War II, a "temporary" defense tax increased estate taxes 10%.

1941 – The progressive rates were increased, and the "temporary" defense tax became permanent. The rates were *increased* to 3% on the first $5,000 bracket, and increased to 77% on amounts over $10 *million*.

1981-99 – During this 19-year period, no less than 126 new estate tax laws were enacted (an average of seven per year).[2]

2001 – EGTRRA 2001 repeals the estate tax for the year 2010.

2010 – The 2010 Tax Relief Act reinstates the estate tax with an increased exemption of $5 million and a maximum rate reduced to 35% (for the years 2011 and 2012). Estates of 2010 decedents may opt for *repeal* of estate tax in favor of modified carryover basis.

---

[1] Portions of this history have been compiled from an exhaustive work by Louis Eisenstein, contained in "The Rise and Decline of the Estate Tax," Tax Law Review, 1956, pages 223-259.

[2] See, Hal Graff, "Estate Tax Law Changes: More Sales Opportunities for Financial Advisors," *Journal of Financial Service Professionals*, July 2001, page 87.

TYPICAL ESTATE DEBTS, COSTS AND TAXES

GROSS ESTATE	DEBTS AND LIABILITIES	+	PROBATE COSTS	+	STATE TAX	=	TOTAL EXPENSES
100,000	5,600		5,000		1,700		12,300
200,000	10,600		9,900		4,400		24,900
300,000	15,600		14,700		6,000		36,300
400,000	20,400		19,600		11,000		51,000
500,000	25,000		22,500		16,600		64,100
600,000	29,400		26,880		21,400		77,680
700,000	33,600		31,220		26,700		91,520
800,000	37,600		35,520		32,600		105,720
900,000	41,400		39,780		38,900		120,080
1,000,000	45,000		44,000		45,800		134,800
1,500,000	62,250		65,250		71,800		199,300
2,000,000	84,000		86,000		100,000		270,000
3,000,000	120,000		126,000		180,000		426,000
4,000,000	154,000		164,000		260,000		578,000
5,000,000	185,000		200,000		350,000		735,000

Explanation of Table. Debts and Liabilities are calculated on a descending scale from 5.6 to 3.7 percent and Probate Costs on a descending scale from 5.0 to 4.0 percent. Both reflect actual government studies involving estates of various sizes. Specific debts, costs, and taxes will differ from those illustrated.

STATE EXEMPTIONS FOR LIFE INSURANCE

The following states, unless otherwise noted, completely exempt from taxation insurance proceeds payable to a named beneficiary, provided the named beneficiary is not the insured's estate. Because of the many variations among state laws, it is recommended that the specific statute be reviewed when developing an individual's estate plan.

Indiana	Nebraska
Iowa	New Jersey
Kentucky	Ohio
Maryland	Pennsylvania[1]

---

[1] All proceeds are exempt, including those paid to estate.

FEDERAL CREDIT STATES[1]

The following states do not have a separate state inheritance or estate tax, but claim only the maximum federal credit.[2]

Alabama	Louisiana	North Dakota
Alaska	Maine	Oregon
Arkansas	Massachusetts	Rhode Island
California	Michigan	South Carolina
Colorado	Minnesota	South Dakota
Connecticut	Mississippi	Texas
Delaware	Missouri	Utah
District of Columbia	Montana	Vermont
Florida	Nevada	Virginia
Georgia	New Hampshire	West Virginia
Hawaii	New Mexico	Wisconsin
Idaho	New York	Wyoming
Illinois	North Carolina	

Although the following states impose an inheritance or estate tax, they do exempt from taxation all transfers to a decedent's spouse (by either an unlimited marital deduction or an exemption).

Indiana	Maryland	Oklahoma
Iowa	Nebraska	Pennsylvania
Kansas	New Jersey	Tennessee
Kentucky	Ohio	Washington

Although the following states impose an inheritance or estate tax, they do exempt from taxation all transfers to a child.

Iowa	Maryland
Kentucky	New Jersey

COMMUNITY PROPERTY STATES[3]

In the following states, community property laws govern the ownership of property between husband and wife.

Alaska[4]	Louisiana	Texas
Arizona	Nevada	Washington
California	New Mexico	Wisconsin
Idaho		

---

[1] Last researched: November 2010.

[2] Under EGTRRA 2001, the credit for federal estate taxes has been replaced with a deduction. See the discussion of Decoupling of State Death Taxes on page 381.

[3] Community property is discussed on pages 365-366.

[4] In Alaska, a married couple must opt into the community property system.

STATE INHERITANCE & ESTATE TAXES

	VALUE OF TOTAL ESTATE PASSING TO ADULT CHILD				
	100,000	250,000	500,000	1,000,000	2,000,000
Indiana	0	3,750	14,250	45,250	132,250
Nebraska	600	2,100	4,600	9,600	19,600
Ohio	0	0	9,700	44,700	114,700
Pennsylvania	4,500	11,250	22,500	45,000	90,000
South Dakota	0	8,287.50	27,037.50	64,537.50	139,537.50
Tennessee	0	0	0	0	83,400
Washington	0	0	0	100,000	240,000

The above calculations are based upon research conducted in November 2010. It is assumed that the "Value of Total Estate" is equal to the Adjusted Gross Estate in common-law states. Exemptions for specific types of property have not been considered. An inheritance tax is levied on the share of each heir at rates which vary according to the heir's relationship with the deceased. An estate tax is levied on the value of the entire estate, normally in a manner similar to the federal estate tax.

Prior to 2001 where the amount of regular state inheritance or estate tax was less than the maximum federal credit amount, most states collected an amount equal to the maximum federal credit. However, under The Economic Growth and Tax Relief Reconciliation Act (EGTRRA 2001) this credit was phased out over the period 2002-2004. Thereafter, from 2005 to 2009 the credit was replaced with a deduction. This repeal of the state death tax credit resulted in significant revenue losses in many states, and lead to the enactment of new state death tax laws designed to recoup the lost revenue (e.g., state laws imposing state death taxes, "equal to the federal credit as it existed prior to EGTRRA 2001"). See the discussion of Decoupling Of State Death Taxes on page 381.

INFLATION ADJUSTER

Additional Life Insurance Required In 2011 To Keep Up With Inflation

Year Policy Purchased	Death Benefit Of Original Life Insurance Policy				
	50,000	100,000	250,000	500,000	1,000,000
2010	50	100	250	500	1,000
2009	0	0	0	0	0
2008	1,744	3,488	8,720	17,441	34,882
2007	3,193	6,386	15,965	31,929	63,859
2006	4,895	9.790	24,476	48,951	97,902
2005	6,762	13,523	33,808	67,615	135,231
2004	8,294	16,588	41,470	82,941	165,882
2003	9,635	19,270	48,174	96,349	192,697
2002	10,589	21,178	52,945	105,890	211,780
2001	12,286	24,571	61,428	122,855	245,710
2000	14,403	28,806	72,016	144,032	288,064
1999	15,820	31,640	79,100	158,201	316,402
1998	16,873	33,746	84,366	168,732	337,464
1997	18,411	36,823	92,056	184,113	368,226
1996	20,464	40,927	102,318	204,636	409,273
1995	22,437	44,873	112,183	224,366	448,732
1994	24,320	48,640	121,600	243,200	486,399
1993	26,550	53,099	132,748	265,496	530,991
1992	28,846	57,692	144,230	288,461	576,921
1991	32,158	64,315	160,788	321,576	643,152

Explanation: This table shows the amount of additional insurance required to maintain a given purchasing power. For example, if $100,000 of insurance had been purchased in 2000, then an additional $28,806 of insurance would have to be available to provide the same purchasing power in 2011 (i.e., what $100,000 would have purchased in 2000 will require $128,806 in 2011). All calculations are based upon the CPI figures set forth on page 314.

OWNERSHIP AND BENEFICIARY ARRANGEMENTS

	Advantages	**Disadvantages**
POLICY OWNER		
Insured	Insured retains control of policy and owns cash values. See page 70.	Proceeds subject to estate tax. Policy transferred within 3 years also included in estate.
Spouse of Insured	Simple to arrange. Insured retains indirect control of policy (provided marriage stable). See footnote 5, page 73.	If spouse predeceases insured, policy ownership could return to insured (by will, intestacy laws, or policy provisions). Proceeds not given away or consumed included in spouse's estate.
Children of Insured	Simple to arrange. Not taxed in estate. No costs to establish. See page 459.	Insured loses control of policy (or never had control if children were applicants). If children minors, must have legal guardian appointed before proceeds paid (time consuming and costly).
Irrevocable Trust	Proceeds not subject to estate tax. Continued maintenance of policy if insured becomes incompetent. See page 50.	Insured does not control policy and cannot change or revoke trust. Costs to establish and trustee fees after death.
POLICY BENEFICIARY		
Individual - paid as lump sum	Simple to arrange. No costs to establish or collect proceeds. No delay in payment of death benefit.	Control of proceeds by beneficiary may lead to loss of funds or refusal to make proceeds available to pay settlement costs and taxes. With minor beneficiary guardian must be appointed.
Individual – paid under settlement option	Simple to arrange. No costs to establish or collect proceeds. Funds remaining with carrier are secure.	Not flexible, insurance company must pay under original option despite beneficiaries changing circumstances. Proceeds not available to pay estate settlement costs and taxes.
Estate of Insured	Simple to arrange. No costs to establish or collect proceeds. Provides liquidity to estate.	Proceeds subject to estate tax and claims of creditors, as well as increasing probate costs.
Irrevocable Trust	Flexible, trust can give trustee broad authority to pay or withhold benefits, provide for successor beneficiaries, and make proceeds available for settlement costs. Provides professional management and investment advice. Not subject to claims of creditors.	Time consuming to establish. Initial costs for drafting of trust and trustee fees after funded by death benefit. Must coordinate with remainder of estate plan.

SURVIVOR CHECKLIST

Check As
Accomplished

1. Request 10 copies of death certificate (funeral director will assist).   ❏
Deceased's date of birth: _____ .

2. Contact employer regarding group insurance and other benefits.   ❏

3. Contact insurance companies (auto, life, and health). Have policy numbers   ❏
available.

4. If deceased was a government retiree or employee, contact Civil Service   ❏
Personal Management Office (1-888-767-6738: www.opm.gov).

5. If deceased was retired from the military, contact Defense Finance and   ❏
Accounting Service (1-800-321-1080: www.dfas.mil).

6. If deceased was a veteran, contact Veterans Administration   ❏
(1-800-827-1000: www4.va.gov/survivors).

7. Notify Social Security Administration (1-800-772-1213: www.ssa.gov).   ❏
Deceased's Social Security number: _____ .
Spouse's Social Security number: _____ .

8. Check items in safe deposit box.   ❏

9. Locate Last Will and Testament and Trust documents.   ❏

10. Notify banks and stock brokerage companies.   ❏

11. Contact credit card companies and other charge accounts.   ❏

12. Check on credit life insurance with all creditors.   ❏

13. Locate personal balance sheet (or similar listing of cash, securities, real estate,   ❏
personal effects, mortgages, and other liabilities).

14. Locate business disposition agreements (buy/sell agreements, partnership   ❏
agreements, etc.).

15. Call attorney and arrange for meeting to discuss probate and other   ❏
matters: _____.

16. As time for filing tax return approaches – call accountant, CPA, or tax preparer.   ❏

17. Other: _____   ❏

_____

EVALUATING THE RISK OF DEATH

One Individual

The following tables provide the odds of death within the next 10 and 20 years for an individual according to age and sex. For example, a male age 38 has a 2.1 percent chance of dying within the next 10 years and a 7.0 percent chance of dying within the next 20 years; whereas a female age 38 has a 1.6 percent chance of dying within the next 10 years and a 5.6 percent chance of dying within the next 20 years.

Odds Of Death Within 10 Years

Age	Male	Female	Age	Male	Female	Age	Male	Female
21	1.1	0.6	36	1.8	1.4	51	6.5	5.4
22	1.1	0.6	37	2.0	1.5	52	7.1	5.9
23	1.1	0.6	38	2.1	1.6	53	7.9	6.4
24	1.1	0.6	39	2.3	1.7	54	8.7	7.0
25	1.1	0.7	40	2.5	1.9	55	9.6	7.6
26	1.1	0.7	41	2.7	2.1	56	10.5	8.2
27	1.2	0.8	42	2.9	2.3	57	11.6	8.9
28	1.2	0.8	43	3.2	2.5	58	12.7	9.6
29	1.2	0.9	44	3.5	2.7	59	13.9	10.3
30	1.2	0.9	45	3.8	3.0	60	15.2	11.1
31	1.3	1.0	46	4.1	3.3	61	16.5	12.0
32	1.4	1.1	47	4.5	3.7	62	18.0	13.0
33	1.4	1.1	48	4.9	4.1	63	19.6	14.0
34	1.5	1.2	49	5.4	4.5	64	21.3	15.1
35	1.7	1.3	50	5.9	4.9	65	23.1	16.4

Odds Of Death Within 20 Years

Age	Male	Female	Age	Male	Female	Age	Male	Female
21	2.4	1.6	36	5.8	4.7	51	21.9	16.7
22	2.4	1.6	37	6.4	5.1	52	23.8	18.1
23	2.5	1.7	38	7.0	5.6	53	25.9	19.5
24	2.6	1.8	39	7.6	6.1	54	28.1	21.1
25	2.8	2.0	40	8.3	6.7	55	30.4	22.7
26	2.9	2.1	41	9.0	7.3	56	32.9	24.5
27	3.1	2.2	42	9.9	8.0	57	35.6	26.4
28	3.3	2.4	43	10.8	8.7	58	38.4	28.4
29	3.5	2.6	44	11.8	9.5	59	41.4	30.5
30	3.7	2.8	45	13.0	10.3	60	44.6	32.8
31	4.0	3.0	46	14.2	11.2	61	48.0	35.3
32	4.3	3.3	47	15.5	12.2	62	51.5	37.9
33	4.6	3.6	48	17.0	13.2	63	55.2	40.8
34	5.0	3.9	49	18.5	14.3	64	58.9	43.8
35	5.4	4.3	50	20.2	15.5	65	62.6	47.0

Source: Calculations are based upon the Commissioners 2001 Standard Ordinary Mortality Table.

(continued on next page)

EVALUATING THE RISK OF DEATH (continued)

Two Individuals

The risk of *at least one of two individuals* dying is substantially greater than the risk of one individual dying. For example, within the next 10 years the risk of a male age 50 dying is 5.9 percent and the risk of a female age 45 dying is 3.0 percent (see page 91, Evaluating The Risk Of Death - One Individual); but the risk of at least one of them dying within the next 10 years is 8.7 percent. And this risk increases considerably with time (i.e., for a male age 50 and a female age 45 the risk of at least one of them dying within the next 20 years increases to 28.4 percent).

Odds Of At Least One Death Within 10 Years

Male Age

Female Age	20	25	30	35	40	45	50	55	60	65
20	1.6	1.7	1.8	2.2	3.1	4.3	6.4	10.1	15.6	23.5
25	1.8	1.8	1.9	2.3	3.2	4.4	6.5	10.2	15.7	23.6
30	2.0	2.1	2.2	2.6	3.4	4.7	6.8	10.4	15.9	23.8
35	2.3	2.4	2.5	2.9	3.8	5.0	7.1	10.7	16.2	24.1
40	2.9	3.0	3.1	3.5	4.4	5.6	7.7	11.3	16.7	24.5
45	4.1	4.1	4.2	4.6	5.5	6.7	8.7	12.3	17.7	25.4
50	5.9	6.0	6.1	6.5	7.3	8.5	10.5	14.0	19.3	26.9
55	8.6	8.6	8.7	9.1	9.9	11.0	13.0	16.4	21.6	28.9
60	12.1	12.1	12.2	12.6	13.4	14.5	16.4	19.6	24.6	31.6
65	17.3	17.3	17.4	17.8	18.5	19.5	21.3	24.4	29.1	35.7

Odds Of At Least One Death Within 20 Years

Male Age

Female Age	20	25	30	35	40	45	50	55	60	65
20	3.7	4.2	5.2	6.8	9.6	14.2	21.3	31.5	45.4	63.2
25	4.2	4.7	5.6	7.2	10.1	14.7	21.7	31.8	45.7	63.4
30	5.0	5.5	6.4	8.0	10.8	15.4	22.4	32.4	46.1	63.7
35	6.5	6.9	7.8	9.4	12.2	16.7	23.6	33.4	47.0	64.2
40	8.8	9.3	10.2	11.7	14.4	18.8	25.5	35.1	48.3	65.1
45	12.4	12.8	13.7	15.2	17.8	22.0	28.4	37.6	50.3	66.5
50	17.4	17.8	18.6	20.0	22.5	26.4	32.5	41.2	53.2	68.4
55	24.5	24.9	25.6	26.9	29.1	32.7	38.3	46.2	57.2	71.1
60	34.4	34.7	35.3	36.4	38.4	41.5	46.4	53.3	62.8	74.9
65	48.2	48.5	49.0	49.8	51.4	53.9	57.7	63.1	70.6	80.2

Source: Calculations are based upon the Commissioners 2001 Standard Ordinary Mortality Table.

FACTS ABOUT . . .

Facts About Fathers

Father's Age When Child Is Born	Fathers Who Will Die Before Child	
	Enters College	Graduates
25	1 in 43	1 in 30
30	1 in 33	1 in 22
35	1 in 23	1 in 15
40	1 in 15	1 in 10

Facts About Mothers

Mother's Age When Child Is Born	Mothers Who Will Die Before Child	
	Enters College	Graduates
25	1 in 61	1 in 43
30	1 in 44	1 in 29
35	1 in 29	1 in 19
40	1 in 19	1 in 12

Facts About Children

The Cost Of Raising A Child To Age 18		The Annual Costs Of A College Education	
Family Income	Costs	Year	Amount
less than $56,870	$165,447	2011	$34,776
$56,870 - $98,470	228,906	2016	44,384
more than $98,470	379,450	2021	56,647
		2026	72,297

Source of facts about fathers and mothers: Calculations based upon the Commissioners 2001 Standard Ordinary Mortality Table (see pages 555-556), and assume that the child enters a 4-year college at age 18.

Source of costs of raising a child to age 18: Calculations based upon data from the 2005-06 Consumer Expenditure Survey updated to 2011 using the Consumer Price Index table on page 314. See *Statistical Abstract of the United States*, 2010, Table 673, Annual Expenditure Per Child by Husband-Wife Families by Family Income and Expenditure Type. College costs are not included.

Source of the annual costs of a college education: Author research of college internet sites during the month of November, 2010, supplemented by direct inquiry when required. College costs are for the 2010-2011 year, and are based upon a representative sampling of 42 state and private colleges in 39 states (see page 97). Projections are based upon cost increases of 5 percent per year. In recent years actual college costs have increased more than 5 percent.

(continued on next page)

FACTS ABOUT . . . (continued)

Facts About The Value Of An Education

Having an education will often determine the economic opportunities available over a lifetime. Persons with a bachelor's degree or more on the average earn 3 times more than those who have completed less than 9th grade, and 2 times more than those who have completed only high school.

| | Median Annual Income | | |
	Less than 9th grade	High school graduate	Bachelor's degree or more
Men	$27,561	$42,042	$88,641
Women	21,320	30,657	58,000

Facts About Funerals

According to the last available survey conducted by the National Funeral Directors Association, in 2001 the average adult funeral cost $6,130. Updated by the consumer price index this would cost $7,421 in 2011. However, the ultimate costs will depend upon the specific items and services.

Item/Service	Cost
Professional service charges	$1,213
Embalming	420
Other preparations (Cosmetology, hair, etc.)	150
Visitation/Viewing	275
Funeral at Funeral Home	350
Transfer of remains to funeral home	154
Hearse (local)	185
Service Car/Van	85
Acknowledgement cards	18
Casket	2,330
Vault	950
Total	$6,130

Source of Facts About The Value Of An Education: Statistical Abstract of the United States, 2010, Table 687, Average Earnings of Year-Round, Full-Time Workers by Educational Attainment.

Source of Facts About Funerals: The National Funeral Directors Association. These costs do not include cemetery charges, such as a grave space, opening and closing grave, crypts and mausoleum, monument or marker.

FACTS ABOUT . . . (continued)

Facts About The Cost Of Child Care

According to the U.S. Census Bureau weekly child care expenses in the year 1999 averaged $94 per week ($4,888 per year) for children under age 5 and $75 per week ($3,900 per year) for children age 5 to 14. As adjusted in 2011 for inflation, this would be $121 per week ($6,296 per year) for children under age 5 and $97 per week ($5,023 per year) for children age 5 to 14.

According to the Children's Defense Fund in the year 2000 for a 4-year-old child:

(1) In *rural* child care centers annual costs ranged from $2,556 in Nebraska to $7,150 in Alaska (from $3,184 to $8,907 in 2011 as adjusted for inflation).

(2) In *urban* child care centers annual costs ranged from $3,640 in Arkansas to $8,121 in Massachusetts (from $4,534 to $10,116 in 2011 as adjusted for inflation). In all states but Vermont, the cost of child care in an urban area center was more than the cost of public college tuition (in over one-quarter of states the average cost of child care was more than *twice* the cost of public college tuition).

Facts About The Value Of A Homemaker

In valuing a homemaker's services two basic methods are used. The "opportunity cost" method seeks to determine the wages that homemakers might have demanded had they opted to follow an alternate career (e.g., a full-time homemaker who is a trained nurse has foregone a nurse's salary). Under the "replacement cost" method, also called the "market alternative" method, valuation is based upon the prevailing wage rates for similar services, taking into consideration the time spent on each task and the wage rates paid for similar jobs in the marketplace, such as:

	Hourly Wage		Hourly Wage
Maid	$ 10.02	Private Household Cook	$ 13.33
Dishwasher	8.81	Lodging Manager	25.72
Child Care Worker	10.07	Concierge	13.83
Interior Designer	24.99	Taxi Driver	11.51
Teacher's Assistant	13.34	Licensed Practical Nurse	19.66
Recreation Worker	12.04	Nonfarm Animal Caretaker	10.50

Source of Facts About The Cost Of Child Care: U.S. Census Bureau, PPL Table 6 (Average Weekly Child Care Expenditures by Employed Mothers), revised to January 2011; and *The High Cost of Child Care Puts Quality Care Out of Reach for Many Families,* Children's Defense Fund, 2000, revised to January 2011.

Source of Facts About The Value Of A Homemaker: Bureau of Labor Statistics, Washington, D.C., National Occupational Employment and Wage Estimates using Standard Occupational Classification (SOC) system, May 2009. See http://www.bls.gov/oes/current/oes_nat.htm. Hourly wage of a teacher's assistant is estimated by dividing average annual wage of $24,280 by assumed 1,820 annual hours.

FACTS ABOUT . . . (continued)

Facts About Human Life Value in the Courtroom

A study of wrongful death case files selected at random revealed the following:

- The average amount of loss was $1,290,000 but the amount of life insurance was only $302,308.
- The average percent of the families' losses covered by life insurance was only 28 percent.
- Only 15.3 percent of the families had more than 50 percent of their loss covered by life insurance.
- Only 53.8 percent of families had more than 25 percent of their loss covered by life insurance.
- The largest percentage of any one family's loss covered by life insurance was 65 percent.

Note: Those cases which contained no life insurance were excluded from the study. The life insurance amounts are net of accidental death benefits and credit card related benefits.

Source of *Facts About Human Life Value in the Courtroom*: Study conducted in 1996 by Litigation Analytics Inc. of Ridgefield, Connecticut, as reported by John E. Scarbrough, PhD, in "Measuring Human Life Value From the Courtroom to the Living Room," *Journal of the American Society of CLU and ChFC* (January 1998), page 68.

COLLEGE COSTS PROJECTED

Yearly Tuition, Fees, Supplies, Room & Board

NAME OF INSTITUTION	LOCATION	Assuming Increases of 5% Per Year			
		2011	2016	2021	2026
Auburn University	Auburn, Ala.	18,630	23,777	30,346	38,730
Bowdoin College	Brunswick, Maine	52,880	67,490	86,136	109,934
Brigham Young University	Provo, Utah	12,440	15,877	20,263	25,862
Bucknell University	Lewisburg, Pa.	52,280	66,724	85,159	108,686
The Citadel	Charleston, S.C.	22,949	29,289	37,382	47,709
Colorado State University	Ft. Collins, Colo.	17,405	22,213	28,351	36,183
Columbia College	New York, N.Y.	57,294	73,123	93,326	119,110
Dartmouth College	Hanover, N.H.	54,005	68,926	87,968	112,273
De Paul University	Chicago, Ill.	36,049	46,009	58,720	74,943
Drake University	Des Moines, Iowa	35,090	44,785	57,158	72,950
Duke University	Durham, N.C.	52,405	66,884	85,362	108,946
Emory University	Atlanta, Ga.	51,456	65,672	83,816	106,973
Florida State University	Tallahassee, Fla.	15,418	19,678	25,114	32,053
George Washington Univ.	Washington, D.C.	54,475	69,525	88,734	113,250
Hamline University	St. Paul, Minn.	40,359	51,509	65,741	83,903
Harvard College	Cambridge, Mass.	49,557	63,249	80,723	103,025
Jackson State University	Jackson, Miss.	11,468	14,636	18,680	23,841
Kansas State University	Manhattan, Kans.	14,986	19,126	24,411	31,155
Loyola University Chicago	Chicago, Ill.	51,610	65,869	84,067	107,293
Marquette University	Milwaukee, Wis.	40,352	51,501	65,729	83,889
Michigan State University	E. Lansing, Mich.	19,542	24,941	31,832	40,626
Middlebury College	Middlebury, Vt.	53,500	68,281	87,146	111,223
Ohio State University	Columbus, Ohio	19,584	24,995	31,900	40,714
Oral Roberts University	Tulsa, Okla.	28,348	36,180	46,176	58,933
Purdue University	W. Lafayette, Ind.	19,460	24,836	31,698	40,456
Rutgers University	New Brunswick, N.J.	23,466	29,949	38,224	48,784
St. Lawrence University	Canton, N.Y.	51,770	66,073	84,328	107,626
Salem International Univ.	Salem, W.Va.	20,700	26,419	33,718	43,034
Seattle University	Seattle, Washington	41,580	53,068	67,729	86,442
Southern Methodist Univ.	Dallas, Tex.	49,965	63,769	81,388	103,874
Stanford University	Stanford, Calif.	52,499	67,004	85,515	109,142
Texas A & M University	College Sta., Tex.	17,775	22,686	28,954	36,953
Tulane University	New Orleans, La.	52,908	67,526	86,182	109,992
University of Arkansas	Fayetteville, Ark.	15,972	20,385	26,017	33,205
University of California	Berkley, Calif.	26,362	33,645	42,941	54,805
University of Louisville	Louisville, Ky.	16,026	20,454	26,105	33,317
University of New Mexico	Albuquerque, N.Mex.	17,150	21,888	27,936	35,654
University of Rhode Island	Kingston, R.I.	21,106	26,937	34,379	43,878
University of Virginia	Charlottesville, Va.	20,593	26,282	33,544	42,811
Vanderbilt University	Nashville, Tenn.	54,332	69,343	88,501	112,952
Yale University	New Haven, Conn.	52,900	67,515	86,169	109,975
Yeshiva University	New York, N.Y.	43,955	56,099	71,598	91,379
Average Cost		34,776	44,384	56,647	72,297

Explanation of Table. Costs for public schools assume the student is a resident of the state. Costs (i.e., tuition) for out-of-state students are generally substantially more then shown. Costs for supplies are included when available. Costs for transportation are not included. Since over the past decade college costs have more than kept pace with the rate of inflation, it seems highly likely that costs will continue to escalate in the years to come. In this regard, see the Consumer Price Index on page 314. Source of 2010-2011 college education costs: Author research of college internet sites during the month of November 2010, supplemented by direct inquiry when required.

HUMAN LIFE VALUE

The value of $10,000 in annual earnings, discounted by 5 percent, according to the number of "working years to retirement" and rates of projected growth.

Working Years To Retirement	Projected Growth In Earnings				
	4%	5%	6%	7%	8%
1	10,000	10,000	10,000	10,000	10,000
2	19,905	20,000	20,095	20,191	20,286
3	29,719	30,000	30,290	30,576	30,862
4	39,436	40,000	40,578	41,157	41,745
5	49,062	50,000	50,960	51,943	52,935
6	58,597	60,000	61,444	62,935	64,444
7	68,037	70,000	72,032	74,136	76,286
8	77,389	80,000	82,721	85,550	88,467
9	86,655	90,000	93,509	97,177	100,995
10	95,828	100,000	104,397	109,025	113,880
11	104,913	110,000	115,392	121,100	127,135
12	113,912	120,000	126,489	133,408	140,770
13	122,826	130,000	137,692	145,947	154,790
14	131,656	140,000	149,003	158,728	169,214
15	140,404	150,000	160,424	171,754	184,049
16	149,067	160,000	171,953	185,025	199,306
17	157,647	170,000	183,589	198,548	215,001
18	166,146	180,000	195,339	212,331	231,144
19	174,564	190,000	207,197	226,375	247,747
20	182,902	200,000	219,171	240,687	264,826
21	191,159	210,000	231,258	255,273	282,393
22	199,339	220,000	243,461	270,135	300,460
23	207,449	230,000	255,779	285,277	319,044
24	215,465	240,000	268,217	300,714	338,160
25	223,413	250,000	280,773	316,442	357,823
26	231,286	260,000	293,447	332,468	378,045
27	239,081	270,000	306,239	348,797	398,843
28	246,802	280,000	319,152	365,438	420,235
29	254,452	290,000	332,193	382,400	442,242
30	262,028	300,000	345,353	399,680	464,873
31	269,532	310,000	358,643	417,294	488,159
32	276,966	320,000	372,061	435,246	512,112
33	284,330	330,000	385,605	453,538	536,748
34	291,622	340,000	399,281	472,179	562,087
35	298,846	350,000	413,086	491,177	588,153
36	306,000	360,000	427,021	510,535	614,958
37	313,088	370,000	441,091	530,264	642,535
38	320,104	380,000	455,289	550,360	670,887
39	327,056	390,000	469,624	570,842	700,054
40	333,938	400,000	484,092	591,708	730,046

Explanation of Table. Footnote 4 on page 17 contains an explanation of how to use this table to calculate human life value.

TRUSTS AND THEIR USES

TYPE	CHARACTERISTICS	Income	Gift	Estate
			TAX IMPLICATIONS	
Revocable	Created during grantor's life. If unfunded, acts as a will substitute. If funded, can manage property for benefit of grantor, spouse, and other beneficiaries. See chart, page 29.	Trust income taxable to grantor.	No gifts, since grantor retains control of property.	No estate tax advantages, but payment of insurance proceeds to trust can provide greater flexibility than settlement options.
Irrevocable	Created during grantor's life. Grantor gives up all control over assets in order to gain estate tax advantages (chart, page 51). Also, see Dynasty Trust, page 395.	Trust pays tax if income accumulated in trust. Beneficiaries pay taxes if income distributed. Income taxed to grantor if certain strings retained.	When property placed in trust there is a gift. With "Crummey powers," gifts are considered present interest gifts that qualify for the annual exclusion (chart, page 47).	Generally not included in estate, except proceeds of life insurance given to trust within 3 years of death (pages 409-410), or if grantor retains interest in trust.
Testamentary	Created upon death pursuant to a will (chart, page 25, and page 450).	None, trust created at death.	None, trust created at death.	Taxable in testator's estate.
Minor's Trust (Section 2503(c))	Created during grantor's life. Trust's accumulated income and principal must be paid to beneficiary upon attaining age 21 (further discussion, page 544).	Trust pays taxes if income accumulated in trust. Beneficiaries pay taxes if income is distributed.	When property placed in trust there is a gift that qualifies for the annual exclusion.	Not included in grantor's estate, except life insurance given within 3 years of death.
Income Trust (Section 2503(b))	Created during grantor's life. Trust must distribute income annually, but principal need not be paid to beneficiary (further discussion, page 544).	Beneficiaries pay taxes when income is distributed.	When property placed in trust there is a gift that qualifies for the annual exclusion.	Not included in grantor's estate, except life insurance given within 3 years of death.

DEGREES OF KINDRED

Solid lines indicate the paths of direct descendancy. Full cousins are to the right of the principal. Cousins above the principal are "cousins in the ascendancy." Cousins below the principal are "cousins in descendancy." Numbers in lower right corners indicate the degree of kindred to principal (e.g., uncle and nephew are both in the 3rd degree of kindred and therefore would likely inherit in equal amounts, if the principal died intes

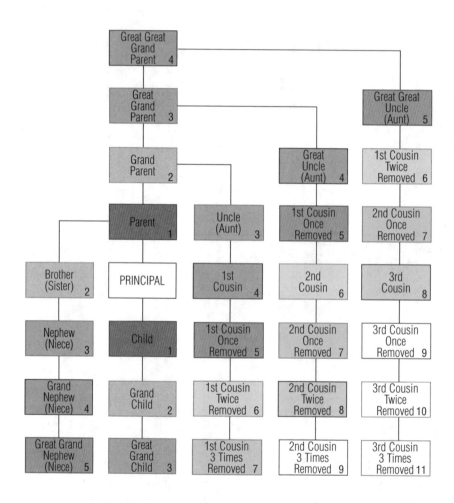

INTESTATE'S "WILL"

Being of sound mind and memory, I _____, do hereby publish this as my Last Will and Testament:

First

I give my wife [husband] only one-third of my possessions, and I give my children the remaining two-thirds.

I appoint my wife [husband] as guardian of my children, but as a safeguard I require that she [he] report to the Probate Court each year and render an accounting of how, why, and where she [he] spent the money necessary for the proper care of my children.

As a further safeguard, I direct my wife [husband] to produce to the Probate Court, a performance bond to guarantee that she [he] guarantee that she [he] exercises proper judgment in the handling, investing, and spending of my children's money. As a final safeguard, my children shall have the right to demand and receive a complete accounting from their mother [father] of all her [his] financial actions with their money as soon as they reach legal age.

When my children reach age 18, they shall have full rights to withdraw and spend their share of my estate. No one shall have any right to question my children's actions on how they decide to spend their respective shares.

Second

Should my wife [husband] remarry, her [his] second husband [wife] shall be entitled to one-third of everything my wife [husband] possesses. Should my children need some of this share for their support, the second husband [wife] shall not be bound to spend any part of his [her] share on my children's behalf.

Such second husband [wife] shall have sole right to decide who is to get his [her] share, even to the exclusion of my children.

Third

Should my wife [husband] predecease me or die while any of my children are minors, I do not wish to exercise my right to nominate the guardian of my children. Rather than nominating a guardian of my preference, I direct my relatives and friends to get together and select a guardian by mutual agreement. In the event that they fail to agree on a guardian, I direct the Probate Court to make the selection. If the court wishes, it may appoint a stranger acceptable to it.

Fourth

Under existing tax law, there are certain legitimate techniques open to me to lower death taxes. Since I prefer to have my money used for government purposes rather than for the benefit of my wife [husband] and children, I direct that no effort be made to lower taxes.

IN WITNESS WHEREOF, I have set my hand to this my LAST WILL AND TESTAMENT this _____ day of _____, 20_____.

_____

STATE LAWS ON INTESTATE SUCCESSION

When someone dies without a will, state law effectively provides a "one-size-fits-all" will through intestate succession statutes. It is important to remember, though, that just as a will may not control all of a decedent's property, state intestate succession statutes may not determine how all of a decedent's property is distributed at his death. Determining how the law will divide the property of a decedent who dies without a will can be complex. Property may pass by title (e.g., joint ownership with rights of survivorship), by contract (e.g., a life insurance beneficiary designation), or by some state statute other than the intestate succession statute.

These "other" statutes include dower and curtesy statutes, homestead statutes, right of election statutes, family allowance and support statutes, and statutes in common law states preserving the community property nature of property previously acquired by a married couple in a community property state. These statutes can be significant in determining the ultimate disposition of an intestate decedent's property.

Nonetheless, the statutes of intestate succession are quite important. The following briefly summarizes the shares into which the various states' intestate succession statutes divide the intestate estate when a decedent dies without a will and *leaves a surviving spouse and child(ren) but no other issue* (i.e., no grandchildren, no great grandchildren, etc.). Special rules may determine whether certain individuals–such as adopted, step or illegitimate children of the decedent–will qualify as "children" of the decedent for purposes of intestate succession.

Unless separately stated, community property includes "quasi-community property" (generally defined as property acquired in another state that would have been considered community property had it been acquired within the community property state). See discussion of community property on pages 365-366. Unless otherwise noted, property passing to the decedent's children is divided equally among them.

One final note of caution! Because state laws can change, the reader should consult local counsel for current law.

Alabama
If all children are issue of the surviving spouse also: spouse gets first $50,000, plus ½ of balance; remainder to child(ren).

If any child is not issue of surviving spouse: ½ to spouse; ½ to child(ren).

Alaska
If all children are issue of the surviving spouse and the decedent leaves no other surviving descendants or parents: all to spouse.

If any child is not issue of the surviving spouse: spouse gets first $100,000 plus ½ of balance; remainder to child(ren).

Arizona
If all children are issue of the surviving spouse also, spouse gets entire estate.

If any child is not issue of surviving spouse: spouse gets ½ of decedent's *separate* property, and none of decedent's share of *community* property; remainder to child(ren).

Arkansas
All property to child(ren).

California
Community property: all to spouse or domestic partner.

Separate property: if one child, then ½ to spouse or domestic partner and ½ to child; if more than one child, then ⅓ to spouse or domestic partner and ⅔ to children.

Colorado
If all children are issue of the surviving spouse also and there are no other issue of the surviving spouse: all to the spouse.

If all of the children are issue of the surviving spouse also but the surviving spouse has one or more surviving issue who are not also issue of the decedent: first $225,000 plus ½ of any balance to the spouse; the rest to the decedent's child(ren).

If one or more of the children is not also issue of the surviving spouse: the first $150,000 plus ½ of any balance to the spouse; the rest to the decedent's child(ren).

Connecticut
If all children are issue of the surviving spouse also: spouse gets first $100,000, plus ½ of balance; remainder to child(ren).

If any child is not issue of surviving spouse: ½ to spouse; ½ to child(ren).

Delaware
If all children are issue of the surviving spouse also: spouse gets first $50,000 of the *personal* estate, plus ½ of balance of the personal estate, plus a life estate in the *real* estate; rest to child(ren).

If any child is not issue of surviving spouse: spouse gets ½ of *personal* estate, plus a life estate in the *real* estate; rest to child(ren).

District of Columbia

If all children are issue of the surviving spouse or domestic partner and the surviving spouse or domestic partner has no other descendants, ⅔ to spouse or domestic partner.

If surviving spouse or domestic partner has one or more surviving descendants who are not descendants of the decedent or if the decedent has one or more surviving descendants who are not descendants of the surviving spouse or domestic partner, spouse or domestic partner takes ½.

Florida

If all children are issue of the surviving spouse also: spouse gets first $60,000 plus ½ of balance; remainder to child(ren).

If any child is not issue of surviving spouse: ½ to spouse; ½ to child(ren).

Georgia

Spouse shares equally with child(ren); but spouse entitled to at least ⅓.

Hawaii

If all children are issue of the surviving spouse also and there are no other issue of the surviving spouse: all to spouse.

If all children are issue of the surviving spouse also but the surviving spouse has one or more surviving issue who are not the issue of the decedent: first $150,000 plus ½ of balance to spouse; the rest to the decedent's child(ren).

If one or more of the children is not also issue of the surviving spouse: the first $100,000 plus ½ of balance to surviving spouse; the remainder to the decedent's child(ren).

Idaho

Community property: all to spouse.

Separate property: spouse gets ½ of estate and ½ goes to child(ren).

Illinois

½ to spouse; ½ to child(ren).

Indiana

½ to spouse; ½ to child(ren). If no child is a child of the surviving spouse, such spouse takes ½ of personal property, remainder of personal property to child(ren); spouse takes ¼ of fair market value of decedent's lands; ¾ to child(ren).

Iowa

If all children are issue of the surviving spouse also: spouse gets all of *real* property, plus all *personal* property that was exempt from execution in hands of decedent as head of family at death, plus all of remainder not necessary for payment of debts and charges.

If any child is not issue of surviving spouse: spouse gets ½ of *real* property, plus all *personal* property that was exempt from execution in hands of decedent as head of family at death, plus ½ of remaining *personal* property not necessary for payment of debts and charges; remainder to child(ren) (but spouse entitled to minimum of $50,000 in value from entire net estate).

Kansas

½ to spouse; ½ to child(ren).

Kentucky

All to child(ren).

Louisiana

Community property: decedent's share to children, but subject to usufruct in favor of surviving spouse (beneficial use until remarriage, unless decedent spouse specifies such use shall be for life or a shorter period).

Separate property: all to children.

Maine

If all children are issue of the surviving spouse or surviving registered domestic partner also: spouse or surviving registered domestic partner gets first $50,000, plus ½ of balance; remainder to child(ren).

If any child is not issue of surviving spouse: ½ to spouse; ½ to child(ren).

Maryland

If a surviving minor child: ½ to spouse; ½ to child(ren).

If no surviving minor child: spouse gets first $15,000, plus ½ of balance; remainder to child(ren).

Massachusetts

½ to spouse; ½ to child(ren).

Michigan

If all children are issue of the surviving spouse also: spouse gets first $150,000 plus ½ of balance; remainder to children.

If any child is not issue of surviving spouse: $100,000 plus ½ of balance to spouse; remainder to children.

Minnesota

If all children are issue of the surviving spouse also and the surviving spouse has no other surviving issue: all to spouse.

If all children are issue of the surviving spouse also but the surviving spouse has one or more surviving issue who are not issue of the decedent, or if any child is not issue of the surviving spouse also: the first $150,000 plus ½ of any balance to the spouse; the rest to the decedent's child(ren).

Mississippi

Spouse shares equally with child(ren).

Missouri

If all children are issue of the surviving spouse also: spouse gets first $20,000, plus ½ of balance; remainder to child(ren).

If any child is not issue of surviving spouse: ½ to spouse; ½ to child(ren).

Montana

If all children are issue of the surviving spouse also and the surviving spouse has no other surviving issue: all to spouse.

If all children are issue of the surviving spouse but the surviving spouse has any surviving issue who is not also issue of the decedent: the spouse gets first $150,000, plus ½ of any balance; the rest to decedent's child(ren).

If any child is not also issue of the surviving spouse: spouse gets first $100,000, plus ½ of balance; the rest to the decedent's child(ren).

Nebraska

If all children are issue of the surviving spouse also: spouse gets first $100,000, plus ½ of balance; remainder to child(ren).

If any child is not issue of surviving spouse: ½ to spouse; ½ to child(ren).

Nevada

Community property: all to spouse.

Separate property: if one child, then ½ to spouse and ½ to child; if more than one child, then ⅓ to spouse and remainder to children equally.

New Hampshire

If all children are issue of the surviving spouse also: spouse gets first $250,000, plus ½ of balance; remainder to child(ren).

If any child is not issue of surviving spouse: the first $100,000 + ½ to spouse; remainder to child(ren). If surviving spouse has issue that are not issue of decedent, first $150,000 + ½ to surviving spouse; remainder to child(ren).

New Jersey

If all children are issue of the surviving spouse also and the surviving spouse has no other surviving issue who are not also issue of the decedent: spouse gets entire estate.

If any child is not issue of surviving spouse or the surviving spouse has surviving issue who are not also issue of the decedent: first 25 percent (but not less than $50,000 nor more than $200,000), plus ½ of the balance to spouse; balance to child(ren).

New Mexico

Community property: all to spouse.

Separate property: ¼ to spouse; ¾ to child(ren).

New York

$50,000 plus ½ of the balance to spouse; the rest to child(ren).

North Carolina

If only one child: *real* property goes ½ to spouse and balance to child; with respect to *personal* property, spouse gets first $30,000 plus ½ of balance, and remainder to child.

If two or more children: *real* property goes ⅓ to spouse and balance to children; with respect to *personal* property, spouse gets first $30,000 plus ⅓ of balance, and remainder to children.

North Dakota

If all children are issue of the surviving spouse also and the surviving spouse has no other surviving issue: all to spouse.

If all children are issue of the surviving spouse also but the surviving spouse has one or more surviving issue who are not issue of the decedent: the first $225,000 plus ½ of any balance to the spouse; the rest to the decedent's child(ren).

If any child is not issue of the surviving spouse also: the first $150,000 plus ½ of any balance to the spouse; the rest to the decedent's child(ren).

Ohio

If only one child: spouse gets all if spouse is natural or adoptive parent of child, or first $20,000 if spouse is not natural or adoptive parent of child, plus ½ of balance; remainder to child.

If two or more children: spouse gets first $60,000 if spouse is natural or adoptive parent of one of the children, but not all, or first $20,000 if spouse is parent of none of children, plus ⅓ of balance; remainder to children.

Oklahoma

If all children are issue of the surviving spouse also: an undivided ½ interest in the property of the estate to spouse; the balance in undivided equal shares to child(ren).

If any child is not issue of surviving spouse: an undivided ½ interest in property acquired by joint industry of husband and wife during marriage to spouse; the spouse and the child(ren) take equal undivided shares in the property of the decedent not acquired by the joint industry of the husband and wife during marriage; the remainder of estate in undivided equal shares to the child(ren).

Oregon

If all children are issue of the surviving spouse also, spouse gets entire estate.

If any child is not issue of surviving spouse: ½ to spouse; ½ to child(ren).

Pennsylvania

If all children are issue of the surviving spouse also: spouse gets first $30,000, plus ½ of balance; remainder to child(ren).

If any child is not issue of surviving spouse: ½ to spouse; ½ to child(ren).

Rhode Island

Real property: all to child(ren).

Personal property: ½ to spouse; ½ to child(ren).

South Carolina
½ to spouse; ½ to child(ren).

South Dakota
If all children are issue of the surviving spouse also, spouse gets entire estate.

If any child is not issue of the surviving spouse: spouse gets first $100,000 plus ½ of any balance, remainder to child(ren).

Tennessee
Spouse shares equally with child(ren); but spouse entitled to at least ⅓.

Texas
Community property: If all children are also issue of the surviving spouse, then all to the surviving spouse; if any child is not issue of the surviving spouse, then ½ of the community estate is retained by the surviving spouse and ½ passes to child(ren).

Separate property: with respect to *personal* property, ⅓ to spouse and balance to child(ren); with respect to *real* property, spouse takes life estate in ⅓, remainder to child(ren) [Presumably by "remainder" the statute means the remainder interest in the spouse's life estate *and* the fee interest in the remaining ⅔ of the real estate].

Utah
If all children are issue of the surviving spouse also, spouse gets entire estate.

If any child is not issue of surviving spouse: spouse gets first $75,000 plus ½ of any remaining balance

Vermont
If all of the decedent's surviving descedants are also descedants of the surviving spouse, spouse gets entire estate.

If one or more of the decedent's descendants are not also descendants of the surviving spouse; ½ to spouse

Virginia
If all children are issue of the surviving spouse also, spouse gets entire estate.

If any child is not issue of surviving spouse: ⅓ to spouse; balance to child(ren).

Washington

Community property: all to spouse or state registered domestic partner.

Separate property: ½ to spouse or state registered domestic partner; ½ to child(ren).

West Virginia

If all children are issue of the surviving spouse also and the surviving spouse has no other surviving issue, spouse gets entire estate.

If all children are issue of the surviving spouse also but the surviving spouse has any surviving issue who is not also issue of the decedent: $^3/_5$ to spouse; $^2/_5$ to decedent's child(ren).

If any child is not issue of the surviving spouse: ½ to spouse; ½ to decedent's child(ren).

Wisconsin

If all children are issue of the surviving spouse also, spouse gets entire net intestate estate.

If any child is not issue of surviving spouse: spouse gets ½ of net intestate estate consisting of decedent's property other than marital property (i.e., property acquired during marriage); remainder to child(ren).

Wyoming

½ to spouse; ½ to child(ren).

TABLE OF CONTENTS

POINTERS

Value And Control.

It is essential for any successful business continuation or disposition plan to consider the factors of value and control. Complete control of a business with no value is worthless; and value in a business you do not control is tenuous. With most successful operating businesses, value and

control are typically fixed and determined. In the small closely-held business it is generally accepted that the same individual, or group of individuals, both control the business and own the value. But what happens to control and value upon the death of the business owner? This is the essential question you must address in developing an effective business succession plan. By charting the interrelationship of these two factors you can better appreciate how control dictates value. Greater control means greater value – less control means less value. But the relationship is not linear! Having a controlling interest (i.e., more than 50 percent) in a closely-held corporation produces a "control premium," as can be seen from the sharp increase in value in the chart. The flip side of the control premium is the discount allowed for a minority interest (page 411).

Continued – Sold – Liquidated.

There is no better place to begin a discussion of business succession planning than by asking the questions set forth on page 119. But before you begin the discussion, visit the chart on page 117. Where would you place your client on this chart? Just as importantly, where would your client place himself on this chart? This insight should enable you to more effectively work with your client in developing *and implementing* a business disposition plan.

Know The Entity.

Before proceeding, it is essential to identify the type, or format, of the business: C corporation, S corporation, partnership, limited liability company, or sole proprietorship. The form of organization is an important consideration in selecting an agreement to be used if it is intended that the business will be sold (e.g., a stock redemption agreement does not work very well with a sole proprietorship). In this regard, you may wish to consult the materials on pages 176-178, 193-194, 445, 465-467, 471, 483, and 510-512. Knowing the type of business is also important when considering employee benefits (pages 286-294).

Retain Control . . . Shift Value.

If your client's business is to be *continued* by a family member, there are many techniques that can be used to reduce estate taxes – while at the same time maintaining control (e.g., family limited partnerships or recapitalizations, see pages 162-169). Implementation of a specific arrangement will often depend not only upon your client's willingness to proceed, but also upon the ability of your client's professional advisors to work as a team.

Compare The Charts.

The cross purchase agreement involves an agreement between the owners to buy and sell their respective interests. You might think of it as a horizontal obligation running from business owner to business owner. On the other hand, the entity purchase agreement, also referred to as a stock redemption agreement if used with a corporation, involves an agreement by the owners to sell their respective interests to the business. You might think of it as a vertical obligation running between the business owners and the business. However, because of changing individual and business circumstances, choosing between a cross purchase agreement and an entity purchase agreement can be difficult. To keep their options open, your clients may prefer to use the highly flexible "wait and see" buy/sell agreement. With this arrangement, the decision as to who will make the purchase is delayed until after the death of an owner. All of these agreements provide for the complete sale of a business interest, and can be used with either a corporation or a partnership, but not with a sole proprietorship. To gain a better understanding of these plans, compare the charts on pages 127, 131 and 139.

Business Valuation Is Art . . . Not Science.

With the business owner the subject of business valuation is a wonderful "ice breaker." However, do not promise more than you can deliver. Business valuation is art, it is not science. The chart on page 123 provides a good place to begin, but a capitalization of earnings approach is not relevant in valuing many businesses (e.g., a medical practice or professional corporation). If appropriate, do not hesitate to advise your client to retain an accredited expert to perform a comprehensive business valuation.

Risk Management.

You should discuss "risk management" with the business owner. As stated by Judge Staley, "The business that insures its buildings and machinery and automobiles from every possible hazard can hardly be expected to exercise less care in protecting itself from the loss of its most vital assets – managerial skill and experience" (see quotable quotes, page 340). The statistics on pages 179 and 180 will help you quantify this risk for your business-owner clients.

Company Owned Life Insurance (COLI)

Employer-owned life insurance contracts must meet certain notice and consent requirements in order for the death proceeds to be excluded from taxable income. Application of a "related persons" provision, together with complicated attribution rules, will likely cast a very wide net (see discussion, pages 367-369). The general rule is that death proceeds from these contracts are taxed as ordinary income. Exceptions to this general rule are based upon the insured's status, or how death proceeds are paid or used. However, to qualify for any exception, it is essential to first meet strict notice and consent requirements. For each tax year the contract(s) is owned a reporting requirement mandates that all employers owning one or more employer-owned life insurance contracts must file Form 8529 (Report of Employer-Owned Life Insurance Contracts). *It is strongly recommended that notice be given, and consent be obtained, at the time an application is taken for virtually any life insurance contract that might conceivably fall within the scope of this law.*

Understand The Attribution Rules.

These rules have been aptly described as "infamous and insidious." While at first they may appear esoteric and difficult, they are important to understand. In family held corporations, if stock owned by one family member is to be sold to the corporation it is extremely important to consider the effect of the attribution rules (pages 170-175). Violation of these rules means that the sale will be treated and taxed as a stock dividend.

Reality Checks . . . They Are Important!

Often your business owner client will want to retain the business for the benefit of a son or daughter. Good planning will usually help this happen, but not if the child is a 2-year-old. Then there is the sole proprietor, who is convinced that his key man will take over the business and run it for the benefit of his survivors. This sounds just fine, until you discover that the "keyman" is a stock clerk hired just a year ago – but he is a "bright" young man. And then there is the physician, who is practicing as a sole proprietor, and who is convinced that his practice is easily worth five or six times annual billings, plus the book value of all the equipment he purchased a few years back. These clients will be well served if you help them perform a "reality check-up."

DEVELOPMENT CYCLE OF A BUSINESS

This chart will help us to better understand the typical life cycle of the owner-managed business. Such businesses are usually owned by rugged individualists who were drafted into business in a variety of ways. Although the growth curve is different for each business, it can generally be separated into four distinct phases, with the first two involving a lot of hard work.

The first stage is best described as the **Wonder Stage**, because sooner or later he will wonder, "How in the world did I get into this mess?" A seven-day workweek is the norm, for which he gets *freedom, power*, and the *last word* on how the job is to be done. Undercapitalized and overextended, he expends maximum energy just to keep creditors at bay, avoid taxes, and end up with a profit to finance future growth. The large majority of new businesses don't survive this stage.

It is during the **Blunder Stage** that the last of the failures quit, while the survivors experience substantial growth, work 18-hour days, learn to trust no one, and become *highly secretive*. This leads to a reluctance to teach the business to others.

By the time the **Thunder Stage** is reached, the business owner has become a respected and substantial member of his community. He enjoys his success! Secrecy and a *total lack of review* of his decisions have become hallmarks of his management style. The creation of myths at this stage is commonplace. These include the notion that the business is too unique for anyone else to run; that his experience is all that counts, and business practices should stay the same; that the business is his, to do what he wants with; that HE is *truly immortal*.

It is now that he draws the collective attention of the community's life underwriters and financial advisers. He desperately needs their services, but proves to be distrustful of advice. This dilemma could have been avoided had a relationship of trust and service been established *before* the thunder stage.

During the **Plunder Stage** the owner may tend to lose his appetite for risk, preferring instead just to keep what he has. He must learn to teach and share, not destroy on the way down what he built on the way up. Such teaching and sharing will allow for a renaissance of wonder, the opportunity for a successor's hard work and continued business growth. All too often the alternative is liquidation!

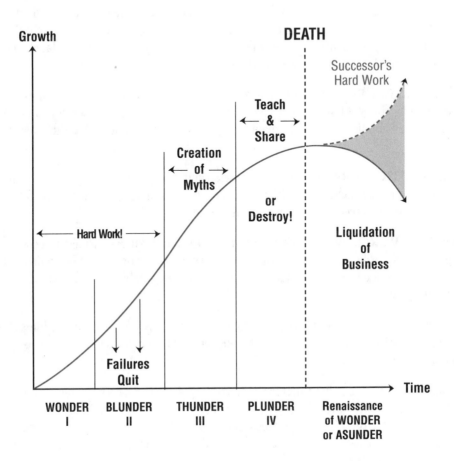

This chart and the accompanying text have been taken from Chapter Three of *Beyond Survival,* by Léon A. Danco, Ph.D., and are reprinted by permission of the publisher. This book has proven to be an invaluable guide to the advisor who desires to understand and effectively communicate with the owner of the closely held business. In addition, Dr. Danco has written *Inside The Family Business,* and *Outside Directors In The Family Owned Business.* Dr. Danco's books may be obtained by writing The Center for Family Business, P.O. Box 24268, Cleveland, Ohio 44124.

DISPOSITION OF A BUSINESS INTEREST

For our purposes, there are essentially three risks facing the business owner: death, disability, and retirement. Likewise, upon the business owner's death, disability, or retirement, only one of three things is going to happen to his business: it will be continued, sold, or liquidated. The planning process should reveal the answers to these questions:

Will **SUCCESSOR MANAGEMENT** be available and willing to operate the business? Such a person could be either a family member or a key employee, but it is important to be realistic about both their abilities and commitment to staying with the business. A *yes* answer will lead to . . .

Would a **SATISFACTORY RETURN** on business capital be provided for the family? The decision as to what is "satisfactory" is a highly subjective determination, but it usually falls within the range of 6 to 20 percent.[1] A *yes* answer will lead to . . .

Could **TAX-FAVORED PROFITS** be withdrawn for the family? If the business is a corporation, then payment of a salary to the stockholder-employee is "tax-favored" as a deductible business expense. However, the same payments to a surviving spouse might be characterized as nondeductible dividends.[2]

If the answers to all three of these questions are *yes*, then it is likely that the business could be successfully **continued**. However, should the answer to any one of these questions be *no*, then this would lead to . . .

Is there a *strong* desire for **CONTINUING FAMILY INVOLVEMENT** in the business? A *yes* answer to this question is often the result of a strong sense of family pride in the business, despite one or more "no" answers to the previous questions. Under such circumstances the business might well be **continued**, provided steps are now taken to assure that continuation is possible.[3] A *no* answer to this question will lead to . . .

Would a **BUYER** be readily available? If the answer is *yes*, then the business should be **sold**, with a binding agreement and adequate funding in order to assure that the sale takes place. A *no* answer to this question means that the business is likely to be **liquidated** and its assets sold for pennies on the dollar.

Footnotes on page 121

UPON DEATH, DISABILITY OR RETIREMENT

THE ANSWERS TO THESE QUESTIONS

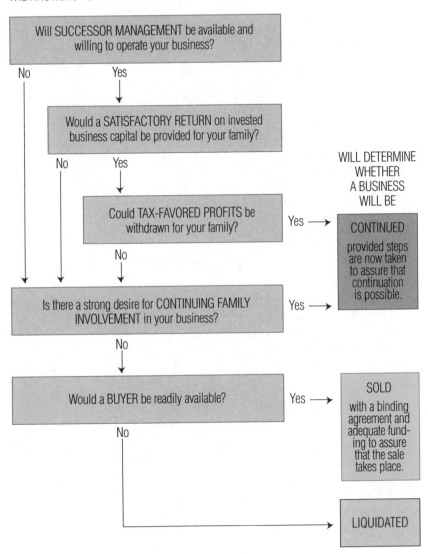

Will SUCCESSOR MANAGEMENT be available and willing to operate your business?

No   Yes

Would a SATISFACTORY RETURN on invested business capital be provided for your family?

No   Yes

Could TAX-FAVORED PROFITS be withdrawn for your family?

Yes →

No

WILL DETERMINE WHETHER A BUSINESS WILL BE

CONTINUED

provided steps are now taken to assure that continuation is possible.

Is there a strong desire for CONTINUING FAMILY INVOLVEMENT in your business?

Yes →

No

Would a BUYER be readily available?

Yes →

No

SOLD

with a binding agreement and adequate funding to assure that the sale takes place.

LIQUIDATED

PLANNING MATRIX

Footnotes

[1] A determination of business value would be a starting point for deciding what would be a "satisfactory" return on business capital. For example, $10,000 of annual income from a business worth $500,000 would probably not be satisfactory. If the business could be sold for $400,000, and the funds invested at 8 percent, the resulting before-tax income would be $32,000 per year, over three times that provided if the business were retained.

[2] There are numerous cases that have held that payments to stockholder-heirs are not deductible to the corporation. In the case of *The Barbourville Brick Company v. Commissioner*, 37 T.C. 7 (1961), the United States Tax Court held that payments to the surviving widow were dividends. Judge Brown, concurring in the denial of any income tax deduction to the corporation, considered the payments nondeductible as not a "reasonable business expense." In his written opinion, Judge Brown observed that:

> "[A]pparently there were no employees, stockholders, or members of [the decedent's] family, qualified to take over the management of petitioner's business. There is neither claim nor evidence that the widow performed any services for [the business]. Finally there is neither claim nor showing that the payments in question were in the nature of extra compensation for past services rendered by petitioner's deceased president . . . income tax deductions are a matter of legislative grace . . . and are to be justified as ordinary and necessary expenses of carrying on a trade or business."

[3] The "steps" relate to preparing for the eventual transfer of a healthy business to other family members or key employees. In this regard, the business planning charts on the following pages demonstrate techniques that will assist in providing the plans and funds for such a smooth transfer of the business. A comparison of life insurance and other sources of estate settlement costs is set forth on page 80.

BUSINESS VALUATION

There are many reasons why the owner of a closely held business must have some idea of the value of his business:

- When *obtaining loans* a higher, yet realistic, value could result in increased credit.
- If the *reasonableness of compensation* to an employee-stockholder is challenged by the IRS, knowing the value of the business will be helpful.[1]
- In *determining a price* for the business when it is sold upon death, disability, or retirement.[2]
- For *estate planning* purposes, the higher the value, the greater the potential estate tax.[3]

Valuation is an art; it is not a science.[4] With the closely held business, the concept of valuation is often elusive. Pat answers rarely exist. However, with many businesses, "capitalizing" expected earnings can be a useful starting point for determining fair market value.

For example, we know that assets, plus the talents of good management, are expected to produce earnings. Assume that a business had assets of $1,400,000 and liabilities of $400,000. By subtracting liabilities from assets, we can determine that book value is $1,000,000.[5] This is the net worth of the business, which is often referred to as stockholder's equity. Also assume that the business has earnings of $220,000.

The first step in capitalizing expected earnings is to determine what rate of return an outside purchaser would expect on his investment. Assume that, after a careful consideration of the risks inherent in this particular business, the *expected* rate of return is determined to be 12 percent.[6] If the sales price were set at book value, or only $1,000,000, expected earnings would then be $120,000. This means that there are *excess* earnings of $100,000, which should be reflected in the sales price as goodwill.

Goodwill is determined by deciding how much a purchaser should pay for these excess earnings, which are the product of such intangibles as reputation and market position. A careful consideration of both the age of the business and the likelihood of continuing excess earnings might reveal that the purchaser should pay for five years of excess earnings, or $500,000. By adding this $500,000 of good will to the $1,000,000 of book value, we get a fair market value for the business of $1,500,000.[7]

Footnotes on page 125

CAPITALIZING EXPECTED EARNINGS

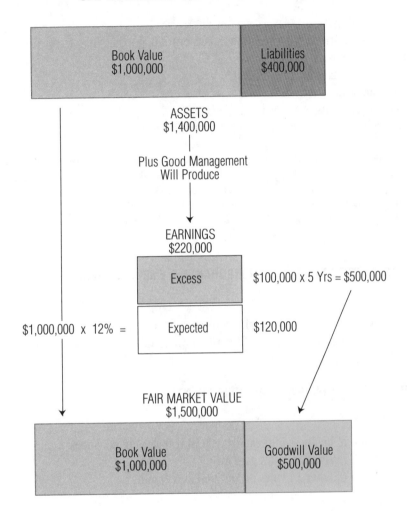

INFORMATION REQUIRED FOR ANALYSIS & PROPOSAL

1. Name of business.
2. Form of organization (C corporation, S corporation, partnership *or* sole proprietorship).
3. Nature of business.
4. Book value (assets minus liabilities).
5. Average earnings (after-tax).
6. Number of years business has been in existence.
7. Salaries of principals in excess of replacement salaries.

Note: Whenever possible, at least a 3-year average of earnings and book value should be used. The salaries of principals in excess of salaries that would be paid to replacements is typically added to average earnings. The nature of the business is relevant to determining the appropriate *expected rate of return* ("12%" in the chart). The number of years the business has been in existence, and thus its stability, reputation and market position, is relevant to determining the appropriate *capitalization of earnings* factor ("5" in the chart). For a further discussion of these rates, see footnote 6, page 125.

CROSS REFERENCES TO TAX FACTS ON INSURANCE & EMPLOYEE BENEFITS (2011)

Estate and Gift Tax

Q 243. Valuation of closely held business interest for federal estate tax purposes.

Q 246. An agreement restricting the lifetime sale of a business interest may be considered for gift tax purposes.

CROSS REFERENCES TO TAX FACTS ON INVESTMENTS (2011)

Estate Tax

Q 7611. Valuation of business interest for federal transfer tax purposes.

Q 7617. Chapter 14 valuation rules generally.

Q 7620. Impact of Chapter 14 rules on buy/sell agreements.

Footnotes

[1] Knowing the value of the business will help defend the reasonableness of salary and other fringe benefits. In this regard, see the expanded discussion of Unreasonable Compensation on page 546.

[2] Common means of selling businesses are set forth in the Entity Purchase Agreement chart on page 127 and the Cross Purchase Agreement chart on page 131.

[3] Under the Chapter 14 special valuation provisions, the value of property for gift and estate tax purposes is determined without regard to any agreement to acquire the property at less than fair market value. However, this rule does not apply if the agreement is: (1) a *bona fide* business arrangement; (2) not a *device* to transfer the property to members of the decedent's family for less than full and adequate consideration; and (3) in its terms, *comparable* to similar arrangements entered into by persons in an arm's length transaction. All three of these tests are presumed to be met if the agreement is between unrelated individuals (i.e., an agreement exclusively among persons who are not the natural objects of each others' bounty).

In agreements between related individuals maintenance of family ownership and control could be a *bona fide* reason for using a particular business value, thereby satisfying the first test. But the stipulated value will not be controlling for estate tax purposes unless the agreement also meets the *device* and *comparable* tests. In order to satisfy all three of these requirements in family held businesses there is likely to be an increased utilization of both *appraisal* and generally accepted *formula* methods of business valuation (see pages 407-408).

For estate tax purposes, the executor of an estate may elect special methods for valuing *real property* used in a farm, trade, or business. A discussion of the strict qualifications and restrictions imposed appears on pages 496-497.

[4] When valuation is left to chance, it opens the door to litigation with the Internal Revenue Service. The table of Contested Business Valuations (pages 186-191) contains a listing of specific types of businesses which ended up being the subjects of extensive litigation when the owners failed to properly plan for their estate tax valuation. The state of the art is at best uncertain for those who fail to "peg" properly the value of their business interests. It is also important to recognize that valuation may mean different things to different people, depending upon the purpose of the valuation. However, as far as the Internal Revenue Service is concerned, it is based upon a consideration of *all relevant facts*, and in particular those eight factors set forth in the expanded discussion of Fair Market Value on page 411. Financial ratio analysis provides another means of determining business value (see page 185).

[5] In using this approach to business valuation, care must be taken to assure that Book Value accurately reflects the true value of business assets (see page 350).

[6] Selection of appropriate *expected rate of return* and *capitalization of earning* factors is very subjective. Nevertheless, the following may provide some idea of the ranges used:

Expected rate of return		Capitalization of earnings	
8-11%	safe business	1-3	volatile earnings
12-17%	average business	4-6	average, variable earnings
18-22%	speculative business	7-9	stable earnings

[7] This chart demonstrates an application of what has come to be known as the "ARM 34" formula. It is most appropriately used with manufacturing firms involving substantial investments of both plant and equipment. The letters "ARM" stand for "Committee on Appeals and Review Memorandum." This committee no longer exists under the present judicial system. Another, more direct, method of capitalizing earnings is sometimes referred to as the "straight capitalization method" and is best demonstrated by the following question: "If a buyer expects to make 12 percent on his investment, and the business is producing earnings of $220,000 per year, what would the buyer be willing to pay for the business?" The calculation required to answer this question produces a substantially higher valuation than the ARM 34 formula shown in the chart:

Value x .12 = $220,000   *or*   Value = $220,000 ÷ .12 = $1,833,333

ENTITY PURCHASE AGREEMENT

The entity purchase agreement is another means of providing for the complete disposition of a business interest. Under such an arrangement the contract is with the business rather than with the other owners.[1]

DURING LIFETIME. To illustrate how it works, assume that we have a corporation that is owned equally by A and B.[2] They would each enter into an agreement with the business for the purchase and sale of their respective interests. Typically, this agreement is *binding*, in that it obligates both A and B, and their estates, to sell, and the business to buy, upon the death, disability or retirement of either one of them.[3]

Rather than relying on its ability to accumulate or borrow sufficient funds to meet its obligations to purchase these interests, the business obtains separate life insurance contracts insuring A and B.[4] The business pays the premiums and is owner and beneficiary of the contracts. In this manner, the business pre-funds its obligations with life insurance. With the use of life insurance to fund an entity purchase agreement the business is in effect *amortizing* the cost of the purchase over the lifetime of the insured.[5]

UPON DEATH. Should A die first, his stock interest passes to his family or estate. At the same time, the insurance company pays a potentially tax-free death benefit to the business as beneficiary of the contract insuring A's life.[6]

Pursuant to the agreement, in return for cash, A's family, or estate, will then transfer A's *entire interest* to the business.[7] In this way a fully funded agreement *guarantees* that the surviving family will receive a fair price for A's interest.[8] If A's estate is subject to estate taxes, the agreement can also serve to help "peg," or establish, the value of the stock for estate tax purposes, thereby avoiding the extensive negotiations and potential litigation with the Internal Revenue Service that may occur when valuation is left to chance.[9]

Footnotes on page 129

DURING LIFETIME

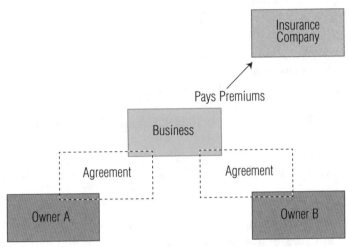

The Business Obtains Life Insurance On Each Owner

UPON DEATH

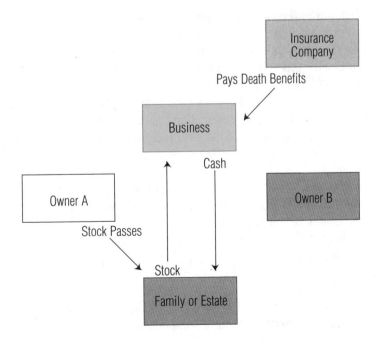

INFORMATION REQUIRED FOR ANALYSIS & PROPOSAL

1. Name of owner to be insured.
2. Sex.
3. Date of birth.
4. Smoker/nonsmoker.
5. Value of ownership interest.
6. Form of organization (C corporation, S corporation *or* partnership).

CROSS REFERENCES TO TAX FACTS ON INSURANCE & EMPLOYEE BENEFITS (2011)

Income Tax

Q 205. When death benefits of business life insurance are exempt from income tax.

Corporation

Q 189. Premiums paid on business life insurance not usually taxable to insured employee.

Q 190. Premiums paid by corporation on policies insuring the life of a stockholder or employee usually not deductible.

Q 194. Premiums paid by corporation to fund stock redemption not taxable to insured stockholder.

Q 225. Amount paid by corporation for decedent's entire stock interest generally not dividend to estate, provided no attribution problems.

Q 226-227. Avoiding attribution of stock ownership.

Q 229. Usually no capital gain to deceased stockholder's estate.

Q 230. Amount paid by corporation for stock usually not taxable as constructive dividend to surviving stockholder(s).

Q 231. Income tax results of funding stock redemption agreement with life insurance.

Q 234. Taxation of payments when redemption by S corporation.

Q 238. Treatment of corporate owned life insurance for purpose of alternative minimum tax.

Partnership

Q 199. Premiums paid by partnership are not deductible.

Q 235. Income tax results when deceased partner's interest is sold or liquidated under a business purchase agreement.

Q 237. Tax treatment of life insurance purchased to fund partnership business purchase agreement.

Estate Tax

Q 242. Life insurance proceeds not directly included in insured owner's estate when partnership or corporation is owner and beneficiary.

Footnotes

[1] Note that in contrast to the cross purchase agreement, the entity agreement requires that the *business* purchase the interest, not the other owners (compare entity purchase agreement with cross purchase agreement using the materials on page 193). The entity agreement can be used by either a partnership or a corporation with more than one stockholder. It is often the preferred method with *multiple* stockholders or partners, since only one policy on the life of each owner is required (but see, First-to-Die Insurance, page 415, which can be used to fund multiple-owner cross purchase agreements). An entity purchase agreement cannot be used by a corporation with only one stockholder or a sole proprietorship, since the corporation cannot own itself and the sole proprietorship is not a separate entity that can make the purchase. When used to fund the purchase of corporate stock, it is usually referred to as a "stock redemption" or "section 302(b)(3) stock redemption" agreement (see footnote 8, page 149). In this sense, the terms "entity purchase" and "stock redemption" are interchangeable.

[2] It is also assumed that A and B are *not* related to each other. If they were, and the business was a corporation, then the attribution rules would have to be considered (attribution is more fully explained on pages 170-175).

[3] If the agreement is binding upon disability as well as death, consideration should also be given to funding the agreement with disability buy-out insurance (see expanded discussion on page 386). The tax treatment of various disability income arrangements is set forth on page 323.

[4] Employer-owned life insurance must meet strict notice and consent requirements if the death benefits are to be received free of income taxes (see Company Owned Life Insurance (COLI), pages 367-369).

[5] By having the corporation purchase and pay the insurance premiums, it is often possible to utilize after-tax "enhanced dollars." A full discussion of Enhanced Dollars is found on page 398. Even if the corporation is not in a lower tax bracket than its stockholders, the entity purchase may still be the preferred method, since the corporate check is usually far easier to obtain for premium payments than a client's personal check. The likelihood that life insurance will be used can be estimated by referring to the Odds of Death tables on pages 179-180. Corporate borrowing as an alternative to life insurance funding is usually unattractive, as can be seen from the Cost of Borrowed Dollars table on page 182.

[6] Under some circumstances a portion of annual cash value increases and death proceeds could be subject to the Corporate Alternative Minimum Tax, as discussed on pages 374-376.

[7] Note that B is now the sole owner of the business. However, B's cost basis for purposes of income taxes has not been increased, because the business, not B, purchased A's interest. If the business were subsequently sold by B, he would have substantially more gain than would have been the case had B previously purchased A's interest under a cross purchase agreement at A's death. With regard to a corporation, once an entity purchase agreement has been funded with life insurance, it *is generally not* possible to use the same policies when changing to a cross purchase agreement. This is because of the Transfer For Value rule, as more fully explained on pages 541-542.

[8] Various means can be used in the agreement to determine the purchase price. A *fixed price* could be established, with a further provision providing for periodic review and redetermination between the business and the owners. Alternatively, a *formula method* could be used, under which specific factors would be employed to calculate a value. For an example of a *capitalization formula*, see the Business Valuation chart on page 123. Another approach to determining a price is to provide for an *appraisal* at the time of sale (i.e., after the first owner's death, or earlier if a lifetime sale is contemplated).

[9] To help "peg" the value of the business for estate tax purposes, the parties must be required to sell during lifetime for the same price as provided for a sale at death. Also, the agreement must specifically *bind* A's estate or family and further comply with the Chapter 14 requirements (see footnote 3, page 125). The listing of Contested Business Valuations on pages 186-191 provides specific examples of what can happen when there is a failure to properly "peg" the value of stock in a closely held corporation. The cases on page 192 demonstrate that a buy/sell agreement really does help fix the value.

CROSS PURCHASE AGREEMENT

The cross purchase agreement is one means of providing for the complete disposition of a business interest.[1] Under this arrangement the owners agree, among themselves, to buy and sell their respective interests.[2]

DURING LIFETIME. To illustrate how this works, assume that we have a corporation equally owned by two individuals, A and B. They enter into an agreement providing for the purchase and sale of their respective interests. Typically, this agreement is *binding* and obligates both parties, or their representatives, to either buy or sell upon the death, disability, or retirement of either one of them.[3]

Rather than trying to accumulate or borrow sufficient funds to buy B's interest, A obtains a life insurance contract insuring B. A applies for this coverage, pays the premiums, and is both owner and beneficiary of the contract. Likewise, B applies for a life insurance contract insuring A, pays the premiums, and is both owner and beneficiary.[4] By this means, A and B can use life insurance to *fully* fund their mutual obligations to each other.[5]

UPON DEATH. Assuming that A dies first, his stock interest would then pass to his family or estate. At the same time, the insurance company pays a death benefit to B, as beneficiary of the contract insuring A's life. B receives these funds free of all income taxes, since they are received as the death benefit of a life insurance contract.[6]

Pursuant to the agreement, A's family, or estate, transfers A's entire stock interest in the corporation to B, in return for which B pays the cash received from the insurance company.

The fully funded agreement will *assure* that A's surviving family receives a fair price for his interest in the business. But such an agreement can also serve another very important function. If the estate had been subject to estate taxes, it is possible that extensive negotiations and even litigation could result if the estate tax value of the business had been left to chance. These problems of delay and litigation can be avoided by having a cross purchase agreement which helps establish, or "peg," the value of the stock.[7]

Footnotes on page 133

DURING LIFETIME

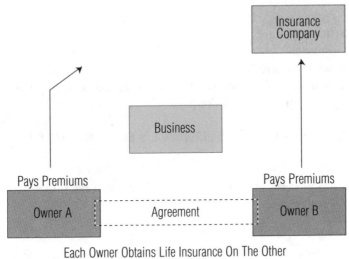

Each Owner Obtains Life Insurance On The Other

UPON DEATH

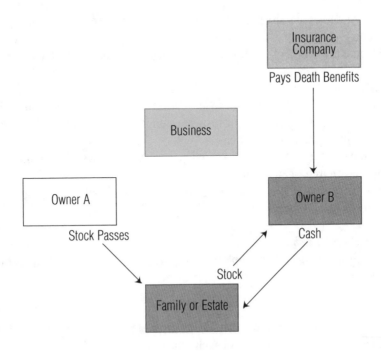

INFORMATION REQUIRED FOR ANALYSIS & PROPOSAL

1. Names of owners to be insured.
2. Sex.
3. Dates of birth.
4. Smoker/nonsmoker.
5. Value of ownership interests.
6. Form of organization (C corporation, S corporation, partnership, or sole proprietorship).
7. Identity of purchaser (stockholder or partner).

CROSS REFERENCES TO TAX FACTS ON INSURANCE & EMPLOYEE BENEFITS (2011)

Income Tax

Q 32.   For death proceeds to be excludable from income, a life insurance policy must meet certain requirements.

Corporation

Q 192.   Stockholder cannot deduct premiums paid on policy purchased on life of another stockholder.

Q 196.   Premiums paid by corporation on policies owned by stockholders are taxable income to stockholders.

Q 223.   Sale of deceased's stock will usually not result in income tax liability to deceased's estate.

Q 224.   Income tax effects of funding stock purchase agreement with life insurance.

Partnership

Q 199.   Premiums paid by partner for insurance on life of copartner are not deductible.

Q 200.   Premiums paid by partner for insurance on his own life are not deductible by him if proceeds payable to copartner.

Q 235.   Income tax results when deceased partner's interest sold or liquidated under a business purchase agreement.

Q 237.   Tax treatment of life insurance purchased to fund partnership business purchase agreement.

Sole Proprietorship

Q 202.   Premiums paid by key employee for insurance on life of sole proprietor are not deductible.

Estate Tax

Q 241.   Life insurance proceeds not included in insured's estate when partners or stockholders purchase insurance on lives of each other.

Footnotes

[1] Compare the cross purchase agreement with the entity purchase agreement using the materials on page 193. The cross purchase agreement can be used with either a corporation or a partnership. With a sole proprietorship, a similar arrangement could be established between the sole proprietor and a key employee (chart, page 143). However, since the key employee has no ownership interest, there are no reciprocal obligations to buy and sell. The sole proprietor would merely be obligated to sell and the key employee obligated to buy. Life insurance funding involves the key employee purchasing a contract on the life of the sole proprietor in order to fund his obligation to purchase. This purchase could be assisted by the split-dollar technique (chart, page 223).

[2] Various means can be used in the agreement to determine a purchase price. A *fixed price* could be established, with a further provision providing for periodic review and redetermination by mutual agreement among the owners. Alternatively, a *formula method* could be employed, under which specific factors would be used to calculate a value. For an example of a *capitalization* formula, refer to the valuation chart on page 123. Another approach to determining a price is to provide for an *appraisal* at the time of sale (i.e., after the first owner's death, or earlier if a lifetime sale is contemplated).

[3] A cross purchase agreement will avoid the attribution problems that can occur in a family held corporation (attribution is more fully explained on pages 170-175). However, a cross purchase agreement with *multiple* stockholders can be cumbersome when the agreement is to be funded with life insurance. For example, with three stockholders, six policies would be required because each stockholder would have to be the owner and beneficiary of a policy on each of the other stockholders. If there were four stockholders, twelve policies would be required. To avoid the problem of multiple policies, preference is often given to using an entity purchase agreement (chart, page 127) or a trusteed cross purchase agreement (chart, page 135 and comparison page 194). However, the death of one owner could create a transfer for value problem with respect to remaining policies insuring the surviving owners (pages 541-542). Funding with first-to-die insurance should avoid these problems (page 415).

[4] In a family-owned business the attribution rules under new Code section 101(j) *may* treat these policies as "employer-owned." This would subject the death benefits to income taxation. To assure the proceeds are received free of income taxes, appropriate notice and consents should be obtained (see Company Owned Life Insurance (COLI) pages 367-369).

[5] When the obligation is not fully funded, borrowing as an alternative to life insurance is usually unattractive, as can be appreciated by referring to the Cost of Borrowed Dollars table (page 183). The real risk of a death among multiple owners of a business can be estimated by using the Odds Of Death figures on pages 179-180. Executive equity or split-dollar could be used to assist A and B in purchasing the life insurance (see charts, pages 211 and 223).

[6] Receipt of the death proceeds allows B to purchase A's business interest *and* obtain an income tax cost basis equal to the purchase price. To illustrate, assume that both A and B originally paid $100,000 for each of their 50 percent stock interests which are now each worth $750,000 (for a total corporate value of $1,500,000). If A dies and the corporation buys A's stock for $750,000, B is then left as the sole stockholder of a corporation valued at $1,500,000. If B then subsequently sells the corporation, his gain on the sale would be $1,400,000 (the $1,500,000 sales price less the $100,000 he originally paid for his stock). However, if upon A's death B had purchased A's stock under a cross purchase agreement, B's basis in his corporate stock would be increased by $750,000. Under these circumstances, B's gain on a later sale of the corporation would be only $650,000 (the $1,500,000 sales price less his basis of $850,000, which includes the $100,000 he paid for his original stock plus the $750,000 he paid for A's shares).

[7] To help "peg" the value, the parties must be required to sell during lifetime for the same price as provided for a sale at death. In addition, the agreement must specifically *bind* A's estate or family and further comply with the Chapter 14 requirements (see footnote 3, page 125 and pages 407-408). The table of Contested Business Valuations on pages 186-191 provides specific examples of what happens when there is a failure to properly "peg" the value of stock in a closely held corporation. The cases on page 192 demonstrate that buy/sell agreements really do help fix the value.

TRUSTEED CROSS PURCHASE AGREEMENT

The trusteed cross purchase agreement is one means of providing for the complete disposition of a business interest.[1] Under this arrangement the owners use a third party to carry out their cross purchase agreement.[2] Although sometimes referred to as a "trustee," this individual is not acting as a trustee in a formal trust sense. Rather, the trusteed cross purchase agreement more closely resembles an escrow arrangement, under which an escrow agent acts as agent for the owners in carrying out their mutual obligations to each other.

DURING LIFETIME. To illustrate how this works, assume that we have a corporation owned by four stockholders, A, B, C and D. They enter into an agreement providing for the purchase and sale of their respective interests.[3] Typically, this agreement is *binding* and obligates all stockholders, or their representatives, to either buy or sell upon their death, disability, or retirement.

To implement the agreement the stockholders transfer their stock certificates to the escrow agent, and further have the escrow agent purchase life insurance on each stockholder.[4] The escrow agent is both owner and beneficiary of these contracts and pays any required premiums.[5] By this means the stockholders can use life insurance to *fully* fund their agreement, while having the assurance that their mutual obligations to each other will be carried out by the escrow agent.[6] Use of an escrow agent can substantially reduce the number of policies required to fund the agreement.[7]

UPON DEATH. Assuming that A dies first, the insurance company pays a death benefit to the escrow agent, as beneficiary of the contract insuring A's life. The escrow agent receives these funds free of all income taxes, since they are received as the death benefit of a life insurance contract. Pursuant to the agreement, the escrow agent then transfers A's entire stock interest in the corporation to the surviving stockholders, in return for which the escrow agent pays the cash received from the insurance company to A's family.[8]

The fully funded agreement will *assure* that A's surviving family receives a fair price for his interest in the business. But such an agreement can also serve another very important function. If the estate had been subject to estate taxes, it is possible that extensive negotiations and even litigation could result if the estate tax value of the business had been left to chance. These problems of delay and litigation can be avoided by having a trusteed cross purchase agreement which helps establish, or "peg," the value of the stock.[9]

Footnotes on page 137

DURING LIFETIME

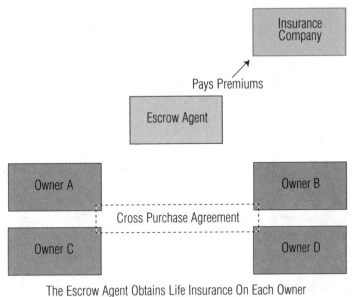

The Escrow Agent Obtains Life Insurance On Each Owner

UPON DEATH

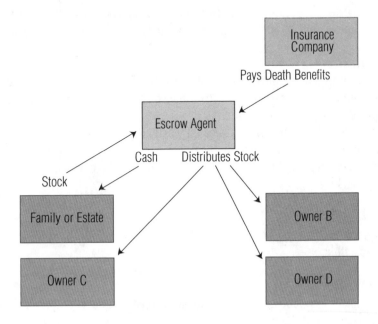

INFORMATION REQUIRED FOR ANALYSIS & PROPOSAL

1. Names of owners to be insured.
2. Sex.
3. Dates of birth.
4. Smoker/nonsmoker.
5. Value of ownership interests.
6. Form of organization (C corporation, S corporation, partnership, or sole proprietorship).
7. Identity of purchaser (stockholder or partner).
8. Identity of escrow agent.

CROSS REFERENCES TO TAX FACTS ON INSURANCE & EMPLOYEE BENEFITS (2011)

Income Tax

Q 32. For death proceeds to be excludable from income, a life insurance policy must meet certain requirements.

Corporation

Q 192. Stockholder cannot deduct premiums paid on policy purchased on life of another stockholder.

Q 196. Premiums paid by corporation on policies owned by stockholders are taxable income to stockholders.

Q 223. Sale of deceased's stock will usually not result in income tax liability to deceased's estate.

Q 224. Income tax effects of funding stock purchase agreement with life insurance.

Partnership

Q 199. Premiums paid by partner for insurance on life of copartner are not deductible.

Q 200. Premiums paid by partner for insurance on his own life are not deductible by him if proceeds payable to copartner.

Q 235. Income tax results when deceased partner's interest sold or liquidated under a business purchase agreement.

Q 237. Tax treatment of life insurance purchased to fund partnership business purchase agreement.

Sole Proprietorship

Q 202. Premiums paid by key employee for insurance on life of sole proprietor are not deductible.

Estate Tax

Q 241. Life insurance proceeds not included in insured's estate when partners or stockholders purchase insurance on lives of each other.

Footnotes

[1] Trusteed cross purchase agreements are also known as "custodian" or "escrowed" agreements. The provisions for an escrow agent can be part of the cross purchase agreement, or provided for in a separate agreement. The trusteed cross purchase agreement can be used with either a corporation or a partnership. With a sole proprietorship, a similar escrowed arrangement could be established between the sole proprietor and a key employee (chart, page 143). However, since the key employee has no ownership interest, there are no reciprocal obligations to buy and sell. The sole proprietor would merely be obligated to sell and the key employee obligated to buy.

[2] In recent years there has been a substantial increase in the use of cross purchase agreements (as opposed to entity purchase agreements). The factors contributing to this include: (1) the introduction of the corporate alternative minimum tax that may claim up to 15 percent of the death proceeds paid to a C corporation (see pages 374-376); (2) the avoidance of the attribution rules with a family-held corporation (see pages 170-175); (3) the increase of cost basis for the surviving stockholders, (see footnote 6, page 133); and (4) the ability to convert to a entity purchase agreement using the same policies without running afoul of the transfer for value rules (see page 541-542).

[3] See footnote 2, page 133, for an explanation of the various means that can be used in the agreement to determine a purchase price.

[4] In a family-owned business the attribution rules under new Code section 101(j) *may* treat these policies as "employer-owned." This would subject the death benefits to income taxation. To assure the proceeds are received free of income taxes, appropriate notice and consents should be obtained (see Company Owned Life Insurance (COLI) pages 367-369).

[5] Since the escrow agent pays the premiums on behalf of the owners he obtains the funds from the owners (e.g., B, C and D benefit from and therefore must pay the premiums for the policy insuring A). Although the premiums are not tax-deductible, split-dollar plans could be used to assist the owners in paying for the life insurance (chart, page 223). As an alternative, consider Executive Equity (chart, page 211).

[6] When the obligation is not fully funded, borrowing as an alternative to life insurance is usually unattractive, as can be appreciated by referring to the Cost of Borrowed Dollars table (page 183). The real risk of a death among multiple owners of a business can be estimated by using the Odds Of Death figures on pages 179-180.

[7] With multiple stockholders the typical cross purchase agreement has the disadvantage of requiring that each stockholder be the owner and beneficiary of a policy on each of the other stockholders. Example 1, below, requires twelve policies to fund a cross purchase agreement involving just four stockholders (i.e., A must own policies insuring B, C, and D, etc.). Example 2 uses an escrow agent under a *trusteed* cross purchase agreement to reduce the number of policies to the number of insured stockholders.

EXAMPLE 1	Owner ⟶	A	B	C	D
	12 policies insuring	B C D	A C D	A B D	A B C
EXAMPLE 2	Owner ⟶		ESCROW AGENT		
	4 policies insuring	A	B	C	D

[8] After the first death there is a potential transfer for value problem upon the transfer of the deceased stockholder's ownership interests in the remaining policies insuring the surviving stockholders (pages 541-542). It has been suggested that this problem could be avoided by using a first-to-die policy (see page 415).

[9] To help "peg" the value, the parties must be required to sell during lifetime for the same price as provided for a sale at death. In addition, the agreement must specifically *bind* A's estate or family and further comply with the Chapter 14 requirements (see footnote 3, page 125 and pages 407-408).

"WAIT AND SEE" BUY/SELL AGREEMENT

Choosing between a cross purchase and entity purchase agreement is often made difficult because of changing individual and business circumstances, as well as the inevitable "reforms" to our tax laws. One answer to this dilemma is the highly flexible "wait and see" buy/sell agreement, under which the owners agree among themselves, and with the business, to buy and sell their respective interests.[1]

DURING LIFETIME. To illustrate how this works, assume that we have a corporation which is owned equally by A and B.[2] As with both cross and entity purchase agreements, the "wait and see" agreement provides for valuation of their interests, sale upon death, disability or retirement, and the specific terms of payment.[3] However, unlike cross and entity purchase agreements, the "wait and see" buy/sell agreement does not specifically identify the purchaser. The purchaser and amounts of purchase are not determined until after the death of either A or B.

Life insurance funding of the agreement can be accomplished in a number of ways.[4] A and B could purchase life insurance contracts on each other (as with cross purchase agreements). Alternatively, the business could purchase life insurance contracts on both A and B (as with entity purchase agreements). A third alternative involves a combination of the first two methods.[5] Our example assumes that A and B purchase life insurance contracts on each other, are the policy owners, premium payors and beneficiaries.[6]

UPON DEATH. Should A die first, his stock passes to his family or estate. At the same time, the insurance company pays a tax-free death benefit to B, as beneficiary of the contract insuring A's life. Pursuant to the agreement the following steps are implemented:

> **1st** - The business has a *first option to purchase* A's stock.[7]
>
> **2nd** - If the business does not exercise its option, or purchases less than all of A's stock, B has a *second option to purchase* A's stock.[8]
>
> **3rd** - The business *is required to purchase* any of A's stock not previously purchased by either the business or B.[9]

Under the 1st and 3rd steps the business could obtain funds for purchasing A's stock by borrowing the death proceeds received by B.[10] As with cross and entity purchase agreements, the "wait and see" buy/sell agreement can also serve to help "peg," or establish, the value of the stock for estate tax purposes.[11]

Footnotes on page 141

DURING LIFETIME

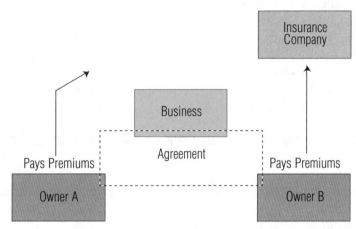

Insurance
Company

Business

Agreement

Pays Premiums

Pays Premiums

Owner A

Owner B

Each Owner Obtains Life Insurance On The Other

UPON DEATH

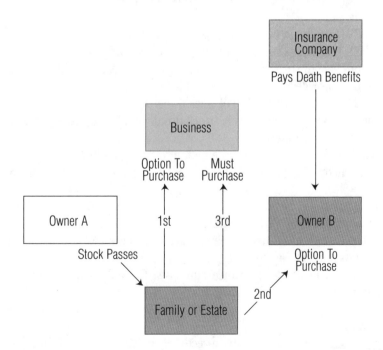

Insurance
Company

Pays Death Benefits

Business

Option To
Purchase

Must
Purchase

Owner A

Owner B

1st

3rd

Stock Passes

Option To
Purchase

Family or Estate

2nd

INFORMATION REQUIRED FOR ANALYSIS & PROPOSAL

1. Names of owners to be insured.
2. Sex.
3. Dates of birth.
4. Smoker/nonsmoker.
5. Value of ownership interests.
6. Form of organization (C corporation, S corporation *or* partnership).
7. Identity of purchaser of insurance.

CROSS REFERENCES TO TAX FACTS ON INSURANCE & EMPLOYEE BENEFITS (2011)

Income Tax

Q 205. When death benefits of business life insurance are exempt from income tax.

Corporation

Q 189. Premiums paid on business life insurance not usually taxable to insured employee.

Q 190. Premiums paid by corporation on policies insuring the life of a stockholder or employee usually not deductible.

Q 194. Premiums paid by corporation to fund stock redemption not taxable to insured stockholder.

Q 223 and 229. Usually no capital gain to deceased stockholder's estate.

Q 224 and 231. Income tax results of funding agreement with life insurance.

Q 225. Amount paid by corporation for decedent's entire stock interest generally not dividend to estate, provided no attribution problems.

Q 226 and 227. Avoiding attribution of stock ownership.

Q 230. Amount paid by corporation for stock usually not taxable as constructive dividend to surviving stockholder(s).

Q 234. Taxation of payments when redemption by S corporation.

Q 238. Treatment of corporate owned life insurance for purpose of alternative minimum tax.

Partnership

Q 199. Premiums paid are not deductible.

Q 235. Income tax results when deceased partner's interest is sold or liquidated under a business purchase agreement.

Q 237. Tax treatment of life insurance purchased to fund partnership business purchase agreement.

Estate Tax

Q 242. Life insurance proceeds not directly included in insured owner's estate when partnership or corporation is owner and beneficiary.

Footnotes

[1] The "wait and see" buy/sell agreement is also referred to as the "option" or "flexible" buy/sell. The agreement is not appropriate when a corporation has only one stockholder, or with a sole proprietorship, since the corporation cannot own itself and the sole proprietorship is not a separate entity that can make the purchase.

[2] It is also assumed that A and B are *not* related to each other. If they were, and the business were a corporation, then the attribution rules would have to be considered if there is a purchase of stock by the business under either the 1st or 3rd step (attribution is more fully explained on pages 170-175).

[3] Various means can be used in the agreement to determine the purchase price. A *fixed price* could be established, with a further provision providing for periodic review and redetermination between the business and the owners. Alternatively, a *formula method* could be used, under which specific factors would be employed to calculate a value. For an example of a *capitalization formula*, see the Business Valuation chart on page 123. Another approach to determining a price is to provide for an *appraisal* at the time of sale (i.e., after the first owner's death, or earlier if a lifetime sale is contemplated).

[4] If the agreement is binding upon disability as well as death, consideration should also be given to funding the agreement with disability buy-out insurance. Such coverage will generally provide a lump-sum payment after a stated period of total and permanent disability. The premiums are nondeductible and the benefits are received free of income taxes. An expanded discussion of disability buy-out insurance is on page 386.

[5] No matter which method is chosen, to assure the death proceeds are received free of income taxes, appropriate notice and consents should be obtained (see Company Owned Life Insurance (COLI), pages 367-369).

[6] Funding of the life insurance owned by A and B could be accomplished with split-dollar (chart, page 223) or executive equity (chart, page 211). Having the stockholders as owners and beneficiaries of the policies avoids any potential corporate alternative minimum tax problem, as discussed on pages 374-376. This also allows the survivor to obtain a stepped-up basis by purchasing some or all of the deceased's stock at the 2nd step (i.e., a cross purchase agreement). The survivor would not have received an increased cost basis if the corporation purchases all of the deceased's stock at the 1st step (i.e., an entity purchase agreement).

[7] Typically the corporation would have from 30 to 90 days to exercise its option at the 1st step. If the corporation purchases all of A's stock the result would be an entity purchase agreement (chart, page 127).

[8] If the corporation does not purchase all of the stock at the 1st step, and B purchases all of A's stock at the 2nd step, the result is a cross purchase agreement (see chart, page 131). Typically B would have from 30 to 90 days to exercise his option. Note that it is important for the surviving stockholder to have an *option*, but not an *obligation*, to purchase stock at the 2nd step. If B had a legal obligation to purchase A's stock, and failed to do so, then the corporation's purchase of stock at the 3rd step would be treated as a dividend to B (i.e., the corporation would be considered as having discharged B's legal obligation).

[9] Note that despite the options involved in the 1st and 2nd steps, the mandatory purchase by the corporation in the 3rd step provides the *binding* agreement that assures A's stock will be sold for the benefit of his family (see footnote 11, below).

[10] Alternatively, the corporation could borrow funds from other sources, or B could make a capital contribution to the corporation, thereby increasing his cost basis in his stock. This also has the advantage of avoiding any problems with the corporate alternative minimum tax, which could occur if the corporation received the death proceeds (see pages 374-376).

[11] To help "peg" the value of the business for estate tax purposes, the parties must be required to sell during lifetime for the same price as provided for a sale at death. In addition, the agreement must specifically *bind* A's estate or family and further comply with the Chapter 14 requirements (see footnote 3, page 125).

KEY PERSON BUY-OUT AGREEMENT

The key person buy-out agreement is one means of providing for the complete disposition of a business interest.[1] Under this arrangement the owner agrees to sell all of his business interest to a key person.[2]

DURING LIFETIME. To illustrate how this works, assume that we have a corporation owned by A. A would enter into an agreement providing for the sale to B, a key person in the business. Typically, this agreement is *binding* and obligates both parties, or their representatives, upon the death, disability, or retirement of A.

Rather than trying to accumulate or borrow sufficient funds to buy A's interest, B obtains a life insurance contract insuring A. B applies for this coverage, pays the premiums, and is both owner and beneficiary of the contract.[3] By this means, B can use life insurance to *fully* fund his obligation to A.[4]

UPON DEATH. Assuming that A dies first, his stock would then pass to his family or estate. At the same time, the insurance company pays a death benefit to B, as beneficiary of the contract insuring A's life. B receives these funds free of all income taxes, since they are received as the death benefit of a life insurance contract.[5]

Pursuant to the agreement, A's family, or estate, transfers A's stock interest in the business to B, in return for which B pays the cash received from the insurance company.

The fully funded agreement will *assure* that A's surviving family receives a fair price for his interest in the business. But such an agreement can also serve another very important function. If the estate had been subject to estate taxes, it is possible that extensive negotiations and even litigation could result if the estate tax value of the business had been left to chance. These problems of delay and litigation can be avoided by having an agreement that helps establish, or "peg," the value of the stock.[6]

Footnotes on page 145

DURING LIFETIME

UPON DEATH

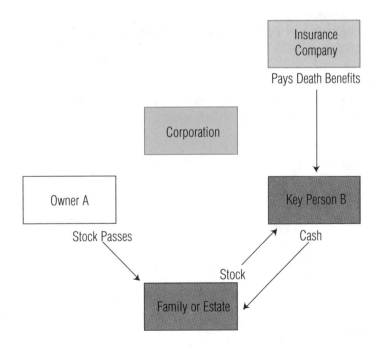

INFORMATION REQUIRED FOR ANALYSIS & PROPOSAL

1. Name of owner to be insured.
2. Sex.
3. Date of birth.
4. Smoker/nonsmoker.
5. Value of ownership interest.
6. Form of organization (C corporation, S corporation, partnership, or sole proprietorship).
7. Identity of key employee.

CROSS REFERENCES TO TAX FACTS ON INSURANCE & EMPLOYEE BENEFITS (2011)

Income Tax

Q 32.   For death proceeds to be excludable from income, a life insurance policy must meet certain requirements.

Corporation

Q 223.   Sale of deceased's stock will usually not result in income tax liability to deceased's estate.

Q 224.   Income tax effects of funding stock purchase agreement with life insurance.

Sole Proprietorship

Q 202.   Premiums paid by key employee for insurance on life of sole proprietor are not deductible.

Estate Tax

Q 241.   Life insurance proceeds not included in insured's estate when partners or stockholders purchase insurance on lives of each other.

Footnotes

[1] Such an agreement can be used with a corporation, a partnership, or a sole proprietorship. Since the key employee has no ownership interest, unlike the cross purchase agreement on page 131, there are no reciprocal obligations to buy and sell. The owner is merely obligated to sell and the key employee obligated to buy. A trusteed key person buy-out agreement might also be considered similar to the trusteed cross purchase agreement (chart, page 135).

[2] Various means can be used in the agreement to determine a purchase price. A *fixed price* could be established, with a further provision providing for periodic review and redetermination by mutual agreement among the owners. Alternatively, a *formula method* could be employed, under which specific factors would be used to calculate a value. For an example of a *capitalization* formula, refer to the valuation chart on page 123. Another approach to determining a price is to provide for an *appraisal* at the time of sale (i.e., after the owner's death, or earlier if a lifetime sale is contemplated).

[3] In a family-owned business it is possible that the reach of the attribution rules under Code section 101(j) *might* treat this policy as "employer-owned." This would subject the death benefit to income taxation. To assure the proceeds are received free of income taxes, appropriate notice and consent should be obtained (see Company Owned Life Insurance (COLI) pages 367-369).

[4] When the obligation is not fully funded, borrowing as an alternative to life insurance is usually unattractive, as can be appreciated by referring to the Cost of Borrowed Dollars table (page 183). Although the premiums paid for this coverage are not tax-deductible, a split-dollar plan could be used to assist B in purchasing the life insurance (chart, page 223). As an alternative, consider Executive Equity (chart, page 211).

[5] Receipt of the death proceeds allows B to purchase A's business interest *and* obtain an income tax cost basis equal to the purchase price. Assume that A originally paid $100,000 for his stock interest that is now worth $750,000. If A dies and B purchases A's stock under a key person buy-out agreement, B's basis in the stock would be equal to the $750,000 purchase price. B's gain on a later sale of the stock would be equal to the amount by which the sales price exceeds $750,000.

[6] To help "peg" the value, A must be required to sell during lifetime for the same price as provided for a sale at death. In addition, the agreement must specifically *bind* A's estate or family and further comply with the Chapter 14 requirements (see footnote 3, page 125 and pages 407-408). The table of Contested Business Valuations on pages 186-191 provides specific examples of what happens when there is a failure to properly "peg" the value of stock in a closely held corporation. The cases on page 192 demonstrate that buy/sell agreements really do help fix the value.

PARTIAL STOCK REDEMPTION

A partial stock redemption under Section 303 offers a very attractive way of paying estate settlement costs, particularly for a corporation that will be continued by the surviving family.[1]

Under most circumstances, a stockholder who has the corporation redeem less than his entire stock interest will be fully taxed on the proceeds as ordinary income. However, under the special provisions of Section 303, his surviving family can do after death what the stockholder generally cannot do during his lifetime . . . namely, sell only a *portion* of his stock interest to the corporation, and have the sale treated as a capital transaction rather than as a dividend.

DURING LIFETIME. If the stock interest will be *more than* 35 percent of the stockholder's adjusted gross estate, then his stock will qualify under Section 303 for a partial redemption at his death.[2] The *amount* of stock which can be purchased is limited to the sum of all federal and state death taxes, funeral, and administrative expenses. The purchase must also be made from whoever has the obligation to pay these costs, usually the family or estate.[3]

Since few corporations can be expected to accumulate sufficient cash for such a purchase, typically the corporation obtains a life insurance contract insuring the stockholder in his capacity as an employee. The corporation pays the premiums and is both owner and beneficiary of the contract.[4] This is generally a much better solution to the funding problem than attempting to accumulate large cash reserves over a period of time, borrowing at high interest rates, or selling corporate assets.[5]

UPON DEATH, the stock passes to the family or estate. At the same time, the insurance company pays a death benefit to the corporation.[6] This money is usually received free of all income taxes.[7] The corporation can then use the cash to purchase *some* of the stock from the family or estate.

The tax-favored treatment under Section 303 has been made available to the family-owned corporation in order to protect it from being sold or liquidated to pay death taxes and other estate settlement costs. When a corporate interest is the bulk of an estate, it only makes sense to use corporate dollars to provide the necessary cash to pay these costs.[8]

Footnotes on page 149

DURING LIFETIME

UPON DEATH

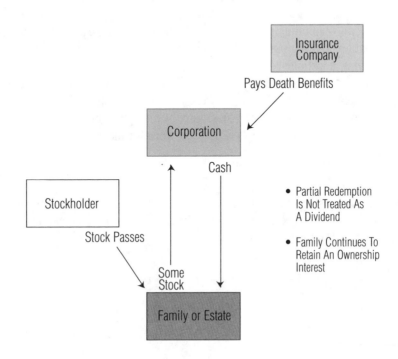

INFORMATION REQUIRED FOR ANALYSIS & PROPOSAL

1. Name of owner to be insured.
2. Sex.
3. Date of birth.
4. Smoker/nonsmoker.
5. Value of ownership interest.
6. Value of adjusted gross estate (see calculation steps, page 83).
7. Form of organization (C corporation *or* S corporation).

CROSS REFERENCES TO TAX FACTS ON INSURANCE & EMPLOYEE BENEFITS (2011)

Income Tax

Q 89.   Income taxation of life insurance policy that insures more than one life.

Q 188.   Premiums paid not deductible.

Q 190.   Premium paid by corporation on policies insuring the life of a stockholder or employee usually not deductible as business expense.

Q 194.   Premium paid by corporation to fund stock redemption not taxable to insured stockholder.

Q 205.   When death benefits of business life insurance are exempt from income tax.

Q 228.   Requirements for a Section 303 stock redemption.

Q 229.   Usually no capital gain to deceased stockholder's estate caused by a redemption.

Q 230.   Amount paid by corporation for stock usually not taxable as constructive dividend to surviving stockholder(s).

Q 231.   Income tax results of funding stock redemption agreement with life insurance.

Q 232.   Accumulated earnings tax and purchase of business life insurance.

Q 234.   Taxation of payments when redemption by S corporation.

Q 238.   Treatment of corporate owned life insurance for purposes of alternative minimum tax.

Estate Tax

Q 141.   Estate taxation of life insurance policy that insures more than one life.

Q 242.   Life insurance proceeds not directly included in insured stockholder's estate when corporation is owner and beneficiary.

Footnotes

[1] Partial stock redemptions are also referred to as "Section 303 Redemptions." Code section 303 authorizes a redemption of less than the entire stock interest of the decedent to be treated as a *sale* of stock, as opposed to a *dividend*. Because of the step-up in basis at death, a sale of stock will generally result in little, if any, taxable gain, since under a capital transaction the seller is not taxed on the basis of the property sold. In contrast, a dividend would be fully taxable as ordinary income (see Stepped-Up Basis, on page 530).

[2] The adjusted gross estate is determined by subtracting debts, funeral, and administrative expenses from the gross estate. This requirement provides you with the opportunity to conduct an estate analysis involving a full review of a client's assets. Without this information, it is not possible to determine whether an estate would qualify for a partial stock redemption (see page 12). If a client has more than one corporation, the stock of two or more corporations may be combined to meet the 35 percent test, provided the stockholder owns 20 percent or more of the value of each corporation, and the stock of the corporation is included in his gross estate. Even though an estate may *presently* be expected to qualify for a partial stock redemption, it is important to monitor estate assets to assure that there is not a subsequent disqualification. For example, the corporate stock could become 35 percent or less of the adjusted gross estate if: (1) other estate assets appreciate more than the stock interests; (2) the stock interests decline in value; (3) stock is either sold or given away.

[3] The redemption can be made only by that party having liability for the federal and state death taxes, funeral, and administrative expenses. It must usually be made within 3 years and 90 days after the estate tax return is filed (the estate tax return must be filed within 9 months after death). The effectiveness of a Section 303 redemption is limited when the unlimited marital deduction is used. See discussion on page 515.

[4] Employer-owned life insurance must meet strict notice and consent requirements if the death benefits are to be received free of income taxes (see Company Owned Life Insurance (COLI), pages 367-369).

[5] It is questionable whether many corporations could accumulate sufficiently large cash reserves for effective partial stock redemptions without running afoul of the prohibition against the unreasonable accumulation of earnings (see page 346, Accumulated Earnings Tax). With the purchase of life insurance to fund a partial stock redemption, the corporation is in effect *amortizing* the cost of the redemption over the lifetime of the insured stockholder. The insurance carried is similar to key person insurance as shown in the chart on page 155. If the corporation is in a relatively low tax bracket, the required premium payments can be made with Enhanced Dollars, as explained on page 398. Another variation of insurance ownership and beneficiary designation is shown in the Reverse Section 303 stock redemption chart, on page 151. Funding a partial stock redemption with survivorship life insurance can be particularly attractive when the unlimited marital deduction is used at the first death, since it provides death proceeds at the second death, when the estate taxes can no longer be deferred.

[6] This death benefit will *increase* the value of the decedent's stock in his gross estate in proportion to the decedent's interest in the corporation. For example, if the decedent owned 100 percent of the stock, a $100,000 death benefit might increase the value of the stock in the estate by $100,000. However, if the decedent owned only 40 percent of the stock, a $100,000 death benefit might increase the value of the stock in the estate by only $40,000. It could always be argued that there was a loss of corporate value caused by the death of a key employee that offsets some or all of the increase in stock value.

[7] Under some circumstances a portion of annual cash value increases and death proceeds could be subject to the Corporate Alternative Minimum Tax, as discussed on pages 374-376.

[8] In this chart, only *some* stock is redeemed, whereas a redemption of *all* stock is referred to as a "Section 302(b)(3) redemption." Section 302(b)(3) is that section of the Code that enables the redemption, or sale to the corporation, of the *entire* stock interest of a stockholder to be treated as a *sale* of stock, as opposed to a *dividend*. The Entity Purchase Agreement chart, on page 127, explains the Section 302(b)(3) redemption. Unlike the entity purchase agreement, in a family held corporation a partial stock redemption does not cause potential attribution problems (see pages 170-175).

REVERSE SECTION 303

A reverse stock redemption under Section 303 offers a very attractive way of paying estate settlement costs by having an entity other than the corporation purchase insurance to fund the redemption.[1]

DURING LIFETIME. If the stock interest will be *more than* 35 percent of the stockholder's adjusted gross estate, then his stock will qualify under Section 303 for a partial redemption at his death.[2] The *amount* of stock that can be purchased is limited to the sum of all federal and state death taxes, funeral, and administrative expenses.[3] However, the purchase must be made from whoever has the obligation to pay these costs, usually the family or estate.

One way to implement a reverse Section 303 is for the stockholder to establish a life insurance trust.[4] A life insurance contract insuring the stockholder is then obtained by the trust.[5] The trust pays the premiums and is both owner and beneficiary of the contract.[6]

UPON DEATH. The stock passes to the family or estate. At the same time, the insurance company pays a death benefit to the trust, which is received free of all income taxes.[7] The trust then loans the money to the corporation, which uses it to purchase *some*, but not all, of the stock from the family or estate.

In repaying this loan the corporation can make tax-deductible interest payments to the trust. Although these interest payments would be taxable income to the trust, repayments of the loan principal would be received by the trust free of income taxes. By this means the family can continue to retain ownership and control of the corporation, while at the same time receiving, as trust beneficiaries, the benefits of the untaxed repayment of loan principal.

Of course, it is not necessary for a trust to be established. Anyone who has substantial funds can loan them to the corporation for the purpose of a partial stock redemption. For example, a son or daughter of the stockholder could be owner and beneficiary of life insurance contracts insuring the parent. After receipt of the death benefit, the proceeds could be loaned by the children to the corporation, which would then repay the loan together with interest.[8]

Footnotes on page 153

DURING LIFETIME

UPON DEATH

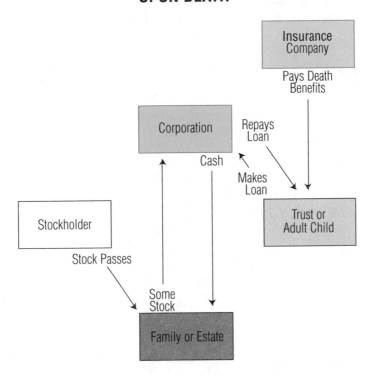

Reverse Section 303

INFORMATION REQUIRED FOR ANALYSIS & PROPOSAL

1. Name of owner to be insured.
2. Sex.
3. Date of birth.
4. Smoker/nonsmoker.
5. Value of ownership interest.
6. Value of adjusted gross estate (see calculation steps, page 83).
7. Form of organization (C corporation *or* S corporation).

CROSS REFERENCES TO TAX FACTS ON INSURANCE & EMPLOYEE BENEFITS (2011)

Q 2.   Premiums paid on life insurance generally not deductible.

Q 89.   Income taxation of life insurance policy that insures more than one life.

Q 141.   Estate taxation of life insurance policy that insures more than one life.

Q 228.   Requirements for a Section 303 stock redemption.

Q 229.   Usually no capital gain to deceased stockholder's estate.

Q 230.   Amount paid by corporation for stock usually not taxable as constructive dividend to surviving stockholder(s).

Q 234.   Taxation of payments when redemption by S corporation.

Footnotes

[1] Section 303 is that section of the Code that authorizes a redemption of less than the entire stock interest of the decedent to be treated as a *sale* of stock, as opposed to a *dividend*. Because of the step-up in basis at death, a sale of stock will generally result in little, if any, taxable gain, since under a capital transaction the seller is not taxed on the basis of the property sold. In contrast, a dividend would be fully taxable as ordinary income (see Stepped-Up Basis, on page 530).

[2] The adjusted gross estate is determined by subtracting debts, funeral, and administrative expenses from the gross estate. This requirement provides you with an opportunity for an estate analysis involving a full review of a client's assets (see page 12). Without this information, it is not possible to determine whether an estate will qualify for a partial stock redemption. If a client has more than one corporation, the stock of two or more corporations may be combined to meet the 35 percent test, provided the stockholder owns 20 percent or more of the value of each corporation, and the stock of the corporation is included in his gross estate. Even though an estate may *presently* be expected to qualify for a Section 303 redemption, it is important to monitor estate assets in order to assure that the estate continues to qualify. For example, the corporate stock could become 35 percent or less of the adjusted gross estate if: (1) other estate assets appreciate more than the stock interests; (2) the stock interests decline in value; (3) some of the stock is either sold or given away.

[3] The reduction of the federal estate tax under EGTRRA 2001 reduced the utility of a Reverse Section 303.

[4] The details of establishing a life insurance trust are set forth in the chart on page 51.

[5] In a family-owned business it is possible that the reach of the attribution rules under Code section 101(j) *might* treat this policy as "employer-owned." This would subject the death benefit to income taxation. To assure the proceeds are received free of income taxes, appropriate notice and consent should be obtained (see Company Owned Life Insurance (COLI) pages 367-369). Funding a reverse Section 303 stock redemption with survivorship life insurance can be particularly attractive when the unlimited marital deduction is used at the first death, since it provides death proceeds at the second death, when the estate taxes can no longer be deferred. If survivorship life insurance is used, then appropriate notice and consents should be obtained from *both* insureds.

[6] Since premiums must come from after-tax dollars, having someone other than the corporation own the insurance contract and pay the premiums could take advantage of a lower tax bracket (see Enhanced Dollars, on page 398).

[7] Use of a reverse Section 303 may be advisable when there is a concern regarding the Corporate Alternative Minimum Tax (see pages 374-376). With the usual Section 303 redemption, as shown in the chart on page 147, the payment of the death benefit to the corporation exposes the corporation to the alternative minimum tax. With a reverse Section 303 redemption the death benefit is paid outside the corporation, meaning that there is no increase in adjusted current earnings, and thus no exposure to the alternative minimum tax.

[8] When the insurance is owned by and payable to either children or a trust, the reverse 303 technique avoids the problem of increasing the value of the deceased's taxable estate, as occurs when death proceeds are paid to a corporation under the usual Section 303 arrangement (see the chart on page 147, and footnote 6 on page 149).

KEY PERSON INSURANCE

Multipurpose key person insurance is designed to help protect a business from the financial losses that can occur when a key employee dies. Such a key employee could be the owner of the business, or a non-owner employee whose very specialized abilities are critical to the operation of the business and difficult or costly to replace.[1] Adequate amounts of key person insurance are essential in any risk management program. Since the existence of business debt "signals a need for insurance," key person insurance can function as a form of commercial loan protection, as well as provide needed funds when a business is to be continued, sold, or liquidated.[2]

DURING LIFETIME. This protection is provided by having the business obtain insurance on the life of the key employee.[3] As both owner and beneficiary of the contract, the business pays the premiums directly to the insurance company.[4] The contract's cash values are carried as a business asset, and are available as collateral for securing commercial loans, or for direct borrowing from the insurance company at generally favorable interest rates.[5]

Many guidelines are used in estimating the *dollar value* of a particular key employee. However, the value can be most easily estimated by using a factor of three to ten times the employee's salary. Other guidelines that have been employed involve either a determination of the employee's replacement cost, or an estimation of lost profits or credit.[6]

UPON DEATH of the key employee the insurance company pays the death benefit directly to the business. The funds are treated as an addition to surplus and are received free of any direct income taxes.[7]

The proceeds can then be used for various purposes. Should it be determined that the business will be *continued*, these can be used to obtain a qualified replacement, replace lost profits, protect its credit position, provide a financial cushion, fund a partial stock redemption or make survivor income payments. If the business is to be *sold*, then there is money available to fund a full stock redemption. In case of *liquidation*, the cash will benefit the surviving family by offsetting lost business value.[8]

Footnotes on page 157

DURING LIFETIME

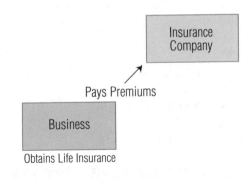

Insurance
Company

Pays Premiums

Business

Obtains Life Insurance

Key Employee

Insured

UPON DEATH

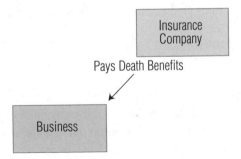

Insurance
Company

Pays Death Benefits

Business

Key Employee

Proceeds Can Be Used To:

- Replace Lost Profits
- Protect Credit Position
- Provide Financial Cushion
- Offset Lost Business Value
- Obtain Qualified Replacement
- Make Survivor Income Payments
- Fund Entity Purchase Agreement (Sec. 302)
- Fund Partial Stock Redemption (Sec. 303)

INFORMATION REQUIRED FOR ANALYSIS & PROPOSAL

1. Name of employee.
2. Sex.
3. Date of birth.
4. Smoker/nonsmoker.

To Determine Amount of Coverage
5. Salary of employee.
6. Position of employee in business.

CROSS REFERENCES TO TAX FACTS ON INSURANCE & EMPLOYEE BENEFITS (2011)

General Rules

Q 3.   Deduction of interest on indebtedness incurred to purchase or carry life insurance contract.

Q 8.   Taxation of distributions from policies classified as modified endowment contracts.

Q 17.   Taxability of policy loans.

Q 18.   Deduction of interest on policy loans.

Q 188.   Premiums paid usually not deductible as business expense.

Q 189.   Premiums paid usually not taxable to insured employee.

Corporation

Q 170.   Tax consequences of attaching disability income rider to key person life insurance policy.

Q 190.   Premiums paid by corporation on policies insuring the life of a stockholder or employee usually not deductible as business expense.

Q 193.   Premiums paid by corporation not taxable to insured employee.

Q 238.   Treatment of corporate owned life insurance for purposes of alternative minimum tax.

Partnership

Q 199.   Premiums paid by partnership are not deductible.

Q 200.   Premiums paid by partner for insurance on his own life not deductible by him if proceeds payable to partnership.

Estate Tax

Q 239.   Life insurance payable to partnership generally not includible in insured partner's estate (but included as part of partnership interest).

Q 240.   Life insurance payable to corporation generally not includible in insured's estate, provided insured had no "incidents of ownership" in policy (but included in valuing corporate stock).

Footnotes

[1] The loss of a good manager can mean the loss of a good business. It has been said that, "debt signals a need for life insurance" (see Quotable Quotes, page 340). The classic statement regarding the need for key person insurance was made by the U.S. Court of Appeals, 3rd Circuit (1951), in the case of *The Emeloid Co., Inc. v. Commissioner*:

> "What corporate purpose could be more essential then key [person] insurance? The business that insures its buildings and machinery and automobiles from every possible hazard can hardly be expected to exercise less care in protecting itself against the loss of two of its most vital assets – managerial skill and experience."

[2] Key person insurance can also be thought of as a "line of credit." As such, it will assure that money is available when needed, without any repayment of the debt, i.e., a forgiveness of the "loan." Relying on borrowed funds may be ill advised, as can be seen by referring to the table, Cost Of Borrowed Dollars, on page 182.

[3] Employer-owned life insurance must meet strict notice and consent requirements if the death benefits are to be received free of income taxes (see Company Owned Life Insurance (COLI), pages 367-369).

[4] The "cost" of key person insurance is sometimes measured as the difference between the premium paid and the cash value increase. This view tends to argue in favor of permanent insurance with cash values, as opposed to term insurance with no cash values (but such an approach ignores the time value of money, as discussed in Interest Adjusted Net Cost on page 430). It should also be recognized that the cash values of permanent insurance, carried for a bona fide business purpose, are not subject to the unreasonable accumulation of earnings tax. An expanded discussion of this subject is contained on page 346. If cash values are borrowed, it would be to the business's advantage to be sure it could deduct interest paid on the borrowed funds (see Minimum Deposit Insurance, on page 458). If borrowing of cash values is contemplated, then it is important to avoid having the policy classified as a Modified Endowment Contract (see expanded discussion on pages 441-442).

[5] Under some circumstances a portion of annual cash value increases and death proceeds could be subject to the Corporate Alternative Minimum Tax, as discussed on pages 374-376. However, this problem is not present in an S corporation, since it is not subject to the alternative minimum tax adjusted current earnings adjustment. In fact, key person insurance in an S corporation may be particularly attractive in view of the opportunity to make tax-free withdrawals of the death proceeds where the S corporation has no accumulated earnings and profits (see S Corporation, pages 510-512). With a C corporation the alternative minimum tax problem can be avoided by using the Reverse Key Person Insurance technique (see chart, page 159).

[6] See page 181 for various formulas used to value a key person. Another approach to the valuation of a key person is to discount all future salary payments to normal retirement age. For example, referring to the Present Value Table on page 565, it can be determined that, using a time value of money assumption of 8 percent, a 45-year-old employee earning $50,000 per year, who is expected to retire in 20 years (age 65), has a present value of $490,900 ($50,000 x 9.818 = $490,900). No matter which approach is used, valuation of a key person is much like valuation of a business, the process may be more art than science. However, application of these guidelines will provide a useful starting point for determining a key person's value to a business.

[7] An explanation and illustration of proper accounting entries for policy premiums and values is set forth in Accounting For Business Life Insurance on pages 344-345.

[8] Whether a business is likely to be continued, sold, or liquidated upon the death of a key employee, will depend upon answers to the questions set forth in the Disposition Of A Business Interest chart on page 119.

REVERSE KEY PERSON INSURANCE

Reverse key person insurance offers an alternative means of providing key employee insurance by having someone other than the business purchase insurance on the life of the key employee. It is particularly useful with C corporations, where the corporate alternative minimum tax can reduce by up to 15 percent the death benefit received by the corporation.[1] With reverse key person insurance there is no exposure to the alternative minimum tax, because the death benefit is not paid to the corporation. If the key employee is also a stockholder, payment of the death benefit outside the corporation also avoids increasing the value of the deceased's stock and thereby avoids any increase in estate taxes.[2]

DURING LIFETIME. Such a program can be established by having the trustee of an irrevocable life insurance trust purchase insurance on the key employee.[3] As both owner and beneficiary of the contract, the trustee pays the premiums directly to the insurance company.[4]

Many guidelines are used in estimating the dollar value of a particular key employee. However, the value can be most easily estimated by using a factor of three to ten times the employee's salary. Other guidelines that have been employed involve either a determination of the employee's replacement cost, or an estimation of lost profits or credit.

UPON DEATH of the key employee the insurance company pays the death benefit directly to the trustee of the trust.[5] The proceeds are received free of income taxes as the death benefit of a life insurance contract.

The funds can then be loaned by the trustee to the corporation.[6] In repaying this loan the corporation makes tax-deductible interest payments to the trust.[7] Although these interest payments are taxable income to the trust, repayments of the loan principal are received by the trust free of income taxes.

Of course, it is not necessary for a trust to be established. Anyone who has the funds can loan them to the corporation for the purpose of key person insurance. For example, an adult child could be the owner and beneficiary of a life insurance contract insuring his parent. After receipt of the death benefit, the proceeds could be loaned by the child to the corporation, which would then repay the loan together with interest.[8]

Footnotes on page 161

DURING LIFETIME

UPON DEATH

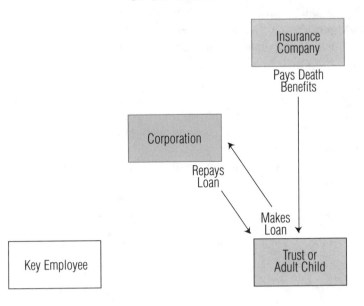

INFORMATION REQUIRED FOR ANALYSIS & PROPOSAL

1. Name of employee.
2. Sex.
3. Date of birth.
4. Smoker/nonsmoker.

To Determine Amount of Coverage
5. Salary of employee.
6. Position of employee in business.

To Determine Party Who Will Own Insurance Contract
7. Availability of irrevocable life insurance trust (including trust language authorizing loan to corporation).
8. Names and ages of children.
9. Degree of involvement of children in business.

CROSS REFERENCES TO TAX FACTS ON INSURANCE & EMPLOYEE BENEFITS (2011)

Income Tax

Q 96. When income taxable to trust or to trust beneficiaries.

Q 98. Death proceeds received by trust free of income taxes.

Q 238. Treatment of corporate owned life insurance for purposes of alternative minimum tax.

Estate Tax

Q 42. Circumstances under which life insurance proceeds are includable in insured's gross estate even though insured has no incident of ownership in policy and proceeds are not payable to estate.

Q 124. Insurance proceeds included in insured's estate when trustee *required* to pay estate debts and taxes.

Footnotes

[1] This reduction is only likely with a C corporation; there is no exposure with an S corporation or a partnership. With Key Person Insurance, as shown in the chart on page 155, the death benefit paid to a C corporation is included in adjusted current earnings as part of the alternative minimum tax calculations. The larger the death benefit relative to anticipated corporate earnings, the greater the likelihood that the corporate alternative minimum tax will reduce the death benefit. Alternatively, the smaller the death benefit relative to anticipated corporate earnings, the lesser the likelihood of a reduction in death benefits on account of the alternative minimum tax. A more detailed explanation of the Corporate Alternative Minimum Tax is contained on pages 375-376. The table on page 376 provides examples of the relationship between the amount of the death benefit and anticipated corporate earnings.

[2] When the insurance is owned by and payable to either a trust or an adult child, the Reverse Key Person Insurance technique also avoids the problem of increasing the value of the deceased's estate, as can occur when death proceeds are paid to a corporation under the typical Key Person Insurance arrangement (see the chart on page 155, and footnote 6 on page 149). In this regard, note the similarity between Reverse Key Person Insurance and Reverse Section 303 (see chart, page 151).

[3] In a family-owned business it is possible that the reach of the attribution rules under new Code section 101(j) *might* treat this policy as "employer-owned." This would subject the death benefit to income taxation. To assure the proceeds are received free of income taxes, appropriate notice and consent should be obtained (see Company Owned Life Insurance (COLI) pages 367-369).

[4] The details of establishing and administering an irrevocable life insurance trust are set forth on pages 50-53.

[5] When considering Reverse Key Person Insurance it is important to determine how the premiums will be paid. With Key Person Insurance the premium is an obligation of the corporation as owner of the insurance contract. In contrast, with *Reverse* Key Person Insurance the contract is owned by a trustee, or an adult child, who has the obligation to make the premium payments. Corporate funds could be used to assist in paying the premiums using either Executive Equity, chart page 211, or Split-Dollar Insurance, chart page 219.

[6] The trustee must have authority to make a loan to the corporation. Although many irrevocable life insurance trusts will give the trustee broad authority to purchase assets and make loans to the estate and others, it would be prudent to give the trustee specific authority to make loans at prevailing interest rates to the corporation. However, the trust language *should not* require the trustee to make such loans, as this would likely cause the death proceeds to be included in the insured's estate. Although the trustee cannot be required to make the loan, preserving the family business for the trust beneficiaries would likely motivate the trustee to make the loan, particularly if the trustee was also responsible for maintaining and preserving the business (see footnote 6, page 53).

[7] Interest payments are deductible by the corporation but taxable to the trust unless distributed and taxed to the trust beneficiaries. Distribution of trust income may be advisable in view of the very high income tax rates applicable to trusts (e.g., the table on page 549 indicates that in 2011 income in excess of $11,350 is subject to a 35.0 percent tax rate). On the other hand, creation of a debt from the corporation to the trustee, or an adult child, offers the advantage of being able to subsequently withdraw the loan principal from the corporation free of income taxes. This is similar to the same advantage offered by the Reverse Section 303 (see chart, page 151).

[8] Because it is not possible to obligate the adult child to loan the death proceeds to the corporation, it is extremely important to be sure the child will be highly motivated to make such a loan (e.g., the child is the "heir apparent" to the business and would suffer financially should the corporation fail to continue operations).

FAMILY LIMITED PARTNERSHIP

The family limited partnership (FLP) is a valuable planning technique offering numerous advantages to the owners of a closely held business.[1] With this technique, business interests and other assets can be transferred to family members at reduced values while maintaining indirect yet effective control.[2]

ESTABLISHING PARTNERSHIP. The FLP is established by an agreement setting forth the partnership's operating rules and the filing of a certificate of limited partnership with state authorities.[3] The typical FLP agreement places restrictions and limitations on ownership of partnership interests, and cannot be changed or terminated for a specified number of years without the concurrence of all partners.[4]

Once the agreement is drawn, the parents then contribute assets to the FLP, which in turn issues both *general* and *limited* partnership interests.[5] Thereafter, the parents make gifts of the limited partnership interests to their children. These gifts can be structured to fall within the gift tax annual exclusion, or the unified credit can be used to immediately transfer large amounts of limited partnership interests.[6]

ADVANTAGES OF PARTNERSHIP. The principal advantages of the FLP are both *control* and *flexibility*.[7] As general partners, the parents have complete power and authority to manage the partnership.[8] As limited partners, the children have no say in the management of the partnership, no liability for partnership debts, and a priority over the general partners in the event of a liquidation.

With a FLP, gifts can be made of assets that are otherwise not easily divisible (e.g., the family farm). Transferring real estate located in another state to the partnership can avoid ancillary probate. Income can be shifted to children in lower income tax brackets.[9] Periodic gifts of limited partnership interests can reduce the parent's taxable estate.[10] Gifts of limited partnership interests are subject to valuation discounts for both minority interests and lack of marketability. Such valuation discounts, which can often range up to 30 percent and more, offer the opportunity to "leverage" these tax-free gifts.[11]

Because the children cannot transfer their limited partnership interests without the consent of all other partners, partnership assets are protected from claims against the individual partners (including those arising out of a divorce). Although creditors might succeed in obtaining a right to partnership distributions, the general partners have the power to withhold distributions by retaining income within the partnership.[12]

Footnotes on page 165

ESTABLISHING PARTNERSHIP

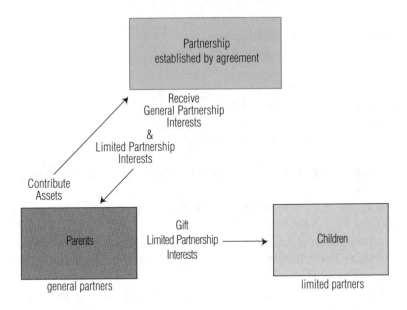

ADVANTAGES OF PARTNERSHIP
Control and Flexibility

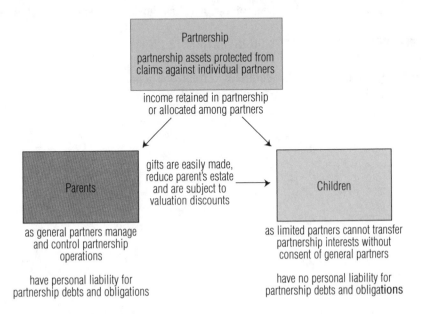

INFORMATION REQUIRED FOR ANALYSIS & PROPOSAL

1. Nature of family business.
2. Other assets in estate (particularly real estate).
3. Value of assets to be contributed to partnership.
4. Marital status.
5. Names and ages of donee(s).
6. Relationship of donee(s) to donor(s).
7. Attitude toward making gifts to family members.
8. Prior gifts made and prior use of unified credit.

CROSS REFERENCE TO TAX FACTS ON INSURANCE & EMPLOYEE BENEFITS (2011)

Q 235. The income tax results when a deceased partner's interest is sold under a business purchase agreement.

Q 239. If a partnership is both policyowner and beneficiary, insurance proceeds are not includable in the insured's estate (but are included in determining the value of the deceased's partnership interest).

Q 241. Proceeds from a policy purchased by a partner on the life of another partner to fund a cross purchase agreement are not included in the insured partner's gross estate.

Q 242. Proceeds from a policy purchased by a partnership on the life of a partner to fund the purchase of the insured partner's interest are not included in the insured's gross estate.

Q 243. How a closely held business interest is valued for federal estate tax purposes.

CROSS REFERENCES TO TAX FACTS ON INVESTMENTS (2011)

Q 7562. When a limited liability company is treated as a partnership.

Q 7563. How the income of a partnership is taxed.

Footnotes

[1] Partnerships are also used as an alternative to the irrevocable life insurance trust and to avoid transfer for value rules, but the latter use appears very aggressive (see page 467).

[2] Although the family limited partnership is an innovative use of existing laws regarding limited partnerships, it should always be established for legitimate business and non-tax estate planning purposes.

[3] The principal requirements for a family limited partnership are: (1) capital must be a material income-producing factor, meaning that a personal service business where income consists primarily of fees or commissions would not qualify for operation as a family limited partnership (i.e., lawyer, doctor, photographer, plumber, etc.); (2) if the partnership has been created by gift, the donor (parent) must be given a reasonable salary for services rendered to the partnership before profits can be allocated among the partners (the concept of "gift" also includes intra-family sales); (3) profits of the partnership must be allocated, or divided, in proportion to each partner's capital investment; and (4) all partners must actually own a "capital interest" (i.e., an interest in partnership assets which is distributable to the partner upon his withdrawal from the partnership or upon partnership liquidation).

[4] Generally, the partnership agreement will limit ownership of partnership interests to family members. The agreement is also likely to contain provisions for settling disputes.

[5] Transfer of assets to the partnership is generally done without recognition of either gain or loss. Alternatively, the parents could make a gift of assets to the children who will then contribute these assets to the family limited partnership in return for limited partnership interests.

[6] Often the ultimate goal is for the parents to eventually own only modest partnership interests, with the bulk of the family limited partnership being held by other family members. Although this example assumes that both parents will be general partners, family limited partnerships are often established with only one spouse as the general partner and the other spouse as a limited partner.

[7] Some disadvantages of the family limited partnership include: (1) the traditional partnership freeze is subject to the impact of the Chapter 14 valuation rules, see pages 407-408 (however, most of the techniques used to reduce the effect of, or to avoid, these rules with respect to recapitalizations will also work with partnerships); (2) much of the ability to reduce taxes by shifting income from parent to younger children has been curtailed by the "kiddie tax" (see discussion on page 545); (3) there are additional expenses associated with establishing and accounting for a FLP (e.g., an information tax return must be filed); (4) gifts do not receive a step-up in income tax basis; and (5) retained partnership interests continue to appreciate in the parent's estate until they are transferred during lifetime or at death.

[8] The general partners also have liability for all partnership debts and obligations.

[9] Effective income shifting requires that the partnership be one in which capital is a material income-producing factor (see also item (2) in footnote 7, above).

[10] These gifts could be made in trust for minor children (see page 544).

[11] Lack of marketability can be established by prohibitions in the partnership agreement against terminating the partnership without the concurrence of all partners (usually limited to 40 years or less). Although valuation discounts of up to 70 percent have been claimed, such overly aggressive discounts are likely to be challenged by the IRS.

[12] The right to partnership distributions is secured by obtaining a charging order. However, because the general partners have the ability to retain profits, the flow-through nature of partnership income taxation gives them the ability to create a tax liability without making cash distributions for tax payments (i.e., an "ugly" asset).

RECAPITALIZATION

A recapitalization through a preferred stock redemption can offer an effective and versatile estate planning technique for corporate stockholders. For example, when combined with a subsequent gifting program, it can:

- Shift substantial future appreciation to children.
- Retain control of the corporation.
- Freeze the value of stock for estate tax purposes.
- Provide an ongoing income stream for retirement.
- Transfer corporate control when, and if, appropriate.
- Motivate younger employees.
- Facilitate distribution of stock at death.

PREFERRED STOCK REDEMPTION. The design of stock to be received in a recapitalization can take many forms. For example, a parent might make a tax-free exchange of *all* his original common stock for a combination of voting cumulative preferred stock and nonvoting common stock.[1] Income would be provided by requiring annual dividends from the preferred stock at a fixed rate.

The voting preferred stock is retained by the parent in order to maintain control of the corporation, and the nonvoting common stock is given to the children, or other donees. As long as the retained preferred stock is entitled to dividends, it will be considered to have a value generally equal to the present value of the right to future payments. Since the value of the common stock is determined by subtracting the value of the preferred stock from the total corporate value, the preferred stock's value has the effect of *decreasing* the value of the common stock, thereby lessening exposure to gift taxes when the common stock is given to the children.[2] However, in order to obtain this increase in value of the retained preferred stock it may be necessary to obligate the corporation to pay substantial cumulative preferred stock dividends.[3]

EFFECT OF SUBSEQUENT APPRECIATION. The prior "freezing" of the value of the preferred stock means that most, if not all, future appreciation is shifted to the common stock owned by the children.[4]

Recapitalizations can be an effective estate planning technique for corporate stockholders who desire to make gifts of stock to children or other heirs.[5] However, they should be undertaken only with the assistance of competent tax counsel.[6]

Footnotes on page 169

PREFERRED STOCK REDEMPTION

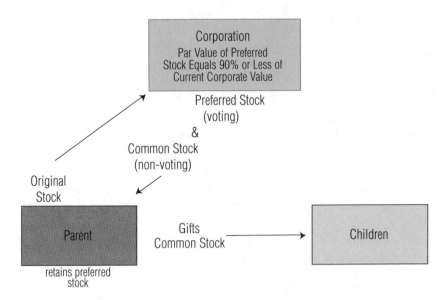

EFFECT OF SUBSEQUENT APPRECIATION

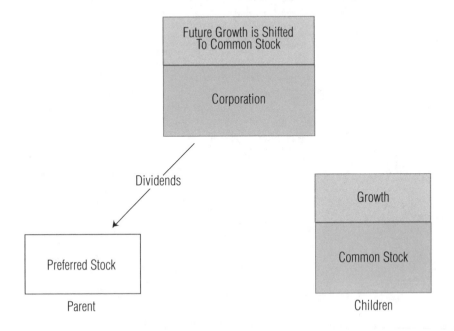

INFORMATION REQUIRED FOR ANALYSIS & PROPOSAL

To Propose Insurance on Life of Donor or Donee
1. Name.
2. Sex.
3. Date of birth.
4. Smoker/nonsmoker.

Attorney Must Also Know
5. Fair market value of corporation performed by qualified appraiser.
6. Capital structure of corporation (type of stock authorized, number of shares outstanding).
7. Number of shares of stock owned by client and value of his holdings.
8. Number of shares of stock owned by client's brothers, sisters, and lineal descendants, and value of their holdings (in order to determine "control" and impact of special valuation rules).
9. Number of people who will be given stock, their ages, relationship to the client, and position in business, if any.

CROSS REFERENCES TO TAX FACTS ON INVESTMENTS (2011)

Q 7618. Effect of Chapter 14 valuation rules on recapitalization.

Footnotes

[1] This chart does not demonstrate a "true" recapitalization in which there is an exchange of *all* of a stockholder's stock (usually common) for a different class of stock (usually preferred). What is demonstrated is essentially a "preferred stock" distribution, under which the stockholder receives another class of stock (the voting preferred) without actually giving up his common stock that represents the future equity growth of the corporation. Although this receipt of preferred stock is non-taxable, it is essentially equivalent to a stock dividend and will likely be considered "Section 306 stock" (see discussion, page 516). If it were then subsequently sold, the proceeds would be treated as ordinary income, not capital gain (capital gains are discussed on page 353).

[2] Because of the special valuation provisions of Chapter 14 all common stock must be given a value of at least 10 percent of the total value of the corporation (e.g., if the corporation had a value of $1,000,000, the common stock value must be at least $100,000, meaning that the retained preferred stock could, at most, be valued at $900,000). For this purpose the total value of the corporation includes the amount of all corporate indebtedness to the transferor and family members (see discussion on pages 407-408). Obtaining an accurate fair market value of the corporation at the time of recapitalization can also avoid unexpected tax problems. For example, if the value placed on the new preferred stock is *greater than* the original common stock, the stockholder may be considered as having received a dividend from the corporation. On the other hand, when a second stockholder exists at the time of the recapitalization, undervaluing the new preferred can lead to either income or gift tax liabilities. If the value placed on the new preferred is *less than* the original common stock the amount of the undervaluation might be treated as taxable income to the co-stockholder (either salary, or worse yet, a nondeductible corporate dividend). It could be treated as a gift if the co-stockholder were a family member.

[3] Under Chapter 14 these cumulative dividends *must actually be paid*, or there will be exposure to *future* gift or estate taxes. If the retained preferred stock is to have a value greater than zero the stock dividend rights must constitute "qualified payments" (i.e., dividends payable on a periodic basis and at a fixed rate or at a variable rate with a fixed relationship to market value). See the expanded discussion of qualified payments on pages 407-408. In the desire to have the retained preferred stock highly valued in order to reduce the exposure to gift taxes when the common is given to children, care must be taken not to obligate the corporation to unrealistic and onerous preferred stock dividends, which are not deductible to the corporation.

[4] Because *future* appreciation is being shifted out of the estate, a recapitalization will generally not reduce *present* estate settlement costs. The value of the stock retained by the donor will still be included in his gross estate. A partial stock redemption under Section 303 can provide an effective means of paying these costs, particularly when funded with life insurance. Dividends paid on the stock transferred by gift can be used by the donee to pay for insurance on the life of the donor using the reverse section 303 technique described in the chart on page 151. However, because of the grantor trust rules, the donee should be an individual, not a trust. Since there is some possibility that the donee will predecease the donor, the donor may wish to insure the donee in order to purchase stock from the donee's estate.

[5] A recapitalization can also be an effective way to accomplish the non-tax objectives of transferring growth and control to one child while providing income for another child. For example, assume that both nonvoting preferred and voting common were issued pursuant to a recapitalization. If Child A were not involved in the business he could be given the *nonvoting* preferred stock (with an income stream provided by dividends). Child B, who is working in the business, might then be given the voting common stock (with both its control and potential for future appreciation).

[6] These less restrictive anti-freeze provisions in the form of special valuation rules are contained in Chapter 14 of the Code.

ATTRIBUTION

When it is intended that continued ownership would be held within a family, it is extremely important to consider the effect of the attribution rules when planning for the sale of stock to a corporation. Unfortunately, all too often the operation of these rules is poorly understood, and the adverse tax consequences can be disastrous (they have been aptly described as "infamous and insidious").

The basic problem arises under Section 302(b)(3) of the Code, that requires that to qualify as a "capital transaction" the sale of stock to a corporation must result in a *complete* disposition of the stockholder's interest (both actually owned and constructively owned). If there is a redemption of *less* than the stockholder's entire interest, then the transaction is likely to be treated and taxed as a stock dividend. However, merely selling all directly owned stock to the corporation, may not satisfy this requirement if stock owned by others is attributed to the selling stockholder or his estate. There are two types of attribution, family attribution and entity attribution. Whereas family attribution can be waived (charts, pages 174-175), entity attribution cannot be waived (charts, page 173). To summarize the rules of family attribution:

1. An individual is deemed (i.e., considered) to own any stock owned directly or *indirectly* by his:
   a. parents
   b. spouse
   c. children
   d. grandchildren

2. There is *no* family attribution with respect to one's grandparent, brother, sister, uncle, aunt, nephew, cousin, or in-law.

3. There is no "secondary" attribution under the family attribution rules (e.g., stock attributed from daughter-in-law to son cannot then be again attributed from the son to his parents).

Depending upon the particular family relationship, an individual may, or may not, be considered to own the stock of other members of his family. For example, assume we have an extended family composed of a husband, his wife, his grandfather, grandmother, father, mother, and brother; as well as his son, daughter-in-law and grandson. In this family the **husband** is considered as owning the stock of *his* father, mother, wife, son and grandson. On the other hand, his **wife** will be considered as owning the stock of only *her* father, mother, husband, son and grandson.

FAMILY ATTRIBUTION

Husband is considered to own the stock of *his* Father,
Mother, Wife, Son and Grandson.

Wife is considered to own the stock of *her* Father,
Mother, Husband, Son and Grandson.

Moving Up One Generation

Father is considered to own the stock of
Grandfather, Grandmother, Mother, Brother, Husband, and Son
(i.e., of *his* father, mother, wife, sons, and grandson).

FAMILY ATTRIBUTION

Moving Down One Generation

Son is considered to own the stock of
Husband, Wife, Daughter-in-law, and Grandson
(i.e., of his father, mother, wife, and son).

Daughter-in-law is considered to own the stock of
Her Parents, Son and Grandson
(i.e., of her parents, husband and son).

GRANDFATHER   GRANDMOTHER
      FATHER   MOTHER
BROTHER   HUSBAND   WIFE   HER PARENTS
            SON   DAUGHTER-IN-LAW
            GRANDSON

CROSS REFERENCES TO TAX FACTS ON INSURANCE & EMPLOYEE BENEFITS (2011)

Q 225. Amount paid by corporation for decedent's entire stock interest generally not dividend to estate, provided no attribution problems.

Q 226. Avoiding attribution of stock ownership among family members.

Q 227. Avoiding attribution of stock ownership from estate beneficiary to estate.

ENTITY ATTRIBUTION

Attribution From An Estate

Stock owned by an Estate is attributed to the Beneficiaries
in proportion to their interests in the estate.

Attribution To An Estate

Stock actually or constructively owned by a beneficiary
is attributed in full to the estate, without regard for the
beneficiaries' percentage of interest in the estate
(the attribution of Son A's 100 shares
to the estate cannot be waived).

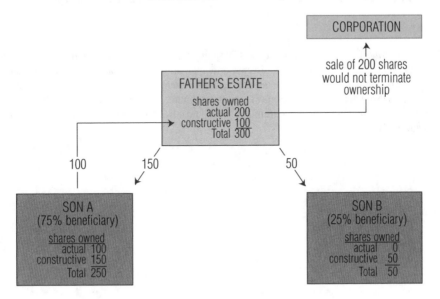

FAMILY & ENTITY ATTRIBUTION

Waiver Of Family Attribution
Sale by Mother

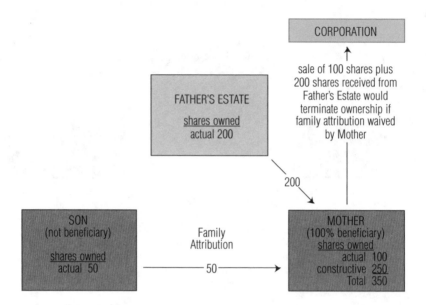

Note: Mother can *waive family attribution* of Son's 50 shares provided she: (1) has no interest in the corporation following the redemption (i.e., as an officer, director, or employee); (2) does not reacquire an interest within 10 years; and (3) agrees to notify the IRS if she does reacquire an interest. Note also the secondary attribution of the Estate's 200 shares through Mother to the Son (i.e., entity attribution followed by family attribution). However, you cannot have entity attribution to the estate from Mother followed by another entity attribution from the Estate to another estate beneficiary.

FAMILY & ENTITY ATTRIBUTION

Waiver Of Family Attribution
Sale by Estate

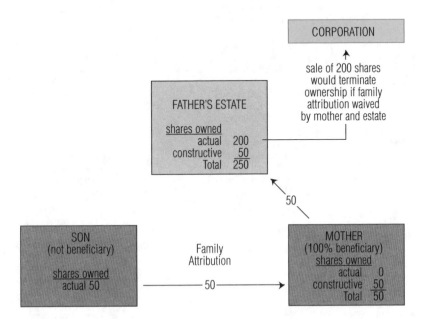

Note: Even though an entity, Father's Estate can *waive* family attribution of Son's 50 shares to Mother. This breaks the chain of secondary attribution from Son to Mother to Father's Estate (i.e., family attribution followed by entity attribution). The waiver by the estate is dependent upon both the entity (i.e., the estate) and those through whom ownership is attributed (i.e., the mother) agreeing to join in the waiver. Both the entity and the beneficiary must hold no interest in the corporation, cannot acquire an interest within 10 years of the redemption, and must agree to notify the Internal Revenue Service should an interest be acquired. If Son predeceased Mother, as an estate beneficiary Son's 50 shares would be attributed in full to the estate (see bottom chart, page 173). There can be no waiver of entity attribution.

BUSINESS COMPARISON

Question	Unincorporated	Incorporated
What is the extent of liability for:		
Contract?	To all business and personal assets of each individual owner.	Usually limited to business assets in most states.
Negligence of owner-employees?	To all business and personal assets of each individual owner.	Generally limited to business assets except professional liability.
Negligence of employees?	To all business and personal assets of each individual owner.	Limited to business assets.
Business debts?	To all business and personal assets of each individual owner (but see discussion of Limited Liability Company, page 445).	Limited to business assets except where owners have personally guaranteed loan by endorsement or otherwise.
To whom are profits taxed?	Individual owners.	To the corporation if retained as earnings. To owner-employees if paid out as reasonable compensation or dividends (page 546).
Can a small portion of the ownership interest have full control?	Not in any practical way (but see Family Limited Partnership chart, page 163).	Yes – by use of voting preferred and non-voting stock (page 166).
Can the business interest be easily transferred to one or more purchasers or recipients?	No – transfer of individual assets or creation of new entity can result in complications.	Yes – stock may be easily transferred to either the corporation, other stock-holders, key persons, or outsiders (pages 126, 130, and 142).
Who pays income taxes on dollars used to pay for life insurance funding a buy/sell agreement?	Individual owners.	Choice of corporation or stockholder-employee.
Can the business purchase a portion of a deceased owner's interest on a tax-favored basis?	No	Yes – under Code section 303 the corporation can purchase some stock, while allowing the surviving family to retain an owner-ship interest (page 146).

Note: "Unincorporated" refers to sole proprietorships and partnerships, but not to limited partners; "incorporated" refers to C corporations, but not to S corporations.

Question	Unincorporated	Incorporated
Does the business entity enjoy any tax-favored investment advantages?	No	Yes – under Code section 243 a corporation can deduct from 70% to 100% of the dividends received from domestic corporations.
Can the business have a different fiscal year than the owners?	Not in any practical way.	Yes
What is the annual cost of Social Security for each owner-employee?	In 2011 10.40% OASDI tax on first $106,800 of self-employment income and 2.90% hospital insurance tax without limit, all paid by the individual owner (normal rate of 12.40% is reduced 2.0% for one year by The 2010 Tax Relief Act).	In 2011 4.20% OASDI tax on first $106,800 of income and 1.45% hospital insurance tax without limit, paid by the owner-employee (normal rate of 6.2% is reduced by 2.0% for one year by The 2010 Tax Relief Act). Rate of 6.20% paid by the corporation, but deductible as a business expense.
What is the cost of unemployment taxes for each owner-employee?	None	In 2011 both state and federal (FUTA) taxes will be at least $434 per employee, i.e., 6.2% of first $7,000 in wages.
What is the cost of worker's compensation?	None	If set by state law, can often be exempt from coverage. If paid, it is considered a deductible business expense.
Is there any extra cost for franchise fees and bookkeeping?	–	A small annual franchise fee is usually payable. Corporate minutes must be kept on an annual basis. Bookkeeping costs may be somewhat higher.
Is there any extra cost to prepare a corporate tax return?	–	Preparation of corporate return can cost more, but usually not much greater than Schedule C (Profit or Loss From Business or Profession) or Form 1065 (U.S. Partnership Return of Income).
Could there be a problem with unreasonable compensation to owner-employees?	No	Yes – under Code section 162 only a reasonable allowance for compensation can be deducted. This is usually not a serious problem, but should be considered (page 546).

Note: "Unincorporated" refers to sole proprietorships and partnerships, but not to limited partners; "incorporated" refers to C corporations, but not to S corporations.

Question	Unincorporated	Incorporated
Is there a potential for double taxation?	No	Yes – if not properly planned there could be a corporate income tax, plus a personal income tax on dividends received.
Could a personal holding company penalty tax of 15% be levied?	No	Yes – a penalty tax could be applied if 60% of income is essentially passive, such as dividends, rents and royalties.
Can individual owner-employees have deferred compensation?	No	Yes – Income may be deferred (Deferred Compensation, page 234).
Can the business pay premiums for personal life insurance, and have the premiums paid tax-free for owner-employees?	No	Yes – up to $50,000 of group insurance is available under Code section 79 (Group Insurance, page 202).
Are tax-favored personal life insurance programs available to owner-employees?	No	Yes – individual plans can be established (Executive Equity, page 210, and Split-Dollar Insurance, page 218).
Is a qualified retirement program available?	Yes – HR-10 permits sole proprietors and partners to be covered under qualified plans.	Yes – under qualified plan rules (Qualified Retirement Plans, pages 258, 354, 384, 513, 524, 531 and 536).
Are other tax-deductible benefits available to owner-employees, such as:		
Disability income plans?	No	Yes – under Code sections 105 and 106 (Disability Income Plan, page 242).
Medical and dental expense reimbursement arrangements?	Not generally, but limited deduction available (footnote 2, page 249).	Yes – under Code sections 105 and 106 (Health Reimbursement Arrangements, page 246).
Survivor income plans?	No	Yes – as a form of salary continuation death benefit (Survivor Income, page 230).

Note: "Unincorporated" refers to sole proprietorships and partnerships, but not to limited partners; "incorporated" refers to C corporations, but not to S corporations.

ODDS OF DEATH BEFORE AGE 65

When a business has two or more owners, the odds of at least one death before age 65 increase dramatically. *The risk is not remote.* Proper planning calls for making provisions for the continuation of the business as well as providing support for the surviving family.

One-Owner Business

Ages	Odds of Death Male	Female		Ages	Odds of Death Male	Female
30	14.9%	11.8%		45	13.0%	10.3%
35	14.4	11.5		50	11.6	9.3
40	13.8	11.0		55	9.6	7.6

Two-Owner Business

Ages	Odds Of One Death Male	Female		Ages	Odds Of One Death Male	Female
30-30	27.6%	22.3%		45-45	24.2%	19.6%
30-35	27.2	22.0		45-50	23.1	18.7
30-40	26.7	21.6		45-55	21.3	17.1
35-35	26.7	21.7		50-50	21.8	17.8
35-40	26.2	21.3		50-55	20.0	16.2
35-45	25.5	20.7		50-60	16.9	13.5
40-40	25.7	20.8		55-55	18.2	14.5
40-45	25.0	20.2		55-60	15.0	11.8
40-50	23.8	19.3		60-60	11.7	9.0

Three-Owner Business

Ages	Odds Of One Death Male	Female		Ages	Odds Of One Death Male	Female
30-30-30	38.4%	31.5%		40-45-50	33.7%	27.7%
30-35-40	37.2	30.6		40-50-60	28.4	23.0
30-40-50	35.2	28.9		45-45-45	34.1	27.9
35-35-35	37.3	30.7		45-50-55	30.4	24.8
35-40-45	35.8	29.4		50-50-50	30.9	25.4
35-45-55	32.6	26.7		50-55-60	24.9	20.1
40-40-40	36.0	29.5		55-55-55	26.0	21.0

Using the following percentages, it is possible to calculate the odds of at least one death before age 65 for any particular group of owners. After multiplying the percent for each owner by the percent for each other owner, subtract the results from 1. For example, the calculations for the odds of at least one death for three male owners, ages 40, 45, and 50: $1 - (.8617 \times .8703 \times .8840) = 1 - .6630 = 33.7\%$.

Age	Living To Age 65 Male	Female	Age	Living To Age 65 Male	Female	Age	Living To Age 65 Male	Female	Age	Living To Age 65 Male	Female
30	85.10%	88.15%	38	85.92%	88.77%	46	87.27%	89.82%	54	89.94%	92.01%
31	85.20	88.21	39	86.04	88.87	47	87.52	90.00	55	90.44	92.44
32	85.29	88.28	40	86.17	88.98	48	87.80	90.21	56	91.00	92.91
33	85.39	88.34	41	86.32	89.10	49	88.09	90.43	57	91.63	93.44
34	85.49	88.42	42	86.47	89.22	50	88.40	90.69	58	92.34	94.02
35	85.59	88.49	43	86.64	89.35	51	88.74	90.97	59	93.11	94.67
36	85.69	88.58	44	86.83	89.50	52	89.10	91.28	60	93.95	95.37
37	85.80	88.67	45	87.03	89.65	53	89.50	91.63			

Source: Commissioners 2001 Standard Ordinary Mortality Table.

ODDS OF DEATH WITHIN 10 AND 20 YEARS

When a business has two or more owners, the odds of at least one death within any given period of time increase dramatically. *The risk is not remote.* Proper planning calls for making provisions for the continuation of the business.

One-Owner Business – MALE
Odds Of Death Within

Age	10 Years	20 Years
30	1.2%	3.7%
35	1.7	5.4
40	2.5	8.3
45	3.8	13.0
50	5.9	20.2
55	9.6	30.4

One-Owner Business – FEMALE
Odds Of Death Within

Age	10 Years	20 Years
30	0.9%	2.8%
35	1.3	4.3
40	1.9	6.7
45	3.0	10.3
50	4.9	15.5
55	7.6	22.7

Two-Owner Business – MALE
Odds Of One Death Within

Ages	10 Years	20 Years
30-30	2.5%	7.3%
30-35	2.9	8.9
30-40	3.7	11.7
35-35	3.3	10.4
35-40	4.1	13.2
35-45	5.4	17.6
40-40	5.0	15.9
40-45	6.2	20.2
40-50	8.3	26.8
45-45	7.4	24.2
45-50	9.4	30.5
45-55	13.0	39.5
50-50	11.5	36.3
50-55	14.9	44.5
50-60	20.2	55.8
55-55	18.2	51.6
55-60	23.3	61.5
55-65	30.4	74.0

Two-Owner Business – FEMALE
Odds Of One Death Within

Ages	10 Years	20 Years
30-30	1.9%	5.5%
30-35	2.2	6.9
30-40	2.8	9.3
35-35	2.6	8.4
35-40	3.1	10.7
35-45	4.3	14.2
40-40	3.7	12.9
40-45	4.8	16.4
40-50	6.7	21.1
45-45	5.9	19.6
45-50	7.8	24.2
45-55	10.3	30.7
50-50	9.6	28.6
50-55	12.1	34.7
50-60	15.5	43.2
55-55	14.5	40.3
55-60	17.8	48.1
55-65	22.7	59.0

Three-Owner Business – MALE
Odds Of One Death Within

Ages	10 Years	20 Years
30-30-30	3.7%	10.8%
30-35-40	5.3	16.4
30-40-50	9.4	29.5
35-35-35	4.9	15.2
35-40-45	7.8	24.5
35-45-55	14.4	42.7
40-40-40	7.4	22.8
40-45-50	11.7	36.3
40-50-60	22.2	59.4
45-45-45	10.9	34.1
45-50-55	18.1	51.7
50-50-50	16.7	49.1
50-55-60	27.8	69.2
55-55-55	26.0	66.3
50-60-70	47.9	91.6

Three-Owner Business – FEMALE
Odds Of One Death Within

Ages	10 Years	20 Years
30-30-30	2.8%	8.2%
30-35-40	4.0	13.2
30-40-50	7.6	23.4
35-35-35	3.8	12.3
35-40-45	6.1	19.9
35-45-55	11.5	33.7
40-40-40	5.5	18.8
40-45-50	9.5	29.3
40-50-60	17.1	47.0
45-45-45	8.8	27.9
45-50-55	14.8	41.4
50-50-50	14.0	39.6
50-55-60	21.9	56.1
55-55-55	21.0	53.8
50-60-70	36.1	80.1

Source: Commissioners 2001 Standard Ordinary Mortality Table.

KEY PERSON VALUATION FORMULAS

No single formula is accepted for valuing a key person or employee. In fact, valuing a key person is much like valuing a business, it is more art than science. Much depends upon the characteristics of the key person (e.g., a sales manager who has a substantial impact upon sales or a financial officer who has access to credit). However, there is little doubt that key persons can have considerable value; and their death or disability can cause substantial financial losses, or even failure of a business. One or more of the following formulas should provide a useful starting point for determining value.

Contribution To Profits. This method evaluates the key person's contributions to profits and then capitalizes this amount to determine value. For example, assume the business has a book value of $500,000, an expected rate of return on book value for this particular type of business is 8 percent and average profits are $120,000. The excess earnings are $80,000 ($500,000 x .08 = $40,000; $120,000 - $40,000 = $80,000). Assuming the key person's contribution to excess earnings is 50 percent, capitalization of the key person's contribution at 12 percent yields a value of $333,200 (.50 x $80,000 = $40,000; 100 ÷ 12 = 8.33 x $40,000 = $333,200). Note that a similar capitalization approach to valuing a business is discussed on page 122. A variation on the contributions to profits method does not capitalize the contribution, but rather reduces the key person's annual contribution as a replacement is recruited, trained, and becomes fully effective. Using this variation, the key person's value would be $120,000, assuming annual contributions to profits of $40,000 and 5 years to complete the replacement. The basic method and the variation are calculated as follows:

Average Profits	$120,000	Variation	
Book Value At 8%	40,000	Year 1	$40,000
Excess Earnings	$80,000	Year 2	32,000
Percent Of Contribution	50	Year 3	24,000
Key Person's Contribution	$40,000	Year 4	16,000
Capitalization Factor	8.33	Year 5	8,000
Key Person Value	$333,200	Key Person Value	$120,000

Business Life Value. This is a variation of the method commonly used to determine human life value. The business estimates its annual loss of earnings if the key person were to die, multiplies that amount by the number of working years to retirement, and then discounts the results by an appropriate interest rate. Assuming annual loss of earnings of $40,000, 15 years to retirement, and 12 percent interest, the value would be calculated as follows:

Loss Of Earnings	$40,000
Present Value Factor	6.811 (from table on page 565)
Key Person Value	$272,440

Multiple Of Salary. This method recognizes that the salaries paid to key persons are an indication of their value. Typically a factor of from 3 to 10 times annual salary is used. Assuming an annual salary of $75,000 and a factor of 5, the value would be calculated as follows:

Annual Salary	$75,000
Factor	5
Key Person Value	$375,000

Discount Of Business. This method simply discounts the value of the business to reflect the loss of the key person. Assuming a business value of $900,000 and a discount of 20 percent, the value would be calculated as follows:

Value Of Business	$900,000
Discount	.20
Key Person Value	$180,000

COST OF BORROWED DOLLARS – CORPORATE

$100,000 Loan to a Corporation

Loan Repaid Over	Interest Rate (%)	Yearly Payment	Total Payments	Income Required By Corporation In Tax Bracket Of		
				15%	25%	34%
5 Years	6	23,740	118,700	136,347	152,033	170,215
	8	25,046	125,230	142,877	158,563	176,745
	10	26,380	131,900	149,547	165,233	183,415
	12	27,741	138,705	156,352	172,038	190,220
	15	29,832	149,160	166,807	182,493	200,675
10 Years	6	13,587	135,870	153,517	169,203	187,385
	8	14,903	149,030	166,677	182,363	200,545
	10	16,275	162,750	180,397	196,083	214,265
	12	17,698	176,980	194,627	210,313	228,495
	15	19,925	199,250	216,897	232,583	250,765
15 Years	6	10,296	154,440	172,087	187,773	205,955
	8	11,683	175,245	192,892	208,578	226,760
	10	13,147	197,205	214,852	230,538	248,720
	12	14,682	220,230	237,877	253,563	271,745
	15	17,102	256,530	274,177	289,863	308,045
20 Years	6	8,718	174,360	192,007	207,693	225,875
	8	10,185	203,700	221,347	237,033	255,215
	10	11,746	234,920	252,567	268,253	286,435
	12	13,388	267,760	285,407	301,093	319,275
	15	15,976	319,520	337,167	352,853	371,035

Explanation of Table. This table is designed to show the income required by a corporation to repay a loan of $100,000 at various rates of interest. For example, assume that to redeem stock under an entity or partial stock redemption plan, the corporation is able to borrow $100,000 to purchase the business interest of a deceased stockholder. If the loan is obtained at 8 percent and is repayable in equal annual payments over 10 years, each yearly payment would be $14,903. Total repayments over the 10-year repayment period would be $149,030. However, if the corporation was in a 25 percent tax bracket, the total *before-tax* income required to repay the loan *principal* is $133,333, which is determined by dividing the loan principal by one minus the borrower's marginal tax bracket ($100,000 ÷ .75 = $133,333). This is because the $100,000 principal must come from after-tax funds. In addition, since the interest payments are deductible, it takes $49,030 of before-tax income to make the interest payments. The total cost to pay the loan is $182,363 ($133,333 + $49,030 = $182,363).

See page 183 for *individual* costs of borrowed dollars.

COST OF BORROWED DOLLARS – INDIVIDUAL

$100,000 Loan To An Individual

Loan Repaid Over	Interest Rate (%)	Yearly Payment	Total Payments	Income Required By Individual In Tax Bracket Of			
				15%	25%	28%	35%
	6	23,740	118,700	139,647	158,267	164,861	182,615
	8	25,046	125,230	147,329	166,973	173,931	192,662
5 Years	10	26,380	131,900	155,176	175,867	183,194	202,923
	12	27,741	138,705	163,182	184,940	192,646	213,392
	15	29,832	149,160	175,482	198,880	207,167	229,477
	6	13,587	135,870	159,847	181,160	188,708	209,031
	8	14,903	149,030	175,329	198,707	206,986	229,277
10 Years	10	16,275	162,750	191,471	217,000	226,042	250,385
	12	17,698	176,980	208,212	235,973	245,806	272,277
	15	19,925	199,250	234,412	265,667	276,736	306,538
	6	10,296	154,440	181,694	205,920	214,500	237,600
	8	11,683	175,245	206,171	233,660	243,396	269,608
15 Years	10	13,147	197,205	232,006	262,940	273,896	303,392
	12	14,682	220,230	259,094	293,640	305,875	338,815
	15	17,102	256,530	301,800	342,040	356,292	394,662
	6	8,718	174,360	205,129	232,480	242,167	268,246
	8	10,185	203,700	239,647	271,600	282,917	313,385
20 Years	10	11,746	234,920	276,376	313,227	326,278	361,415
	12	13,388	267,760	315,012	357,013	371,889	411,938
	15	15,976	319,520	375,906	426,027	443,778	491,569

Explanation of Table. This table is designed to show the income required by an individual to repay a loan of $100,000 at various rates of interest. For example, assume that an executor, or a surviving stockholder, must borrow $100,000 to pay estate settlement costs or purchase a business interest of a deceased co-stockholder. If the loan is obtained at 8 percent and is repayable in equal annual payments over 10 years, each yearly payment would be $14,903. Total repayments over the 10-year repayment period would be $149,030. However, if the borrower was in a 25 percent tax bracket, the total before-tax income required to repay the loan is $198,707, which is determined by dividing the total payments by 1 minus borrower's marginal tax bracket ($149,030 ÷ .75 = $198,707). This assumes that the $100,000 principal must come from after-tax funds, and that interest payments are not deductible (i.e., no deduction is allowed for "personal" interest, and it is assumed there is no "net investment income" available in order to take a deduction for "investment" interest).

See page 182 for *corporate* costs of borrowed dollars.

INTEREST RATES

	2008	2007	2006	2005	2004	2003
Prime Rate Charged by Banks	5.09	8.05	7.96	6.19	4.34	4.12
U.S. Government Securities						
3-Month Treasury Bills	1.37	4.36	4.73	3.15	1.37	1.01
6-Month Treasury Bills	1.62	4.44	4.81	3.39	1.58	1.05
Mortgage Rates						
New-home mortgage yields	6.05	6.41	6.63	5.94	5.77	5.80
Conventional, 15 yr. fixed	5.83	6.11	6.13	5.50	5.23	5.25
Conventional, 30 yr. fixed	6.23	6.40	6.47	5.93	5.86	5.89
Installment Credit						
New Automobiles	7.02	7.77	7.72	7.08	6.60	6.93
Other Consumer Goods	11.35	12.39	12.41	12.05	11.89	11.95
Credit Card Plans	12.07	13.38	13.21	12.51	12.72	12.30

Source: Statistical Abstract of the United States, 2010, Table 1153, Consumer Credit Outstanding and Finance Rates, and Table 1160, Money Market Interest Rates and Mortage Rates.

FINANCIAL RATIOS

Current Ratio =

$$\frac{\text{Total Current Assets}}{\text{Total Current Liabilities}}$$

Also called the "working capital" ratio. The question addressed by this ratio: "Does the business have enough current assets to meet the payment schedule of its current debts with a margin of safety for possible losses in current assets?" A 2 to 1 ratio is generally acceptable.

Quick Ratio =

$$\frac{\text{Cash + Gov't Securities + Receivables}}{\text{Total Current Liabilities}}$$

Also called the "acid-test" ratio and "quick current" test. The question addressed by this ratio: "If all sales revenues disappeared, could the business meet its current obligations with the readily convertible 'quick' funds at hand?" An acid-test of 1 to 1 is typical. Quick funds are current assets minus inventory.

Working Capital =

Total Current Assets - Total Current Liabilities

A measure of cash flow. Considered an indication of the ability to withstand financial crises.

Debt/Worth Ratio =

$$\frac{\text{Total Liabilities}}{\text{Net Worth}}$$

Indicates the extent to which the business is reliant on debt financing.

Gross Margin Ratio =

$$\frac{\text{Gross Profit}}{\text{Net Sales}}$$

Gross profit equals net sales minus cost of goods sold. This ratio measures the percentage of sales dollars remaining to pay overhead expenses.

Net Profit Margin Ratio =

$$\frac{\text{Net Profit Before Tax}}{\text{Net Sales}}$$

This ratio measures "return on sales" and can be used to evaluate performance in comparison with similar businesses.

Inventory Turnover =

$$\frac{\text{Net Sales}}{\text{Average Inventory At Cost}}$$

Measures how well inventory is managed. The more inventory is turned in a given operating cycle, the greater is the profit.

Return On Assets Ratio =

$$\frac{\text{Net Profit Before Tax}}{\text{Total Assets}}$$

Measures how efficiently profits are being generated from the assets employed in the business when compared with ratios of similar firms. A comparatively low ratio indicates an inefficient use of business assets.

Return On Investment =

$$\frac{\text{Net Profit Before Tax}}{\text{Net Worth}}$$

A measure of the percentage of return on funds invested in the business. A very important ratio. If the ROI is less than the rate of return on an alternative, risk-free investment, the owner may wish to sell and invest elsewhere.

Note: Current Ratio, Quick Ratio, and Working Capital are **liquidity** ratios which indicate the ease of turning assets into cash. Debt/Worth Ratio is a **leverage** ratio which measures how dependant the business is on debt financing. Gross Margin Ratio and Net Profit Margin Ratio are **profitability** ratios. Inventory Turnover, Return On Assets Ratio, and Return On Investment are **management** ratios.

CONTESTED BUSINESS VALUATIONS

The Higher The Value – The Greater The Tax

Type of Business	Name of Case	Value Per Share			Delay from Date of Death to Closing of Case		
		Estate's Value on Return	IRS Challenge	Court's Decision			
advertising agency	Katz, Estate of Sidney L. 27 T.C.M. 825	$ 290.00	$ 600.00	$ 300.00	6 yrs	11 mo	11 days
automobile dealer	Leyman, Estate of Harry S. 40 T.C. 100	536.00	700.00	630.00	8 yrs	11 mo	0 days
bank	Davis, Estate of John F. 78,069 P-H Memo T.C.	36.00	75.00	45.00	5 yrs	11 mo	0 days
brewery	Baltimore National Bank v. U.S. 136 F. Supp. 642	1,542.50	2,500.00	2,300.00	8 yrs	5 mo	19 days
brewery equipment manufacturer	Korslin v. U.S. 31 AFTR 2d 1390	25.67	36.72	66.19	6 yrs	11 mo	9 days
carpet manufacturer	Ewing, Estate of Anna C. 9 T.C.M. 1096	2,400.00	6,530.00	4,750.00	7 yrs	6 mo	24 days
citrus grower	Maxcy, Estate of Gregg 28 T.C.M. 783	10,593.79	12,463.28	10,593.79	8 yrs	11 mo	21 days

Type of Business	Name of Case	Value Per Share			Delay from Date of Death to Closing of Case		
		Estate's Value on Return	IRS Challenge	Court's Decision			
cleaning products manufacturer	Louis v. U.S. 369 F. 2d 263	$ 3.25	$ 20.00	$ 5.34	7 yrs	8 mo	27 days
cold storage	Sundquist et al. v. U.S. 74-2 USTC 13,035	270.00	500.00	270.00	7 yrs	9 mo	18 days
construction & paving	Tully, Estate of Edward A. v. U.S. 78-1 USTC 13,228	100.00	344.00	164.77	13 yrs	10 mo	18 days
crude oil processing	Vandenhoeck, Estate of Paul M. 4 T.C. 125	14.00	85.00	40.00	5 yrs	6 mo	9 days
department store	Holmes, Estate of Sue E. 22 B.T.A. 757	160.00	400.00	245.00	4 yrs	10 mo	17 days
dry goods wholesaler	Fitts' Estate v. Commissioner 237 F. 2d 729	150.00	600.00	375.00	7 yrs	9 mo	23 days
electrical parts supplier	Goodall, Estate of Robert A. 24 T.C.M. 807	7.44	10.30	10.30	11 yrs	7 mo	13 days
electric systems manufacturer	Damon, Estate of Robert H. 46 T.C. 108	3.00	6.00	3.75	7 yrs	10 mo	11 days
elevator manufacturer	Heinold, Estate of Matthew I. 24 T.C.M. 26, aff'd 363 F. 2d 329	3.17	10.00	8.00	7 yrs	9 mo	4 days
embalming fluid manufacturer	Yeazel v. Coyle, Jr. 21 AFTR 2d 1681	304.01	450.00	400.00	8 yrs	11 mo	15 days

Type of Business	Name of Case	Estate's Value on Return	Value Per Share		Delay from Date of Death to Closing of Case		
			IRS Challenge	Court's Decision			
farmer	Wilson, Estate of S.A. Regenold 51,247 P-H Memo T.C.	$ 353.92	$ 753.05	$ 395.00	8 yrs	1 mo	23 days
fertilizer manufacturer	Bradley, Estate of Mrs. Sarah H. 2 T.C.M. 609	200.00	430.00	275.00	6 yrs	7 mo	7 days
flour & grain milling	Gwinn, Estate of D. Byrd 25 T.C. 31	40.00	195.00	60.00	4 yrs	9 mo	3 days
furniture sales	Helmers, Estate of George J. 9 T.C.M. 524	500.00	1,000.00	900.00	5 yrs	4 mo	0 days
games manufacturer	Richter v. U.S. 27 AFTR 2d 1691	424.90	1,000.00	700.00	9 yrs	10 mo	23 days
gas company	McIlhenny, Estate of John D. 22 B.T.A. 1093	46.66	62.50	50.00	5 yrs	4 mo	16 days
glass container manufacturer	Hazelton, Estate of Ben F. Jr. 2 T.C.M. 450	41.25	46.25	43.00	3 yrs	5 mo	11 days
grain feed storage	Bader v. U.S. 172 F. Supp. 833	521.83	1,250.00	642.00	7 yrs	9 mo	24 days
grocery wholesaler	Pendleton, Estate of A. S. 20 B.T.A. 618	150.00	400.00	400.00	5 yrs	4 mo	14 days
hair shampoo manufacturer	Goar, Estate of Joseph E. 9 T.C.M. 854	200.00	447.31	275.00	3 yrs	7 mo	8 days

Type of Business	Name of Case	Estate's Value on Return	Value Per Share IRS Challenge	Court's Decision		Delay from Date of Death to Closing of Case	
hardware store	Anderson, Estate of J. Macfie 72,125 P-H Memo T.C.	$ 2,500.00	$ 3,000.00	$ 3,000.00	5 yrs	9 mo	30 days
holding company	Smith, Estate of Loyd R. 9 T.C.M. 907	3,350.00	7,317.28	5,700.00	5 yrs	9 mo	24 days
hotel	McDermott, Estate of James D. 12 T.C.M. 481	50.00	150.00	50.00	6 yrs	0 mo	8 days
insurance company	Maxwell, Estate of William 3 T.C.M. 1207	49.00	52.75	52.75	5 yrs	3 mo	7 days
intercom systems installer	Sobel, Estate of Ephraim F. 10 T.C.M. 613	55.83	187.35	65.00	5 yrs	0 mo	1 day
kitchen appliance manufacturer	Johnson, Estate of Herbert L. 2 T.C.M. 299	31.00	50.00	36.00	5 yrs	5 mo	1 day
laundry supply company	Hogan, Estate of James 3 T.C.M. 315	1,125.00	2,100.00	1,459.00	3 yrs	10 mo	11 days
loading equipment manufacturer	Houghton v. U.S. 15 AFTR 2d 1359	195.00	450.00	375.00	8 yrs	11 mo	25 days
logging company	Garrett, Estate of Jessie R. 12 T.C.M. 1142	50.39	285.65	285.65	6 yrs	6 mo	15 days
meat packing company	Russell v. U.S. 18 AFTR 2d 6278	1,360.00	2,100.00	2,100.00	6 yrs	6 mo	27 days

Type of Business	Name of Case	Estate's Value on Return	Value Per Share		Delay from Date of Death to Closing of Case		
			IRS Challenge	Court's Decision			
mining equipment manufacturer	Schneider-Pass, Est. of Alfred J. 28 T.C.M. 81	$ 4,761.90	$ 38,500.00	$ 23,809.00	11 yrs	1 mo	19 days
motel & restaurant	Wallace Estate v. U.S. 31 AFTR 2d 1395	64.23	147.00	91.50	8 yrs	7 mo	6 days
mushroom grower & supplier	Thompson, Estate of Barbara F. 18 T.C.M. 801	225.00	535.00	283.50	7 yrs	9 mo	27 days
newspaper	S. Carolina Nat'l Bank v. McLeod 256 F. Supp. 913	700.00	980.00	800.00	5 yrs	7 mo	25 days
oil drilling supply sales	Burda, Estate of L.J. 2 T.C.M. 497	3.00	10.00	5.00	1 yrs	6 mo	7 days
paper products wholesaler	Worthen v. U.S. 7 AFTR 2d 1801	100.00	175.00	104.00	7 yrs	6 mo	4 days
ranching	O'Connell, Estate of J.E. 78,191 P-H Memo T.C.	485.33	1,631.00	1,000.00	5 yrs	7 mo	17 days
real estate development	Hanscom, Estate of Edward E. 24 B.T.A. 173	50.00	100.00	100.00	5 yrs	1 mo	18 days
retail shops	Kessler, Estate of Bernard 78,491 P-H Memo T.C.	.50	4.96	3.67	6 yrs	7 mo	20 days
sawmill & finishing plant	Brooks v. Willcuts 78 F. 2d 270	140.00	175.00	175.00	5 yrs	4 mo	22 days

Type of Business	Name of Case	Value Per Share			Delay from Date of Death to Closing of Case		
		Estate's Value on Return	IRS Challenge	Court's Decision			
shipping firm	Brush, Estate of Marjorie G. 22 T.C.M. 900	$ 3.00	$ 7.37	$ 5.50	5 yrs	3 mo	2 days
shoe store	Patton, Estate of Walter L. 10 T.C.M. 1066	300.00	414.25	365.00	7 yrs	2 mo	16 days
steel fabrication	Huntsman, Estate of John L. 66 T.C. 861	18.40	36.64	29.00	5 yrs	6 mo	12 days
steel mill equipment manufacturer	Harrison, Estate of Florence M. 17 T.C.M. 776	4.00	5.85	5.85	5 yrs	7 mo	3 days
tobacco dealer	Nienhuys, Jan W. 17 T.C. 1149	115.00	285.00	172.68	5 yrs	9 mo	6 days
woolen textile manufacturer	Olney, Estate of Lizzie F. 46,138 P-H Memo T.C.	676.00	1,100.00	855.00	3 yrs	10 mo	17 days

AVERAGES IN THE PREVIOUS 54 CASES

Value Per Share			Delay from Date of Death to Closing of Case		
Estate's Value on Return	IRS Challenge	Court's Decision			
$ 654.28	$ 1,680.82	$ 1,202.32	6 yrs	7 mo	20 days

Even in those cases in which the court agreed with the estate, it took an average of 7 years, 7 months and 5 days to resolve the dispute.

BUY/SELL AGREEMENTS HELP FIX THE VALUE

In Each of These Cases the Court Upheld the Value as Established in the Agreement

Type of Business	Name of Case	Value As Provided In Agreement	Value Per Share IRS Challenge	Court's Decision
advertising agency	Mitchell, Estate of John T. H. 37 B.T.A. 1	$ 123.45	$ 348.63	$ 123.45
coal wholesaler	May et al., v. McGowan 194 F. 2d 396	-0-	100.00	-0-
electrical parts wholesaler	Salt, Albert B. 17 T.C. 92	20.00	60.00	20.00
mental hospital	Slocum v. U.S. 256 F. Supp. 753	100.00	1,108.62	100.00
newspaper	Littick, Orville B. 31 T.C. 181	298.50	384.94	298.50
optical & lens manufacturer	Lomb v. Sugden 82 F.2d 166	69.44	100.00	69.44
real estate development	Fieux's Estate 149 N.E. 857	100.00	200.50	100.00
shoe store	Third National Bank v. U.S. 64 F. Supp. 198	100.00	150.00	100.00
soft drink bottler	Strange, Estate of John Q. 42,247 P-H Memo T.C.	250.00	5,953.16	250.00

COMPARISON
CROSS PURCHASE & ENTITY PURCHASE

	Cross Purchase	Entity Purchase
Purchaser	Surviving stockholders (see charts, pages 131, 135 and 139).	Corporation (see charts, pages 127 and 139).
Seller	Deceased stockholder's estate.	Deceased stockholder's estate.
Policy Owner	Individual stockholders (or trustee, see chart page 135).	Corporation.
Number of Policies Required	Multiple policies depending upon number of stockholders (unless trusteed cross purchase, or funded with first-to-die insurance, see chart page 135 and page 415).	One policy on each stockholder.
Premiums	Paid by individual stockholders and not deductible (but could use split-dollar, see chart, page 223).	Paid by corporation and not deductible.
Taxation of Life Insurance Death Benefits	Received tax-free by surviving stockholders (but may be subject to notice and consent requirements, see pages 367-369).	Received tax-free provided notice and consent requirements have been met (see pages 367-369). Could be subject to corporate alternative minimum tax (see page 374).
Effect on Surviving Stockholders	Stockholder's basis increases in an amount equal to price paid for deceased's stock.	Value of stock owned by survivors increases if corporation retires stock (but no increase in stockholder's basis).
Impact of Attribution	No effect.	Redemption is subject to attribution rules (see pages 170-175).
Taxation of Deceased Stockholder's Heirs	Basis is stepped-up at death and no gain recognized (see page 530).	Basis is stepped-up at death and no gain recognized, provided redemption meets either Code section 302(b)(3) or Code section 303 requirements. (see footnote 1, page 149 and page 530).
Legality of Arrangement	No problem, unless professional corporation and state law restricts sale to other professionals.	Must meet state laws regarding corporate purchase of own stock.
Flexibility to Change Plans	Transfer of existing policies to corporation could be an exception to transfer for value rules (see page 541).	Transfer of corporate owned policies to co-stockholder violates transfer for value rules, unless co-stockholder is also a partner of the insured (see page 541).

COMPARISON
CROSS PURCHASE & TRUSTEED CROSS PURCHASE

	Cross Purchase	Trusteed Cross Purchase
Purchaser	Surviving stockholders (see chart, page 131).	Trustee as escrow agent for surviving stockholders (see chart, page 135).
Seller	Deceased stockholder's estate.	Deceased stockholder's estate. Stock certificates held in escrow by trustee are transferred to surviving stockholders.
Policy Owner	Individual stockholders.	Trustee as agent for stockholders.
Policy Beneficiary	Individual stockholders.	Trustee as agent for surviving stockholders. Trustee transfers funds to deceased's estate in return for deceased's stock interest.
Number of Policies Required	Multiple policies depending upon number of stockholders (see footnote 3, page 133).	One policy on each stockholder (see footnote 7, page 137).
Premiums	Paid by individual stockholders.	Paid by trustee from funds obtained from stockholders (see footnote 5, page 137).
Taxation of Life Insurance Death Benefits	Received tax-free by surviving stockholders (but may be subject to notice and consent requirements, see pages 367-369).	Received tax-free by trustee as agent for surviving stockholders (but may be subject to notice and consent requirements, see pages 367-369).
Effect on Surviving Stockholders	Surviving stockholder's basis in stock increases in an amount equal to price paid for deceased's interest.	Surviving stockholder's basis in stock increases in an amount equal to price paid for deceased's interest.
Taxation of Deceased Stockholder's Heirs	Basis is stepped-up at death and no gain recognized (see page 530).	Basis is stepped-up at death and no gain recognized (see page 530).
Flexibility to Change Plans	Transfer of existing policies to corporation could be an exception to transfer for value rules (see pages 541-542).	Transfer of existing policies to corporation could be an exception to transfer for value rules. However, there is a potential transfer-for-value problem after the first death (see footnote 8, page 137 and pages 541-542).

Note: A trusteed cross purchase agreement can also be used with a partnership (see footnote 1, page 137).

TABLE OF CONTENTS

Page

POINTERS

New Laws Enacted In 2010.

The Patient Protection And Affordable Care Act that was signed into law on March 23, 2010, is both complex and far reaching. Of immediate interest to the small business owner are the following:

Self-insured health reimbursement arrangements. These arrangements must comply with many of the requirements of the new law, but grandfathered plans are exempt from some additional requirements that apply to new and non-grandfathered plans. See chart on page 247 and **Q 320-321**, *Tax Facts on Insurance & Employee Benefits (2011)*.

Insured health reimbursement arrangements. These arrangements can no longer benefit only a select class of employees (but those in existence on March 23, 2010 are grandfathered). See the chart on page 247.

Tax credit for health insurance costs. Generally, beginning in 2010 businesses with 24 or fewer employees, whose average compensation is less than $50,000, may receive a 35 percent income tax credit for the cost of qualifying health insurance costs in 2010 through 2013, provided they pay 50 percent of the cost of health care coverage. The credit is increased to 50 percent of qualifying expenses for any two consecutive years beginning in 2014 (resulting in a maximum of six years that an employer can take advantage of the credit). See **Q 313-316**, *Tax Facts on Insurance & Employee Benefits (2011)*.

SIMPLE Cafeteria Plans. Beginning in 2011, SIMPLE cafeteria plans may be established by employers who employed an average of 100 or fewer employees for either of the prior two years (the concept is similar to the SIMPLE 401(k) and SIMPLE-IRA). See the discussion on page 523.

The Tax Relief, Unemployment Insurance Reauthorization, and Job Creation Act of 2010 provided tax cuts and tax extenders for everyone. Some that should not be overlooked include:

Educational Benefits. Among the many educational tax benefits that were extended through December 31, 2012 are: The American Opportunity Tax Credit (including enhanced income limitations); the $5,250 education assistance exclusion; the enhancements to the $2,500 above-the-line student loan interest deduction (including a modified AGI phase-out range); the $2,000 maximum contribution to Coverdell Education Savings Accounts (including elementary school expenses as qualified expenses); and the $2,000/$4,000 higher education interest deduction. See pages 361-363.

IRA Charitable Rollover. The IRA charitable rollover was restored for 2010 and may be used for all of 2012. The IRA owner must be age 70½ or older, the amount cannot exceed $100,000 total in one year, and the rollover must be a trustee-to-charity transfer. Transfers qualify as required minimum distributions.

Time Can Work For You . . . And Against You.

Dollars can grow, but they need time. Some people have more time, and some people have less time. If you are just starting out, time is your friend; the stock market will go up, maybe not today, tomorrow, next week, next month, or even next year, but it will go up. If you are about to retire, time is *not* your friend, particularly if you did not take advantage of time when it was your friend. By allowing before-tax dollars to grow tax-deferred, tax-favored retirement plans offer a very effective way of using time to secure your retirement years. The materials on pages 258-261, 315-320, 560 and 561, will help you better understand and explain concepts involving the time value of money.

Providing For Retirement.

Retirement income planning. Retirees are living longer, healthier, and more active lives (see table, Healthy Life Expectancy, page 557). No longer is it adequate to merely help clients save for retirement. Your soon-to-retire clients must have a plan that will provide an inflation-adjusted stream of income that will not be outlived (pages 501-502). In this regard, see the Longevity In Retirement table on pages 558-559. This table can be used to estimate the odds of living to a specific retirement age. For example, a 65-year-old male has a 55.6 percent chance of living to age 80, and a 34.6 percent chance of living to age 85; but only a 15.5 percent chance of living to age 90. Given those odds, a healthy 65-year-old male should be very concerned about having sufficient retirement funds for at least the next 20 years (age 85), if not the next 25 years (age 90).

Self-Employed Individuals. A variety of retirement plans are available for the self-employed. The discussion on page 521 generally lists them in the order of amount of maximum annual contribution, costs to set up, complexity, and difficulty of administration.

Minimum distribution rules. With qualified retirement plans, there are strict rules regarding when, how much, and for how long money can be put away (pages 262-277, 303-309, 427, 433-434, and 524-525). The minimum distribution rules allow your clients to significantly defer income taxes with post-retirement and post-death distribution planning, particularly with regards to IRAs (pages 433-434 and 551). Under rollover rules, your clients have a great deal of flexibility to transfer, or consolidate, their retirement funds between IRAs, 403(b) plans, 457 plans, and qualified plans including 401(k) plans.

Will The Plan Fit?

Employers and employees come in many shapes and forms. Before proceeding with recommendations as to a specific benefit plan, it is essential to ascertain whether your client is doing business as a C corporation, S corporation, partnership, limited liability company, or sole proprietor (pages 286-294, 412, 445, 465-467, 471, 483, and 510-512). In general, the S corporation, partnership, and sole proprietorship provide limited opportunities for creative employee benefit plans for the owner/employee (pages 176-178).

In contrast, C corporations are taxable entities, separate and apart from their stockholders. They offer attractive opportunities for using tax-advantaged employee benefits for employee/stockholders. For example, a deferred compensation plan can be used in the medium to large sized corporation to reward key executives who are stockholders in the corporation (page 235). However, deferred compensation is not appropriate if your client is a sole proprietor. The threshold question is simple: are your client and his business separate taxable entities? If they are, then your client is able to use a "business check" for funding employee benefits, and can take advantage of any tax leverage provided by the difference between employer and employee income tax brackets (pages 200-201 and 398).

You should refer to the following footnotes for guidance regarding the appropriateness of specific employee benefits: group insurance (footnote 1, page 205); executive equity (footnote 2, page 213); split-dollar insurance (footnote 2, page 221); deferred compensation (footnotes 1 and 7, page 237); disability income plan (footnote 1, page 245); and health reimbursement arrangements (footnote 1, page 249).

With Whom Are You Working?

It is also important to consider *whom* you are working with and what their objectives are. Is your client the owner of a small closely-held business who wants to fund his corporate buy/sell agreement with split-dollar life insurance, or is your client the chief financial officer of a larger corporation charged with the responsibility of assembling a selective supplemental retirement plan for a group of key executives? Is the benefit for a "pure" employee (i.e., a nonowner)? Is the nonowner/employee related to your client? Is it expected that the nonowner/employee will eventually become an owner? Answers to these questions will help you design an employee benefit plan that is responsive to your client's objectives. A relevant and responsive plan improves your credibility with your client, and is far more likely to be accepted and implemented.

Disability, Long-Term Care, And IRAs.

As with retirement planning concepts, disability income, long-term care, and IRAs are included in this employee benefits section. However, these important needs may well be provided for outside the context of an employer-employee relationship. For example, some of your clients will establish IRAs that have nothing to do with their employer, while other clients may participate in Simple IRAs established by their employer (pages 427 and 524). Likewise, many clients acquire individual disability income contracts outside of a formal disability income plan; while other clients are covered by plans with varying degrees of employer participation (pages 238-241, 242-248, 323, and 387).

TAXATION OF EMPLOYEE BENEFITS

Employee benefits, once considered an "addition" to wages, have now become an integral part of virtually all compensation packages. Because the rapid increase in their variety and value has made it difficult to evaluate them, this overview is designed to review some of their tax advantages and disadvantages.[1]

Characterization of a benefit as either bad, better, or best, can be made according to its effect upon the income taxes of the employer and the employee. For example, assume that in 2011 we have an employer in a 34 percent marginal tax bracket and an employee in a 25 percent tax bracket.

BAD. A bad employee benefit is one that is *nondeductible* to the employer yet *taxable* to the employee, such as one that results in unreasonable compensation or is treated as a dividend. Because it is nondeductible, on each $1.00 of income the employer must pay 34 cents in taxes. Since the remaining 66 cents is taxable to the employee, 17 cents of employee taxes will further reduce the original $1.00 to only 49 cents. That's bad!

BETTER. A better employee benefit is one that is *deductible* to the employer, although still *taxable* to the employee. Since there are no employer taxes, the full $1.00 is taxable income to the employee. Now 25 cents goes to pay employee taxes, and the remaining 75 cents actually benefits the employee. That's better!

Better benefits include salary allotment plans, executive equity plans, split-dollar insurance, survivor income plans, disability income plans, and deferred compensation.

BEST. The best employee benefit is one that is *deductible* to the employer and either *nontaxable* or *tax deferred* to the employee. Now the entire $1.00 benefits the employee, without any current reduction for either employer or employee taxes. That's the best!

"Best" benefits include group term insurance, medical expense reimbursement plans, SIMPLE IRAs, and qualified retirement plans, including 401(k) plans.[2]

---

[1] The checklist on pages 286-294 describes many employee benefits and the income tax effect on employees.

[2] Specific benefits may not be available to all employees and employers. Although SIMPLE IRAs and qualified retirement plans, including 401(k) plans, are listed among the "best," it must be recognized that the employee pays taxes when retirement income is actually received. Tax-free group term insurance is limited to $50,000 of coverage. The term "leveraged benefit" can be used to describe some of the best employee benefits, as discussed further on page 437.

BAD

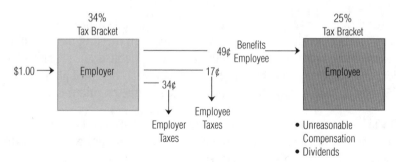

34%
Tax Bracket

$1.00 →   Employer

                                           49¢ Benefits
                                               Employee

                                           17¢

           34¢

        Employer   Employee
         Taxes   Taxes

25%
Tax Bracket

        Employee

• Unreasonable
  Compensation
• Dividends

BETTER

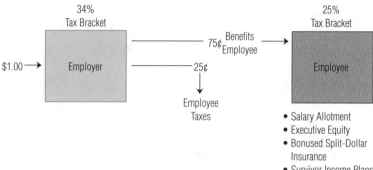

34%
Tax Bracket

$1.00 →   Employer

                                           75¢ Benefits
                                               Employee

                                           25¢

                                        Employee
                                          Taxes

25%
Tax Bracket

        Employee

• Salary Allotment
• Executive Equity
• Bonused Split-Dollar
  Insurance
• Survivor Income Plans
• Disability Income Plans
• Deferred Compensation

BEST

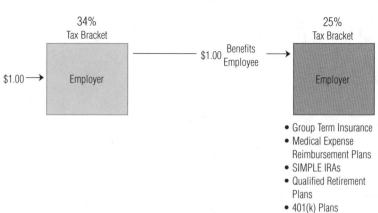

34%
Tax Bracket

$1.00 →   Employer

                                        $1.00 Benefits
                                              Employee

25%
Tax Bracket

        Employer

• Group Term Insurance
• Medical Expense
  Reimbursement Plans
• SIMPLE IRAs
• Qualified Retirement
  Plans
• 401(k) Plans

GROUP INSURANCE

Group insurance has gained wide acceptance as a tax-favored benefit that an employer can provide for his employees, including stockholder-employees.[1] In meeting the twin objectives of family security and reduced cost, most plans offer group term life insurance together with group hospital, surgical, and major medical coverage. Under a properly designed plan, employees can receive up to $50,000 of life coverage, free of income taxes on the premium payments.[2]

DURING LIFETIME. To provide this benefit, an employer will arrange for the insurance coverage and pay the premiums to the insurance company. These premiums are tax-deductible to the employer, but not taxable to the covered employee.

Group term life insurance must meet four basic requirements:

1. The plan must provide a general death benefit that is excludable from income.
2. It must be provided to a group of employees as compensation for personal services as an employee.
3. The insurance must be provided under a policy carried directly or indirectly by the employer.
4. The amount of insurance provided each employee must be computed under a formula that precludes individual selection of such amounts. This formula must be based upon factors such as age, years of service, compensation or position.[3]

If a group insurance plan discriminates in favor of "key employees," then these particular employees may not exclude the cost of the first $50,000 of coverage.[4]

UPON DEATH. When the employee dies, the insurance company pays the death benefit directly to the employee's family or estate, as beneficiary of the insurance.[5] This payment is also free of income taxes as the death benefit of a life insurance contract.[6]

Footnotes on page 205

DURING LIFETIME

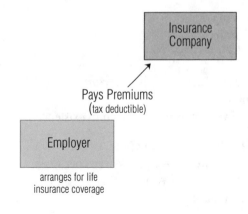

Insurance
Company

Pays Premiums
(tax deductible)

Employer

arranges for life
insurance coverage

Employee

can receive up to
$50,000 of coverage
free of income taxes

UPON DEATH

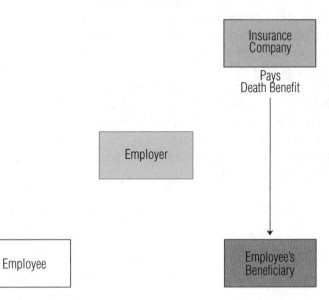

Insurance
Company

Pays
Death Benefit

Employer

Employee

Employee's
Beneficiary

INFORMATION REQUIRED FOR ANALYSIS & PROPOSAL

1. Names of employees.
2. Dates of birth.
3. Salary schedule.

To Determine Eligibility for Program
4. Nature of business.
5. Number of years business has been in existence.

To Exclude Ineligible Employees
6. Status of employees   – hours worked per week.
                – months worked per year.
7. Employment dates.

Note: It is also possible to exclude employees who are: (1) covered by a collective bargaining agreement; and (2) nonresident aliens who received no earned income from the employer from sources within the United States.

CROSS REFERENCES TO TAX FACTS ON INSURANCE & EMPLOYEE BENEFITS (2011)

Q 171. Tax benefits of group term life insurance.
Q 172. Requirements of group term life insurance.
Q 173. Groups of fewer than 10 employees can be covered.
Q 174. Premiums paid are deductible business expenses.
Q 175. Taxation of cost of coverage to insured employee.
Q 176. Taxation of key employees when plan discriminates in favor of them as to eligibility, kinds or amounts of benefits (including definition of "key employee").
Q 177. When cost of coverage is subject to social security tax.
Q 178. What information returns must be filed by employer.
Q 179. Advantages of group carve-out plans.
Q 224. Use of group term life insurance to fund buy/sell agreement will likely cause denial of deduction to employer.

Footnotes

[1] The tax advantages of group insurance can be made available to the *employees* of a corporation, a partnership, or a sole proprietorship. However, this *does not include* the stockholder-employees of an S corporation who own more than 2 percent of the stock, the partners of a partnership, and the sole proprietor. They are not treated as "employees" for this purpose. Stockholders of a regular C corporation, who are also employees, can be covered by the plan as employees. Insurance provided for a non-employee corporate director does not qualify as group insurance.

[2] It is surprising to find how often corporate owners have failed to provide the maximum amount of tax-free coverage for themselves and their key employees. Although federal law allows up to $50,000, state law may set lower limits on the amount of coverage that can be provided by group life insurance. The coverage in excess of $50,000 is taxable income to the employee. To determine the value of this excess coverage, refer to the Table I Rates on page 552. This table is specifically provided by IRS Regulations to measure the value of group term insurance in excess of $50,000. In Notice 89-110 (1989-2 C.B. 447) the IRS has indicated that up to $2,000 of coverage on spouse and dependents will also be income tax-free to the employee as a "de minimis" fringe benefit. Although retired employees are generally subject to the same limits as active employees, the $50,000 limit does not apply to disabled retirees.

[3] Generally, there must be at least 10 full-time employees for a plan to qualify as group term life insurance. However, insurance for *fewer than* 10 employees may also qualify as group term life insurance if: (1) it is provided for all full-time employees; and (2) the amount of protection is computed either as a uniform percentage of compensation or on the basis of coverage brackets established by the insurer under which no bracket exceeds 2½ times the next lower bracket, and the lowest bracket is at least 10 percent of the highest bracket.

[4] Discrimination as to either *eligibility to participate*, or with respect to the *kind or amount of benefits*, will result in "key employees" having to include in income the higher of actual cost or Table I cost of the entire amount of coverage (see the definition of "key employee" on page 304).

[5] One note of caution regarding group term life insurance – do not attempt to use the death benefits to fund an obligation to purchase the insured's business interest. The adverse tax consequences can be very costly. For example, if there is an attempt to fund an entity purchase agreement (chart, page 127) by making the employer a beneficiary of the policy, the Code specifically prohibits any deduction for the cost of coverage on the life of an employee. In addition, state laws often prohibit the employer from being named beneficiary of group insurance. If there is an attempt to fund a cross purchase agreement (chart, page 131) by naming a co-owner beneficiary of the policy, the arrangement is likely to run afoul of the transfer for value rules (discussion, pages 541-542). Group term insurance is an *employee* fringe benefit, the death benefit of which should be paid to the employee's personal beneficiary. Such a personal beneficiary could properly include the trustee of an irrevocable life insurance trust, to which the insured had assigned ownership of the coverage in order to exclude the death proceeds from his taxable estate. In this regard, refer to the Life Insurance Trust chart on page 51.

[6] Over the years a variety of benefits have been offered as "group" term insurance. Included among these were Retired Lives Reserves (RLR) and "Section 79." RLR was a fund established for continuing group life insurance for retired employees, whereas Section 79 was used to describe the use of individual permanent policies, often by superimposing them on top of existing group coverage, to provide group term life insurance. Neither variation is viable today, as is further discussed under Retired Lives Reserves on page 500.

SALARY ALLOTMENT

The compensation provided to most employees consists of both salary and benefits. Benefits can often equal 30 percent or more of direct payroll costs.[1] With a salary allotment plan, it is possible to contain these expenses, while at the same time offering a valuable benefit with *no direct cost* to the employer.[2]

A salary allotment plan can also be very attractive to employees. By purchasing a base of permanent life insurance during his working years, an employee can avoid the prohibitive costs often associated with converting group life insurance upon retirement. This then guarantees that some life insurance will always be available, whether death occurs before or after retirement.

Under the typical salary allotment plan, employees are given the opportunity to supplement their existing group and other coverages with life insurance, disability income insurance, long-term care insurance, or annuity benefits. This is a purely voluntary program, which each employee can take advantage of through an individual pay allotment to the insurance company.

The advantages of such plans often include:

- Discounted premiums from group billing efficiencies.
- No physical examinations.
- Level premiums that do not increase.
- No lapse of policy upon retirement.
- Convenient payroll deduction of premiums.[3]

To make these benefits available, the insurance carrier will usually require the employer to:

- Provide notice of enrollment opportunity.
- Allow for enrollment at work during business hours.[4]
- Arrange for payroll deductions.

Most employers have found that their employees are grateful for the opportunity to enroll in such plans, since they are often viewed as an extension of existing benefits packages. These plans offer a relatively painless means by which employees pay modest premiums in order to provide substantial life, disability, and annuity benefits for themselves and their families.[5]

Footnotes on page 209

COMPENSATION

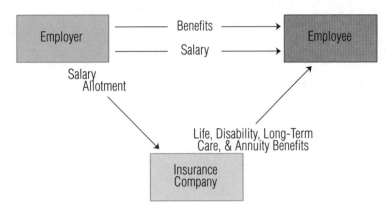

THE ADVANTAGES

- Discounted Premiums
- No Physical Examinations
- Level Premiums
- Permanent Coverage
- Payroll Deduction

INFORMATION REQUIRED FOR ANALYSIS & PROPOSAL

To Determine Eligibility for Program
1. Nature of business.
2. Number of years business has been in existence.

To Exclude Ineligible Employees
3. Status of employees (full time *or* part time).
4. Employment dates.
5. Current employment status (i.e., at work for prior 30 days).

To Prepare Individual Proposals
6. Names of employees.
7. Dates of birth.
8. Smoker/nonsmoker.
9. Salary schedule (if appropriate).

To Administer Program
10. Payroll dates.
11. Payroll cycle (weekly, biweekly, bifortnightly, *or* monthly).
12. Payroll clerk's name and telephone number.

CROSS REFERENCES TO TAX FACTS ON INSURANCE & EMPLOYEE BENEFITS (2011)

Q 190. Life insurance premiums are deductible by corporation as additional compensation provided it has no ownership rights or beneficial interest in policy.

Q 195. Premiums paid by employer on policy owned by employee are taxable income to employee.

Q 255. Disability income benefits received from personally paid policy are tax-free.

Q 347. Within certain limits, benefits received from qualified long-term care policy are tax-free.

Footnotes

[1] The Employee Benefit Statistics, on page 295, indicate that of the companies surveyed in 2008, Total Employee Benefits amounted to 29.2 percent of payroll. Among the best prospects for salary allotment plans are existing group insurance clients. As to the employer, the tax treatment of salary allotment plans is similar to group insurance, in that the amounts paid for insurance are *deductible* (as a compensation expense). However, employee *after-tax* dollars are used to pay for the coverage.

[2] The terms "salary allotment," "salary deduction," and "payroll deduction" are interchangeable. In discussing this market, the terms "voluntary insurance" and "worksite marketing" are also used. If desired, there is no reason why an employer cannot contribute a portion of the premium. Contributions toward *life insurance* coverage are fully included in the employee's income. However, the employee may choose either to include or exclude employer contributions for *disability insurance* (see footnote 5, on page 245, and the table on page 323).

[3] The deduction of premium payments from payroll checks means that the employee will never have to sit down and write a check to the insurance company. A salary allotment plan provides an effective means by which the rank and file employee can set aside for emergencies or retirement some of the earnings projected in the table on page 315.

[4] Favorable enrollment conditions are required in order to obtain high levels of participation. Higher participation enables the insurance carrier to absorb increased losses, which often occur on account of underwriting concessions (i.e., guaranteed standard issue, simplified underwriting, etc.).

[5] Spouse and children riders are frequently available with life insurance offered in salary allotment plans. With disability insurance, the coverage will not necessarily offer level premiums, level benefits, and a guarantee of no policy cancellation. Annuity benefits would likely come from using accumulated life insurance cash values.

EXECUTIVE EQUITY

Executive equity is an employee benefit plan that allows an employer to provide valuable life insurance protection for a *selected* employee on a tax deductible basis to the employer.[1] The employer has total discretion to select the employee, or employees, to be covered by the agreement, and the amounts of insurance to be provided. It can be made available to both the stockholder-employee and the nonstockholder-employee.[2]

DURING LIFETIME. Under the agreement, the employee purchases and owns a permanent life insurance contract on his life.[3] The employer pays premiums to the insurance company, which are fully tax-deductible by the employer as compensation to the employee.[4]

These premiums are considered taxable income to the employee, upon which the employee is responsible for paying taxes to the IRS.[5] However, the *employee owns* the life insurance contract, including all policy cash values, and the annual increase in these values usually more than offsets any taxes paid by the employee. If desired, these taxes could be paid with borrowed or withdrawn policy cash values, or dividends, if funded with a participating policy.[6]

UPON DEATH. At the employee's death, the insurance company pays the total death benefit directly to the employee's beneficiary. Because it is the death benefit of a life insurance contract, this payment is received free of all income taxes.

Executive equity offers something for everyone – tax deductibility to the employer, cash value accumulations for the employee, ease of installation, and premium payments with a business check.[7] If the employee-stockholder's marginal tax bracket is less than his corporation's marginal tax bracket, then executive equity should be attractive to the employee-stockholder who wishes to withdraw profits from the corporation.

Footnotes on page 213

DURING LIFETIME

UPON DEATH

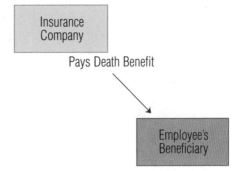

INFORMATION REQUIRED FOR ANALYSIS & PROPOSAL

1. Name of employee.
2. Sex.
3. Date of birth.
4. Smoker/nonsmoker.
5. Employee's tax bracket – to calculate taxes on bonuses (i.e., premium payments made for employee by employer).
6. Employer's tax bracket – to calculate after-tax cost of bonuses.
7. Projected bonuses or premiums to be paid by employer each year.

CROSS REFERENCES TO TAX FACTS ON INSURANCE & EMPLOYEE BENEFITS (2011)

Q 188. General discussion of when premiums paid are either deductible or nondeductible.

Q 190. Life insurance premiums are deductible by corporation as additional compensation provided it has no ownership rights or beneficial interest in policy.

Q 195. Premiums paid by employer on policy owned by employee are taxable income to employee.

Q 197. Income tax consequences of Section 162 Bonus Plan.

Footnotes

[1] Executive Equity plans are also referred to as "Executive Bonus Plans," "Executive Retirement Bonus Plans," and "Section 162 Bonus Plans" (after Section 162(a)(1) of the Internal Revenue Code, which authorizes a business to deduct a "reasonable allowance" for salaries or other compensation for personal services actually rendered).

[2] If executive equity is to be effective with owner-employees, it must usually be used in a regular C corporation (not an S corporation). Neither the sole proprietorship nor the partnership provides the separate taxable entity that is essential for the concept to be an attractive benefit for owner-employees.

[3] Because the contract is entirely owned by the employee, it is not essential that the agreement be in writing, as it is with split-dollar insurance. However, it is good practice to have the terms of any important agreement in writing; and the agreement could help defend against an IRS attempt to characterize the bonuses as nondeductible dividends.

[4] In 2011 married couples filing jointly with $212,300 or less of taxable income, and single taxpayers with $174,400 or less of taxable income, are in a 28 percent or lower tax bracket (see tax rates on page 549). For these individuals, executive equity is an attractive benefit (i.e., "enhanced" individual after-tax dollars are available to pay premiums, whereas a corporation with over $75,000 of taxable income is in a minimum 34 percent tax bracket). For an expanded discussion of Enhanced Dollars, see page 398.

[5] The premiums paid by the employer are reported as "other compensation" on the employee's W-2 form. Likewise, this compensation is subject to both the Social Security Tax (FICA) and the Federal Unemployment Tax (FUTA). Underlying any discussion of employee benefits is the assumption that, if challenged by the Internal Revenue Service, the increased compensation would be considered "reasonable." For an expanded discussion of Unreasonable Compensation, see page 546.

[6] In designing the column arrangements of executive equity illustrations, it is particularly important to emphasize the direct comparison between the yearly *income taxes* paid by the employee and the annual *cash value increases*, all of which are owned by the employee. For example, if the employer pays a premium of $2,500 for $100,000 of insurance protection, this $2,500 will constitute taxable income to the employee. Assuming in 2011 the employee is in a 25 percent tax bracket, he will have to pay $625 of additional income taxes (.25 x $2,500). However, if the cash values *owned* by the employee increased by $1,300 in that year, this more than offsets the taxes paid.

[7] Note that with executive equity, the employer has no interest in either the cash values or the death benefits. This contrasts with a split-dollar arrangement, under which the employer usually owns most, if not all, of the cash values, and receives a portion of the death benefits. To better appreciate these differences, see the Split-Dollar Insurance chart on page 219, and the comparison of Executive Equity and Split-Dollar Insurance on page 300. The Restrictive Bonus Plan discussed in the chart on page 215 provides an interesting alternative to both Executive Equity and Split-Dollar plans.

RESTRICTIVE BONUS PLAN

The restrictive bonus plan is an employee benefit that allows an employer to provide valuable life insurance protection for a *selected* employee on a tax deductible basis to the employer.[1] The employer has total discretion to select the employee, or employees, to be covered by the agreement, and the amounts of insurance to be provided. It is typically made available to the non-stockholder-employee.

DURING LIFETIME. Under the agreement, the employee purchases and owns a permanent life insurance contract on his life. Added to the policy is a restrictive endorsement that requires the employer's consent for the employee to: (1) surrender the policy; (2) assign or pledge the policy for a loan; (3) change ownership of the policy; or (4) borrow the cash values of the policy.[2] The endorsement will typically provide for these restrictions to expire upon the earliest to occur of: (1) the retirement of the employee; (2) attainment of a specific age; (3) release by the employer; or (4) the bankruptcy or dissolution of the employer.

By *separate* written agreement, the employer agrees to provide a bonus to the employee by paying all premiums to the insurance company, which are fully tax-deductible by the employer as compensation to the employee.[3] These premiums are considered taxable income to the employee, upon which the employee is responsible for paying taxes to the IRS.[4]

UPON DEATH. At the employee's death, the insurance company pays the total death benefit directly to the employee's beneficiary. Because it is the death benefit of a life insurance contract, this payment is received free of all income taxes.[5]

The restrictive bonus plan offers something for everyone – tax deductibility to the employer, a simple yet attractive "golden handcuff" for attracting and retaining a key employee, life insurance protection together with cash value accumulations available to the employee upon retirement, ease of installation, and premium payments with a business check.[6]

Footnotes on page 217

DURING LIFETIME

UPON DEATH

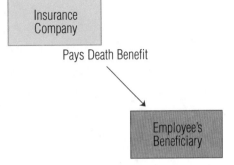

INFORMATION REQUIRED FOR ANALYSIS & PROPOSAL

1. Name of employee.
2. Sex.
3. Date of birth.
4. Smoker/nonsmoker.
5. Employee's tax bracket – to calculate taxes on bonuses (i.e., premium payments made for employee by employer).
6. Employer's tax bracket – to calculate after-tax cost of bonuses.
7. Projected bonuses or premiums to be paid by employer each year.

CROSS REFERENCES TO TAX FACTS ON INSURANCE & EMPLOYEE BENEFITS (2011)

Q 188. General discussion of when premiums paid are either deductible or nondeductible.

Q 190. Life insurance premiums are deductible by corporation as additional compensation, provided it has no ownership rights or beneficial interest in policy.

Q 195. Premiums paid by employer on policy owned by employee are taxable income to employee.

Footnotes

[1] The restrictive bonus plan is also referred to as a "Restrictive Endorsement Bonus Arrangement (REBA)," a "Golden Executive Bonus Arrangement (GEBA)" and a "Controlled Executive Bonus Plan."

[2] One objection to executive equity plans is that the employee can terminate employment at any time, yet have full access to the cash values of the life insurance contract (see chart, page 211). The restrictive bonus plan is an extension of the executive equity concept that in part answers this objection by giving the employer some measure of control over the employee's use and enjoyment of the policy (i.e., a "golden handcuff").

[3] If desired, a "double bonus" could be given (i.e. the bonus is large enough to pay not only the premium, but also the tax on the bonus). The premiums paid by the employer are reported as "other compensation" on the employee's W-2 form. Likewise, this compensation is subject to both the Social Security Tax (FICA) and the Federal Unemployment Tax (FUTA). Underlying any discussion of employee benefits is the assumption that, if challenged by the Internal Revenue Service, the increased compensation would be considered as "reasonable." For an expanded discussion of Unreasonable Compensation, see page 546.

[4] A more aggressive plan design requires the employee to reimburse the employer for some or all of the premiums paid, should the employee terminate employment prior to normal retirement date (or within a certain period of time). While the tax results of this reimbursement are not entirely clear, it seems likely the employee would not be allowed to deduct the repayment and the employer would be required to include the repayment in income. Also, see footnote 6 below regarding the need for the employee's interest to fully vest (i.e., not subject to a substantial risk of forfeiture, thus taxed on bonus).

[5] Note that with both the restrictive bonus plan and executive equity, the employer has no interest in either the cash values or the death benefits. This contrasts with a split-dollar arrangement, under which the employer usually owns most, if not all, of the cash values, and receives a portion of the death benefits.

[6] It is important that the employer have no interest in the life insurance contract, because Code section 264 would disallow the employer's tax deductions for the bonuses if the employer is directly or indirectly a beneficiary under the policy. It is also important to keep the written agreement entirely separate from the policy endorsement, particularly if the employer has a right to be reimbursed for bonuses given the employee. Code section 83 provides, in effect, that the employee is not taxed on property "transferred in connection with the performance of services," if the property: (1) is not transferable by the employee; *and* (2) is subject to a substantial risk of forfeiture. It is clear that the first condition is met since the endorsement prohibits the employee from transferring the policy. Therefore, if the second condition is met, the employee is not taxed and the employer cannot take a current tax deduction. However, most authorities agree that there is no substantial risk of forfeiture if the employer has no interest in the policy and employee's agreement to repay bonuses is nothing more than a bare promise set forth in a separate agreement.

SPLIT-DOLLAR INSURANCE

Split-dollar insurance is an agreement between two parties to *allocate* between them the costs and benefits of a life insurance policy.[1] It is *not* a particular type of life insurance policy. When adopted by an employer split-dollar insurance allows the employer to provide valuable life insurance protection for *selected* employees.[2]

Under regulations issued by the IRS there are two ways for an employer to establish a new split-dollar plan.[3]

(1) **Loan regime.** Under this method the *employee* purchases and is the owner of a life insurance contract. The employee-purchased policy is then collateral assigned to the employer to secure employer premium payments. Each employer premium payment is treated as a loan from the employer to the employee. The employee will either: (a) pay to the employer a market rate of interest on these loans; or (b) receive additional compensation equal to the foregone interest.[4]

(2) **Economic benefit regime.** This method offers a straightforward means of providing to the employee a supplemental executive life insurance death benefit during the years prior to retirement. It can be implemented as follows:

DURING LIFETIME. The *employer* purchases and owns a permanent life insurance policy insuring the employee's life.[5] Pursuant to the split-dollar agreement the employer typically pays the entire premium (an "employer pay all" plan) and owns all cash values.[6] Each year income is imputed to the employee in an amount equal to the "economic benefit" of the insurance protection received by the employee.[7] The employee is responsible for paying taxes to the IRS on this imputed income. There are no tax deductions to the employer (i.e., income imputed to the employee cannot be deducted by the employer). However, provided it is reasonable compensation, the employer could consider paying a bonus to assist the employee in paying taxes on the imputed income.

UPON DEATH. The death benefit payable to the employer can vary according to the provisions of the split-dollar agreement. Typically, the employer is entitled to a death benefit equal to the *greater* of the cash values or the cumulative premiums paid. By endorsement to the policy the employee's personal beneficiary is entitled to the death benefits in excess of the amount paid to the employer.[8]

Footnotes on page 221

DURING LIFETIME

UPON DEATH

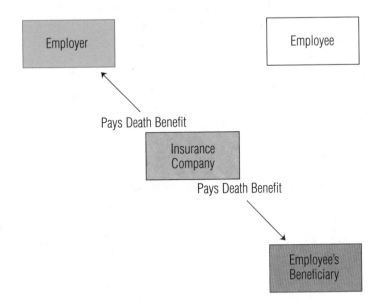

INFORMATION REQUIRED FOR ANALYSIS & PROPOSAL

1. Name of employee.
2. Sex.
3. Date of birth.
4. Smoker/nonsmoker.
5. Amount of desired death benefit.

To Design Plan
6. Position of employee.
7. Is the employee a stockholder?
8. Purpose of the employee's insurance need – family income, estate liquidity, etc. (i.e., how long is the death benefit needed?).
9. Employee's tax bracket – to calculate employee's after-tax cost of imputed income.

CROSS REFERENCES TO TAX FACTS ON INSURANCE & EMPLOYEE BENEFITS (2011)

Q 64. Gift taxation of split-dollar.
Q 245. Estate taxation of split-dollar.
Q 3789. Description of split-dollar.
Q 3790. Income tax results of traditional split-dollar plan.
Q 3791. Treatment of split-dollar plans under final regulations.
Q 3792. Income tax consequences of transfer or "rollout" of split-dollar policy.
Q 3794. Description of private split-dollar and how it is taxed.

Footnotes

[1] The split-dollar plan described in this chart is intended to comply with the requirements of the final split-dollar regulations (effective for plans established after September 17, 2003). Given that the employer pays *all* life insurance premiums and is entitled to *all* cash values, it is better to use the word "allocate" rather than the word "share" (i.e., the premiums and the cash values are allocated to the employer, they are not shared with the employee). See tables A and B on pages 296-297 concerning the treatment of Employer/Employee Split-Dollar Plans established on and before September 17, 2003.

[2] Split-dollar insurance can be provided for the employees of a corporation, a partnership, or a sole proprietorship (sole proprietors cannot be covered because there is no separate taxable entity). Split-dollar is generally not appropriate for partners or employee-stockholders of S corporations because of the pass-through nature of taxation (except to reallocate premiums among owners and when used with a life insurance trust to reduce the value of gifts to the trust, see footnote 5, page 229, and pages 510-512). In contrast, Private Split-Dollar involves an agreement between individuals, or between an individual and a trust (see chart on page 63).

[3] Based upon policy ownership the split-dollar regulations use a formalistic, yet straight forward, approach in providing two "mutually exclusive regimes" (or methods) for the taxation of split-dollar plans. The **economic benefit regime** which is illustrated in this chart (as in the typical endorsement arrangement) applies where the employer owns the contract. The **loan regime** (as in the typical collateral assignment arrangement) applies where the employee owns the contract. However, as an exception to the general rule, even if the employee owns the contract the split-dollar plan is subject to the economic benefit regime if all cash values belong to the employer. This is useful in majority stockholder situations when it is desired to remove all employer death benefits from the insured's estate (see the discussion of Controlling Stockholder on page 373).

[4] In contrast to the chart on page 219 illustrating a split-dollar plan under the economic benefit regime, see the chart on page 401 illustrating a split-dollar plan under the loan regime (the "during lifetime" portion of the chart looks quite different). See also the discussion of Equity Split-Dollar on pages 400-401 for an explanation of the complicated tax treatment of imputed loans.

[5] If the employer could receive a death benefit in excess of cumulative premiums paid it is essential to meet strict notice and consent requirements to preserve the employer's income tax-free death benefit (see Company Owned Life Insurance (COLI), pages 367-369).

[6] These employer-owned cash values can be used to informally fund a nonqualified deferred compensation plan (see chart, page 235). Under the economic benefit regime any direct or indirect access to the cash values is immediately taxable to the employee-nonowner, who cannot obtain any income tax bases in a policy owned by the employer (meaning equity endorsement plans will rarely be adopted). Also, the employee does not share in the premium payments, since under the split-dollar regulations any premiums paid by the *employee* under the economic benefit regime are considered taxable income to the *employer* (under the theory that the employee is paying premiums on a contract owned by the employer). This means that the old "single bonus" plan no longer offers any advantage since this taxable income offsets the employer's deduction for the bonus given the employee.

[7] Under the regulations this "economic benefit" is measured by "life insurance premium factors" to be published by the IRS. Until these factors become available, the Table 2001 rates on page 552 are permissible. Failure of the employee to report this economic benefit, or to contribute an equal amount of premiums, will result in the death benefits being taxed as ordinary income to his beneficiary (i.e., they will not qualify as tax-free life insurance death benefits). Assuming the employee will live to normal retirement age or beyond the taxable economic benefit will get very expensive. This means that an "exit strategy" must be in place if the employee's death benefit is to be maintained after retirement (see Split-Dollar Rollout, page 528).

[8] Provided the employer is willing to have no interest in either the cash values or the death benefit, Executive Equity offers a simpler approach to obtaining needed life insurance protection. It is easier to install, in that there is no required formal agreement between the employer and the employee (see chart, page 211, and comparison, page 300). The Restrictive Bonus Plan in the chart on page 215 provides an interesting alternative.

SPLIT-DOLLAR FUNDING CROSS PURCHASE

Split-dollar insurance is not limited to merely funding the personal insurance needs of an employee. For example, the employee could chose to enter into a split-dollar agreement insuring someone other than himself, such as a spouse or a child. Alternatively, the employee could chose to enter into a split-dollar agreement insuring another stockholder whose stock he is obligated to purchase.[1]

DURING LIFETIME. Assume that we have a corporation owned by two individuals, Employee A and Employee B. They enter into a cross-purchase agreement providing for the purchase and sale of their respective interests.[2]

The *corporation* purchases and owns a permanent life insurance policy insuring the life of each employee.[3] In order to fund their mutual obligations to each other, A and B enter into split-dollar agreements with the corporation providing for the allocation of premiums, cash values and death benefits. In contrast to the typical employer/employee split-dollar plan that provides death benefits for the insured's personal beneficiary, these agreements provide for A to received the death proceeds from the policy insuring B, and for B to receive the death proceeds from the policy insuring A.[4]

The corporation typically pays the entire premium for each policy ("employer pay all" plans) and owns all cash values.[5] Each year income is imputed to the employee in an amount equal to the "economic benefit" of the insurance protection received by the employee on the life of the other employee.[6] Rather than having to come up with expensive after-tax dollars to pay premiums, A and B pay taxes to the IRS on only this imputed income.[7]

UPON DEATH. Assuming that A dies first, his stock interest would then pass to his family or estate. At the same time, the insurance company pays a portion of the death benefit to the corporation to reimburse it under the terms of the split-dollar agreement. The remainder of the death benefit is paid income tax-free to B, which is then used by B to purchase A's entire stock interest from A's family or estate.[8]

Footnotes on page 225

DURING LIFETIME

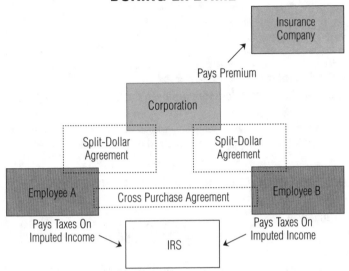

Corporation Obtains Life Insurance On Each Employee

UPON DEATH

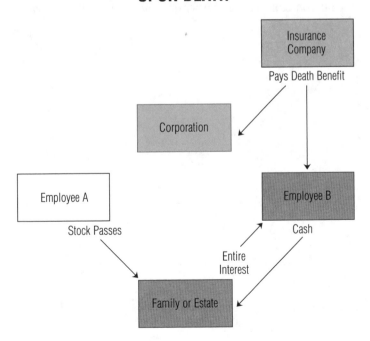

INFORMATION REQUIRED FOR ANALYSIS & PROPOSAL

1. Name of stockholder to be insured.
2. Sex.
3. Date of birth.
4. Value of ownership interest.
5. Employee's tax bracket – to calculate employee's after-tax cost of imputed income.

Note: The "employee's tax bracket" is that of the employee who is entering into the split-dollar agreement with the corporation, *not* the tax bracket of the employee-stockholder who is the insured.

CROSS REFERENCES TO TAX FACTS ON INSURANCE & EMPLOYEE BENEFITS (2011)

Footnotes

[1] In working with a business client it is important to remember that it is usually far easier to obtain payment of premiums with the *corporate* check than the *personal* check. Split-dollar enables employee-stockholders to use a corporate check to pay for life insurance to fund their cross purchase agreement. (Where there is a disparity in ages between the insureds, split-dollar can also help to de-emphasize the difference because substantial portions of the premiums are paid with corporate dollars.) To fund a cross purchase agreement between employee-stockholders, in some situations executive equity may offer a simpler solution, provided there is no requirement that the corporation have any interest in either the cash values or the death benefits (see the Executive Equity chart, page 211).

[2] See the Cross Purchase Agreement chart, page 131. To be viable, split-dollar usually requires that the employer and employee each be a separate taxable entity. Therefore, funding a cross purchase agreement between two owners of a business is generally limited to a regular C corporation, and would *not* be applicable to an S corporation or a partnership. However, it would be feasible to use split-dollar to fund a *key employee* purchase of a stockholder's interest in a corporation, a partnership, or even a sole proprietorship, since in each of these situations the key employee represents a separate taxpayer from his employer (see the Key Person Buy-Out Agreement chart, page 143).

[3] The corporation's ownership of the policy under an endorsement split-dollar plan (see footnote 5, below) could result in a prohibited "transfer for value" if the policy is subsequently transferred to a co-stockholder (e.g., the split-dollar arrangement is terminated and the policy is transferred to a co-stockholder to fund an ongoing cross purchase obligation). This problem only occurs if the transfer does not fit within any of the transfer for value exceptions (see the expanded discussion on page 541). If it is considered important to avoid this *latent* transfer for value problem, the split-dollar agreement could be implemented using the loan regime (i.e., the policy is *owned by the co-stockholder* who collaterally assigns the cash values to the corporation, see the expanded discussion on pages 400-401).

[4] If there is any possibility that the employer could receive a death benefit in excess of cumulative premiums paid, it is essential to meet strict notice and consent requirements to preserve the employer's income tax-free death benefit (see Company Owned Life Insurance (COLI), pages 367-369).

[5] Under the split-dollar regulations this is a "nonequity endorsement plan" intended to be taxed under the economic benefit regime (see the Split-Dollar Insurance chart, page 219). Under the economic benefit regime any direct or indirect access to the cash values is immediately taxable to the employee-nonowner (see also footnote 6, page 221). However, these employer-owned cash values could be used to informally fund a nonqualified deferred compensation plan (see the Deferred Compensation chart, page 235).

[6] Note that the life used to measure the "economic benefit" is that of the insured co-stockholder, not the employee-stockholder who enters into the split-dollar agreement with the corporation. Under the regulations this "economic benefit" is measured by "life insurance premium factors" to be published by the IRS. Until these factors become available, the Table 2001 rates on page 552 are permissible.

[7] The typical corporate split-dollar agreement involving an employee/stockholder is intended to provide an *employee benefit*, not a stockholder benefit. However, lowered maximum tax rates on qualified corporate dividends (reduced to 15 percent through 2012 except for taxpayers in the 10 and 15 percent ordinary income tax brackets, whose rates are reduced to 0 percent through 2012, as extended by The 2010 Tax Relief Act) may cause some split-dollar agreements to be established as stockholder plans, with the stockholder's imputed income taxed at these lower dividend tax rates. Of course, any imputed dividends would not be deductible by the corporation.

[8] Failure of the employee to report this economic benefit, or to contribute an equal amount of premiums, will result in the death benefits being taxed as ordinary income (i.e., they will not qualify as tax-free life insurance death benefits).

SPLIT-DOLLAR FUNDING
LIFE INSURANCE TRUST

Split-dollar offers a means of using employer-provided dollars to pay premiums for life insurance used for a variety of purposes, to include family income needs, estate taxes and other estate settlement costs. When combined with an irrevocable life insurance trust, it is possible to take advantage of the gift tax laws while at the same time assuring that the proceeds will be received free of estate taxes.[1]

These plans will likely be structured as: (1) a "nonequity endorsement plan" using a employer-owned policy with the employee taxed under the *economic benefit regime* (all cash values owned by the employer); (2) a "equity collateral assignment plan" using a trust-owned policy with employer-paid premiums treated as loans to the employee under the *loan regime* (cash values owned by the trust but assigned to the employer as security for the loans); or (3) a "nonequity collateral assignment" plan using a trust-owned policy with the employee taxed under the *economic benefit regime* (employer entitled to all cash values).[2] This last design offers the most flexibility and can be implemented as follows:[3]

DURING LIFETIME, the employee establishes a trust and the trustee applies for, or obtains, insurance on the employee's life.[4] Thereafter, at the employee's request, the employer and trustee enter into a split-dollar agreement providing for the allocation of premiums, cash values and death benefits on the trust-owned insurance policy.[5] Under this agreement the employer pays all premiums and is entitled to all cash values (by virtue of a limited collateral assignment from the trust).[6]

Each year *income* is imputed to the employee in an amount equal to the "economic benefit" of the insurance protection received by the trust.[7] This same amount is then imputed as a *gift* by the employee to the trust. Provided the trust is properly funded, and the beneficiaries given appropriate withdrawal powers, these imputed gifts will qualify for the gift tax annual exclusion of $13,000 in 2011.[8] Of course, it is unlikely that they would exercise these powers, since to do so would defeat the purpose of the trust.

UPON DEATH of the employee, the policy proceeds are split between the employer and the trust. The employer is entitled to a death benefit equal to the *greater of* the cash values or the cumulative premiums paid. Under the split-dollar agreement the balance of the proceeds are paid directly to the trust and are both income and estate tax free.[9] The funds are then available to be used or disbursed by the trustee pursuant to the trust provisions, which could include purchase of estate assets, loans to the estate or others, payment of income to beneficiaries, and eventual distribution of trust corpus to beneficiaries.

Footnotes on page 229

Split-Dollar Funding Life Insurance Trust

DURING LIFETIME

UPON DEATH

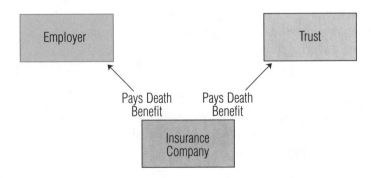

INFORMATION REQUIRED FOR ANALYSIS & PROPOSAL

1. Name of individual or individuals to be insured.
2. Sex.
3. Date of birth.
4. Smoker/nonsmoker.
5. Amount of desired death benefit.

To Design Split-Dollar Plan
6. Position of employee.
7. Is employee a stockholder?

Attorney Drafting Trust Instrument Must Also Know
8. Trustee during insured's lifetime.
9. Trustee after insured's death.
10. Names of beneficiaries.
11. Ages of minor beneficiaries.
12. To who, in what amount, and when trust income is to be paid.
13. To who, in what amount, and when trust corpus is to be paid.

CROSS REFERENCES TO TAX FACTS ON INSURANCE & EMPLOYEE BENEFITS (2011)

Income Tax
Q 98. Death proceeds received by trust free of income taxes.
Q 3789. Description of split-dollar.
Q 3790. Income tax results of traditional split-dollar plan.
Q 3792. Income tax consequences of transfer or "rollout" of split-dollar policy.

Estate Tax
Q 121. When proceeds either included or excluded from insured's estate.
Q 245. Estate taxation of split-dollar.

Gift Tax
Q 64. Gift taxation of split-dollar.
Q 104. Qualification for annual gift tax exclusion.
Q 106. Qualification for annual gift tax exclusion when gifts made to trust for premium payments (Crummey rules).

See also cross references to life insurance trusts on page 52.

Footnotes

[1] If the insured is a majority stockholder the corporation can have no ownership interest in the policy if it is desired to remove the death benefits from his estate. It is important that the corporation not own the policy and have only a *limited* collateral assignment (see discussion, page 373).

[2] These regimes, or methods, are set forth in IRS regulations and are used to determine the tax treatment of *new* split-dollar plans (see Table C on page 298). Regarding the treatment of split-dollar plans established on or before September 17, 2003, see Tables A and B on pages 296-297.

[3] As an insured grows older the endorsement and nonequity collateral assignment plans taxed under the economic benefit regime can become very costly to maintain. This is due to the increasing "economic benefit" amount that is imputed as income to the employee and a gift to the trust. For example, using Table 2001 rates, $1,000,000 of insurance is valued at only $1,530/year for a male age 45, but this increases to $11,900/year for a male age 65, and to $88,760/year for a male age 85 (see table, page 552. When there is a permanent need for life insurance coverage, such as to pay estate taxes, it is important to establish some means of maintaining the policy (often described as an "exit strategy"). The split-dollar regulations have ushered in a new world of split-dollar taxation that makes it important to adopt flexible plans. For example, in order to be more cost effective the illustrated *nonequity* collateral assignment plan, taxed under the economic benefit regime, might be converted to a *equity* collateral assignment plan, taxed under the loan regime (i.e., at older ages reporting or paying loan interest costs less than paying income and gift taxes on imputed economic benefit). See the discussion of Equity Split-Dollar on pages 399-402. However, if the conversion occurs after the accrual of policy cash values, this equity will be taxable income to the employee and a gift to the trust. Other exit strategies providing for a *termination* of the split-dollar plan should also be considered (see footnote 6, below).

[4] In a family-owned business it is possible that the reach of the attribution rules under new Code section 101(j) *might* treat this policy as "employer-owned." This could subject the death benefits to income taxation. To assure the proceeds are received free of income taxes, appropriate notice and consent should be obtained (see Company Owned Life Insurance (COLI) pages 367-369).

[5] When large amounts of insurance are required on older individuals, the premium requirements can often exceed the annual exclusion limits for present interest gifts (see footnote 4, page 53, and page 379). Split-dollar funding survivorship life insurance payable at the second death can substantially reduce the annual gifts to the trust, thereby allowing larger amounts of insurance to be purchased within these "present interest" limits (see Survivorship Life Insurance, page 535).

[6] If the split-dollar agreement is terminated and the employer releases the trust's assignment of cash values under a split-dollar "rollout," all cash values would then be owned by the trust. This release of employer-owned cash values would be treated as both taxable income to the employee and a gift by the employee to the trust (see Split-Dollar Rollout, page 526).

[7] Under the regulations this "economic benefit" is measured by "life insurance premium factors" to be published by the IRS. Until these factors become available the Table 2001 rates on page 552 should be permissible.

[8] Note that gifts to the trust are *imputed*, funds are not actually transferred to the trust. Also, unlike the typical life insurance trust, the trustee does not have any ownership interest in the policy cash values (see Life Insurance Trust chart, page 51). To qualify for the annual gift tax exclusion the trust beneficiaries must actually have an opportunity to withdraw funds from the trust. Partial funding of the trust with other liquid assets would allow the trustee to satisfy potential present interest demands of trust beneficiaries. See page 379 for a discussion of these withdrawal rights, which are often referred to as "Crummey" powers.

[9] Failure of the employee to report this economic benefit, or to contribute an equal amount of premiums, will result in the death benefits being taxed as ordinary income to his beneficiary (i.e., they will not qualify as income tax-free life insurance death benefits).

SURVIVOR INCOME

The sudden loss of income at the death of a breadearner can be devastating to a surviving family.[1] A survivor income plan can assure that continuing income will be available and is based upon a written agreement between the employer and the employee.

Benefits under such a plan usually take the form of ongoing and periodic payments for a specified number of years following the employee's death. Typically, such benefits might be set at 50 percent of pay, per year, for 10 years.[2]

DURING LIFETIME, the employer and employee enter into an agreement providing for the employer to make periodic payments to the employee's beneficiary following the employee's death. In order to provide the funds to meet its obligation, the employer purchases a life insurance contract insuring the employee.[3] Neither the employee nor his family has any rights whatsoever in this policy. Because the employer is both owner and beneficiary of this contract, the premium payments are not tax-deductible to the employer. Nor will the premiums be taxable to the employee provided the contract is clearly not tied to the promise to pay the survivor benefit. In this sense, the contract is carried in the same manner as key person insurance, the difference being the *purpose* for which the death benefit will be used.

UPON DEATH, the insurance company pays a death benefit directly to the employer, as beneficiary of the contract insuring the employee.[4] Under the pre-existing agreement, the employer then provides a survivor income benefit to the family. While these payments are fully tax-deductible by the employer, they will be received as taxable income by the family.

Using life insurance to help meet the obligation under a survivor income plan offers tax-leverage to the employer, in that *receipt* of the death benefit by the employer is potentially tax-free, whereas *payments* made to the surviving family are fully tax-deductible. For an employer in a 34 percent marginal tax bracket, payment of $1.00 in benefits will generate a tax savings of 34 cents.[5]

The *insured* survivor income plan provides the security of continuing income to the employee's family, while offering tax-leverage to the employer.[6]

Footnotes on page 233

DURING LIFETIME

UPON DEATH

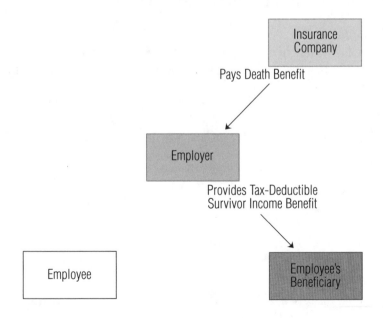

INFORMATION REQUIRED FOR ANALYSIS & PROPOSAL

1. Name of employee.
2. Sex.
3. Date of birth.
4. Smoker/nonsmoker.
5. Employer's tax bracket.
6. Amount of insurance coverage.
7. Method of payment to surviving family (i.e., lump-sum, period certain, annuity purchase, etc.).

CROSS REFERENCES TO TAX FACTS ON INSURANCE & EMPLOYEE BENEFITS (2011)

Income Tax

Q 193. Premiums paid by corporation not taxable to insured employee (provided corporation is owner and beneficiary).

Q 195. Uncertain tax results if family is named as revocable beneficiary of life insurance contract.

Q 216. Proceeds paid to widow are taxable as compensation for past services of deceased employee.

Q 3608. Taxation of contractual death benefits to surviving spouse.

Q 3609. Employer's deduction of survivor income payments.

Estate Tax

Q 54. Estate tax treatment when only benefit is survivor income.

Q 55. Estate tax treatment when employee has no rights to income (death benefit only plan).

Gift Tax

Q 66. Gift tax treatment of survivor income benefit.

Footnotes

[1] To better appreciate the total amount of future income lost when a breadearner dies, refer to the table of Projected Earnings on page 315. Human Life Value is also dealt with in the table Life Insurance Needs As a Percentage Of Earnings on page 16. While many surviving families can expect to receive benefits from Social Security, it is probably not advisable for them to rely on the system for the greater part of their financial security. For example, in 2010 the *maximum* monthly survivor's benefits available under Social Security was:

Age of Worker	Surviving Spouse & 1 Child; or 2 Children	Surviving Spouse & 2 Children; or 3 Children	One Child (no parent)	Widow Age 60	or	Widower Age 66
25	$3,834	$4,473	$1,917	$1,827		$2,556
30	3,826	4,464	1,913	1,823		2,550
35	3,777	4,407	1,888	1,800		2,518
40	3,766	4,394	1,883	1,795		2,511
45	3,750	4,375	1,875	1,787		2,500
50	3,735	4,358	1,867	1,780		2,490
55	3,720	4,340	1,860	1,773		2,480
60	3,672	4,284	1,836	1,750		2,448

The above table has been extracted from Social Security Table 11, Social Security Source Book (National Underwriter Company). Note that a surviving family is entitled to payments provided one or more children are under age 18. Once all children are 18 or over, no social security benefits are available until the surviving spouse is age 60. This period between the youngest child's age 18 and spouse's age 60 is often referred to as the Social Security "blackout period."

[2] Although a lump-sum payment could be made, it is usually preferable to provide the family with an income stream more suited to its needs. This will also allow for spreading out of the family's income tax liability and the employer's tax deductions.

[3] Employer-owned life insurance must meet strict notice and consent requirements if the death benefits are to be received free of income taxes (see Company Owned Life Insurance (COLI), pages 367-369).

[4] Under some circumstances the corporate alternative minimum tax could result in the indirect taxation of life insurance proceeds received by a corporation (see pages 374-376).

[5] For each $1.00 received as a tax-free death benefit by the employer, this employer could afford to pay $1.52 in benefits. The calculations are as follows:

Desired After-Tax Cost	$ 1.00
Reciprocal Of Tax Bracket	÷ .66
Tax-Deductible Payment To Family	$ 1.52
Less Taxes Saved (34% tax bracket)	(.52)
After-Tax Cost	$ 1.00
Less Tax-Free Death Benefit	(1.00)
Cost To Make Payment	$ 0.00

Alternatively, the employer might prefer a return of all premiums, plus a tax-free gain to corporate surplus. For example, assume the tax-free death benefit from a $100,000 policy was invested in tax-free 6.6 percent municipal bonds. The employer could then afford to pay a survivor $10,000 per year for life, and eventually receive a return of all premiums and a tax-free gain. The yearly after-tax cost of the $10,000 payment would be covered by the $6,600 of tax-free income ($100,000 x .066). Of course, the above calculations would have to be adjusted downward if the death proceeds were subject to the corporate alternative minimum tax (see page 374-376).

[6] "Death benefit only" plans allow payments from a survivor income plan to be excluded from the employee's federal taxable estate (see Death Benefit Only plan on page 380).

DEFERRED COMPENSATION

In allowing *selected* management or highly compensated employees to defer income until after retirement, deferred compensation offers *multiple tax advantages* to both the employer and the participant.[1]

CORPORATE OBLIGATION. To illustrate, assume we have a key corporate manager who is currently age 45. Under its terms, the plan would provide for retirement payments, at age 65, of $10,000 per year for 10 years.[2] These payments would be *tax-deductible* to the corporation when made, and, although *taxable* to the retired employee, presumably he would pay less in taxes due to a reduced retirement income and resulting lower marginal tax bracket.

Typically, such plans also provide for survivor payments if the employee dies prior to retirement. For example, should the employee die at age 55, a typical plan might pay his surviving family $10,000 per year for 10 years. Since these payments would be tax-deductible to the corporation, each $10,000 payment would cost only $6,600 (assuming a 34 percent corporate marginal tax bracket). However, these payments would be taxable income to the family.[3]

The plan can also be structured to provide disability benefits to the employee. To assure itself of funds to meet its obligation, the employer could purchase a disability income contract, or it could *partially* protect itself by adding a waiver of premium rider to any life insurance contract on the employee's life.[4]

LIFE INSURANCE on the employee can assure the employer that it will have the funds to meet its obligation.[5] Using life insurance for this purpose requires a corporate commitment to spend $4,000 per year during the first 20 years, and $6,600 per year during the 10 years following the employee's retirement (all after taxes).[6] The *cumulative* outlay by the corporation would be $80,000 during the 20 years prior to retirement at age 65, and $146,000 by time the employee reaches age 75.[7]

If life insurance with an increasing death benefit is purchased, it will likely produce a *gain* to corporate surplus when the employee dies, which amount can then be used to make the survivor payments. This gain is the amount by which the death benefit *exceeds* the cumulative outlay by the corporation (i.e., the sum of the premium payments prior to retirement and the after-tax cost of the retirement payments). For example, if the employee died at age 55, payment of a $120,000 death benefit would produce a gain to corporate surplus of $80,000 ($120,000 - $40,000 = $80,000).[8]

Footnotes on page 237

CORPORATE OBLIGATION

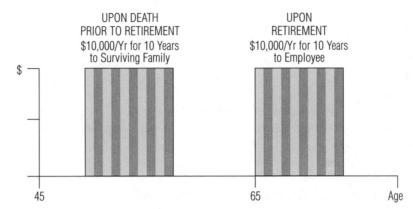

UPON DEATH
PRIOR TO RETIREMENT
$10,000/Yr for 10 Years
to Surviving Family

UPON
RETIREMENT
$10,000/Yr for 10 Years
to Employee

LIFE INSURANCE FUNDING

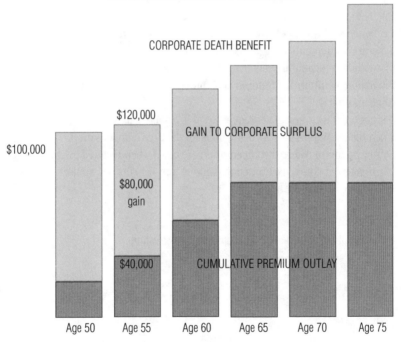

CORPORATE DEATH BENEFIT

$120,000

GAIN TO CORPORATE SURPLUS

$100,000

$80,000
gain

$40,000

CUMULATIVE PREMIUM OUTLAY

Age 50   Age 55   Age 60   Age 65   Age 70   Age 75

ASSUMPTIONS

Current Age 45 - Premium Outlay $4,000/year for 20 Years
Insurance Contract Provides Increasing Death Benefit
Retirement Outlay $10,000/year for 10 Years Beginning at Age 65
After-Tax Cost of Retirement Outlay is $6,600/year
(34% Tax Bracket)

INFORMATION REQUIRED FOR ANALYSIS & PROPOSAL

1. Name of executive.
2. Sex.
3. Date of birth.
4. Smoker/nonsmoker.
5. Retirement age.
6. Retirement benefit *or* amount of contribution.
7. Method of payment for pre-retirement death benefit (i.e., lump-sum, period certain, annuity purchase, etc.).
8. Employer's tax bracket.

CROSS REFERENCES TO TAX FACTS ON INSURANCE & EMPLOYEE BENEFITS (2011)

Income Tax

Q 3585. Discussion of income tax consequences of a "secular" trust.

Q 3588. Tax benefits of informally funded deferred compensation.

Q 3589. General requirements for deferred compensation.

Q 3590. Discussion of "economic benefit" theory.

Q 3591. Discussion of informal funding and other security devices in connection with deferred compensation.

Q 3592. Discussion of income tax consequences of a "rabbi" trust.

Q 3594. When the employer can take deductions for deferred compensation.

Q 3595. How payments of deferred compensation are taxed when received by employee or beneficiary.

Q 3596. When deferred compensation contributions and benefits are subject to social security and federal unemployment taxes.

Estate Tax

Q 55. Inclusion of survivor benefit in employee's gross estate.

Footnotes

[1] The corporate owner who is also an employee will find many planning opportunities with deferred compensation that are not subject to the rules of "qualified" retirement plans. For example: (1) deferred reasonable compensation payments to a retired employee-stockholder are deductible to the corporation, whereas inflated payments for stock are not deductible; (2) the cash values of a life insurance contract, carried on the books and intended for deferred compensation, are usually considered to be for the reasonable needs of the business and thus immune from the accumulated earnings tax; (3) the liability for deferred payments to a surviving widow can have the effect of depressing the value of a deceased's stock for estate tax purposes; and (4) corporate owned cash values under a split-dollar arrangement can be used to provide the employer with funds to make deferred compensation payments (see comparison of split-dollar and deferred compensation on page 301).

[2] There are two types of deferred compensation plans: "pure" deferred compensation plans and salary continuation plans. Under a pure deferred compensation plan, the employee agrees to defer receipt of some portion of his present compensation. This deferral of compensation is not currently taxable to the employee, provided it is subject to a substantial risk of forfeiture (see the discussion of Section 409A on page 517 and Constructive Receipt on page 370). Under a salary continuation plan, the employer provides a benefit in addition to all other forms of compensation (i.e., there is no reduction in the employee's present compensation). When used with a vesting schedule or a non-competition agreement, a deferred compensation plan provides the "golden handcuffs" to retain a valued employee.

[3] Benefits paid to survivors are generally not subject to FICA and FUTA taxes. However, these taxes can be currently imposed upon participants if the plan provides nonforfeitable benefits. This will not be too great a problem for the executive whose other wages exceed the OASDI wage base.

[4] Backing up the plan with a life insurance contract containing the waiver of premium benefit would relieve the employer of having to make premium payments in case of the employee's disability. Assuming a premium of $4,000, a corporation in a 34 percent tax bracket could pay $6,060 per year to the disabled employee, since the after-tax cost of these payments is equal to the nondeductible premiums being waived ($4,000 divided by one minus the employer's tax bracket, or $4,000 ÷ .66 = $6,060).

[5] Employer-owned life insurance must meet strict notice and consent requirements if the death benefits are to be received free of income taxes (see Company Owned Life Insurance (COLI), pages 367-369).

[6] During the first 20 years, it is assumed that $4,000 purchases either a universal life insurance contract providing for a death benefit equal to the face plus the cash values (Option 2), or a paid-up at age 65 participating contract (with dividends typically being used to purchase paid-up additions). Once the employee reaches age 65, the chart assumes that the corporation will make retirement payments from *current* cash flow, as opposed to utilizing the contract's cash values. By maintaining the contract, the corporation will eventually receive the death benefit, which may more than offset its cumulative outlay. Assuming a 34 percent tax bracket and no alternative minimum tax, the after-tax cost of making a $10,000 payment is $6,600 (for sample calculations see footnote 5, page 233). Use of computer-prepared illustrations can provide a variety of funding options and schedules.

[7] Because the corporation is both owner and beneficiary of the life insurance contract, the premium payments that it makes are *not* tax-deductible. In this sense, the contract is carried in the same manner as key person insurance, the difference being the *purpose* for which the death benefit will be used. To avoid any current tax liability to the employee, it is essential that the employee have no vested interest in a fund or any investments intended to secure the deferred compensation payments. The life insurance contract must remain the unrestricted asset of the employer, available to general creditors of the employer, and the employee can have no interest in the contract (see discussion on page 386). Despite this, it is generally recognized that the use of life insurance to back up a deferred compensation agreement provides some psychological security to the employee, in the sense that the employer is preparing to follow through on its commitment. Alternatives such as a Restrictive Bonus Plan, a Rabbi Trust or a Secular Trust might also be considered (see pages 214, 493 and 519).

[8] Under some circumstances, the cash values and death benefits could be subject to the corporate alternative minimum tax, as discussed on pages 374-376.

DISABILITY – THE LIVING DEATH

No estate or financial plan can be considered complete unless there has been an evaluation of the risks of disability. *Planning to live* is as important as *planning to die*, and the risk is greater. For example, for a male age 40, long-term disability is 2.9 times more likely than death.

Before disability, most people are able to acquire savings to the extent income exceeds expenses. However, **after disability** caused by a sickness or injury, income will *fall* and expenses will *rise*.[1]

WITHOUT PLANNING, the expenses of a disability can quickly exhaust the family's savings and create substantial debt. This is true despite the availability of Social Security after six months of continuous and total disability. For most people these payments will rarely fill the gap created between falling income and increasing expenses. When available, Social Security disability payments to a disabled wage earner with children will be substantially more than those to a disabled wage earner without children. The fact that a disabled wage earner is married – and often responsible for the financial needs of a spouse – does not result in an increase in Social Security payments.[2]

Attempting to reduce expenses by selling personal possessions, a car, or even the family home, is unlikely to eliminate the substantial debt which is created by a long-term disability, which is often referred to as "the living death."

WITH PLANNING, the cornerstone of any disability plan is **disability insurance**. Just as life insurance protects a family in case of the insured's death, disability income insurance protects *both* the insured and his family in case of the insured's disability. In addition, before disability strikes, the purchase of a comprehensive **major medical expense plan** offers one of the most effective ways of paying the major expenses of many disabilities. A **waiver of premium rider** on existing or new life insurance policies will provide for payment of premiums after a stated period of disability.[3]

Footnotes on page 241

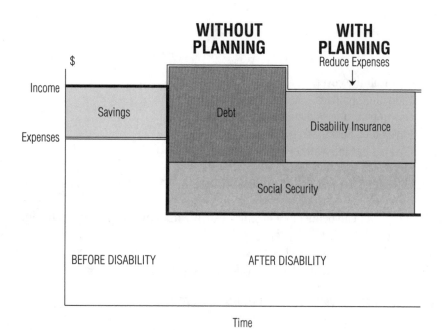

RISK OF LONG-TERM DISABILITY - RISK OF DEATH

	Male	Female
Age 30 –	4.0 times more likely	7.6 times more likely
Age 40 –	2.9 times more likely	5.9 times more likely
Age 50 –	2.3 times more likely	3.8 times more likely

INFORMATION REQUIRED FOR ANALYSIS & PROPOSAL

1. Name.
2. Sex.
3. Date of birth.
4. Smoker/nonsmoker.
5. Annual earned income.
6. Occupation.
7. Present disability coverage:
   a.   Individual policies – benefits and duration.
   b.   Group insurance – benefits and duration.
   c.   Covered by Social Security?
   d.   Covered by state worker's compensation?

CROSS REFERENCES TO TAX FACTS ON INSURANCE & EMPLOYEE BENEFITS (2011)

Q 247. Employer can deduct as a business expense amounts paid for disability income policy for employee.

Q 255. Disability income benefits received from personally paid policies are tax free.

Q 258. Taxation of benefits when provided for stockholder-employees only.

CROSS REFERENCES TO TAX FACTS ON INVESTMENTS (2011)

Q 7544. Tax credit for the permanently and totally disabled.

Footnotes

[1] The expenses associated with a long-term disability can be devastating. With death, the funds required are those needed to support a surviving family. With disability, the living death, not only is there a need to provide for the family, but the living and medical expenses of the disabled person must also be provided. The advances of modern medicine and equipment, which have enabled many more people to survive crippling accidents and illnesses, have further added to the expenses of long-term care. See the chart on page 255 regarding the risk and costs of long-term care.

[2] In 2010, after six months of total and continuous disability, the maximum Social Security disability benefit a typical wage earner could have expected ranged from $2,434 per month (age 60) to $2,506 per month (age 25). With a spouse and children this maximum benefit ranged from $3,651 per month (age 60) to $3,759 per month (age 25). The specific amount of payment depends upon age when disabled and previous contributions to the system. A complete description of coverage, benefits, and benefit computations is contained in Social Security Table 12, *Social Security Source Book* (National Underwriter Company). All benefits are subject to income taxes, as described on page 526. Qualifying for Social Security disability requires that no less than nine separate tests be met, as set forth on page 388.

[3] In addition to disability income insurance, the owners of a business should consider funding their buy/sell agreements with disability buy-out insurance (see page 386). Also, business overhead expense insurance can provide for payment of specific business expenses during a period of disability (see discussion, page 349).

DISABILITY INCOME PLAN

When a disabled employee is faced with increasing expenses and decreasing income, often many corporations will informally continue his salary for an extended period of time. Such an approach can be unwise when the disabled employee is a stockholder. To illustrate, assume that a corporation's income is $150,000 before paying a $50,000 salary to its employee-stockholder.[1]

NO PLAN. If this employee-stockholder becomes disabled without a pre-existing plan, continued salary payments of $50,000 will likely be treated by the IRS as *nondeductible dividends*, which must come from after-tax profits. Taxable income would then be $150,000, upon which $41,750 of taxes must be paid, with $58,250 remaining after-tax and after payment to the disabled stockholder-employee.

PLAN. A pre-existing disability income plan would enable the corporation to preserve the tax-deductibility of these continued salary payments to the disabled employee-stockholder. This would place the corporation in the same position as existed prior to the employee-stockholder's disability.

To establish a plan, three things are required: (1) a corporate resolution must be adopted; (2) a plan document must be prepared; and (3) notification of the plan's existence must be given to the covered employee.[2] By doing this, the corporation could deduct continued salary payments and retain $77,750 after paying taxes of $22,250. Compared to "no plan," this represents a saving of $19,500 per year. Such plans may be *highly selective*, and a class may consist of just one employee, provided it is a "reasonable" classification. If stockholders are covered, it must be in their capacity as employees.

REDUCED RISK PLAN. Under the reduced risk plan, the corporation shifts a part of its liability to an insurance company.[3] With an individual disability income contract, an insured benefit of $25,000 per year could be paid directly to the disabled employee-stockholder.[4] The corporation would deduct a continued salary payment of $25,000, with $125,000 of taxable income remaining with the corporation. After paying taxes of $32,000, the corporation then retains $93,000. When compared to "no plan," this represents a saving of $34,750 per year.

With a reduced risk plan the premium is deductible by the corporation, yet not taxable to the employee, who is *assured* of receiving disability payments if the corporation should fail.[5]

Footnotes on page 245

NO PLAN

$150,000
Corporate Income

$41,750
Taxes

$50,000
Dividend

$58,250
Retained

$150,000
Taxable Income

PLAN

$50,000
Salary

$22,250
Taxes

$77,750
Retained

$100,000
Taxable Income

REDUCED RISK PLAN

$25,000
Insured Benefit

$25,000
Salary

$32,000
Taxes

$93,000
Retained

$125,000
Taxable Income

REQUIREMENTS FOR A "PLAN"

- Corporate Resolution
- Plan Document
- Notification to Employee

KEY FEATURES OF THE "REDUCED RISK PLAN"

- Premiums Deductible by Corporation
- Premiums Not Taxable to Employee
- Employee is Assured of Payments

INFORMATION REQUIRED FOR ANALYSIS & PROPOSAL

1. Name.
2. Sex.
3. Date of birth.
4. Smoker/nonsmoker.

To Demonstrate Benefit of Insured Plan
5. Annual earned income of employee-stockholder.
6. Corporate income (to calculate taxes and retained earnings, as demonstrated in chart).

To Determine Amount of Coverage
7. Occupation.
8. Present disability coverage:
    a.   Individual policies – benefits and duration.
    b.   Group insurance – benefits and duration.
    c.   Covered by social security?
    d.   Covered by state worker's compensation?

CROSS REFERENCES TO TAX FACTS ON INSURANCE & EMPLOYEE BENEFITS (2011)

Q 247. Employer can deduct as a business expense amounts paid for disability income policy on employee.

Q 249. Premiums paid by employer are not taxable income to employee.

Q 250. Disability income payments are fully taxable to employee (except portion of income attributable to employee's contributions, if any).

Q 255. Disability income benefits received from personally paid policy are tax-free.

Q 258. Taxation of benefits when provided for employee-stockholders only.

CROSS REFERENCES TO TAX FACTS ON INVESTMENTS (2011)

Q 7544. Tax credit for the permanently and totally disabled.

Footnotes

[1] Although a corporation has been selected to demonstrate the tax problems that can occur when a employee-stockholder becomes disabled, a disability income plan can be established for the *employees* of a partnership or a sole proprietorship. However, the partners and the sole proprietor are not "employees" and cannot exclude from their incomes premiums paid for disability income insurance. On the positive side, benefits received by a partner or sole proprietor are totally free of income taxes, because premiums are paid with after-tax dollars. For this purpose, the stockholder who owns more than two percent of an S corporation will be treated the same as a partner in a partnership (see pages 510-512).

[2] Notification given by himself as an officer, to himself as an employee, that the board of directors, on which he serves, has established a disability income plan for him, may appear unnecessary, but that is what is required. For appearance sake, it would be preferable to have another officer sign the letter of authorization.

[3] Despite the tax advantages of having a pre-existing plan, it alone *will not guarantee* that salary continuation payments will be made to a disabled employee. This is particularly true if the corporation is liquidated because of the extended absence of the owner during a long-term disability.

[4] The maximum coverage that most insurers will issue for long-term disability is generally limited to 60 percent of pre-disability earned income, reduced to account for other disability insurance and anticipated Social Security or state lump-sum benefits. However, reliance upon Social Security to provide the needed disability benefits may be ill-advised in view of the strict qualification requirements (see Disability Under Social Security, page 388).

[5] Provided they are *reasonable*, corporate premium payments are deductible as a business expense. Although the *premium* is not taxable to the employee, if and when disability *payments* are received by the employee, they will be taxed as salary. In order for the employee to receive tax-free payments, he must have paid the premiums. By including the premiums paid by the employer in his taxable income, the employee will be considered as having paid the premiums with his own after-tax dollars. He can then receive the disability payments tax-free. This is a decision to be made by the employee, and it will not affect the deductibility of the amount equal to the premium paid by the employer. The concept is sometimes referred to as a "Section 162 Bonus Plan," and is similar to that described in the Executive Equity chart on page 211. To determine the various tax ramifications of premium and benefit payments under different arrangements, see the table on page 323.

The calculations of the figures used in this chart:

			No Plan	Plan	Reduced Risk Plan
Corporate Income			$150,000	$150,000	$150,000
Less Salary			0	(50,000)	(25,000)
Taxable Income			$150,000	$100,000	$125,000
Tax on:	first	$ 50,000 (15%)	$ 7,500	$ 7,500	$ 7,500
	next	25,000 (25%)	6,250	6,250	6,250
	next	25,000 (34%)	8,500	8,500	8,500
	amount over	100,000 (39%)	19,500	0	9,750
Total Tax			$41,750	$22,250	$32,000

The 5 percent surtax on income between $100,000 and $335,000 is reflected in the 39 percent rate used in this table (see income tax table on page 549).

HEALTH REIMBURSEMENT ARRANGEMENTS

Under a health reimbursement arrangement, it is possible to pay for the medical expenses of an employee and the employee's dependents.[1]

MEDICAL EXPENSES include items such as doctor bills, dentist bills, hospital bills, transportation, prescription drugs, dentures, nursing services, eyeglasses, and hearing aids. The ideal plan has the cost of the benefit tax deductible to the employer and not includable in the employee's income.

SELF-INSURED ARRANGEMENTS will cause highly compensated individuals to be taxed on part or all of any reimbursements, unless the arrangement is nondiscriminatory as to benefits provided and meets one of three eligibility requirements:[2]

1. The IRS has found specific eligibility classifications within the arrangement to be nondiscriminatory;
2. 70 percent or more of employees benefit from the arrangement; or
3. 70 percent or more of all employees are eligible, and at least 80 percent of the 70 percent actually benefit from the arrangement.

If a self-insured arrangement does not meet one of these three requirements, then the highly compensated individuals who will be taxed include:

- Any stockholder who owns more than 10 percent of the stock.
- The 5 highest paid officers.
- Any employee who is among the 25 percent highest paid of all employees.

These arrangements must also comply with many of the requirements of the Patient Protection and Affordable Care Act (the Health Care Act). Some of the more significant include: (1) prohibition of preexisting condition exclusions; (2) prohibition on excessive waiting periods; (3) no lifetime or annual limits; (4) prohibition on rescissions; (5) coverage of preventive health services; and (6) extension of dependent coverage.

INSURED ARRANGEMENTS in the past have not been subject to any nondiscrimination requirements and could be established to benefit only a select class of employees. However, under the Health Care Act, policies purchased on or after September 23, 2010, will be subject to nondiscrimination requirements (i.e., these arrangements can no longer be used to provide tax benefits to stockholder-employees or officers who can be segregated from other employees).[3]

Footnotes on page 249

MEDICAL EXPENSES

Doctor Bills - Dentist Bills - Hospital Bills
Transportation - Prescription Drugs - Dentures
Nursing Services - Eyeglasses - Hearing Aids

SELF-INSURED ARRANGEMENTS

will cause highly compensated
individuals to be taxed, unless
plan is nondiscriminatory as to benefits
and

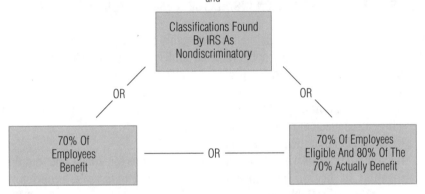

Classifications Found
By IRS As
Nondiscriminatory

OR   OR

70% Of
Employees
Benefit

OR

70% Of Employees
Eligible And 80% Of The
70% Actually Benefit

HIGHLY COMPENSATED INDIVIDUALS INCLUDE

Stockholder Who
Owns More Than
10% Of Stock

5 Highest Paid
Officers

25% Highest Paid
Employees

INSURED ARRANGEMENTS

Cannot Benefit
A Select Class
of Employees

INFORMATION REQUIRED FOR ANALYSIS & PROPOSAL

1. Name of employee.
2. Date of birth.
3. Smoker/nonsmoker.
4. Salary.
5. Status of employee (full time or part time).
6. Employment date.
7. Employer's tax bracket.

CROSS REFERENCES TO TAX FACTS ON INSURANCE & EMPLOYEE BENEFITS (2011)

Q 249. Value of health coverage not generally taxable to employee.

Q 250. Employee taxation of payments received under employer provided health insurance.

Q 251. Employee taxation of benefits provided under employer's noninsured plan.

Q 252. Nondiscrimination requirements that apply to employer provided health benefits.

Q 253. Taxation of amounts paid to highly compensated employees under a discriminatory self-insured medical reimbursement plan.

Q 257. Taxation of "domestic partnership" benefits.

Q 258. Taxation of benefits when provided by C corporations for stockholder-employees only.

Q 259. Taxation of health insurance coverage for partners, sole proprietors, and S corporation stockholders.

Q 265. Coverage continuation requirements under "COBRA."

Q 317. New health insurance nondiscrimination rules affect on insured plans.

Q 318. How to determine if a health plan is discriminatory.

Q 319. The consequences of violating the nondiscrimination rules.

Q 321. Application of health reform to self-insured plans.

Footnotes

[1] A health reimbursement arrangement can be provided for the *employees* of a C corporation, a partnership, or a sole proprietorship. However, the partners of a partnership and the sole proprietor cannot be covered and receive the same tax benefits, as they are not considered "employees." Only the stockholders of a corporation who are also employees of the corporation can be covered and receive the tax benefits. For this purpose, the stockholder-employees of an S corporation who own more than 2 percent of the outstanding stock or voting power are treated the same as partners (see pages 510-512). In 2010 and 2011, sole proprietors, partners, and stockholders of S corporations can deduct 100 percent of amounts paid during the taxable year for medical insurance for themselves and their dependents. To take the deduction, the individual must not be eligible to participate in any subsidized health plan maintained by his employer or his spouse's employer. The deduction is allowable in determining adjusted gross income (but is limited to the amount of the individual's income from the business for which the plan was established).

[2] Routine physical examinations, blood tests, and X-rays (that are not for a known illness or symptom) are not subject to the nondiscrimination requirements (i.e., the "medical diagnostic procedures" exception). In addition, despite having to include in income reimbursements under a discriminatory self-insured plan, a "highly compensated individual" may be able to claim a portion of his reimbursements as an itemized deduction. Medical and dental expenses, prescription drugs, and medical insurance premiums, which in total exceed 7.5 percent of adjusted gross income, may be deducted if the taxpayer itemizes deductions. For example, assume we have two employees, each of whom had $4,000 of medical expenses, which were fully reimbursed under a *discriminatory* medical reimbursement plan:

	Employee A	*Employee B*
Adjusted Gross Income	$ 25,000	$ 50,000
	x 7.5%	x 7.5%
Amount That Cannot Be Deducted	$ 1,875	$ 3,750
Medical Expenses Reimbursed	$ 4,000	$ 4,000
Less: Amount That *Cannot Be Deducted*	(1,875)	(3,750)
Amount That *Can Be Deducted*	$ 2,125	$ 250

[3] The Patient Protection and Affordable Care Act generally extended the *nondiscrimination rules* applicable to non-insured plans to insured plans. However, employer-provided health insurance policies in existence on March 23, 2010 were grandfathered and may continue to discriminate in favor of highly compensated employees. Policies purchased after March 23, 2010, and before September 23, 2010, will be subject to the nondiscrimination requirements beginning with the first plan year beginning after September 23, 2010. Failure to satisfy the nondiscrimination requirements will subject the employer to a $100 per day/per affected participant excise tax.

HEALTH SAVINGS ACCOUNTS

Offering an attractive means of funding future health care costs, a health savings account (HSA) can be established by eligible individuals covered by a high deductible health plan (HDHP), provided they are not claimed as a dependent on another person's income tax return and are not entitled to benefits under Medicare (i.e., have not reached age 65).[1] The required HDHP must provide for a *minimum* annual deductible of at least $1,200 for individual coverage and $2,400 for family coverage; and *maximum* annual out-of-pocket expenses must be limited to $5,950 for individual coverage and $11,900 for family coverage (as adjusted in 2011 for inflation). As an exception to these deductibles, preventative care services may be covered on a first-dollar basis.[2]

Annual contributions to the HSA are limited to a maximum of $3,050 for an individual, or $6,150 for a family (as adjusted in 2011 for inflation). Account holders and covered spouses, aged 55 and over, may each make additional contributions of $1,000 in 2009 and thereafter.[3] Both the account holders and their employers can make contributions, but total contributions cannot exceed these annual limits.[4] Employer contributions for all similarly situated employees must be "comparable" (i.e., the same dollar amount or percentage of the annual deductible limit). The account is entirely owned by the employee. Because unused funds may be carried over from year-to-year, for many individuals it may be possible to accumulate substantial amounts prior to retirement.[5]

HSAs offer substantial tax advantages.[6] **Contributions** made by an individual are fully deductible from income as an "above the line" deduction (i.e., without regard to whether deductions are itemized). Employer contributions are deductible by the employer, are not taxable to the employee, and are not subject to Social Security and federal unemployment taxes. **Earnings** within the account are tax-deferred. **Distributions** are tax-free, provided they are for "qualified medical expenses," a term that is broadly construed to include items such as braces and nursing home costs (but not over-the-counter medications or cosmetic surgery). Distributions other than for qualified medical expenses are taxable and subject to a 20-percent-penalty tax.[7]

Although payments of health insurance premiums are not considered qualified medical expenses, exceptions allow tax-free reimbursements for premiums paid for a qualified long-term care insurance contract, premiums for COBRA continuation coverage, and premiums for health-care while receiving unemployment compensation. For those who are eligible for Medicare, tax-free distributions can be made for post-age 65 health insurance such as Medicare Parts A, B, C, and D, and employer-sponsored retiree health insurance (but not for a Medicare supplement policy).[8]

Footnotes on page 253

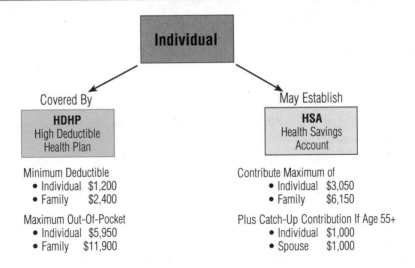

Individual

Covered By

HDHP
High Deductible
Health Plan

Minimum Deductible
- Individual $1,200
- Family $2,400

Maximum Out-Of-Pocket
- Individual $5,950
- Family $11,900

May Establish

HSA
Health Savings
Account

Contribute Maximum of
- Individual $3,050
- Family $6,150

Plus Catch-Up Contribution If Age 55+
- Individual $1,000
- Spouse $1,000

TAX ADVANTAGES OF HSA

CONTRIBUTIONS
Tax-Deductible

EARNING
Tax-Deferred

DISTRIBUTIONS
Tax-Free

TAX-FREE DISTRIBUTION MUST BE FOR
"QUALIFIED MEDICAL EXPENSES"

- Medical Care For Individual, Spouse & Dependent
- Premiums For Qualified Long-Term Care Insurance
- Premiums For Health Insurance During Period:
    - Of COBRA Continuation Coverage
    - Receiving Unemployment Compensation
- Premiums For Post-Age 65 Health Insurance Such As:
    - Medicare Part A, Part B, Part C, or Part D Coverage
    - Employer-Sponsored Retiree Health Insurance

INFORMATION REQUIRED FOR ANALYSIS & PROPOSAL

1. Name of individual.
2. Date of birth.
3. Annual income.
4. Names and ages of dependants.
5. Details regarding current health insurance (to include coverage, deductibles, and maximum out-of-pocket expense).
6. Employment status (i.e., employee of another or self-employed).

CROSS REFERENCES TO TAX FACTS ON INSURANCE & EMPLOYEE BENEFITS (2011)

Q 292. Description of a Health Savings Account (HSA) and how it can be established.

Q 293. Definition of an "eligible individual" for purposes of a HSA.

Q 294. Definition of a "high deductible health plan" for purposes of a HSA.

Q 295. Limits on contributions to a HSA.

Q 296. An employer offering a HSA to its employees must make "comparable" contributions for comparable employees.

Q 297. Penalty for making excess contributions to a HSA. Treatment of excess contributions.

Q 298. Taxation of funds accumulated in a HSA prior to distribution.

Q 299. Taxation of amounts distributed from a HSA.

Q 300. Transfer of funds into a HSA.

Q 301. Transfer of an individual's interest in a HSA as part of a divorce or separation.

Q 302. Disposition of a HSA upon the death of the account holder. Treatment of a surviving spouse as account owner.

Q 303. Amounts contributed to a HSA are not subject to social security taxes.

Q 304. Employer contributions to a HSA on behalf of an employee are not subject to withholding.

Q 305. Tax reporting requirements that apply to a HSA.

Q 328. Distributions from a HSA that do not qualify as medical expenses under the Patient Protection and Affordable Care Act (i.e., nonprescription drugs).

Footnotes

[1] HDHPs can also include self-insured medical reimbursement plans that are sponsored by an employer. See chart on page 247.

[2] The "preventative care" safe harbor allows HDHP coverage for items such as periodic physical exams, routine prenatal and well-child care, immunizations, tobacco cessation programs, obesity weight-loss programs, and a long list of health screening services that includes, among others, mammograms and PSA tests (i.e., these services can be provided without regard to the $1,200 and $2,400 deductibles). If prescription drug coverage provides a benefit before satisfying the required deductible it would prevent tax-deductible contributions to a HSA. Permitted is insurance for a specific disease or illness, accident and disability insurance, and coverage for dental care and vision care. In sum, only preventive care services, permitted insurance and permitted coverages are allowed in conjunction with a HDHP.

[3] Calendar year taxpayers have until April 15 of the following year to make contributions for the previous year (filing extensions do not extend the time). The additional contribution for age 55 and over increased from $900 in 2008 to $1,000 in 2009 and thereafter. No contributions are allowed once an individual has reached age 65.

[4] For tax years beginning before 2012, a participant in a health reimbursement arrangement (HRA), or a health flexible spending account (FSA), may, one time per arrangement, make an employer-to-trustee transfer to a HSA (see overview of Medical Expense Programs, on page 322). This transfer will be treated as a rollover contribution to the HSA (i.e., it will not count toward the annual HSA contribution limit). In addition, individuals who own either a traditional or a Roth IRA may make a one-time trustee-to-trustee transfer from their IRA to a HSA (referred to as an "IRA-HSA rollover"). This transfer will not be included in the individual's income, nor will it be subject to the 10-percent penalty tax for premature withdrawals. However, the amount cannot exceed the individual's maximum HSA contribution limit for the year (in 2011, $3,050 for individuals and $6,150 for families).

[5] Tax-deferred accumulation of earnings and no requirement to withdraw funds at any particular time makes the HSA particularly advantageous as a savings vehicle for future health care expenses (e.g., expenses incurred after age 65). For example, assume a family is covered by a HDHP. In 2011 this allows a maximum annual deposit into the HSA of $6,150. Ignoring possible future indexed increases in the maximum deposit, investing $6,150 per year at 5 percent return would accumulate to $81,222 in 10 years (multiply $6,150 by 13.207, as found in the table on page 563). Assuming the account holder and spouse were both age 55, and also made maximum catch-up contributions, they would accumulate $107,635 in 10 years. Contributions to a HSA may be invested in the same manner as contributions to an IRA (e.g., in stocks and bonds). Of course, the HSA is also available for spending on current medical costs or to reimburse the account holder for incurred health care costs.

[6] Lower-paid employees in the lowest tax brackets are less likely to benefit from these tax-deductions. Critics of HSAs maintain that for lower-paid employees with substantial health care costs these tax benefits may prove largely illusory. The perceived cost-shifting of the cost of health care to workers is also of concern when an employer switches from a comprehensive coverage program to a high-deductible health plan in order to reduce premium costs. In response, proponents of HSAs maintain that increases in health care costs have excluded many people (particularly the self-employed) from having any health care insurance; and HSAs, together with HDHPs, will make insurance more affordable. It is also argued that savings will come from engaging the health care consumer in health care choices (see the discussion of Consumer Direct Health Plans on page 371).

[7] Under the Patient Protection and Affordable Care Act of 2010 the penalty-tax was increased from 10 percent to 20 percent for distributions made on and after January 1, 2011. The penalty tax does not apply if the distribution is on account of the beneficiary's death, disability, or after reaching age 65 (i.e., has become eligible for Medicare).

[8] Prior to age 65, HSAs cannot be used to make tax-free reimbursements of an employee's share of health insurance premiums.

LONG-TERM CARE

Planning for long-term care is an integral part of retirement and financial planning. Long-term care consists of a continuum of services including nursing home care, assisted living, home health and adult day care. The need can arise from an accident, illness, or advanced age.

THE RISK. Statistics make a very good case for long-term care planning. For example, a 65-year-old woman can expect to live another 20.1 years, and a 65-year-old man can expect to live another 16.8 years.[1] During these years it is estimated that the risk of entering a nursing home ranges anywhere from 20 to 49 percent.

THE COST. Nursing care is expensive. Although there is a large variation from one region to another, the average nursing home cost was $75,190 per year in 2010.[2]

MANAGING THE RISK. For an individual with substantial retirement income and assets self-insurance may be a realistic option.[3] However, for those who cannot self-insure reliance upon government programs may be ill advised. For example, after a minimum three-day hospital stay Medicare will only pay for the first 20 days of *skilled nursing* care. From days 21 through 100 the patient must pay in 2011 the first $141.50 per day, and all costs after 100 days. Medicare does not pay for *custodial* care.[4] Although Medicaid will pay for custodial care, the patient must first "spend down" assets in order to qualify.[5] Private insurance is often considered by those desiring independence and choice of care and benefits.[6] It also provides asset protection from the Medicaid spend down requirements.

PRIVATE INSURANCE provides flexibility by allowing individuals to obtain care in various settings and at different levels (skilled nursing, intermediate and custodial care). Contracts do not require prior hospitalization, are guaranteed renewable and offer level premiums.[7] Daily benefits run from $50 to $300 or more. The benefit periods are typically 2, 3, 4, or 5 years, or lifetime. Benefits are paid when the insured has a cognitive impairment or is unable to perform certain activities called "benefit triggers."[8] A deductible, in the form of an elimination period, will generally last from 0 to 180 days. Provisions for home health care and adult day care will allow the beneficiary to remain in the community. Of particular importance is waiver of premiums to limit premium costs and inflation protection to ensure an adequate daily benefit in the future.[9]

In addition to these basic components, other benefits are often available. These features include spousal discounts, respite care, hospice care, caregiver training, bed reservation, medical equipment, cognitive reinstatement, non-forfeiture benefits, case management and referral services.[10] Choosing from such a range of contract options requires a balancing of benefits and flexibility against premium costs.

Footnotes on page 257

THE RISK

The estimated risk of a 65-year-old person entering a nursing home at some time in his or her life ranges from 20% to 49%, depending upon the study and methodology used.

THE COST

Nursing home care can cost $75,190 or more per year. There is, however, a large variation from one region to another around this national average.

MANAGING THE RISK

Government Programs
- Medicare
- Medicaid

Self-Insurance
- Income
- Assets

Private Insurance
- Independence & Choice
- Protection Of Assets

PRIVATE INSURANCE

- Daily Benefit Amount
- Benefit Period
- When Benefits Paid
- Elimination Period
- Home Health Care
- Adult Day Care
- Waiver Of Premium
- Inflation Protection

- Spousal Discounts
- Respite Care
- Hospice Care
- Caregiver Training
- Bed Reservation

- Medical Equipment
- Cognitive Reinstatement
- Non-Forfeiture Benefits
- Case Management
- Referral Services

INFORMATION REQUIRED FOR ANALYSIS & PROPOSAL

1. Name of individual to be insured.
2. Sex.
3. Date of birth (and spouse's date of birth).
4. Has individual or spouse been hospitalized in the last 5 years?
5. Has individual or spouse had any health problems?
6. What medications is the individual or spouse currently taking (include both dosage and frequency)?
7. What is the current monthly income and what monthly income is anticipated in retirement?
8. What is the net worth of the individual and spouse? (see page 12).

CROSS REFERENCES TO TAX FACTS ON INSURANCE & EMPLOYEE BENEFITS (2011)

Q 340.   Description of a "qualified" long-term care insurance contract.

Q 341.   Description of "qualified" long-term care services.

Q 342.   Grandfathering of long-term care contracts issued prior to 1997.

Q 343.   Within limitation premiums for a qualified long-term care insurance contract are deductible as medical expenses.

Q 344.   Subject to a dollar limitation the self-employed may deduct premiums for a qualified long-term care insurance contract.

Q 345.   Premiums paid by an employer for a qualified long-term care insurance contract should be excludable from the employee's gross income.

Q 346.   Premiums paid by an employer for a qualified long-term care insurance contract for employees should be deductible by the employer.

Q 347.   Description of limitations on the amount of benefits received under a qualified long-term care insurance contract that may be excluded from income.

Q 348.   Taxation of a "nonqualified" long-term care insurance contract.

Q 349.   Reporting requirements applicable to long-term care benefits.

Footnotes

[1] See Commissioners 2001 Standard Ordinary Mortality Table on pages 555-556.

[2] Source of 2010 nursing home costs for a private room with skilled nursing care 24 hours a day: Genworth Financial 2010 Cost Of Care Survey (www.genworth.com/costofcare). Because of the wide range of charges a local cost survey of various levels of care is strongly recommended. The "cost of waiting" to buy long-term care insurance can be considerable. Not only are premiums substantially more at older ages but additional coverage must be purchased to cover inflation (see footnote 9, below).

[3] How much in assets or income does it take to self-insure? *Consumer Reports* in October of 1997 suggested that setting aside "roughly $160,000" at 5 percent compound interest would cover "about four years of care" (adjusted for inflation this would be $218,697 in 2011). That is $320,000 for a married couple (adjusted for inflation this would be $437,832 in 2011).

[4] Medicare will pay for medically necessary home health visits that are restorative in nature (i.e., the patient must be improving). However, Medicare will not pay for intermediate care or custodial care (see page 454). It should also be noted that Medigap coverage only pays Medicare deductibles or coinsurance, it does not extend the basic coverage.

[5] Simply put, "spend down" means liquidating assets to pay for long-term care until a level of financial indigence is reached and it is possible to qualify for Medicaid. When does such a "financial meltdown" become significant? The answer depends upon marital status. In most states a single individual cannot have more than $2,000 in countable assets. But the "indigent spouse rules" provide better treatment to a married couple with an at-home spouse. In 2011, many states allow them to retain up to $109,560, plus the home, automobile, household goods and personal belongings (and a minimum monthly income of $1,821.25 for the at-home spouse, as changed annually in July of each year). Amounts over these allowances are referred to as the "Medicaid deductibles."

[6] If an individual needs 24-hour-a-day custodial care, under Medicaid there is little or no provision for "community based care" (i.e., home care, assisted living or adult day care). It is understood that, on average, Medicaid pays about two-thirds as much as the private pay patient. Although a nursing home cannot, by law, treat patients differently depending on who is paying the bills, quality of care remains an issue. The Medicaid patients do not get private rooms. If the quality of care deteriorates, the family of a private pay patient can move him to a different facility.

[7] Premiums can be raised on a class basis. These features are offered either within the base contract or by contract rider. Long-term care insurance is also available on a group basis or as permanent life insurance that advances the death benefit.

[8] Typically, benefit payments are triggered by the loss of two or more activities of daily living (ADLs). These activities include eating, toileting, transferring, bathing, dressing and continence. There has been considerable debate over the quality of benefits under tax qualified versus nontax qualified products (e.g., the nontax qualified products will pay a benefit using the more liberal "medical necessity" standard). See the discussion of Qualified Long-Term Care Insurance on page 489.

[9] For younger insureds inflation protection is particularly important (e.g., a 50-year-old will not likely need coverage as soon as a 70-year-old, thus with inflation his care will cost more). Assuming 5 percent inflation per year, care that costs $3,750 a month today will cost $6,108 in 10 years and $9,948 in 20 years (see Future Value Table on page 562).

[10] It has been observed that eldercare may soon replace childcare as the number one dependent care issue. Good prospects for long-term care insurance are individuals in the so called "sandwich generation" (i.e., persons in their forties and fifties who still have children living at home, *and* are also providing for their own parents). In taking care of their parents these individuals have come to fully appreciate the problems of long-term care and generally do not want to be a burden on their own children.

TAX-FAVORED RETIREMENT PLANS

Tax-favored retirement plans can be established in a variety of ways.

- Qualified retirement plans such as defined benefit pension plans, money-purchase pension plans, and 401(k) plans, can be installed in a corporation, a partnership or a sole proprietorship.[1]
- Individual retirement arrangements (IRAs), including both individual retirement accounts and individual retirement annuities, can be established by many taxpayers. With a simplified employee pension plan (SEP) or a SIMPLE IRA, employer contributions can also be made to individual retirement accounts.
- Section 403(b) plans are available to employees of public schools and colleges, and certain non-profit hospitals, charitable, religious, scientific and educational organizations.
- Section 457 plans are available to employees of state and local governments and tax-exempt organizations.

To better appreciate the advantages of tax-favored retirement plans, we can compare the growth of a tax-favored account to the results obtained when after-tax funds are invested outside a tax-favored plan . . . for example, in certificates of deposit, savings accounts, or treasury bills.[2] Assume that there are $1,000 of before-tax funds available for investment per year over the next 20 years.[3]

Taxable Growth. If after-tax dollars were invested outside of a tax-favored plan, assuming a 25 percent tax bracket, of the original $1,000 only $750 per year would remain after-taxes for investment.[4] The earnings will also be taxed, which means that although the investment might pay 8 percent interest, it would yield only 6 percent after-taxes. The reduced after-tax funds available for investment, combined with the reduced after-tax yield, means that in 10 years $10,478 will have accumulated, and in 20 years $29,245.

Tax-Deferred Growth. The tax leverage provided by a tax-favored plan offers the opportunity for substantially increased accumulations, because there are no current taxes on contributions, and no current taxes on investment earnings. This means that each year $1,000 will actually be invested, and a full 8 percent rate of return will actually be credited, neither being subject to current income taxation. A tax-deferred growth of 8 percent will accumulate $15,645 in 10 years, and $49,423 in 20 years. Although payments received during retirement will be taxable, after-tax income will usually far exceed that available with investments that are not tax-favored.[5]

Footnotes on page 261

TAX LEVERAGE

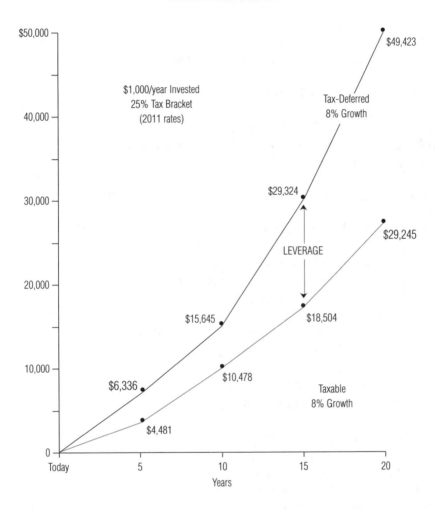

$1,000/year Invested
25% Tax Bracket
(2011 rates)

Tax-Deferred
8% Growth

$49,423

$29,324

LEVERAGE

$29,245

$15,645

$18,504

$10,478

$6,336

Taxable
8% Growth

$4,481

Today   5   10   15   20

Years

NO CURRENT TAXATION ON CONTRIBUTIONS & INVESTMENT EARNINGS

- Money Purchase Pension Plans
- Target Benefit Plans
- Profit Sharing Plans
- 401(k) Plans
- ESOPs
- Stock Bonus Plans
- Age-Weighted Profit Sharing Plans
- Thrift Plans

- Defined Benefit Plans
- Cash Balance Plans
- Keogh Plans For Self Employed (HR-10)
- Individual Retirement Arrangements (IRAs)
- SIMPLE IRAs
- Simplified Employee Pension Plans (SEPs)
- 403(b) Plans
- 412(i) Plans
- 457 Plans

INFORMATION REQUIRED FOR ANALYSIS & PROPOSAL

1. Names of employees.
2. Dates of birth.
3. Smoker/nonsmoker – when life insurance is to be used.
4. Salary schedule.
5. Status of employees – full time *or* part time.
6. Employment dates.
7. Retirement benefit – if defined benefit; *or*
   Dollar or percent contribution – if defined contribution.
8. Employer's tax bracket.

CROSS REFERENCES TO TAX FACTS ON INSURANCE & EMPLOYEE BENEFITS (2011)

Q 3597. Nonqualified deferred compensation tax benefits that are available to employees of state or local governments and other tax-exempt employers.

Q 3598. Requirements that a Section 457 plan must satisfy.

Q 3611. Description of individual retirement plan (IRA).

Q 3612. Description of a "deemed IRA."

Q 3622. Description of Roth IRA.

Q 3623. Rollover or conversion from traditional IRA to Roth IRA.

Q 3641. Description of simplified employee pension plan (SEP).

Q 3643. Description of SIMPLE IRA plan.

Q 3648. Description of defined benefit plan.

Q 3653. Description of defined contribution plan.

Q 3659. Description of pension plan.

Q 3670. Description of profit sharing plan.

Q 3673. Description of 401(k) plan.

Q 3677. Description of solo 401(k) plan.

Q 3680. Description of SIMPLE 401(k) plan.

Q 3690. Description of a 412(i) plan.

Q 3701. Description of Keogh (HR-10) plan.

Q 3705. Tax advantages of qualified pension and profit sharing plans.

Q 3706. Requirements for a plan to be "qualified."

Q 3795. Tax benefits of 403(b) tax sheltered annuities.

Q 3796. Organizations that can make 403(b) tax sheltered annuities available to their employees.

Q 3798. Requirements that must be met by 403(b) tax sheltered annuities.

Footnotes

[1] The Qualified Plans Checklist on pages 303-304 provides a brief overview of some of the characteristics of qualified plans. Although many plans allow contributions of after-tax dollars, the chart on page 259 assumes all contributions are made from pre-tax dollars.

[2] Most individuals are already paying after-tax dollars into the Social Security System. Contributions to this system are substantial, as can be seen from the table on page 312. Individuals covered by Social Security can anticipate receiving some benefits upon retirement. For example, assume a worker had maximum Social Security earnings, in 2010 the projected *maximum* monthly Social Security retirement payments were:

Current Age of Worker	Worker	Normal Retirement Spouse	Total	Current Age of Worker	Worker	Normal Retirement Spouse	Total
25	$2,556	$1,278	$3,834	45	$2,537	$1,268	$3,805
30	2,556	1,278	3,834	50	2,525	1,262	3,787
35	2,555	1,277	3,832	55	2,506	1,253	3,759
40	2,548	1,274	3,822	60	2,484	1,242	3,726

The above table has been extracted from Social Security Table 10, *Social Security Source Book* (National Underwriter Company). A gradual increase in the retirement age when full benefits are available – previously age 65 and progressing to age 67 – began in 2000. If you were born between 1943 and 1959, your retirement age for full benefits is your 66th birthday plus two months for every year by which your year of birth exceeds 1954. If you were born in 1960 or after, your retirement age for full benefits is 67. These Social Security benefits are subject to income tax if your income exceeds a "base" amount (see page 526). See also, the table on page 313, Social Security Retirement Benefits – When To Take.

[3] To estimate the total before-tax dollars that a wage earner can expect to receive assuming annual increases in earnings of either 5 percent or 8 percent, refer to the tables of Projected Earnings on page 315. To demonstrate the importance of starting early to save for retirement, refer to the Penalty Of Waiting table on page 316. The table entitled Early Saver vs. Late Saver on page 317 also illustrates the advantage of saving early for retirement. The table entitled How Money Grows on page 319 provides the accumulations for given amounts of monthly savings. How long these savings will last during retirement can be demonstrated using the table How Money Goes on page 320. See also, Facts About Retirement on page 324.

[4] In return for *nondeductible contributions*, the Roth 401(k) feature permits *tax-free distributions* (see discussion on page 505). In contrast to the traditional IRA, the Roth IRA also permits tax-free distributions in return for nondeductible contributions (see discussions and analysis on pages 307, 308, 427, 433 and 506).

[5] Assuming a marginal federal tax bracket of 25 percent and a lump-sum distribution of $49,423, payment of $12,356 in taxes would be required, with $37,067 remaining after-taxes. This result is substantially better than the $29,245 available with the non-qualified investment. However, assuming 2011 tax rates, the *worst possible* assumption involves a maximum marginal federal tax bracket of 35 percent that would require payment of $17,298 in taxes, with only $32,125 remaining after taxes. The calculations are as follows:

	25% Tax Bracket	28% Tax Bracket	35% Tax Bracket
Qualified Plan Accumulation In 20 Years	$49,423	$49,423	$49,423
Less: Tax On Distribution	(12,356)	(13,838)	(17,298)
Qualified Plan Net	37,067	35,585	32,125
Less: Nonqualified Accumulation In 20 Years	(29,245)	(27,299)	(23,094)
Advantage Of Qualified Plan	$ 7,823	$ 8,285	$ 9,031

This table does not reflect the sunset provisions of EGTRRA 2001 (i.e., reversion to 2001 rates in 2013 and thereafter). Higher tax rates would result in a lesser amount remaining after taxes.

401(k) PLAN

These plans allow eligible employees to defer compensation or bonuses and contribute the funds to an employer-sponsored profit sharing plan.[1] Known as cash or deferred arrangements (CODAs), they are funded entirely or in part through salary reductions elected by the employees.[2] Because employee participation in 401(k) plans is entirely voluntary, employers will often encourage participation by matching employee contributions. These matching contributions are typically limited to a maximum percentage and/or maximum dollar amount.[3]

One of the better ways of explaining the advantages of participating in a 401(k) plan is to contrast current nonparticipation with the benefits of participation (i.e., a "before and after" presentation).

WITHOUT PARTICIPATION. Assume that in 2011 a 35-year-old married employee with an annual salary of $52,000 currently pays $2,990 in federal income taxes, $1,560 in state income taxes and $3,978 in Social Security taxes. This leaves $43,472 of "take-home pay," with nothing set aside for retirement. (Calculation assumes: joint filing, four personal exemptions, standard deduction, and 3% of federal AGI state income tax.)

WITH PARTICIPATION. Now assume that this same employee has the opportunity to participate in a plan with a 50 percent employer match, (i.e., the employer will contribute one dollar for every two dollars of employee elective deferral).[4] If the employee elects to defer 6 percent of salary ($3,120 per year), the employer would then make a matching contribution of $1,560.[5] The total annual deposits to the employee's account are $4,680, consisting of the employee's elective deferral of $3,120 and his employer's matching contribution of $1,560. Because his contributions are before tax, the employee's federal income taxes are reduced to $2,522 and his state income taxes are reduced to $1,466. Social Security taxes are not affected by employee elective deferrals.[6]

Note that a reduction in take-home pay of only $2,558 has produced a deposit of $4,680 into the employee's retirement account. Because he pays $562 less in federal and state income taxes, take-home pay has been reduced by only $2,558, despite having contributed $3,120 to the plan (43,472 – 40,914 = 2,558).

A 35-year-old employee can accumulate $393,720 by age 65; assuming level plan contributions of $390 at the beginning of each month and 6 percent interest on plan assets. Over the same 30-year period, total employee contributions amount to only $93,600. Waiting just 5 years to begin participation would reduce age 65 projected accumulations to $271,619, which is $122,101 less than would accumulate assuming immediate participation (393,720 - 271,619 = 122,101).[7]

Footnotes on page 265

WITHOUT PARTICIPATION

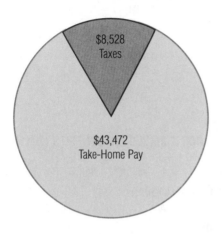

$8,528
Taxes

$43,472
Take-Home Pay

Annual Salary	$52,000
Less: Federal Income Tax	2,990
State Income Tax	1,560
Social Security	3,978
Take-Home Pay	$43,472

WITH PARTICIPATION

Assuming 6% Deferral and 50% Employer Match

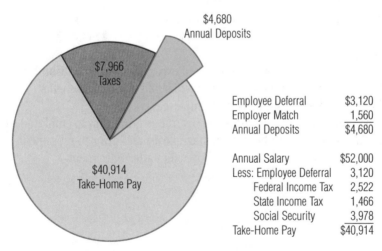

$4,680
Annual Deposits

$7,966
Taxes

$40,914
Take-Home Pay

Employee Deferral	$3,120
Employer Match	1,560
Annual Deposits	$4,680
Annual Salary	$52,000
Less: Employee Deferral	3,120
Federal Income Tax	2,522
State Income Tax	1,466
Social Security	3,978
Take-Home Pay	$40,914

An annual reduction in Take-Home Pay of
$2,558 produces Annual Deposits of $4,680.

Assuming 6.00% interest and level contribution levels,
an employee age 35 would accumulate $393,720 by age 65.
Total employee contributions would be $93,600.

Waiting 5 years to begin participation would
reduce age 65 projected accumulations to $271,619.

INFORMATION REQUIRED FOR ANALYSIS & PROPOSAL

1. Names of employees.
2. Dates of birth.
3. Smoker/nonsmoker – when life insurance is to be used.
4. Salary schedule.
5. Status of employees – full time *or* part time.
6. Employment dates.

CROSS REFERENCES TO TAX FACTS ON INSURANCE & EMPLOYEE BENEFITS (2011)

Q 3673. General description of 401(k) plan.

Q 3674. Special qualification requirements for 401(k) plans.

Q 3675. Limits on elective deferrals.

Q 3676. Description of catch-up contributions.

Q 3677. Description of a solo 401(k) plan.

Q 3678. Description of an automatic enrollment safe harbor 401(k) plan.

Q 3679. Requirements for a 401(k) safe harbor plan.

Q 3680. Requirements for a SIMPLE 401(k) plan.

Q 3681. Requirements for Roth 401(k) feature.

Q 3685. Restrictions that apply to distributions from a 401(k) plan.

Q 3686. When hardship withdrawals may be made from a 401(k) plan.

Q 3687-3688. The ADP and ACP tests.

Q 3689. Distributions of excess contributions and excess aggregate contributions.

Q 3703. Extent to which a qualified plan can provide life insurance benefits.

Q 3740. Definition of "highly compensated" employees.

Q 3754. Method used to determine cost of life insurance protection to employee participant.

Q 3765-3766. Taxation of death benefit when employee dies prior to retirement.

Q 3767. Taxation of death benefit when employee dies after retirement.

Footnotes

[1] In addition to meeting the requirements necessary to qualify as a profit sharing or stock bonus plan, traditional 401(k) plans must: (1) limit the forfeitability and distribution of employee elective deferrals; (2) permit participation by the later of age 21 or one year of service; (3) limit elective deferrals to $16,500 in 2010 and 2011; and (4) meet an annual nondiscrimination requirement (the ADP test), by comparing ratios of elective deferrals for highly compensated and nonhighly compensated employees. In contrast, employers can avoid the nondiscrimination testing required of traditional 401(k) plans if they are willing to make required contributions and meet other design requirements. See 401(k) Plan Designs, page 305.

[2] These amounts are referred to as "elective deferrals." It is helpful to remember that 401(k) plans can contain the following:

    a. **Employee elective deferrals** – amounts the employee elects to have the employer contribute instead of receiving cash (the source might be existing salary, salary increases, or bonuses).

    b. **Employer matching contributions** – made by the employer in some ratio to employee elective deferrals (if immediately 100 percent vested and subject to certain withdrawal restrictions, they are known as "qualified matching contributions").

    c. **Employer nonelective contributions** – made by the employer on behalf of employees and not conditioned upon employee elective deferrals (if immediately 100 percent vested and subject to certain withdrawal restrictions, they are known as "qualified nonelective contributions").

    d. **Catch-up contributions** – made by employees age 50 or over (see page 306).

[3] In 2011 the employer's tax deduction is 25 percent of total compensation. The typical plan design provides for the employer to match from 25 to 100 percent of employee *contributions* to a maximum of 5 to 10 percent of employee compensation.

[4] The employee elective deferral is limited to $16,500 in 2010 and 2011 for traditional and safe harbor plans. Amounts deferred in excess of this limit (other than catch-up contributions) are not excludable from income, and, if not timely corrected by distribution, will be taxed a second time when distributed from the plan.

[5] Unless the plan is a safe harbor design (see page 305), the amount of elective deferrals must satisfy the ADP test. Matching contributions are often used to improve ADP results. The Actual Deferral Percentage (ADP) test is applied by dividing employees into two groups . . . the *highly* compensated, and the *nonhighly* compensated. The ADP test is met if either: (1) the deferral percentage for eligible highly compensated employees during the year does not exceed the deferral percentage of all other eligible employees in the *preceding* year multiplied by 1.25; *or* (2) the deferral percentage for eligible highly compensated employees during the year is not more than 2 percent higher than, nor more than 2 times, the deferral percentage for all other eligible employees in the *preceding* year (in either case, an election is available to compare current instead of preceding year results). An employee is potentially within the group of "highly compensated employees" if he:

    a. Was a 5 percent owner at any time during the current or preceding year, or

    b. Earned from his employer more than $110,000 for the preceding year (in 2010 and 2011, as indexed for inflation) and, if the employer elects to apply this clause, was in the top 20 percent in relation to compensation for that year.

[6] Although most states allow an employee to exclude 401(k) contributions from taxable income, it would be advisable to check with individual state authorities.

[7] Provided it is an "incidental benefit," life insurance can be purchased within a 401(k) plan. Up to 49.9 percent of annual contributions can be used to purchase whole life insurance (24.9 percent if used to purchase universal life). The participant must include in gross income the "cost" of the insurance coverage (measured by multiplying the difference between the face amount and the cash surrender value by either the Table 2001 rates or the insurance companies rates for individual 1-year term life insurance). If the employee dies prior to retirement, death proceeds in excess of cash surrender values are received free of income taxes.

403(b) PLANS

403(b) plans are available to employees of public schools and colleges, and certain non-profit hospitals, charitable, religious, scientific and educational organizations.[1] The employee may supply the funds by agreeing to a salary reduction, or by foregoing a salary increase, or the employer may make contributions as additional compensation to the employee.[2] Contributions are *before taxes*, meaning that a participant is able to exclude the contributions from his current taxable income.[3]

Generally, with a salary reduction plan the lowest of these two limits may be excluded from income each year:

- A limit of $16,500 in 2010 and 2011, which also includes total salary reduction contributions to Section 401(k) Plans, Simplified Employee Pension Plans and SIMPLE IRAs. "Catch up" provisions allow: (1) certain employees with 15 years of service to increase this amount by an additional $3,000; and (2) employees who have attained age 50 to increase this amount by an additional $5,500 in 2011.

- The lesser of $49,000 in 2010 and 2011, or 100 percent of compensation, made to all 403(b) plans and, under some circumstances, retirement plans.

The compounding effect of before tax contributions and tax-deferred growth may result in substantially increased accumulations.[4] Since the annuity is generally portable to another qualified employer, contributions may be continued when changing employment.

Distributions from tax deferred annuities are subject to ordinary income taxes, unless rolled over into a traditional Individual Retirement Arrangement (IRA), another 403(b) plan, a 401(k) plan, a 457 government plan, or a 401(a) qualified retirement plan.[5] In addition, withdrawals may be subject to a 10-percent penalty tax. However, penalty-free withdrawals are allowed once the participant has attained age 59½, separated from service after attaining age 55, or under other specific circumstances.[6] With some restrictions, tax-free loans are also available.[7]

Required distributions of amounts accruing after 1986 generally must begin by April 1st of the year following the year in which the employee retires or attains age 70½, whichever is later.[8] Payments made under an annuity contract may be for the life of the employee (or lives of the employee and his beneficiary), or a period certain not longer than the life expectancy of the employee (or joint and last survivor life expectancy of the employee and his beneficiary).

Footnotes on page 269

SALARY REDUCTION PLAN

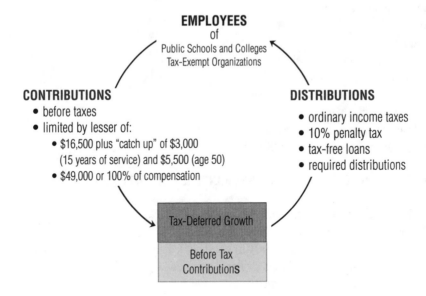

EMPLOYEES
of
Public Schools and Colleges
Tax-Exempt Organizations

CONTRIBUTIONS
- before taxes
- limited by lesser of:
    - $16,500 plus "catch up" of $3,000
      (15 years of service) and $5,500 (age 50)
    - $49,000 or 100% of compensation

DISTRIBUTIONS
- ordinary income taxes
- 10% penalty tax
- tax-free loans
- required distributions

Tax-Deferred Growth

Before Tax
Contributions

INFORMATION REQUIRED FOR ANALYSIS & PROPOSAL

1. Name of employee.
2. Date of birth.
3. Marital status.
4. Salary (annual, monthly, weekly).
5. Assumed current tax bracket.
6. Employment date.
7. Projected retirement age.
8. Prior participation in tax deferred annuity plan.
9. Current participation in any qualified plan.

CROSS REFERENCES TO TAX FACTS ON INSURANCE & EMPLOYEE BENEFITS (2011)

Q 3783. Rollovers from 403(b) tax sheltered annuities.

Q 3795. Tax benefits of 403(b) tax sheltered annuities.

Q 3796. Organizations that can make 403(b) tax sheltered annuities available to their employees.

Q 3797. Methods of funding 403(b) tax sheltered annuities.

Q 3798. Requirements that must be met.

Q 3800. Minimum nondiscrimination requirements.

Q 3801. Limits on excludable contributions.

Q 3802. Section 415 overall limits.

Q 3804. Salary reduction limits.

Q 3813. Taxation of incidental life insurance protection.

Q 3815. Loans under a 403(b) tax sheltered annuity.

Q 3817. Distributions subject to penalties.

Q 3818-3821. Required distributions.

Q 3822. Taxation of payments received by employee.

Q 3823. Taxation of death benefits received by employee's beneficiary.

Q 3824. Effect of salary reduction on social security tax and income tax withholding.

Footnotes

[1] A 403(b) plan is also referred to as a "tax sheltered annuity," or "TSA." Rather than "tax *sheltered* annuity," the Securities and Exchange Commission prefers the term "tax *deferred* annuity." Many companies now use the terms "tax deferred annuity" and "TDA," particularly when marketing variable annuities (see footnote 3, page 285, regarding licensing and prospectus requirements). 403(b) plans are also referred to as: (1) "qualified" annuity plans; and (2) "501(c)(3) plans" or "501(c)(3) pensions" (Section 501(c)(3) describes certain tax-exempt organizations).

[2] Nondiscrimination rules may apply to both salary reduction and employer contributions.

[3] Where a reduction in salary is taken to provide the premium payments for a 403(b) plan, Social Security taxes and benefits are based upon the *unreduced* salary (i.e., although income taxes are reduced, there is no reduction in Social Security taxes).

[4] The chart on page 259 demonstrates the leverage afforded by the typical tax-favored retirement plan. Investing in a *variable* 403(b) plan provides a particularly attractive opportunity for dollar cost averaging (see graph, page 318).

[5] However, if the employee has an investment in the contract, he is allowed a tax-free recovery of his investment. Examples of an employee's *investment in the contract* include: (1) any premiums that he has paid with nondeductible dollars; (2) any employer contributions that were taxable to him by virtue of having exceeded his exclusion allowance in years before 2002 or the overall limit; (3) the sum of the annual one-year term costs that were taxable to him (where the contract provided life insurance protection); and (4) the amount of any loans included in income as a taxable distribution. When benefits are received in installments, or as a life income, the employee's investment in the contract requires the calculation of an exclusion ratio. The method used to determine the exclusion ratio depends upon the annuity starting date. Distributions are generally subject to mandatory withholding of 20 percent unless the employee elects a direct rollover.

[6] These additional specific circumstances include: (1) death; (2) disability; (3) as a part of substantially equal periodic payments beginning after separation from service; (4) when used for medical expenses exceeding 7.5 percent of adjusted gross income; (5) distribution of excess contributions within the same calendar year; (6) payments to an alternate payee under a qualified domestic relations order; and (7) penalty-free withdrawals for military reservists.

[7] The maximum tax-free loan is generally one-half the contract value, or $50,000, whichever is less. However, an exception is available for the first $10,000 of cash value, all of which may be borrowed. Loan repayments must be made at least quarterly and in amounts that allow for amortization over five years, except for loans to purchase a primary residence, which may be repaid over a longer "reasonable" period.

[8] These rules apply whether the distribution is calculated under the 1987, 2001, or 2002 regulations. However, different rules apply when distributions are not made as an annuity. See pages 433-434.

412(i) PLANS

A 412(i) plan is a defined benefit plan that is funded by life insurance and annuities.[1] These plans provide high-earning business owners who have stable cash flow an opportunity to make maximum deductible retirement contributions while offering a high degree of security to plan participants. They are most appropriate for risk-averse employers with five or fewer employees, one or more of which are owners who are at least 50 years of age.

PLAN REQUIREMENTS. 412(i) plans are subject to all the requirements that apply to other defined benefit plans, including nondiscrimination, vesting and benefit limitations.[2] In addition, they must generally meet the following six additional requirements: (1) the plan must be funded exclusively by life insurance policies and/or annuities guaranteed by a state licensed insurance company; (2) contracts must have level premiums; (3) benefits must be provided entirely by these contracts; (4) premiums must be paid without lapse; (5) contract rights cannot be subject to a security interest; and (6) no policy loans are allowed.[3]

FUNDING. Known as "fully insured" plans, 412(i) plans are typically funded with a combination of life insurance and annuities.[4] The primary purpose of the plan must be to provide retirement income. Therefore, when life insurance is used it must provide participants with no more than an "incidental" death benefit. To satisfy this requirement defined benefit plans often limit the insured death benefit to not more than 100 times the expected monthly benefit.[5] Excessive funding may result in nondeductible contributions and "listed transaction" status. Each plan participant has the right to name the beneficiary of this death benefit and must include in income an amount equal to the "economic benefit" of the life insurance benefit.[6]

THE TRADEOFFS. Because **412(i) plans** are exempt from the full funding limit that otherwise applies to defined benefit plans, they offer (within limits) the opportunity to make accelerated contributions resulting in large upfront tax deductions. Simplicity is achieved with conservative low-risk life insurance and annuity contracts that shift investment risks from the employer to the insurance company. These "fully insured" plans offer pre-retirement death benefits that are easy to calculate and plan benefits that are easier to understand.[7]

In contrast, **other defined benefit plans** provide more flexibility in both plan design and investment options. This offers the potential for high investment returns, but this entails fewer guarantees and increased risk (i.e., risk and return go hand in hand). Initial costs tend to be lower, but ongoing administrative and actuarial costs tend to be higher in comparison to 412(i) plans.[8]

Footnotes on page 273

PLAN REQUIREMENTS

Subject to the same qualification requirements as any other defined benefit plan, including:

- Nondiscrimination
- Vesting
- Benefit Limits

Must also meet the following additional requirements:

- Funded exclusively by life insurance contracts and/or annuities
- Level annual premiums
- Benefits guaranteed by insurance company
- Premiums paid without lapse
- Not subject to security interests
- No policy loans

FUNDING

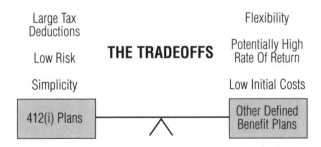

INFORMATION REQUIRED FOR ANALYSIS & PROPOSAL

1. Names of employees.
2. Sex.
3. Dates of birth.
4. Dates of employment.
5. W-2 salary.
6. Hours worked per year.
7. Tax status of business (sole proprietor, C corporation, S corporation, professional corporation, partnership, limited liability company).
8. Ownership percentage.
9. Projected retirement age.
10. Other pension plans in force.

CROSS REFERENCES TO TAX FACTS ON INSURANCE & EMPLOYEE BENEFITS (2011)

Q 3649. Special qualification requirements that apply to defined benefit pension plans.

Q 3663. Minimum funding standard for pension plans.

Q 3690. Basic description of 412(i) plans.

Q 3691. Requirements a Section 412(i) fully insured plan must meet in order to be exempt from the minimum funding requirements.

Q 3703. Extent to which a qualified plan can provide life insurance benefits for its participants.

Q 3754. Description of the method used to determine the cost of current life insurance protection taxed to common law employee participants.

Q 3755. The cost of life insurance protection can be recovered tax free from plan benefits.

Q 3765. When employee dies *before* retirement – how beneficiary is taxed on a single sum cash payment of the death benefit.

Q 3766. When employee dies *before* retirement – how beneficiary is taxed on life income or installment payments of the death benefit.

Q 3767. When employee dies *after* retirement – how beneficiary is taxed on payments of the death benefit.

Footnotes

[1] In consolidating the funding rules of Section 412, the Pension Protection Act of 2006 eliminated Section 412(i) and moved its provisions without substantive changes to Section 412(e)(3). Although Section 412(i) no longer exists, it is expected that the fully insured plans described in this chart will continue to be known as "412(i) plans."

[2] For example, the plan must generally include all full-time non-union employees, except for employees younger than 21 and those with less than one year of service. See the Qualified Plan Checklist, page 303 (but 412(i) plans are exempt from the stated "maximum limits").

[3] It is important to recognize that a defined benefit plan entails an obligation on the part of the employer to fund the plan each and every year. Failure to make regular premium payments could cause it to fail the IRS requirement that the plan be "permanent."

[4] Most 412(i) plans provide a death benefit, but it is not required. Guidance released by the IRS in 2004 announced a crackdown on 412(i) plans in three major areas: (1) **valuation of life contracts** – regulations require that a contract's fair market value be included in the distributee's income, not merely the cash value (a safe harbor definition of fair market value is provided); (2) **discrimination in the types of contracts provided to highly compensated employees** – discrimination against nonhighly compensated employees with respect to purchase or surrender rights, cash value growth terms, exchange features, or other benefits rights and features, will be considered to violate the nondiscrimination requirement; and (3) **deduction of premiums for "excessive" amounts of life insurance** – premiums attributable to excessive coverage will not be deductible, a 10 percent excise tax on nondeductible contributions may be applied, and the plan may be classified as a "listed transaction."

[5] This "incidental" death benefit requirement is also satisfied if: (1) the cost of the benefit is less than 25 percent of the cost of all benefits provided under the plan (the 25 percent rule); or (2) less than 50 percent of the employer contribution credited to each participant's account is used to purchase "ordinary life insurance" (if either *term* insurance or *universal life* insurance is purchased the 50 percent is reduced to 25 percent).

[6] This value is taxed at the lower of the Table 2001 rates (page 552) or the life insurance company's actual term rates for standard risks (beginning in 2004 the use of the insurance company's term rates was more restricted). When life insurance protection under a plan is provided by a cash value policy the aggregate costs taxed to the employee are considered to be a part of the employee's basis and may be recovered tax free from the *retirement benefits* received under the policy. Income taxation of this *death benefit* is as follows: (1) the pure insurance element (death benefit less cash values) is received free of taxes; (2) the total of "economic benefit" costs paid by participant are also received free of taxes; and (3) any remaining death benefit is taxed as a qualified plan distribution (generally as ordinary income). Qualified plan death benefits are included in the decedent's estate for estate tax purposes unless the participant avoids having any "incidents of ownership" in the policy (see page 409).

[7] If there are excess earnings they must be used to reduce future contributions that fund plan benefits. 412(i) plans also avoid both excise and income taxes on reversions to the employer, since they are fully funded by the annuity values and life insurance cash vales that determine the retirement benefit.

[8] When compared to other funding vehicles, such as variable annuities or equity investments, the question of whether the large and accelerated tax deductions produced by 412(i) plans adequately compensate for their comparatively low guaranteed rates of return is controversial. Ultimately the decision may be more influenced by a desire to: (1) fund life insurance on a tax deductible basis; and (2) avoid the risks associated with equity investments.

457 PLANS

Section 457 plans are nonqualified deferred compensation plans available to employees of state and local governments and tax-exempt organizations.[1] By deferring income, employees are able to reduce current income taxes while saving more for retirement than they would with the typical after-tax savings plan.[2]

ELIGIBLE PLANS. Under "eligible" plans, in 2010 and 2011 deferrals are limited to the lesser of $16,500, or 100 percent of includable compensation.[3] Benefits usually are not subject to forfeiture. Eligible plans are most often used for the "rank and file" employees of state and local governments, who desire to defer *limited* amounts of compensation on an attractive tax deferred basis.[4] Employees of *state and local governments* are not taxed until benefits are actually paid. In contrast, employees of *tax-exempt organizations* are not taxed until the benefits are actually paid *or* otherwise made available to them. Tax-exempt organizations can only make eligible plans available to a select group of management or highly compensated employees.[5] (These higher paid employees of tax-exempt organizations often prefer "ineligible plans" providing for greater deferrals.) The *earliest* plan distributions can be made is at severance of employment, death, an "unforeseeable emergency," or in the calendar year in which the participant reaches age 70½. Plan distributions must generally begin by April 1 of the year following the year in which the employee retires or attains age 70½, whichever is later. Distributions from Section 457 plans are subject to ordinary income taxes. Rollovers are permitted to and from an eligible Section 457 plan of a state or local government, a qualified plan, a Section 403(b) tax sheltered annuity, or an IRA.

INELIGIBLE PLANS. Under "ineligible" plans, employees may make *unlimited* deferrals of compensation, provided the benefits are subject to a "substantial risk of forfeiture."[6] These plans are most often used by tax-exempt organizations to provide substantial deferrals for a *select* group of management or highly compensated employees (the "top hat" group). Use of ineligible plans by state and local governments is generally limited to highly paid employees who can accept a risk of forfeiture, since such a risk is often unacceptable to the "rank and file" employee. Because employees are taxed when there is no longer a substantial risk of forfeiture, vesting provisions must be carefully drafted.[7] Ineligible plans are not required to comply with any specific distribution requirements.

Both eligible and ineligible plans may not be formally funded, except for eligible governmental plans. However, it is customary and desirable for employers to "informally" fund their obligations through the purchase of annuities or investment products.[8] Any deferrals, and assets purchased with the deferrals, must remain the property of the employer and are subject to the employer's general creditors.

Footnotes on page 277

EMPLOYEES

of

State and Local Governments
Tax-Exempt Organizations

ELIGIBLE PLANS

- Deferrals limited to lesser of:
  $16,500,
  or 100% of compensation

- Benefits not subject to forfeiture

- Coverage - State and Local Governments
  have no specific coverage
  requirements (Tax-Exempt
  Organizations must limit
  coverage to "top hat" group)

- Employee taxed when benefits
  actually paid or otherwise
  made available

- Distribution requirements:
  o seperation from service
  o unforeseeable emergency
  o age 70½

INELIGIBLE PLANS

- Deferrals unlimited

- Benefits subject to a "substantial
  risk of forfeiture"

- Coverage - Tax-Exempt Organizations
  must limit coverage to
  "top hat" group (State and
  Local Governments have no
  specific coverage requirements)

- Employee taxed when there is no
  substantial risk or forfeiture

- No distribution requirements

- May not be formally funded except
  for eligible governmental plans

- Deferrals subject to employer's creditors
  except for eligible governmental plans

INFORMATION REQUIRED FOR ANALYSIS & PROPOSAL

1. Name of employee.
2. Date of birth.
3. Marital status.
4. Salary (annual, monthly, weekly).
5. Assumed current tax bracket.
6. Projected retirement age.
7. Prior and current participation in any qualified plans (including state teacher's retirement plans), 403(b) plans, and Section 457 plans.

CROSS REFERENCES TO TAX FACTS ON INSURANCE & EMPLOYEE BENEFITS (2011)

Q 3597. Nonqualified deferred compensation tax benefits that are available to employees of state or local governments and other tax-exempt employers.

Q 3598. Requirements that a Section 457 plan must satisfy.

Q 3599. Taxation of cost of life insurance protection and death benefits provided under Section 457 plans.

Q 3600. Taxation of participants in eligible Section 457 plans, and "ineligible" plans.

Footnotes

[1] "State and local governments" include a state, a political subdivision of a state, or any agency or instrumentality of either of them (e.g., a school district or sewage authority). Tax-exempt organizations include those types of nongovernmental organizations exempt from tax under Code Section 501 (i.e., most nonprofit organizations that serve their members or some public or charitable purpose, but not a church or synagogue). Under "eligible" plans, only individuals may participate, not partnerships or corporations. Partnerships and corporations may participate in "ineligible" plans (see footnote 5, below). Section 457 plans can also be made available to independent contractors, but under somewhat different rules.

[2] The chart on page 259 can be used to demonstrate the leverage afforded by the typical tax-favored retirement plan. Investing in a *variable* tax deferred annuity provides a particularly attractive opportunity for dollar cost averaging (see graph, page 318).

[3] The dollar limit on deferrals to a Section 457 plan is $16,500 for 2011 (the same as in 2009 and 2010). When appropriate, cost-of-living adjustments are made in $500 increments. This conforms to the elective deferral limits for 401(k) plans and Section 403(b) plans. "Catch-up" provisions may permit larger deferrals. See the table of Employee Benefit Limits on page 306.

[4] The term "eligible plans" is used to describe the deferred compensation plans of state and local governments and tax-exempt organizations that comply with the provisions of Section 457. When a plan provides for deferrals in *excess* of the lesser of $16,500 or 100 percent of compensation, Section 457(f) states, "compensation shall be included in the gross income of the participant or beneficiary for the 1st taxable year in which there is no substantial risk of forfeiture." Plans falling under Section 457(f) are variously referred to as "ineligible" plans and "Section 457(f)" plans.

[5] Unlike plans of state and local governments, plans of tax-exempt organizations can be subject to the participation, vesting, and funding requirements of ERISA (see page 405). These ERISA requirements are in conflict with the "no funding" requirements of Section 457 for tax-exempt organizations. This prevents most tax-exempt organizations from having a Section 457 plan unless the plan fits within the ERISA "top hat" exemption (i.e., an unfunded plan for a select group of management or highly compensated employees). This also means that "rank and file" employees of tax-exempt organizations cannot participate in Section 457 plans.

[6] A "substantial risk of forfeiture" is said to exist if a participant's right to the compensation is conditioned upon the future performance of substantial services. The risk of forfeiture must be both real and substantial.

[7] For example, payment of compensation might be conditioned upon the continued employment of the participant for a specified period, measured by a pre-established service completion date. At the end of the service completion date, when there are no longer any future service requirements, and therefore no risk of forfeiture, the deferred amount (including earnings accumulated prior to the lapse of the risk) is included in the participant's taxable income. However, the *earnings* credited to the participant's account after the substantial risk of forfeiture ends generally will not be taxable as compensation until actually paid or otherwise made available. It may be desirable to release compensation over a specific period of years in order to reduce the tax burden as the contract conditions are met.

[8] If life insurance is purchased with amounts deferred, the premiums are not taxed to the participant as long as the employer remains the owner and beneficiary of the contract. However, upon the employee's death, payment of the proceeds to the employee's beneficiary would be taxed under the normal annuity rules and would not be treated as tax-free death proceeds.

PENSION MAXIMIZATION

Upon retirement under a qualified pension plan, married workers and their spouses are often faced with making a difficult decision regarding the desired payout election.[1] Basically one of two elections may be made: (1) to take a reduced monthly income with a survivor income benefit providing for payments during the lifetimes of both the retiree and his spouse;[2] or (2) to take an increased monthly income for the lifetime of the retiree without provisions for a survivor income benefit. Although plans differ, typically when the survivor income benefit is elected there is a reduction of 25 to 30 percent.[3]

CURRENT PENSION PLAN. For example, assume that the election under the current pension plan involves a choice between a retirement benefit of $1,600 per month to both husband and wife, or $2,100 per month for the retiree only. This difference of $500 per month can be viewed as the "cost" of securing a survivor benefit for the retiree's spouse. The election must be made prior to retirement and under most plans it is irrevocable once retirement begins.[4]

The retiree and his spouse are faced with a dilemma! If the survivor income benefit is elected they will receive only $1,600 per month. And, if his spouse dies first, he will continue to receive only this reduced monthly income. On the other hand, if he elects to receive $2,100 per month and dies before his spouse, no further payments will be made to the surviving spouse.

PURCHASE OF LIFE INSURANCE can provide an alternative means of providing for the surviving spouse.[5] If life insurance is purchased upon retirement, it may be possible, depending upon the particular plan of insurance, for the increased monthly after-tax income to pay for this coverage.[6] However, it is generally better to obtain the insurance some years prior to retirement, when premiums are lower and the worker more likely to be insurable.[7] In either case, the amount of insurance should be sufficient to provide an income in replacement of the survivor benefit that was not elected.[8]

AFTER RETIREMENT the contract insuring the retiree provides great flexibility. If the *retiree* dies first, then the death benefit can be used to pay a lifetime annuity to the surviving spouse. If the *spouse* dies first, then accumulated cash values are available to the retiree.[9] By either terminating the contract, or placing it in a "paid-up" status, the retiree could then stop premium payments and retain his full retirement income of $2,100 per month.[10]

Footnotes on page 281

CURRENT PENSION PLAN

AN ELECTION

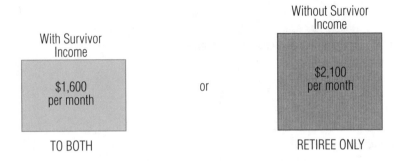

With Survivor
Income

$1,600
per month

TO BOTH

or

Without Survivor
Income

$2,100
per month

RETIREE ONLY

PURCHASE LIFE INSURANCE

Prior To Retirement   or   Upon Retirement

AFTER RETIREMENT

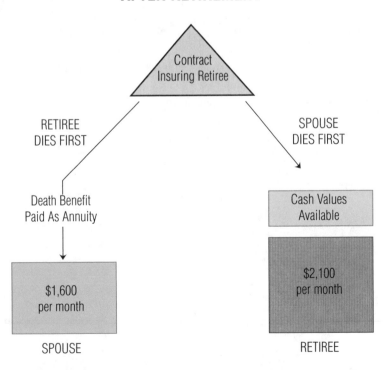

Contract
Insuring Retiree

RETIREE
DIES FIRST

SPOUSE
DIES FIRST

Death Benefit
Paid As Annuity

$1,600
per month

SPOUSE

Cash Values
Available

$2,100
per month

RETIREE

INFORMATION REQUIRED FOR ANALYSIS & PROPOSAL

1. Name.
2. Sex.
3. Date of birth.
4. Smoker/nonsmoker.
5. Anticipated marginal tax bracket during retirement.
6. Spouse's date of birth.
7. Spouse's health.

With Regard to Current Pension Plan

8. What survivor elections are available (joint and full survivor, joint and two-thirds survivor, joint and one-half survivor, etc.)?
9. What is the monthly dollar amount payable under the preferred survivor election?
10. What is the monthly dollar amount payable if no survivor income is elected (i.e., a straight-life annuity is paid to the retiree)?
11. Does the plan provide cost-of-living increases? If so, what annual rate of increase is anticipated?
12. Does the plan require surviving spouse election in order to maintain medical benefits?

CROSS REFERENCES TO TAX FACTS ON INSURANCE & EMPLOYEE BENEFITS (2011)

Q 177. Advantages of group carve-out plans.

Q 3720-3721. Forms of survivor benefits that must be provided under qualified plans and when they may be waived.

Q 3767. Taxation of employee's beneficiary on death benefit payments when employee dies after retirement.

Q 3768. Withholding of income taxes from qualified retirement plan benefits.

Footnotes

[1] "Pension maximization" is also referred to as pension maximizer, pension expander, pension trap, pension predicament, and retirement dilemma.

[2] In the chart it is assumed that survivor payments will be in the same amount as those made while both the retiree and spouse are living. This option is known as a "joint and full survivor" annuity. Another option often made available is known as a "joint and two-thirds" annuity (e.g., $2,100 per month to both husband and wife, with $1,400 per month to the survivor). In order to protect surviving spouses, the law requires that qualified pension plans must provide as a minimum a joint and one-half annuity (e.g., $1,800 per month to both husband and wife, with $900 to the survivor). The retiree's *spouse must join* with the retiree in agreeing to waive the minimum joint and survivor annuity in order to obtain the increased benefit for the life of the retiree only.

[3] The reduction will depend upon the survivor option selected. For example, if a straight-life benefit pays $2,100 per month, a joint and full survivor benefit might pay $1,600 per month, whereas a joint and one-half survivor benefit might pay $1,800 per month to both retiree and spouse and $900 per month to the survivor. Typically these options are said to be "actuarially equivalent," in that at retirement they annuitize the value of the retiree's pension benefit according to actuarial tables.

[4] Occasionally a plan may provide for reinstatement of the retiree's full benefits upon the death of his spouse. However, such a "bounce-back" provision will not recapture benefits lost prior to the spouse's death.

[5] Pension maximization may be particularly useful to the retiree who is reluctant to accept a permanently reduced retirement income to assure a survivor income to his terminally ill spouse. However, as with any pension maximization proposal, it is *absolutely essential* to ascertain whether any medical benefits would be lost to the surviving spouse if no survivor option were elected.

[6] Note that the full increase in retirement income will not be available for making premium payments, since these payments must be made with after-tax retirement dollars. On the other hand, if the surviving spouse takes an annuity payout of the tax-free death benefits, less of each payment will be subject to income tax than post-retirement survivor benefits received under a noncontributory pension plan (i.e., less death benefits will be required to provide the surviving spouse a given after-tax income).

[7] When proposed some years prior to retirement, it is appropriate to consider the time value of money, since initial premium payments will come from other than additional after-tax retirement funds. However, the pension maximization concept can be particularly useful in demonstrating the need for ongoing insurance coverage after retirement. In fact, a discussion of the concept may *demonstrate the need for permanent insurance* to a breadwinner who is considering term insurance to meet a family income need (e.g., once children are grown the same insurance can be used to provide protection for a spouse during retirement, thus there is an ongoing but different need for permanent insurance). See also, First-To-Die Insurance, page 415.

[8] When a plan provides cost-of-living adjustments this potential for increasing survivor income would be lost by electing an option providing for no survivor income. However, to some degree this would be offset by the increased annuity payments available to his spouse from a level death benefit (i.e., the longer the retiree lives, the older the surviving spouse; the older the surviving spouse, the larger the annuity payments from a given death benefit). Availability of an *increasing* death benefit might more than make up for such cost-of-living adjustments.

[9] If taken as a lump-sum, cash values in excess of net premiums paid would be subject to income taxation. Alternatively, the retiree might obtain additional income by exercising a settlement option under the contract by receiving existing cash values as an annuity.

[10] Maintaining the policy or taking "paid-up" insurance would preserve the death benefit for children or other heirs.

DEFERRED ANNUITY

It has been said that three things can happen to you. You can die too soon, you can become disabled, or you can live too long. The last of these requires that each of us make advance plans to assure sufficient funds for our retirement years.[1]

Deferred annuities provide an opportunity to accumulate these funds on a tax-favored basis.[2] As a flexible cash accumulation vehicle, these annuities are available with either a *single* payment or *multiple* payments over a number of years (often referred to as a modal annuity). In either case, prior to the annuity starting date, the cash values of the annuity accumulate tax-deferred, with specific contractual guarantees and at generally competitive rates of interest.[3]

LIVE. For the annuitant who lives to retirement, the annuity can provide a guaranteed income for life. The actual amount of each payment will depend upon the values that have accumulated prior to retirement and the desired frequency of payments. When the deferred annuity matures, payments can be taken in a variety of ways, to include "full" annuity payments for the life of one person (the annuitant) or "reduced" annuity payments for the lives of the annuitant and another person (e.g., a joint and survivor annuity).

DIE. If the annuitant dies *prior* to the annuity starting date, the then existing values could be used to provide either a lump-sum payment or an ongoing income to one or more beneficiaries. The specific amount and duration of these payments will depend upon the particular settlement option selected.

QUIT. Should the annuitant decide to surrender the contract prior to the annuity starting date, the then existing values, minus any surrender charges, could be taken in a lump-sum cash payment, or applied towards a settlement option providing ongoing income payments. Before making a decision, the tax implications of each of these options should be carefully considered.[4]

Of course, it is possible that the annuitant might die *after* the annuity starting date. To protect a surviving spouse, or other beneficiary, the annuitant can elect a settlement option providing somewhat reduced annuity payments in return for ongoing payments to a survivor. Other options are also available:

- Payments could be elected to begin prior to normal retirement age;
- Payments could be guaranteed for a minimum number of years;
- Payments could be elected for a fixed number of years.[5]

Footnotes on page 285

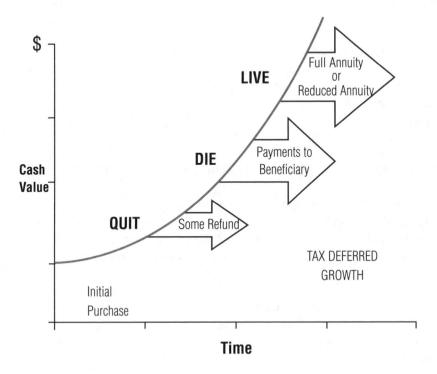

INFORMATION REQUIRED FOR ANALYSIS & PROPOSAL

1. Name of annuitant.
2. Sex.
3. Date of birth.
4. Funds available for purchase.

   To Determine Suitability for Variable Product
5. Attitude toward risk.
6. Income.
7. Net worth.

CROSS REFERENCES TO TAX FACTS ON INSURANCE & EMPLOYEE BENEFITS (2011)

Q 3501. General rules governing taxation of annuity payments.

Q 3503. Basic rule for taxing amounts received prior to annuity starting date.

Q 3504. Penalties that apply to "premature" distributions under annuity contracts.

Q 3542. Amount payable upon death prior to maturity subject to income taxation.

   See Generally

Q 3507-3520. Annuity rules: fixed annuities.

Q 3521-3524. Annuity rules: variable annuities.

Q 3534-3537. Gift tax annuity rules.

Q 3562-3569. Estate tax annuity rules.

Footnotes

[1] The Penalty Of Waiting table on page 316 gives the monthly deposit required to save $100,000 by age 65, assuming 6 percent interest. The table also shows the additional savings required if there is a delay of one or 5 years in starting to save for retirement. This same concept is illustrated another way in the table entitled Early Saver vs. Late Saver on page 317.

[2] Annuities are either immediate or deferred. *Immediate* annuities, by definition, are single-premium contracts that begin paying installments immediately. (Immediate annuities are also often referred to as "income annuities.") For example, an immediate monthly annuity would begin paying to the annuitant one month after the premium was paid and the contract issued. A *deferred* annuity is one in which payments to the annuitant are delayed to a specified future date more than one payment period in the future. See also, the Annuity Matrix, page 302.

[3] Deferred annuities are also available as *variable* annuities (see the expanded discussion on page 547). With the variable annuity, the cash accumulations reflect the performance of an underlying portfolio of investments such as stocks and bonds. While these investments can provide a hedge against inflation and an increased opportunity for growth, there is also the risk that investment performance will be poor and that an annuity's value will decrease or be lost (in contrast, see the discussion of the equity-indexed annuity on pages 403-404). As an alternative to annuitization, the guaranteed minimum withdrawal benefit ensures the owner of a minimum income stream (see page 421). Since it is a security, in order to sell variable annuities you must hold a valid federal securities license and state license where required. In addition, *a prospectus must be delivered* with or preceding a proposal to a prospect or client. This chart refers to a *nonqualified* annuity, which is purchased with after-tax dollars. A *qualified* annuity is described in the chart entitled 403(b) Plans, on page 267.

[4] An early withdrawal of funds from an annuity can cause serious tax consequences. For example, taxable interest is considered to be distributed first when there is a partial withdrawal from an annuity contract purchased after August 13, 1982. This means that with such a contract a tax-free return of the amount invested in the annuity cannot be received until all accrued interest earnings have been withdrawn. If amounts are invested after August 13, 1982 in a preexisting annuity contract, amounts withdrawn are treated first as return of pre-August 14, 1982 investment, then as income on pre-August 14, 1982 investment, then as income on investment made after August 13, 1982, and finally as return of post-August 13, 1982 investment. In addition, there is a 10-percent-penalty tax applied to all taxable withdrawals from the annuity, with certain specific exceptions: such as withdrawals made after age 59½, or on account of disability, or of earnings on investment made before August 14, 1982, or as part of a series of substantially equal payments for life and not modified before age 59½ or within 60 months if modified after age 59½.

[5] These settlement options are similar to those available with most life insurance cash values.

EMPLOYEE BENEFITS CHECKLIST

Benefit	Description	Taxation of Employee
Athletic Facilities	Provided on premises and used by employees, their spouses, and dependent children.	Not included in income.
Automobile	Used for business purpose.	Not included in income.
	Used for personal benefit (including travel from home to office).	Taxable as additional noncash compensation.
Cafeteria Plans	Permit employees to choose between cash and certain tax favored benefits, but not including deferred compensation other than 401(k). The plan must be written, cover only employees or former employees, and may provide benefits for beneficiaries of participants (see page 352).	A participant will not be taxed just because plan offers a choice between cash and non-taxable benefits to extent he selects nontaxable benefits. Plans are subject to special nondiscrimination rules.
Charitable Contributions	Made by employer to organizations designated by key employees.	Not included in income provided contributions made and deducted by employer.
Club Memberships	Used for business purpose or used for both business and personal purposes.	Included in income and not deductible by employee.
Conventions, Meetings, and Business Trips	Attended for a business purpose.	Not included in income.
	When made primarily for a business purpose, but including a nonbusiness side trip.	Meeting and travel expenses to and from meetings are not included in income (if foreign convention, may have to prorate travel expenses).
Deferred Compensation	See chart on page 235.	Not included in income until payments actually or constructively received.
Dependent Care Expenses	Provided to employees to enable them to be gainfully employed. Employee must have at least one dependent under 13 years old or dependent or spouse who cannot care for self and resides with employee. Although plan does not have to be funded, it must be in writing.	Up to $5,000 (not more than employee's earned income, or, if less, the employee's spouse's earned income) excluded from income. Plan must meet non-discrimination and notice requirements for exclusions by highly compensated. No more than 25% of benefits can be paid to more-than-5% stockholder-employees.
Disability Income	See charts on pages 239 and 243.	Refer to table on page 323 and discussion on page 387.

Benefit	Description	Taxation of Employee
Discounts	Discounts made available to employees, spouses, and children. Discount limited to 20% of the selling price of a service, or the gross profit percentage multiplied by the selling price of merchandise.	Not included in income provided nondiscriminatory.
Eating Facilities	Providing subsidized meals on or near premises.	Not included in income (provided revenue employer receives equals or exceeds direct operating costs).
Educational Expenses	Reimbursed to an employee for maintaining or improving skills required in employment.	Included in income, but deductible. See table on page 310.
	Reimbursed to an employee for meeting minimum requirements for employment or qualifying for a new trade or business.	Included in income and not deductible. See table on page 310.
	Provided under a nondiscriminatory Educational Assistance Program. Education need not be job related or lead to a degree (includes graduate level courses). Covered expenses include tuition, fees, books, and supplies.	Up to $5,250 not included in income. Amounts over $5,250 are included in income and subject to employment and income tax withholding.
Executive Equity Life Insurance	See chart on page 211.	Taxable as additional compensation.
Financial Counseling & Estate Planning	Provided to key employees for personal investment and estate planning.	Included as additional wages, but deductible to the extent that they are for tax or investment counseling (subject to 2% floor).
401(k) Plans	See chart on page 263.	Employer contributions not included in income. Employee elective deferrals not included in income but limited to $16,500 in 2010 and 2011 ($11,500 for SIMPLE 401(k) plans). Roth 401(k) elective deferrals are included in income (see page 505).
403(b) Plans	See chart on page 267.	Compensation not currently included in income (employees of public schools and colleges, and certain non-profit organizations), but generally limited to $16,500 in 2010 and 2011.

Benefit	Description	Taxation of Employee
412(i) Plans	See chart on page 271.	Premiums paid by employer for life insurance or annuities are not included in income, but employee must include in income an amount equal to the "economic benefit" of life insurance benefit.
457 Plans	See chart on page 275.	Compensation not currently included in income (employees of state and local governments and tax-exempt organizations), but limited, in "eligible" plans to $16,500 for 2010 and 2011.
Gifts	Gifts to employees (but not managers, administrators, and other professional employees) if for safety or achievement.	Not included in income provided given in recognition of length of service or safety achievement. Value of award generally limited to $400.
Group Permanent Life Insurance (Section 79)	Superimposed on an existing group term plan, providing whole life insurance for employees (also referred to as "Group Ordinary Life Insurance").	Premium attributable to permanent insurance and term coverage over $50,000 are both taxable as additional compensation.
Group Term Life Insurance	See chart on page 203.	First $50,000 of coverage not included in income and amounts over $50,000 are taxable at the Table I Rates (rates, page 552). Up to $2,000 on spouse and children can be provided tax-free.
Health Savings Account	For individuals covered under high deductible health plans these accounts allow contributions by employers and employees for payment of medical expenses. Balances may be carried forward.	Contributions are deductible up to an annual contribution limit. Distributions for "qualified medical expenses" are not taxable. See chart, page 251.
Holidays	Granting time off from work on specific dates during the year. Most holidays are set, but employees may be given a number of discretionary paid holiday days.	Wages paid during holidays are included in income.
Individual 401(k) Plans	Allows owner-only small businesses, partnerships, and sole proprietors to make maximum contributions to a 401(k) plan.	Maximum of $49,000 annual additions in 2010 and 2011. Employee pre-tax deferral of $16,500 (plus catch-up of $5,500 if age 50 or older). See page 426.

Benefit	Description	Taxation of Employee
Interest-Free Loans	Provided to key employees in amounts of $10,000 or less.	Not taxable and no deemed interest provided tax avoidance is not a principal purpose. If loan exceeds $10,000, employee is deemed to have income in an amount equal to foregone interest (page 432). There may be no deduction for the deemed interest payment (page 431).
IRA Contributions	Contributions to the Individual Retirement Accounts of selected key employees.	Taxation depends upon whether employee is covered by certain other plans (see pages 304 and 427).
Keogh Plans (HR-10)	These are qualified retirement plans for the self-employed. Although such individuals (sole proprietors or partners operating a trade, business, or profession) are not employees in the commonly accepted sense of the term, they are treated as "employees" for the purpose of allowing them to participate in qualified plans ("employees" include any individuals who have net earnings from self-employment in a trade or business).	Virtually no distinction is made between pension, profit sharing, and other retirement plans established by the self-employed and those established by corporations.
Legal Expense Benefit	Providing legal services to employees for a variety of legal matters. Most plans offer scheduled benefits provided by a specified group of lawyers.	Benefits should be received tax-free. If employer pays "premiums" on employee's behalf, employee must include that amount in income. See discussion on page 436.
Meals and Lodging	Provided on the employer's premises and "for the convenience of the employer." There must also be a "substantial noncompensatory business reason." Acceptance of lodging must be a condition of employment.	Not included in income.
	Provided off the employer's premises while the employee is traveling to and attending a business convention or meeting, or on a business trip.	Not included in income.
Medical Benefits (continued on next page)	Providing hospitalization, surgical and major medical expenses for employees and their dependents.	Not included in income. Non-discrimination requirements apply to self-insured plans.

Benefit	Description	Taxation of Employee
Medical Benefits (continued)	Providing reimbursement for medical, dental, and drug expenses (usually expenses not covered under a group plan). See chart on page 247.	Not included in income. Non-discrimination requirements apply to self-insured plans.
Medical or Physical Examinations	Made available on a periodic basis to executives and key employees, including blood tests and x-rays.	Not included in income. In discriminatory self-insured plan, included in income if for specific illness or symptom.
Moving Expenses to New Principal Place of Work	Reimbursed to an employee for direct expenses, including moving household goods, cars, and family, as well as indirect expenses such as pre-move house hunting trips, temporary living expenses while waiting to move into a new home, and certain expenses of selling, pur-chasing, and leasing an old home or new home.	Direct expenses are included in income but deductible from gross income, provided requirements as to length of service and distance from former home are met. Indirect expenses are included in income and are not deductible by employee.
Parking	Provided to an employee on or near the business premises or on or near a location from which the employee commutes to work by mass transit, in a commuter highway vehicle, or by carpool.	May exclude from gross income up to $230 per month for value of employer-provided qualified parking in 2010 and 2011.
Pension Plans	Providing guaranteed retire-ment benefits to employees based upon a nondiscrimina-tory formula or formulas. Such formulas utilize either a defined benefit or a defined contribution approach (e.g., either a specific dollar benefit to the employee at retirement, or a specific dollar contribu-tion each year by the employer).	Employer contributions not included in income until pay-ments received. If the plan contains insurance, each employee reports the value of coverage using Table 2001 rates as set forth on page 552. See discussions on pages 354, 384, 460 and 491.
Per Diem	Paid to employees as a fixed reimbursement for subsis-tence items such as meals, lodging, laundry, tips, etc., while on business trips.	Rate authorized to be paid by the federal government for the area in which the travel is authorized may be excluded from income, as well as an additional amount per mile for transportation expenses.
Professional Dues and Publications	Paid by an employer for the benefit of key employees.	Usually taxable as additional compensation, but deductible by the employee as a miscel-laneous itemized deduction (subject to 2% floor).

Benefit	Description	Taxation of Employee
Profit Sharing Plans	Providing retirement benefits based upon a nondiscriminatory formula for allocating contributions among participants. There is no requirement to have a predetermined formula for calculating contributions (permissible maximum employer deduction is generally 25% of total compensation of plan participants).	Employer contributions not included in income until payments received, and payments are then subject to favorable tax treatment. See discussions on pages 347, 484, 491 and 531.
Retired Lives Reserves (RLR)	See discussion on page 500.	Contributions not currently taxed; after retirement, cost of coverage is taxable in year provided.
Sabbaticals	Allowing key executives to undertake independent work and study for periods of 3 to 12 months. The expected benefits are expanded horizons, life-goal reassessments, and renewed commitment to job performance.	Wages paid during sabbaticals are considered income.
Salary Allotment Plans	See chart on page 207.	Employee allotments come from after-tax income.
Salary Deferral SEP (SAR-SEP)	New plans may not be established after 1996. These plans were established by employers with 25 or fewer employees (at least 50% of employees must participate). Contributions to existing plans are made on a cash or deferred basis. In 2010 and 2011 the maximum annual employee elective deferral is $16,500, plus $5,500 catch-up if over age 50.	Employee elective deferrals are not included in income. Employer nonelective and matching contributions are also not included in the employee's income. Distributions are subject to the same rules as IRAs. Nondiscrimination rules apply. See discussion on page 525.
Sick Leave	Paid to employees while absent from work due to sickness or accident.	Amounts paid are included in income. A tax credit is available if the employee is permanently and totally disabled (page 387).
SIMPLE IRA	A simplified tax-favored retirement plan for small employers providing for elective contributions by employees. Within limits, employer can match employee contributions.	Both employee and employer contributions are not included in income until payments are received. See discussion on page 524.

Benefit	Description	Taxation of Employee
Simplified Employee Pension (SEP)	Providing for employer contributions to the employee's IRA on a nondiscriminatory basis and under a written allocation formula. See discussion on page 525.	Employee may exclude up to lesser of 25% of compensation or $49,000 in 2010 and 2011.
Social Security	Contributions to the Old-Age, Survivors, and Disability Insurance programs (FICA taxes). Refer to pages 311-312.	Employer contributions not included in income. However, retirement and disability payments may be partially or fully taxed (see page 526).
Split-Dollar Insurance	See chart on page 219.	Value of employer-provided coverage is taxable as additional compensation See chart on page 219 and discussion on page 400.
Split-Dollar Rollout	See discussion on page 528.	Generally included in income to extent of policy's interpolated terminal reserve, roughly equivalent to the cash values. Not taxed if converted to a loan under two-regime taxation of split-dollar (see page 528).
Stock Options –Incentive	Granted to key executives under a plan specifying the number of shares to be offered and the employees to be included. Certain requirements must be met, but stockholder-employees can be issued options (if more than 10% of stock is owned, additional limitations are imposed).	When option is exercised, no tax is paid, even on bargain element (i.e., the difference between the exercise price and the stock's value at time of exercise) if holding period and employment requirements are met. Sale of stock by the employee results in capital gain.
Stock Options –Nonqualified	May be granted to key executives, including stockholder-employees, with virtually no IRS imposed restrictions regarding time within which they must be exercised, exercise price, or period stock must be held before sale (also known as "nonstatutory stock options"). See discussion on page 464.	When option is granted, no tax is paid provided option does not have an ascertainable fair market value (closely held stock). When option is exercised, the spread between the option price and market value, at the time of exercise, is taxed as ordinary income (at same time company gets deduction).

Benefit	Description	Taxation of Employee
Stock Options –Phantom	Providing selected employees a form of deferred compensation by awarding "units of participation." Each unit is equivalent to a share of stock. As the stock appreciates, so do the participation units. On retirement, the employee receives appreciation that occurred in the comparable stock, plus previously credited dividend equivalents. Also known as phantom stock plans (see discussion on page 473).	Not included in income until payments actually received for participation units and dividend equivalents, at which time all payments would be taxed as ordinary income, not as capital gains. Employee must have no rights in units. Could be used by S corporation without creating a second class of stock.
Stock Ownership Plan (ESOP)	Established on a nondiscriminatory basis, covering a wide range of employees. Stock is currently contributed to a trust to be eventually distributed to retiring employees. Not practical unless corporate payroll is at least $500,000 and the owner has a real desire to eventually transfer ownership to employees.	Not included in income at time the stock is contributed to trust. Taxable as ordinary income when the stock, or cash payment for stock, is transferred to the employee upon retirement. However, taxation may be deferred if the distribution is an "eligible rollover distribution." See discussion on pages 396-397.
Stock Purchase Plan	Providing employees the opportunity to purchase limited amounts of stock at a discount from fair market value. Purchases cannot be made by employees owning 5% or more of the voting control or value of all classes of stock.	Purchase is made with after-tax dollars. Subsequent appreciation will qualify as capital gain on sale if certain holding period and employment requirements are met.
Supper Money	Paid to employees who voluntarily stay overtime, when furnished for the employer's convenience.	Not included in income.
Survivor Income Benefit Plan	See chart on page 231.	Pre-death "informal" funding of plan by employer is not included in employee's income. Benefits received by surviving family are taxable income.

Benefit	Description	Taxation of Employee
Thrift Plans	Permit employees to make contributions to a pension, profit sharing, or stock bonus plan. The employer's contributions are usually geared to the amount or rate of the employee's contributions. Both employer and employee contributions are limited by nondiscrimination requirements.	Employee contributions are made with after-tax dollars. Employer contributions are not included in income until withdrawn from the plan. All accruals are tax-deferred. See discussion on page 513.
Transportation	Provided to an employee in the form of transit passes or vanpooling in a "commuter highway vehicle."	May exclude from gross income a maximum of $230 per month in value of employer-provided qualified transportation in 2010 and 2011.
Travel Accident Life Insurance	Provided to employees and covering accidental death while traveling on company business. Other variations can provide 24-hour accident coverage on and off the job.	Not included in income.
Unemployment Compensation	Benefits paid to unemployed workers who were previously employed by contributors to the system.	Included in income (also subject to substantial downward adjustments depending upon other income).
Vacation Travel	Combined with a trip made "primarily" for business purposes.	Business expenses including travel to and from business meetings are not taxable. Expenses associated with vacation would be taxable.
Vacations	Providing a paid rest from work and usually based upon years of service.	Wages paid during vacations are included in income.
Worker's Compensation	Providing both medical expense and direct payments to workers injured on the job, as well as survivors of workers who are killed on the job.	Premiums paid by employer and benefits received are not included in income.

EMPLOYEE BENEFIT STATISTICS

Total Employee Benefits

As Percent of Payroll	29.2%
As Dollars per Payroll Hour	$7.28
As Dollars per Year per Employee	$14,919

	Benefit as Percent of Payroll		Annual Dollars per Employee
Legally Required			
Federally required payroll taxes	6.6		$2,883
Unemployment payments	0.4		177
Compensation payments	0.7		292
Other	0.0		22
		7.7%	$3,375
Payments for Time Not Worked		5.5	2,851
Medically Related Payments			
STD, sickness or accident insurance	0.2		140
LTD or wage continuation	0.2		94
Major medical	6.2		3,201
Dental	0.3		176
Vision	0.0		4
Retiree heath insurance	0.5		344
Life insurance premiums & death benefits	0.2		87
Prescription drug coverage	0.9		514
Administration costs	0.9		29
Other	0.0		5
		8.6	4,595
Retirement & Savings			
401(k) & similar	1.3		773
Defined benefit pension plan	2.1		1,492
Cash balance or other hybrid plan	0.0		20
Plan administration costs	0.1		84
Profit sharing	0.1		60
Stock bonus/ESOP	1.9		565
Other	0.9		557
		6.5	3,551
Miscellaneous Benefit Pay			
Severance pay	0.1		93
Dependent care	0.0		1
Employee tuition reimbursement	0.2		106
Employee relocation reimbursement	0.5		275
Other	0.1		73
		0.9	548

Source: U.S. Chamber of Commerce, *The 2008 Employee Benefits Study*, Table 1, page 10. Dollar expenditures amounting to less than 0.1 percent of payroll are shown as 0.0. Totals given are subject to rounding differences.

EMPLOYER/EMPLOYEE SPLIT-DOLLAR PLANS

In light of Notice 2002-8 & Final Regulations

Table A - Plans Entered Into *Before* January 28, 2002		
	Taxation of Cash Values	Economic Benefit
Plan Terminated Before January 1, 2004	**SH1:** Employee not taxed on cash value in excess of employer's interest (referred to as the rollout safe harbor). See Planning Point 1, bottom page 297.	n/a
Plan Terminated On Or After January 1, 2004	**SH2:** Employee not taxed on equity if plan converted to a loan from employer to employee for all periods beginning January 1, 2004 (pre-2004 employer outlays considered beginning loan balance, and subsequent employer premiums added to loan balance). After conversion to a loan there is no reportable economic benefit.	1. Use insurer's published term premium rates (Notice 2002-8 appears to indicate that these rates are grandfathered and can be used indefinitely, but this may not be true, see Section 2.02 of Notice 2002-59), or 2. Until further IRS guidance use Table 2001 rates as first set forth in Notice 2001-10, or 3. If specified by split-dollar agreement, may use P.S. 58 rates.
	SH3: Employee taxed on existing employee equity if plan **converted** to a loan on or after January 1, 2004. However, employee not taxed on equity accruing after conversion.	
	Upon termination employee subject to being taxed on all equity if plan **not previously converted** to a loan from employer to employee. Would have to rely on interpretation of prior split-dollar rulings (i.e., Revenue rulings, Technical Advice Memorandums, Private Letter Rulings, etc.). Under no inference language of Notice 2002-8 would ignore Notice 2001-10 And Notice 2002-8.	
Plan Not Terminated (and not materially modified)	**SH4:** Employee not taxed on equity provided the employee continues to report the receipt of the economic benefit and the employer retains some economic interest	
	SH5: Employee not currently taxed on equity merely because cash surrender value exceeds the amount payable to employer.	

SH1: This safe harbor (SH) provides that, as long as the employer is entitled to receive full repayment of premiums, if plans entered into before January 28, 2002, are terminated before January 1, 2004, (i.e., are rolled out) the IRS will not assert that there is a taxable transfer (under Section 83). Interestingly, this appears to apply to endorsement plans as well as collateral assignment plans.

SH2-SH5: See bottom of page 297.

EMPLOYER/EMPLOYEE SPLIT-DOLLAR PLANS (cont'd)

Table B - Plans Entered Into *After* January 28, 2002 & *Before* September 18, 2003		
	Taxation of Cash Values	Economic Benefit
Plan **Terminated**	**SH3:** If plan **converted** to a loan emplyee *not taxed* on equity accruing after conversion. However, any existing emplyee equity at time of conversion would be taxable. See Planning Point 2, bottom page 298.	n/a
Plan **Terminated**	Employee subject to being taxed on all equity if plan **not coverted** to a loan. Would have to rely on interpretation of prior split-dollar rulings (i.e., Revenue Rulings, Technical Advice Memorandums, Private Letter Rulings, etc.). According to the no inference of Notice 2002-8 would not consider Notices 2001-10 and 2002-8.	1. Use insurer's published premiums rates, but for periods after December 31, 2003, insurer must actually make known and sell term insurance at these rates language (Notice 2002-8 appears to indicate that these rates are grandfathered and can be used indefinitely, but this may not be true, see Section 2.02 of Notice 2002-59), or
Plan **Not Terminated** (and not materially modified)	**SH4:** Employee not taxed on equity *provided* the employee continues to report the receipt of the economic benefit and the employer retains some economic interest.	2. Until further IRS guidance use Table 2001 rates as first set forth in Notice 2001-10.
Plan **Not Terminated** (and not materially modified)	**SH5:** Employee not currently taxed on equity merely because cash surrender value exceeds the amount payable to employer.	

SH2: This safe harbor provides that, as long as the employer is entitled to receive full repayment of premiums, if the plan is converted to loan treatment the IRS will not assert that there is a taxable transfer (under Section 83) upon eventual termination.

SH3: This safe harbor allows taxation under the Loan Regime (see Table C, page 298).

SH4: This safe harbor provides that, as long as the plan is maintained by having the employee continue to report the economic benefit, the IRS will not challenge the arrangement as terminated (with resulting transfer of equity to employee).

SH5: This safe harbor provides that there will be no deemed transfer under Section 83 of a portion of the cash surrender value that exceeds the amount payable to the employer

Planning Point 1: SH1 is probably the safe harbor of choice for plans with large amounts of employee equity. It appears to allow the unwinding of virtually any split-dollar plan without having to recognize income on the employee's interest in cash values as property transferred in connection with the performance of services. However, under some circumstances the split-dollar agreement might be maintained in order to continue using the lower insurer's published term premium rates (assuming they continue to be available). This decision will also depend upon the age of insured and the need for ongoing insurance coverage

EMPLOYER/EMPLOYEE SPLIT-DOLLAR PLANS (cont'd)

Table C - Plans Entered Into *After* September 17, 2003		
Plan Structured As	Taxation of Cash Values	Economic Benefit
Economic Benefit Regime: *emplyer* owns policy (endorsement method).	Employee *taxed* on annual increase in cash values (not just at rollout). This is likely to present a difficult problem of valuation, particularly, regarding variable life. Employee *taxed* on equity upon transfer of policy from employer to employee (i.e., when there is a "rollout"). But "taxable equity" is reduced by amounts paid at time of transer and amounts of equity previously included in employee's income.	According to final regulations the IRS will issue new "life insurance premium factors." Until then, use Table 2001 rates as first set forth in Notice 2001-10. Under proposed regulations the economic benefit: 1. Reported or paid by employee does not give the employee any *basis* in the policy, and 2. Paid by employee is considered *income to employer* (i.e., under the theory that employee is "renting" death benefit from employer).
Loan Regime: *employee* owns policy (collateral assignment method).	Employee *not taxed* on equity (i.e., employee owns the policy, is obligated to repay the employer, and the policy is subject to the employer's security interest for loans made to employee). Note: if employee owns policy, but employer is entitled to all cash values (a non-equity collateral assignment arrangement), the IRS will treat it as employer-owned under the economic benefit regime. See Planning Point 3.	n/a (all employer outlays are treated as loans to employee)

Planning Point 2: In order to secure potentially lower economic benefit reporting (as opposed to assumed higher cost of loan interest) a plan might be established under SH4 and SH5 as collateral assignment split-dollar until such time as the employee is about to acquire an equity interest (employee equity = cash value - employer interest - employee basis, if any). At that time the plan could be switched to SH3 (referred to as "switch dollar"). This would avoid taxation of any employee interest at time of switch (i.e., none exists) and avoid taxation of future employee equity interests (unless cash value withdrawals exceed employee's basis). Also, might consider switching to SH3 if cost of economic benefit exceeds cost of nondeductible loan interest (i.e., the crossover point).

Planning Point 3: This could be useful in *controlling stockholder* situations when using a limited collateral assignment to keep corporate employer from having prohibited incidents of ownership (see Controlling Stockholder, page 373).

SPLIT-DOLLAR – APPLICABLE CODE SECTIONS

Code Section	Relates To	Used In Reference To
61	Taxation of **all income** rom whatever source derived (a catch-allprovision).	Valuation of life insurance protection under the economic benefit principle (annual economic benefit measured by Table 2001 rates).
83	Taxation of **property transferred** in connection with the performance of services (this approach not taken in final regulations).	Transfer of an existing policy from the employer to the employee, to include partial transfers of interests in policy cash values. Concept of "deemed transfer."
1271-1275	Taxation of **original issue discount** loans.	These sections would only be applicable if: 1. Loan is subject to Section 7872 because no or an inadequate rate of interest is charged, <u>and</u> 2. Loan is considered a *term* loan under Section 7872, therefore deemed payment to employer treated as original issue discount (not applicable to employment-related *demand* loans payable upon termination of employment).
7872	Taxation of **below market interest** loans.	Imputing interest when loans charge no interest, or if interest is charged at less than the appropriate applicable federal rate (AFR). But interest-bearing loans at the appropriate AFR are not taxed under the imputed interest rules of Section 7872.

COMPARISON

SPLIT-DOLLAR & EXECUTIVE EQUITY

	Split-Dollar	**Executive Equity**
Premium Payments	Allocated between employer and employee under various arrangements.	Employer pays full premium and employee includes amount of premium in income.
Death Benefits	Usually divided between employer and employee, with employer death benefit equal to outstanding loans to employee (loan regime) or greater of cumulative premium payments or cash values (economic benefit regime).	All paid to employee's beneficiary.
Cash Values	*Loan regime:* cash values are owned by employee but assigned to employer to secure repayment of loans. *Economic benefit regime:* generally cash values are owned by employer (employee interest in cash values is immediately included in income).	All owned by employee.
Contract Ownership	*Loan regime:* contact is owned by employee with limited assignment to employer. *Economic benefit regime:* contract is owned by employer.	Owned by employee.

Note: See charts on pages 211 and 219. A private split-dollar arrangement between individuals or between an individual and a trust is described in the chart on page 63.

COMPARISON

SPLIT-DOLLAR & DEFERRED COMPENSATION

	Split-Dollar	**Deferred Compensation**
Premium Payments	Allocated between employer and employee under various arrangements.	All premiums are paid by employer and are not deductible (see footnote 7, page 237).
Death Benefits	Paid income tax-free and usually divided between employer and employee, with employer death benefit equal to outstanding loans to employee (loan regime) or greater of cumulative premium payments or cash values (economic benefit regime).	Usually paid tax-free to employer (provided strict notice and consent requirements are met, see pages 367-369). However, if employer is a C corporation, then could be subject to the corporate alternative minimum tax (see pages 374-376). Proceeds can be used to make survivor income payments to employee's beneficiaries or offset costs of plan.
Cash Values	*Loan regime:* cash values are owned by employee but assigned to employer to secure repayment of loans. *Economic benefit regime:* generally cash values are owned by employer (employee interest in cash values is immediately included in income).	Owned by employer and considered part of the employer's general assets, which are subject to the claims of the employer's creditors. Cash values are often used to informally fund retirement payments to employee.
Contract Ownership	*Loan regime:* contact is owned by employee with limited assignment to employer. *Economic benefit regime:* contract is owned by employer.	Entirely owned by employer. Employee has no interest in the contract.

Note: See charts on pages 219 and 235. A private split-dollar arrangement between individuals or between an individual and a trust is described in the chart on page 63.

ANNUITY MATRIX

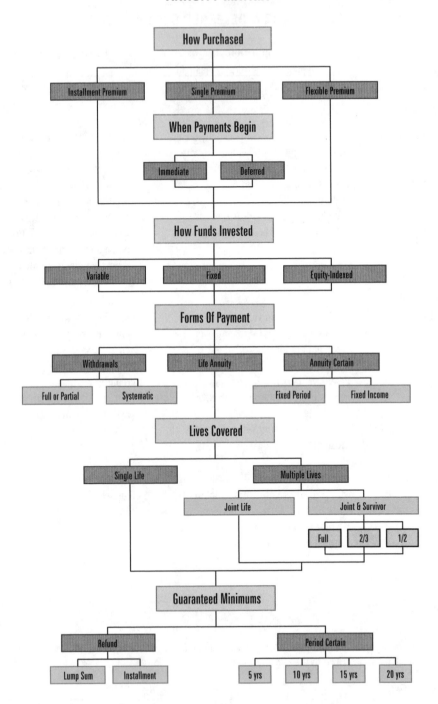

QUALIFIED PLANS CHECKLIST

Element	Limitation
Maximum limits	**Defined Benefit Plan:** Benefits are limited to the lesser of 100% of pay, or $195,000 (as indexed for 2010 and 2011).
	Defined Contribution Plan: The annual additions limit is the lesser of 100% of salary, or $49,000 (as indexed for 2010 and 2011). In a profit sharing plan the total annual employerdeduction is 25% of total compensation of plan participants.
	401(k) Plans (traditional or safe harbor): During calendar years 2010 and 2011, the allowable employee deferral is $16,500 (during 2010 and 2011 participants who are age 50 or over may be permitted to make additional catch-up contributions of $5,500). SIMPLE 401(k) plans are limited in 2010 and 2011 to $11,500 elective deferrals and $2,500 catch-up.
Eligibility to participate	Exclusions are permitted for age and years of service (maximum of age 21 and 1 year service).
Integration with Social Security	A plan integrated with Social Security will often permit significantly higher benefits for higher paid employees within certain limits.
	Defined *contribution* plans may provide additional contributions of up to 5.7% of pay in excess of current Social Security wage base ($106,800 in 2010 and 2011).
	Defined *benefit* plans may provide additional monthly benefits of up to the lesser of .75% of earnings, or the base benefit percentage for the plan year.
	In either type of plan the percentage of total contributions/benefits for those above the "integration level" may not be more than two times the percentage of contributions/benefits below that level. In addition, the disparity between the two percentages must be uniform with respect to all participants. If additional requirements are met, the "integration level" may be lower than the Social Security wage base.
Employee vesting	Employer contributions need not become immediately and irrevocably vested, but may be contingent upon continued employment. Thus, costs to the employer may be reduced or benefits increased for employees who continue their employment.
	"Top-heavy" plans, and certain employer matching contributions, are subject to special rapid vesting rules.

Element	Limitation
Definition of a "top heavy" plan	A plan is top heavy if for "key employees" the present value of accrued benefits in a defined benefit plan or account balances in a defined contribution plan exceeds 60% of accrued benefits or account balances for all employees. Key employees include: (1) officers earning more than $160,000 (as indexed for 2010 and 2011), (2) any 5% owner of the employer, and (3) any 1% owner who earns more than $150,000 per year.
For top-heavy plan purposes, definition of the term "officer"	The term "officer" has a very special meaning. Officers of any employer include no more than either: (1) 50 employees; or, if *less*, (2) the greater of 3 employees or 10% of the employee group. In other words, the maximum number of employees considered officers is 10% of the employee group, up to 50.
Fund investment flexibility	Trustee may direct the investments into nearly any type of investment media. Strict fiduciary standards apply.
Distributions	Generally, distributions to a non-5%-owner must be started by April 1 of the year following the year the individual attains age 70½ or retires, whichever is later. Distributions to a 5%-owner cannot be delayed until retirement.
Premature distributions	Distributions prior to age 59½ will be subject to a 10% penalty tax (25% during first two years with SIMPLE IRA) unless distribution is due to death, disability, separation from service after age 55, or in the event of certain specified hardships. The penalty tax is also waived if the distribution is annuitized or to the extent needed to pay family medical expenses in excess of 7½% of adjusted gross income
Federal estate tax status of death benefits	Fully included in estate.
Availability of $5,000 IRA deduction (in 2011)	Not available if covered by pension, profit sharing or stock bonus plan, a 403(b) plan, a SIMPLE IRA, a SEP, or a government plan and adjusted gross income in 2011 exceeds: (1) $66,000 – individual return (2) $110,000 – joint return *Partially* deductible if covered by plan (listed above) and adjusted gross income ranges from: (1) $56,000-$66,000 – individual return. (2) $90,000-$110,000 – joint return *Fully* available if not covered by listed plan. See discussions on page 427 and page 506.

401(k) PLAN DESIGNS

Traditional 401(k) Plan

Maximum salary deferral is $16,500 in 2010 and 2011, plus $5,500 if age 50 or over.

Employer can sponsor other qualified retirement plans.

Employer contribution is not required. Overall maximum contribution per employee limited to 100% of compensation and not to exceed $49,000 in 2010 and 2011.

Graduated vesting allowed on employer contributions, but immediate vesting required on employee contributions.

Subject to both ADP/ACP tests and top heavy rules.

See also, chart on page 263.

Safe Harbor 401(k) Plan

Maximum salary deferral is $16,500 in 2010 and 2011, plus $5,500 if age 50 or over.

Employer can sponsor other qualified retirement plans.

Employer contribution is required, either:

- 100% on first 3% of employee deferral, plus 50% of next 2% of employee deferral (total of 4%), or
- 3% of compensation to all eligible employees (i.e., nonelective).

Immediate vesting is required.

Deemed to satisfy ADP/ACP tests and generally not subject to top heavy rules.

SIMPLE 401(k) Plan

Maximum salary deferral is $11,500 in 2010 and 2011, plus $2,500 if age 50 or over.

Employer cannot sponsor other qualified retirement plans. Employer limited to 100 or fewer eligible employees.

Employer contribution is required, either:

- 100% on up to 3% of employee's compensation, or
- 2% of compensation to all eligible employees (i.e., nonelective).

Immediate vesting is required.

Deemed to satisfy ADP/ACP tests and not subject to top heavy rules.

Automatic Enrollment Safe Harbor 401(k) Plan
(available for plan years beginning on or after January 1, 2008)

Default elective deferral must be at least 3% the 1st year, 4% the 2nd year, 5% the 3rd year, and 6% the 4th year (not to exceed 10% in any year).

Employer contribution is required, either:

- 100% on first 1% of compensation, plus 50% on next 5% (maximum of 3½%), or
- 3% of compensation to all eligible employees (i.e., nonelective).

Vesting after two years of service is allowed on employer contributions.

Deemed to satisfy ADP/ACP tests and not subject to top-heavy rules.

- **Roth 401(k) Feature**
  1. This is a separate account to which after-tax contributions may be designated.
  2. Distributions are potentially tax-free, if certain requirements are met.
  3. Subject to the same salary deferral limit as overall plan ($16,500 in 2010 and 2011, plus $5,500 if age 50 or over).
  4. See also, discussion on page 505.
- **Individual 401(k) Plan**
  1. Also referred to as a solo or mini-401(k) plan.
  2. This is a single-participant profit sharing plan with 401(k) features (the name itself has been created by the marketplace, it is not found in the Code).
  3. Requirements depend on which of the four designs above is used.
  4. See also, discussion on page 426.

EMPLOYEE BENEFIT LIMITS

Type of Limit	Year			
	2008	2009	2010	2011
Defined Benefit Section 415	185,000	195,000	195,000	195,000[1]
Defined Contribution Section 415	46,000 or 100% of salary	49,000 or 100% of salary	49,000 or 100% of salary	49,000[2] or 100% of salary
Elective Deferral for traditional and safe harbor 401(k) Plans, 403(b) Plans (TDAs), & SEPs	15,500	16,500	16,500	16,500[3]
Catch-Up for traditional and safe harbor 401(k) Plans (age 50 and over)[4]	5,000	5,500	5,500	5,500[3]
Catch-Up for 403(b) Plans (TDAs)[4]				
age 50 and over	5,000	5,500	5,500	5,500[3]
15 years of service	3,000	3,000	3,000	3,000
Elective Deferral Limit for Section 457	15,500	16,500	16,500	16,500[4]
Catch-Up for Section 457 Plans - age 50 and over[4]				
other than last 3 years before retirement[5]	5,000	5,500	5,500	5,500[3]
during last 3 years before retirement	15,500	16,500	16,500	16,500[3]
Elective Deferral Limit for SIMPLE IRAs and SIMPLE 401(k) Plans	10,500	11,500	11,500	11,500[4]
Catch-Up for SIMPLE IRAs and SIMPLE 401(k) Plans[4]	2,500	2,500	2,500	2,500[3]
Highly Compensated Employee Definitional Limit	105,000	110,000	110,000	110,000[1]
Maximum Compensation for Qualified Plans, SEPs, TSAs, & VEBAs	230,000	245,000	245,000	245,000[1]

[1] Subject to indexing in $5,000 increments.

[2] Subject to indexing in $1,000 increments.

[3] Subject to indexing in $500 increments.

[4] Catch-up amounts are in addition to the elective deferral limit.

[5] Use the participant's compensation, reduced by any other elective deferrals made that year, if less than the applicable dollar amount shown in the table.

THE IRA SPECTRUM

Type	Eligibility For Plan	Limits On Contributions[1]	Deductible	Tax Advantages	Withdrawals/Distributions
Roth (page 506)	Individual: In 2011 AGI[2] less than $122,000 (phase-out $107,000–$122,000) Married filing jointly: In 2011 AGI[2] less than $179,000 (phase-out $169,000–$179,000)	Individual: $5,000. Married filing jointly: $10,000. Contributions allowed after age 70½. Catch-up for individuals who have reached age 50 is $1,000.	No	Tax-free earnings. Early withdrawals of contributions tax-free and penalty-free.	Tax-free if after 5 years and: after age 59½, for first home, disability, or upon death. Distribution *not* required at age 70½.
Traditional - deductible (page 427)	Not active participant in employer-sponsored retirement plan, or Individual: In 2011 AGI[2] less than $66,000 (phase-out $56,000–$66,000). Married filing jointly: In 2011 AGI[2] less than $110,000 (phase-out $90,000–$110,000).	Individual: $5,000. Married filing jointly: $10,000. Contributions *not* allowed after age 70½. Catch-up for individuals who have reached age 50 is $1,000.	Yes	Tax-deferred earnings, but taxable upon withdrawal.	Penalty-free if after age 59½, for first home, higher education, or upon death. Distribution required at age 70½.
SIMPLE (page 524)	Self-employed or employed by company with 100 employees or less.	Employer: 3% matching or 2% non-elective. Employee: $11,500. Catch-up for individuals who have reached age 50 is $2,500.	Contributions are before taxes.	Tax-deferred earnings, but withdrawals taxable.	Distribution required at age 70½.
SEP (page 525)	Self-employed or employed by sponsoring employer.	Up to 25% of employees salary or $49,000 maximum. See also SEP-IRA, page 525.	Contributions are before taxes.	Tax-deferred earnings, but withdrawals taxable.	Distribution required at age 70½.

[1] Combined annual contributions to both Roth IRA and Traditional IRA are limited to $5,000 (effectively, $10,000 for a married couple).

[2] AGI stands for adjusted gross income.

WHICH IRA — ROTH OR TRADITIONAL?

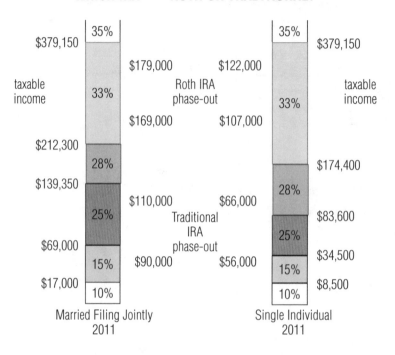

Married Filing Jointly
2011

Single Individual
2011

A Roth IRA offers the following potential advantages: (1) distributions are not required at age 70½; (2) contributions may continue after reaching age 70½; (3) phaseout limits are higher than those for deductible contributions to a Traditional IRA; and (4) tax-free retirement distributions will not push modified adjusted gross income above the threshold that triggers taxation of Social Security benefits (see page 526). This analysis focuses on after-tax accumulations and requires assumptions regarding tax rates prior to and after retirement (the above chart may help).

Assuming the same tax rate prior to and after retirement: (1) there is no difference between the after-tax distributions from a Roth IRA and a Traditional IRA if all funds can be deposited in a Traditional IRA, or other tax deductible fund (see Table A, page 309); (2) the Roth IRA offers the advantage of larger after-tax distributions if before-tax funds exceed the $5,000 limit that can be deposited in a Traditional IRA and the excess must be placed in a nondeductible side fund (see Table B, page 309). Further, the Roth IRA advantage increases if the side fund earnings are currently taxed.

Assuming a lower tax rate after retirement, the Traditional IRA generally provides larger after-tax distributions (i.e., 25 percent prior to retirement and 15 percent after retirement). For active participants, no comparison need be made assuming a tax rate higher than 25 percent since deductible contributions to a Traditional IRA are phased out before reaching the 28 percent tax rate (i.e., no deduction is allowed in 2011 for "married filing jointly" once modified adjusted gross income exceeds $110,000 and for a "single individual" once modified adjusted gross income exceeds $66,000). Note that marginal tax rates in the above chart vary according to taxable income, whereas IRA contributions are phased out according to modified adjusted gross income (see pages 304, 307, 427, 506 and 519). Taxable income is equal to adjusted gross income less deductions and personal exemptions.

Assuming a higher tax rate after retirement, the Roth IRA provides larger after-tax distributions (e.g., 25 percent prior to retirement and 28 percent after retirement).

WHICH IRA — ROTH OR TRADITIONAL? (continued)

Table A – This table assumes an 8 percent interest rate and 25 percent tax rate. The nondeductible Roth IRA deposit requires $1,333 before taxes (1,000/(1 - .25) = 1,333). This is the same as making a deductible deposit of $1,333 to a Traditional IRA. There is no Roth IRA advantage.

	Roth IRA				Traditional IRA		
Year	Deposit	Plus Interest	Value		Deposit	Plus Interest	Value
1	1,000	80	1,080		1,333	107	1,440
2	1,000	166	2,246		1,333	222	2,995
3	1,000	260	3,506		1,333	346	4,675
4	1,000	360	4,867		1,333	481	6,489
5	1,000	469	6,336		1,333	626	8,448
6	1,000	587	7,923		1,333	782	10,564
7	1,000	714	9,637		1,333	952	12,849
8	1,000	851	11,488		1,333	1,135	15,317
9	1,000	999	13,487		1,333	1,332	17,982
10	1,000	1,159	15,645		1,333	1,545	20,861
11	1,000	1,332	17,977		1,333	1,776	23,970
12	1,000	1,518	20,495		1,333	2,024	27,327
13	1,000	1,720	23,215		1,333	2,293	30,953
14	1,000	1,937	26,152		1,333	2,583	34,869
15	1,000	2,172	29,324		1,333	2,896	39,099
16	1,000	2,426	32,750		1,333	3,235	43,667
17	1,000	2,700	36,450		1,333	3,600	48,600
18	1,000	2,996	40,446		1,333	3,995	53,928
19	1,000	3,316	44,762		1,333	4,421	59,683
20	1,000	3,661	49,423		1,333	4,881	65,897
Less Taxes			0				16,474
Net Distribution			49,423				49,423

Table B – This table assumes an 8 percent interest rate and 25 percent tax rate. The nondeductible Roth IRA deposit requires $6,667 before taxes (5,000/(1 - .25) = 6,667). This is the same as making a deductible deposit of $5,000 to a Traditional IRA *plus* a nondeductible deposit of $1,250 to a Side Fund (5,000 + 1,250/(1 - .25) = 6,667). The Roth IRA advantage is $13,038 when compared to a currently taxed side fund (247,115 - 185,336 - 48,741 = 13,038) and $9,195 when compared to a tax deferred side fund (247,115 - 185,336 - 52,584 = 9,195).

	Roth IRA		Traditional IRA		Side Fund		
Year	Deposit	Value	Deposit	Value	Deposit	Currently Taxed	Tax Deferred
1	5,000	5,400	5,000	5,400	1,250	1,325	1,350
2	5,000	11,232	5,000	11,232	1,250	2,730	2,808
3	5,000	17,531	5,000	17,531	1,250	4,218	4,383
4	5,000	24,333	5,000	24,333	1,250	5,796	6,083
5	5,000	31,680	5,000	31,680	1,250	7,469	7,920
6	5,000	39,614	5,000	39,614	1,250	9,242	9,904
7	5,000	48,183	5,000	48,183	1,250	11,122	12,046
8	5,000	57,438	5,000	57,438	1,250	13,114	14,359
9	5,000	67,433	5,000	67,433	1,250	15,226	16,858
10	5,000	78,227	5,000	78,227	1,250	17,465	19,557
11	5,000	89,886	5,000	89,886	1,250	19,837	22,471
12	5,000	102,476	5,000	102,476	1,250	22,353	25,619
13	5,000	116,075	5,000	116,075	1,250	25,019	29,019
14	5,000	130,761	5,000	130,761	1,250	27,845	32,690
15	5,000	146,621	5,000	146,621	1,250	30,841	36,655
16	5,000	163,751	5,000	163,751	1,250	34,016	40,938
17	5,000	182,251	5,000	182,251	1,250	37,382	45,563
18	5,000	202,231	5,000	202,231	1,250	40,950	50,558
19	5,000	223,810	5,000	223,810	1,250	44,732	55,952
20	5,000	247,115	5,000	247,115	1,250	48,741	61,779
Less Taxes		0		61,779		0	9,195
Net Distribution		247,115		185,336		48,741	52,584

EDUCATIONAL TAX INCENTIVES

Contributions, Benefits & Offsets

Incentive	Limit	Tax Nature	Covers	AGI Phaseout[1]	Note
American Opportunity Credit (§25A)[2]	2,500	Credit against taxes (refundable in part).	First *four* years of post-secondary education.	S: 80,000-90,000 J: 160,000-180,000	ABCD
Lifetime Learning Credit (§25A)	2,000	Credit against taxes.	Unlimited number of years.	S: 51,000-61,000 J: 102,000-122,000	ABCD
Trade or Business Expense (§162)	None.	Below-line deduction (must itemize).	Employee expenses in maintaining or improving skills.	None.	n/a
Education Expense (§222)	4,000/ 2,000	Above the line deduction (need not itemize).	Qualified educational espenses paid through 2012.	S: 65,000-80,000 J: 130,000-160,000 (see page 363)	A
Employer Tuition Reimbursement (§127)	5,250	Not included in income.	Covers both undergraduate and graduate programs.	None.	B
Coverdell Education Savings Account (§530)	2,000	Contributions not deductible; but earnings are tax-free.	Qualified education expenses.[3]	S: 95,000-110,000 J: 190,000-220,000	C
Student Loans (§221)	2,500	Above-line deduction for interest (need not itemize).	Student loan interest.	S: 60,000-75,000 J: 120,000-150,000	n/a
Section 529 Plans	Varies.	Contributions not deductible; but distributions are tax-free.	Tuition, fees, special-needs services, room, board, books, supplies and equipment.	None.	D
Educational Savings Bonds (§135)	Varies.	Interest tax-free.	Qualified educational expenses.	S: 71,100-86,100 J: 106,650-136,650	n/a

A – American Opportunity Credit (AOTC) and Lifetime Learning Credits are not available if Education Expense (§222) deduction is taken.

B – American Opportunity and Lifetime Learning Credits are not available for the same expense excluded as an Employer Tuition Reimbursement.

C – Earnings on Coverdell Education Savings Account are not tax-free if used for same expenses as American Opportunity and Lifetime Learning Credits.

D – Section 529 qualifying expenses are reduced to the extent they are used in determining American Opportunity and Lifetime Learning Credits.

[1] S – single taxpayer; J – married filing joint return.

[2] American Opportunity Credit (AOTC) is a modification of the Hope Scholarship Credit through 2012.

[3] Includes elementary and secondary education (K-12) at private, public, or religious institutions, and post secondary education at accredited public, nonprofit, and proprietary institutions (college and graduate programs).

HISTORICAL INCREASES OF SOCIAL SECURITY TAXES

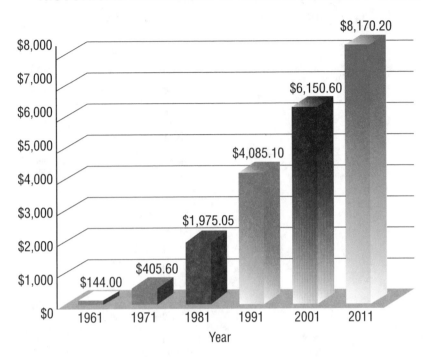

Social Security Tax. The Social Security Tax (FICA) is paid by both the employer and the employee. For example, in 2011 an employer who pays an employee wages of $106,800 per year will pay an additional $8,170.20 (Social Security Taxes equal to 7.65% of $106,800). The employee would normally pay an equal amount, but The 2010 Tax Relief Act reduced the employee OASDI rate by 2.0% to 4.2% for one year and the overall rate for the employee is 5.65% (4.2% OASDI plus 1.45% hospital insurance tax). In 2011 the employee pays $6,034.20 (Social Security Taxes equal to 5.65% of $106,800). The maximum amount of wages in 2011 on which the OASDI tax is paid by both the employer and the employee is $106,800. However, there is no maximum amount for the 1.45% hospital insurance tax; all wages are subject to that tax.

Federal Unemployment Tax. In addition to these Social Security Taxes, Unemployment Taxes may have to be paid. In 2011, the Federal Unemployment Tax (FUTA) is 6.2% of the first $7,000 of wages paid to each employee, or $434 (credit is given to employers for contributions to state unemployment funds).

Self-Employment Tax. An individual who is self-employed must pay a Self-Employment Tax on net earnings from self-employment when these earnings are $400 or more. The tax is equal to the combined employer-employee Social Security tax and would normally be 12.40%, but The 2010 Tax Relief Act reduced the OASDI tax rate by 2.0% to 10.2% for one year. In 2011 the rate of 10.2% is paid on the first $106,800 of self-employment income, or a maximum tax of $11,107.20, plus 2.90% hospital insurance tax on all self-employment income. Self-employed individuals may deduct one-half of their self-employment taxes for income tax purposes as a trade or business expense. This is the "Social Security Tax" for people who work for themselves.

SOCIAL SECURITY PAYROLL TAXES

Taxes in Future Years Subject to Change, Generally Upward!

Year	Maximum Tax Rate	Maximum Taxable Earnings	Tax
1974	5.85	13,200	772.20
1975	5.85	14,100	824.85
1976	5.85	15,300	895.05
1977	5.85	16,500	965.25
1978	6.05	17,700	1,070.85
1979	6.13	22,900	1,403.77
1980	6.13	25,900	1,587.67
1981	6.65	29,700	1,975.05
1982	6.7	32,400	2,170.80
1983	6.7	35,700	2,391.90
1984	7.0	37,800	2,532.60
1985	7.05	39,600	2,791.80
1986	7.15	42,000	3,003.00
1987	7.15	43,800	3,131.70
1988	7.51	45,000	3,379.50
1989	7.51	48,000	3,604.80
1990	7.65	51,300	3,924.45
1991	7.65	53,400	4,085.10
1992	7.65	55,500	4,245.75
1993	7.65	57,600	4,406.40
1994	7.65	60,600	4,635.90
1995	7.65	61,200	4,681.80
1996	7.65	62,700	4,796.55
1997	7.65	65,400	5,003.10
1998	7.65	68,400	5,232.60
1999	7.65	72,600	5,553.90
2000	7.65	76,200	5,829.30
2001	7.65	80,400	6,150.60
2002	7.65	84,900	6,494.85
2003	7.65	87,000	6,655.50
2004	7.65	87,900	6,724.35
2005	7.65	90,000	6,885.00
2006	7.65	94,200	7,206.30
2007	7.65	97,500	7,458.75
2008	7.65	102,000	7,803.00
2009	7.65	106,800	8,170.20
2010	7.65	106,800	8,170.20
2011	5.65	106,800	6,034.20

Note: The 2011 rate of 5.65% reflects a 2.0% reduction in the OASDI tax rate by The 2010 Tax Relief Act (i.e., 4.2% OASDI tax plus 1.45% hospital insurance tax). All earnings above $106,800 are subject to an additional 1.45% hospital insurance tax (see page 311). The first tax was imposed in 1937. The rate was 1.0% on maximum taxable earnings of $3,000, producing a tax of $30.00.

SOCIAL SECURITY RETIREMENT BENEFITS

When To Take

Social Security retirement benefits are based upon the worker's primary insurance amount (PIA). The PIA is the monthly amount that would be paid to a worker who receives benefits at normal retirement age. The normal retirement age differs, depending upon the worker's year of birth.

Year of birth	Normal Retirement Age	Year of birth	Normal Retirement Age
Before 1938	65 years	1955	66 years, 2 months
1939	65 years, 2 months	1956	66 years, 4 months
1940	65 years, 6 months	1957	66 years, 6 months
1941	65 years, 8 months	1958	66 years, 8 months
1942	65 years, 10 months	1959	66 years, 10 months
1943-1954	66 years	1960 and after	67 years

A worker can take retirement benefits as early as age 62, but the amount received is calculated by *reducing* the PIA by 5/9 of 1 percent per month for the first 36 months, plus 5/12 of 1 percent for any additional months. For example, a worker taking payments three years prior to normal retirement age will receive only 80 percent of his PIA (i.e., 100 - (5/9 x 36) = 80). In addition, a worker who no longer pays social security taxes fails to *increase* his PIA.

Many authorities agree that, for the average worker, it is best to wait until normal retirement age in order to take full (unreduced) retirement benefits. Despite this, Social Security records indicate that well over 50 percent of retiring workers take early (reduced) benefits. Clearly, if life expectancy is less than average, then taking an early benefit is indicated. However, if an individual is in good health, and does not require the money to provide for retirement, the following table may assist in making the decision:

Cross-Over Point Based Upon Life Expectancy*			
Discount Rate	When Reached	Discount Rate	When Reached
0%	13 years, 3 months	6%	20 years, 0 months
2%	14 years, 9 months	8%	26 years, 7 months
4%	16 years, 9 months	10%	Never

This table compares the present values of the income streams produced by reduced (early) and unreduced (normal) retirement benefits. For example, using a discount rate of 4%, for the first 16 years and 9 months the present value of reduced retirement payments are greater than the present value of unreduced retirement payments (assuming retirement three years prior to normal retirement age, and 2.4% annual increases in retirement benefits); when the cross-over point is reached at 16 years and 9 months, the present value of the unreduced benefits will finally exceed the present value of the reduced benefits. Absent other considerations, a person who views the time value of money at 4% should consider early retirement if he expects to live *less than* 16 years and 9 months. On the other hand, if he expects to live *at least* 16 years and 9 months, he should wait until normal retirement. See also, Compound Interest & Present Value of Money, page 561.

* Assumes payments begin 36 months prior to normal retirement age, and Social Security benefit increases of 2.4% per year (the average increase during the 10-year period 2002-2011).

CONSUMER PRICE INDEX

(annual average)

Year	Yearly Increase	Cumulative Increase	Purchasing Power of the Dollar
1981	10.3	90.9	1.10
1982	6.2	96.5	1.04
1983	3.2	99.6	1.00
1984	4.3	103.9	.96
1985	3.6	107.6	.93
1986	1.9	109.6	.91
1987	3.6	113.6	.88
1988	4.1	118.3	.85
1989	4.8	124.0	.81
1990	5.4	130.7	.77
1991	4.2	136.2	.73
1992	3.0	140.3	.71
1993	3.0	144.5	.69
1994	2.6	148.2	.68
1995	2.8	152.4	.66
1996	3.0	156.9	.64
1997	2.3	160.5	.62
1998	1.6	163.0	.61
1999	2.2	166.6	.60
2000	3.4	172.2	.58
2001	2.8	177.1	.56
2002	1.6	179.9	.56
2003	2.3	184.0	.54
2004	2.7	188.9	.53
2005	3.4	195.3	.51
2006	3.2	201.6	.50
2007	2.8	207.3	.48
2008	3.8	215.3	.46
2009	-0.4	214.5	.47
2010	0.1	214.7	.47

Source: Bureau of Labor Statistics, Washington, D.C., and *Statistical Abstract of the United States*, 2010, Table 708, Purchasing Power of the Dollar, and Table 709, Consumer Price Indexes (CPI-U) by Major Groups. The Consumer Price Index is a measure of the average change in prices over time in a fixed "market basket" of goods and services purchased by urban consumers. The items include food, clothing, shelter, fuels, transportation, fares, charges for doctors' and dental services, drugs, etc. purchased for day-to-living. The reference base year is the 1982-84 period (i.e., 1982-84 = 100). The figures projected for 2010 are based on January through September 2010 monthly numbers.

PROJECTED EARNINGS

5% Annual Increase In Earnings

Present Earnings	Yearly Earnings In				Total Earning Over Next	
	5 Years	10 Years	15 Years	20 Years	10 Years	20 Years
10,000	12,763	16,289	20,789	26,533	125,779	330,660
12,000	15,315	19,547	24,947	31,840	150,935	396,791
14,000	17,868	22,805	29,105	37,146	176,090	462,923
16,000	20,421	26,062	33,263	42,453	201,246	529,055
18,000	22,973	29,320	37,421	47,759	226,402	595,187
20,000	25,526	32,578	41,579	53,066	251,558	661,319
25,000	31,907	40,722	51,973	66,332	314,447	826,649
30,000	38,288	48,867	62,368	79,599	377,337	991,979
35,000	44,670	57,011	72,762	92,865	440,226	1,157,308
40,000	51,051	65,156	83,157	106,132	503,116	1,322,638
45,000	57,433	73,300	93,552	119,398	566,005	1,487,968
50,000	63,814	81,445	103,946	132,665	628,895	1,653,298
60,000	76,577	97,734	124,736	159,198	754,674	1,983,957
70,000	89,340	114,023	145,525	185,731	880,452	2,314,617
80,000	102,103	130,312	166,314	212,264	1,006,231	2,645,276
90,000	114,865	146,601	187,104	238,797	1,132,010	2,975,936
100,000	127,628	162,889	207,893	265,330	1,257,789	3,306,595

8% Annual Increase In Earnings

Present Earnings	Yearly Earnings In				Total Earnings Over Next	
	5 Years	10 Years	15 Years	20 Years	10 Years	20 Years
10,000	14,693	21,589	31,722	46,610	144,866	457,620
12,000	17,632	25,907	38,066	55,931	173,839	549,144
14,000	20,571	30,225	44,410	65,253	202,812	640,667
16,000	23,509	34,543	50,755	74,575	231,785	732,191
18,000	26,448	38,861	57,099	83,897	260,758	823,715
20,000	29,387	43,178	63,443	93,219	289,731	915,239
25,000	36,733	53,973	79,304	116,524	362,164	1,144,049
30,000	44,080	64,768	95,165	139,829	434,597	1,372,859
35,000	51,426	75,562	111,026	163,133	507,030	1,601,669
40,000	58,773	86,357	126,887	186,438	579,462	1,830,479
45,000	66,120	97,152	142,748	209,743	651,895	2,059,288
50,000	73,466	107,946	158,608	233,048	724,328	2,288,098
60,000	88,160	129,535	190,330	279,657	869,194	2,745,718
70,000	102,853	151,125	222,052	326,267	1,014,059	3,203,337
80,000	117,546	172,714	253,774	372,877	1,158,925	3,660,957
90,000	132,240	194,303	285,495	419,486	1,303,791	4,118,577
100,000	146,933	215,892	317,217	466,096	1,448,656	4,576,196

Explanation of Tables. These tables assume that earnings increase at an annual rate of either 5 or 8 percent. For example, at annual increases of 5 percent an individual earning $50,000 today would be earning $81,445 in 10 Years, and total earnings over 10 Years would be $628,895. Projected earnings are also considered in the discussion of Human Life Value on page 14.

PENALTY OF WAITING

What It Takes To Save $100,000 By Age 65
Assuming 6% Interest

Current Age	Monthly Deposit	Total Deposits	Penalty of Waiting	
			1 Year	5 Years
21	40.42	21,342	877	4,707
22	43.06	22,219	905	4,867
23	45.88	23,124	945	5,043
24	48.92	24,069	973	5,208
25	52.17	25,042	1,007	5,387
26	55.66	26,049	1,037	5,567
27	59.40	27,086	1,081	5,758
28	63.44	28,167	1,110	5,944
29	67.77	29,277	1,152	6,137
30	72.45	30,429	1,187	6,334
31	77.49	31,616	1,228	6,535
32	82.94	32,844	1,267	6,740
33	88.83	34,111	1,303	6,950
34	95.20	35,414	1,349	7,168
35	102.12	36,763	1,388	7,382
36	109.63	38,151	1,433	7,604
37	117.81	39,584	1,477	7,830
38	126.73	41,061	1,521	8,059
39	136.48	42,582	1,563	8,289
40	147.15	44,145	1,610	8,528
41	158.87	45,755	1,659	8,769
42	171.79	47,414	1,706	9,010
43	186.06	49,120	1,751	9,257
44	201.87	50,871	1,802	9,507
45	219.47	52,673	1,851	9,760
46	239.14	54,524	1,900	10,017
47	261.22	56,424	1,953	10,277
48	286.16	58,377	2,001	10,536
49	314.47	60,378	2,055	10,800
50	346.85	62,433	2,108	11,067
51	384.17	64,541	2,160	11,338
52	427.57	66,701	2,212	11,610
53	478.56	68,913	2,265	11,878
54	539.23	71,178	2,322	12,160
55	612.50	73,500	2,379	12,433
56	702.58	75,879	2,432	12,697
57	815.74	78,311	2,480	12,971
58	961.80	80,791	2,547	13,268
59	1,157.47	83,338	2,595	13,542
60	1,432.21	85,933	2,643	14,067

Explanation of Table: This table shows the amount of money which must be deposited at the beginning of each month in order to accumulate $100,000 by age 65. Interest is credited at a 6 percent net annual rate and is compounded monthly (i.e., it is credited at the end of each month assuming a 6 percent annual after tax or untaxed growth). The Penalty Of Waiting 1 Year is calculated by subtracting total deposits at the current age from total deposits one year later (e.g., at age 45 the penalty of waiting one year is $54,524 - $52,673, or $1,851). The Penalty Of Waiting 5 Years is calculated by subtracting total deposits at the current age from total deposits five years later (e.g., at age 45 the penalty of waiting five years is $62,433 - $52,673, or $9,760).

EARLY SAVER vs. LATE SAVER
The Advantage Of Saving Early For Retirement
Assuming 8% Interest

Age	Early Saver	Late Saver	Age	Early Saver	Late Saver	Age	Early Saver	Late Saver
30	$2,000	0						
31	2,000	0						
32	2,000	0						
33	2,000	0						
34	2,000	0						
35	2,000	0						
36	2,000	0						
37	2,000	0						
38	2,000	0						
39	2,000	0						
40	0	$2,000	40	$2,000	0			
41	0	2,000	41	2,000	0			
42	0	2,000	42	2,000	0			
43	0	2,000	43	2,000	0			
44	0	2,000	44	2,000	0			
45	0	2,000	45	2,000	0			
46	0	2,000	46	2,000	0			
47	0	2,000	47	2,000	0			
48	0	2,000	48	0	$2,000			
49	0	2,000	49	0	2,000			
50	0	2,000	50	0	2,000	50	$2,000	0
51	0	2,000	51	0	2,000	51	2,000	0
52	0	2,000	52	0	2,000	52	2,000	0
53	0	2,000	53	0	2,000	53	2,000	0
54	0	2,000	54	0	2,000	54	2,000	0
55	0	2,000	55	0	2,000	55	2,000	0
56	0	2,000	56	0	2,000	56	0	$2,000
57	0	2,000	57	0	2,000	57	0	2,000
58	0	2,000	58	0	2,000	58	0	2,000
59	0	2,000	59	0	2,000	59	0	2,000
60	0	2,000	60	0	2,000	60	0	2,000
61	0	2,000	61	0	2,000	61	0	2,000
62	0	2,000	62	0	2,000	62	0	2,000
63	0	2,000	63	0	2,000	63	0	2,000
64	0	2,000	64	0	2,000	64	0	2,000
Total Invested	$20,000	$50,000		$16,000	$34,000		$12,000	$18,00
Amount at Age 65	$214,296	$157,909		$85,008	$72,900		$31,676	$26,973

Explanation of Table: This table demonstrates the advantage of beginning to save early for retirement. For example, a 40-year-old Early Saver who saves $2,000 per year for eight years, and earns 8 percent per year on his savings, will accumulate $85,008 by age 65. In comparison, a 48-year-old Late Saver who saves $2,000 per year until age 65, will accumulate only $72,900. Whereas the Late Saver has invested $18,000 more than the Early Saver, he has accumulated $12,108 less than the Early Saver ($34,000 - $16,000 = $18,000; $85,008 - $72,900 = $12,108). If savings had been placed in a tax deferred investment, then the Amount At Age 65 will likely be reduced by income taxes.

DOLLAR COST AVERAGING

Investing A Fixed Sum At Regular Intervals
means that

More Shares Are Bought At Low Prices Than High Prices
and

Average Cost Is Lower Than Average Share Price

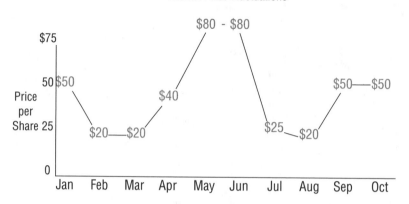

Market Price Fluctuations

INVESTING FIXED SUM - DOLLAR COST AVERAGING

											Totals
Cost	$100	$100	$100	$100	$100	$100	$100	$100	$100	$100	$1,000
Shares	2	5	5	2.5	1.25	1.25	4	5	2	2	30

Average Cost Per Share $33.33

↑
end up
with same
number of
shares
↓

BUYING FIXED NUMBER OF SHARES

Shares	3	3	3	3	3	3	3	3	3	3	30
Cost	$150	$60	$60	$120	$240	$240	$75	$60	$150	$150	$1,305

Average Cost Per Share $43.50

Note. Dollar cost averaging neither guarantees a profit nor protects against a loss.

HOW MONEY GROWS

How Much Monthly Savings Will Accumulate To

Save Per Month	Accumulated At 5%		
	5 Years	10 Years	20 Years
50	3,414	7,796	20,637
100	6,829	15,593	41,275
250	17,072	38,982	103,187
500	34,145	77,965	206,373
1,000	68,289	155,929	412,746

Save Per Month	Accumulated At 8%		
	5 Years	10 Years	20 Years
50	3,698	9,208	29,647
100	7,397	18,417	59,295
250	18,492	46,041	148,237
500	36,983	92,083	296,474
1,000	73,967	184,166	592,947

Save Per Month	Accumulated At 10%		
	5 Years	10 Years	20 Years
50	3,904	10,328	38,285
100	7,808	20,655	76,570
250	19,521	51,638	191,424
500	39,041	103,276	382,848
1,000	78,082	206,552	765,697

Explanation of Table. All accumulations assume monthly contributions are made on the first day of the month with interest compounded monthly. All results are rounded to the nearest whole dollar. Accumulated amounts assume the funds are invested at a rate of 5, 8, or 10 percent before taxes (i.e., during the accumulation phase appreciation is not subject to current income taxation). For example, if an individual invested $100 per month and earned 8 percent compounded monthly, at the end of 10 years the funds would accumulate to $18,417. Referring to the table How Money Goes on page 320, if this $18,417 were invested at 5 percent per year compounded monthly, it would provide $195 per month for 10 years or $121 per month for 20 years. Withdrawing interest only, without invading principal, would provide $77 per month. All withdrawal amounts are before taxes.

HOW MONEY GOES

How Much Can Be Withdrawn Monthly From A Given Accumulation

Amount Accumulated	At 5% Interest			At 8% Interest		
	10 years	20 Years	Forever	10 Years	20 Years	Forever
3,414	36	22	14	41	28	23
3,698	39	24	15	45	31	25
3,904	41	26	16	47	32	26
6,829	72	45	28	82	57	46
7,397	78	49	31	89	61	49
7,796	82	51	32	94	65	52
7,808	82	51	33	94	65	52
9,208	97	61	38	111	77	61
10,328	109	68	43	124	86	69
15,593	165	102	65	188	130	104
17,072	180	112	71	206	142	114
18,417	195	121	77	222	153	123
18,492	195	122	77	223	154	123
19,521	206	128	81	235	162	130
20,637	218	136	86	249	171	138
20,655	218	136	86	249	172	138
29,647	313	195	124	357	246	198
34,145	361	224	142	412	284	228
36,983	391	243	154	446	307	247
38,285	404	252	160	461	318	255
38,982	412	256	162	470	324	260
39,041	412	257	163	471	324	260
41,275	436	271	172	497	343	275
46,041	486	303	192	555	383	307
51,638	545	339	215	622	429	344
59,295	626	390	247	715	493	395
68,289	721	449	285	823	567	455
73,967	781	486	308	891	615	493
76,570	809	503	319	923	636	510
77,965	824	512	325	940	648	520
78,082	825	513	325	941	649	521
92,083	973	605	384	1,110	765	614
103,187	1,090	678	430	1,244	857	688
103,276	1,091	679	430	1,245	858	689
148,237	1,566	974	618	1,787	1,232	988
155,929	1,647	1,025	650	1,879	1,296	1,040
184,166	1,945	1,210	767	2,220	1,530	1,228
191,424	2,022	1,258	798	2,307	1,591	1,276
206,373	2,180	1,356	860	2,487	1,715	1,376
206,552	2,182	1,357	861	2,489	1,716	1,377
296,474	3,132	1,948	1,235	3,573	2,463	1,976
382,848	4,044	2,516	1,595	4,614	3,181	2,552
412,746	4,360	2,713	1,720	4,975	3,430	2,752
592,947	6,263	3,897	2,471	7,146	4,927	3,953
765,697	8,088	5,032	3,190	9,228	6,362	5,105

Explanation of Table. Withdrawals are assumed to be made at the beginning of each month with interest compounded monthly on the remaining funds invested at either 5 or 8 percent interest. Results are rounded to the nearest whole dollar. All calculations and amounts are before taxes. It is intended that this table be used with the table How Money Grows on page 319 (i.e., first obtain the amount accumulated from How Money Grows, then enter this table). See explanation at the bottom of page 319.

MEDICAL EXPENSE PROGRAMS

A confusing array of medical expense programs are available, with varying features, benefits and tax implications (similar to the many and varied educational tax incentives, see page 310). This matrix is intended to provide a general overview of their essential characteristics.

Health Reimbursement Arrangement HRA

This is an "arrangement"; it is not an account. Allows tax-free reimbursement to employees for qualified health care expenses, including the employee's purchase of health insurance (e.g., long-term care premiums). Plans are either insured or self-insured. Governed by IRC Section 105, it is funded and owned by the employer.

Formal guidance from the IRS allows a carryover of unused amounts to later years. Not available to the self-employed.

See Health Reimbursements Arrangements chart, page 247.

Flexible Spending Account FSA

A health FSA allows employees to make pre-tax contributions to an account to pay for health care expenses or their share of health insurance premiums (dependent care FSAs allow payment of qualifying child care expenses). Reimbursement for over-the-counter drugs is not allowed. Governed by IRC Section 125.

Can only be set up by employers (not available to the self-employed). Typically included under cafeteria plans, but may stand-alone. Any unused balance is forfeited at the end of the year (the infamous use-it-or-lose-it provision).

See Cafeteria Plans, page 352.

Health Savings Account HSA

The HSA is similar to the now outdated Medical Savings Account (MSA), but without the restrictions or limits on participation. Any "eligible individual" with a "high deductible health plan" can contribute. Generally allows reimbursement for "qualified medical expenses," to include long-term care insurance premiums but not over-the-counter drugs. May be included under cafeteria plans. Governed by new IRC Section 223. Contributions may be invested like IRAs (e.g., in stocks and bonds). Undistributed amounts may be carried forward. In 2011 deductible contributions cannot exceed $3,050 for an individual and $6,150 for a family. See Health Savings Accounts chart, page 251.

Consumer-Directed Health Plan

Also referred to as a "Consumer-Driven" Health Plan, this is a catch-all term that can include Health Reimbursement Arrangement (HRAs), Flexible Spending Accounts (FSAs), and Health Savings Accounts (HSAs). See page 371.

DISABILITY STATISTICS

Odds This Year For Different Risks Covered By Insurance
1 out of 5 that your auto will be damaged in an accident (National Safety Council).

1 out of 21 that you will have a disabling accident (National Safety Council).

1 out of 96 that you will have a fire (National Safety Council).

1 out of 114 that you will die (World Almanac).

Income Lost Through Disability Is
2 times as great as auto accident losses.

3 times as great as fire losses.

Risk of Disability Is Substantially Greater Than Risk Of Death (Male)
At age 30, long-term disability is 4.0 times more likely than death.

At age 40, long-term disability is 2.9 times more likely than death.

At age 50, long-term disability is 2.3 times more likely than death.

Risk Of Disability Within Groups Of People
The following chart indicates the odds of at least one long-term (90-day) disability occurring before age 65 to any one person out of one, two, or three persons.

Age of Each Person	Chances out of 1,000 of Disability Occurring Prior to Age 65		
	To Any One Person	To Any One Person out of Any Two People	To Any One Person out of Any Three People
30	467	716	849
35	451	699	835
40	430	675	815
45	401	641	785
50	360	590	738

From the chart we can conclude, for example, that 43 percent of all people age 40 will have a long-term disability prior to age 65.

Long-Term Disabilities

If a long-term (90-day) disability has lasted two years, it will probably continue longer – even for life.

Age When Disabled For 90 Days	Percentage Of People Still Disabled At End Of 2 Years And 90 Days	Percentage Of People Still Disabled At End Of 5 Years And 90 Days
25	63.5%	44.2%
35	69.7	52.6
45	73.6	58.0
55	77.6	59.6

Source: Figures based upon Commissioners Disability Table and Commissioners 1980 Standard Ordinary Mortality Table.

DISABILITY INCOME - TAX CONSIDERATIONS

	PREMIUM PAYMENTS Income Tax Effects As To		PROCEEDS Income Tax Effects As To	
	Employer	Insured	Employer	Insured
NONCONTRIBUTORY PLANS				
Employer				
pays premium	deductible IRC §162(a)		no effect	
Insured				
owns policy receives benefit		not taxable IRC §106(a)		taxable
Employer				
pays premium owns policy receives benefit	not deductible IRC §265		proceeds subject to corporate AMT (see pages 374-376) but deductible when paid to employee	
Insured				
receives benefit		not taxable IRC §106(a)		taxable when received from employer
CONTRIBUTORY PLAN				
Employer				
pays part of each premium	deductible IRC §162(a)		no effect	
Insured				
owns policy pays balance of premium receives benefit		not taxable on employer's contribution		taxable on amount attributable to employer contribution but not taxable on amount attributable to own contribution
NO PLAN NECESSARY				
Employer				
pays bonus to insured	deductible IRC §162(a)		no effect	
Insured				
pays premium owns policy receives benefit		taxable as salary IRC §61		not taxable IRC§104(a)(3)

Note: Insured is assumed to be an employee (not partner or sole proprietor).

FACTS ABOUT . . .

Facts About Long-Term Care

An individual who turns age 65 has a 43 percent chance of spending some time in a nursing home. Once in a nursing home, 21 percent will stay for at least five years.

Two-thirds of single people and one-third of married people exhaust their funds after just 13 weeks in a nursing home. Within two years 90 percent will bankrupt themselves.

From East to West, in 2010, nursing home costs for a semi-private room ranged from $304.00 per day ($110,960 per year) in Boston, Massachusetts, to $175.00 per day ($63,875 per year) in Chicago, Illinois, to $205.00 per day ($74,875 per year) in San Diego, California.

Facts About Retirement

In 2004 just under half of all families had a retirement account of any type. In 2006, far less than half (43.2 percent) of private sector workers had an employer-sponsored retirement plan, either a traditional pension or a retirement savings plan.

To maintain his or her standard of living, a worker earning $50,000 at retirement will need to replace 81 percent of that amount ($40,500). Social Security will provide 51 percent, while the worker's own savings and/or retirement plan must provide the remaining 30 percent ($15,000). In contrast, to maintain his or her standard of living a worker earning $150,000 at retirement will need to replace 84 percent of that amount ($126,000). Social Security will provide 23 percent, while the worker's own savings and/or retirement plan must provide the remaining 61 percent ($91,500).

According to the Social Security Administration, the ratio of "covered workers" (those paying into the system) to each beneficiary will drop from 8.6 in 1955 to 2.1 in 2031. This means that by 2040: (1) payroll taxes will have to be increased by over 20 percent, or; (2) cash benefits will have to be decreased by 22 to 25 percent, or; (3) some combination of (1) and (2).

Source of Facts About Long Term Care: Jeff Sadler, *The Long Term Care Handbook*, 3rd ed., Cincinnati: The National Underwriter Company, 2003; Jeff Sadler, *How To Sell Long-Term Care Insurance*, 3rd ed., Cincinnati: The National Underwriter Company, 2006; and *Genworth Financial 2010 Cost Of Care Survey*, Genworth Financial, Inc., April 2010, pages 74, 77 and 78.

Sources of Facts About Retirement: John M. Berry, *Many Workers' Finances Not Improving Under Bush*, News & Commentary, www.bloomberg.com, March 7, 2006; Michael Ettlinger, *Challenges Facing American Workers*, testimony before Subcommittee on Income Security and Financial Support, U.S. House of Representatives, September 11, 2008; *Aon Consulting's 2008 Replacement Ratio Study*, Aon Corporation news release, August 11, 2008.

TABLE OF CONTENTS

Motivational

"A man's success is measured by the amount he can borrow. When he dies, his measure of success is now the amount his widow is able to repay."

> Judge Michael A. Telesca, "Estate Planning: A View From The *Bench*," *National Underwriter*, July 10, 1976, page 17.

"Two weeks of solid work on his estate may be worth more to an executive than his financial gains of the past ten to fifteen years."

> Joseph D. Coughlan, "Executive Blindspot," *Price Waterhouse Review*, Autumn 1966, pages 38-39.

"The legal right of a taxpayer to decrease the amount of what otherwise would be his taxes, or altogether avoid them, by means which the law permits, cannot be doubted."

> Mr. Justice Sutherland in the United States Supreme Court case *of Gregory v. Helvering*, 293 U.S. 465 (1935), page 469.

"As a teacher, advisor and consultant to many closely held businesses, I am convinced that the privately held company is an endangered species. The threat lies not so much from competition, regulatory legislation, consumer movement or other outside forces. The real threat to the private business lies primarily within the business practices and policies of its owners."

> Léon A. Danco, *Beyond Survival – A Business Owner's Guide For Success*, Cleveland: The University Press, 1975, pages 4-5.

"The Robbie family likely must sell part of the Miami Dolphins to pay hefty estate taxes due this summer, a lawyer for two of Joe Robbie's children told a judge Thursday. . . . '[T]he biggest issue facing the Robbie children is not who gets what. . . . The fundamental problem here is taxes, and not enough money to pay them. . . . Selling part of the Dolphins is a likely probability unless we can find some money.' . . . [N]ow that both parents are dead, the Robbie children now must divide the estate and pay federal estate taxes. Estate taxes can be as high as 55 percent."

> David Satterfield, "Robbie Tax Bill May Force Sale Of Dolphin Stake," *The Miami Herald*, January 10, 1992, page 1C.

Motivational

"Kentucky could lose a multi-million-dollar collection of John Audubon's artwork if the state can't find a way to buy it from the famed naturalist's heirs. Audubon's four great-great-great-granddaughters face crushing inheritance taxes and plan to sell the rare paintings, which their family has leased to the state's Audubon Park Museum in Henderson, Ky., for decades. The possible dispersal of the treasures has auction houses drooling and state officials scrambling for money in the middle of a severe budget crunch. Losing the art would be devastating to the Henderson museum, which is finishing a $2.2 million renovation project aimed at protecting and preserving Audubon's works."

> Eric Gregory, "Tax Bill Imperils Art Collection," *The Atlanta Constitution,* February 10, 1993, page A3.

"If the debtor be insolvent to serve creditors, let his body be cut in pieces on the third market day. It may be cut into more or fewer pieces with impunity. Or, if his creditors consent to it, let him be sold to foreigners beyond the Tiber."

> Twelve Tables, Table III, 6 (ca. 450 B.C.) as quoted in "Illness And Injury As Contributors To Bankruptcy," published by *Health Affairs Journal* (www.healthaffairs.org). Many versions of this ancient code have been published, this appears to be one of the more graphic.

"When there is an income tax, the just man will pay more and the unjust less on the same amount of income." – Plato, circa 390 B.C.

"The art of taxation consists in so plucking the goose as to obtain the largest possible amount of feathers with the smallest possible amount of hissing." – Jean Baptiste Colbert, attributed, circa 1665.

"If Patrick Henry thought that taxation without representation was bad, he should see how bad it is with representation." – The Old Farmer's Almanac.

"I'm proud to be paying taxes in the United States. The only thing is – I could be just as proud for half the money." – Arthur Godfrey, 1951.

"In this world nothing is certain but death and taxes." – Benjamin Franklin, 1789.

> Obtained from: Al Cole, "Presidents and Tax Reform," *Modern Maturity,* April-May, 1993, page 11.

Motivational

"The taxpayer – that's someone who works for the federal government but doesn't have to take a civil service examination." – President Ronald Reagan.

"Don't tax you, don't tax me; Tax the fellow behind the tree." – Senator Russell B. Long.

"There's nothing wrong with the younger generation that becoming taxpayers won't cure." – Comedian Dan Bennett.

> Obtained from: www.tax.org/quotes/quotations.htm.

"The survival rate for family firms for a first to second-generation transfer runs about 30%. For firms that stay in the family from the second to third generation, that number drops to 4%. For the fourth-generation transfer that put the company in my hands, it's a fraction of 1%. . . . According to a recent Gallup Poll, one-third of all small-business owners will have to sell outright or liquidate a part of their firm to pay estate taxes. Of those who have to liquidate to pay the Internal Revenue Service, half expect they'll have to eliminate 30 or more jobs. Another 20% of those firms put the number of employees they'll have to let go as high as 100 or more."

> David Pankonin, "Will Uncle Sam Inherit the Family Business?," *The Wall Street Journal*, November 28, 1995, page A15.

"[Having just won $770,000 in a double or nothing payoff at a craps table of the Horseshoe Club in Las Vegas, the gambler was heard to say:] 'You know . . . this damned inflation was just eroding this money. I figured I might as well double it or lose it.' Having protected himself against the ravages of inflation, he drove off into the night."

> "Double or Nothing – $770,000 Rides on a Roll of the Dice," *The Washington Post*, September 26, 1980, page A1.

"'Would you tell me, please, which way I ought to go from here?' 'That depends a good deal on where you want to get to,' said the Cat. 'I don't much care where –' said Alice. 'Then it doesn't matter which way you go,' said the Cat."

> Lewis Carroll, Alice's Adventures in Wonderland, 1865.

Motivational

"Certainly, emphatically nothing should be left for the government to come in and plunder. . . . the idea that some clown in Washington will lay claim to the product of my life's energies, just because I wasn't smart or careful enough to divest myself of my property (to my family and chosen charities), fills me with horror. . . . I feel no debt of gratitude to the IRS for their gentle shepherding through life, and I choose passionately to leave nothing for them to pick over."

> Walter M. Bortz II, M.D., *Dare To Be 100*, New York: Simon & Schuster, 1996, pages 192 and 263.

"If you get up early, work late, and pay your taxes, you will get ahead – if you strike oil."

> J. Paul Getty, oil billionaire reputed to be the richest man in the world at the time of his death in 1976.

"As a Fed governor, Edward Gramlich helps set interest rates for the nation's financial markets. . . . How did Mr. Gramlich, also the Fed's point person on economic education for the public, get his kids to understand about taxes? He bought them ice cream, and then took a lick."

> Jon E. Hilsenrath, "Tricks Of the Trade – A Fed Chief's Finances," *The Wall Street Journal*, September 18, 2002, page D1.

"It's bad enough when a loved one dies, and it will get even worse if the person died without a will. Dying intestate leaves heirs with a bundle of legal, administrative and tax headaches. And even if you get an inheritance, there might be little you can do about crushing tax consequences. Beyond these practical problems, if husband and wife die together without wills, the decision of who will raise minor children is left to the court – not as you might have wished. These nightmares notwithstanding, more than half of American adults die without a will."

> Adrienne Sanders, "Willful Omission," *Forbes Magazine*, December 27, 1999.

"Bum advice and basic mistakes by banks, brokers and mutual funds are wrecking havoc with many people's individual retirement accounts. The result: Their heirs may end up loosing a bundle."

> Lynn Asinof, "Oops…How a Variety of Basic Foul-Ups Are Bedeviling the Beneficiaries of IRAs," *The Wall Street Journal*, March 29, 1999.

The "Estate Tax" Reality

"The estate tax has numerous strengths. It is by far the most progressive source of federal revenue. Despite the perception that advocates of repeal have created, the vast majority of estates are not subject to the estate tax. Only 2 percent of deaths result in any estate payments at all. About half of all estate taxes are paid by the wealthiest 1 out of every 1,000 estates. By 2009, couples with less than $7 million in wealth will pay nothing at all. Repeal would be a massive giveaway to the nation's wealthiest dynasties."

> William G. Gale, Senior Fellow, Economic Studies, The Brookings Institution, "Estate Tax: Tax Needs Reform, But Repeal Would be a Giveaway to the Wealthy," *Spartanburg Herald-Journal*, July 27, 2003.

"[EGTRRA 2001 is] the strangest, most reckless, most -- well -- hilarious estate tax law ever. Laughter is the only rational response."

> Jane Bryant Quinn, "The Estate Tax That Won't Stand Still," The Washington Post, June 24, 2001, page H2.

Imagine . . . .

"Imagine a story about tax policy created by horror writer Stephen King. A fictional Congress, divided between anti-tax ideology and fiscal responsibility, amends the inheritance tax on the very wealthy so that it disappears entirely one year and then returns at steeper rates the following year. Over the 'zero year,' death rates skyrocket in the nation's most affluent ZIP codes. Seemingly robust and healthy billionaires perish in mysterious accidents. Lexus wheels fall off from Bloomfield Hills to Scarsdale to Beverly Hills. Sailboats and yachts inexplicably crash in calm coastal and Caribbean waters. Tainted champagne wipes out clusters of prosperous alumni at class reunions from dozens of elite prep schools from Groton to Choate. Meanwhile, thousands of infirmed elders take their own lives in organized rituals called 'legacy sacrifices.' Pledging unlimited inheritances to their heirs, these multi-millionaires die with smiles on their faces knowing they've outfoxed Uncle Sam one last time."

> Bill Gates Sr. and Chuck Collins, "Death and life of the estate tax," Raleigh, *The News & Observer*, December 26, 2009, page 15A.

And It Came To Pass . . . .

"Nothing's certain except death and taxes – but a temporary lapse in the estate tax is causing a few wealthy Americans to try to bend those rules. Starting Jan. 1 the estate tax – which can erase nearly half of a wealthy person's estate – goes away for a year. . . . 'I have two clients on life support, and the families are struggling with whether to continue heroic measures for a few more days,' says Joshua Rubenstein, a lawyer with Katten Muchin Rosenman LLP in New York. . . .

Of course, plenty of taxpayers themselves are eager to live to see the new year. One wealthy, terminally ill real-estate entrepreneur has told his doctors he is determined to live until the law changes. 'Whenever he wakes up,' says his lawyer, 'He says: 'What day is it? Is it Jan. 1 yet?'"

Estate-tax experts didn't expect Congress to allow the tax to lapse, and are flabbergasted that it is actually happening. . . . Prof. Michael Graetz of Columbia University . . . calls the lapse 'congressional malpractice.'"

> Laura Saunders, "Rich Cling to Life to Beat Tax Man," *The Wall Street Journal*, December 30, 2009, page A1.

And Now Back To The Real World . . . Of Good Planning

"The death of Wellington Mara yesterday does not mean that the Mara family's 50 percent stake in the team will be sold to an outsider. . . . As recently as two years ago, John Mara said the family had taken the steps to structure the team's ownership so that federal estate taxes would not be so onerous that they would prompt the sale of the team. The goal was to avoid what happened in Miami, where estate taxes and feuding among the trustees of Joe Robbie's estate led to the sale of the Dolphins to H. Wayne Huizenga in 1994. . . . [According to Cheryl Hader, a tax specialist at the law firm of Drinker Biddle & Reath in Manhattan,] 'The basic technique is trusts . . . but I'd be surprised if there weren't a lot of life insurance to pay the taxes.'"

> Richard Sandomir, "Mara Family Plans to Follow Its Patriarch in Ownership," *The New York Times*, October 26, 2005.

. . . And No Planning

"When La Caravelle and Lutèce closed their doors for good last year, there was much lamentation over 'the end of an era' in New York dining. [After Saturday night's last-hurrah open house for the regulars, they will be joined by] The Beatrice Inn, a cozy, subterranean Italian place in the West Village. The Cardia family, which has owned the restaurant since 1955 . . . is selling the property. . . . Aldo Cardia is aware of his customers' unmoored feelings, but insists that selling the building now is the right thing to do for his family. His mother, Elsie, shrewdly bought lots of Greenwich Village real estate when it was affordable, in the 50's, 60's and 70's. But her death in January left her children in the position of owing a huge amount of estate tax."

> David Kamp, "Regulars Prepare for a Last Hurrah," *The New York Times*, October 26, 2005.

The Public Will Of A Private Man!

"In courtrooms, judges' chambers, Denver's high-society party circuit and other rarefied venues, his widow, his two grown sons and a rich supporting cast of lawyers and business heavyweights are fighting for control of the biggest estate in Colorado history. At stake in this ugly personal dispute is more than $1 billion generated by a man dead from cancer barely a year. It's happening because, in the end, Bob Magness, a beloved Colorado tycoon and philanthropist, didn't take care of business. The three antagonists in the fight are widow Sharon Magness on one side and brothers Gary and Kim Magness on the other . . . . It's a situation that folksy patriarch Bob Magness would have abhorred. . . . In an era of aggressive tax planning, Magness appeared to have had a momentous lapse in judgment. He had made surprisingly little use of charitable trusts, family partnerships and other tax-sheltered gifts to transfer wealth to heirs. Executors somberly informed Kim and Gary that most of their father's TCI stock would probably have to be sold to pay an estimated $400 million-to-$500 million tax bill. . . . People who knew him . . . said Magness, even with rapidly progressing cancer, might have put off detailed estate planning because he believed there would be a better time later."

> "Fighting Over A Fortune - Second Wife Vs. The Sons," *Scripps Howard News Service*, December 16, 1997.

In Just Two Short Months!

"Make no mistake, Forbes Inc. Chairman and chief shareholder Malcolm S. Forbes is rich. Experts value his company's flagship business magazine as high as $600 million, while its American Heritage magazine, suburban newspaper, real estate and art holdings almost certainly add $100 million or more to the Forbes family fortune. . . . On [his] death, Steve Forbes [his son] will inherit 51% voting control of the Forbes empire – along with a potential tax nightmare, because state and federal taxes on big estates are levied at approximately 55% . . . . According to Malcolm, much of his company's income is being used to purchase 'enormous sums of life insurance,' a device that can legally transfer millions of dollars in cash to his beneficiaries without an estate tax assessment."

> Michael Cieply, "The Wary Capitalist," *Los Angeles Times,* December 31, 1989, page D1.

"The change of command at Forbes Inc. with the death on Saturday of Malcolm S. Forbes comes at a time when the Forbes publishing empire . . . has been flourishing and bent on diversification. . . . Steve Forbes was entrusted with control to fulfill his father's desire that the company remain a family business. [Steve Forbes said that his father] 'saw what happened at other family businesses where one person didn't have control, and would lose control and sometimes ultimately lose the company . . .' He [also] said that while the transfer of assets would require payment of substantial inheritance taxes, considerable estate planning had been done using several possibilities. He added that he believed there was enough cash available to pay the taxes without having to sell any assets or causing any disruption in business."

> N. R. Kleinfield, "At Forbes, the Family Still Reigns," *The New York Times,* February 27, 1990, page D1.

"A line in the obituaries of Malcolm Forbes, the owner of Forbes Magazine who died last weekend, may have started many Americans thinking about their own family finances. Forbes' sons will inherit the family's business magazine, the article said, but also a potential tax liability of 55% of the firm's value. . . . [T]houghts of estate taxes . . . might occur these days to surprisingly large numbers [of people]. . . . What do they do about it? Do what Malcolm Forbes did, say financial planners. Buy life insurance."

> James Flanigan, "Malcolm Forbes' Lesson on Estate Taxes," *Los Angeles Times*, March 4, 1990, page D1.

The Very Short Will Of A Supreme Court Justice

"LAST WILL AND TESTAMENT OF WARREN E. BURGER.

I hereby make and declare the following to be my last will and testament. 1. My executors will first pay all claims against my estate; 2. The remainder of my estate will be distributed as follows: one-third to my daughter, Margaret Elizabeth Burger Rose and two-thirds to my son, Wade A. Burger; 3. I designate and appoint as executors of this will, Wade A. Burger and J. Michael Luttig.

IN WITNESS WHEREOF, I have hereunto set my hand to this my Last Will and Testament this 9th day of June, 1994."

> Warren E. Burger, served as 15th chief justice of the United States, 1969-1986.
>
> source: www.courttv.com/legaldocs/newsmakers/wills/

An Even Shorter Distribution Plan

"Whoever's in the house when I die gets it."

> Bill Cosby, *Fatherhood*, Garden City, New York: Doubleday, 1986, page 145.

How Far We Have Come!

In holding that a full time homemaker could recover damages for injuries, the court stated: "While the evidence does not show that plaintiff was engaged in any direct gainful employment for which she received a specific wage, it does show that she was capable of and did perform her family and household duties. Such services have value."

> From an opinion of the California Appelate Court in the case of: *Gotsch v. Market Street Railway*, 265 P. 268 (Cal. App. 1928).

Did They Really Say That?

"Profiles in noncourage: 'Everything is off the record,' a government official said at a recent conference on estate and gift taxes. 'So if I said anything quotable, it was a mistake or you heard it wrong.'"

> Tom Herman, "Tax Report," *The Wall Street Journal*, May 24, 2000, page 1.

"Every good citizen . . . should be willing to devote a brief time during some one day in the year, when necessary, to the making up of a listing of his income for taxes . . . to contribute to his government, not the scriptural tithe, but a small percentage of his net profits."

> Cordell Hull, addressing the U.S. House of Representatives, April 26, 1913 (appointed secretary of state by President Franklin D. Roosevelt and served in that position 1933-1944).

"We don't pay taxes. Only the little people pay taxes."

> Leona Helmsley, (her tax evasion convictions were affirmed by the Second Circuit Court of Appeals on July 30, 1991).

"An accountant in the Washington, D.C., area called the IRS about an estate-tax issue. He says the IRS representative asked him: 'Are you the decedent?'. . ."

> Tom Herman, "Tax Report," *The Wall Street Journal*, March 6, 1996, page A1.

IRS Agent – "We've got what it takes to take what you've got."

IRS Auditor – "The trick is to stop thinking of it as 'your' money."

> Obtained from:
>
> http://207.218.245.80/~taxform/index.html?05quotes.

Did It Really Happen?

"A tax office official in Finland who died at his desk was not found by his colleagues for two days. The man in his 60s died last Tuesday while checking tax returns, but no-one realized he was dead until Thursday. . . . According to [a Finnish newspaper] co-workers had assumed the dead man . . . was silently poring over returns."

> "Finns miss death in tax office," BBC News (International Edition) – Monday, 19 January 2004, 17:00 GMT.

Life Insurance

"Will Rogers once said, 'If a man doesn't believe in life insurance, let him die once without it. That will teach him a lesson.' Such a lesson could be expensive to the survivors."

> J. W. Looney, *Estate Planning For Business Owners*, Reston: Reston Publishing Company, 1979, page 100.

"[I]nsurance, which appears to be just another form of gambling, has actually exactly the opposite effects. For the same reasons that gambling is bad, insurance is economically advantageous. Whereas gambling creates risk, insurance helps to lessen and spread risks."

> Paul A. Samuelson, Economics, New York: McGraw-Hill Book Company, 1980, pages 424-25.

"Life insurance is not very sophisticated. You do not talk about making a killing on your life insurance, or selling your policy short. Life insurance is a necessity and a responsibility, not a conversation piece. Perhaps you can make more money in the market. Some people do, some people do not. But, we are not talking about your making money in the stock market – we are concerned with a family spending money in the supermarket. Money is not an investment. It is the measure of an investment. Life insurance is not an investment. It is the measure of a person."

> John J. O'Connell, LL.M., J.D., CLU, "More Thoughts On Life And Life Insurance," *Techniques*, January 1979, Hartford: Aetna Life Insurance Company.

"As noted attorney Jonathan Blattmachr has said, 'Life insurance is the only asset that is certain to work in a time of great uncertainty.'"

> Stephan R. Leimberg and Albert E. Gibbons, "Dealing With EGTRRA's Impact on an Insurance Professional's Practice," *Estate Planning*, August 2001, page 404.

"How much life insurance do you need? . . . James Hunt, a director of the National Insurance Consumer Organization, or NICO, has a rule of thumb. A four-person family, with one wage earner and two young children, should buy five times the wage earner's annual income. If you're making $40,000 a year, for example, you need $200,000 worth of coverage. This assumes the wage earner also has coverage through his or her company, equal to two or three year's salary, Hunt says. If not, you should buy a policy equal to seven to eight times income."

> Jane Bryant Quinn, "Insurance Rule Of Thumb Signals How Much To Buy," *The Richmond Times-Dispatch*, April 13, 1992, page 16.

Life Insurance

"The most common purchase of life insurance is to cushion a family financially if the primary wage earner dies prematurely. In short, life insurance is a security blanket — something to replace your paycheck and to wrap around your dependents when you die. The funds from an insurance death benefit payable to a specified beneficiary are immediately and automatically available, while other funds may be held up in probate. . . . Life insurance benefits can be tailored to virtually any of your requirements or those of your beneficiaries."

Leonard Sloane, The New York Times Book Of Personal Finance, New York: Times Books, 1985, page 96.

"In a capitalistic society, where credit is the life blood of that system, debt signals a need for life insurance."

Judge Michael A. Telesca, "Estate Planning: A View From The Bench," *National Underwriter*, July 10, 1976, page 17.

"There is probably no type of property more appealing as the subject of a gift than life insurance. The gift, made currently, involves only perhaps a premium or two or, perhaps, some small amount of cash. But the value removed from the insured's estate is the full face proceeds. And, of course, the fundamental combination of maximum death tax reduction with minimum current gift cost is almost irresistible."

Lawrence G. Knecht, "The Human Equation In Estate Planning," *Trusts & Estates*, December 1975, page 855.

"It is possible to pass along millions of dollars' worth of insurance to your children or other heirs tax-free . . . . The device for doing so is the irrevocable life insurance trust. . . . 'Anyone potentially subject to federal estate taxes is a good candidate for a life-insurance trust. It's probably one of the last, best estate-planning opportunities available.'"

"Irrevocable Life Insurance Trust Passes On Money To Heirs Tax-Free," *The Atlanta Constitution*, March 20, 1989, page 4C.

Life Insurance

"Advisers should suggest to clients planning opportunities that have the greatest likelihood of success in each of the possible scenarios: increasing estate tax exemptions, no estate tax and carryover basis."

"Life insurance is the only asset that provides absolute certainty in all three cases. If a client purchased a policy for estate tax liquidity, the policy can remain in effect until the estate tax disappears. If the estate tax remains, the client will have the policy for liquidity purposes. If the estate tax does disappear, the client will have the only leveraged asset that is income tax deferred or tax free and that receives a full basis step-up at the insured's death. Given the options, life insurance provides a "win-win" for clients and the advisers who recommend it."

> Robert A. Esperti, J.D. et. al., "Post-EGTRRA Life Insurance Planning," *The Tax Adviser*, August, 2002.

"Most people know the proceeds of their life insurance policy, in most cases, pass to their beneficiaries free from income tax. However, few realize that the same policy adds to their taxable estate for estate tax purposes. . . . It's not uncommon for people to own life insurance policies with death benefits exceeding $500,000 . . . Thus, even if you think you have a modest estate, your life insurance may put your estate into a taxable level . . . . The solution to these problems is not to get rid of the life insurance, but rather to create an irrevocable life insurance trust (ILIT). An ILIT takes advantage of certain tax laws that allow your existing life insurance policy to be removed from your taxable estate or treat a new policy as never having been a part of your taxable estate. . . . ILITs are a well-tested tool in estate planning, and are easily implemented and maintained. The tax savings, control of the proceeds and leveraging of annual gifting all make ILITs an important part of any estate plan."

> Brandon Culter, "Life Insurance Increases the Value of Your Estate," *Denver Business* Journal, September 5, 2008.

"The cash value of a life insurance contract may be exempt under Florida law. Cash value life insurance is exempt . . . to the extent of life insurance owned by the debtor insuring his own life. The exemption does not hinge on whether to debtor, his estate, or some other person is the beneficiary of the insurance policy."

> Posted by Jonathan Alper, "Cash Value Life Insurance Owned Jointly With Non-Filing Spouse," *Florida Bankruptcy Law Blog*, August 29, 2008. www.bankruptcyorlando. com/2008/08/cash-value-life.html.

Annuity

"A dozen of the lawyers contesting the estate of the ice cream magnate Thomas Carvel have gathered before Judge Albert J. Emanuelli . . . . 'I came here in 1991, and this case is still being litigated,' the judge told the assembled attorneys. 'Seven years of litigation. I think it's tragic.' . . . Carvel died childless at the age of 84 in October 1990. He left behind most of the $80 million proceeds from selling his namesake ice cream chain . . . . [Today] the Thomas and Agnes Carvel Foundation has but $12 million, and has managed to distribute less than $6 million . . . . The widow isn't doing particularly well, either. Although she was supposed to receive income from her husband's fortune, she hasn't seen a penny from this part of the estate . . . . Carvel's probate case involves six entities that we know of . . . . He didn't need to be so complicated. His needs were simple: Set aside enough for his widow to live comfortably and leave the rest to charity. He could have accomplished all this very cleanly by purchasing an annuity for Agnes from an insurance company and leaving the whole estate to charity."

> Thomas Easton, "Meltdown Of An Ice Cream Fortune," *Forbes Magazine,* June 15, 1998.

Long-Term Care Insurance

"Given a choice, most people prefer to receive care in their own homes – another option seldom covered by Medicaid. Purchasing long-term care insurance with the right benefits means you can decide where you will receive care while protecting your life savings."

> Mary Beth Franklin, "Insuring Against Life's Frailties," *Kiplinger's Personal Finance Magazine,* July, 1999.

Business Valuation

"[Fair market] value is a fact, the determination of which is, at least, generally difficult. The result is rarely satisfactory."

> United States Board of Tax Appeals in the case of *Estate of Leonard B. McKitterick,* 42 B.T.A. 130, page 136.

"The valuation of stock, like many questions of fact, cannot be completely rationalized."

> United States Tax Court in the case of *Estate of Paul M. Vandenhoeck,* 4 T.C. 125, page 138.

Business Valuation

"The determination of the fair market value of stock in a closely held corporation absent previous sales of the stock at arm's length is an arduous task. It is an uncertain art at best . . . ."

> Judge Fay in the United States Tax Court case of *Dale F. Miller*, 77,039 P-H Memo TC, page 172.

Key Person Insurance

"What corporate purpose could be considered more essential than key man insurance? The business that insures its buildings and machinery and automobiles from every possible hazard can hardly be expected to exercise less care in protecting itself against the loss of two of its most vital assets – managerial skill and experience."

> From an opinion by Circuit Judge Staley in the 3rd Circuit of the U.S. Court of Appeals, *Emeloid Co., Inc. v. Commissioner of Internal Revenue*, 189 F.2d 230, page 233.

"In a capitalistic society, where credit is the life blood of that system, debt signals a need for life insurance . . . . The corporate or partnership debt, personally guaranteed by the deceased, makes the widow and his family absolutely vulnerable to the forced sale of assets. Everybody knows that 'a sale to settle an estate' means bargain prices."

> Judge Michael A. Telesca, "Estate Planning: A View From The Bench," *National Underwriter*, July 10, 1976, page 17.

"Take away my factories, my plants; take away my railroads, my ships, my transportation; take away my money; strip me of all these, but leave me my men, and in two or three years I will have them all again."

> Andrew Carnegie, Industrialist, as quoted in: Edward A. Stoeber, *How To Use* Life *and Health Insurance In Business And Estate Planning*, Cincinnati: The National Underwriter Company, 1980, page 57.

"Losses of key personnel are among the most serious setbacks a firm can have – particularly when the major asset of a firm, especially a small one, is the skills and training of its managers."

> Mark R. Greene, *Insurance and Risk Management for Small Business*, Washington: U.S. Small Business Administration, Third Edition, page 69.

Buy/Sell Agreements.

"Q: 'Is there anything I can do to help the sale of my business after I die so that my daughters are not penalized by estate taxes?'

A. 'Yes. Buy life insurance to provide the liquidity your business will need while it is being sold as well as for its tax advantage. More and more small business people are taking this step these days for precisely your reasons . . . . A widely preferred arrangement is the stock retirement agreement, under which your business itself buys your interest, pays the insurance premiums, and carries the insurance on its books as an asset. Buy-sell agreements guarantee your business will be sold at a fair price and that your estate will have sufficient assets to pay taxes and other expenses."

> Sylvia Porter, "Spending Your Money," *Ladies' Home Journal*, July 1979, page 39.

"The contract established a market value for the stock and at the same time fixed its value to testator's estate for tax purposes as well as for all other purposes. Resort to methods of estimating and computing the value of closely held stock is wholly unnecessary and improper when its actual value has been fixed and determined by a bona fide contract entered into by the testator."

> From an opinion of the Surrogate's Court Monroe County, New York, in the case of: *Matter of Miller*, 191 N.Y. Misc. 784, page 786.

"Because each type of buy-sell agreement either requires or provides the corporation or the remaining shareholders with an opportunity to purchase a retiring shareholder's stock, the purchasing party (or parties) must have funding in place to finance the purchase. However, without adequate planning, most businesses and/or shareholders would not likely have sufficient liquid assets to make such a purchase. Consequently, insurance (most commonly, life insurance) is often used to fund both redemption and cross-purchase agreements."

> George Jackson III, MS, J.D. & David M. Maloney, Ph.D., CPA, "Buy-Sell Agreements An Invaluable Tool," *The Tax Adviser*, April, 2003.

ACCELERATED DEATH BENEFIT

An accelerated death benefit (ADB) is a portion of a life insurance death benefit that is paid to the insured after he has been diagnosed as either chronically or terminally ill. Provided certain conditions are met, payments received may be excluded from federal taxable income.

A person is considered *terminally* ill if certified by a physician to have an illness or physical condition that is reasonably expected to result in death within 24 months. A person is considered *chronically* ill if certified by a health care professional as unable to perform for a period of at least 90 days, without substantial assistance, at least two activities of daily living (i.e., eating, toileting, transferring, bathing, dressing and continence) or requires substantial supervision to protect himself from threats to health and safety due to severe cognitive impairment (i.e., a deterioration or loss of intellectual capacity that places the individual in jeopardy of harming self or others). These standards for the chronically ill also apply to long-term care benefits (see chart, page 255).

There is no limitation on the amount or use of payments made to a *terminally* ill person. However, payments made to a *chronically* ill individual must be for the actual costs incurred that have not been compensated for by insurance or otherwise. Amounts received from a qualified long-term care contract in 2011 are generally not includable in income up to the greater of $300 per day or actual costs incurred (see discussion on page 489). The terms of the contract must comply with certain provisions of the Internal Revenue Code, standards adopted by the National Association of Insurance Commissioners (NAIC) and standards adopted by the state in which the policyowner resides. These are the same limits and requirements that apply to payments for long-term care (see chart, page 255).

As an exception to these rules, payments are included in income if made to someone other than the insured and the payee has an insurable interest in the insured's life because the insured is a director, officer or employee of the payee, or because the insured is financially interested in any trade or business carried on by the payee (i.e., business insurance).

In contrast to an accelerated death benefit *received* under a life insurance policy, when a chronically or terminally ill insured *sells* his death benefit at a discount to a third party it is known as a life settlement or viatical settlement (see discussion, pages 443-444).

ACCOUNTING FOR BUSINESS LIFE INSURANCE

Premium Payments. With cash value insurance the excess of net premiums paid (i.e., the premiums paid less dividends declared, if any) over the increase in cash surrender values is considered an insurance expense. Because premium payments are generally *not* deductible as a business expense, they are usually considered an "Extraordinary Item" and placed on the profit and loss statement before "Net Income Before Taxes," as at **B** on page 345. Alternatively, the insurance expense could be shown on the balance sheet as a direct charge to capital, with no entry being made on the profit and loss statement (note that this method highlights the non-tax-deductible nature of the expense).

Cash Values. The general rule is that cash values are carried on the balance sheet under "Noncurrent Assets," as at **A** on page 345 ("noncurrent assets" are also referred to as "other assets"). It has been suggested that with universal life containing surrender charges the full cash values should be carried as an asset. However, this is not consistent with the position taken by the Financial Accounting Standards Board in FASB Technical Bulletin No. 85-4, entitled "Accounting for Purchases of Life Insurance." When responding to the question of how to account for an investment in life insurance, the bulletin states: *"The amount that could be realized* under the insurance contract *as of the date of the statement* of financial position should be reported as an asset. . . . the current capacity to realize contract benefits is limited to settlement amounts specified in the contract" [emphasis added]. When it is intended to surrender a universal life policy value during the normal operating cycle, the *surrender* values might be carried on the balance sheet as a "Current Asset," as opposed to a "Noncurrent Asset."

Policy Loans. Usually there is no intention of repaying the policy loan within the current year, in which case the loan should be reflected on the balance sheet as a deduction from the cash surrender value (i.e., net cash surrender values should be shown). If there is an intention to repay within the current year, the loan should be carried as a current liability and the full cash surrender value shown as an asset.

Death Benefits. The amount of the death benefit in excess of the cash surrender values is considered a gain to corporate surplus. The entry can be made as a negative expense under Extraordinary Items on the profit and loss statement (**B** on page 345). Assuming cash surrender values of $36,000 and a death benefit of $250,000, the actual entry would read, "Plus: proceeds of officers life insurance in excess of cash surrender value . . . 214,000."

(continued on next page)

ACCOUNTING FOR BUSINESS LIFE INSURANCE (continued)

BALANCE SHEET

ASSETS

CURRENT ASSETS:

Cash	$450,000	
Notes and accounts receivable	850,000	

FIXED ASSETS:

Land	300,000	
Buildings	550,000	
Machinery and equipment	220,000	

NONCURRENT ASSETS:

Prepaid insurance, taxes, etc.	18,500	
Life insurance cash surrender values	36,000 **A**	
Total Assets		$2,424,500

LIABILITIES AND STOCKHOLDER EQUITY

CURRENT LIABILITIES:

Notes and loans payable banks	$145,000	
Accounts payable	85,000	
Liability for income taxes	42,500	

LONG-TERM LIABILITIES:

Mortgages	735,000	
Total Liabilities	$1,007,500	

STOCKHOLDER EQUITY:

Common stock authorized and issued	$900,000	
Retained earnings	517,000	
Total Stockholder Equity	1,417,000	
Total Liabilities and Stockholder Equity		$2,424,500

PROFIT AND LOSS STATEMENT

Net Sales	$ 869,000	

Less: Cost of Sales and Operating Expenses

Cost of goods sold	$260,000	
Depreciation	95,000	
Selling and administrating expenses	184,000	
	(539,000)	
Operating Profit		$ 330,000

Other Income		
Interest and dividends		5,000
Total Income		$ 335,000
Extraordinary Item		
Less: life insurance expense		(7,000)**B**
Net Income Before Taxes		$ 328,000
Provision for Income Tax		(113,900)
Net Profit for Year		$ 214,100

ACCUMULATED EARNINGS TAX

Accumulating corporate earnings and profits in excess of the reasonable needs of the business and for the purpose of avoiding income tax can in 2011 result in a surtax of 15 percent of accumulated taxable income. This surtax is imposed on the current year's earnings, and once taxed, accumulated earnings are not again taxed in subsequent years during which the accumulation is retained.

However, a corporation is allowed to accumulate at least $250,000 without being subject to this surtax. This figure is reduced to $150,000 for personal service corporations, whose principal business consists of the performance of services in the fields of health, law, engineering, architecture, accounting, actuarial science, performing arts, or consulting.

Reasonable needs of the business can include: (1) providing for plant expansion; (2) acquiring another business through purchase of either stock or assets; (3) retiring indebtedness; and (4) making loans to suppliers or customers in order to maintain the business of the corporation. Insurance carried as *key person insurance*, or to help meet an employer's obligation under a *deferred compensation plan* or *entity purchase agreement (§302)*, is generally considered as carried for reasonable business needs. However, under Section 303 (partial stock redemption) only accruals in the year of death or thereafter are considered as carried for reasonable needs of the business.

For example, if a corporation in its first year of existence in 2011 has $425,000 of retained earnings for which no reasonable need exists, it would be subject to a penalty tax of $26,250. It is calculated as follows:

First $250,000   is exempt from tax
Excess $175,000   is subject in 2011 to a tax of 15 percent, or $26,250

The penalty tax is imposed *in addition to* the regular corporate income tax.

AGE-WEIGHTED PROFIT SHARING PLAN

Pension plans, both defined contribution (money purchase and target benefit) and defined benefit, require that the employer make recurring annual contributions. These annual obligations can be avoided with profit sharing plans. Under a traditional profit sharing plan employer contributions are generally allocated each year to employees in proportion to relative compensation, either with or without Social Security integration. However, with an age-weighted profit sharing plan the participant's age is taken into account when making these allocations. The results are similar to those produced in target plans, with significantly larger allocations (as a percentage of compensation) to older employees, but with the added flexibility of a profit sharing plan (e.g., fixed annual contributions are required under a target plan, but there is no such requirement under an age-weighted profit sharing plan).

One of the most common types of age-weighted profit sharing plans is the "cross tested" or "new comparability" plan. The name is derived from the cross testing that is used in order to satisfy the nondiscrimination regulations. An age-weighted plan that discriminates as to contributions may be permissible, provided it does not discriminate when compared to benefits that could be provided using the benefits testing. With respect to defined contribution plans, cross testing is an "end justifies the means" or "benefit justifies the contribution" test. It is permissible for a profit sharing plan to fail the nondiscrimination tests for defined contribution plans, provided it actually produces nondiscriminatory benefits using the nondiscrimination tests applicable to defined benefit plans. Final regulations define three methods under which a cross tested defined contribution plan can satisfy the nondiscrimination in amount requirement.

To summarize, compared to defined benefit plans and other pension plans (both money purchase and target benefit), profit sharing plans offer the flexibility of not having to make annual contributions, but age-weighted profit sharing plans offer the additional advantage of providing significantly larger allocations to older employees.

See also, the discussion of qualified retirement plans on page 491.

ASSET PROTECTION

The term "asset protection" has traditionally been used in referring to techniques that offer protection from the claims of personal and business creditors. However, today the term is used to describe a wide array of planning techniques, including those intended to reduce or eliminate income and estate taxes.

These techniques can range from the fairly simple to the very complicated. For example, in some states, much, if not all, of a personal residence is protected from creditors. Many states exempt annuity values, substantial life insurance cash values, and all death benefits. The assets of most retirement plans covered by ERISA are also protected (but not from tax deficiency claims or divorce disputes). The Supreme Court has strengthened IRA protection, and the Bankruptcy Abuse Prevention and Consumer Protection Act of 2005 provides increased protection for most retirement plan assets. Gifts can be made to family members or charitable organizations, provided they are not made with intent to defraud specific creditors (see charts on pages 47 and 55). Gifts may also be made to an irrevocable trust or custodial account (see charts on pages 51 and 67, and discussions on pages 543-545). However, making substantial gifts to a spouse may no longer isolate assets from creditors and could eventually increase estate taxes (see chart, page 25).

More sophisticated techniques include limited liability companies and family limited partnerships (see chart on page 163, and discussions on page 450 and pages 468-469). Trusts can be established with "spendthrift" provisions to prevent the creditors of trust beneficiaries from reaching trust assets (see discussion of self-settled trusts on page 522). But this technique does not provide protection from existing creditors.

The most sophisticated of all asset protection techniques is probably the offshore or asset protection trust (APT). See discussion of Self-Settled Trust on page 522. It is thought that using an APT to remove assets to a foreign jurisdiction will lead to more favorable terms in disputes with creditors. Just as some states have laws that are more favorable to asset protection, certain countries have gained similar reputations. Jurisdictions considered most favorable as a situs for APTs do not recognize foreign judgments (thereby forcing a retrial of claims), have weakened or no fraudulent conveyance laws, and permit a trust settlor to retain trust powers and benefits without subjecting the trust to the claims of creditors. APTs are not intended to avoid income taxes.

In our litigious society, it is understandable why monied individuals and high-risk professionals have long been interested in adopting asset protection techniques. However, a few words of caution: not only will the concealment of assets from a known creditor be set aside by the courts, but assisting a debtor will likely subject both the debtor and his advisor to ethical, civil, and criminal liability (e.g., Code section 7206, see page 468). Therefore, asset protection techniques must be implemented long *before* there is a need. Also, state laws vary widely in the protection they offer and should be specifically consulted.

BANK OWNED LIFE INSURANCE (BOLI)

In many respects, Bank Owned Life Insurance (BOLI) is similar to Company Owned Life Insurance (COLI), in that BOLI enables banks to recover, or to informally fund, the costs of nonqualified benefit plans (see page 367). However, there are important differences.

Banks are considered highly "balance sheet sensitive." From a bank investment perspective, the life insurance contract has been described as "a perpetual municipal with a yield that resets to the market." From a bank accounting perspective, the purchase of life insurance has been described as a "repositioning" of assets on the balance sheet, "from the securities portfolio to the BOLI portfolio," that generates "incremental income." Unlike traditional taxable investments, the cash value increases of BOLI are reflected on the balance sheet as "other non-interest income," without any reduction for income taxes (accounting for BOLI policies is subject to FASB Technical Bulletin 85-5, see page 344). When compared to currently taxed investments, BOLI can produce improved after-tax yields and a positive impact on earnings per share.

Unlike COLI, the purchase of BOLI by national banks is very tightly regulated by the Office of Comptroller of the Currency (OCC) (FDIC regulated state-chartered banks are typically subject to similar regulation). When purchasing BOLI, OCC Bulletin 2000-23 requires an informed decision "consistent with safe and sound banking practices." To that end, the bank must perform a *pre-purchase analysis* that includes determination of need, quantification of amount, vendor and carrier selection, review of insurance product characteristics, determination of reasonableness of compensation, analysis of benefits and risks, and alternatives. The purchase of BOLI, ". . . must address a legitimate need of the bank for life insurance. Life insurance may not be purchased to generate funds for the bank's normal operating expenses [or for] speculation . . ." However, the purchase of "key-person insurance, insurance on borrowers, insurance purchased in connection with employee compensation and benefit plans, and insurance taken as security for loans," are all found to fall within the "incidental powers [that are] necessary to carry on the business of banking."

BOLI policies are typically issued as either annual or single premium contracts. If purchased with a single premium, a BOLI policy is classified as a modified endowment contract (MEC), with the resulting LIFO taxation of policy withdrawals, loans and surrenders; and application of a 10-percent-penalty tax on amounts includable in gross income (see Life Insurance Premium Limitations, page 441). However, if the contract is held until the insured's death, the policy proceeds are received income tax-free (provided strict notice and consent requirements are met, see pages 367-369, and there is no prior "transfer-for-value," see page 541). Banks may purchase variable life insurance, provided it is for the purpose of "hedging their obligations under employee compensation and benefit plans." In selecting the employees to be insured, a bank must be mindful of the state "insurable interest" requirements (see discussion, page 429).

BOOK VALUE

Many approaches to valuation require a consideration of book value. Simply stated, book value is assets less liabilities, or the net worth of the business. However, because assets are often carried at substantially *below* their fair market value, care must be taken to assure that book value is adjusted upward to reflect accurately the value of these underlying assets. This adjustment in book value results in an *adjusted book value*.

For example, land purchased many years ago is likely to have appreciated in value, yet it is often carried on the books at the original purchase price. Machinery and equipment may be depreciated for income tax purposes, yet be worth substantially more than is shown on the books (when carried at its depreciated value). If the LIFO (last in, first out) method of inventory valuation is used, the value of inventory will likely be carried at below market value. This can be seen in the following example:

1000 units purchased at $1.00 on June 1	$1,000
1000 units purchased at $1.50 on July 1	1,500
1000 units purchased at $2.00 on August 1	2,000
Total cost of inventory	$4,500
Less 1000 units sold on August 2 (charged to inventory at $2.00 per unit)	(2,000)
Remaining 2000 units carried at	$2,500
But to replace these units it would cost	$4,000
Inventory is undervalued by	$1,500

BUSINESS OVERHEAD EXPENSE INSURANCE

Business overhead expense insurance is designed to provide funds to cover overhead expenses during a business owner's disability. Business overhead expense insurance is intended to help maintain the business; it is not intended to replace disability income insurance (see chart, page 243) or disability buy-out insurance (see discussion, page 386).

Covered expenses include those that are tax deductible to the business. Typically these expenses include employee salaries, utilities, professional fees, rent, mortgage payments, lease payments for furniture and equipment, premiums for health, property and liability insurance, laundry services, janitorial services, and maintenance services. Not included are the insured's salary, salaries of co-workers who perform the same duties as the insured, salaries of family members, and depreciation.

Monthly benefits are paid upon the insured's total and continuous disability, and are limited to a maximum amount. Partial disability benefits are also available. During disability a "carry-forward" provision allows unused benefits to be carried forward from month to month. Extension of the benefit period allows unused benefits to be received beyond the original benefit period.

Waiting periods are typically either 30, 60, or 90 days. The cash flow requirements of the business are considered when selecting an appropriate waiting period.

Benefit periods are typically limited to 12, 18, or 24 months. Limited benefit periods assume that the insured will dispose of the business interest if disability lasts longer then the benefit period (see disability buy-out insurance, page 386).

Optional coverages are often similar to individual disability income policies (e.g., partial disability riders, guaranteed insurability riders, and lump-sum survivor benefits). Other optional coverages are unique to business overhead expense insurance (e.g., a professional replacement rider covering the cost of hiring someone to perform the insured's duties).

Eligible businesses include regular C corporations, S corporations, limited liability companies, partnerships, and sole proprietorships. The business must have been in operation for a minimum period of time (e.g., 3 years). The business cannot have more than a specific number of owners (e.g., 5 professionals working in the business). This requirement recognizes that a substantial loss of revenue is less likely if the business has a large number of owner-employees. There are specific issue ages and medical underwriting requirements; and the insured must be actively at work full time (e.g., a minimum of 30 hours per week).

Premiums are deductible as a business expense. Although the *proceeds* are taxable, they are used for tax-deductible business expenses (i.e., taxable proceeds are offset by deductible business expenses).

CAFETERIA PLANS

Cafeteria plans, also described as "flexible benefit" plans or Section 125 plans, allow participating employees to choose between a number of non-taxable qualified benefits or taxable cash. Plans typically offer participants a "cafeteria menu" of items, including group term life insurance, medical expense insurance, dependent group term life insurance, child care, and dental expense coverage.

Among the advantages to an *employer* that establishes such a plan are reductions in FICA (Federal Insurance Contributions Act) and FUTA (Federal Unemployment Tax Act) taxes, expansion of employee benefits, and enhanced employee appreciation of the benefit package.

Employee advantages include the opportunity: (1) to select benefits most suited to individual needs; (2) to pay for these benefits with before-tax rather than after-tax dollars; (3) to obtain benefits that may not be available for individual purchase; and (4) to pay less FICA taxes by reducing taxable income.

The design of cafeteria plans can range from simple "premium only" plans to full-blown flexible benefit plans including flexible spending accounts. **Premium-only plans**, which are also referred to as "premium-conversion" plans, merely allow employees to use their before-tax, rather than after-tax, dollars for plan contributions. In contrast, **flexible spending accounts** allow employees to defer before-tax dollars to pay for dependent care expenses and unreimbursed medical expenses (such as deductibles and coinsurance payments, glasses, and eye exams).

The election to defer dollars must be made in advance of the plan year and can be changed only under limited circumstances. With flexible spending accounts, employees forfeit fund balances that are not used up by the end of the plan year, except for a 2½ month grace period if permitted by the plan (regarding a one-time opportunity to make a rollover contribution from a health flexible spending account to a health savings account, see footnote 4, page 253). An additional period is allowed after the close of the plan year for submission of claims incurred during the plan year. Forfeitures may be used to offset the employer's cost of administering the plan, reallocated proportionately to other employees, or given to charity.

Former employees may participate, but self-employed individuals may not. All plans are subject to special nondiscrimination rules. Proper administration of cafeteria plans requires preparing plan documents, conducting annual enrollments, tracking claims and benefit payments, and filing yearly 5500 reports.

See also, Consumer-Directed Health Plans, page 371, Defined Contribution Health Plan, page 385, and SIMPLE Cafeteria Plans, page 523.

CAPITAL GAINS

If property is classified as a "capital asset," then, upon its sale, any gain generally is considered a capital gain. Gain is the excess of the amount realized upon the sale over the basis (adjusted downward for depreciation or upward for additions to the property). Gains and losses from the sale or exchange of capital assets are either short-term or long-term. Generally, in order for gain or loss to be long-term, the asset must have been held for more than one year. The excess of net long-term capital gain over net short-term capital loss (if any) is net capital gain.

"Adjusted net capital gain" is net capital gain reduced (but not below zero) by the sum of: (1) unrecaptured IRC Section 1250 gain; and (2) 28 percent rate gain; plus (3) "qualified dividend income."

For taxpayers in the 25 percent tax bracket and higher, the rate on long-term capital gains is 15 percent through 2012. For taxpayers in the 15 percent and 10 percent tax brackets, the rate on long-term capital gains is 0 percent through 2012. (In the following paragraph at (D) these are described as 15 percent and 5 percent capital assets.) After December 31, 2012, for taxpayers in the 25 percent tax bracket and higher, the rate on long-term capital gains is scheduled to be increased from 15 percent to 20 percent and for taxpayers in the 15 percent and 10 percent tax brackets, the rate on long-term capital gains is scheduled to be increased from 0 percent to 10 percent.

In summary, there are essentially four groups of capital assets: (A) short-term capital assets which are taxed at normal rates; (B) 28 percent capital assets, generally consisting of collectibles gain or loss, and IRC Section 1202 gain (qualified small business stock, see page 491); (C) 25 percent capital assets, consisting of assets that generate unrecaptured IRC Section 1250 gain; and (D) 15 percent and 5 percent capital assets, consisting of all other long-term capital assets. After netting gains and losses within each group, if there is a net loss from group A, it is applied to reduce any net gain from B, C, or D, in that order. If there is a net loss from B it is applied to reduce any net gain from C or D, in that order. If there is a net loss from D, it is applied to reduce any net gain from B or C, in that order. If there are net losses after the above netting, up to $3,000 ($1,500 in the case of married individuals filing separately) of losses can be deducted against ordinary income. Any remaining net losses are carried over to other taxable years while retaining their group classifications.

The tax rate on collectibles gain and IRC Section 1202 gain is 28 percent, and unrecaptured IRC Section 1250 gain is taxed at 25 percent.

See also, the discussion of Net Unrealized Appreciation on page 459.

CASH BALANCE PENSION PLAN

A cash balance plan is a defined benefit plan that calculates benefits in a manner similar to defined contribution plans. Each employee has a hypothetical account or "cash balance" to which contributions and interest payments are credited. Under the typical plan a fixed percentage of each employee's salary is contributed each year, and both the level of contribution and a minimum rate of return are *guaranteed* by the employer (i.e., the employer bears the investment risk). Contributions may be weighted for age or years of service. Unlike a true defined contribution plan, individual accounts are not maintained and participants may not direct the investments in their accounts. As with the defined benefit pension plan the plan benefits are guaranteed up to specific limits by the Pension Benefit Guaranty Corporation (PBGC). See page 469.

Compared with traditional defined benefit plans cash balance plans generally provide greater benefits to younger employees and those with shorter service (but at a higher cost), and lower benefits to older, longer service employees (at lower cost).

In an effort to reduce the costs of employee retirement plans, and offer more attractive plans to younger workers with few years of service, employers can convert their traditional defined benefit plans into cash balance plans. This conversion benefits younger workers, who not only can accrue benefits more rapidly, but will also enjoy the added advantages of portability (i.e., if the employee leaves prior to normal retirement age vested account values can be taken in a lump sum, rolled over into an IRA, or otherwise invested). However, these conversions are generally detrimental to older employees, since they occur just as these workers are reaching the age where the defined benefit formulas began to sharply raise the value of their future pension payouts. The effect is that some cash balance conversions have arguably lowered the rate of future benefit accruals. In response to this concern, the Pension Protection Act of 2006 required that future conversions of defined benefit plans to cash balance plans preclude the possibility of "wear-away" (i.e., a time after conversion during which additional benefits do not accrue).

Controversy over cash balance conversions has resulted in many employers giving employees the option of staying with the old defined benefit plan, or providing other incentives in order to mitigate loss of anticipated benefits.

See also, the discussion of qualified retirement plans on page 491.

CHARITABLE GIFT ANNUITY

A charitable gift annuity is received pursuant to a contractual obligation by a charity to make annuity payments to a donor in exchange for the transfer of property to the charity. In comparison to charitable trusts they are less costly and relatively simple to adopt, typically requiring only an application and a one or two page agreement. The donor's tax-deductible gift is measured by the difference between the market value of the gift and the value of the retained life annuity. The annuity can be immediate or deferred and for a single life or the joint lives of two annuitants.

The actual rates used to calculate the annuity payout are typically based upon those published by the American Council of Gift Annuities. The council meets periodically in order to review interest rates and mortality assumptions and update the annuity rates. Although these rates are published in an attempt to avoid "rate bidding wars" between charities, the council has no enforcement authority. However, charities using the rates need not retain their own actuaries and have the assurance that the underlying actuarial assumptions will likely produce an ultimate charitable benefit.

The annuity receives favorable tax treatment. A portion of each payment is received tax-free as a return of principal (but excludable only until the investment has been recovered, thereafter taxed as ordinary income). The remaining portion is taxed as ordinary income. However, if the donor has transferred appreciated property to the charity, the donor has a gain (either capital gain or ordinary income depending on the property) to the extent the fair market value exceeds the donor's adjusted basis. The basis in the property must then be allocated between the charitable gift and the donor's investment in the annuity contract. As a result the return of principal element of each annuity payment is divided into two parts, one representing a return of gain (taxed as capital or ordinary gain) and the other representing a return of basis (excluded from income).

The contractual obligation to the annuitant is solely the charity's and the annuity payments are dependent upon the continuing financial stability of the charity. If desired, the charity can reinsure its obligation to the donor by purchasing a commercial annuity. This relieves the charity of the burden of investing the proceeds to assure that all payments will be made to the annuitant. To the extent that the cost of a commercial annuity is less than the amount realized from the gift the excess funds become immediately available to the charity.

CHARITABLE GIFTS OF LIFE INSURANCE

Gifts of life insurance policies and premiums have become a popular way of providing substantial gifts to a donor's favored charity. When properly implemented, the donor should receive charitable deductions for the value of the insurance contract and for all future premium payments.

In order to obtain the anticipated income, gift and estate tax deductions, the donor must make a gift of his *entire* interest in the policy. The donor will not qualify for these deductions if he retains the right to name or change the beneficiary, or gives less than his entire interest (e.g., assignment of death benefit but retention of cash values).

However, even when the donor appears to have given his entire interest in the policy to a charity, or where the charity originally applies for the insurance, a 1991 private letter ruling (withdrawn when state law changed) provided that the charity's lack of an insurable interest under state law would be a basis for denying the income, gift and estate tax deductions, since state law would also allow the insured's executor to sue for the proceeds (i.e., there would be a transfer of less than the donor's entire interest in the policy and premiums, since the threat of a suit by the executor renders the gifts incomplete). Even if the proceeds were actually received and retained by the charity, the Service would likely deny an estate tax deduction, because the charitable contribution would be deemed a result of the executor's action or inaction, rather than a transfer by the decedent-insured.

This could jeopardize a donor's income, gift and estate tax deductions (i.e., charity did not have an insurable interest, and executor could sue to recover life insurance proceeds paid to one not having an insurable interest). Following this ruling virtually all states have passed legislation that specifically provides that charities have an insurable interest in the lives of their donors.

The variety of state laws and likely changes to these laws make it imperative that specific state statutes be consulted prior to making gifts of life insurance and premiums, or having a charitable organization apply for life insurance (for an expanded discussion of insurable interest, see page 429).

Do not confuse charitable gifts of life insurance with "charitable split-dollar," a highly aggressive planning technique that provided the donor with an improper financial benefit in exchange for his charitable contributions. Charitable split-dollar is no longer viable due to legislation passed in 1999.

Likewise, do not confuse charitable gifts of life insurance with "stranger-originated life insurance" involving the questionable use of a charity's insurable interest to promote a speculative life insurance arrangement (see discussion on page 532).

CHARITABLE TRUSTS

Charitable trusts can be established for both individual and charitable beneficiaries. The requirements for charitable remainder trusts are specific and detailed in order to assure that an accurate determination can be made of the benefit the charity will eventually receive. Such trusts can offer both income and estate tax benefits, and include:

1. **Charitable Remainder Annuity Trusts (CRATs)** are trusts under which a *fixed amount* of at least 5 percent and no more than 50 percent of the initial fair market value of trust assets is paid annually to a noncharitable beneficiary. Payments to the noncharitable beneficiary may be for a set term not exceeding 20 years or for the life of the beneficiary. The amount of the grantor's tax deduction is measured by the present value of the charity's remainder interest at the time property is given to the trust. The value of the remainder interest must be at least 10 percent of the initial fair market value of all property placed in the trust. If the trust income is insufficient to make the required payments to the noncharitable beneficiary, then capital gains or trust principal must be used. If the trust income is more than required to make the payments, the excess is reinvested in the trust. See chart on page 55.

2. **Charitable Remainder UniTrusts (CRUTs)** are trusts under which a *fixed percentage* of the net fair market value of the trust (valued annually) is paid at least annually to a noncharitable beneficiary. This percentage cannot be less than 5 percent and no more than 50 percent. Payments to the noncharitable beneficiary may be for a term not exceeding 20 years or for life. The amount of the grantor's tax deduction is the present value of the charity's remainder interest. The value of the remainder interest must be at least 10 percent of the net fair market value of each contribution as of the date the property is contributed to the trust. See chart on page 55 and discussion of NIMCRUT on page 462.

3. **Pooled income funds** are trusts created by public charities rather than private donors. The donors, or other income beneficiaries, receive from the commingled funds in the trust an income for life that is based upon the earnings of the trust. The amount of the grantor's tax deduction is the present value of the charity's remainder interest.

4. **Charitable lead trusts** allow a grantor to place funds in trust with an annuity or unitrust interest going to a charitable beneficiary and the remainder interest returning to the grantor or some other noncharitable beneficiaries. Although the grantor continues to be taxed on trust income under the grantor trust rules, he is entitled to an income tax deduction at the time of the gift equal to the present value of the charity's annuity or unitrust interest.

CHARITY AS DESIGNATED BENEFICIARY OF RETIREMENT PLAN

Naming a charity as beneficiary of some or all of a retirement plan can be a simple and tax-efficient way to make a charitable bequest. The many benefits include the following:

1. Payments made from a tax-deferred retirement account to individual beneficiaries are considered "income in respect of a decedent" and taxed as ordinary income (see page 425). However, charities are exempt from state and federal income taxes and can receive retirement funds without any reduction for taxes paid.

2. Payments made to a charity are deductible from the gross estate and not subject to estate taxes. With larger estates this can save substantial amounts of estate taxes. (But an income tax credit is available to the beneficiaries for any estates tax paid.)

3. By satisfying charitable objectives with retirement account assets the decedent can then pass appreciated property to non-charitable beneficiaries. Since this property is entitled to a stepped-up basis at death, it can then be sold at fair market value without paying income taxes (see page 530).

Before making a charity a beneficiary, it should be determined if: (1) the plan contains any restrictions against naming a charity as beneficiary; and (2) the account holder is married (retirement plans other than IRAs require that the spouse waive his or her rights under the retirement plan). The mere naming of a charity as beneficiary will not adversely impact the calculations of the owner's required minimum distributions (RMDs) during his or her lifetime (prior rules would have prevented using the joint life expectancy of the owner and another person if a charity was a named beneficiary).

A "designated beneficiary" must be determined for the purpose of calculating the required post-death distributions from a retirement account. Designated beneficiaries are living persons for whom a life expectancy can be calculated. (An exception to this rule allows some trusts to qualify as designated beneficiaries provided they meet specific requirements.) A charity is considered to be a "non-designated beneficiary" since it has no life expectancy.

When the **charity is the only beneficiary**, the RMD is determined as if there were no designated beneficiary and there is limited flexibility as to when distributions may be taken (see page 435). However, this is rarely a concern as most charities have no tax incentive to delay distribution and want to receive the funds as soon as they are available.

When there are **multiple individual beneficiaries** (i.e., multiple "designated beneficiaries") the RMD calculation is based upon the oldest beneficiary, unless separate accounts are established before September 30th of the year following the owner's death, in which case each individual beneficiary should be able to calculate his or her own RMD (based upon their individual life expectancies).

(continued on next page)

CHARITY AS DESIGNATED BENEFICIARY (continued)

When a **charity is among the beneficiaries**, the individual beneficiaries will be unable to use their life expectancies to calculate RMDs if the charity is included among the beneficiaries on September 30th of the calendar year following the year of the account owner's death (the deadline for determining the identity of account beneficiaries for the purpose of determining RMDs). The reason for this is that an account that has both designated and non-designated beneficiaries is treated as if it has no designated beneficiaries. However, the problem can be avoided and the individual beneficiaries can preserve their ability to stretch out annual withdrawals over the course of their lifetime by either:

1. Establishing separate accounts for the charitable and the non-charitable beneficiaries after the death of the account owner, but not later than the September 30th deadline.

2. Paying out the charity's share prior to the September 30th deadline. Unlike individual beneficiaries, a charity has no incentive to stretch out distributions from the retirement account. The individual beneficiaries may then take minimum distributions over the life expectancy of the oldest remaining beneficiary or over their individual life expectancies if the account is divided into separate accounts for each remaining individual beneficiary.

A retired married couple might wish to make a charity a partial beneficiary of their retirement assets, but be reluctant to do so because of a need to provide for the surviving spouse and a desire to leave the bulk of the account to adult children. The following beneficiary designation addresses that concern and passes a ten percent interest (a tithe) in the retirement account to a charity, with the remaining ninety percent to any surviving children, but only upon the death of the surviving spouse: "In the event of my death, transfer ownership of my Account to <u>my spouse if he/she survives me. If my spouse predeceases me, transfer ownership of my Account to</u> the following beneficiaries who survive me and make payment in the following proportions: Son A – 30%; Son B – 30%; Daughter C – 30%; XYZ Charity – 10%. If any of my Individual Beneficiaries predeceases me, his or her share shall be divided among the other individual beneficiary(ies) who survive me in the relative proportions assigned to each such surviving Individual Beneficiary. If there is no surviving Individual Beneficiary(ies) at the time of my death, transfer ownership of my Account to my estate (unless otherwise required by the laws of my state of residence)."

Should the **account owner's spouse die first,** then the charity would receive a ten percent interest and the adult children would receive their ninety percent interest in the retirement account. Should the **account owner die first**, the spouse would either remain a beneficiary of the account or transfer the funds to the spouse's IRA. In this event, the spouse should consider using the same beneficiary designation as above, but with the underlined text deleted. In either case, if the individual beneficiaries desire to delay receipt of their distributions over the longest possible time, it is important to take the actions set forth in paragraphs 1 or 2 above.

CHILDREN'S LIFE INSURANCE

Children's insurance, also referred to as "juvenile insurance," offers many advantages. The death proceeds can be used to pay medical bills and funeral expenses, provide a financial cushion for a grieving family or establish a lasting memorial (e.g., a scholarship fund in the child's name). Loans or withdrawals from policy cash values can be used for educational expenses, as a down payment on the purchase of a home, to start a business, or for emergency expenses. Adding a guaranteed purchase option will assure that in future years the child can purchase additional death benefits without evidence of insurability (see discussion on page 422).

Despite these advantages, placing insurance on a child's life is not without controversy. Opponents maintain that the lack of an underlying economic risk makes the purchase inappropriate and, further, that the wrong person is being insured. Clearly, if family resources are limited they should first be used to obtain adequate amounts of insurance on a child's parents (upon whom the child is economically dependent). Opponents also contend that if cash accumulations are desired it is better to save outside of a life insurance contract, thereby avoiding charges for the death benefit. Obviously, insuring a child can raise different issues than those encountered when insuring a spouse, parent, estate owner, employee or stockholder.

Since a minor cannot directly own a policy on his own life, it is important that the individual applying for the insurance have an insurable interest in the child's life (see discussion on page 429). Initially the contract will typically be owned by a parent, grandparent, trust, or obtained as a custodial gift under the Uniform Transfers to Minors Act or Uniform Gifts to Minors Act (see discussions on pages 459 and 545).

A grandparent's purchase of insurance on the life of a grandchild can provide a meaningful gift to the grandchild while taking advantage of the gift tax laws (see chart on page 47). Virtually any form of permanent life insurance policy can be used. Single premium or limited payment plans are often used, or additional funds can be placed in a prepaid premium account (also referred to as a "premium deposit fund").

The amount of death benefit that can be purchased may be limited by state law and will be limited by insurance company underwriting standards. Purchase of a low death benefit with higher premiums will produce larger cash values. However, in making premium payments it is important to avoid classification as a modified endowment contract, since loans or surrenders of cash values could be subject to less favorable income taxation (see discussion on pages 441-442). It should also be recognized that a lower initial death benefit means that smaller amounts of additional insurance can be purchased under the guaranteed purchase option.

See also, the discussion of Life Insurance Default Risk on page 438.

COLLEGE EDUCATION FUNDING

1. **Financial Aid.** In order to determine who qualifies for financial aid, a formula provided by the federal government subtracts the expected family contribution from the cost of attendance. Among other factors, this formula takes into consideration the assets and income of the parents and child. Because the formula gives substantially greater weight to the child's income and assets, large gifts should not be made to a child if financial aid is likely to be sought.

2. **Life Insurance And Annuities.** One advantage of life insurance cash values and annuities is that they are not included in the formula used by the government in determining eligibility for financial aid. Tax-deferred cash value accumulations, favorable loan provisions and a preferred status under the financial aid laws make permanent life insurance attractive for funding a college education. But there should be a real need for the insurance; otherwise, funds might better be invested where there would be no charges for a death benefit. And since a parent is most likely to be paying for college, it makes sense that a parent be the insured (with parent or trust the owner). Provided the parents are adequately insured, life insurance on the child might also be considered. However, a minor child should not be the owner of an annuity or life insurance contract (see page 459). Note also, that when the owner of an annuity is under age 59½, there is a 10-percent-penalty tax upon surrender.

3. **Gifts.** Gifts can be made to a minor under either the Uniform Transfers to Minors Act or in trust (see page 545). However, most authorities agree that the actual payment of college costs falls within a parent's obligation to support a child; therefore, such payments are not subject to gift taxation. Grandparents can take advantage of the annual exclusion to make gifts to the parents or grandchildren (see chart, page 47). Tuition costs paid directly to a university are free of gift and estate taxes.

4. **Section 529 Plans.** Also known as Qualified Tuition Programs, initial contributions to these plans must come from after-tax income. Contributions must be in cash, are not tax deductible, and are treated as completed gifts eligible for the gift tax annual exclusion ($13,000 in 2011). See the table of Educational Tax Incentives on page 310, and the discussion of Section 529 Plans on page 518.

5. **American Opportunity Credit.** This credit, extended by The 2010 Tax Relief Act through 2012, expands and replaces the Hope Scholarship tax credit. It provides an income tax credit of up to $2,500 per year for each of the first *four* years of college, calculated as 100 percent of the first $2,000 of qualifying expenses and 25 percent of the next $2,000. Up to 40 percent of the credit is refundable (i.e., low income students without a federal income tax liability can receive up to $1,000 a year). Books and course materials are included among eligible expenses.

(continued on next page)

COLLEGE EDUCATION FUNDING (continued)

The student must be enrolled at least half-time in a qualifying educational institution and may be the taxpayer, his spouse or any dependent. However, the credit may not be taken by an individual who is eligible to be claimed as a dependent on another taxpayer's return. Nor may the credit be taken if the student has ever been convicted of a state or federal charge of felony drug possession or distribution. There is no limit in any given year as to the number of American Opportunity Credits a taxpayer may claim as to his or her dependents (i.e., the limit is on a per-student basis). The credit is phased out ratably between modified adjusted gross income of $80,000 to $90,000 for unmarried taxpayers and $160,000 to $180,000 for married taxpayers filing joint returns.

6. **Lifetime Learning Credit.** The Lifetime Learning Credit is 20 percent of the first $10,000 of qualifying education expenses (i.e., a maximum of $2,000 per year). The Lifetime Learning Credit limit is on a per-return basis, meaning that only $10,000 of educational expenses covering all students in the household qualifies each year. In 2011 the credit is phased out ratably between modified adjusted gross income of $51,000 to $61,000 for unmarried taxpayers and $102,000 to $122,000 for married taxpayers filing joint returns. Unlike the Hope Scholarship Credit, the Lifetime Learning Credit can be taken for any year of post-secondary education (except a year in which the Hope Scholarship Credit is claimed for the same student), does not require at least half-time enrollment, and study may be intended to improve the student's job skills and need not lead to a degree.

7. **Deducting Interest On Education Loans.** This deduction allows the taxpayer to deduct up to $2,500 of interest paid on any qualified education loan (the debt must be incurred solely to pay qualified higher education expenses). In 2011, the deduction is phased out ratably between modified adjusted gross income of $60,000 to $75,000 for unmarried taxpayers, and $120,000 to $150,000 for married taxpayers filing joint returns (as indexed for inflation). It is an "above the line" deduction, meaning that the taxpayer does not have to itemize in order to claim the deduction.

8. **Coverdell Education Savings Account.** The 2010 Tax Relief Act extended through 2012 the annual non-deductible contributions of $2,000 per beneficiary that can be made to these accounts (it was scheduled to be reduced to $500). This contribution limit is phased out ratably for individual taxpayers with modified AGI between $95,000 and $110,000, and for married taxpayers filing jointly with modified AGI between $190,000 and $220,000. Funds distributed to pay qualified education expenses are income tax-free (see page 377). These accounts had previously been known as "Education IRAs."

9. **Penalty-Free Withdrawals From Traditional IRAs.** Withdrawals from an IRA for qualified higher education expenses of the taxpayer are not subject to the 10-percent-penalty tax for premature distributions (but are subject to regular income taxes).

(continued on next page)

COLLEGE EDUCATION FUNDING (continued)

10. **Series EE Bonds and Series I Bonds.** The purchase of these bonds can provide tax-free interest if the proceeds are used for the tuition and fees of a dependent. However, there is a phase-out of this exclusion once modified adjusted gross income exceeds a designated amount (in 2011 for single taxpayers the phase-out is between $71,100 and $86,100; for joint tax return filers the phase-out is between $106,650 and $136,650).

11. **Education Expense Deduction.** The 2010 Tax Relief Act extended this deduction through 2012. It provides an above-the-line $4,000 deduction for qualified educational expenses for taxpayers in certain income ranges. The expenses must be for tuition and fees at an eligible post-secondary educational institution. For expenses paid through 2012 a maximum deduction of $4,000 is available for employees who file a single return with adjusted gross income of $65,000 or less and for those who file jointly with adjusted gross income of $130,000 or less. The deduction decreases to $2,000 for employees who file a single return with adjusted gross income that is greater than $65,000 but less than or equal to $80,000, and for those who file jointly with adjusted gross income that is greater than $130,000 but less than or equal to $160,000.

12. **Employer Tuition Reimbursement.** Also known as "educational assistance plans," or "Section 127 plans," under these nondiscriminatory programs an employee may exclude up to $5,250 of employer-provided educational assistance each calendar year. Amounts over $5,250 are included in income and subject to employment and income tax withholding (but expenses related to the employee's current job may be deductible, see paragraph 13 below). The education expenses need not be job related or lead to a degree. Covered expenses include tuition, fees, books, and supplies. Expenses for both undergraduate and graduate-level courses are covered.

13. **Trade Or Business Expense.** Reimbursements to an employee outside of an educational assistance plan are included in the employee's income. These reimbursements are *deductible* if the education expense was incurred for maintaining or improving skills required in employment – but this is a below-line deduction, meaning that the employee must itemize and the deduction is subject to a "2-percent-floor" (i.e., it is only useful to the extent that miscellaneous itemized deductions exceed 2 percent of adjusted gross income). These reimbursements are *not deductible* if the education expense was incurred for meeting minimum requirements for employment or qualifying for a new trade or business.

COMMON DISASTER CLAUSE

The term "common disaster clause," also known as a "simultaneous death provision," has been loosely used to describe a variety of clauses dealing with presumptions as to the order of death of the insured and the beneficiary. The basic intent of these clauses is to prevent the death benefit from passing to a named beneficiary if that person dies at the same time or shortly after the insured. Thus, it is an attempt by the deceased to better control the disposition of property after death. Although this discussion refers to an insured and the death benefit paid from a life insurance contract, the same concepts apply to a testator and the transfer of property under a will.

Under a "true" common disaster clause, when the beneficiary and the insured die as a result of a common disaster there is a *conclusive* presumption that the insured was the last to die, despite the fact that the beneficiary might survive the insured by days, or even months. Under the Uniform Simultaneous Death Act, enacted in almost all states, there is a *nonconclusive* presumption that the insured survived the beneficiary. However, if it can be shown that the beneficiary survived the insured, even for a moment, then the beneficiary receives the death proceeds. A "reverse common disaster clause" is used to assure that the marital deduction will be available. This clause assumes that a beneficiary-spouse survives the insured and therefore the death benefit passes to the estate of the beneficiary-spouse.

A "time clause" (or "short term survivorship clause"), on the other hand, refers not to the cause of death, but to the length of time the beneficiary must survive the insured. The time period is typically 30 days, but may be as long as six months. Periods longer than six months should be avoided if a surviving spouse is the beneficiary and the insured desires to take advantage of the marital deduction (see page 450). This is because property that does not vest in the surviving spouse within six months does not qualify for the marital deduction. For example, assume a time clause requires the spouse to survive for nine months after the insured's death. Once the spouse has survived the required nine months the death benefit is paid, but since it did not vest within six months, it does not qualify for the marital deduction, and will likely be subject to estate taxes.

Because of the difficulty of determining what time period to specify, it is often better to name contingent beneficiaries and have the insurance proceeds paid under a settlement option (other than a life income option that would terminate upon the beneficiary's death). Under such an arrangement, the primary beneficiary might receive a few payments, but the bulk of the death benefits would pass to the contingent beneficiaries upon the death of the primary beneficiary (which occurs after the death of the insured). Providing the primary beneficiary with an unlimited right of withdrawal under the settlement option would qualify the death proceeds for the marital deduction.

COMMUNITY PROPERTY

Community property is a specialized form of property ownership that exists only between a husband and wife who are considered to have an undivided one-half interest in such property during marriage. In most community property states, both spouses have an equal right and duty to manage community property, but neither spouse has the right to convert to his separate use or give away any substantial amount of community property without the other's consent (the gift can be voided by the nondonor spouse). In case of divorce, each spouse becomes a tenant in common of his share of the former community property (see footnote 1, page 13). Upon death, each may dispose of his own share of community property however he wishes. Without a will, community property passes by state law (often to the surviving spouse), with the deceased spouse's separate property passing according to the state's intestacy statute.

The ten states that have adopted some form of community property law are: Alaska, Arizona, California, Idaho, Louisiana, Nevada, New Mexico, Texas, Washington, and Wisconsin (Wisconsin uses the term "marital property"). However, community property laws are not exactly the same in each of these states. A married couple living in a community property state does not have the option of being governed by the state's community property law (except Alaska, where they may opt into the community property system). However, all community property states have provisions allowing for the partition of existing community property into separate property by gift from one spouse to the other, but this must be evidenced by a clear intention (retitling of assets will not suffice). During marriage, merely placing newly acquired property in the name of either spouse is not enough to assure that it will be treated as separate property. Prenuptial and postnuptial agreements can be used to fix the property rights of existing or after-acquired property (but are considered invalid in some states).

Community property generally consists of: (1) property purchased during the marriage; (2) earned income during marriage; (3) fringe benefits derived from employment; (4) dividends, interest, and capital gains earned on community property; and (5) dividends and interest earned on separate property during the marriage (Texas, Louisiana, and Idaho). In addition, property that is otherwise separate property can become community property if it becomes so commingled with community property that it cannot be identified.

Separate property consists of: (1) property owned by either spouse before marriage; (2) earned income from work before marriage; (3) gifts and inheritances received before or during marriage; (4) capital gains on separate property; and (5) dividends and interest earned on separate property during the marriage (Arizona, California, Nevada, New Mexico, and Washington).

(continued on next page)

COMMUNITY PROPERTY (continued)

A particular asset can be a mixture of both community property and separate property (e.g., purchase of home using funds earned before marriage and subsequent mortgage payments with community funds). Many community property states provide for other forms of co-ownership, such as joint tenancy and tenancy in common. For example, owning a home in joint tenancy rather than as community property avoids probate (but must be titled using explicit language). On the other hand, community property enjoys the specific advantage of getting a full step-up in income tax basis upon the death of one of the spouses (not available in common law states). There are also advantages to maintaining separate property, since it is generally not subject to pre-marriage debt or debt connected with the other spouse's separate property (but separate property could be subject to claims arising from "community debt").

Problems can occur when married couples move between community property and common law states. Common law property rights have been addressed by California's "quasi-community property" laws, whereas community property interests in common law states have been addressed by the Uniform Disposition of Community Property Rights at Death Act (adopted in a number of common law states).

When a life insurance policy is considered community property, generally one-half of the proceeds will be included in the insured's estate. But unique problems can arise when life insurance is community property. If the insured spouse dies first and the beneficiary is someone other than the surviving spouse, then one-half of the proceeds received by the beneficiary will be deemed a gift by the surviving spouse to the beneficiary, and subject to gift taxes on the surviving spouse's community share of the proceeds. If the noninsured spouse dies first, the deceased's one-half interest in the policy is included in his probate estate.

Merely naming the noninsured spouse owner of a newly issued policy will likely not avoid the policy becoming community property. The ownership designation should read: "John Doe as his sole and separate property and for his sole use and benefit," or words to that effect. With an existing policy, a transfer can be made to the noninsured spouse using a formal release of the community property interest. Thereafter, all premiums should be paid from the noninsured spouse's separate funds. If premiums are paid with both separate and community funds, one of two approaches will be used to determine the amount included in the insured's estate, either the "premium tracing" rule or the "inception of title" doctrine (see **Q 112**, *Tax Facts on Insurance & Employee Benefits (2011)*).

Buy-sell agreements involving community property business interests should contain the written consent of both spouses to be bound by the agreement. They should also include provisions limiting the disposition of stock or partnership interests upon death or divorce.

COMPANY OWNED LIFE INSURANCE (COLI)

The term company owned life insurance (COLI), also referred to as corporate owned life insurance, or employer-owned life insurance, is used to describe a wide variety of life insurance products that are purchased to fund both employee benefit plans and business insurance needs. These products include virtually all forms of permanent life insurance, including participating whole life, interest sensitive whole life, universal life, and variable life.

Employee benefit plans. COLI products are purchased on the lives of key employees to fund survivor income plans (chart, page 231), deferred compensation plans (chart, page 235), post-retirement medical benefits, and supplemental executive retirement plans (SERPs) (discussion, page 534). When used for funding employee benefit plans, key features of COLI products include: (1) high early cash values ranging from 50 to 90 percent of premiums; (2) underwriting considerations providing either guaranteed issue or guaranteed standard issue; (3) flexibility in funding variable benefits from both cash values and death proceeds; (4) change of insured provisions; (5) levelized commissions; (6) limited pay or vanish features; and (7) contract guarantees relating to mortality charges, expense charges, credited interest rates, and interest rates charged on borrowed funds. Tax and investment considerations often weigh heavily in the design and implementation of these plans.

Business insurance needs. COLI products are also purchased on the lives of business owners and key employees to fund a wide variety of needs related to risk planning, business continuation, and succession planning. These include entity purchase agreements (chart, page 127), "wait and see" buy/sell agreements (chart, page 139), partial stock redemptions (chart, pages 147), and key person insurance (chart, page 155).

Income Taxation Of COLI Death Benefits

In response to the regrettable practice of insuring rank-and-file workers, without their knowledge and consent, Congress included in the Pension Protection Act of 2006, major provisions impacting the income tax treatment of COLI death benefits. Employer-owned life insurance contracts, entered into after August 17, 2006, must meet certain requirements in order for the death proceeds to be excluded from taxable income. The general rule is that death proceeds from these contracts are taxed as ordinary income, except to the extent of any premiums paid for the policy. Exceptions to this general rule are based upon the insured's status, or how death proceeds are paid or used.

Exceptions to the general rule. Provided specific notice and consent requirements are met (see below), under these exceptions *the following death proceeds will generally be received free of income taxes*:

(continued on next page)

COMPANY OWNED LIFE INSURANCE (COLI) (continued)

1. Proceeds from a life insurance contract insuring the life of an employee who was employed at time of death, or was employed within 12 months of death (this includes rank-and-file employees).

2. Proceeds from a life insurance contract insuring the life of an individual who was (at the time the contract was issued):

   a. Among the highest-paid 35-percent of all employees, or
   b. One of the five highest-paid officers, or
   c. Received in the preceding year compensation in excess of $110,000 (as adjusted for inflation in 2011), or
   d. A 5-percent or greater owner of the business at any time during the preceding year, or
   e. A director.

3. Proceeds paid to the insured's heirs, to include:

   a. A member of the insured's family (i.e., spouse, brother, sister, ancestor, or lineal descendant).
   b. An individual who is the insured's designated beneficiary (other than the employer).
   c. A trust established for a member of the insured's family or such designated beneficiary.
   d. The estate of the insured.
   e. Proceeds used to purchase an interest (including partnership capital, or profits) in the employer from any of the above individuals or entities.

Under the statute, an "employer-owned life insurance contract" is a life insurance contract owned by a person or entity engaged in a trade or business, that person or entity (or certain *related persons*) is a beneficiary under the contract, and the contract covers the life of an insured who is an employee when the contract is issued. Clearly, using life insurance to fund the following concepts falls within the definition of employer-owner life insurance: (1) entity purchase agreement (chart, page 127); (2) "wait and see" buy/sell agreement, if the business purchases the insurance (chart, page 139); (3) partial stock redemption (chart, page 147); (4) key person insurance (chart, page 155); (5) split-dollar insurance, if the employer purchases the insurance under the economic benefit regime (chart, page 219); (6) split-dollar funding cross purchase, if the employer purchases the insurance (chart, page 223); (7) survivor income (chart, page 231); and (8) deferred compensation (chart, page 235). However, note that when the employer's death benefit is limited to recovering the employer's premium outlays, there is no actual taxation (e.g., as under many split-dollar agreements). Likewise, there is no income taxation of the employer's death benefit when proceeds are paid out to a member of the insured's family or a designated beneficiary (e.g., as under deferred compensation arrangements).

(continued on next page)

COMPANY OWNED LIFE INSURANCE (COLI) (continued)

The above concepts are obvious examples of "employer-owned" life insurance. Not so obvious is the application of the "related persons" provision, which treats individuals as "related" if they own more than 50 percent of a corporation (i.e., life insurance contracts owned by a majority stockholder are treated as "employer-owned"). For example, in the cross purchase agreement on page 131, assume that Owner A is a 60 percent stockholder, and Owner B is both a stockholder and an employee of the business. Insurance purchased by Owner A on Owner B's life to fund their cross purchase agreement is treated as employer-owned, and the death benefit is subject to income taxation. Payment of the proceeds to B's heirs would provide relief from taxation, but only if there had been the required notice and consent (see below).

The "related persons" provision is further complicated by application of the attribution rules. For example, assume Owner A is a 40 percent owner, Owner B (A's brother) is a 35 percent owner, and Owner C is a 25 percent owner. By family attribution B's stock is attributed to A, making A a majority stockholder (A's 40 percent + B's 35 percent = 75 percent). Insurance A owns on C is treated as employer-owned, and the death benefit is subject to income taxation. These attribution rules may even cause life insurance contracts owned by individuals, who themselves are not business owners, to be treated as employer-owned (e.g., insurance on A owned by A's spouse treated as employer-owned). Hopefully, the IRS will clarify and limit the scope of these rules. Until then, it is essential to fall within the exceptions by first meeting the following notice and consent requirements.

Notice and consent requirements. To qualify for an exception, it is essential to first meet strict notice and consent requirements. Under these requirements, the employee must: (1) be notified in writing that the employer intends to insure the employee's life and the maximum face amount to be issued; (2) be informed that the employer will be the policy beneficiary; and (3) give written consent, before the policy is issued, to being insured and consent to the coverage continuing after the insured employee terminates employment. *It is strongly recommended that notice be given, and consent be obtained, at the time an application is taken for virtually any life insurance contract that might conceivably fall within the scope of this law.* The statute provides no means of obtaining relief from these requirements. The potential cost of noncompliance is income taxation of the death proceeds in excess of premiums paid.

Reporting requirements. Every employer (technically referred to as the "applicable policyholder"), owning one or more employer-owned life insurance contracts issued after August 17, 2006, must file a return showing for each year: (1) the number of employees at the end of the year; (2) the number of employees insured under such contracts at the end of the year; (3) the total amount of insurance in force at the end of the year under such contracts; (4) the employer's name, address, and taxpayer identification number, and the employer's type of business; and (5) that the employer has a valid consent for each insured employee (if any consents were not obtained, the number of insured employees for whom such consent was not obtained).

CONSTRUCTIVE RECEIPT

A general rule of taxation is that income becomes taxable when it is "made available" to the taxpayer. The constructive receipt doctrine is used to currently tax cash basis taxpayers on income that is available to them, but which they have not actually received. The purpose of the rule is to prevent taxpayers from turning their backs on available income and thereby avoiding current taxation on that income. However, even though the taxpayer could, under some circumstances, currently receive the money, he will not be taxed provided his control of its receipt is subject to substantial limitations or restrictions. For example, a substantial limitation or restriction might be a forfeiture of the right to continued participation in the plan, a suspension of plan participation for a period of time, or a reduction in plan benefits.

If an employee's rights to deferred compensation are *forfeitable*, there is no constructive receipt. Even where the employee's rights are *nonforfeitable*, there will be no constructive receipt, provided (1) the agreement to defer compensation is entered into before the services are performed, and (2) the employer's promise to pay is not secured in any way.

Employers will often informally fund a deferred compensation plan through the purchase of a life insurance contract. This can be done without adverse tax consequences to the employee provided the employee has no interest in the contract and it remains the unrestricted asset of the employer and, as such, subject to the employer's general creditors. The employer should be the applicant, owner, and beneficiary of the contract. If the employee has any interest in the contract, he may be subject to current taxation.

Code section 409A has tightened up the deferral and distribution rules that apply to nonqualified deferred compensation plans. Under prior law the constructive receipt doctrine was the only restriction on the time and manner of deferred compensation *distributions* (e.g., provided a significant penalty was imposed, an employee could be given the right to withdraw funds at any time). Now a participant must make the *deferral* election before the start of the year in which the compensation is earned (prior law required that the election be made before the compensation was payable). See the expanded discussion of Section 409A on page 517.

See also, the discussion of Rabbi Trusts on page 493.

CONSUMER-DIRECTED HEALTH PLANS

Also known as "consumer-driven" health plans, these plans are a response to the escalating costs of health care and employee demands for more choice and better access to providers (i.e., the "healthcare backlash"). Under the managed care system the co-payments made by patients gave them little appreciation of the real cost of the health care services they were receiving. Consequently, patients had little or no incentive to hold costs down. Underlying consumer-directed health plans is the expectation that more cost-effective healthcare choices will be made by informed buyers who are motivated, price-sensitive, quality-minded, and actively involved in selecting healthcare providers and services.

Financial incentives are provided by employer-paid funds, carry forward of unused employer-paid fund balances, and first-dollar coverage for routine visits and preventive care (e.g., 100 percent of first $300 per covered individual with excess subject to a deductible). These plans are evolving in many different forms. A common plan design combines a high-deductible preferred provider organization (PPO) with an individual HRA out of which plan participants pay for routine care (see page 321).

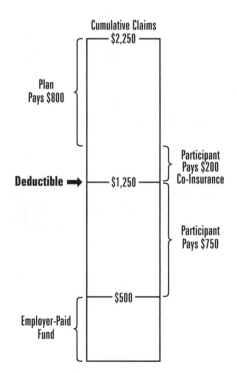

Cumulative Claims
$2,250
Plan Pays $800
Participant Pays $200 Co-Insurance
Deductible ➡ $1,250
Participant Pays $750
$500
Employer-Paid Fund

This chart illustrates a plan containing a $500 employer-provided fund, a deductible of $1,250 and a co-payment of 20 percent. For example, assume the plan participant submits a claim for $1,250. The first $500 of this claim is paid with the $500 employer-paid fund (it may be used toward both the deductible and coinsurance). The remaining $750 must be paid by the participant (the $1,250 deductible has now been satisfied). Assume the participant then submits a subsequent claim for $1,000. Since the annual $1,250 deductible has already been satisfied, the participant pays $200 (the 20 percent co-insurance) and the plan pays the remaining $800. Protection from more serious health conditions is provided by co-insurance limits and out-of-pocket maximums above which all expenses are paid by the plan.

The Patient Protection and Affordable Care Act applies to high-deductible and low-premium consumer-directed health plans that are linked to Health Reimbursement Arrangements (chart page 247) and Health Savings Accounts (chart page 251).

CONTINGENT OWNERSHIP

In planning their estates, clients are sometimes reluctant to give up control of policy values and death benefits. In these situations, "contingent" ownership of a survivorship life policy insuring both husband and wife can be used to provide some measure of flexibility. However, with this technique there is ongoing estate tax exposure that could be avoided by using a third party as the original policy owner (see Life Insurance Trust chart, page 51). Flexibility is achieved by maintaining individual ownership of the life insurance policy and designating an irrevocable trust as contingent owner of the policy (which could subsequently be changed to a new irrevocable trust with different provisions and beneficiaries).

Assume that husband and wife need life insurance to cover estate taxes and other estate settlement costs. They apply for a survivorship life insurance contract paying a death benefit at the death of the second spouse to die (see page 535). The policy owner should be that person who is most likely to die first. Since the husband is older than his wife, he is named policy owner (see table, pages 555-556). An irrevocable life insurance trust is designated as both beneficiary and "contingent" owner (e.g., by endorsement to the contract specifying the trust as owner upon the husband's death). One of three scenarios is likely to occur:

1. **Husband dies first.** The trust becomes policy owner and the value of the policy at the time of death is its interpolated terminal reserve (approximately the cash values). This is the value of the policy to be included in the husband's gross estate (because many survivorship policies provide for a large cash value increase upon the first death this amount could be substantial). Since the wife never owned the policy, upon her subsequent death the policy proceeds paid to the trust are not included in her estate.

2. **Wife dies first.** If the husband continues to own the policy, the death proceeds will be included in his estate upon his subsequent death. However, the husband could give the policy to the irrevocable trust (or to any third party), in which case the proceeds will be excluded from his estate *provided* he lives for more than three years after the gift (see pages 409-410). Although this exposure to estate taxation is aptly described as "estate planning roulette," with some clients it may be an acceptable risk if they are unwilling to give up control from the inception of the policy.

3. **Husband and wife die in a common disaster.** A "reverse common disaster" clause might be used to establish a conclusive presumption that the wife survives her husband (i.e., husband dies first). See discussion on page 364.

It is strongly recommended that this technique only be resorted to when a client is unwilling to have the insurance policy owned by an irrevocable life insurance trust. Such a trust can *assure* that both cash values and death proceeds are not subject to estate taxation (see chart, page 51).

CONTROLLING STOCKHOLDER

The concept of a controlling stockholder, also referred to as a "majority stockholder," is important with respect to split-dollar plans in which the death benefit is shared between the corporation and the insured's personal beneficiary. As with any key person insurance, that part of the *death benefit received by the corporation* on a policy insuring a controlling stockholder is included with other assets in valuing the corporation, and thus in determining the value of stock in the controlling stockholder's estate. But that part of the *death benefit received outside of the corporation* by a personal beneficiary or a trust will also be included in the insured's estate where the insured was a controlling stockholder, since any incidents of ownership held by the corporation are attributed to the insured through his stock ownership as a controlling stockholder. A person is considered a controlling stockholder when, at the time of his death, he owns more than 50 percent of the voting stock of a corporation.

Assume a split-dollar plan is funded by a $500,000 policy paying $100,000 to the corporation and $400,000 to the employee's beneficiary. Because corporate ownership is attributed to the controlling stockholder, the $400,000 death benefit paid to the personal beneficiary is included in the estate. The concept can be illustrated as follows:

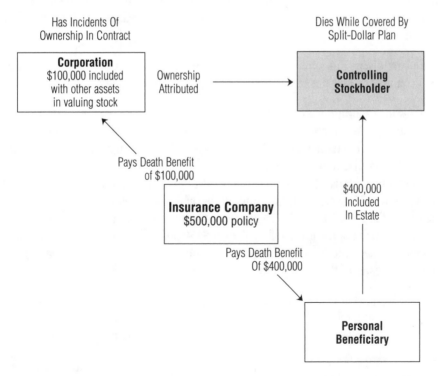

Note: See the Life Insurance As Property chart on page 71, discussion in footnote 3 on page 221, and **Q 245**, *Tax Facts on Insurance & Employee Benefits (2011)*.

CORPORATE ALTERNATIVE MINIMUM TAX

The corporate alternative minimum tax (AMT) is designed to assure that the taxpayer with substantial economic income will not be able to avoid taxes merely by using available tax exclusions, deductions, and credits.

A corporation qualifying as a "small corporation" is not subject to the alternative minimum tax. A small corporation is a corporation that for its first tax year beginning after 1996 has average annual gross receipts not exceeding $5,000,000 for the preceding three-year period (if the corporation was in existence less than three years, then the test will be applied to whatever period it was in existence). Annualization of receipts is required for any short taxable year. Once a corporation qualifies as a small corporation, it will continue to be treated as a small corporation as long as its average gross receipts for the three-year period preceding the taxable year do not exceed $7,500,000.

Gross receipts include total sales (net of returns and allowances) and all amounts received for services. In addition, gross receipts include any income from investments, and from incidental or outside sources. For example, gross receipts include interest, dividends, rents, royalties, and annuities, regardless of whether such amounts are derived in the ordinary course of the taxpayer's trade or business. Gross receipts are generally not reduced by the cost of goods or property sold.

The following discussion applies only to those corporations that do not qualify as a "small corporation" and therefore are subject to the alternative minimum tax.

As it applies to corporations, the AMT requires that the corporate tax base be determined with certain adjustments and increased by specific tax preferences. Two of the more common tax preference items are accelerated depreciation and certain tax-exempt interest. In the process of determining the alternative minimum taxable income (AMTI) of a C corporation, 75 percent of the amount by which adjusted current earnings (ACE) exceed the tentative AMTI is added to the tentative AMTI (or 75 percent of the amount by which the tentative AMTI exceeds ACE is subtracted from the tentative AMTI). The resulting amount is then reduced by an exemption of $40,000 less 25 percent of the excess of AMTI over $150,000. The resulting tax base is multiplied by 20 percent to determine the tentative minimum tax. The corporation then pays a tax equal, in effect, to the greater of this amount or its regular tax.

Although ACE is not equivalent to current earnings and profits (E&P), some of the adjustments used in computing ACE rely on E&P concepts. For example, life insurance will increase ACE, since under generally accepted accounting principles E&P are increased by: (1) yearly cash value

(continued on next page)

CORPORATE ALTERNATIVE MINIMUM TAX (continued)

increases in excess of annual premiums; and (2) death proceeds (including outstanding loans) in excess of basis increased for cash value increases previously included in AMTI. Proceeds from disability income and buy-out policies payable to the corporation are also included in ACE.

Conversely, if premiums are paid for term insurance, or the cash value increase is less than the annual premium, there is a *decrease* of ACE that reduces exposure to the AMT. However, redemption of the deceased or disabled owner's stock in the same year as the proceeds are received will not avoid an increase in ACE.

The existence of the AMT does not mean that all, or even most, life insurance cash values or death proceeds will be subject to the tax. Much depends upon the corporation's taxable income, tax preference items, and other factors (e.g., S corporations are not subject to the ACE adjustment). Only a portion of cash value increases and death proceeds will be potentially exposed to this tax, since cash value increases will be partially offset by premiums; and death proceeds will be offset by cash values. Even when there is exposure, generally **the maximum rate is 15 percent** (i.e., a 20 percent tax on 75 percent of ACE). With many corporations payment of the tax will be an *acceleration of* rather than an *increase of* tax liability, since it then becomes a credit available to offset a portion of the corporation's tax liability in future years (unlimited carry forward). However, this credit may be useless to the closely held or professional corporation that will have little, if any, taxable income.

(continued on next page)

CORPORATE ALTERNATIVE MINIMUM TAX (continued)

Impact Of Alternative Minimum Tax
On Life Insurance Death Benefits
Payable To C Corporation

Taxable Income	Death Benefit				
	100,000	250,000	1,000,000	2,500,000	5,000,000
0	**7,000**	**31,375**	**150,000**	**375,000**	**750,000**
	7,000	31,375	150,000	375,000	750,000
25,000	**12,000**	**37,625**	**155,000**	**380,000**	**755,000**
	8,250	33,875	151,250	376,250	751,250
50,000	**17,000**	**43,875**	**160,000**	**385,000**	**760,000**
	9,500	36,375	152,500	377,500	752,500
100,000	**28,250**	**56,375**	**170,000**	**395,000**	**770,000**
	6,000	34,125	147,750	372,750	747,750
250,000	80,750	**87,500**	**200,000**	**425,000**	**800,000**
		6,750	119,250	344,250	719,250
500,000	170,000	170,000	**250,000**	**475,000**	**850,000**
			80,000	305,000	680,000
1,000,000	340,000	340,000	**350,000**	**575,000**	**950,000**
			10,000	235,000	610,000
2,000,000	680,000	680,000	680,000	**775,000**	**1,150,000**
				95,000	470,000

Note: This chart assumes the C corporation is not exempt from the alternative minimum tax (AMT) as a "small corporation." Small figure represents that portion of the income tax that is attributable to the death benefit (i.e., additional tax imposed under the AMT calculations). The corporation is assumed to have no tax preference items. No adjustments are made for cumulative premiums paid and for possible annual cash value increases in excess of premiums paid (i.e., "basis for ACE"). As an example of how to use this chart, assume a corporation has $500,000 of taxable income in a given year and also receives a death benefit payment of $1,000,000. The corporation will owe federal income taxes of $250,000 of which $80,000 is attributable to the effect of the AMT and the receipt of the life insurance death benefit. If this corporation received the same $1,000,000 death benefit but had $2,000,000 of taxable income, the corporation would owe $680,000 in taxes, none of which would be attributable to the death benefit and the AMT. This chart also indicates that a corporation with taxable income of $1,000,000 could consider increasing its key person life insurance on a key employee from $100,000 to $250,000 without additional exposure to the AMT (i.e., the income taxes remain at $340,000).

COVERDELL EDUCATION SAVINGS ACCOUNT

A Coverdell Education Savings Account, originally called an "Education IRA," may be created for the purpose of paying the qualified education expenses of a designated beneficiary. The 2010 Tax Relief Act extended through 2012 the annual non-deductible contributions of $2,000 per beneficiary that can be made to these accounts (it was scheduled to be reduced to $500). The beneficiary must be under age 18 (except in the case of a special needs beneficiary). This $2,000 annual contribution limit is phased out ratably for individual taxpayers with modified AGI between $95,000 and $110,000, and for married taxpayers filing jointly with modified AGI between $190,000 and $220,000. Contributors with modified AGI above this phase-out range are not allowed to make contributions to an Education Savings Account. This contribution limit is per beneficiary, meaning that multiple contributors cannot exceed the $2,000 per beneficiary per year limit (e.g., if grandfather contributes $1,800 for grandson then grandmother is limited to contributing an additional $200 for grandson).

Contributions to an Education Savings Account are not tax deductible, but will be treated as completed present interest gifts from the contributor to the beneficiary at the time of the contribution. A taxpayer may claim a American Opportunity Credit or Lifetime Learning Credit for the same taxable year there are distributions from an Education Savings Account, provided the distributions are used to pay for different education costs.

When the funds are distributed to pay the beneficiary's qualified education expenses, *neither the principal nor the earnings will be included in the beneficiary's income*. Qualified education expenses include elementary and secondary school tuition, expenses of special needs beneficiaries, post-secondary tuition, fees, books, supplies, uniforms, equipment, and certain room and board expenses. The earnings portion of distributions that are not used to pay for qualified education expenses is not only taxed to the beneficiary, but is also subject to an additional 10-percent-penalty tax. For this purpose, the "earnings portion" means any growth in the funds in excess of the nondeductible contributions.

Any balance remaining in an Education Savings Account at the time a beneficiary becomes 30 years old (except in the case of a special needs beneficiary) or dies, if earlier, must be distributed. The earnings portion of such a distribution will be includable in gross income of the beneficiary and will be subject to the additional 10-percent-penalty tax because the distribution was not for educational purposes. However, it is possible to avoid taxation by rolling the account balance over to another Education Savings Account benefiting a different beneficiary, who is a member of the family of the original beneficiary and who has not attained age 30 as of such date (except in the case of a special needs beneficiary).

CRITICAL ILLNESS INSURANCE

Major advances in medical sciences in recent years have resulted in substantial increases in the number of people surviving a critical illness. Survival periods have also been increasing. For example, in 2006, the American Heart Association reported that 75 percent of men and 62 percent of women suffering a heart attack would be alive one year later. Advancements in treatment have caused more forms of cancer to be viewed as chronic illnesses rather than terminal diseases. Critical illness insurance is designed to provide for those suffering from, and surviving, such illnesses.

Critical illness insurance typically pays a benefit upon the *diagnosis* of the first occurrence of a named critical illness or condition. Some products provide for payments for a limited number of conditions, such as heart attack, stroke, or cancer. Other products pay upon such wide ranging conditions as Alzheimer's Disease, multiple sclerosis, major organ transplant, kidney failure, loss of sight, loss of use of two or more limbs, any terminal illness, or death.

Although often resembling the more common "dreaded disease" products, critical illness insurance typically offers substantially greater coverages and benefits. For example, proceeds might be used to provide for home health care needs, replace lost wages of the insured or a care-giver, provide for housekeeping or child care services, pay for "experimental" treatment or drugs, pay medical copayments and deductibles, or make modifications to automobiles and homes for a disabled survivor. Benefits can vary widely. The amount can be either a fixed sum or a percentage of a life insurance death benefit. Payments can be made as a lump sum or over a number of years. Typically, coverage terminates at age 65 or 70.

While critical illness insurance has apparently gained wide acceptance in the United Kingdom, Australia, and Japan, within the United States it is not available in all states. The product is likely to have wide application, not just to the married couple or business owner but also to the single person, who, after suffering a critical illness becomes his or her own dependent (traditionally a difficult market for life insurance). The increase of consumer-directed health plans, larger medical deductibles and lower reimbursement caps, are all likely to increase interest in the product.

It is currently offered in the form of a stand-alone product, as a rider to a life insurance policy, as group insurance, or as part of a health, term life, or universal life policy. However, payment of critical illness benefits from a life insurance policy could reduce death benefits and reduce or eliminate accumulated cash values.

There is debate as to whether critical illness insurance can give the purchaser a false sense of security (i.e., the product covers only specific illnesses when there is a need for comprehensive health insurance).

CRUMMEY POWERS

By using the gift tax annual exclusion, in 2011 up to $13,000, as adjusted for inflation, can be given tax free each year to as many people (donees) as desired. However, this exclusion is available only when the donee has a right to the immediate use, possession, or enjoyment of the property that is the subject of the gift (i.e., a "present interest" in the property as opposed to a "future interest").

Although outright gifts present no difficulty with this requirement, gifts made to trusts are often subject to substantial restrictions on the beneficiaries' (donees') rights to the trust property. Under these circumstances, in order to assure the availability of the annual exclusion it is important for the beneficiaries to be given powers to withdraw gifts placed in a trust. These powers are often referred to as "Crummey powers." The term is derived from the case of D. Clifford Crummey v. Commissioner, 397 F.2d 82 (9th Cir. 1968). A trust containing such powers is often referred to as a Crummey Trust.

Typically these withdrawal rights, or "Crummey powers," are exercisable only during a specific period of time (e.g., for 30 days after receiving notice of the gift to the trust). For the power to be effective, the beneficiary must receive timely notice of the gifts, but the withdrawal rights are noncumulative and will lapse after the designated period of time.

For example, an irrevocable life insurance trust might provide for each beneficiary to have "the right to demand up to $5,000, not to exceed the amount placed in the trust during the calendar year." Note that the power is usually limited to $5,000, rather than the full $13,000 allowed as the annual exclusion or the $26,000 allowed as a split-gift (the $13,000 annual exclusion is subject to indexing for inflation). Such a limitation avoids creating adverse gift and estate tax consequences for the beneficiaries of the trust (for a further explanation, see page 46). A "hanging" Crummey power used to avoid a lapse of a power of withdrawal in excess of the greater of $5,000 or 5 percent of the trust corpus should be drafted by reference to such "5-or-5" limitation and not as a tax savings clause (see footnote 4, page 53).

An alternative to the Crummey power is the cumulative power, which is a vested withdrawal right that does not lapse. Use of a cumulative power enables the trust grantor to make annual gifts of $13,000 (subject to indexing) per beneficiary without causing problems with lapsing powers of withdrawal. However, these nonlapsing withdrawal powers are always subject to being exercised in case of bankruptcy or divorce, and would be included in the beneficiary's estate.

DEATH BENEFIT ONLY PLAN

Under the usual survivor income plan, the present value of the survivor income payments is considered to be a part of the employee's taxable estate. With a larger estate, the "death benefit only plan" (DBO plan) offers a particular type of survivor income plan that can be designed to keep these benefits out of the employee's taxable estate and thereby avoid federal estate taxes. However, because of the unlimited marital deduction, there is no exposure to federal estate taxes unless benefits are payable to someone other than the surviving spouse (e.g., children or other heirs).

In order to establish a death benefit only plan, it is essential that the employee have no right to any post-retirement or disability benefits from his employer, other than those which would be made available under a qualified pension or profit sharing plan. Nor can the employee have any right to alter, amend, revoke, or terminate the survivor income agreement or change the beneficiary, either alone or with the consent of any other person.

Typically, the employer and employee enter into a legally binding agreement under which the employer agrees to provide a specified payment, or payments, to a named beneficiary of the employee. In the agreement, it is the employer, not the employee, who names the beneficiary, and the employee cannot thereafter change the beneficiary. The actual payments are usually either a fixed amount or based upon some multiple of salary.

If life insurance is used to provide the employer with funds to meet his obligation under the agreement, the policy should be carried as key person insurance and the agreement itself should contain no specific mention of the insurance funding. Although, as with all key person insurance, the premiums paid by the employer come from after-tax dollars, none of the premiums are included in the employee's income. Should the employee die, the employer's payments to the employee's beneficiary under the DBO plan are received as ordinary income and are deductible by the employer, provided they are considered as "reasonable compensation" for the employee's services (see page 546).

There may be some question as to whether a DBO plan would be successful in removing the death benefit from the estate of a controlling stockholder, since his voting control of the corporation gives him the right to alter, amend, or terminate the agreement.

DECOUPLING OF STATE DEATH TAXES

Prior to the Economic and Tax Relief Act of 2001 (EGTRRA), the majority of states imposed a state death tax that was equal in amount to the allowable state death tax credit under federal law (known as a pick-up or sponge tax). Other states, that maintained an independent state death tax system, imposed a tax at least equal to the state death tax credit (i.e., the tax imposed was the greater of the state death tax credit or the separately computed state tax). Under this system of revenue-sharing, all states imposed a tax at least equal to the federal credit. For example, in 2001 the maximum federal estate tax of 55 percent was effectively split into two parts, with 39 percent paid to the federal government and 16 percent paid to the state government (lesser percentages were provided in a table for taxable estates under $10,100,000).

Under EGTRRA, the state death tax credit was eliminated and replaced with a deduction from 2005 to 2009 (for the taxpayer a deduction provides less than half the benefit of a credit). This elimination of the state death tax credit effectively repealed the state inheritance tax in those states that levied a tax exactly equal to the state death tax credit. Threatened with the loss of significant revenue, many states responded by "decoupling" from the federal estate tax. The laws designed to recoup lost revenues have taken a number of different forms, to include:

(1) **Decoupling as to the tax rate but not the exempt amount.** For example, in the chart on page 25, no state tax would be imposed on up to $5,000,000 going to the family trust (state exemption is equal to federal exemption), but upon the second death the amount in excess of $5,000,000 would be subject to a maximum tax of 16 percent.

(2) **Decoupling as to both the tax rate and the exempt amount.** For example, assume a pick-up state decouples by imposing a tax based on the law immediately prior to EGTRRA 2001 (i.e., $675,000 is exempt and the top rate is 16 percent). In the chart on page 35, placing $5,000,000 in the family trust to take full advantage of the federal unified credit would expose $4,325,000 to *state* death taxes (5,000,000 - 675,000 = 4,325,000).

Sunset provisions provided for return of the state death tax credit in 2011, as it existed in 2001. However, The 2010 Tax Relief Act extended the deduction through the end of 2012, effectively denying a return of the revenue-sharing income to the states.

To cope with the lack of uniformity from state to state and the ongoing uncertainty of the federal estate tax, additional flexibility should be added to estate plans (e.g., post mortem planning with disclaimers, see page 389). See also the planning pointers on pages 5-7 and the discussion of post mortem planning on 476.

DEEMED IRA

With deemed IRAs, also referred to as "sidecar IRAs," the participants in qualified plans, Section 403(b) plans, and eligible 457 plans are allowed to make traditional and Roth IRA contributions to a separate account or annuity established under their employer's plan. As to timing and limits on *contribution*, timing and taxation of *distributions*, and *reporting/disclosure* requirements, deemed IRAs are subject to the same rules governing traditional and Roth IRAs (see pages 307, 308, 427 and 506). Compliance with the rules for traditional IRAs under Section 408, or for Roth IRAs under Section 408A, means that the account (or annuity) will be "deemed" an IRA and not a qualified employer plan.

It remains to be seen how popular deemed IRAs will become. Initially, they appear to offer the following *employee advantages*: (1) they may encourage retirement savings by facilitating the coordination of pension and IRA investments (i.e., "one-stop shopping" for retirement savings); (2) they provide the convenience of consolidation of IRA contributions, both traditional and Roth, in the same investment options as employer plan assets (i.e., for investment purposes IRA funds can be commingled with other funds in the qualified plan, but the contributions and earnings must be separately accounted for); (3) they are potentially less expensive than stand-alone IRAs; and (4) as compared to a stand-alone IRA the employer's qualified plan offers better protection from the employee's creditors. Additionally, it is also to the employee's advantage that deemed IRAs will be subject to the general fiduciary rules and claims procedures applicable to qualified retirement plans, but this is likely to be viewed as a disadvantage to employers.

The deemed IRA was originally scheduled to be terminated in 2010 under the "sunset" provisions of EGTRRA 2001, but was subsequently made permanent by the Pension Protection Act of 2006.

DEFERRAL OF ESTATE TAX

The federal estate tax is normally due and payable in cash within nine months after death. However, special deferral provisions are available for a "closely held" business, provided: (1) the business interest exceeds 35 percent of the adjusted gross estate; and (2) the decedent was a sole proprietor, a partner in a partnership with 45 or fewer partners (or owning 20 percent or more of the partnership capital interest), or a stockholder in a corporation with 45 or fewer stockholders (or owning 20 percent or more of the voting stock in a corporation).

If an estate meets these requirements, then the estate taxes attributable to the business interest may be deferred for 4 years during which interest only is payable. Thereafter, there is a maximum period of 10 years during which annual installments of principal and interest must be paid (Code section 6166).

The interest rate was only 2 percent on the tax attributable to the first $1,360,000 in business value (as indexed in 2011 for inflation) in excess of the "applicable exclusion amount." Under prior law the applicable exclusion amount was known as the "exemption equivalent." In 2011 the applicable exclusion amount is $5,000,000 and the unified credit is $1,730,800. The tax on $6,360,000 of assumed business value is $2,206,800 and the tax on the first $5,000,000 of business value is $1,730,800 (i.e., the unified credit). Therefore, the maximum amount of tax deferrable at the 2 percent rate is $476,000 ($2,206,800 − $1,730,800 = $476,000). Any estate tax that is attributable to the business interest in excess of $476,000 is deferrable at 45 percent of the rate applicable to underpayment of tax (4 percent in the last quarter of 2010).

Before relying on the Section 6166 deferral provisions as an alternative to life insurance, a business owner should give serious consideration to **the following qualifications and restrictions**:

1. **The business** interest **must meet strict qualification standards and percentages** in order for the deferred payment provision to be available.

2. **Not all settlement costs can be deferred**. For example, federal estate taxes on non-business assets, state death taxes, income taxes, debts, and administrative expenses must normally be paid in cash when due.

3. **The interest** payments **are not deductible**.

4. **Only a limited** amount **of tax** can qualify for the 2 percent interest rate (in 2011 the amount is limited to $476,000).

5. **All remaining** payments **may be accelerated** if either installment or interest payments are not made within 6 months of the due date, in addition to the payment of a 5 percent per month penalty.

6. **The executor is** personally **liable** for payment of the tax and must post a bond of up to twice the amount of the deferred tax unless a special IRS tax lien is placed on the estate.

7. **Extensive delays** in the final disposition of the estate will often occur when there is a deferral of the estate tax.

8. **The** tax must be paid. The deferral provisions only allow the business to continue with another creditor (the IRS) making demands on cash flow.

9. **After-tax dollars must be used to pay the tax**. For example, an individual in a 35 percent bracket would require $1.54 of before-tax income in order to pay $1.00 of estate taxes ($1.54 - ($1.54 × .35) = $1.00).

DEFINED BENEFIT PENSION PLAN

Under the defined benefit pension plan the employer guarantees a specified benefit at "normal retirement age." Based upon actuarial calculations the employer is required to maintain a level of "minimum funding" such as will assure that funds will be available to pay this guaranteed retirement benefit. In contrast to defined contribution pensions, such as the money purchase pension plan, there are no individual accounts.

The maximum amount of the projected annual benefit at age 65 (paid as a life annuity or as a joint and survivor benefit) is limited to the lesser of $195,000 (as indexed in 2010 and 2011), or 100 percent of compensation averaged over the three highest-earning consecutive years (if normal retirement age is earlier than age 62 these maximum limits are reduced). In contrast to the money purchase pension plan, a defined benefit pension plan has maximum benefit limits but not maximum contribution limits (i.e., the regulatory concern is directed toward assuring that minimum funding standards are met). However, plan contributions must be suspended if the plan is found to be overfunded. In determining the specified benefit integration with Social Security is allowed.

Under a defined benefit pension plan the employer bears the investment risk of the plan (i.e., the employer is obligated to pay a specified benefit upon the employee's retirement). Up to specific limits the benefits of a defined benefit pension plan are guaranteed by the Pension Benefit Guaranty Corporation. See page 469.)

Various formulas are used to determine the employee's benefit: (1) **Flat amount formula** – all employees receive the same stated dollar monthly benefit without regard to the employee's level of compensation (e.g., $600 per month for life beginning at age 65). However, some minimum years of employment might be required for the maximum monthly benefit, with reduced benefits for lesser years of employment. (2) **Flat percentage formula** – each employee receives a benefit that is based upon a percentage of his average earnings (e.g., 50 percent of average earnings for life beginning at age 65). However, some minimum years of employment might be required for the maximum monthly benefit, with reduced percentages for lesser years of employment. (3) **Unit credit formula** – each employee receives a benefit that is based upon his years of employment (e.g., assuming 1¼ percent credit for each year of service an employee with 20 years of service and $100,000 of average earnings would receive a benefit of $25,000, calculated as 1.25 x 20 = 25 x .01 = .25 x 100,000 = 25,000).

Defined benefit pension plans entail high installation and administration costs, are complex to design, and are often difficult to understand. Despite these disadvantages they generally offer the older and more highly compensated employee a higher level of tax-deferred retirement savings and income.

See also, the discussion of qualified retirement plans on page 491, and the discussion of life insurance in qualified plans on pages 439-440.

DEFINED CONTRIBUTION HEALTH PLAN

The term "defined contribution health plan" describes a funding mechanism under which the employer pays a fixed amount of medical expenses on behalf of each employee. Beyond that, there appears to be little agreement among insurers, benefit managers, and commentators on how the term should be used. Under the simplest model the employer merely gives all employees a set amount of money and they are left to assemble their own health plans. But such direct cash payments to employees would undoubtedly be subject to being included in taxable income, since the employees would be under no obligation to use these funds for qualified medical expenses.

The term is more frequently used to describe various health plan models that allow employees to make decisions regarding the allocation of whatever dollars their employers are willing to contribute to an employee health plan. Under a "health reimbursement arrangement" the employer would merely reimburse the employee for medical expenses incurred by the employee from whatever source chosen by the employee (see Health Reimbursement Arrangements chart, page 247). Under other programs the employer prescreens and selects carriers and coverage parameters, and then presents employees with a menu of health care suppliers and options. See Medical Expense Programs, page 321.

Although the term "defined contribution" is often used interchangeably with "consumer-directed" health plans, it is not synonymous. Defined contribution only describes a contribution strategy, whereas consumer-directed more broadly describes the design features of a health care plan. See expanded discussion of Consumer-Directed Health Plans, page 371.

DISABILITY BUY-OUT INSURANCE

Disability buy-out insurance is designed to provide funds for the purchase of a disabled owner's interest in a corporation or partnership after an extended period of *permanent and total* disability. The benefits of such insurance include: (1) providing funds for the purchase, which funds are not tied to the continued success of the business; and (2) assuring that the disabled owner will no longer be a drain on business income and assets. In contrast, see the discussion of business overhead expense insurance on page 351.

A business is usually not eligible for coverage until it has been in existence for two years, although exceptions can be found (e.g., professional corporations). Maximum amounts of coverage typically range from $300,000 to $1,000,000, with specific amounts limited to a percentage of the owner's interest (e.g., 80 percent of fair market value). As with disability income insurance, definitions of disability vary widely, from inability to engage in one's "own occupation," to inability to perform the duties of "any other occupation" for which one is reasonably suited. It is *absolutely essential* that the provisions of the purchase agreement be consistent with the definitions and terms of the disability buy-out policy.

Because a disabled individual's chances of recovery are highest in the early months of his disability, the waiting period is extended and typically lasts from 12 months to three years (see disability statistics, page 322). This attempts to avoid the forced sale of a business interest while the disabled owner might reasonably expect to return to work. Benefits are paid to the "loss payee," who is that individual or business entity having the contractual obligation to purchase the disabled owner's interest (i.e., entity purchase or cross purchase, see charts on pages 127 and 131). Payment of proceeds can vary from lump sum to installment, with lump sum having the advantage of simplicity, but losing the tax advantage of spreading gain over a number of years.

Successive disabilities can cause a problem when the insured returns to work after being disabled for less than the waiting period, and thereafter suffers a second period of disability. Some policies require satisfaction of a new waiting period, while others consider both disabilities to be "continuous," provided the gap between them does not exceed a certain period. If the insured recovers after the end of the waiting period, but prior to the last indemnity payment, some policies will stop all future payments, while others disregard the recovery and make payments as originally scheduled (i.e., a form of "presumptive" disability).

Although the premiums are not tax deductible, the benefits are received tax-free by the loss payee. As with any other lifetime sale of a business interest, the disabled owner is subject to capital gains taxation of any gain on the sale of his business interest.

DISABILITY INCOME TAXATION

The general rule is that disability income payments under an employer's plan are included in gross income and fully taxable to the disabled employee, including both pre-retirement and post-retirement payments. However, if the payments have been received under a plan to which the employee has contributed part of the premium, that portion of the benefit attributable to the employee's contributions will be received free of income taxes. The tax treatment is the same, whether such payments are characterized as disability payments, salary continuation, wage continuation, or sick pay. See page 526 for an explanation of the taxation of Social Security disability payments.

Under some circumstances, there is a tax *credit* available to individuals who are: (1) age 65 or older; or (2) under age 65 and retired on permanent and total disability. The credit is equal to 15 percent of the taxpayer's "Section 22" amount of income for the year: $5,000 for single taxpayers or married taxpayers filing jointly when only one spouse qualifies for the credit (i.e., $750 credit), and $7,500 for married taxpayers when both qualify for the credit (i.e., $1,125 credit). If the taxpayer is under age 65, the base amount is limited to the amount of taxable disability income.

The base amount used to figure the credit must also be reduced: (1) for nontaxable pension or disability benefits received under social security, railroad retirement and certain other nontax laws; and (2) by one-half of the amount by which adjusted gross income exceeds $7,500 for single taxpayers, and $10,000 for married taxpayers filing jointly. The impact of these rules means that *no credit is available* if a taxpayer receives more than the following amounts of income:

	Nontaxable Social Security, pension, or disability benefits	or	Adjusted gross income
Single	$ 5,000		$ 17,500
Married filing jointly with one spouse qualified*	5,000		20,000
Married filing jointly with both spouses qualified*	7,500		25,000

* A qualified individual is one who is either age 65 or older, or under age 65 and retired on permanent and total disability.

DISABILITY UNDER SOCIAL SECURITY

In order to qualify for Social Security disability benefits an applicant must meet *all* nine of the following tests:

1. He is fully insured by: (1) accumulating 40 quarters of coverage (a total of ten years of covered work); or (2) accumulating at least six quarters of coverage provided he has acquired at least as many quarters of coverage as there are years elapsing after 1950 (or, if later, after the year in which he reaches age 21) and before the year in which he becomes disabled.

2. He has worked under Social Security for at least five of the 10 years (20 out of 40 quarters) just before becoming disabled, or if disability begins before age 31 but after age 23, for at least one-half of the quarters after reaching age 21 and before becoming disabled (but not less than six).

3. He is unable to engage in "any substantial gainful work that exists in the national economy," whether or not such work exists in the area, a specific vacancy exists, or the applicant would be hired if he or she applied for the work (however, consideration is given to age, education, and work experience).

4. Such inability results from "a medically determinable physical or mental impairment" which is expected to result in death, or which has lasted (or can be expected to last) for a continuous period of not less than 12 months. A special definition of the term "disability" is provided for individuals age 55 or over who are blind.

5. He is under 65 years of age.

6. He has filed an application.

7. He has furnished the required proof of disability.

8. He has fulfilled a five-month waiting period.

9. He accepts state vocational rehabilitation services or has good cause for refusal.

DISCLAIMER

The use of disclaimers in estate planning can often result in obtaining greater flexibility by providing the opportunity for post mortem decisions when more facts are likely to be available regarding assets, taxes, and beneficiaries. Disclaimers can be used for both tax and nontax purposes. For example, an individual might disclaim an inheritance in order to avoid losing eligibility for public benefits. Under limited circumstances disclaimers are sometimes used to benefit a charity and produce an estate tax charitable deduction. Disclaimers can also be employed outside an estate with respect to gifts, employee benefits, or life insurance proceeds.

To be effective, disclaimers must comply with state as well as federal tax law, must be made in writing prior to acceptance of the property or any of its benefits, contain an irrevocable and unqualified refusal to accept an interest in the property, and must be given to the holder of legal title to the property within nine months after the date that the transfer was made which created the interest (i.e., after death or date of gift). Because of their inherent flexibility, disclaimers have been increasingly used to deal with uncertainty (e.g., to allow a surviving spouse the opportunity to make post death adjustments to the amount placed in the family or non-marital trust under a Trust Will, see chart on page 25).

For example, the chart on page 25 shows an example of a trust will under which the testator directs that an amount equal to or less than the applicable exclusion amount be placed in the family trust ("B" Trust). Similar results could be obtained by passing all property to the surviving spouse, but with provision for a "disclaimer trust." The disclaimer trust would come into being only if the surviving spouse disclaimed, or refused to accept, a portion of the estate under the will. When funded as a result of such a disclaimer, the trust would function in exactly the same way as the family trust illustrated in the chart, except that the surviving spouse would decide exactly how much property, if any, was to go into the trust.

DIVORCE AND LIFE INSURANCE

Transfer of an existing policy incident to a divorce can generally be made without recognition of gain to the husband (this discussion assumes that property or income is being transferred from husband to wife, but the same principles apply if the transfer is from wife to husband). Because the wife is treated as having acquired the property by gift, the husband's cost basis is carried over to the wife, and since the transfer is within an exception to the transfer for value rule, the death proceeds can be received by the wife (or former wife) free of income taxes. A transfer is "incident to a divorce" if it is made within one year after the marriage is terminated or is made within six years after the divorce and pursuant to a divorce or separation instrument.

Payment of premiums pursuant to a divorce or separation agreement that qualify as alimony payments are deductible to the husband and taxable to the wife, provided the wife is owner of the policy. To qualify as "alimony": (1) the payment must be made in cash; (2) the divorce or separation instrument must not stipulate that the payments are not alimony; (3) there must be no liability to make payments after the death of the payee (wife); and (4) the parties must not be members of the same household.

Payment of death benefits to the divorced wife would be taxable as income if the policy had been owned and maintained by the husband pursuant to a divorce decree or agreement as security for post-death payments. However, if the policy had been owned by and payable to the divorced wife, the death benefits would be received free of income taxes.

DOMESTIC PARTNERS

Also referred to as nontraditional couples and unmarried partners, the term "domestic partners" includes both opposite-sex and same-sex couples. There currently exists a legal patchwork. Rights and benefits afforded to domestic partners in some jurisdictions may not be available or recognized elsewhere. This is particularly true with respect to same-sex couples.

Same-sex marriages are not recognized by most states and the federal government. The Defense of Marriage Act (DOMA) for all federal purposes defines "marriage" as a legal union between a man and a woman as husband and wife, and "spouse" as a person of the opposite sex who is a husband or wife. This law further mandates that all federal agencies not recognize same-sex marriages and civil unions; and additionally provides that no state is required to recognize another state's laws as to same-sex marriage. The reach of this law is substantial. For example, domestic partners are not entitled to federal benefits extended to married couples relating to income taxes, gift taxes, estate taxes, Social Security entitlements, IRAs, and retirement plans under ERISA. (Interestingly, a Private Letter Ruling has stated that the medical and dental benefits for a dependant domestic partner are not included in an employee's income.) A majority of states have enacted their own DOMAs denying recognition to same-sex marriages. The U.S. Constitution requires each state to give "full faith and credit" to the laws of the other states, except when it would violate the state's strongly held public policy. Same-sex marriages fall within the exception.

Vermont was the first state to recognize same-sex marriage by legislation. The Massachusetts Supreme Court ruled in 2004 that under the state constitution two individuals of the same sex have a right to the protections, benefits, and obligations conferred by civil marriage. In 2008 the Connecticut Supreme Court ruled that denying gays the right to marry was against the equality and liberty rules in the Connecticut Constitution. Iowa became the fourth state to recognize same-sex marriage when the Supreme Court of Iowa held that civil unions would violate the equal protection clause of the Iowa Constitution. New Hampshire recognized same-sex marriage effective January 1, 2010. California voters approved Proposition 8 eliminating the right of same-sex couples to marry. The District of Columbia began performing same-sex marriages in March of 2010.

California, Colorado, Maine, Maryland, Nevada, New Jersey, Oregon, Washington, and Wisconsin have enacted legislation recognizing either domestic partnerships or granting varying rights to same-sex unions. Other states and employers provide survivor and health care benefits to domestic partners, including same-sex couples (see News/Publications at www.lambdalegal.org). Differences between state separate and community property laws only add further complexity.

Despite this complex and evolving legal environment and the unique issues facing domestic partners, both same sex and opposite sex, there are effective techniques that domestic partners can use in planning their financial affairs and estate plans. As with a marriage, every domestic partner-ship or other non-marital relationship will sooner or later end with either separation or death.

(continued on next page)

DOMESTIC PARTNERS (continued)

Domestic partnership agreement. It is generally acknowledged that individuals can contract for most anything, provided it is legal and not against public policy. Domestice partnership agreements, also called cohabitation agreements, are similar to premarital (antenuptial) agreements in that they provide for a division of income, expenses, and assets, as well as provisions relating to termination of the relationship.

Wills. Domestic partners generally have no right to take under state intestacy laws (but California allows a surviving domestic partner to inherit a portion of the estate when a partner dies intestate). See pages 102-109. A will, or will substitute, assuring that property passes to a domestic partner should cover issues relating to qualification of a survivor to take under the will (e.g., defining the beneficiary as "that person living with me at my death," and disqualify a survivor from taking in case of "separation due to domestic disharmony"). It is also important to define exactly those children or other heirs that are to take under the will (e.g., children born or adopted prior to or after the domestic partnership agreement).

Revocable living trusts. As a will substitute, the living trust is particularly attractive to domestic partners, as it avoids probate and reduces the chances of a successful will challenge by the decedent's relatives (see page 28). However, unlike the exemption trust will on page 24, a "marital trust" will not shield assets from the estate tax (i.e., the federal unlimited marital deduction is not available).

Gifts. In 2011, present interest gifts of $13,000 and gifts that use the $5,000,000 gift tax applicable exclusion amount are both effective with domestic partners (see page 48). However, under federal law, split-gifts are available only to a married man and woman (see page 46).

Life insurance. It is generally required that an individual who is issued a life insurance contract on another person's life has an insurable interest (see page 429). In most states, domestic partners can avoid insurable interest problems by having the policy initially issued to the insured, and then later transferring the policy by gift to the other partner. An irrevocable life insurance trust offers many advantages to domestic partners (see page 50).

Joint tenancy. Although the simplicity of joint ownership is attractive, the following should be considered: (1) federal law includes the entire value in the first decedent's estate, unless the survivor can prove contributions; (2) the account is subject to the creditors of both partners; and (3) to pass the asset at death, the title must include the words "rights of survivorship."

Other techniques that should be considered include parenting agreements, direct payments for tuition and medical expenses (footnote 4, page 49), and financial and health care durable powers of attorney (page 394). Because the federal government does not recognize their relationship, same-sex couples may have greater flexibility in utilizing some estate planning techniques (e.g., under federal law, a GRIT can pass assets to a less wealthy "nonfamily" partner at a reduced transfer cost, see page 419).

DOMICILE

Domicile is the place that an individual has freely chosen as the center of his domestic and legal relations. It is the place he intends to remain indefinitely. However, residence without this intention to remain indefinitely does not constitute domicile. A person can have a number of residences, but only one domicile. Once acquired, a domicile is presumed to continue until it is shown to have been changed.

The impact of establishing domicile is far reaching. It determines a person's liability for state and local income taxes; liability for state and local gift and estate taxes; potential limitations on the right to choose fiduciaries such as executors or trustees; rights of surviving spouses to take against a will; community property rights between spouses; divorce and child custody issues; availability of homestead exemptions or similar laws that reduce real estate taxes on a primary residence; where wills must be probated; how property is passed if there is no will; liability for intangible personal property tax on stocks, bonds, and savings accounts; and the ability to vote in state and local elections.

To demonstrate the intent to establish a new domicile, the following actions should be taken: (1) register to vote in state and local elections; (2) obtain a new driver's license; (3) change automobile and boat registrations; (4) file for a homestead exemption on the new residence; (5) file a declaration of domicile, if the procedure is available in the new state; (6) remain physically present in the state for over one-half of the year; (7) file federal income tax with the Internal Revenue Service Center servicing the state and include new address on returns; (8) file state and local income tax returns for the new location; (9) file state and local intangible personal property tax returns, if imposed; (10) use the new address on all legal documents (e.g., contracts, wills, bills of sale, and deeds); (11) adopt new wills and trusts; (12) provide notice of the new address to banks, credit card companies, professional associations, insurance companies, publishers, friends, relatives, and others; (13) establish new relationships with doctors and dentists and have medical records transferred to them; (14) establish new relationships with professional advisers; (15) move stock brokerage accounts to local offices; (16) open checking and savings accounts at a local bank; (17) obtain a safe deposit box and place valuables and legal documents in it; (18) apply for a passport using the new address; and (19) become active in local social, civic, and religious organizations.

See also the discussion of noncitizen estate planning on page 463.

DURABLE POWER OF ATTORNEY

A power of attorney is a written document executed by one individual, the "principal," authorizing another person, the "attorney-in-fact," to act on his behalf. Under a *general* power of attorney, the powers are very broad and authorize the attorney-in-fact to enter into and discharge virtually all legal obligations on behalf of his principal. Under a *special* power of attorney, the powers are very limited and authorize the attorney-in-fact to perform only specific functions on behalf of the principal. Typically, either power of attorney is limited to acts being performed at a time when the principal himself has legal capacity (e.g., is not deceased, disabled, mentally incompetent, or under some other incapacity).

A *durable* power of attorney authorizes the attorney-in-fact to act even if the principal is incapacitated. The durable power of attorney has been recognized in some form in all states. Such powers of attorney may be either *immediate*, giving the attorney-in-fact power to act prior to an incapacity, or *contingent*, giving the attorney-in-fact power to act only when the principal has become incapacitated. This is particularly useful in estate planning situations where it may be desired to make gifts, file tax returns, or provide for the lifetime management of assets.

See also, Health Care Power Of Attorney, page 423, and Living Will, page 446.

DYNASTY TRUST

The term "dynasty" trust is often used to describe a trust created for the benefit of multiple generations. Such trusts are also referred to as "generation-skipping," "legacy," "mega," "dynastic," or "super" trusts. They are often similar to the typical irrevocable life insurance trust, but adapted to take advantage of the generation-skipping transfer tax (GSTT) exemption.

The federal transfer tax system is designed to tax property each time it is passed from one generation to the next. To assist in accomplishing this objective, the GSTT applies an additional tax to the normal gift or estate tax whenever property is transferred to persons two or more generations younger than the transferor, or whenever there are taxable distributions or terminations from a trust (see chart, page 39). However, a GSTT exemption is available which allows aggregate transfers of $5,000,000, in 2011, to be exempt from this tax ($10,000,000 total for both husband and wife).

A dynasty trust can be created during lifetime or upon death. In order to avoid the GSTT, the donor will typically allocate a portion of his GSTT exemption each time there is a transfer to the trust. Purchase of life insurance upon the life of the grantor, or upon the lives of trust beneficiaries, can result in a leveraging of trust assets through life insurance. Once assets are placed in the trust, and shielded from the GSTT, a properly drafted trust document would avoid subjecting the trust corpus to estate and gift taxes applicable to the trust beneficiaries (e.g., the trust beneficiaries would have no powers over trust assets such as would cause inclusion in their estates). However, a disinterested trustee could be given authority to make discretionary distributions of both trust income and corpus. Trust assets could be made available for use by trust beneficiaries and spendthrift provisions could protect trust assets from a beneficiary's estranged spouse and creditors. Special powers of appointments held by trust beneficiaries could also provide added flexibility (see page 477).

In its purest form, a dynasty trust would forever avoid application of the federal estate tax by providing that trust beneficiaries in each generation never have anything more than an income interest in trust property. However, this is generally prevented by the rule against perpetuities, which requires that trust assets must vest in the trust beneficiaries after a certain period of time (see page 509). Apparently even this limitation can be avoided by establishing a trust in those states where the rule has been eliminated by state statute.

The complexity of both the GSTT and state statutes effecting property interests make it extremely important to seek the advice of knowledgeable legal counsel when considering a dynasty trust.

EMPLOYEE STOCK OWNERSHIP PLAN (ESOP)

An employee stock ownership plan, or ESOP, is a stock bonus plan, or a stock bonus plan combined with a money purchase plan, that is designed to invest primarily in the common stock of the employer (see pages 457 and 525). However, unlike a pure stock bonus plan, the ESOP is typically used as a device for implementing the business continuation and estate planning objectives of its stockholders. The benefits provided by an ESOP are similar to those provided by a profit sharing plan, but they are distributable in stock of the employer, and contributions are not dependent upon employer profits.

An ESOP must meet specific requirements pertaining to coverage, nondiscrimination in contributions, limits on contributions, diversification of investments, and nonforfeiture of rights upon termination of employment. If these requirements are met, then the plan can be useful in:

1. Motivating employees toward increased productivity (the value of corporate stock held by the trust is dependent upon the corporate profitability).

2. Providing retirement income as a supplement to Social Security and other retirement benefits.

3. Generating liquidity for principal stockholders through the sale of stock to the ESOP during lifetime or after death.

4. Securing funds for corporate growth and expansion with untaxed dollars.

5. Avoiding taxation of accumulated earnings.

6. Securing income tax deductions for an employer with little or no cash outlay.

7. Paying for life insurance on key employees with before-tax dollars.

Leveraged ESOP. A "leveraged" ESOP can be used to borrow money from a financial institution based on the credit (and guarantee) of the employer. (Normally, loans or extensions of credit between an employer and its plans are "prohibited transactions," but the ESOP is exempt from these restrictions.) The borrowed funds are then used by the ESOP trustee to purchase stock from the employer. In turn, the employer typically uses these funds to finance expansion and capital purchases.

(continued on next page)

EMPLOYEE STOCK OWNERSHIP PLAN (ESOP) (continued)

Subsequent employer *contributions* to the ESOP are used by the ESOP trustee to repay the debt. In effect, provided employer contributions to the ESOP are within the annual additions limitations, this technique has enabled an employer to: (1) obtain funds for expansion by selling shares to the ESOP; and (2) repay the ESOP's bank loan with fully tax deductible dollars (i.e., in the form of deductible contributions to the ESOP). Had the employer borrowed the funds directly the interest payments would have been deductible, but repayment of principal would not have been deductible.

Distributions to employees may be made entirely in cash or partly in cash and partly in employer securities. Participants must be given the right to demand the entire distribution in the form of employer stock. If the stock is not readily tradable on an established market the participants must also be given the right to require the *employer* to purchase any distributions of employer stock made to them (a "put option").

It has been suggested that the complexity of establishing a leveraged ESOP is usually not necessary since the same tax benefit can be accomplished if the employer borrows funds directly from a financial institution and contributes an amount of its stock to a stock bonus plan each year equal in value to the amount of its loan repayment.

Non-Leveraged ESOP. ESOPs are also used to purchase an owner's stock interest on death (sometimes referred to as a "non-leveraged ESOP"). These arrangements entail giving the ESOP an *option* to purchase stock upon the stockholder's death. To fund the purchase the trustee of the ESOP acquires life insurance on the life of the stockholder. However, requiring the ESOP to purchase the stock under a formal stock purchase plan should be avoided, since it is likely that this purchase would be treated as a fully taxable stock dividend paid by the corporation to the estate. In contrast, if treated as a sale the transaction would likely produce little or no taxable gain due to the estate's stepped-up basis in the stock (see page 530).

ENHANCED DOLLARS

If a particular expenditure will not qualify as a tax-deductible business or personal expense, then it makes sense to use the lowest bracket taxpayer to make the payment. Understanding the concept of enhanced dollars will help in weighing the relative merits of executive equity or split-dollar, and cross purchase or stock redemption agreements (i.e., a corporate entity purchase agreement).

Enhanced after-tax dollars would be utilized when a corporation making less than $50,000 annually, and, therefore, in a 15 percent tax bracket, purchases and pays for insurance to fund a stock redemption agreement (chart, page 127). Although premium payments must be made with after-tax dollars, they will be made with enhanced 85 cent dollars, since the corporation gets to keep 85 cents of each dollar of taxable profit. This can be compared to a cross purchase agreement, under which the stockholders might have to pay premiums with their own after-tax dollars. In 2011, a married stockholder filing a joint tax return with taxable income over $139,350, and less than $212,300, is in a 28 percent marginal tax bracket, thus having 72 cent dollars available to pay premiums. Most clients would prefer to use 85 cent dollars rather than 72 cent dollars.

On the other hand, if the corporation was in a 34 percent tax bracket, only 66 cents of each corporate before-tax dollar is available to pay insurance premiums, as compared to the stockholder's 72 cent dollars. Under such circumstances a cross purchase agreement might be favored (chart, page 131).

See also, the tax rates set forth on page 549, and the Cost of Borrowed Dollars figures that appear on pages 182 and 183.

EQUITY SPLIT-DOLLAR

Under a split-dollar plan the term "equity split-dollar" is derived from the employee's interest in policy cash values (i.e., the employee has an "equity" interest). By sharing the ownership of cash values and limiting the employer's interest in the policy to its cumulative premium payments it was often possible for the employee to accrue substantial interests in the remaining cash values, with little or no adverse income taxation.

Until the final split-dollar regulations issued in 2003 there had been a great deal of uncertainty surrounding the tax treatment of equity split-dollar. However, Notice 2002-8 (issued in January of 2002) and proposed regulations (REG-164754-01 released in July of 2002) appeared to provide workable transition rules, safe harbors, and limited grandfathering of existing plans. The final split-dollar regulations (Treasury Decision 9092 issued in September of 2003) generally adopted the proposed regulations and dramatically altered the tax treatment of split-dollar plans. The tax treatment of new split-dollar plans is now governed by policy ownership.

Plans Established Prior To September 18, 2003

To better understand the transition rules for existing split-dollar plans and the application of the regulations to new split-dollar plans, it is helpful to break plans out according to the date they were entered into:

1. In split-dollar plans *entered into before January 28, 2002, and terminated before January 1, 2004*, the employee's equity will not be taxed. In split-dollar plans entered into before January 28, 2002, and terminated on or after January 1, 2004, the employee's equity will not be taxed, provided the plan is converted to a loan from the employer to the employee for all periods beginning on or after January 1, 2004 (if the plan is not converted to a loan, the employee will be taxed on all equity if the plan is eventually terminated). See the treatment of Employer/Employee Split-Dollar Plans (Table A) on page 296.

2. In split-dollar plans *entered into on or after January 28, 2002 and before September 18, 2003*, if the plan has not been converted to a loan the employee is subject to taxation on all equity in excess of the employee's basis when the plan is terminated (employee basis does not include amounts reported or paid for life insurance protection). But if the plan is not terminated the employee will not be currently taxed on equity as it builds up, provided the employee continues to report the receipt of the economic benefit and the employer retains some economic interest in the policy. See the treatment of Employer/Employee Split-Dollar Plans (Table B) on page 297.

(continued on next page)

EQUITY SPLIT-DOLLAR (continued)

Plans Established After September 17, 2003

In split-dollar plans entered into after September 17, 2003 (or prior plans that are "materially modified") taxation of employee equity depends upon how the plan is structured. Based upon policy ownership the split-dollar regulations use a formalistic, yet straight forward, approach in providing two "mutually exclusive regimes" (or methods) for the taxation of split-dollar plans (see also Table C on page 298).

Economic Benefit Regime. This regime applies when the *employer* owns the contract and the employee's death benefit is accomplished by a policy endorsement (known as endorsement split-dollar). (By exception this regime also applies when the employee owns the contract but the employer owns all cash values - see Split-Dollar Insurance chart, page 219.) In addition to being taxed for the value of the life insurance protection (i.e., the "economic benefit" as imputed income), the employee is also taxed on any increased interest in policy cash values (not just at rollout). Also, if the policy is subsequently transferred from the employer to the employee the employee is taxed on any employer equity (see Split-Dollar Rollout, page 528). The employee's basis in the policy is equal to the amount paid at the time of transfer, but *does not* include amounts that had been taxed to the employee on account of prior increases in policy cash values and amounts reported or paid for life insurance protection. Any premium amounts contributed by the employee are taxable income to the employer. Given these harsh rules it is doubtful whether the employee should be given an equity interest in plans established and taxed under the economic benefit regime. However, nonequity endorsement plans taxed under the economic benefit regime avoid many of these adverse tax consequences (see Split-Dollar Insurance chart, page 219).

Loan Regime. This regime applies when the *employee* owns the contract and collaterally assigns the policy cash values to the employer in order to secure repayment of the employer's premium advances (known as collateral assignment split-dollar). Because he already owns the policy and is obligated to repay any employer loans the employee is not taxed on the equity interest in policy cash values.

Each premium payment by the employer is treated as a separate loan to the employee ("deemed loan" in the chart below). If the employee fails to pay an adequate rate of interest they are classified as below-market split-dollar loans and he is considered to have received compensation equal to the foregone interest (taxable to the employee and deductible by the employer). This foregone interest is then imputed back to the employer (taxable to the employer but not deductible to the employee since it is considered personal in nature). The complexity of *loan regime* taxation, as illustrated in the following chart, should be compared with the simplicity of *economic benefit regime* taxation, as illustrated in the chart on page 219.

(continued on next page)

EQUITY SPLIT-DOLLAR (continued)

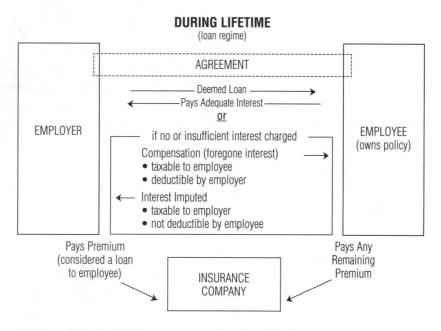

DURING LIFETIME
(loan regime)

For the purpose determining whether the employee has paid an adequate rate of interest loans are generally classified as either demand loans or term loans.

1. **Demand loan.** A split-dollar demand loan is due in full upon demand of the employer. If the employer reserves the right to terminate the split-dollar plan it is a demand loan (e.g., upon the employee's terminating his employment). These loans are tested each year for adequate interest by comparing the interest rate to the *blended* applicable federal rate (AFR) published in July of each year (in 2010 this rate was 0.59 percent). The foregone interest for that particular year is taxed as shown in the chart above. Classification as loan offers the advantages of being relatively easy to calculate with taxation spread over the term of the agreement, but has the disadvantage of being subject to yearly changes in the blended AFR.

   For example, assume the employer advances a $10,000 premium payment without interest in a year in which the blended AFR is 6 percent. The employee includes $600 in income ($10,000 x .06). Each employer premium payment is considered a separate loan and each loan must be tested every year for adequate interest rates.

(continued on next page)

EQUITY SPLIT-DOLLAR (continued)

2. **Term loan.** A split-dollar term loan is any loan that is not a demand loan (e.g., a loan payable in full in 15 years). Loans payable upon the death of the insured are also treated as term loans. The amount of the interest over the period of the loan is discounted to present value and then all of the interest is taxed in the very first year (i.e., all up-front). Classification as a term loan offers the advantage of knowing the interest rate for the loan's duration (it is not redetermined annually), but has the distinct disadvantage of being accelerated to the first tax year in which the loan is created (i.e., borrower must include all of foregone interest in the very first year, but lender reports interest income ratably over the term of the loan). The appropriate applicable federal rate (AFR) is based upon the original term of the loan (short-term for loans of 3 years or less, mid-term for loans between 3 and 9 years, and long-term for loans greater than 9 years). These AFR rates change monthly (in November of 2010 the AFR was 0.35 percent for short-term loans, 1.59 percent for mid-term loans, and 3.35 percent for long-term loans).

   For example, assume the employer advances a $10,000 premium payment repayable in 15 years without interest. Also assume that the AFR for a long-term loan is 5 percent. Discounted at 5 percent the present value of $10,000 payable in 15 years is approximately $4,810 ($10,000 times the factor of .4810 as obtained from the table on page 564). The employee is taxed on $5,190 (the difference between the $10,000 loan and the present value of the $4,810 repayment amount).

Sarbanes-Oxley Act. This law generally makes it a *crime* for any publicly-traded company to make loans to officers or directors (the law does not apply to closely-held companies). Enforcement of the Act falls within the jurisdiction of the Securities and Exchange Commission (SEC) and the SEC has yet to provide any guidance regarding its impact on split-dollar plans.

It is likely that new split-dollar plans taxed under the loan regime (employer premium payments considered employee loans) are prohibited, whereas new split-dollar plans taxed under the economic benefit regime are not prohibited (i.e., plans providing only death benefit protection for the employee). As to existing split-dollar plans, it is not clear whether the "grandfathering" provisions of this Act will apply (e.g., employer-paid premiums secured by employee-owned cash values considered as extensions of outstanding credit). Pending clarification, it may be prudent to consider: (1) using existing cash values to pay premiums; (2) reducing coverage to obtain a paid-up policy; or (3) paying premiums with employee bonuses.

EQUITY-INDEXED ANNUITY

This is an annuity that guarantees minimum interest earnings but links excess earnings to increases in an identified equity index. Equity-indexed annuities may be sold by individuals who are not equity licensed (see footnote 6, page 77). The Securities and Exchange Commission (SEC) has withdrawn proposed Rule 151A after the rule was vacated by the U.S. Court of Appeals for the District of Columbia in July of 2010. Under proposed Rule 151A the SEC could have considered an annuity a security that would have required selling agents to be equity licensed.

The workings of an EIA can be quite complicated and it is important to fully understand the product. Market conduct and disclosure are important issues with respect to EIAs. Because they can have so many "moving parts," the following discussion provides, at best, only a general outline of EIAs. Individual contracts can vary greatly. Second and third generation products are being introduced with new features and new complexities.

The EIA is particularly attractive to individuals who are concerned about the safety of principal but who want the opportunity to experience market related gains. Ideally, they should have available an easily understood product that provides the benefits of market appreciation without the risk of losing principal. In reality, they are likely to be faced with an array of products that are not easy to understand.

The minimum purchase amount is typically $5,000, but this can vary widely and is less for products sold in qualified markets. Both single premium and flexible premium contracts have been introduced. There are usually no sales charges (front-end loads), management fees or mortality costs. However, there are often large penalties for early withdrawals. Both level and declining surrender charges are used.

Contracts are linked to the growth of an index over a period that can range from one to ten years, although four to seven years appear most popular. This is referred to as the "term" of the contract or the policy period. While growth can be linked to the performance of virtually any equity index, the large majority of EIAs use Standard & Poor's 500 stock index (the S&P 500 Index). Virtually all EIAs that use the S&P 500 Index refer to the price-level version that excludes dividends. The other is the total-return version and it is determined using dividend reinvestment.

Central to the indexed annuity is a guarantee of principal at the end of the term. This is done by taking a set percentage of the purchase amount and accruing interest at a given percent for the contract term (e.g., 90 percent of a $100,000 deposit plus 3 percent over seven years provides a $111,000 end-of-term guarantee; $.90 \times \$100,000 = \$90,000$; $.03 \times \$100,000 = \$3,000 \times 7 = \$21,000$; $\$90,000 + \$21,000 = \$111,000$). The reason that most contracts use 90 percent of deposit and 3 percent for earnings is due to state law minimum guarantee requirements for fixed annuities.

(continued on next page)

EQUITY-INDEXED ANNUITY (continued)

Most contracts use one of three different methods to determine gain in the contract. For example, assume that upon issue of a contract with a six-year term the S&P Index was 700. Thereafter the index stood as follows:

End Of Year	1	2	3	4	5	6
S&P Index	781	834	823	871	904	880
Point-To-Point	-	-	-	-	-	25.71%
High-Water Mark	-	-	-	-	29.14%	-
Ratchet (27.98%)	11.57%	6.79%	0%	5.83%	3.79%	0%

Using the point-to-point method the gain is calculated using the beginning point of 700 and ending point of 880 (880 - 700 = 180 ÷ 700 = .2571). In contrast, the high-water mark method, also known as the discrete look-back method, uses the highest point of 904 (904 - 700 = 204 ÷ 700 = .2914). The ratchet method, also known as the annual reset method, calculates gain by adding up the sum of annual gains (11.57 + 6.79 + 0 + 5.83 + 3.79 + 0 = 27.98). A drop in the index is counted as zero. Unlike the other methods, this has the effect of locking in gains and annually resetting the starting point of the index. Earnings are typically not credited until the end of the term, thus there is no compounding of interest earned. Averaging can be done daily, monthly or annually. The usual effect of averaging is to increase the rate in a decreasing market and reduce the rate in a rising market (e.g., averaging the monthly gains the first year would likely result in less than 11.57 percent gain).

A cap (maximum rate) may be set on annual gains in the contract. The participation rate is the percentage of the index movement that will be credited (this can vary widely from 60 to over 100 percent). Some contracts guarantee the participation rate for the term of the contract, while other contracts reserve the right to change the participation rate or even lower the cap.

Liquidity features can include nursing home/hospitalization/terminal illness waivers, partial surrenders and penalty-free withdrawals (e.g., 10 percent per year). However, loans are not usually allowed. At the end of the contract term the owner can: (1) renew for another term; (2) make a tax-free exchange for another fixed or variable annuity; (3) surrender the contract without penalty; or (4) annuitize the contract.

Insurance companies fund indexed products by investing in high grade bonds in order to cover the end-of-term guarantee of principal, pay commissions and make a profit. The remaining funds are used to purchase S&P 500 Index call options (i.e., the right to purchase stock at a fixed price at some future time). If the market goes up selling the call options provides funds for meeting the contract obligations.

See also, the discussion of Guaranteed Minimum Withdrawal Benefit on page 421.

ERISA

The purpose of the Employee Retirement Income Security Act of 1974 (ERISA) is to protect the interests of workers and their beneficiaries who depend on benefits from employee pension and welfare plans. Among other things, the law requires disclosure of plan provisions and financial information, establishes standards of conduct for trustees and administrators, and sets up funding, participation, and vesting requirements for pension plans.

ERISA covers employee pension and welfare plans that are established or maintained: (1) by any employer engaged in commerce or in any industry or activity affecting commerce; or (2) by an employee organization or organizations representing employees of such employers.

A **pension plan** includes any plan that provides *retirement income* to employees or results in a *deferral of income* by employees to the termination of employment or beyond.

A **welfare plan** includes any plan that provides medical, surgical or hospital care, or benefits in the event of sickness, accident, *disability*, *death* or unemployment (other miscellaneous benefits are also covered).

Title I, Subtitle B, of ERISA contains requirements relating to the following:

Part 1 - Reporting and Disclosure
Part 2 - Participation and Vesting
Part 3 - Funding
Part 4 - Fiduciary Responsibility
Part 5 - Administration and Enforcement

Deferred Compensation Plans

Unfunded deferred compensation plans for a select group of management or highly compensated employees are generally considered pension plans and are subject to the following requirements:

Part 1 - Reporting and Disclosure. Can comply with by: (1) providing a letter to the Secretary of Labor giving the employer's name and address, IRS identification number, a statement that the employer maintains a plan or plans primarily for the purpose of providing deferred benefits for a select group of management or highly compensated employees, and the number of plans and number of employees in each plan; and (2) providing plan documents to the Secretary of Labor upon request.

Part 2 - Participation and Vesting. Not applicable.

Part 3 - Funding. Not applicable.

(continued on next page)

ERISA (continued)

Part 4 - Fiduciary Responsibility. Not applicable, unless considered a welfare benefit plan because death or disability benefits are provided. Can then comply by naming the employer, through one of its officers, as the plan's fiduciary. These requirements may be met in a properly drafted deferred compensation agreement.

Part 5 - Administration and Enforcement. Can comply by providing a definite procedure for handling claims, including providing a written explanation of any denial of benefits. These requirements may be met in a properly drafted deferred compensation agreement.

Split-Dollar Plans

Plans providing split-dollar insurance are generally considered welfare benefit plans under ERISA and are subject to the following requirements:

Part 1 - Reporting and Disclosure. Compliance is generally dependent upon the type of split-dollar plan, for example:

1. A noncontributory split-dollar plan (e.g., an endorsement employer-pay-all plan) for a select group of management or highly-compensated employees is exempt from these requirements, except for the requirement that plan documents be provided to the Secretary of Labor upon request.

2. A contributory split-dollar plan (e.g., a collateral assignment plan) having less than 100 participants is also exempt from these requirements, except for the requirement that plan documents be provided to the Secretary of Labor upon request and the need to provide the employee with a summary plan description. Generally, the summary plan description requirement can be satisfied by providing the employee with a copy of the split-dollar agreement and any policy ledgers prepared as part of the proposal.

Part 2 - Participation and Vesting. Not applicable.

Part 3 - Funding. Not applicable.

Part 4 - Fiduciary Responsibility. Can comply by naming the employer, through one of its officers, as the plan's fiduciary. Additionally, the plan documents must set forth procedures for funding the plan, allocating operational responsibilities, amending the plan, and making payments from the plan. These requirements may be met in a properly drafted split-dollar agreement.

Part 5 - Administration and Enforcement. Can comply by providing a definite procedure for handling claims, including providing a written explanation of any denial of benefits. These requirements may be met in a properly drafted split-dollar agreement.

ESTATE FREEZES

Code sections 2701-2704, together referred to as "Chapter 14," contain special valuation rules that maximize the gift tax value of many intra-family transfers by assigning zero value to specific retained interests (unless the retained interest is entitled to "qualified payments").

With Chapter 14 it is possible for a stockholder to freeze the value of a retained corporate interest (the preferred stock) and have a minimal gift tax value assigned to the common stock given to family members (see chart on page 167). However, recapture rules insure that the stockholder actually receives the anticipated dividends that are claimed to increase the value of the retained preferred stock (similar rules apply to partnership interests).

These valuation rules affect three categories of retained rights:

1. A cumulative distribution right with a preference upon liquidation is generally valued as the present right to future "qualified payments."

2. A noncumulative distribution right, or one that lacks preference upon liquidation, is valued at zero unless a "qualified payment" election is made.

3. A retained liquidation, put, call, or conversion right is valued at zero, unless the right must be exercised at a specific time and amount, or the right contains certain provisions which insure that its holder can share in appreciation.

For example, assume that pursuant to a recapitalization a stockholder transfers common stock to a family member and retains *noncumulative* preferred stock (a noncumulative distribution right under #2 above). Since the preferred stock (the retained interest) does not encompass a "qualified payment" (cumulative rights), it is valued at zero, meaning that the common stock represents the entire value of the corporation and is subject to gift taxes on that amount (to avoid this result, the transferor could elect into "qualified payment" treatment, with dividends to be paid in the amounts and at the times specified in the election). Alternatively, assume that after the transfer of common stock to a family member the transferor retains *cumulative* preferred stock with a liquidation preference (a cumulative distribution right under #1 above). In this instance, the transferor has retained a right to a "qualified payment" (i.e., to a dividend payable on a periodic basis and at a fixed rate or at a variable rate with a fixed relationship to market value). The value of the gift of common stock is then determined by subtracting the value of the qualified payment/preferred stock interests from the total value of the corporation (meaning that the common stock will have substantially less gift tax value). However, this reduction in the value of the common stock is limited by an additional provision requiring that all common stock (termed the "junior equity" interest) be given a value of at least 10 percent of the total value of the corporation (which, for this purpose, includes a gross-up equal to the total amount of corporate indebtedness to the transferor and family members).

(continued on next page)

ESTATE FREEZES (continued)

For the statute to apply: (1) the transfer must be to the transferor's spouse, lineal descendants of the transferor or the transferor's spouse, and the spouses of such descendants; and (2) the transferor and applicable family members immediately before the transfer must "control" the entity by owning, by vote or value, 50 percent of the stock. For purposes of "control" a person is treated as holding any interest held by his ancestor or his spouse's ancestor, or a spouse of such ancestor, or a lineal descendant of his parent or his spouse's parent (see Degrees Of Kindred chart, page 100).

The valuation rules assume that payments on the cumulative preferred will be made as scheduled. If payments are not made in accordance with a statutorily provided grace period, the rules provide for additional gift tax to be paid at the time of a subsequent lifetime transfer, or for additional estate tax at the death of the transferor (i.e., recapture). The increase in the taxable gift or taxable estate is the compounded value of the unpaid dividends using the same discount rate employed in determining the preferred stock's value.

Excluded from the scope of these valuation rules are interests in publicly traded stock, interests of the same class as the transferred interest, and interests that are proportionately the same (without regard to differences relating to nonlapsing voting power).

Affected by Chapter 14 are Buy/Sell Agreements (discussion in footnote 3, page 125), Family Holding Companies (discussion on page 410), Family Limited Partnerships (chart, page 163, and discussion on pages 465-466), Grantor Retained Annuity Trusts (chart, page 59), Grantor Retained Income Trusts (discussion on page 419), Personal Holding Companies (discussion on page 472), Recapitalizations (chart, page 167), and Remainder Interest Transactions (discussion on page 499).

Not affected are Deferred Compensation (chart, page 235), Installment Sales (chart, page 43), Life Insurance Trusts (chart page 51), and Private Annuities (chart, page 43). For a further discussion of the impact of Chapter 14 on specific techniques, see **Q 7617-7621**, *Tax Facts on Investments (2011)*.

ESTATE TAXATION OF LIFE INSURANCE

Section 2042 Proceeds of Life Insurance.

Incidents of ownership – Any incidents of ownership in a policy held by decedent at the time of death will cause the proceeds to be included in his estate. The regulations under Section 2042 state that the term "incidents of ownership" is not limited in its meaning to ownership of the policy in the technical legal sense. These rights include the power to: (1) the economic benefit of the policy, including the power to change the beneficiary; (2) surrender or cancel the policy; (3) assign the policy; (4) revoke an assignment; (5) pledge the policy for a loan; or (6) obtain a policy loan. However, direct or indirect payment of premiums is not an incident of ownership. See also, Life Insurance in Qualified Plans, pages 439-440.

Proceeds payable to estate – When proceeds are payable to or for the benefit of the deceased's estate they are subject to taxation in the insured's estate (e.g., when a trustee or third party is required to use the proceeds to pay estate taxes or other estate obligations).

Controlling stockholder – If the insured is a controlling stockholder and the corporation has any incidents of ownership in the policy, then proceeds paid to someone other than the corporation will be included in the estate of the insured. Under a split-dollar plan, an incident of ownership includes the right to borrow cash values (see expanded discussion and chart on page 373).

Fiduciary capacity – Under the regulations, an individual is considered to have an "incident of ownership" in an insurance policy on his life which is held in trust if he (either alone or in conjunction with another person or persons) has the power (as trustee or otherwise) to change the beneficial ownership of the policy or its proceeds, or the time or manner of enjoyment of the policy or its proceeds, even if he has no beneficial interest in the trust. It has been held that a co-trustee who has the right to elect a settlement option has a power to effect the time and manner of enjoyment of the policy proceeds insuring himself (i.e., he has an economic benefit). The courts are not consistent in their interpretation of the regulations (see **Q** 46 *Tax Facts on Insurance & Employee Benefits (2011)*).

Section 2035 Transfers of Life Insurance.

Transfer of a policy by an insured within three years of his death will cause the proceeds to be included in his gross estate. It is not necessary that the insured have outright ownership of the policy, since transfer within three years of death of any of the above "incidents of ownership" is sufficient to cause the policy proceeds to be included in his estate.

(continued on next page)

ESTATE TAXATION OF LIFE INSURANCE (continued)

Under the pre-1982 versions of Section 2035, using a "beamed transfer" theory the courts found constructive transfers of life insurance policies by insureds within three years of death where: (1) the policy was purchased on the initiative of the insured; (2) the insured supplied the funds used to purchase the insurance; and (3) the insured died within three years of the purchase. However, after the change to Section 2035 in 1981, the courts have refused to extend this beamed transfer theory to insureds dying after 1981 (*Estate of Leder*, 10th Cir. 1989, *Estate of Headrick*, 6th Cir. 1990, and *Estate of Perry*, 5th Cir. 1991).

In July of 1991, the IRS issued an action on decision in which the Service announced that it would no longer litigate the issue of whether life insurance proceeds are includable in the insured's estate where the life insurance policy is procured by a third party at the instance of the insured, the insured pays the premiums, and the insured dies within three years of procurement of the policy by the third person (i.e., the "beamed transfer" theory). This means that the incidents of ownership in a policy on the decedent's life that is issued to a trustee of an irrevocable life insurance trust will not be imputed to the decedent by reason of the fact that the decedent initiated the procurement of the policy, paid the premiums, or filled out the application for the policy in his capacity as the prospective *insured* (as distinguished from the prospective *owner* of the policy).

Recommended method of purchase and ownership. Despite the Service's favorable decision, it is recommended that whenever possible: (1) a third party be the original applicant, owner, and premium payer; (2) premiums come from an account held in the name of someone other than the insured, i.e., a trustee or adult child; (3) gifts should not be in the same amount as the premiums; (4) the gifts should be made at times other than premium due dates; (5) the insured not be named trustee of an irrevocable trust which owns a policy on his life; and (6) split-dollar plans involving controlling stockholders should avoid giving the corporation any incidents of policy ownership (see page 373). See also, table of ownership and beneficiary arrangements, page 89.

Section 2036 Retained Life Estate.
Section 2037 Reversionary Interests.
Section 2038 Revocable Transfers.

Property given away is still included in the decedent's estate if he: (1) retained the income from, use or enjoyment of, or the right to designate who will ultimately receive the property or its income; or (2) had a reversionary interest worth more than 5 percent of the value of the property at his death, and the person to whom the gift was made could obtain possession or enjoyment only by surviving the decedent; or (3) reserved the power to alter, amend, revoke, or terminate the gift.

FAIR MARKET VALUE

Property included in a decedent's gross estate is valued at its fair market value on the date of the decedent's death or, if the executor elects, its fair market value 6 months after death (i.e., the "alternate valuation date"). Fair market value is defined in Treasury regulations as the price at which an item of property, or a business interest, would change hands between a willing buyer and a willing seller, neither of whom is under any compulsion to buy or sell, and both of whom have a reasonable knowledge of all the relevant facts.

When it comes to valuing an interest in a closely held business, the above definition of fair market value is often of little practical assistance. In Revenue Ruling 59-60, the Internal Revenue Service set forth the following eight factors that are considered essential in valuing a closely held corporation:

1. The nature of the business and the history of the enterprise from its inception.

2. The economic outlook in general and the condition and outlook of the specific industry in particular.

3. The book value of the stock and the financial condition of the business.

4. The earning capacity of the company.

5. The dividend-paying capacity.

6. Whether the enterprise has goodwill or other intangible value.

7. Sales of stock and the size of the block to be valued.

8. The market price of stocks of corporations engaged in the same or a similar line of business having their stocks actively traded in a free and open market, either on an exchange or over the counter.

It is interesting to note that factor number 6 is goodwill, and that four of the other factors play a part in the capitalization of earnings formula demonstrated in the chart on page 123.

In determining fair market value, discounts are allowed for minority interests and lack of marketability. For publicly traded stock, it is also possible to obtain discounts using the "blockage" theory, which recognizes that placing a large block of stock on the market would likely have a depressing effect on its price. However, a "control premium" might increase the stock value of a person owning more than 50 percent of the business.

FAMILY HOLDING COMPANY

The family holding company, or asset holding company, which is a method of recapitalization, should not be confused with the personal holding company. When a new family holding company is formed, it is authorized to issue both voting preferred stock and non-voting common stock. The business owner then transfers his common stock in the original operating corporation to the family holding company in exchange for the voting preferred stock and the non-voting common stock.

Traditionally, the intention is to "freeze" the interest of the business owner in the operating corporation by subsequent gifts of the non-voting common stock of the family holding company. Although gifts of family holding company stock would be subject to the impact of Chapter 14, the techniques used to reduce or avoid the effect of these valuation rules will also work with a family holding company (see pages 407-408, and **Q 7617-7618**, *Tax Facts on Investments (2011))*.

The problems with Section 306 stock do not exist with respect to the formation of the family holding company. A family holding company could become a personal holding company if it generates personal holding company income (i.e., passive income such as dividends, rents, and royalties). If there were personal holding company income, a distribution could avoid the personal holding company tax of 15 percent in 2011.

As with a recapitalization, there is a definite need to establish an accurate fair market value of the operating corporation prior to a transfer of its common stock to the family holding company.

FIDUCIARY

A fiduciary is an individual or organization who stands in a relationship of trust with another. The law imposes the highest standard of care upon fiduciaries, who must have complete loyalty to their principals in exercising their fiduciary duty. Attorneys, accountants, trust officers, physicians, registered investment advisers, trustees who manage money, and company directors and officers are all fiduciaries.

Under ERISA, a person who exercises discretionary control over plan management or plan assets, or regularly provides investment advice for a fee, is considered to be a fiduciary. When found to have exercised "functional control" over the plan's insurance decisions, life insurance salespersons have been held to be "inadvertent fiduciaries" under ERISA (e.g., when an unsophisticated fund trustee relies on the salesperson's advice as the primary basis for insurance decisions).

In contrast, as suggested by their state licenses, stock brokers and insurance sales agents who act only in a traditional sales capacity by limiting their advice to recommended purchases are typically considered salespersons, not fiduciaries. In declining to offer an opinion regarding an agent's alleged "fiduciary duty for recommending one policy over another," the State of New York Insurance Department has stated that: "the suitability of an insurance policy is a business decision for the insured to make based upon the insured's unique situation." However, under New York law, insurance agents and brokers are responsible in a fiduciary capacity for all funds received or collected from their customers.

Even if not a fiduciary, the agent or broker who undertakes to obtain insurance for a client owes a duty to exercise reasonable skill, care, and diligence in obtaining the coverage. Insurance agents and brokers can be held liable to their clients if they: (1) commit a fraud by either making a fraudulent statement or by withholding material information; (2) violate a state insurance code or other state statute; or (3) breach an express or implied contract.

The line between *sales* activities and *fiduciary* activities is not always clear. Insurance producers who hold themselves out as professionals, with numerous credentials and high levels of expertise, may well be taking the first steps toward creating fiduciary relationships. It has been argued that fiduciary relationships are created when unsophisticated clients rely on these professionals for advice regarding complex insurance products and tax planning. If the facts and circumstances establish that fiduciary relationships exist, then these professionals will be held to fiduciary standards. Insurance professionals, particularly those holding themselves out as "financial planners," are well advised to maintain a high level of expertise through continuing study and education, and to further protect themselves with appropriate levels of errors and omissions insurance.

FINANCIAL UNDERWRITING

Underwriting is the process of risk selection. In addition to *medical* underwriting it is also important to consider *financial* underwriting, where the objective is to issue an amount of insurance that indemnifies but does not enrich the beneficiary.

The key to good financial underwriting is good communication and information. The more information that can be supplied the more likely that a case will be fairly and efficiently underwritten. Typically, the following kinds of information will be required: (1) sales proposals establishing reasons for the life insurance; (2) W-2 forms or latest income tax returns; (3) certified personal financial statements; (4) audited reports of assets, liabilities and operating income of the business; (5) business purchase agreements; and (6) letters of transmittal setting forth reasons for the insurance, details of the agent's knowledge of the applicant and other pertinent information about the case.

When applying for life insurance it is important to be familiar with the insurance company's specific financial underwriting guidelines. Although different carriers may have similar guidelines, carriers will often differ in their published standards and the application of these standards.

Personal life insurance is intended to provide ongoing income to a surviving family by replacing human life value (see chart, page 15). The maximum amount is typically based upon the insured's age and annual *earned* income (but not including *unearned* income such as interest, dividends, rents and royalties). For example, between ages 50 and 54 the amount might be 8 times income, whereas between ages 20 and 30 the amount might be increased to 15 times income. These guidelines are sometimes exceeded when the proposed insured has a potential for substantially increased future income (e.g., the young medical intern).

Key person life insurance is intended to protect a business from the loss of technical and business talent and the resulting loss of profits (see chart, page 155). The amount of insurance is typically limited to some multiple of the insured's compensation (e.g., from three to ten times annual compensation). For a discussion of these formulas, see page 181.

Estate liquidity life insurance provides for final expenses, debts and estate taxes (see charts, pages 19, 23 and 25). Projections of liquidity needs at reasonable rates of estate growth for 5 to 10 years are often allowed (e.g., 8 percent growth over 10 years).

Buy/sell life insurance is issued to fund the purchase of a business interest. Determining the amount of insurance requires a consideration of the reasonableness of the value placed upon the business under the agreement. Insurance will likely be required on all owners, but not necessarily with the same carrier (see charts, pages 127, 131, 135 and 139).

FIRST-TO-DIE LIFE INSURANCE

First-to-die life insurance, also known as "joint life insurance," insures two or more lives, and pays a benefit upon the *first* death. Generally, the premium required for a permanent product is substantially less than those for individual policies on each insured.

Uses for first-to-die life insurance include: (1) income replacement in two wage-earner families (e.g., to pay off mortgage); (2) social security replacement for retirees; (3) estate tax payment to facilitate early transfer of appreciating assets to heirs; (4) key person insurance (chart, page 155); (5) funding split-dollar rollout of survivorship life insurance (page 528); and (6) funding both entity purchase and cross purchase agreements (charts, pages 127 and 131).

When funding a cross purchase agreement it is appropriate to have joint *ownership* of the contract. With equal ownership interests an appropriate *beneficiary* designation would be: "surviving insureds, equally." With unequal interests an appropriate designation would be: "surviving insureds as their interests may appear in the cross purchase agreement dated ____."

First-to-die life insurance is very effective in reducing the number of policies required to fund multiple-owner cross purchase agreements. For example, funding of a four stockholder cross purchase agreement requires twelve individual policies, but only four first-to-die policies (Options 1 and 2 below). A trusteed cross purchase agreement using an escrow agent requires four individual policies, but only one first-to-die policy (Option 3 below). If available, a survivor purchase option provides an effective means of acquiring ongoing insurance for surviving stockholders. Exercising this option appears to resolve the "transfer for value" problem caused by a transfer of policy interests following the death of a stockholder under a trusteed cross purchase agreement funded with individual policies (see footnote 8 on page 137, and pages 541-542).

OPTION 1	Owner ⟶	**A**	**B**	**C**	**D**
	12 individual policies insuring	B C D	A C D	A B D	A B C

OPTION 2	Owner ⟶	**A**	**B**	**C**	**D**
	4 first-to-die policies insuring	B C D	A C D	A B D	A B C

OPTION 3	Owner ⟶	**ESCROW AGENT**
	1 first-to-die policy insuring	A B C D

FUNERAL TRUSTS

A funeral trust is an arrangement under which an individual, during his lifetime, purchases funeral services or merchandise from the provider of funeral and burial services. Pursuant to a contract between the individual and the provider, the individual selects the services and merchandise to be provided at death and agrees to make payments during lifetime into a trust.

A "qualified funeral trust" is a trust arising out of a contract with a person in the business of providing funeral or burial services, the sole purpose of which is to hold, invest, and reinvest funds in the trust and to use such funds to make payments for the funeral or burial services of beneficiaries under the trust. Contributions to the trust can only be made for the benefit of beneficiaries. There is no dollar limit on contributions to funeral trusts for taxable years beginning after August 29, 2008. Contributions to the trust are not deductible for income tax purposes. However, the trustee of the trust can elect to have the trust earnings taxed to the trust and payable by the trustee (i.e., elect exemption from the grantor trust rules that would cause trust income to be taxed to the grantor). Each beneficiary's interest is treated as a separate trust for this purpose. However, a qualified funeral trust is not allowed a personal exemption.

GOLDEN PARACHUTE RULES

Under these rules, a corporation is barred from taking an income tax deduction for an "excess parachute payment" made to an officer, shareholder or highly compensated individual when the payment is contingent upon a change in ownership or control of the corporation. In addition, a nondeductible 20 percent excise tax is imposed on the employee's excess payment.

Parachute payments are generally defined as any payments in the nature of compensation, which are contingent upon a change of ownership or effective control of the corporation when the present value of such payments equals or exceeds three times the individual's average annual compensation in the five taxable years ending before the date of the change. If the individual has been employed by the corporation for fewer than five years, then average annual compensation is determined by using the years actually employed.

These rules can adversely impact a *supplemental* deferred compensation plan if the plan calls for an acceleration of vesting or payment of benefits due to a change in control. However, these rules do not impact a pure *deferral* plan under which the executive has made an election to actually defer income previously earned. There are also limited exceptions for payments made by closely held corporations.

The golden parachute rules should not be confused with the $1,000,000 compensation deduction limitation placed upon publicly-held corporations (i.e., those that issue stock required to be registered under the Securities Exchange Act of 1934). Under this limitation, such corporations may not deduct compensation in excess of $1,000,000 paid to the chief executive officer and the four highest paid officers of the corporation. In effect, this limitation declares such excess compensation to be unreasonable per se, and therefore not deductible. Both split-dollar and executive bonus plans for this group of executives could be impacted. However, excluded from the limitation are: (1) amounts paid by reason of worker's compensation, medical or hospitalization expenses, or payments made to any qualified plan or SEP; (2) commission payments; (3) performance-based compensation meeting strict qualifications and standards; and (4) stock options and stock appreciation rights. A $500,000 compensation deduction limit applies to executives of employers who sold assets to the Troubled Asset Relief Program and employees of certain health insurers or service providers (after 2012).

GRANTOR TRUST RULES

Under the grantor trust rules, a grantor who retains interests in a trust created by the grantor may be treated as the owner of all or part of the trust and thus taxed on all or a portion of the trust income. Retention of the following powers or interests can cause a trust to be considered a grantor trust: (1) reversionary interests in the income or principal of any portion of a trust that exceed five percent of the value of the trust; (2) the power to control the beneficial enjoyment of any portion of the trust that can be exercised without the approval of an adverse party (excepted is the power to limit distributions of principal to a beneficiary using a "reasonable definite standard"); (3) administrative powers, including the power to deal with trust funds for less than full and adequate consideration and to borrow without adequate interest or security; (4) power to revoke the trust; and (5) income of the trust is *or may be* distributed to or held for the future use of the grantor or the grantor's spouse, used to discharge a legal obligation of the grantor, or used to purchase life insurance on the life of the grantor or the grantor's spouse.

Thus, transfer of income-producing property to a trust and the subsequent use of that income to pay life insurance premiums will result in the income being taxed to the grantor. The results are less clear when a trust merely authorizes the payment of premiums from trust income but does not use trust income for this purpose. In order to avoid grantor trust status, most authorities recommend that the trust language specifically prohibit the use of trust income to pay life insurance premiums on the life of the grantor or the grantor's spouse.

A "defective" trust is an *irrevocable* trust that intentionally violates one or more or the grantor trust rules (see chart, page 67). With a defective trust, application of the grantor trust rules can work to the taxpayer's advantage: (1) *To take an income tax deduction for interest paid on a life insurance policy loan.* An irrevocable life insurance trust considered a grantor trust enables the grantor to take an income tax deduction (if available) for loans on policies held by the trust, with no estate tax inclusion. (2) *To transfer additional amounts to trust beneficiaries without gift tax consequences.* Income taxes paid by the grantor on trust income distributed to beneficiaries may not be included in the value of gifts made by the grantor. (3) *To avoid the transfer for value rules.* A grantor trust that is taxed as if owned by the grantor/insured can purchase or obtain existing policies on the grantor's life without adverse tax consequences (i.e., the transaction falls within the "transfer to the insured" exception, see page 541). (4) *To avoid disqualification of the S corporation election.* An irrevocable grantor trust can be a stockholder, but limited to 2 years after the grantor's death.

It is important that any powers or interests retained by the grantor not cause the trust to be included in the grantor's taxable estate. Clearly, application of the grantor trust rules can be very complicated and the advice of competent tax counsel should always be sought.

GRITs, GRUTs, AND GRATs

GRITs. Prior to the changes brought about by the special valuation rules of Chapter 14, a grantor retained *income* trust (GRIT) was an effective technique for transferring property between generations. For example, a GRIT was created by having a grantor establish an irrevocable trust from which he retained the right to trust income for a specified period. At the end of this period, the succeeding trust beneficiaries (or remainderpersons) received the trust principal. Because of the reserved income interest, the gift tax value of the transferred remainder interest was usually substantially less than the current value of the property. However, except for a personal residence, Chapter 14 effectively eliminated the GRIT as a viable estate planning tool, since the grantor's right to trust income is deemed to have no value, meaning that the gift tax value of the remainder interest is equal to the *entire* value of the trust property (see pages 407-408). The gift tax cost is exactly the same as if the grantor had made a direct gift of the property to the remainderpersons. In place of a GRIT, the grantor retained unitrust (GRUT) and the grantor retained *annuity* trust (GRAT) are available to leverage gifts between generations.

GRUTs. The GRUT is an irrevocable trust in which the grantor retains the right to receive a *fixed percentage* of the trust's assets payable at least annually for life or for a term of years (and which must be revalued annually). However, in contrast to the GRAT, the GRUT will provide increasing payments to the grantor if the value of the trust increases (or decreasing payments if the value of the trust decreases). The GRUT is actuarially similar to the charitable remainder unitrust (see page 54).

GRATs. The GRAT is an irrevocable trust in which the grantor retains the right to receive *fixed payments* payable at least annually for life or for a term of years (see chart, page 59). In contrast to the GRIT, the GRAT *must pay* a fixed annual payment to the grantor, regardless of the income earned (whereas the GRIT often experienced substantial appreciation while yielding only a modest income). The GRAT is actuarially similar to the charitable remainder annuity trust (see page 54).

With both the GRAT and the GRUT, the value of the transferred remainder interest is equal to the value of the entire property reduced by the value of the retained interest. If the grantor is seeking to reduce his estate, additional smaller gifts that qualify for the annual exclusion can be made with the funds provided by trust payments. See the discussion of recessionary estate planning on pages 494-495.

GROUP CARVE OUT

The term "group carve out" is often used to describe the *replacement* of group term insurance for a selected class of executives with individual permanent insurance policies. Increased popularity of this concept has been due to the prohibition against individual selection in providing amounts of coverage to key employees.

Although a variety of plans are used to fund a group carve out, the more popular include Executive Equity (chart, page 211) and Split-Dollar Insurance (chart, page 219). The advantages of group carve outs include: (1) the provision of permanent post retirement insurance for the executive; (2) lower long term cost for the employer; (3) elimination of the increasing long term cost after retirement to both the executive and the employer; (4) flexible structure with no ERISA or nondiscrimination requirements; (5) cost recovery options for the employer; and (6) portability of the policy for the executive.

The design of individual illustrations will differ widely depending upon the circumstances of the existing group program and the proposed method of funding the group carve out. However, it is essential to compare annual costs to both the employer and executive, both before and after the carve out. This includes estimates of the current and projected group premiums for the executive's coverage under the group plan, together with the after-tax costs of bonuses, if any, given the executive to cover his tax cost of amounts of coverage in excess of $50,000. These same employer after-tax dollars are then placed in an executive equity or split-dollar program. Should the group carve out plan require additional executive costs (i.e., either direct premium payments or increased tax costs), then it is important to make a direct year-by-year comparison of this cost to the executive's ownership of policy cash values.

GUARANTEED MINIMUM WITHDRAWAL BENEFIT

When an annuity is annuitized, the owner losses all control over the underlying funds, has no right to make investment decisions, and gives up any rights to accelerated payments. The owner's only right is to receive the periodic payments as stipulated in the contract. The guaranteed minimum withdrawal benefit (GMWB) is a variable annuity living benefit that allows the contract owner to retain control.

The GMWB guarantees the contract owner can withdraw each year a fixed percentage of the premiums, *until all premiums have been completely recovered*, regardless of the actual account value. The amount against which this percentage is applied is variously referred to as the total premiums, the principal, the protected value, or the benefit base. Although annual withdrawals can be stopped and started at any time, failure to make a withdrawal does not entitle the contract owner to subsequently recover the amount not withdrawn. If a withdrawal in any one year exceeds the guaranteed percentage, the benefit base can be reset, which in a declining market could result in a lower guaranteed payment (i.e., same percentage applied to a lower benefit base). The contract can be surrendered at any time, provided the underlying funds are positive (i.e., a form of liquidity guarantee). The GMWB addresses the fear of losing control, but it does nothing to protect the contract owner from running out of money.

The GMWB "for life," or guaranteed lifetime withdrawal benefit (GLWB), addresses the fear of running out of money. Whereas the GMWB is essentially a money-back guarantee for the original premium, the GLWB guarantees a lifetime of income, regardless of the performance of the underlying funds (both single and joint spousal lifetime withdrawal options are available). In order to control risk, the owner is contractually limited as to the types of investments in the annuity subaccounts. A "step-up," or "ratchet-up," feature in many contracts allow the withdrawal amount to be increased on specified contract anniversaries, provided the actual account value is higher than the benefit base. Withdrawing more than the annual guaranteed percentage will generally void the lifetime guarantee.

Although the GLWB guarantees an income stream that may appear similar to annuitization, there are substantial differences between withdrawals and annuitization. For example, *withdrawals* from an annuity are first taxed at ordinary income tax rates on any growth within the annuity (first-in last-out), whereas when a contract is *annuitized*, use of an exclusion ratio allows a portion of each payment to escape taxation as a return of principal.

It is important to recognize that the "guarantees" offered by these living benefits (GMWB and GLWB) are subject to the claims-paying ability of the issuing life insurance company (i.e., guaranteed may not *really* mean guaranteed). See Life Insurance Default Risk, page 438. The evolving nature and variety of contract provisions make these complex products. This makes it essential that the agent fully understand the product and the purchaser carefully read the prospectus.

GUARANTEED PURCHASE OPTION

At the time a life insurance policy is issued it is often possible to purchase an option that provides the policyowner with the right to purchase, without evidence of insurability, additional amounts of permanent insurance at stated intervals or upon stated events. This option is usually issued as a rider to the basic policy and terminates at a specified policy anniversary. Some options provide an overall limit on the amount of additional insurance that may be purchased. Premiums for the option are based upon the insured's attained age and are payable until the rider terminates. Guaranteed purchase options are also referred to as "insurability options." Use of a guaranteed purchase option is particularly attractive when insurance is issued on the life of a child (see the discussion of children's life insurance on page 360).

When the option is exercised the insurance purchased does not have to be the same plan as the basic policy. Premiums for the additional insurance are at standard rates. For example, a typical rider might provide for the option to purchase $20,000 of additional insurance every 3 years until the policy anniversary nearest the insured's age 40. Additional option dates might also include the insured's marriage and the birth of each of the insured's children.

Other forms of guaranteed purchase options offer guaranteed insurance under cost-of-living adjustments that are tied to increases in an economic inflation indicator, such as the Consumer Price Index. Another variation, known as a "beneficiary purchase option," allows the beneficiary, upon the death of the insured, to elect to use part or all of the proceeds to purchase insurance without evidence of insurability. However, at the time the underlying policy is issued the beneficiary must prove insurability. This option is used as a substitute for survivorship life insurance and may offer greater flexibility (i.e., the surviving spouse uses some of the proceeds to pay estate taxes at the first death and the remaining proceeds to exercise the "last to die" option). Still another variation, known as a "surviving spouse option," is used with survivorship insurance (see the discussion of survivorship life insurance on page 535). This option allows the policyowner to purchase an additional amount of insurance on the primary insured following the death of his or her spouse.

HEALTH CARE POWER OF ATTORNEY

A health care power of attorney is a document that allows an individual to designate another person to make health care decisions when the individual is unconscious or mentally incompetent. The powers given include the power to consent to the giving, withholding, or stopping of medical treatment, service, or diagnostic procedures, including the withdrawal of life support. (The privacy rules of the Health Insurance Portability and Accountability Act of 1996, or HIPAA, make it important that the power-holder also be given the right to obtain and review medical records.) The power does not become effective until the individual has been declared by an attending physician to be incapacitated. In order to avoid conflicts between power-holders, it is best that only one power-holder be appointed at a time, but successor power-holders should be named. In general, a subsequent marriage automatically revokes a health care power of attorney held by someone other than the new spouse. Likewise, a subsequent divorce or separation usually revokes a health care power of attorney held by the divorced or estranged spouse. While there may be slight distinctions from state to state, the health care power of attorney is also referred to as a:

- Durable Power Of Attorney For Health Care
- Medical Power Of Attorney
- Health Care Proxy
- Health Care Surrogate Designation

In various ways, virtually all states recognize the right of a person to designate another person to make end-of-life choices for them in case of their mental incapacity. Other documents used for these purposes include:

1. **Living Wills** that merely express individuals' wishes with regard to life-sustaining procedures. They do not appoint another person to make specific health care decisions (see page 446).

2. **Advanced Health Care Directives** that provide instructions as to what should be done if grantors are unable to make future health care decisions. Health care power of attorneys and living wills are both considered to be advanced health care directives (AHCDs). In some states, documents referred to as AHCDs contain elements of both the health care power of attorney and the living will.

3. **Medical Directives** that contain elements of both the health care power of **attorney** and the living will, by allowing individuals to state their wishes regarding various types of specific medical treatments, appoint a proxy, and record wishes regarding organ donation (see www.caringinfo.org).

Because of potential differences between states, it is strongly recommended that individual state laws be consulted.

INCENTIVE TRUST

The dilemma faced by many wealthy individuals is how to pass down the family fortune without taking away their children's ambition, drive, and willingness to lead productive lives. Recent creation of substantial wealth in the stock market and the large inheritances being passed to today's "baby boomers" has only added to the number of families facing the challenge of "financial parenting." The incentive trust is a response to these concerns.

In contrast to the traditional trust, with its set distribution times and amounts, the incentive trust goes beyond the age-linked distribution formulas by attaching conditions to distributions. For example, the incentive trust might contain provisions that tie the timing and size of distributions to the achievement of certain goals by the beneficiaries, such as receipt of good grades, graduation from college, obtaining a graduate degree, a first job, or the attainment of specific levels of income. More controlling provisions might reward certain conduct or community service, such as staying at home to take care of children, serving as a missionary, or remaining alcohol or drug free (i.e., "tough love" when there has been a prior history of abuse).

The potentially restrictive and controlling nature of such trusts is a matter of some debate. To some, incentive trusts might be seen as nothing more than an attempt to unduly "control from the grave." Yet it seems most laudable when parents desire to teach their children to be good stewards of family wealth. Establishing such a values-oriented trust will likely require a great deal more thought and effort then is required of the typical tax-savings and distribution trust (see charts on pages 25 and 51).

When creating an incentive trust, a "one size fits all" approach is not appropriate. Ideally, the trust will accomplish the grantor's objectives without unduly restricting the trustee's ability to respond to changing circumstances, such as a beneficiary's marriage, medical emergency, or behavior. A good trust must be carefully drafted. While encouraging positive social goals and distributing income, the trust should also act as an economic safety net for children and other heirs.

Use of an institutional trustee together with an individual co-trustee who is either a family member or friend will avoid the undue pressure that can be placed on an individual trustee by beneficiaries demanding distributions that are inconsistent with trust objectives. It also seems quite reasonable to include provisions for the replacement of an unsatisfactory trustee by the beneficiaries.

In addition to the incentive trust, private foundations and family limited partnerships are also used as a means of involving children and other heirs in the responsible charitable distribution of a family's wealth.

INCOME IN RESPECT OF A DECEDENT

The term "income in respect of a decedent" (IRD) refers to those amounts which a decedent was entitled to as gross income, but which were not includable in his taxable income for the year of his death. For example, the following are considered IRD: (1) payments to a surviving spouse under an individual deferred compensation agreement; (2) compensation for services rendered before death; (3) renewal commissions of a life insurance agent; (4) dividends declared but unpaid to a stockholder prior to his death; (5) interest owed the decedent at the time of his death; (6) the decedent's distributive share of partnership income; (7) amounts paid for unrealized receivables upon the sale or liquidation of a partnership interest; (8) distributions from a 403(b) plan; (9) distributions from a decedent's individual retirement account; and (10) proceeds from sales on the installment method.

It is important to recognize that, unlike other property included in an estate, the recipient of IRD does not receive a stepped-up basis for the purpose of computing gain or loss (see the discussion of stepped-up basis on page 530). Thus, the estate or beneficiary who receives IRD will pay tax on that income in the same manner as the decedent. If the income would have been ordinary income to the decedent, then it is ordinary income to the estate or beneficiary. Likewise, if the income would have been treated as capital gains to the decedent, then it is treated as capital gains to the estate or beneficiary.

However, an income tax deduction is available which somewhat alleviates this "double" taxation (i.e., subjecting the IRD to both estate taxation and income taxation). The recipient of IRD generally may take an income tax deduction for any estate taxes paid by the estate on the IRD. The amount of the deduction is determined by comparing the actual estate tax paid with the amount of estate tax that would have been paid had the IRD not been included in the estate (i.e., the deduction is determined at the highest estate tax rates to which the estate was subject). The deduction can also be taken for generation-skipping taxes paid on the IRD. This is a *deduction* to be used in determining the income taxes of the estate or beneficiary receiving the IRD, it is not a *credit* against the income tax due.

INDIVIDUAL 401(k) PLAN

Also referred to as a "Solo 401(k) Plan," the Individual 401(k) Plan is a regular 401(k) plan combined with a single-participant profit sharing plan (the name itself has been created by the marketplace, it is not found in the Code). Individual 401(k) Plans are limited to self-employed individuals or small business owners who have no other full-time employees (an exception allows coverage of both the self-employed individual or business owner and his or her spouse who is employed full time).

Individual 401(k) Plans can provide for increased retirement contributions without many of the complex administrative rules and nondiscrimination testing required of 401(k) plans and profit sharing plans covering multiple employees. (Should the sponsoring employer add additional employees to the plan, it is subject to the same minimum participation, coverage, nondiscrimination, and other requirements that apply to any other qualified defined contribution plan.) Other advantages include availability of loans, year-to-year contribution flexibility, availability of hardship withdrawals, rollovers from other retirement arrangements, and the ability to purchase permanent life insurance (see pages 439-440).

In 2010 and 2011, the Individual 401(k) Plan contribution limit is effectively the lesser of 100 percent of compensation or $49,000 ($54,500 if age 50 or over). Annual contributions to an Individual 401(k) Plan consist of two parts: a tax deductible salary deferral contribution plus an additional tax deductible profit sharing contribution.

Salary Deferral Contribution. In 2010 and 2011, 100 percent of compensation up to a maximum of $16,500, or $22,000 if age 50 or older ($16,500 plus $5,500 catch-up), can be contributed in salary deferrals. For S and C corporations compensation is based on W-2 wages. For businesses taxed as sole proprietorships and partnerships compensation is based on net earnings (net profit less the deduction taken for one-half of the self-employment tax).

Profit Sharing Contribution. For S and C corporations profit sharing contributions can be made up to 25 percent of W-2 wages. For sole proprietorships and partnerships profit sharing contributions can be made up to 20 percent of net earnings.

The sum of the salary deferral and profit sharing contributions cannot exceed the 2011 Individual 401(k) Plan contribution limit. For example, a self-employed individual age 45 (limit of $49,000) doing business as a sole proprietor and having $100,000 in net earnings can contribute $36,500 ($16,500 of salary deferrals plus 20 percent of $100,000 in net earnings). Likewise, a self-employed individual age 52 (limit of $54,500) doing business as an S corporation and having $100,000 in W-2 wages can contribute $47,000 ($22,000 of salary deferrals plus 25 percent of $100,000 in W-2 wages). Deferral contributions reduce taxable W-2 wages (or net earnings) and profit sharing contributions are generally tax deductible as a business expense. See also, simplified employee pension (SEP) on page 525.

INDIVIDUAL RETIREMENT ARRANGEMENTS (IRAs)

There are two types of regular individual retirement arrangements, individual retirement accounts and individual retirement annuities. Each is often referred to as an "IRA" (see also pages 308-309, 506 and 540). Generally an individual retirement *account* is set up as a trust or custodial account with a bank, a federally insured credit union, or a savings and loan association, whereas an individual retirement *annuity* is established by purchasing an annuity contract from a life insurance company. Life insurance may not be purchased by the IRA.

Contributions may be made up to the time when the individual's tax return is due (excluding extensions). In order to deduct contributions an individual must: (1) have compensation (including earned income as an employee or self-employed person, or alimony); and (2) not have attained age 70½ during the taxable year for which the contribution is made.

In 2010 and 2011 a deduction may be taken for amounts contributed up to the lesser of $5,000 or 100 percent of compensation includable in gross income. An additional "catch-up" contribution of $1,000 is allowed in 2010 and 2011 for individuals who attain age 50 before the close of the taxable year. Deductions may be reduced or eliminated if the individual is an "active participant" in a qualified plan. In 2011 the phase-out range for a *married couple filing jointly* is between $169,000 and $179,000 for a spouse who is not an active participant and between $90,000 and $110,000 for a spouse who is an active participant. The phase-out range for a *single individual* who is an active participant is between $56,000 and $66,000. Similar deductions may be taken for contributions to the IRA of a lesser-compensated spouse.

Generally, funds accumulated in a plan are not taxable until they are actually distributed. However, amounts distributed prior to age 59½ are considered early distributions and are subject to a 10-percent-penalty tax. Exceptions to the penalty tax include distributions: (1) made on or after death; (2) attributable to disability; (3) which are part of a series of substantially equal periodic payments made (at least annually) for the life or life expectancy of the individual or the joint lives or joint life expectancy of the individual and a designated beneficiary (e.g., an annuity payout); (4) for medical expenses in excess of 7.5 percent of adjusted gross income; (5) for health insurance premiums for those receiving unemployment compensation; (6) to pay for a first home; or (7) to pay for qualified higher education expenses. Distributions from a plan must usually begin by April 1 of the year after the year in which the individual reaches age 70½.

In order to prevent current taxation IRAs are frequently used for "rollovers" of distributions from qualified plans, 403(b) plans, or eligible 457 government plans. An IRA that meets certain requirements may accept an expanded rate of contribution as a simplified employee pension (SEP). SEPs are discussed on page 525.

INSTALLMENT SALE

An installment sale provides a method by which the gain on the sale of property, and the income tax on that gain, can be spread over a period of time. No payment is required in the year of sale; the only requirement is that at least one payment be made in a taxable year after the year of the sale. Payments can be tailored to fit both the seller's income and tax requirements, since gain and the payment of tax on that gain is prorated according to the amount received each year.

When there is a sale between related parties (spouses, children, etc.), any resale by the buyer within 2 years accelerates the gain to the seller unless such resale occurs after the death of either of the related parties. The seller's gain will also be accelerated if the seller cancels the buyer's obligation (this may also include a cancellation by bequest or by the seller's executor). However, it appears that this technique of making gifts is available with an installment sale, provided there is a forgiving of each installment payment as it comes due. See the expanded discussion of self-cancelling installment notes, page 520.

If the amount of debt does not exceed $5,201,300 (as adjusted in 2011 for inflation) and the installment sale does not provide for a *minimum* interest rate equal to the "applicable federal rate," the IRS will generally impute an interest rate at the lower of the applicable federal rate or 9 percent, compounded semiannually. However, with intra-family aggregate sales of land of not more than $500,000 during a calendar year, the imputed interest rate would be the lower of the applicable federal rate or 6 percent. Applicable federal rates are determined by the Secretary of the Treasury on a monthly basis (for this purpose it is the lowest rate in effect during the 3-month period ending with the month in which there is a written contract).

Unless it can be shown that avoidance of income tax was not a principal purpose, the sale of *depreciable property* to a controlled entity may not be reported on the installment basis. Accrual method taxpayers generally may once again use the installment method for sales or other dispositions retroactive to December 17, 1999 (except in the case of property used in the trade or business of farming, timeshares, and residential lots).

INSURABLE INTEREST

The issuance of an insurance contract to someone who does not have an insurable interest in the life of the insured is void as a matter of public policy. Generally stated, an insurable interest arises from the relation of the party obtaining the insurance to the insured, provided there is a reasonable expectation of advantage or benefit from the continuance of the insured's life. An insurable interest is based upon relationships which involve: (1) pecuniary or economic advantage through the continued life of the insured or loss by reason of his death; or (2) love and affection in case of individuals closely related by blood or marriage.

The following are generally considered to have insurable interests: (1) a person on his own life; (2) a wife in her husband's life and a husband in his wife's life; (3) a fiancée in her fiancé's life and a fiancée in his fiancée's life; (4) a parent on a minor child's life (but not necessarily on an adult child's life); (5) a creditor in the life of his debtor; (6) an employer in the life of a key employee (but not a rank and file employee); (7) each of the partners, and the partnership itself, in the life of a partner whose death would result in a substantial loss; (8) each of the partners to a buy/sell agreement in the life of another partner, provided the beneficiaries do not stand to gain upon the death of the insured; and (9) among stockholders in a closely held corporation to the extent, and on the same basis, that an insurable interest exists among partners. See page 356 regarding charities having an insurable interest in the lives of donors.

Provided the insurable interest requirements are satisfied at the *inception* of the contract, in most states a policy remains valid thereafter even if at the insured's death the policyowner-beneficiary no longer has an insurable interest (but Texas requires that the beneficiary have an insurable interest at the time of death).

In most states there can be a valid *subsequent assignment* of a policy even if the assignee does not have an insurable interest in the life of the insured (but in Kentucky and Kansas, the assignment to one having no insurable interest in the life of the insured, other than charitable, benevolent, educational or religious institutions that are irrevocable beneficiaries, is void as contrary to public policy.

If the applicant has no insurable interest at the time a policy is taken out, the proceeds will be taxed as gain from a wagering contract. If a policy is found to be void for lack of an insurable interest, the insurance company is generally required to refund premiums paid plus interest. Since the existence of an insurable interest is governed by the case and statutory law of each state, it is essential to refer to these specific state laws for answers to questions regarding an insurable interest.

See Stranger-Originated Life Insurance (STOLI), page 532, for a discussion of the controversy surrounding using the insurable interest of a charity for the benefit of third-party investors.

INTEREST ADJUSTED NET COST

Net Cost Method. Prior to introduction of the interest adjusted net cost method, the cost of life insurance was frequently determined by the "net cost" method, which consisted of simply adding up the net premiums (premiums less dividends), subtracting out any cash values, dividing by the number of years, and then dividing by the number of thousands of insurance. For example, assume a $150,000 nonparticipating contract with premiums of $900 per year yields $6,000 of cash values in the 10th year:

Premiums per year	900
Number of years	x 10
Total premiums paid	9,000
Less cash values	(6,000)
	3,000
Number of years	÷ 10
Cost per year	300
Number of thousands	÷ 150
Cost per year per thousand	2.00

Interest Adjusted Net Cost Method. But the above calculation fails to account for the time value of money. The *interest adjusted* net cost (IANC) method has been adopted by most states in order to provide some index for comparing one life insurance contract with another, and is particularly useful where there is a difference in amount and timing of premiums, availability of dividends, and amounts of cash values. The IANC method assumes that the purchaser would be helped by comparing the results of his purchase to those that he could obtain by investing his money in a 5 percent savings account, with interest compounded annually. The basic question involves determining what amount of annual deposit would be required to end up with the same cash accumulation. Assuming the same $150,000 nonparticipating contract:

Life Insurance Contract		
Premiums per year		900.00
Cash values in 10 years	6,000	
5% Savings Account		
Cash value objective	6,000	
Future Value factor (table, page 562)	÷ 13.207	
Annual deposit required		(454.30)
Cost per year for insurance		445.70
Number of thousands of coverage		÷ 150
Cost per year per thousand		2.97

INTEREST DEDUCTION

The deductibility of interest depends on its classification. For example, *investment interest* is generally deductible only to the extent of investment income, *qualified residence interest* is generally deductible in full, *trade or business interest* is generally deductible as a business expense, and *personal interest* is not deductible at all (except student loan interest; see page 362).

Personal interest includes interest on personal loans and interest on personal life insurance policy loans used to pay premiums on the policy. Investment interest may be deducted to the extent of net investment income. There are no limitations on deductibility of interest on amounts borrowed for ordinary and necessary business purposes.

For policies that are minimum deposited (i.e., carried with loans from the cash values) the inability to deduct the interest paid on these loans means that it will cost the individual policy owner more to maintain the policy. If this cost is unacceptable, then the following alternatives might be considered:

1. Borrow from a home equity mortgage and use the proceeds to pay off the life insurance loan (assuming that payments on the home equity mortgage would be deductible).

2. For those who are officers or 20-percent-stockholders of a corporation, if there is a need for key person insurance, transfer the policy to the corporation and allow the corporation to take the interest deduction on debt up to $50,000 (but subject to strict limits, see Minimum Deposit Insurance, page 458). There would be no taxable gain to the transferor provided the loan does not exceed his basis in the contract. The interest payments must be a reasonable business expense (e.g., the corporation must have a need for key person insurance) and the contract must be "tax qualified" (again, see page 458). Such a transfer would be an exception to the transfer for value rules (see page 541).

INTEREST-FREE LOANS

At one time the use of interest-free, or below market, loans between parent and child, or employer and employee, was generally considered an effective means of transferring income that offered many tax advantages. The Supreme Court decision in *Dickman* (1984), the introduction by the Deficit Reduction Act of 1984 of the concept of "forgone interest" and the phasing out of the deduction for personal interest by the 1986 Tax Reform Act limited these tax advantages. Nevertheless, there may still be circumstances in which such loans would be appropriate to accomplishing nontax objectives (parent loans to child to buy life insurance, or corporation loans to nonstockholder-employee as a form of "golden handcuffs").

Gift Loans. When a below market or term loan is treated as a "gift loan" the lender is deemed to have transferred (imputed gift) to the borrower, and the borrower is deemed to have retransferred to the lender, an amount equal to the forgone interest. The effect of this retransfer is that the forgone interest is included in the gross income of the lender, and the borrower is considered as having paid the interest (for individuals, there is no deduction for personal interest, as discussed on page 431).

Compensation-Related Loans. The same transfer and retransfer of forgone interest is deemed to have occurred with loans between employers and employees, or corporations and stockholders, as with gift-loans. The employer will be deemed to have interest income in the amount of the forgone interest, which would be offset by a corresponding deduction for compensation paid (if reasonable). The employee is considered as having paid the interest. However, with stockholder-employees, the forgone interest will be treated as a nondeductible dividend payment. The Sarbanes-Oxley Act of 2002 adopted new securities law provisions that prohibit below-market loans made by a *public* corporation to its executives. Note in this regard the split-dollar regulations that consider some split-dollar arrangements as employee-loans subject to deemed loan and imputed interest treatment (see pages 401-402).

Exceptions. There is a $10,000 de minimis exception for compensation-related or corporation-stockholder loans that do not have tax avoidance as a principal purpose. Another exception is available when the total loans between individuals (husband and wife are considered one individual) do not exceed $10,000 unless the gift loans are directly attributable to the purchase or carrying of income-producing assets. These exceptions may protect low interest loans used to purchase life insurance, unless the life insurance is considered an income-producing asset in the case of a gift loan, or there is a tax avoidance purpose in the case of a corporation-employee or corporation-stockholder loan.

IRA DISTRIBUTION PLANNING

Funds cannot be kept in an IRA indefinitely. Eventually they must be distributed. Effective distribution planning requires a careful consideration of both tax and nontax issues. The first and most important consideration should be the owner's need for income. If funds are required before age 59½, the early distribution penalty tax must be avoided. If funds are left to accumulate after age 70½, the 50 percent excise tax on undistributed minimum required distributions must be avoided. And finally, selection of beneficiaries not only determines those individuals who will inherit the IRA, but how and when the IRA will be subject to income taxation.

Early Distribution Penalty Tax

Distributions prior to the owner's age 59½ are subject to an additional 10 percent early distribution penalty tax, unless an exception applies (see pages 427 and 514). With a SIMPLE IRA, early distributions within two years of beginning participation are subject to a 25 percent penalty tax (see page 524). Beneficiaries of inherited IRAs are not subject to this tax.

Required Minimum Distributions

Distributions that are less than the required minimum are subject to a 50 percent excise tax (i.e., it is levied on any amount not distributed as required). The amount and timing of these distributions will vary, and is dependent upon a number of factors, to include, the attained age of the owner, when the owner dies, the existence of a surviving spouse or designated beneficiaries, and the ages of these individuals. Roth IRA owners are generally not subject to these distribution requirements during their lifetimes (and are treated as dying before their RBD, see below).

Owner during lifetime. The owner of a traditional IRA must start receiving distributions by April 1st of the year following the owner's attaining age 70½. This date is referred to as the required beginning date (RBD). Although this first distribution can be delayed, distributions for the second and future years must be made by December 31st (e.g., two distributions would have to be made in a single year if the first distribution was not made until April 1st). If the IRA owner dies after reaching age 70½, but before April 1st of the next year, no distribution is required (i.e., death occurred before the RBD).

The amount of the required minimum distribution (RMD) is calculated by dividing the IRA account balance at the end of the previous year by the life expectancy of the IRA owner and another person. This is also referred to as the applicable distribution period, or the RMD factor.

(continued on next page)

IRA DISTRIBUTION PLANNING (continued)

For example, assume that an IRA owner is age 75 and has an account balance of $100,000. The RMD uniform lifetime table on page 555 provides an RMD factor of 22.9. The required minimum distribution is $4,367 (100,000 ÷ 22.9 = 4,367). This table is used when the owner is alive, and there is no designated beneficiary or the designated beneficiary is either: (1) a spouse not more than ten years younger than the owner; or (2) a nonspouse beneficiary of any age. Under the incidental benefit rule, this table treats a nonspouse beneficiary as no more than 10 years younger than the IRA owner, thereby assuring that distributions are primarily for the benefit of the IRA owner.

When the owner is alive, and a spouse more than ten years younger than the owner is the sole beneficiary, then the RMD joint and last survivor table can be used (see Appendix F of *Tax Facts on Insurance & Employee Benefits (2011)*). Use of this table is particularly helpful if the spouse is substantially younger than the IRA owner (i.e., a longer joint life expectancy reduces the amount of the annual required minimum distribution). For example, assume that an IRA owner age 75 is married to a spouse age 45, and the account balance is $100,000. The RMD factor from this table is 39.2, and the required minimum distribution is $2,551 (100,000 ÷ 39.2 = 2,551).

Surviving spouse as beneficiary. A surviving spouse who is the sole primary beneficiary of the deceased's IRA can either:

1. Elect to be *designated as the account owner* of the IRA (or use a "spousal rollover" to transfer assets to the spouse's traditional IRA). This allows for using the surviving spouse's age in determining required minimum distributions, and for the naming of new designated beneficiaries (i.e., the so-called "stretch IRA," see page 435). However, if withdrawn by a surviving spouse under age 59½, these funds may be subject to the 10 percent early distribution penalty tax (a spouse who remains a beneficiary is not subject to this tax), or

2. Remain a *beneficiary* of the IRA, with the following results:

   a. Distributions must generally be taken over the surviving spouse's lifetime (using the single life expectancy of the spouse). The first distribution must be made by the end of the year following the owner's death.
   b. If the IRA owner dies on or after the RBD, the life expectancy of the owner can be used for any year if it is greater than the spouse's life expectancy.

Non-spouse as beneficiary. Distributions to a designated beneficiary (see definition on page 435) are determined by whether the IRA owner dies before the required beginning date (RBD):

(continued on next page)

IRA DISTRIBUTION PLANNING (continued)

1. If the owner dies *before* the RBD, distributions must be made using the beneficiary's life expectancy under the RMD single life table (see Appendix F of *Tax Facts on Insurance & Employee Benefits (2011)*). This life expectancy is determined by using the beneficiary's age in the year following the owner's death, reduced by one for each year after the year of death. For example, assume the owner died in 2008 and the beneficiary was age 50 in 2009. Using the single life table, the factor is 34.2 in 2009, 33.2 in 2010, and 32.2 in 2011 (applying the subtract-one method).

2. If the owner dies *on* or *after* the RBD, distributions are generally based upon the longer of:

   a. The life expectancy of the beneficiary under the RMD single life table, or
   b. The life expectancy of the owner under the RMD single life table using the owner's age as of his or her birthday in the year of death, reduced by one for each year after the year of death.

No designated beneficiary. Distributions are again determined by whether the IRA owner dies before the required beginning date (RBD):

1. If the owner dies *before* the RBD, distributions must be made under the five-year rule. The entire account must be distributed by the end of the fifth year (sixth year, if 2009 is one of the five years) after the owner's death, but no distribution is required before then.

2. If the owner dies *on* or *after* the RBD, distributions continue to made based upon the life expectancy of the owner under the RMD single life table using the owner's age as of his or her birthday in the year of death, reduced by one for each year after the year of death.

Trust as beneficiary. A trust cannot technically be a designated beneficiary for RMD purposes, but the oldest beneficiary of a trust will be treated as the designated beneficiary if the trust meets certain specific requirements. (This is commonly known as a "see-through" trust.) If the trust fails to meet these requirements, then distributions must be made under the five-year rule. Before making a trust the beneficiary of an IRA, the advice of qualified counsel should be sought.

Designated beneficiary. This is the individual (or certain trusts) who is designated to receive the IRA proceeds by the terms of the IRA document. Generally, the designated beneficiary will be determined as of September 30th of the calendar year following the year of the owner's death.

Stretch IRA. This concept uses a combination of beneficiary designations and life expectancy elections to delay receipt of distributions (also referred to as a "multi-generation IRA").

LEGAL EXPENSE BENEFIT

Given our litigious society, it is hardly surprising that the legal expense benefit has grown in popularity as an employee benefit. Intended to provide affordable access to legal services, these benefits are referred to as "legal service plans," "prepaid legal services," and "discount legal plans." Plans providing legal expense benefits are offered in a variety of forms, including legal referral networks, prepayment plans, and indemnity plans.

Prepayment plans are similar in concept to HMOs, and provide for services from specific groups of lawyers employed by or under contract to the plan, specific lists of attorneys, or attorneys of choice. Less common are indemnity plans that provide benefits by reimbursing employees for specific legal services, with reimbursements limited to flat amounts, hourly rates, and maximum annual benefits.

Benefits are provided on either a comprehensive or scheduled basis. Plans providing comprehensive benefits typically provide full legal services, with specific services excluded. More common are plans providing only scheduled services. Typical of all plans is their emphasis on preventative law.

A variety of services are available. Most plans offer telephone consultations, document review, phone calls on the client's behalf, letter writing, and contract review. While many services are available without limit, limits are likely to be placed on some services (e.g., contract review limited to 10 pages; trial preparation and representation limited to 75 hours of attorney time). Excess time is typically charged at reduced rates.

Covered are family law matters such as divorce, adoption, child custody, will services, and estate planning; property rights such as real estate and probate matters; IRS audit representation; and trial defense on civil matters. Criminal defense work is excluded, except for moving vehicle violations and work-related criminal charges. Generally no coverage is provided for plaintiff actions, and virtually all nonunion plans specifically exclude actions against the sponsoring employer.

In evaluating a plan, it is important to determine the availability of attorneys, as well as the specific services offered (e.g., attorneys may not be available for face-to-face consultations, or appointments may be difficult to get).

Most plans are enrolled by payroll deduction, with the individual employee paying for his share of plan costs. These costs are not deductible, but the benefits are tax-free. If the plan is paid for by the employer, the costs are deductible by the employer, provided the employee's total compensation is reasonable. Although the employee must include in income his prorata share of these costs, any benefits received are tax-free.

LEVERAGED BENEFIT

The "best" type of fringe benefit is one that is not taxable to the employee, or at least not currently taxable, yet currently deductible by the employer. Because of this favorable tax treatment, it can be considered a leveraged benefit.

For example, assume that in 2011 an *employee* in a 25 percent marginal tax bracket is in need of $30,000 of additional life insurance protection and is presently receiving only $20,000 of group term coverage. If insurance were individually purchased by the employee for $200, the employer could pay for the benefit by giving the employee a salary of $267 ($200 ÷ .75 = $267). The tax cost of the additional salary of $267 is $67, leaving the employee with $200 to pay the insurance premium. Assuming an *employer* in a 34 percent marginal tax bracket, the after-tax cost to the employer of the salary increase is $176 ($267 × .66 = $176).

To provide a leveraged benefit, the employer could increase the group term coverage by $30,000, which would be tax-free to the employee. Assuming this would cost the employer $200, the after-tax cost of providing the same benefit to the employee is now only $132 ($200 × .66 = $132). The employee gets the needed $30,000 of additional life insurance protection, but the employer has saved $44 by using a leveraged benefit.

Other leveraged benefits include physical examinations, increased mileage allowances, medical expense reimbursement, and employer paid premiums for disability income insurance.

LIFE INSURANCE DEFAULT RISK

Life insurance default risk refers to the possibility that an insurance company might default on its obligations to individual policyholders. It is important to recognize that after the near financial meltdown of the banking industry in 2008, and its potential spillover into the insurance industry, the life insurance purchaser will likely be far more interested in understanding the nature of this risk (see Insurance Company Ratings, page 567).

Life insurance companies are subject to strict regulation by state regulatory agencies. This regulation includes conservative accounting rules, mandatory annual CPA audits, minimum capital/surplus requirements, and investment regulations/limitations (e.g., they are not allowed to invest in complex financial instruments). As a result, in down-market cycles life insurance companies are better positioned to handle greater losses than other companies in the financial sector, and thus better able to maintain adequate reserves to cover their financial obligations to policyholders.

If an insurance company does become financially unstable the insurance department in its home state takes control of the company in a "receivership process." The first step in this process involves an attempt to *rehabilitate* the company by improving its financial status. Sale of the distressed company is often brokered to a stronger company that assumes policyholder obligations. If rehabilitation is not successful, then the company is declared insolvent and the receivership process moves into the *liquidation* stage. Here the receiver attempts to maximize the company's assets in order to pay off as many creditors as possible, including individual policyholders who are given priority over other creditors.

Insolvent insurance companies frequently do not have enough funds to meet their obligations to policyholders. When this occurs state guarantee associations provide policyholders with benefits up to specified limits. The amount varies from state to state, but most states provide at least $100,000 in cash surrender or withdrawal values for life insurance and $300,000 in life insurance death benefits (a quick link to each individual state association website is available by going to www.nolhga.com/policyholderinfo/main.cfm/location/ga). Unfortunately, 100 percent of policyholder benefits are not covered in full, particularly as to high-dollar policies.

It is important to distinguish between separate account products and general account products. Assets backing variable products, such as variable life insurance, are held in separate accounts that are insulated from the general creditors of the company. In contrast, assets backing fixed products, such as whole life and universal life insurance, are held in the company's *general* account, which is subject to the claims of all the creditors of the insurance company. (The general account also backs guaranteed death benefits and other available riders and endorsements.) Although this credit-risk exposure may be low, it nevertheless exists.

LIFE INSURANCE IN QUALIFIED PLANS

Qualified plans can offer an attractive way of using pretax dollars to purchase life insurance for the benefit of plan participants. In pension plans the plan trustee determines to purchase life insurance as a plan asset; plan participants do not have the power to direct plan investments. In defined contribution plans, such as profit sharing and 401(k) plans, each participant has the ability to elect to purchase life insurance with part of his or her account (e.g., from a self-directed account). Qualification rules do not require that all employees actually purchase life insurance. Discrimination against non-highly compensated employees is prohibited and if life insurance benefits are available to the highly compensated employees they must be available to all employees. Generally, the plan trustee is named owner and beneficiary of the life insurance policy.

Amount of insurance. Pension plans exist primarily to provide retirement benefits and profit sharing plans are primarily plans of deferred compensation. When these plans provide life insurance coverage for plan participants the life insurance must be an "incidental benefit" under the plan. This incidental benefit limitation is satisfied if the cost of providing a current life insurance benefit is less than 25 percent of the cost of providing all the benefits under the plan (both deferred and current). Staying within either of the following will satisfy this incidental benefit limitation:

1. The death benefit is no more than 100 times the expected monthly retirement benefit, or

2. At all times over the life of the plan total premiums paid for the insurance death benefit are less than the following percentages allocated to that participant:

    50% - for ordinary life insurance or variable life insurance

    25% - for term life insurance or universal life insurance

These limits may be used by any type of plan, although the "100 times" limit has typically been used by defined benefit plans and the "percentage limit" by defined contribution plans (e.g., profit sharing plans). See table, Types Of Qualified Retirement Plans, on page 491.

Profit sharing plans are an exception to these limits. There is no limit on the amount of life insurance that may be purchased with trust funds that have accumulated for two or more years, provided the plan requires that only such funds can be used to purchase life insurance (i.e., the "seasoned money" concept).

Premiums. With a defined benefit plan the additional cost associated with the purchase of life insurance increases the total amount deductible as a plan contribution (i.e., the cost of life insurance is on top of the maximum funding limits). In contrast, with a defined contribution

(continued on next page)

LIFE INSURANCE IN QUALIFIED PLANS (continued)

plan premiums are paid from the participant's account without increasing the annual additions limit (in 2010 and 2011, the lesser of 100 percent of compensation, or $49,000).

Insured. Insurance is generally provided on the life of the plan participant for family protection or estate needs. However, in profit sharing plans where life insurance is purchased in self-directed accounts, insurance may be purchased on the lives of third parties (e.g., a spouse for family protection, a business partner to fund a buy/sell agreement, or a survivorship life policy on both the participant and spouse for estate liquidity needs).

Taxation. Each year the plan participant must include in income the economic value of the current life insurance protection (i.e., death benefit less cash values, if any). This includable cost is calculated using the lower of (a) the Table 2001 rates on page 552, or (b) the insurer's published rates for initial issue one-year term for standard risks. Except for owner-employees of unincorporated businesses, the cumulative value of these taxable amounts constitutes the participant's "basis" in the contract. (This can be a substantial benefit for the highly rated individual who reports an economic benefit based upon standard rates.) If the insured dies while the policy is held within the plan, the death benefit in excess of the policy's cash value (the amount "at risk") is received by the beneficiary free of income taxes. The remaining distribution, reduced by the participant's basis in the contract, is taxed as a qualified plan distribution. Death benefits from a qualified plan are generally includable in a decedent's estate for federal estate tax purposes, under the theory that the participant has an "incidents of ownership" in the policy (see page 409). Regarding the controversial and untested "subtrust" technique employed for avoiding estate taxation, see Stephan R. Leimberg et al., *Tools & Techniques of Life Insurance Planning*, 4th ed. (Cincinnati: The National Underwriter Company, 2007), pages 489-490. Account values payable at death to a named beneficiary are classified as income in respect of a decedent and are subject to both income and estate taxes (see page 425).

Disposition of policy. If the insured does not die prior to retirement, the life insurance policy must be either surrendered, distributed, or sold. In making transfers from the plan to third parties, it is important to fall within the parameters set forth in Prohibited Transaction Exemption 92-6 (e.g., sold for "fair marker value"). To avoid current income taxation, a policy with cash values may be sold to the insured and then passed by gift from the insured to a third party. If estate taxation is a concern, the policy may be sold directly to an irrevocable life insurance trust established by the insured (see chart, page 51). Provided this trust is considered a grantor trust, this sale would not violate the transfer for value rules (see discussions on pages 418 and 541-542).

See also, the fully insured 412(i) plan, pages 270-273.

LIFE INSURANCE PREMIUM LIMITATIONS

TAMRA limitations. Under TAMRA (Technical and Miscellaneous Revenue Act) a life insurance contract issued on or after June 21, 1988, is subject to being classified as a modified endowment contract (MEC) if cumulative premiums paid during the first seven contract years exceed the sum of "net level premiums" (the seven-pay test). Net level premiums are determined by each carrier and reflect the premiums required to pay up the contract during the first seven years using guaranteed mortality costs and interest rates. Distributions from a MEC are subject to "gain first" taxation to the extent there is gain in the contract (i.e., cash values exceed investment in the contract). Such distributions include withdrawals, loans, and use of the policy as collateral for a loan. Generally, the investment in the contract is the sum of premiums paid, less dividends received, plus prior taxable loans (but not prior taxable withdrawals).

Additionally, a 10-percent-penalty tax is imposed on amounts includable in gross income if the distribution is made prior to the contract owner's attaining age 59½, unless the owner is disabled or receives the cash values under a life annuity settlement option. However, the penalty tax is always applicable if the contract owner is a "non-natural person" (e.g., a corporation or trust).

For example, assume that the "net level premium" for a particular contract is $2,500 and the following payment plans are being considered:

Year	Cumulative Net Level Premium	Plan A Annual	Plan A Cumulative	Plan B Annual	Plan B Cumulative
1	2,500	2,000	2,000	2,500	2,500
2	5,000	1,000	3,000	2,500	5,000
3	7,500	1,500	4,500	3,000	8,000
4	10,000	5,500	10,000	2,000	10,000

Plan A is not a MEC, since at no time did the cumulative amount paid exceed the cumulative net level premiums. However, Plan B became a MEC in year 3, since the cumulative amount paid ($8,000) exceeded the allowable cumulative net level premium ($7,500). In summary, a policyowner can "catch up" after falling behind, but he cannot "get ahead" by paying premiums in advance.

Now assume premiums are paid according to Plan B, and at the end of year 4 the cash values are $11,000. A withdrawal of $2,500 would result in a taxable gain of $1,000, since there is gain of $1,000 in the contract (cash values of $11,000 less cumulative premiums of $10,000).

(continued on next page)

LIFE INSURANCE PREMIUM LIMITATIONS (continued)

Once a contract becomes a MEC, it forever stays a MEC (except for limited opportunities given insurance companies to correct procedural errors). In addition, even though a contract is "grandfathered" because it was issued prior to June 21, 1988, it can become a MEC if a "material change" occurs with respect to its benefits or terms. Since it is very broadly defined, virtually any alteration in benefits is likely to be treated as a material change, except for death benefit increases of up to $150,000 (or cost of living increases tied to a broad-based index). Potential material changes can occur when: (1) exchanging an old contract for a new contract; (2) converting term insurance to permanent cash value insurance; (3) adding a new insured to the contract; and (4) increasing the death benefit voluntarily. Contracts issued after June 21, 1988 are also subject to the material change rules.

While it is important to be aware of the potential adverse tax implications of TAMRA, there will be no adverse effect if: (1) the contract was issued prior to June 21, 1988; (2) the death proceeds are the only payments received under the contract; (3) the premium payments do not exceed the seven-pay limits; or (4) the only payment received is pursuant to a complete surrender of the contract after age 59½.

DEFRA limitations. In contrast to TAMRA, it is *absolutely essential* to comply with the guideline premium and corridor test or meet the cash value accumulation test of DEFRA (Deficit Reduction Act). A failure to abide by these limitations will produce disastrous tax results since the contract will immediately lose its status as life insurance, all cash value increases will be subject to current income taxation, and the death benefit will be taxed as ordinary income (to the extent it exceeds cumulative net premiums paid).

For example, assume Plan A is being tested for DEFRA compliance:

	TAMRA	DEFRA		Plan A	
	Cumulative	Guideline	Cumulative		
Year	Net Level	Single	Annual	Annual	Cumulative
1	2,500	9,000	1,000	2,000	2,000
2	5,000		2,000	1,000	3,000
3	7,500		3,000	1,500	4,500
4	10,000		4,000	5,500	10,000

In year 4, Plan A violates both DEFRA guideline premium tests. Under this test the cumulative annual premiums cannot exceed either the greater of: (1) the guideline single premium ($9,000); or (2) the guideline cumulative annual premiums ($1,000 per year). Although the cumulative annual premiums were exceeded beginning year 1, Plan A cumulative premiums fell within the guideline single premium ($9,000) until year 4.

LIFE SETTLEMENTS

The term "life settlement" generally refers to the sale to an investor of a life insurance contract when the insured is age 65 or older and *is not* terminally or chronically ill (i.e., the insured is expected to live more than two years). Life settlements are also variously referred to as "senior settlements," "high net worth settlements," and "high net worth transactions." In contrast, the term "viatical settlement" is used to describe the sale of life insurance contract when the insured *is* terminally or chronically ill and expected to die within two years (see below). However, these terms are not consistently used, particularly in state laws and regulations. Life settlements typically require that the policy have a minimum face value of between $100,000 and $250,000, be beyond the contestability period, and be fully renewable. Policies that can be sold include convertible term life, whole life, universal life, variable life and survivorship life insurance. The prices paid are more than the current cash values, but less than the net death benefit.

When an application for a settlement is taken many states require that a disclosure statement be presented to the viator. (A "viator" is the owner of a life insurance policy who enters into a contract to sell the policy to a third party, usually a viatical settlement provider.) These statements typically inform the policy owner that: other alternatives may be available, such as loans and accelerated death benefits (see page 343); sale proceeds may be subject to income taxes and claims of creditors; other rights and benefits contained within the policy could be lost; sale proceeds may adversely affect eligibility for Medicaid and other government benefits; and the contract contains a rescission provision. The owner of the policy does not have to be the insured (e.g., a policy owned by one spouse on the life of the other spouse). Insureds should also be informed that the sale of the policy could negatively affect their ability to obtain *future* life insurance coverage, since the outstanding investor-owned policy will likely be considered in the underwriting process (see the discussion of financial underwriting on page 414).

Before selling a life insurance policy the owner should give careful consideration to the impact that the loss of the death benefit will have upon family income requirements and existing estate plans. Life settlements are most appropriately considered when *changing circumstances* cause the owner to consider surrendering a policy for its cash value. (This should be distinguished from the regrettable practice of stranger-originated life insurance that is intended to evade the insurable interest laws, see discussion on page 532.) The following are examples of those changing circumstances which can lead to life settlements: (1) business is sold and policies purchased to fund buy/sell agreement are no longer needed; (2) executive leaves business or retires and there is no need for policy intended for key person insurance; (3) premiums are no longer affordable (due to change in financial condition or failure of policy to perform as originally projected); (4) large policy loans make it very expensive to maintain policy; (5) changing family circumstances reduce or eliminate need for insurance coverage (e.g., death of spouse, divorce or newly acquired wealth); (6) desire to replace individual policy with last-to-die policy; and (7) decrease in size of estate or increase in tax credits or exemptions result in lowered estate taxes.

(continued on next page)

LIFE SETTLEMENTS (continued)

When the insured is expected to live 24 months or less the proceeds from the sale of a policy to a viatical settlement provider may be excluded from income. To obtain this favorable income tax treatment the viatical provider must be licensed in the state in which the insured resides. If the insured resides in a state not requiring such licensing, then there must be compliance with certain provisions of the Viatical Settlements Model Act (the Model Act) and requirements of the National Association of Insurance Commissioners (NAIC) relating to standards for evaluating the reasonableness of payments. To protect the viator (the individual selling the policy) the Model Act sets standards for evaluation of reasonable payments for terminally or chronically ill insureds. One alternative standard sets forth minimum percentages of the policy face that must be paid (ranging from 80 percent when the insured's life expectancy is less than six months, to 60 percent when the insured's life expectancy is at least eighteen but less than twenty five months).

Proceeds from a sale will be subject to income taxation. In Revenue Ruling 2009-13, the Service ruled that when a life insurance contract is *sold*, the cost of insurance protection must be subtracted from the net premiums paid in order to determine the owner's tax basis. The Service also ruled that a life insurance contract is a capital asset, and income recognized can qualify as long-term capital gain. (Basis is reduced by cost of insurance; the amount received in excess of basis up to cash surrender value is ordinary income; and the amount received in excess of cash surrender value is capital gain.) This ruling will not be adversely applied to sales before August 26, 2009.

In an effort to regulate the sale of life insurance policies, over half the states have enacted statutes based upon the Model Act. In keeping with the ongoing evolution of that Act, in 2004 the NAIC voted to not require a separate viatical broker's license for certain licensed insurance producers. However, in some states life and viatical settlements are considered *securities*, their sale is formally regulated and agents must be separately licensed. Further complicating the regulatory environment is the fact that states often do not distinguish between life settlements and viatical settlements. In view of these inconsistencies, and ongoing changes in state regulation, the agent should contact the appropriate state insurance or securities departments before engaging in the solicitation or sale of life and viatical settlements.

In 2006, the NASD issued a notice to members reminding firms and associated persons that life settlements involving *variable* insurance policies are securities transactions subject to NASD rules. The NASD has been consolidated with the enforcement arm of the New York Stock Exchange, and is now called the Financial Industry Regulatory Authority (FINRA). In July of 2010 the Life Settlements Staff of the U.S. Securities and Exchange Commission submitted a report recommending that the definition of a security be amended by Congress to include life settlements. Their report also observed that with respect to state securities laws, 48 states now treat life settlements as securities under state laws, although some states exclude from the definition of security the original sale from the insured or the policy owner to the provider.

LIMITED LIABILITY COMPANY

The increasingly popular limited liability company (LLC) offers owners the limited liability of C corporations together with the tax and management advantages of partnerships, without the restrictions and complexities of S corporations. An LLC is created by filing articles of organization and complying with the relevant state law. The participants are called "members" and the rules governing the operation of an LLC are usually set forth in an "operating agreement."

The LLC form of business was first established by Wyoming in 1977 and has now been adopted by statute in all 50 states and the District of Columbia. However, due to a lack of uniformity between the various state statutes, the LLC is most attractive to the smaller business operating within just one or two states.

The primary *advantages* of the LLC include: (1) no liability of owners for business debts (enjoyed by corporations and S corporations but not by general partnerships); (2) flow through of income and expenses to the individual owners (enjoyed by S corporations and partnerships but not by corporations); (3) the ability to allocate income and losses among members and include business liabilities in cost basis (enjoyed by partnerships but not by corporations and S corporations); and (4) freedom from the stringent requirements and restrictions of S corporations in the formation, operation and disposition of the business. For further discussions of partnerships and S corporations see the chart on page 163, pages 465-467 and pages 510-512. It has also been suggested that the LLC could serve as a viable alternative to the irrevocable life insurance trust, by affording the insured greater control and flexibility, in much the same way as the limited partnership (see discussion, page 467).

An LLC formed *after* December 31, 1996, will generally be taxed as a partnership if it has more than two owners, or as a sole proprietorship if it has only one owner, unless it elects to be taxed as a corporation. This election can be made under the "check the box" regulations by filing Form 8832 (Entity Classification Election). An LLC formed *before* January 1, 1997, will generally be treated as it was prior to January 1, 1997, unless it elects otherwise.

LIVING WILL

The living will is a legal document that allows an individual to state in advance his unwillingness to be subjected to life-sustaining medical measures once there is no chance of recovery. Such a document relieves others of the legal and emotional burden of making such decisions.

For example, it can ease a doctor's fears of civil or criminal liability, since he is abiding by his patient's wishes in withholding or withdrawing life-prolonging treatment. It can ease the stress and emotional pain for the family, which might otherwise be faced with having to make a most difficult decision as to what their loved one would have wanted. Further, it offers some hope of avoiding the legal battles that have occurred when a medical facility is unsure of its responsibility to the patient, and thus provides the family some protection from the financial devastation that a protracted death can cause.

Almost all of the states have some form of legislation governing living wills. Generally such a document must be in writing, dated, and witnessed by two persons who are not family members or possible heirs. The document must usually be notarized if a durable power of attorney is included giving another person the power to make medical treatment decisions (see discussion, page 394). In addition, language can be included providing for organ donation.

Copies of the living will should be given to close relatives, the family doctor and the family attorney. Both the living will and the durable power of attorney can be revoked at any time by either destroying all copies or by executing a signed and notarized statement revoking the prior document.

See also, Health Care Power Of Attorney, page 423.

LONG-TERM CARE COMBINATION PRODUCT

The risk of needing long-term care (LTC) is substantial and the costs of providing such care can be overwhelming (see chart on page 255). Despite the need, sales of the stand-alone LTC insurance products have been negatively impacted by both product costs and the client's fears of paying premiums for a product from which they will never derive a benefit (i.e., the fear of "use it or lose it"). Hybrid, or so-called combination products, address both of these concerns and can involve either life insurance or annuity policies.

With a cash value **life insurance policy** the death benefits can be accelerated to make either per diem payments or expense reimbursements upon the insured's chronic illness. A rider is often added to provide additional coverage in order to extend the LTC benefits once the contract cash values and death benefits had been exhausted. This effectively allows the consumer to purchase at an attractive cost one policy to insure against two risks. However, it must be recognized that LTC payments from the contract could reduce or even eliminate the life insurance death benefit. (The use of cash values and death benefits for LTC payments is considered a form of "self-funding.") The accelerated benefit, whether paid from the net amount at risk or from the rider providing separate LTC coverage, will be entitled to favorable tax treatment provided the contract is a "*qualified* long-term care insurance contract" (QLTCI). See discussion on page 489. Charges against policy cash values are not taxable even if there is gain in the contract.

With a **non-qualified annuity** LTC benefits can be paid from a tax-qualified LTC rider provided the rider complies with the requirements of a QLTCI. Benefits received after January 1, 2010 are entitled to favorable tax treatment (see page 489). Such coupling of a LTC rider with a non-qualified annuity provides a unique opportunity to use a non-qualified annuity for LTC needs since this favorable tax treatment is available even though the benefit payment reduces the annuity contract's cash values (i.e., untaxed inside buildup within the annuity may be paid out tax-free for LTC expenses).

Both life insurance and non-qualified annuities can be exchanged tax-free under Section 1035 for a QLTCI (see page 537). This would allow for an exchange of an existing life policy that has outlived its purpose into a combination life/LTC plan (i.e., gain in the policy would not be subject to current taxation). Likewise, one QLTCI can be exchanged for another QLTCI.

LONG-TERM CARE PARTNERSHIP PROGRAM

The Long-Term Care Partnership Program is a joint effort between the states and private insurance companies to reduce state long-term care (LTC) expenditures by encouraging moderate-income individuals, who are most likely to rely on Medicaid for potential LTC needs, to purchase private insurance. With the assistance of the Robert Wood Johnson Foundation the original demonstration model was begin in the early 1990's. Although originally limited to only four states, the Deficit Reduction Act of 2005 allowed expansion of the program to the remaining states.

A LTC policy must meet special conditions to be considered a "Qualified Partnership Policy." The policy must: (1) insure a person who was a resident of the Partnership State when coverage first became effective; (2) have an issue date that is not earlier than the approval date of the required state plan amendments; (3) comply with specific rules of the National Association of Insurance Commissioners; (4) provide inflation protection (e.g., 3 or 5 percent per year); and (5) meet the IRS definition of a "qualified LTC insurance policy" (see page 489). The inflation protection requirements are: (1) for purchasers under 61 years old, compound annual inflation protection (e.g., 3 percent or 5 percent per year); (2) for purchasers 61 to 76 years old, some level of inflation protection; and (3) for purchasers 76 years or older, inflation protection may be offered but is not required.

As an exception to the estate recovery provisions the Partnership programs allow individuals who purchase Partnership LTC insurance policies to exempt some or all of their personal assets from Medicaid eligibility requirements (see pages 451-452). Under the *dollar-for-dollar model* the amount of insurance coverage purchased equals the amount of assets protected from consideration if and when the consumer needs to apply for Medicaid (e.g., a consumer who bought a policy with a benefit of $100,000 would be entitled to up to $100,000 worth of nursing home or community-based). Under the *total asset protection model* all assets can be protected when applying for Medicaid when a more comprehensive and expensive benefit package is purchased.

When consumers purchase private LTC insurance, States avoid the entire burden of long-term-care costs. When States exclude from estate recovery the amount of LTC benefits paid under a qualified LTC policy, consumers are protected from becoming impoverished in order to qualify for Medicaid.

Premiums paid for LTC insurance can be itemized together with other medical expenses as deductions from taxable income (to the extent they exceed 7.5% of adjusted gross income) and *proceeds received* can be from excluded income when used to pay for LTC expenses.

Insurance agent training and consumer education are generally an important part of each State Partnership program. An excellent resource is contained at the Long-Term Care Partnership Program Technical Assistance Website at www.dehpg.net/ltcpartnership/map.aspx.

MANAGED CARE

Managed care is a comprehensive approach to health care with the intent of lowering costs by arranging for care at predetermined or discounted rates, specifying which doctors and hospitals the patient can use and overseeing physicians' treatments and referrals. The basic variations of managed care plans include:

1. **Health Maintenance Organization (HMO):** A health plan that combines coverages of health-care costs and delivery of health care for a prepaid premium. Members receive services from individuals employed by or under contract to the HMO. HMOs generally require patients to select a primary-care physician (PCP) who coordinates the patient's care. Patients usually need referrals from the PCP before going to a specialist or a hospital. The PCP is often referred to as a "gatekeeper." In return for accepting these restrictions, patients are relieved of deductible or coinsurance payments and copayments are typically only $5 to $10 per visit to the doctor. This is in contrast to the traditional major medical plan or fee-for-service plan under which patients can choose both their doctors and hospitals, but must pay 20 percent of the costs (subject to caps). In HMOs the direct relationship between the financing and delivery of health care has generated criticism of: (1) the existence of "gag rules" that prohibit physicians from discussing all possible treatment options with patients; (2) the denial of access to specialists; (3) the denial of reimbursements for emergency room charges in hospitals outside the plan; (4) limits placed on hospital stays for certain procedures; and (5) treatment decisions designed to save money and adverse to the patient's health.

2. **Point-Of-Service (POS):** A managed-care option that allows members to seek care outside the HMO network, but at a higher cost (usually in the form of higher premiums, co-payments and deductibles).

3. **Preferred Provider Organization (PPO):** A network of independent physicians, hospitals, and other healthcare providers who contract with insurance companies to provide care at discounted rates. Members are given incentives to use the PPO physicians but for a higher cost are allowed to use doctors and hospitals outside the network. This is also referred to as a "managed indemnity" plan.

MARITAL DEDUCTION

By taking advantage of the marital deduction, unlimited amounts of property can be passed between spouses, during lifetime or at death, and free of gift taxes and estate taxes. However, the marital deduction is generally not allowed if the property represents a terminable interest (i.e., an ownership right that will come to an end after a period of time or upon the occurrence of some specified event in the future).

The marital deduction can be obtained through the use of any of the following techniques:

1. **Outright** transfer – passes property directly to the surviving spouse. This can be accomplished in a variety of ways, to include: joint ownership with rights of survivorship; beneficiary designation; bequest or devise; inheritance; and dower or curtesy (or under state intestate succession laws).

2. **Power of appointment trust** – gives the surviving spouse a right to all income for life and general power of appointment over the trust assets (i.e., the unlimited right to withdraw property during lifetime or appoint property at death). In the chart on page 25, the "A" trust represents a power of appointment trust, which is also referred to as a "marital deduction trust." An expanded discussion of "general power of appointment" is contained on page 477.

3. **QTIP trust** – gives the surviving spouse a right to all income for life, with principal to children, or others, upon death of the surviving spouse (the executor or executrix must make this election, it cannot be mandated in the will). In larger estates, property placed in a QTIP trust is subject to being taxed in the surviving spouse's estate. See the discussion and chart on pages 34-35.

4. **Estate trust** – can accumulate income without payments to the surviving spouse, but must be paid to the estate of the surviving spouse (i.e., surviving spouse determines who eventually receives property placed in this trust, plus any accumulated income).

5. **Qualified domestic trust** – assures collection of the federal estate tax when the surviving spouse is a non-citizen. An expanded discussion is contained on page 488.

MEDICAID

This state-run public assistance program provides medical benefits to groups of low-income people, some who may have no medical insurance or inadequate medical insurance. Although the Federal government establishes general guidelines for the program, the Medicaid program requirements are actually established by each State. A State is required to include certain types of individuals or eligibility groups under its Medicaid plan and the plan may include others. States' eligibility groups include: *categorically needy* such as Supplemental Security Income (SSI) recipients, *medically needy* such as blind persons, and *special groups* such as community Long Term Care services for individuals who are Medicaid eligible and qualify for institutional care.

Qualifying For Medicaid. Basic to qualifying for Medicaid assistance is the requirement that applicants do not have sufficient *income* to provide for their own care. Most states permit individuals with excess income to qualify for Medicaid, provided they "spend down" this income by incurring medical expenses (but some "income cap" states deny benefits whenever there is excess income). Medicaid qualification also requires that the applicant have very limited amounts of personal *resources* (spousal impoverishment rules allow a non-institutionalized spouse to maintain separate property). Home equity that is exempt is limited to $500,000, although states may raise this to $750,000. See also, page 452. There is no limit for homes occupied by a stay-at-home spouse (referred to as a "community spouse"). To discourage applicants from making transfers for inadequate consideration, transfers during a "look-back" period can delay eligibility for a period equal to the amount of the transfers divided by the average costs to a private patient in a nursing facility in the state.

(1) **Transfers prior to February 8, 2006.** The look-back period is the *36 months* before application for Medicaid benefits, and any penalty begins to run the *month after* the transfer is made (in some states the penalty begins to run in the month of transfer). For example, assume a Medicaid applicant transferred to his children by gift a home valued at $140,000 in June of 2003. If the average cost for nursing home care was $3,500, the period of ineligibility for Medicaid would be 40 months ($140,000 ÷ $3,500 = 40). This period begins to run in July of 2003. If the applicant entered a nursing home on February 1, 2006, he would have to pay for the first 9 months of care (July 2003 through January 2006 = 31 months; 40 - 31 = 9).

(2) **Transfers on and after February 8, 2006.** The look-back period is the *60 months* before application for Medicaid benefits, and any penalty begins to run the *later of* the date of the transfer, or the date of first possible eligibility for Medicaid. Again, assume a Medicaid applicant transfers a gift to his children in June of 2006, and the ineligibility period is 40 months. If the applicant enters a nursing home on February 1, 2011, he would have to pay for the first 40 months of care after financially qualifying for Medicaid (i.e., there is no prior tolling of the ineligibility period).

MEDICAID PLANNING

Medicaid long-term care benefits require that an institutionalized individual can have countable assets of no more than $2,000. If married, the non-institutionalized spouse can retain countable assets within limits set by the Federal government (the specific amount varies from state to state, but is limited to a maximum of $109,560 in 2011). Countable assets include virtually all investments, savings, and real estate owned by the applicant and his or her spouse. See also, page 451.

Annuities. An immediate annuity can be used as a means of transforming "countable" assets into an income stream that does not affect Medicaid eligibility. To qualify the annuity must be: (1) irrevocable – periodic payments cannot be changed, (2) non-transferable – benefits cannot be changed to another beneficiary, (3) "actuarially sound" – a term certain annuity cannot be payable for longer than the annuitant's actuarial life expectancy; and (4) the state must be named the first remainder beneficiary up to the amount of Medicaid benefits paid on the annuitant's behalf (if a surviving spouse or blind or disabled child is named as the primary beneficiary, then the state may be named the secondary beneficiary).

Purchase of life estate. The purchase of a life estate is not considered a transfer of assets provided the purchaser resides in the home for a period of at least one year after the date of purchase (e.g., father living in son's home purchases from the son a life estate in the home, lives there for at least one year, and then enters a nursing home). This transforms a countable resource (cash) into a non-countable resource (the life estate), provided payment for the life estate does not exceed its fair market value as calculated in accordance with certain tables. Before entering into such an arrangement the capital gains tax consequences to both the parent and the child should be carefully considered (e.g., potential elimination of capital gains tax exemption upon a subsequent sale of the home).

Transfer in trust for disabled child. Transfers to a supplemental needs trust for the "sole benefit" of the applicant's permanently and totally disabled (or blind) child do not affect Medicaid eligibility (see page 527).

Planning for the home. The value of the applicant's home is important in determining eligibility for Medicaid benefits to pay the costs of long-term care. Home equity that is exempt is limited to $500,000, although states may raise this to $750,000. However, this limitation on home equity does not apply if any of the following persons reside in the home: (1) the individual's spouse; (2) the individual's child under 21; (3) the individual's blind or disabled child; (4) a sibling who has an ownership interest in the home and was residing in the home for a period of at least one year immediately before the individual became institutionalized; or (5) a caregiver child who resided in the home for a period of at least two years immediately before the individual became institutionalized and whose care permitted such individual to reside at home. Further, Medicaid eligibility is not compromised if the individual receiving Medicaid *transfers* the home to any of these same people (e.g., the home is given to the caregiver child). Once transferred, the home is no longer subject to a Medicare reimbursement claim, as such claim can only be asserted against the recipient's estate.

MEDICAL INFORMATION BUREAU

The Medical Information Bureau (MIB) is a nonprofit trade association of over 700 life insurance companies that was first organized in 1902 to conduct a confidential interchange of underwriting information among its members as an alert against fraud. This interchange enables MIB member companies to protect the interests of both insurance consumers and life and health insurance providers. MIB's basic purpose is to detect and deter fraud and misrepresentation in connection with the underwriting of life and health insurance and claims.

Upon receipt of an application accompanied by a suitable authorization, member companies conduct a search of MIB records as part of their usual underwriting procedure. Members are also required to report relevant results of their underwriting evaluation to the MIB; that is, of conditions that are significant to health or longevity. Both favorable and unfavorable medical information is reported. Certain nonmedical information of a very restricted nature regarding insurability is also reported (e.g., confirmed adverse driving record, hazardous sports activity and aviation activity). In order to help preserve confidentiality the information is reported and maintained in code symbols. Members may not report codes based on claim information.

MIB information is used only to alert member companies to the possible need for further information. It *may not* be used as a basis for establishing eligibility for insurance. An MIB report does not indicate either the underwriting action of the reporting company or how much coverage was applied for.

Only member companies have access to MIB information and then only after receiving written authorization from the proposed insured in the course of the application process. The proposed insured's spouse cannot give this authorization. MIB information is not released to nonmember companies, credit or consumer reporting agencies, or governmental agencies, except pursuant to court order or authorization from the consumer.

The consumer who applies for life, health or disability insurance receives a brief written notice which describes MIB and its function. In addition, this notice tells how the consumer can access and correct his MIB record when needed. To obtain a copy of their MIB record, if one exists, or to seek correction of the MIB record, consumers can contact the MIB toll-free at 866-692-6901. Their web site is located at www.mib.com.

MEDICARE

Medicare is a federal health insurance program for persons 65 or older, persons of any age with permanent kidney failure, and certain disabled persons. The program is administered by the Centers for Medicare & Medicaid Services (CMS). Medicare claims are processed and paid by various commercial insurance companies under contract with CMS.

Part A – Hospital Insurance protection provides institutional care, including inpatient hospital care, skilled nursing home care, post-hospital home health care, and, under certain circumstances, hospice care.

(a) **Enrollment.** Any person eligible for Social Security monthly benefits is automatically eligible for Hospital Insurance protection, beginning with the first day of the month in which the person turns age 65. An individual who is *already receiving* Social Security monthly benefits need not file again to receive Medicare Part A benefits. A person *eligible for, but not yet receiving*, Social Security monthly benefits may apply separately for Medicare Part A benefits. Most retired individuals pay no Part A premium (see premium summary on page 456).

(b) **Coverage.** For the first 60 days, all covered hospital expenses are paid in full except for an initial inpatient deductible ($1,132 in 2011). For the next 30 days, the patient must pay a daily coinsurance charge ($283 per day in 2011). Thereafter, the patient has available an additional lifetime reserve of 60 hospital days, during which the patient must pay a daily coinsurance charge ($566 per day in 2011). Skilled nursing facility care, home health care, and hospice care, are also covered, but intermediate and *custodial care* are not covered. Beyond 150 days there is no coverage. See benefits summary on page 457.

Part B – Medical Insurance protection is a voluntary program of health insurance, which covers physician services, outpatient hospital care, physical therapy, ambulance trips, medical equipment, prosthetics, and a number of other services not covered under Part A. This is also known as "Supplementary Medical Insurance (SMI)."

(a) **Enrollment.** Those who are receiving Social Security benefits are enrolled automatically at the time they become entitled to Hospital Insurance, unless they elect not to be covered for Medical Insurance. For persons born after 1938 normal retirement age is not age 65 (see page 313). These persons must enroll before the beginning of the month in which age 65 is reached, in order to obtain coverage at the earliest possible date (unless they have elected early retirement, in which case they are enrolled automatically). See premium summary on page 456.

(continued on next page)

MEDICARE (continued)

(b) **Coverage.** Medical Insurance helps pay for covered services received from a doctor in the doctor's office, in a hospital, in a skilled nursing facility, in the patient's home, or any other location. After the patient pays the first $162 of covered services in each calendar year, Medicare usually pays 80 percent of the approved charges for doctors' services and the cost of other services. See benefits summary on page 457. Medical Insurance under Medicare *does not cover*: (1) most routine physical examinations and tests directly related to such examinations; (2) most routine foot care and dental care; (3) examinations for prescribing or fitting eyeglasses or hearing aids, and most eyeglasses and hearing aids; (4) immunizations (except annual flu shots and limited vaccinations for certain persons at risk); (5) most cosmetic surgery; and (6) custodial care at home or in a nursing home. (Although Medicare does provide a limited benefit for home health care, it is the Medicaid system that provides for nursing home care.)

Part C – Medicare Advantage, previously known as Medicare+Choice, permits contracts between CMS and a variety of different managed care and fee-for-service organizations. These plans must provide all current Medicare-covered items and services, and they may incorporate extra benefits in a basic package, and they may offer supplemental benefits priced separately from the basic package. Most Medicare beneficiaries can choose to receive benefits through the original Medicare fee-for-service program, or through a coordinated care plan (including Health Maintenance Organizations (HMOs), Preferred Provider Organizations (PPOs), and Provider-Sponsored Organizations (PSOs)), or a private fee-for-service plan that reimburses providers on a fee-for-service basis.

Part D – Prescription drug plans, provides a comprehensive voluntary prescription drug benefit available to everyone with Medicare. The plans are provided by insurance companies and other private companies approved by Medicare. Coverage is available under stand-alone plans, or through Medicare Advantage plans that integrate with health care coverage provided under Part C of Medicare. In 2011 the average premium is expected to be about $30 a month.

(a) **Enrollment.** There is an opportunity to enroll when joining Medicare, or during an annual open enrollment period running from November 15th to December 31st. Although enrollment is optional, those who fail to enroll will pay a penalty of about 1 percent for each month of delay (e.g., delaying enrollment for 14 months will result in a 14 percent lifetime increase in premiums). Persons who have prescription drug coverage "at least as good" as the basic plan (see next paragraph) will not incur a penalty. However, not all drugs are available in every plan.

In selecting a plan the enrollee must balance the three Cs of cost, coverage, and convenience. For example, plans may charge a higher monthly premium in return for enhanced

(continued on next page)

MEDICARE (continued)

coverage offering a greater selection of drugs (set out in a "formulary"), lower deductibles, lower co-pays, and greater geographic coverage. Plan selection has been made difficult by the sheer number and variety of plans offered. A drug finder program can be found at www.medicare.gov.

(b) **Coverage.** All plans must provide coverage "at least as good" as the standard coverage set by Medicare. Under standard coverage, once the enrollee has paid a $310 annual deductible, the enrollee pays 25 percent and Medicare pays 75 percent of drugs costs on the next $2,530. The enrollee then pays 93 percent for generic drugs and 50 percent for brand name drugs on the next $3,607.50 (this represents the beginning of the phase out of the donut hole coverage gap under The Patient Protection and Affordable Care Act of 2010). Thereafter, the enrollee pays 5 percent, and Medicare pays 95 percent of drug costs. Plans cover both generic and brand-name drugs. Low-income subsidies provide for no gap in coverage, and reduce, or eliminate, premiums, deductibles, and co-payments.

For those individuals who have retiree prescription drug benefits from their employers, substantial direct subsidies, and tax benefits, are offered to employers who maintain drug coverage for retired workers. The previous Medicare-approved drug discount cards have been phased out.

Premium Summary
2011

HOSPITAL (Part A)

Monthly Premium*	Quarters of Medicare-Covered Employment
$0	40 or more
$248	30-39
$450	less than 30 (and not otherwise eligible for premium-free hospital insurance)

MEDICAL (Part B)

	Income Of Beneficiaries Who File			
	Joint Tax Return		Other Tax Return	
Monthly Premium	Over	To	Over	To
$115.40**	0	170,000	0	85,000
$161.50	170,000	214,000	85,000	107,000
$230.70	214,000	320,000	107,000	160,000
$299.90	320,000	428,000	160,000	214,000
$369.10	428,000	-	214,000	-

* Most retired individuals pay no Part A premium.

** As a result of the "hold harmless" provision of the law beneficiaries who currently have the Social Security Administration withhold their Part B premium and have incomes of $85,000 of less (or $170,000 or less for joint filers) will not have an increase in their Part B premium for 2011 (i.e., the premium will remain at $96.40 per month – the 2010 rate).

(continued on next page)

MEDICARE (continued)

Benefits Summary
2011

HOSPITAL (Part A)	Benefit	Individual Pays	Medicare Pays
Hospitalization	first 60 days	$1,132	balance
	61st to 90th day	$283 a day	balance
	91st to 150th day	$566 a day	balance
	beyond 150 days	all costs	nothing
Skilled Nursing Facility Care	first 20 days	nothing	all (as approved)
	next 80 days	$141.50 a day	balance
	beyond 100 days	all	nothing
Home Health Care	first 100 days in spell of illness	nothing for services 20% for durable medical equipment	all balance
Hospice Care	unlimited (doctor must certify)	outpatient drugs and inpatient respite care	balance
MEDICAL (Part B)			
Medical Expenses	unlimited	$162 deductible plus 20% of remaining	balance
Clinical Laboratory Services	unlimited	nothing	all
Home Health Care	unlimited (but covers only what is not covered under Part A)	nothing for services 20% for equipment	all balance
Outpatient Hospital Treatment	unlimited	$162 deductible plus 20% of remaining	balance

Benefits must be medically necessary. Under Part A hospitalization benefits from 91st to 150th day are the 60 "reserve" days that may be used only once in a lifetime.

MINIMUM DEPOSIT INSURANCE

This term is used to describe the payment of premiums for a life insurance contract with borrowed cash values from the policy (in contrast, see the discussion of Premium Financing on page 478). It is not a particular type of life insurance contract.

Because consumer interest is not deductible, minimum deposit insurance is unattractive for most individual policy owners (see page 431). Nevertheless, within strict limits a business (including a corporation, partnership, or sole proprietorship) can deduct interest payments that are reasonable business expenses on a policy that is "tax qualified." This deduction is limited to loan interest paid on policies insuring a "key person" for up to $50,000 of indebtedness. A key person is an officer or a 20-percent owner of the business. The number of individuals who may be treated as key persons is limited to the greater of: (1) five persons; or (2) the lesser of five percent of the total officers and employees or 20 individuals (i.e., no more than 20 persons can be treated as key persons).

In addition, interest in excess of an "applicable rate" cannot be deducted (referred to as an interest rate "cap"). The applicable rate is that rate described in Moody's Corporate Bond Yield Average - Monthly Average Corporates, as published by Moody's Investors Service.

Except for application of a modified interest rate cap, contracts issued prior to June 21, 1986, are "grandfathered" (e.g., they are not subject to the key person provisions described above). Loans taken on nongrandfathered policies before 1996 are subject to a phase-in of the disallowance of the interest deduction. No deduction is allowed for the part of the taxpayer's interest expense which is "allocable to unborrowed policy cash values," which are defined as the excess of the cash surrender values (determined without regard to surrender charges) over the amount of any policy loans. However, there is an exception which applies to policies and contracts owned by entities if the policy covers only one individual who, at the time first covered by the policy, is: (1) a 20-percent-owner of the entity; or (2) an individual who is an officer, director or employee of the trade or business. See **Q 18**, *Tax Facts on Insurance & Employee Benefits (2011)* for a more complete explanation of the above limits on policy loan interest.

Most plans of minimum deposit insurance can be best explained as follows: (1) cash values are borrowed at a relatively low rate of interest; (2) borrowed cash values are used to pay premiums; (3) if any 4 out of the first 7 years' premiums are paid from unborrowed funds and borrowing in the other 3 years does not exceed the annual premiums, the policy is considered "tax qualified" and the interest paid on the borrowed cash values is deductible within the limits established under IRS regulations; (4) if the interest is deductible, after-tax cost is reduced; (5) if desired, beginning in the 8th year, both the premium and the after-tax cost of interest payments can be borrowed.

MINORS AND LIFE INSURANCE

Insurance companies will not knowingly accept a minor as the direct owner or beneficiary of a life insurance contract (for minor as insured, see page 360). Although trusts provide the most flexible way of managing policies and proceeds, establishing and administering them involves both time and expense. Ownership and beneficiary arrangements involving minors are governed by either the Uniform Transfers to Minors Act (UTMA) or the Uniform Gifts to Minors Act (UGMA) (see page 545). At the end of 2010, 48 states had statutes based upon the UTMA. The older and more restrictive UGMA was still in effect in the states of South Carolina and Vermont. It is important to consult individual state laws, since states typically alter the text of the uniform versions.

If the beneficiary designation includes a custodial nomination, the proceeds can be transferred to a custodian without appointing a guardian. Any trust company or adult other than the insured can be nominated custodian (an adult under state UTMAs is usually age 21). A designation paying a death benefit to a child of the insured might read: "to [name of child], child of the insured; provided that if any proceeds become payable when [name of child] is a minor as defined in the [state] Uniform Transfers to Minors Act, such proceeds shall be paid to [name of adult] as custodian for [name of child] under the [state] Uniform Transfers to Minors Act." Note that this language covers the possibility that the child might become an adult by the time a death benefit is paid. A substitute custodian should be named in case the primary custodian cannot serve.

Without a custodial nomination, it is likely that the insurance company will require appointment of a guardian of the minor's property prior to making payment of death proceeds. The only exception allows for payment of small amounts, usually $10,000, to either a trust company or an adult member of the minor's family (a no-nomination transfer).

To give an *existing* policy to a minor, the owner merely signs a change of ownership form. To give a *new* policy, the custodian is designated as owner on the application. In either situation the ownership designation might read: "to [name of adult] as custodian for [name of child] under the [state] Uniform Transfers to Minors Act." In contrast, the purchase of a policy using custodial funds is a reinvestment of funds. If the minor is the insured then the minor's estate should be named beneficiary. If someone else is the insured then the beneficiary must be the minor, the minor's estate, or a custodian, and the designation must be irrevocable so long as the custodianship remains in effect. In this situation the beneficiary designation might read: "to [name of child], child of the insured, if living, otherwise to the estate of [name of child]; provided that the proceeds shall be paid to [name of adult] as custodian for [name of child] under the [state] Uniform Transfers to Minors Act if the proceeds become payable while such custodianship remains in effect; without the right to change while such custodianship remains in effect."

MONEY PURCHASE PENSION PLAN

Under the money purchase pension plan each employee/participant has an individual account into which the employer makes annual contributions pursuant to the plan's contribution formula. These employer contributions are required and the employer is subject to a minimum funding penalty if they are not made. The formula used to determine contribution amounts must be nondiscriminatory and typically sets employer contributions at a specific percentage of the employee's annual compensation. Only the first $245,000 (in 2010 and 2011, as indexed) of each employee's compensation can be taken into consideration. The maximum annual addition that can be contributed to a money purchase plan is the lesser of 100 percent of the participant's compensation, or $49,000 (in 2010 and 2011, as indexed). In determining the level of employer contributions, integration with Social Security is allowed.

The maximum amount an employer may deduct for money purchase plan contributions is 25 percent of compensation (i.e., generally payroll, but subject to the $245,000 per participant limit). Prior to 2002 this 25 percent limit provided money purchase pension plans with an advantage over profit sharing plans, since the deduction for profit sharing contributions was limited to 15 percent of payroll. Without this advantage, employers have increasingly chosen to establish the more flexible profit sharing plan, rather than a money purchase pension plan that requires annual employer contributions.

Unlike the defined benefit pension plan, under a money purchase pension plan the employee bears the investment risk of the plan (i.e., the employer is obligated only to make the initial contribution, after that *the risk of poor investment performance is borne by the participant*). The employee also bears the risk that the amounts accumulated at retirement might be insufficient to fund retirement needs. Upon retirement the participant's account balance can be paid in a lump sum, paid in installments for a number of years, or used to purchase an annuity providing an income for life (this is the origin of the term "money purchase"). Of all qualified plans the money purchase pension plan is generally considered the simplest to design, explain, install and administer.

See also, the discussions of Qualified Retirement Plans on page 491 and Life Insurance in Qualified Plans on pages 439-440.

NET UNREALIZED APPRECIATION

With certain exceptions, distributions from qualified retirement plans are subject to taxation as ordinary income. To avoid current taxation, it is common for an individual receiving a lump sum distribution from a qualified retirement plan to make a tax-free rollover to a traditional IRA. However, if the distribution includes *appreciated employer stock*, then the employee should consider taking distribution of the stock (i.e., not rolling it over into an IRA). By doing this, the stock's net unrealized appreciation (NUA) will qualify for long-term capital gains rates whenever the stock is sold; by the employee, by the employee's spouse, or by the employee's heirs. NUA is the stock's fair market value in excess of basis. Basis is generally the value of the stock at the time that it was acquired by the plan. Subsequent appreciation of the stock in excess of NUA is taxed as either short-term or long-term capital gains, depending upon how long the stock is held after it is distributed from the plan. See capital gains, page 353.

To take advantage of this favorable tax treatment, the employee must receive the stock as part of a "lump sum distribution" from a qualified retirement plan (i.e., payment within one year of the entire account balance as a result of the employee's separation from service, attaining age 59½, disability, or death). The employee must also pay ordinary income taxes on the cost basis of the stock distributed (i.e., the value of the stock at the time that it was acquired by the plan). The decision for the employee comes down to this: Is it worth paying current ordinary income taxes on the stock's basis in return for obtaining long-term capital gains treatment for the stock's NUA?

The employee may also make a tax-free rollover to a traditional IRA of some, but not all, of the employer stock. (The NUA within the stock rolled over to the IRA would end up being taxed as ordinary income.) Likewise, when a distribution consists of both employer stock and other assets, these other assets may be rolled into an IRA to avoid current taxation. All rollovers must be made within 60 days of the distribution.

For example, assume an employee receives a lump-sum distribution from his 401(k) plan of $600,000 in employer stock with a cost basis of $125,000, pays ordinary income taxes on the $125,000, and sells the stock six years later for $850,000. Of this amount, the cost basis of $125,000 is not taxed (it was taxed upon distribution), NUA of $475,000 is taxed as long-term capital gains, and the after-distribution gain of $250,000 is taxed as either short-term or long-term capital gains – depending upon the holding period (long-term in this example).

If the stock with NUA remains unsold at death, the NUA is treated as income in respect of a decedent and it is not entitled to a step-up in basis (but it is entitled to capital gains treatment when sold by the heirs). See income in respect of a decedent, page 425, and stepped-up basis, page 530.

NIMCRUT

The term NIMCRUT stands for Net Income with Make-up Charitable Remainder UniTrust. As a form of charitable remainder unitrust (CRUT), the trust assets are valued annually creating a unitrust amount (variable annuity payment) made at least annually to one or more trust beneficiaries. Distributions consist of the *lesser of*: (1) a fixed percentage (not less than 5 percent) of the value of the trust assets (valued annually); or (2) the net income of the trust for the current year. Unlike the CRUT, a make-up account is created in any year that income earned is less than the fixed percentage allowed. The make-up account is then paid out in any future year in which the income earned exceeds the fixed percentage payout for that specific year (i.e., the NIMCRUT provides for "make-up" distributions). No adjustment for the time value of money is allowed for these make-up distributions. *Pre-contribution* capital gains are generally not available for distribution. *Post-contribution* capital gains may be classified as income, provided this does not conflict with state law (see the discussion of the Prudent Investor Rule on page 485).

A NIMCRUT provides a great deal of flexibility for the donor who wishes to defer income for retirement. Trust income can be deferred by having the trustee make appropriate investment selections (e.g., a deferred annuity), or by donating to the trust low-income or non-income producing assets (e.g., growth stocks, closely held stock, or real estate). Unlike the CRUT, if trust income is not adequate, the trustee has no obligation to pay out the unitrust amount and the donor can be positioned to receive larger make-up payments after retirement. Also, as with the CRUT, a donor may make multiple gifts to the same NIMCRUT. However, before making gifts to any NIMCRUT, it is essential that the donor fully understand that payments are contingent upon the trust earning income.

For the donor who desires greater flexibility, a FLIP unitrust might be considered. This technique begins with a NIMCRUT, or a NICRUT (similar to a NIMCRUT but without the makeup provisions), that is converted to a standard CRUT upon the occurrence of an approved triggering event. Approved triggering events cannot be controlled by the donor, unitrust beneficiary, trustee, or any other person. For example, the beneficiary's 65th birthday is an approved triggering event, but not the beneficiary's retirement, as that event is controlled by the beneficiary. Unfortunately, when a NIMCRUT flips to a standard CRUT, any outstanding make-up amounts are forfeited.

See also, Charitable Remainder Trust chart on page 55.

NONCITIZEN ESTATE PLANNING

For the purpose of estate and gift tax planning, it is helpful to recognize three categories of individuals: (1) United States citizens; (2) resident aliens (i.e., non-citizens who are resident in the United States); and (3) nonresident aliens (i.e., non-citizens who are resident in another country).

Resident aliens. The property of a resident alien is subject to United States estate and gift tax laws, no matter where it is located. For estate and gift tax purposes, residency means that the person is actually "domiciled" in the United States. Generally, a person acquires a domicile by living in a place, even for a brief period of time, with no definite present intention of leaving and living elsewhere. This is a rather subjective determination that is influenced by where the individual's time is spent, as well as the location of other family members, business interests, social activities, driver's license, and financial and tax relationships. It is important to recognize that although a person can have more than one "residence," they can have only one domicile (i.e., do not confuse the terms "residence" and "residency"). See the expanded discussion of domicile on page 393.

Although a resident alien is generally subject to the same estate and gift taxes rules and rates as a United States citizen, the unlimited marital deduction is unavailable if the surviving spouse is not a United States citizen (in 2011 gifts to foreign spouses are limited to $136,000, see page 488). Because of the unified gift and estate tax system, gifts made prior to becoming a resident may also be included in the resident alien's estate. However, resident aliens can take advantage of the full unified credit (page 19), annual exclusion gifts (page 47), split-gifts with spouses (page 47), and irrevocable life insurance trusts (page 51).

Nonresident aliens. Property located within the United States is subject to both gift and estate taxes (i.e., it has a "situs" within the United States and is therefore taxed). Only the first $60,000 of property is free of transfer taxes and the unlimited marital deduction is not available unless the surviving spouse is a United States citizen (in 2011 gifts to foreign spouses are limited to $136,000, see page 488). Gifts of *tangible* property and *real estate* are subject to gift taxes (but gifts of *intangible* property are generally free of gift taxes). However, bank deposits and life insurance are specifically excluded from both gift and estate taxation (i.e., they are deemed not to have a "situs" within the United States). Thus, the proceeds of a life insurance policy on the life of a nonresident alien are not subject to estate taxes, even though the beneficiary is a resident or citizen of the United States.

A foreign death tax credit is available for estate taxes actually paid to a foreign country or United States possession in which the property is located (but there is no credit for foreign *gift* taxes). Foreign death and gift tax treaties can also offer relief from the double taxation often imposed upon both resident and nonresident aliens. However, such planning can be very complicated, and the advice of competent tax counsel should be sought.

NONQUALIFIED STOCK OPTIONS

Nonqualified stock options (NQSOs), also referred to as "nonstatutory stock options," are rights to purchase a certain number of shares of stock at a fixed exercise price within a specified period of time. With NQSOs a corporation is able to provide selected employees with the opportunity to share in the future growth of the company, without having to make any current cash outlays for salary or bonuses. Because there are few regulatory restrictions on how they may be designed, NQSOs offer a great deal of flexibility in meeting specific corporate objectives.

The option's exercise price is often referred to as the grant price or strike price. It may be set at the full fair market value (FMV) of the stock as of the date of the grant, at a price below FMV (at a "discount"), or at a price above FMV (at a "premium"). Options may be exercised after the passage of a set period, upon the occurrence of a certain event, and may even be immediately exercisable, although this is not usual. They can also be subject to vesting rules (e.g., after 3 years of continuous employment).

At the time they are granted NQSOs are generally not taxed to the employee, provided they do not have a "readily ascertainable fair market value." In contrast to options for stock actively traded on an established market, an option to acquire closely held stock has no readily ascertainable fair market value. (Note that it is the option itself that must be tradable, not the underlying stock.) When the option is exercised the difference between the exercise price and the market value, referred to as the bargain element, is taxed to the employee as ordinary income. At the time of exercise the employer is entitled to a corresponding compensation deduction.

NQSOs are referred to as "nonqualified" stock options because they do not meet the requirements of the Code to be qualified as "incentive" stock options (ISOs). Although ISOs offer income tax advantages that are not available to NQSOs, the Code imposes limitations and restrictions upon ISOs that are not applicable to NQSOs. For example, ISO gains may be taxed at favorable capital gains rates, but ISOs are not transferable during lifetime.

In contrast to ISOs, if permitted by the underlying stock option agreement or plan, NQSOs are transferable during the employee's lifetime. Provided the option is vested, its transfer to a child or other heir is treated as a completed gift (see chart, page 47). However, the donor-employee remains liable for any income taxes when the option is subsequently exercised by the donee-child (i.e., the income tax consequences cannot be transferred). This tax treatment is similar to that imposed upon the trust income of a Intentionally Defective Trust (see chart, page 67).

PARTNERSHIPS

Family Limited Partnership

A chart describing the family limited partnership (FLP) is on page 163. The following advantages, disadvantages, and requirements will help in better understanding this important planning technique.

The principal *advantages* of the FLP include:

1. **Retention of control** by the general partner, who has property which he is willing to transfer to family members but is reluctant to lose control over the property. A general partner operating under a well drafted partnership agreement can maintain indirect control without adverse income and estate tax consequences.

2. **Shifting of income** within certain family partnership limits. The general partner often has the power to retain current profits for investment and reasonable business needs.

3. **Protection of partnership assets** from the creditors of limited partners by restricting the limited partners ability to dispose of their limited partnership interests. Because the general partner has the ability to retain profits, the flow through nature of partnership income taxation gives him the ability to create a tax liability without making cash distributions for tax payments (i.e., an "ugly" asset).

4. **Reduction of value** through minority discounts and lack of marketability. The typical limited partnership gift represents a minority interest. Lack of marketability can be established by prohibitions against terminating the partnership without the concurrence of all partners (this prohibition is usually limited to 40 years or less). Valuation discounts can range from 30 to 70 percent.

5. **Facilitating gifts** of assets which otherwise are not easily divisible (e.g., the family farm). Often the ultimate goal is for the parent to eventually own only modest partnership interests, with the bulk of the FLP being held by other family members.

Some *disadvantages* of the FLP include:

1. The traditional partnership freeze is subject to the impact of the Chapter 14 valuation rules (see pages 407-408). However, most of the techniques used to reduce the effect of, or to avoid, these rules with respect to recapitalizations will also work with partnerships.

2. Much of the ability to reduce taxes by shifting income from parent to younger children has been curtailed by the "kiddie tax" (see discussion on page 545).

(continued on next page)

PARTNERSHIPS (continued)

3. There are additional expenses associated with establishing and accounting for an FLP (e.g., an information tax return must be filed).

4. Gifts do not receive a step-up in income tax basis.

5. Retained partnership interests continue to appreciate in the parent's estate until they are transferred during lifetime or at death.

The principal *requirements* for an FLP are:

1. Capital must be a material income-producing factor. A personal service business where income consists primarily of fees or commissions would not qualify for operation as a family partnership (i.e., lawyer, doctor, photographer, plumber, etc.).

2. If the partnership has been created by gift, the donor (parent) must be given a reasonable salary for services rendered to the partnership before profits can be allocated among the partners (the concept of "gift" also includes intra-family sales).

3. Profits of the partnership must be allocated, or divided, in proportion to each partner's capital investment.

4. All partners must actually own a "capital interest" (i.e., an interest in partnership assets which is distributable to the partner upon his withdrawal from the partnership or upon partnership liquidation).

5. In order to avoid inclusion under Code section 2036 (i.e., prohibition against retained life estates) of the underlying partnership assets (rather than the partnership itself) a donor or decedent should adhere to all partnership formalities and *should not*: (1) put virtually everything they own in the partnership; (2) retain complete control over the income of the partnership; and (3) use the partnership to pay personal expenses (see also, page 410).

(continued on next page)

PARTNERSHIPS (continued)

Partnership Used As Alternative To
Irrevocable Life Insurance Trust

Partnerships are increasingly being used as a substitute for the irrevocable life insurance trust. When contrasted to the irrevocable life insurance trust the primary advantages of a partnership are the *control* that a general partner can exercise over the partnership, which is not available with a trust since the grantor cannot be a trustee, and the *flexibility* a partnership offers to adjust to changing circumstances, which is not available with the irrevocable life insurance trust. Implementation of the technique involves creation of either a general or limited partnership of which the insured is the managing or general partner. Limited partnership interests are obtained by family members either by having the insured make cash gifts to them, after which the funds are contributed to the partnership in return for partnership interests, or by having the insured contribute cash to the partnership in return for partnership interests which are then given to family members. Assuming the insured holds no incidents of ownership, and the death proceeds are paid to the partnership, only his proportionate partnership share, including the insurance proceeds, will be in his estate.

Partnership Created To Avoid
Transfer For Value Problem

Insurance death benefits paid to a C corporation to fund a stock redemption agreement may be subject to the corporate alternative minimum tax (see pages 374-376). Although the AMT can be avoided by converting to a cross purchase agreement, transferring existing corporate owned policies to co-stockholders of the insured can run afoul of the transfer for value rules, meaning that the death benefits would be subject to ordinary income taxes (see pages 541-542). Transfers to a partnership of which the insured is a partner are exempt from the transfer for value rules. In a private letter ruling, the IRS has approved the creation of a partnership for the purpose of receiving corporate-owned policies. Although a partnership must be for a valid business purpose, and not just for avoiding taxes, this ruling appears to approve a partnership whose sole purpose is to "engage in the purchase and acquisition of life insurance policies on the lives of the partners." However, use of this technique might cause the proceeds received by the partnership to be taxed in the insured's estate, since the proceeds are not being retained by the partnership, but rather distributed to the surviving partners to fund a cross purchase agreement (i.e., as a partner the insured possesses an incident of ownership in the policy on his own life and there may be no double taxation issue since the value of the proceeds are not included in valuing the insured's partnership interest). It is probably advisable to avoid using such a "sole purpose" partnership until this estate taxation issue is resolved.

PENALTIES – ESTATE AND GIFT TAXES

Failure to file return. A 5 percent penalty if the failure is for not more than 1 month, with an additional 5 percent for each additional month, not to exceed a total of 25 percent; unless it is shown that the failure was due to reasonable cause and not due to willful neglect. If the failure to file is fraudulent then the monthly penalty is increased from 5 percent to 15 percent, and the total penalty from 25 percent to 75 percent. *Section 6651.*

Failure to pay tax. A 0.5 percent penalty if the failure is for not more than 1 month, with an additional 0.5 percent for each additional month, not to exceed a total of 25 percent; unless it is shown that the failure was due to reasonable cause and not due to willful neglect. *Section 6651.*

Fraud penalty. Penalty is 75 percent of the underpayment attributable to fraud. If the IRS establishes that any portion of an underpayment is attributable to fraud, the entire underpayment will be treated as such. The taxpayer must establish the part not attributable to fraud. *Section 6663.*

Accuracy related penalty. A 20 percent penalty is imposed on any underpayment attributable to negligence or a *substantial* valuation understatement. A substantial valuation understatement exists if the value of property on the return is 65 percent or less of the amount determined to be correct (penalty is 40 percent if property on return is 40 percent or less of correct amount). No penalty for a substantial valuation understatement is imposed if the underpayment is no more than $5,000. Also, no penalty is imposed if the taxpayer acts with reasonable cause and good faith. *Sections 6662 and 6664.*

Statute of limitations on assessment. Generally, 3 years after return filed. If the taxpayer omits items that exceed 25 percent of total amounts stated on return, statute of limitations is 6 years after date of return. There is no statute of limitations if no return is filed, or if return was false or fraudulent and filed with intent to evade tax. *Section 6501.*

False statement as crime. Any person who under the penalties of perjury willfully makes and subscribes a return, statement, or other document, and who does not believe it to be true and correct, is guilty of a felony, and will be fined not more than $100,000 or imprisoned not more than 3 years, or both, together with the costs of prosecution. *Section 7206.*

Removal or concealment as crime. Any person who removes or conceals any goods with intent to evade or defeat the assessment or collection of taxes is guilty of a felony, and will be fined not more than $100,000 or imprisoned not more than 3 years, or both, together with the costs of prosecution. *Section 7206.*

Statute of limitations on criminal prosecutions. If the taxpayer willfully attempts to evade any payment or willfully fails to make a return or pay a tax, the statute of limitations is 6 years. *Section 6531.*

PENSION BENEFIT GUARANTY CORPORATION (PBGC)

The PBGC is a federal agency created by the Employee Retirement Income Security Act of 1974 (ERISA) to protect defined benefit pension plans (defined contribution plans are not covered). Plans sponsored by churches, governmental bodies, and small professional employers with fewer than 26 employees are generally not covered by the PBGC. The PBGC guarantees "basic benefits" earned before a plan has been terminated, which include: (1) pension benefits at normal retirement age; (2) most early retirement benefits; (3) annuity benefits for survivors of plan participants; and (4) disability benefits for disabilities that occurred before the plan ended. Benefits are not adjusted for inflation (i.e., there are no cost-of-living increases). Health care, vacation pay, and severance pay are not guaranteed. (But recipients age 55 or over who are covered by qualified health insurance may be eligible for the Health Coverage Tax Credit administered by the IRS.)

Although most people receive the full benefit they earn before the plan ends, there is a maximum benefit guaranteed by the PGBC according to the year the plan is terminated. For example, with pension plans ending in 2011, the maximum guaranteed amount is $4,500 per month ($54,000 per year) for workers who retire at age 65. The maximum guaranteed amount is lower if the participant receives payments before age 65, or if the pension includes benefits for a survivor or other beneficiary (e.g., a joint and survivor annuity). The following shows the maximum monthly guarantees for plans terminating in the years 2007-2011 (i.e., a straight-life annuity).

Year Plan Terminated	Maximum Monthly Guarantee			
	Age 65	Age 62	Age 60	Age 55
2011	$4,500.00	$3,555.00	$2,925.00	$2,025.00
2010	$4,500.00	$3,555.00	$2,925.00	$2,025.00
2009	$4,500.00	$3,555.00	$2,925.00	$2,025.00
2008	$4,312.50	$3,406.88	$2,803.13	$1,940.63
2007	$4,125.00	$3,258.75	$2,681.25	$1,856.25

The full table can be seen at: www.pbgc.gov/benefits-information/find-your-pension-plan/content/page789.html.

Benefits may be further limited if a plan was created or amended to increase benefits within five years before it ended, or if the participant owned more than 10 percent of the business. It is possible to receive more than these guaranteed amounts if the plan has enough assets.

PER STIRPES – PER CAPITA

These terms are used in making beneficiary designations in life insurance policies, wills, and trusts.

The term **per stirpes** is used when it is desired that the share of a deceased beneficiary go to the beneficiary's children (in Latin it means "by the trunk," "by right of representation," or "by roots or stocks"). For example, assume John Smith desires to name his wife primary beneficiary of his life insurance policy with his children as contingent beneficiaries. However, should one of his children predecease him, John wants the children of that child (i.e., his grandchildren) to share equally their deceased parent's share. The following beneficiary wording might be used: "Sally Smith, wife of the insured, if she survives the insured, otherwise in equal shares to the surviving children of the insured, and to the surviving children of any deceased children of the insured, per stirpes." If Sally died before John and upon his subsequent death John had two children who were alive (A and B) and one child who had previously died leaving two children (deceased child C who left John's grandchildren D and E), then A and B would each take one-third of the proceeds and D and E would each take one-sixth of the proceeds (i.e., they would share their deceased parents one-third). In some jurisdictions the term "by representation" is used in lieu of "per stirpes."

The term **per capita** is used when it is desired that the children of a deceased beneficiary share equally with the surviving members of the original group of beneficiaries (in Latin it means "by the head," "according to the number of individuals," or "share and share alike"). Again, assume that John Smith desires to name his wife primary beneficiary of his life insurance policy with his children as contingent beneficiaries. However, should one of his children predecease him, John wants the children of that child (i.e., his grandchildren) to share equally with all other beneficiaries. The following beneficiary wording might be used: "Sally Smith, wife of the insured, if she survives the insured, otherwise in equal shares to the surviving children of the insured, and to the surviving children of any deceased children of the insured, per capita." Again, if Sally died before John and upon his subsequent death John had two children who were alive (A and B) and one child who had previously died leaving two children (deceased child C who left John's grandchildren D and E), then A, B, D and E would each take one-fourth of the proceeds (i.e., all beneficiaries would share equally).

For an expended discussion of beneficiary designations involving minors, see page 459.

PERSONAL HOLDING COMPANY

A personal holding company exists when more than 50 percent of a corporation's outstanding stock is owned by 5 or fewer individuals, directly or indirectly, and 60 percent of the corporation's adjusted ordinary gross income is personal holding company income. Personal holding company income is essentially passive income such as dividends, rents and royalties. If this income is not distributed during the year it will be subject to a 15 percent penalty tax in 2011.

Because of the limited marketability of personal holding company stock, courts have often allowed substantial valuation discounts (i.e., the stock of the personal holding company is held to be worth less than the value of its underlying assets). Because of this, under some circumstances personal holding companies can function as a particularly effective means of transferring future appreciation to other family members.

For example, an individual with a large estate containing a portfolio of stock that is expected to appreciate substantially would form a corporation with both voting and nonvoting common stock. His portfolio of stock is transferred to the personal holding company in return for the voting and nonvoting common stock. Thereafter, the nonvoting common is transferred by gift, or by sale, to other family members, and all future appreciation of this stock is shifted outside the stockholder's estate. By retaining ownership of the voting common the stockholder maintains control of the personal holding company (and of the investment decisions).

In addition to the penalty tax on undistributed income, a personal holding company can result in double taxation if appreciated assets are sold and the proceeds distributed to stockholders. Also, it is important to avoid running afoul of the special valuation provisions of Chapter 14 (see discussion on pages 407-408).

The penalty tax can be avoided with regard to a personal service contract by having the corporation reserve to itself the right to designate the professional who is to render services rather than giving the client the right to make the choice. In that case the income from such a personal service contract is not treated as personal holding company income.

PET ESTATE PLANNING

The law treats a pet as tangible personal property. The simplest way of providing for a pet after the owner's death is to identify a relative or close friend to whom a testamentary transfer of both the pet and sufficient funds to care for the pet can be made. While this method may be the least expensive, it is subject to will challenges by disgruntled relatives, does not become effective until the will is probated, and is not legally enforceable.

Trusts. The vast majority of states have passed laws that enable pet owners to set up trusts providing funds for the care of pets after the owner has died (see www.estateplanningforpets.org/legal-statutes.htm). While these statutes vary widely, they commonly recognize pet trusts as valid and enforceable and provide for termination of the trust upon the death of the pet (see www.professorbeyer.com/Articles/Animal_Statutes.htm). Under most of these statutes, the courts are authorized to reduce the amount transferred in trust if it is determined that the trust property substantially exceeds the amount needed for pet care (e.g., Leona Helmsley's bequest of $12 million to her aptly-named dog Trouble). Both inter vivos and testamentary pet trusts are used. An inter vivos trust offers the advantage that it becomes effective immediately and the trustee is empowered to use trust assets to care for a pet immediately upon the owner's disability or death. However, inter vivos trusts typically entail additional start-up costs and administration fees. Although pet trusts often have a separate trustee and caretaker, many pet trusts simply use a single caretaker-trustee.

Caretaker organizations. There are numerous organizations that have established formal programs for the care of pets after the death of the owner. Typically these charities and perpetual care programs involve payments or donations to the organization prior to or after the owner's death (see www.professorbeyer.com/Articles/Animals_More_Information.htm).

Power of attorney. Language may be included in a pet owner's durable power of attorney that gives the owner's agent express authority to care for the pet (see page 394). Such authority should include permission to take possession of the pet and to further utilize the funds provided to provide for the health, care, and welfare of the pet.

Living will. This document provides direction to the veterinarian and other pet care providers regarding the owner's feeling about end-of-life treatment and euthanasia.

Pet card. This is a card carried in the owner's wallet or purse for the purpose of providing information about the pet. The information provided includes the pet's name, location, breed, sex, and veterinarian. Availability of the card helps assure that the animal survives to the time when the owner's plans for the pet's care can take effect.

PHANTOM STOCK PLAN

Phantom stock plans are a form of nonqualified deferred compensation made available to select employees. They are also referred to as "shadow stock plans" or "as if" deferred compensation (i.e., the amount deferred is treated as if invested in the employer's stock).

The advantage to the employee is that his efforts and loyalty are rewarded by having an economic interest or stake in the business similar to that of the owners. The advantage to the owners of a small and closely held family business is that they are able to retain a valued employee without diminishing their percentage of ownership. Phantom stock plans are used in both regular C corporations and S corporations, limited liability companies, partnerships, and sole proprietorships.

To implement a phantom stock plan, a bookkeeping account in the name of the employee is established. This account is then credited with hypothetical shares of stock (when used with a noncorporate employer, the business equity credited to the employee is referred to as a "participation unit"). Periodically, the account can be credited with additional stock, as well as with dividends and stock splits. The deferral period is usually set at a specific number of years or upon the employee's retirement. At the end of the deferral period, the employee is entitled to receive cash payments equal to the excess of the market value of the stock on that date over its value on the date awarded. If appropriate, a vesting schedule can be used that provides for nonforfeitable appreciation rights prior to the end of the deferral period.

The terms "stock appreciation right" and SAR have been used to describe a benefit under which the employee receives only the appreciation of the stock, but not the stock value itself. For example, assume that ten shares of stock are awarded to an employee, with a current value of $150 each. If, at the end of the deferral period, the stock has increased in value to $275 per share, the employee is entitled to a payment of $1,250 ($275 - $150 = $125 appreciation per share; $125 x 10 shares = $1,250). Alternatively, in addition to any appreciation, the plan could provide for the employee to receive the underlying value of the stock. Assuming such a design, the employee would be entitled to a payment of $2,750 ($1,500 initial stock value plus $1,250 appreciation).

As with other nonqualified deferred compensation plans, the employer's obligation to the employee is unsecured. Income is not recognized by the employee until the benefits are actually paid or made available. The employer then deducts the payment made to the employee (assuming compensation is reasonable, see page 546). Phantom stock plans are often informally funded with cash value life insurance. Life insurance also allows the employer to provide a preretirement death benefit payable to the employee's family (see chart entitled Deferred Compensation on page 235, and footnotes 6 and 7 on page 237).

PLANNED GIVING

The term "planned giving" can be defined in terms of the **sources of funds** which donors use to make charitable gifts. In contrast to the annual gifts made from the donor's *disposable income* in support of the operational needs of a charitable or religious organization, the concept of planned giving involves gifts of the donor's *accumulated assets* to ensure the organization's long-term financial viability. The process often requires that donors make decisions regarding the distribution of significant portions of their estates. In recognizing that planned gifts must be coordinated with the donor's overall financial and estate plans, one definition simply describes planned giving as involving "any charitable gift that requires assistance by a qualified professional to complete." The terms "deferred giving" and "gift planning" are also used.

Planned giving can also be defined in terms of the **techniques and products** used when making charitable gifts. In addition to providing for a substantial charitable gift, the donor and his family also often enjoy both income and estate tax benefits and an ongoing income. These techniques and products include:

1. **Wills** that transfer assets by *outright* bequests of named assets (e.g., cash or real estate), *residuary* bequests of property remaining after payment of debts, estate costs, devises, bequests, and legacies, and *contingent* bequests (e.g., "I direct payment of $100,000 to XYZ Charity provided my spouse dies before me").

2. **Retirement plan assets** transferred at death from both IRAs and qualified retirement plans – see pages 307, 358-359, and 491.

3. **Charitable gift** annuities providing income as a general obligation of the charity and **pooled income funds** providing income from co-mingled investments – see page 357.

4. **Charitable trusts**, including:

   a. **Charitable remainder annuity trust** paying a fixed amount annually to the donor or other beneficiary – see pages 54 and 357.
   b. **Charitable remainder unitrust** paying a fixed percentage of the trust's value, as determined yearly. Variations of the unitrust include net income with makeup unitrusts (NIMCRUT), net income unitrusts (NICRUT), FLIP unitrusts, and charitable lead trusts (CLT) – see pages 54, 357 and 462.

5. **Life insurance** by transferring ownership directly or by irrevocably designating the charity as owner and beneficiary – see page 356.

6. **Private foundations** and **donor-advised funds** allowing for limited donor influence over fund disbursements – see page 480.

PORTABILITY

Historically, each individual has had the right to leave to the next generation a specific amount of property free of the federal estate tax. In 2009 that amount, described as an exemption, was $3,500,000. This could be done during lifetime by gift, or upon death, but the right could not be passed to a surviving spouse (i.e., you either used it during lifetime or upon death, or you lost it). It required prior planning to take advantage of the exemption.

The 2010 Tax Relief Act allows any unused exemption to be passed to a surviving spouse without the need to re-title assets and establish complex wills and trusts (e.g., by the use of QTIP, credit shelter, by-pass, or family trusts). The unused exemption is called the "Deceased Spousal Unused Exclusion Amount," or DSUEA. In order to take advantage of this portability, the executor of the estate of the deceased spouse must file an estate tax return and make a DSUEA election.

Under The 2010 Tax Relief Act, the exemption was increased to $5,000,000 per person and indexed for inflation beginning in 2012. Assuming none of the $5,000,000 was used, adding the $5,000,000 DSUEA to the surviving spouse's "basic exclusion amount" of $5,000,000 produces an "applicable exclusion amount" of $10,000,000. This is the amount that can be passed during lifetime or at death by the surviving spouse free of federal gift or estate taxes. The DSUEA is limited to that of the *last* deceased spouse. It is not clear that the DSUEA would be indexed for inflation (but it would be indexed up to the decease spouse's date of death).

Despite the advent of portability, there remain many non-tax reasons to use trust wills in estate plans. Surviving families require asset management, parents require assurance that assets will pass to their children and not to subsequent spouses, professionals require asset protection from civil suits, blended and nontraditional families have special needs, business interests must be continued, and incapacity planning often can best be accomplished with trusts.

It may be ill advised to rely solely on the portability of the federal estate tax exemption to plan an estate, as many states have their own *state death taxes* and virtually all states are continually seeking new sources of income in a financially challenging economy. Likewise, Congress can, and has, changed the estate tax laws with some regularity (see page 84). Portability does not apply to generation-skipping transfers (i.e., a surviving spouse cannot receive the deceased spouse's unused GST exemption).

Although the estate tax provisions of The 2010 Tax Relief Act are set to expire at the end of 2012, the portability and indexing provisions will most likely be a permanent feature of the estate tax laws. Taken together, portability and indexing of the exemption will likely result in a major transformation in the estate planning community.

POST MORTEM PLANNING

Post mortem (after death) planning is not limited to merely "picking up the pieces" for the families of decedents who have failed to plan in advance. In fact, rather than being a substitute for good planning, post mortem planning is best used as a means of effectively implementing plans that had been set in motion during the decedent's life, or of adapting to changing circumstances prior to or after the decedent's death. No matter how well an estate is planned, changing family and business circumstances, not to mention estate tax laws that are ever mutating, make it essential to build flexibility into every estate plan (see page 5). Such flexibility anticipates the use of both tax and nontax post mortem planning options and elections. The following are examples of some of these techniques:

Disclaimers. The use of disclaimers in estate planning can often result in obtaining greater flexibility by providing the opportunity for post mortem decisions, when more facts are likely to be available regarding assets, taxes, and beneficiaries. Disclaimers can be used with respect to gifts, wills, or even life insurance proceeds. The disclaimant has no authority to direct the distribution of the property, and it passes as though the disclaimant had predeceased the decedent. See Disclaimer on page 389.

Section 6166 election. Estate taxes attributable to an interest in a closely held business may be paid in installments, provided certain conditions are met. See Deferral of Estate Tax on page 383.

QTIP election. Not only gives the executor the power to determine how much, if any, of the estate will be taxed at the first death, but also provides great flexibility for post death planning based upon changing circumstances. See the QTIP Trust chart on page 35.

Alternate valuation date. Electing to value the gross estate 6 months after death can lower estate taxes. See Fair Market Value on page 411.

Special use valuation. Lower valuations can help to minimize federal estate taxes, provided the estate qualifies and the required restrictions are acceptable to the heirs. See Reduced Valuation on pages 496-497.

Donation of conservation easements. Allowing for a donation to be made after the decedent's death, but before the estate tax return is filed, can significantly reduce estate taxes, while allowing a family to retain their lands. See Qualified Conservation Easement on page 486.

Section 303 redemptions. These after-death sales of partial stock interests to a corporation receive tax-favored treatment as capital transactions, rather than as dividends. See the Partial Stock Redemption chart on page 147.

POWER OF APPOINTMENT

A power of appointment is the delegation of authority from one individual (the donor) to another individual (the donee) to direct the transfer, use, benefit, or enjoyment of property, both real and personal. A power exercisable in favor of the power-holder, his estate, his creditors, or the creditors of his estate is a *general* power of appointment. Any other power of appointment is a *special* power of appointment.

Whether a power of appointment is general or special is important, since a general power of appointment will cause the assets subject to the power to be included in the power-holder's estate, whereas a special power of appointment is generally excluded for estate tax purposes. The existence, release, or lapse of a general power of appointment all have the potential of causing the property subject to such power to be included in the estate of the power-holder.

With the exemption trust will, as shown in the chart on page 25, property placed in the marital trust ("A" trust) will qualify for the marital deduction only if the surviving spouse has a general power of appointment over the property (an exception to this statement would be a trust that qualified as a QTIP trust). This assures that even though the property was not taxed at the first death it will eventually be subject to estate taxes upon the subsequent death of the surviving spouse.

If the power to consume, invade, or appropriate property from a trust is limited to *ascertainable standards*, it will not be considered to be a general power of appointment (e.g., for "health, education, maintenance, or support," but not for "comfort, welfare, or happiness"). Again referring to the chart on page 25, a surviving spouse can be given the right to invade the family or nonmarital trust ("B" trust) without causing the trust property to be included in her estate, provided the power is limited to such ascertainable standards, and therefore not treated as a general power of appointment.

Even though it might be considered a general power of appointment, a noncumulative power of appointment that does not exceed the greater of $5,000 or 5 percent of the corpus of a trust will not cause the lapse of such a power to be treated as a gift or included in the power-holder's estate. However, such a power held at death would be included in the power-holder's estate. See also, the expanded discussion of the Marital Deduction on page 450.

PREMIUM FINANCING

The term "premium financing" is often used to describe a method of purchasing large life insurance contracts with money borrowed from a commercial bank or lender. In contrast, the term "minimum deposit insurance" is used to describe the payment of premiums for a life insurance contract with borrowed cash values from the policy (see Minimum Deposit Insurance, page 458).

The low interest rates of the past few years have brought increased attention to premium financing as a means of funding the termination of split-dollar plans (see Split-Dollar Rollout, page 528). Premium financing is also used to fund company owned life insurance (see discussion on page 367) and trust-owned life insurance. With an irrevocable life insurance trust, the loan is entered into between the trustee and the lender, and interest payments are made from gifts to the trust by the trust grantor or others (see Life Insurance Trust chart, page 51).

Where a policy is purchased using premium financing the loan is typically collateralized by the underlying life insurance policy, but additional collateral may be required. It is important to recognize that there are no tax advantages to premium financing, since the interest paid will *not* be tax deductible (i.e., 4 out of 7 years premiums will not have been paid from unborrowed funds, see page 458).

The rate of interest is often based upon commercial loan rates using the one-year LIBOR (London Interbank Offered Rate), plus a spread and loan origination free totaling perhaps 1.5 to 2.0 percent. As of November 2010, the one-year LIBOR was 0.76 percent, meaning that for current premium financing the effective interest rate would be approximately 2.8 percent. Although the spread is typically guaranteed for the loans duration, because the underlying LIBOR rate is subject to annual adjustments the loan interest rate can increase substantially (e.g., in November of 2006 the one-year LIBOR was 5.24 percent, or 4.48 percent *higher*). Also, unlike the loan provisions provided in most life insurance contracts, if the underlying insurance contract requires ongoing premium payments, commercial lenders are unlikely to guarantee rates to be charged on future loans. However, lenders may not provide assurance that future loans will be made.

In order for premium financing to work over a period of years, it is essential that the rate of return on policy values (cash values and death benefit that are intended to repay the loan) exceed the interest rate paid on the loan. With interest rates at or near historic lows, there is often a differential between these loan rates and higher current (or projected, but not guaranteed) policy earnings rates. This arbitrage opportunity may at first appear attractive, but there are many variables that can negatively impact the results obtained. They should be carefully evaluated.

PRIVATE ANNUITY

The private annuity has been most effectively used in family situations where it is desired to make a transfer of a business interest, or other asset, from one generation to the next free of estate taxes (see chart, page 43). Under a typical private annuity transaction, a parent will sell part or all of the business interest, or other asset, to his child or children. In return, the children would promise to pay the parent an income for life (called a "straight life" annuity). While the annuity obligation cannot be secured, it does represent a contractual obligation that is legally enforceable. Since payments terminate at the parent's death, the annuity has generally been considered to have no value and to escape taxation in the parent's estate.

The amount of the annual payment is determined by use of annuity valuation factors. The entire amount of the gain or loss must be recognized at the time of the transaction. Annuity payments are made up of interest income and a nontaxable recovery of basis. If it is desired to provide an ongoing income to *both* surviving parents, a reduced income can be paid for as long as either parent is alive (called a "joint and survivor" annuity). Although the value of the survivorship benefit is includable in the estate of the first parent to die, it should escape taxation because of the unlimited marital deduction. At the time the annuity is established, the child receives a "temporary basis" equal to the value used in calculating the annuity. After the parent's death, this temporary basis is adjusted to reflect the amount actually paid.

It would be best to avoid stipulating lower annual payments than those calculated under the annuity tables. Such annuity payments result in a gift from the parent to the child (i.e., the child is not paying full value from his separate funds). If there is a gift element, then its value is the difference between the fair market value of the asset and the present value of the annuity payments.

Furthermore, if the child does not pay full value, the property transferred for the private annuity could be included in the parent's estate as a gift with a retained life estate.

PRIVATE FOUNDATION

A private foundation is a not-for-profit organization established by an individual charitable donor that operates as either a trust or a corporation. (It is referred to by the IRS as a "private non-operating foundation.") The foundation is controlled by the foundation's board or trustees, who may be selected by the founder. Private foundations are particularly suited to those individuals who wish to make substantial donations while providing a lasting legacy in the family name. Unlike outright gifts to public charities, the founder and his family are able to maintain control over assets given to the foundation and retain the flexibility to redirect charitable gifts with changing community needs. Active involvement of the founder's children and other family members as board members has the ancillary benefit of teaching others how to share the family wealth consistent with the founder's values and vision.

To assure that private foundations adequately serve a public purpose, there are very strict rules and regulations governing their operation. In particular, a prohibition against "self-dealing" prevents any transactions, with certain exceptions, between the foundation and "disqualified persons." Such disqualified persons include the founder, the founder's spouse, and lineal descendants, as well as the foundation managers and others involved in business relationships with a substantial contributor to the foundation. Compliance with these rules is essential and penalties for self-dealing are substantial. One exception to these rules allows disqualified persons to be paid by the foundation for reasonable and necessary work performed for the foundation, provided the compensation is reasonable.

Although the earnings on investments held by private foundations are not subject to income taxes, they are subject to an excise tax of 2 percent on investment income. Income on investments must be distributed to qualified charities each year. Regardless of income, approximately 5 percent of its "net investment assets" are required to be distributed within 12 months of the close of the fiscal year. Specific steps must be taken to verify the tax-exempt status of grant recipients. Added to these requirements are annual information tax returns, corporate filings, documentation of gifts received,and requirements for public inspection and disclosure.

The maximum amount a donor may deduct in one year for gifts to a private foundation is 30 percent of his contribution base, generally equal to adjusted gross income. This is reduced to 20 percent for appreciated capital gain property (see footnote 4, page 57). Private foundations cannot receive gifts of interests in a closely held or family-owned business stock under the rules governing "excess business holdings."

PRIVATE PENSION

The term "private pension" is occasionally used in describing life insurance products that offer investment elements in addition to death benefits. For the following reasons it is recommended that agents and their companies avoid using the term in the marketing and sales of individual life insurance policies.

It is suggested that to the average consumer the term "pension" implies a plan that is sponsored by an employer and qualified under the tax code as to the deductibility of employer contributions, without current taxation to the employee. *Webster's New Dictionary* defines a "pension" as "a stated allowance to a person for past services; an allowance to one who has retired or has been disabled or reached old age, or has been widowed, orphaned, etc." The term "private pension plan" can be found in section 2(c) of the Findings And Declaration Section of ERISA, which states: "It is hereby further declared to be the policy of this Act to protect . . . the interests of participants in *private pension plans* and their beneficiaries by improving the equitable character and the soundness of such plans . . . [emphasis added]." Clearly, the individual life insurance policy does not fall within either of these definitions or usages of the term "pension."

An illustration which fails to inform a prospect that life insurance is being offered is considered a misrepresentation and false advertising of life insurance in violation of the National Association Of Insurance Commissioners (NAIC) Model Laws entitled Unfair Trade Practices Act and Rules Governing The Advertising Of Life Insurance, which have been adopted in many states. Determining what constitutes a "failure to inform" can be difficult. For example, it may not be sufficient to include a short reference to life insurance at the bottom of page seven of an eight page "Private Pension Plan" proposal. While this may be subject to some debate, a more important concern should be how regulators will view such sales illustrations in light of industry difficulties concerning the marketing of life insurance as a retirement plan without adequate disclosure.

The unique benefit of life insurance is its ability to provide food and clothing for a surviving family, keep them secure in their home and educate the children. Business life insurance enables a business to continue after the death of an owner and can provide funds for purchase of the deceased's business interest by the surviving owners. These noble objectives have more than justified the current tax deferred nature of the internal cash value buildup of the permanent life insurance contract. This tax deferred status should not be threatened by placing an unwarranted emphasis on its tax benefits.

PROBATE

Although the term is now used in referring to the entire estate settlement process, "probate" originally referred to the act of proving a will before a court or other authorized person. Courts having jurisdiction over probate matters are called probate courts, surrogates courts, or orphans courts. The first step in settling an estate is to offer the will for probate. If the will is not likely to be contested, informal proceedings, usually called probate in *common form*, establish that the document offered is the valid last will of the decedent. However, if there is any doubt regarding validity, formal probate proceedings, usually known as probate in *solemn form*, are required.

After admission of the will to probate, the court appoints an executor (male) or executrix (female) and provides them with letters testamentary as evidence of their appointment. If there is no will, the court appoints an administrator (male) or adminstratrix (female) and provides them with letters of administration. The personal representative (a term including an executor, executrix, and administrator) is then qualified to carry out his duties. Typically, the personal representative will hire an attorney to advise and assist in settling the estate.

The personal representative then collects, safeguards, and manages estate assets, has assets appraised, prepares lists of assets, converts personal property into cash, distributes assets as directed by the decedent (pursuant to specific bequests in the will), disposes of business interests, publishes notices giving creditors of the estate an opportunity to file their claims, and pays death taxes, income taxes, property taxes, court costs, appraisal fees, and fees and reimbursement expenses of the personal representative and the attorney. After a court accounting (called a judicial settlement of the account) is made and accepted by the court, the personal representative makes a distribution of the net estate to the heirs as required by either the will or the statute of intestate succession (see pages 102-109).

In recent years, much has been written about the benefits of "avoiding probate." The advantages cited include avoiding fees associated with the probate process, maintaining confidentiality, better control of assets, reduction in delays, and avoiding ancillary probate of property located in another state. However, there are some distinct advantages to having an estate go through probate. For example, protection is provided beneficiaries by having a court oversee the collection and distribution of assets. By giving creditors notice and the opportunity to make claims against the estate, beneficiaries are provided with clear title to estate assets. In addition, the Uniform Probate Code, as enacted by many states, simplifies and streamlines the probate process by providing for self-proved wills, proof of a will by affidavit of witnesses, waiver of bond, and unsupervised administration.

PROFESSIONAL CORPORATION

Professional corporations are closely held corporations formed by doctors, dentists, optometrists, lawyers, and others. They may be established by an individual or by a group of professionals and are organized primarily to take advantage of the tax deductible benefits available to employees of corporations but not to sole proprietors or partners. Typically they are organized under state professional corporation and professional association acts.

A professional in a high personal tax bracket incorporates, becomes an employee of the corporation (as well as an owner-stockholder) and receives a salary from the corporation. The usual business deductions are allowed, including salaries for stockholder-employees, as well as special corporation deductions.

Professional corporations are taxed under the same rules as other corporations. However, professional corporations in which substantially all of the activities involve the performance of services in the fields of health, law, engineering, architecture, accounting, actuarial science, performing arts, or consulting are considered qualified personal service corporations and corporate income is taxed at a flax rate of 35 percent.

A wide variety of employee benefits are available to the stockholder-employees of a professional corporation, including accident and health plans, group term life insurance (chart page 203), salary allotment (chart page 207), executive equity (chart page 211), split-dollar insurance (chart page 219), survivor income (chart page 231), deferred compensation (chart page 235), disability income plans (chart page 243), health reimbursement arrangements (chart page 247) and tax-favored retirement plans (chart page 259).

State laws generally restrict ownership of stock in professional corporations to qualified professionals (as a condition of continued authorization to provide professional services). Therefore, with professional corporations it is most important to implement buy-sell agreements that prevent the transfer of stock to anyone who is a nonprofessional. In addition to providing for the sale of stock upon death, such agreements should also contain provisions for sale in the event of retirement, permanent disability, and termination of employment or professional disqualification.

While the typical choice involves either a entity purchase agreement (chart page 127) or a cross purchase agreement (chart page 131), hybrid arrangements involving "wait and see" buy/sell agreements (chart page 139) and partial stock redemptions (chart page 147) are also used. Whichever method is chosen, adequate funding with life insurance will provide funds to meet the underlying obligations.

PROFIT SHARING PLAN

Profit sharing plans are often used by employers to distribute profits to their employees. Employer contributions to a profit sharing plan can be entirely discretionary, made according to a formula provision, or a combination of both. If on a discretionary basis, then the employer determines each year whether or not to make contributions to the plan (but a failure to make "recurring and substantial" contributions could result in disqualification of the plan). It is not necessary that the employer actually have current or accumulated profits. If on a formula basis, then contributions are made under a formula typically tied to employer profits (e.g., 5 percent of net profits after taxes, 10 percent of gross profits in excess of $100,000, or some other profit-driven formula). In either case, the employer can deduct up to 25 percent of total payroll of plan participants.

Once the amount of contribution is determined, it is then allocated among the participants' individual accounts under a nondiscriminatory formula that must be definite and predetermined. For example, each participant might receive an allocation of a percentage determined by comparing his compensation to the total compensation of all plan participants. If the employer's total contribution to the plan was $100,000, and the participant's $150,000 of compensation represented 15 percent of the $1,000,000 total payroll, then the allocation to his account would be $15,000 ($100,000 x .15 = $15,000). For 2010 and 2011, the maximum compensation base for any participant is limited to $245,000. An overall "annual additions" limit for defined contribution plans limits each participant to the lesser of $49,000 or 100 percent of compensation. In determining this allocation formula integration with Social Security is allowed under most plans.

Upon the participant's termination or retirement, benefits under the plan consist of the participant's account value. This account value reflects total employer contributions, forfeitures from other plan participants, and returns on plan investments (i.e., interest, dividends and capital gains). As with a money purchase pension plan, the employee/participant bears the risks associated with investment performance. In addition, because employer contributions and profits are not assured, unlike defined benefit or money purchase pension plans, the employee is unable to project with any certainty his account values at retirement. In contrast to pension plans, certain profit sharing plans can offer participants the opportunity to take "in-service distributions" prior to retirement (subject to a 10-percent early withdrawal tax penalty prior to age 59½). In order to avoid this penalty, profit sharing plans sometimes allow participants access to account funds through plan loans at reasonable rates of interest and within specified limits.

See also, the discussion of Qualified Retirement Plans on page 491, and Life Insurance in Qualified Plans on pages 439-440.

PRUDENT INVESTOR RULE

Under the Uniform Prudent Investor Act of 1994, the prudent *investor* rule replaced the prudent *person* rule (the prudent person rule is also known as the prudent *man* rule). A majority of states have now enacted some form of the prudent investor rule.

With its focus on minimizing risk, the prudent person rule forces trustees to adopt conservative fixed-income approaches to investing trust assets. Such a conservative approach may well be appropriate for the small-to-mid-size trust whose primary function is to provide support for the current beneficiary (e.g., a marital deduction trust for the support of a surviving spouse, as in the chart on page 25). However, with larger trusts, application of the rule often results in underperforming investments and dissatisfied life and remainder beneficiaries (amusingly referred to as the trustee's duty to "disappoint equally").

State Principal and Income Acts further compounded the problem. These statutes defined "income" to include dividends, interest, and rents, but not capital gains. As a result, investment decisions were often driven by the character of the return, rather then the rate of return (e.g., trustees could distribute to income beneficiaries interest from low-yield certificates of deposit, but were prohibited from using capital gain from highly appreciated stock). The Uniform Principal and Income Act of 1997 gives trustees the authority to allocate principal to income, but it has not been adopted in many states.

Under the prudent investor rule, a trustee is required to develop an overall investment strategy having risk and return objectives reasonably suited to the trust and its beneficiaries. The trustee is to be judged by considering the performance of the portfolio as a whole, rather than individual investments. Although the trustee may delegate investment functions, there remains a duty to review and monitor overall performance. Consistent with modern portfolio analysis, the trustee may invest for capital appreciation in a diversified portfolio of equity and growth stocks. A reduction in the risk of loss is achieved by a reasonable diversification of investments. Because the trustee has a positive duty to reduce investment costs, passive investment strategies are permitted (e.g., the purchase of indexed mutual funds). It is appropriate for the trustee to seek to maintain the beneficiaries' purchasing power, and the tax implications of trust investments and distributions may be considered. Clearly, the flexibility provided by the prudent investor rule enables a trustee to better serve all beneficiaries and sizes of trusts.

Some planners have suggested that a total return unitrust can take maximum advantage of this flexibility. As with the charitable remainder unitrust, the total return unitrust requires the trustee to pay a fixed percentage of the trust principal to the life beneficiary each year. See the discussion of the total return unitrust on page 539.

QUALIFIED CONSERVATION EASEMENT

The executor of a decedent may elect on the estate tax return to exclude from the decedent's taxable estate up to 40 percent of the value of any land subject to a "qualified conservation easement." In addition to meeting the requirements of a "qualified conservation contribution," the land must be located within the United States or its possessions and must have been owned by the decedent or a member of his family for 3 years. The 2010 Tax Relief Act removed geographic limitations within the United States that otherwise would have limited the exclusion in 2011 and 2012. The exclusion is generally not available when the property is debt-financed or the donor has retained development rights (i.e., the donor cannot retain the right to develop property for general recreational use by the public, such as a ski resort). The granting of the easement can be made by the decedent before death or by the decedent's executor.

The exclusion amount is limited to $500,000. The 40-percent exclusion percentage is reduced by 2 percent for each percentage point by which the value of the qualified conservation is less than 30 percent of the value of the land. For example, assume that property with a basis of $500,000 has a value of $1,000,000 before an easement is granted and the easement reduces the value of the property to $750,000, a reduction of 25 percent. This is 5 percent less than the minimum 30 percent threshold. Therefore, the 40 percent exclusion must be reduced by 10 percent to 30 percent (40 - (5 × 2)). The property is included in the estate at a reduced value of $525,000 ($750,000 × .30 = $225,000 reduction; $750,000 - $225,000 = $525,000 reduced value). The value of the property excluded from the decedent's estate under this provision does not receive a step-up in basis. This means the new basis is $675,000 ($525,000 stepped-up basis plus $150,000 carryover basis attributable to fact that 30 percent of the property was excluded from the gross estate; $500,000 × .30 = $150,000).

A "qualified conservation contribution" requires that the donor convey a qualified real property interest to a qualified organization exclusively for conservation purposes. A taxpayer who makes such a contribution may take a charitable income tax deduction equal to the difference in the value of the land immediately before and after the easement is placed on the property (i.e., the loss of value due to the placement of the easement). A portion of the income tax savings might be used to fund a wealth replacement trust for family members (as in the chart on page 55).

Granting a conservation easement during lifetime can provide the property owner with an income tax deduction plus a potential estate tax savings attributable to both the easement's depressing the value of the property and to the partial exclusion of that reduced value from the gross estate. However, because the exclusion reduces the adjusted gross estate, it could affect qualification for a partial stock redemption (page 146), estate tax deferral (page 383), and special use valuation (page 496).

QUALIFIED DOMESTIC RELATIONS ORDER (QDRO)

ERISA and the Code generally do not permit retirement benefits under a qualified retirement plan to be assigned or transferred to another person. As an exception to this rule, in order to satisfy family support or marital property obligations, a qualified domestic relations order (QDRO) is allowed to create or recognize the existence of an alternate payee's right to receive benefits under a pension plan. An alternate payee can be a spouse, former spouse, child, or other dependent.

A QDRO must contain the following information: (1) the name and last known mailing address of the participant and each alternate payee; (2) the name of each plan to which the order applies; (3) the dollar amount or percentage (or the method of determining the amount or percentage) of the benefit to be paid to the alternate payee; and (4) the number of payments or time period to which the order applies. A QDRO may be included as part of a divorce decree or court-approved property settlement, or issued as a separate order. It cannot provide for benefits that are not otherwise available under the plan, nor can it increase benefits payable under the plan.

Pension plans are required to establish written procedures relating to QDROs. The administrator of the pension plan that provides the benefits affected by an order is initially responsible for determining whether a domestic relations order is a QDRO. Intervening events, such as a participant's retirement, remarriage, or death, or the death of a nonparticipant spouse, can complicate the division of property interests and even result in a loss of anticipated benefits. Therefore, it is very important that a QDRO be filed in a complete and timely manner.

Under the Code transfers "incident to a divorce" are generally not taxable to either spouse. Distributions made to an alternate payee under a QDRO are not subject to the 10-percent-penalty tax normally applied to *premature distributions* from qualified retirement plans (i.e., distributions before the participant reaches age 59½). For the purpose of determining required *minimum distributions*, if the nonparticipant spouse's share is segregated (i.e., accounted for separately), the required distributions will be calculated without regard to the participant's portion of the account, except that distributions must begin by the participant's required beginning date. See pages 433-434 and 514.

The Department of Labor is a very good resource for information and forms pertaining to QDROs. For example, see www.dol.gov/ebsa/Publications/qdros.html.

QUALIFIED DOMESTIC TRUST

The federal estate tax is imposed on the taxable estate of every resident of the United States, wherever the property is located, and whether the decedent is a citizen or a noncitizen. In order to prevent a noncitizen surviving spouse from leaving and removing property from the United States, the unlimited marital deduction is not available, unless: (1) the noncitizen surviving spouse becomes a citizen prior to the time for filing the deceased spouse's federal estate tax return; or (2) the property is passed to a qualified domestic trust (QDOT). In short, no federal estate tax marital deduction is available when the surviving spouse is a noncitizen, unless use is made of a QDOT.

Both probate and nonprobate property will qualify for QDOT treatment if transferred directly from the decedent to the QDOT, or irrevocably assigned to the QDOT prior to the time that the federal estate tax return is filed. However, it is not necessary that property be placed in the QDOT in any particular fashion or by any particular person.

The requirements for a QDOT are: (1) there must be an irrevocable election for QDOT treatment; (2) the trust must require that at least one trustee be a U.S. citizen and that no distribution can be made unless such trustee has the right to withhold any estate tax which may become due; (3) the transfer must otherwise qualify as one which would be eligible for the marital deduction; and (4) specific additional procedural requirements must be met in order to ensure collection of the estate tax.

Events that trigger an estate tax on assets placed in a QDOT include: (1) failure of the QDOT to meet any of the above requirements; (2) the surviving spouse's death; or (3) any payment to the surviving spouse other than income or a "hardship" distribution. The surviving spouse cannot be given a power to invade the trust unless the U.S. trustee can withhold any estate tax from the distribution (compare chart on page 25).

When property previously placed in a QDOT becomes subject to estate taxes, it is taxed using the marginal estate tax rate of the deceased citizen spouse. This means that although the unified credit is available to the surviving noncitizen spouse, it cannot be used unless the surviving spouse dies in possession of a separate estate.

There is available a gift tax exclusion which allows for annual tax-free transfers of up to $136,000 (as indexed in 2011 for inflation) to a noncitizen spouse. Taking advantage of this annual exclusion will create a separate estate for the noncitizen spouse, part of which could be used to purchase life insurance on the citizen spouse. Provided the noncitizen spouse was both policy owner and beneficiary, the life insurance proceeds would not be included in the estate of the insured citizen spouse. This would diminish the need to fund a QDOT in order to provide support for the surviving noncitizen spouse.

See also, Noncitizen Estate Planning, page 463.

QUALIFIED LONG-TERM CARE INSURANCE

A "qualified" long-term care insurance contract: (1) must provide only coverage for "qualified long-term care services"; (2) cannot pay or reimburse for services covered under Medicare; (3) must be guaranteed renewable; (4) cannot provide a cash surrender value; (5) must apply premium refunds or dividends to either reduce future premiums or increase future benefits; and (6) must satisfy consumer protection provisions, disclosure and nonforfeitability requirements as set forth by the National Association of Insurance Commissioners (NAIC).

Qualified long-term care services are defined as necessary diagnostic, preventive, therapeutic, curing, treating, mitigating, and rehabilitative services, and maintenance or personal care services, which are required by a chronically ill individual and are provided under a plan of care set forth by a licensed health care practitioner. A person is considered "chronically ill" if certified by a health care professional as unable to perform for a period of at least 90 days, without substantial assistance, at least two activities of daily living (i.e., eating, toileting, transferring, bathing, dressing, and continence) or requires substantial supervision to protect himself from threats to health and safety due to a "severe cognitive impairment" (i.e., a deterioration or loss of intellectual capacity that places the individual in jeopardy of harming self or others).

Beneficial tax treatment is afforded to a *qualified* long-term care insurance contract. (There is uncertainty regarding the tax treatment of *nonqualified* long-term care contracts issued after the enactment of the Health Insurance Portability and Accountability Act of 1996.)

Premiums. *Individuals* can deduct premiums as medical expenses, but the deduction is limited to expenses in excess of 7.5 percent of adjusted gross income. This deduction for premiums paid is further subject in 2011 to the following age-based limits: $340 if age 40 or less; $640 if age 41 through 50; $1,270 if age 51 through 60; $3,390 if age 61 through 70; and $4,240 if age 71 and over (these limits are indexed for inflation). Subject to these age-based limits, *self-employed individuals* can deduct 100 percent of premiums. Apparently premiums paid by an *employer* for a nonowner employee are fully deductible by the employer, are not includable in the employee's income, and are subject only to "reasonable compensation" limits.

Benefits. Amounts received from a qualified long-term care contract in 2011 are generally not included in income up to the greater of $300 per day or the actual costs incurred. It is not necessary to prove a need for medical care in order to deduct unreimbursed long-term care expenses for nursing homes, assisted-living facilities, adult homes and home care. This is very much to the taxpayer's advantage.

QUALIFIED PERSONAL RESIDENCE TRUST

A qualified personal residence trust, also referred to as a "residence GRIT," is created by transferring a residence, or a second home, into a split interest trust for a specific period of time, typically between 10 and 20 years. The principal advantages of such a trust include transfer of the property at a low gift tax value and shifting of future appreciation out of the grantor's estate, provided he lives to the end of the trust term.

At the time of the transfer, the value of the gift is determined by the value of the remainder interest in the residence calculated using actuarial tables (i.e., the value of the property is discounted for the fact that it will not be available to the remainderperson for many years). The grantor can also transfer limited amounts of cash to the trust in order to service debt and maintain the residence. The grantor can serve as trustee. Although a taxable gift is made when establishing a qualified personal residence trust, the value of the gift is minimized by the remainder interest calculations, and the grantor can avoid actually paying gift taxes by utilizing unused unified credit. However, because the gift is of a future interest, the annual exclusion is not available (see page 46).

Unlike other transfers with a retained interest, the grantor can continue to use the residence throughout the term of years established by the trust, yet the property will be removed from his estate provided he lives to the end of the term (the same as a GRIT, see page 419). Although death prior to the termination of the trust would cause the full date of death value to be brought back into the grantor's estate, purchase of life insurance on the grantor's life could provide for payment of any estate taxes. A desire to lengthen the trust term in order to lower gift tax exposure upon establishing the trust must be balanced against the loss of all estate tax benefits if the grantor dies before the end of the trust term.

The trust can also give the grantor a contingent reversionary interest, which will cause the residence to revert back into his estate in case of death before the end of the term. With such a provision, the grantor could utilize the marital deduction by passing the residence to a surviving spouse, thereby postponing estate taxes, while at the same time causing the trust to be classified a "grantor trust," which would allow the grantor to deduct property taxes and mortgage interest on his own tax return during the term of the trust. The existence of such a reversionary interest would also cause a further reduction in the value of the gift, measured by the probability that the grantor would not survive the term of the trust.

Upon the termination of the trust, the grantor may wish to continue living in the residence. To accomplish this, he can either rent the residence from the remainderperson, or purchase the residence prior to the expiration of the trust term (for a fair rental rate or a fair market value). However, regulations prohibit a sale of the residence to the grantor or the grantor's spouse during the original term or while a grantor trust.

QUALIFIED RETIREMENT PLANS

A qualified retirement plan, also referred to as a "qualified plan," is a tax-favored retirement arrangement established by an employer that is designed to satisfy the requirements of Section 401 of the Internal Revenue Code. The employer may be a corporation, a partnership or a sole proprietorship. The "plan" is the document that sets forth in writing the rules by which the plan operates, such as how employees become participants and the method of calculating the benefits to which they become entitled. Contributions to the plan are transferred to a trustee or insurance company that holds and invests them until they are distributed upon the participant's termination of employment, retirement, or death. Assuming the necessary requirements are met, contributions are deductible to the employer (within limits) and are not currently taxable to the employee/participant. Earnings on plan investments grow tax-deferred and are not taxable to the employee until withdrawn or distributed.

Types Of Qualified Retirement Plans*		
	Defined Contribution	Defined Benefit
Pension	Money Purchase Pension Plan [460] Target Benefit Plan [536]	Defined Benefit Pension Plan [384] Cash Balance Pension Plan [354] 412 (i) Plan [270]
Profit Sharing	Profit Sharing Plan 484] 401(k) Plan [262] Stock Bonus Plan [531] ESOP [396] Age-Weighted Profit Sharing Plan [347] Savings/Thrift Plan [513]	n/a
* Numbers in brackets [ ] indicate page numbers.		

Qualified retirement plans can be categorized in a number of ways. One method distinguishes between plans according to the nature of the employer's obligation. Under a **defined contribution** plan the employer makes specific contributions to the plan, after which the participant's retirement benefits are determined by the account value at retirement (i.e., the *employee* bears the investment risk). In contrast, under a **defined benefit** plan the employer is obligated to provide a specific retirement benefit to the participant (i.e., the *employer* bears the investment risk).

Another way of categorizing plans distinguishes between them according to whether employer contributions can be tied to employer profits. Under a **pension** plan the employer is obligated to provide a "definitely determinable benefit." However, under a **profit sharing** plan employer contributions can be completely discretionary and based on employer profits.

QUALIFIED SMALL BUSINESS STOCK

In order to raise capital, small businesses may designate certain stock as "qualified small business stock." The 2010 Small Business Jobs Act together with The 2010 Tax Relief Act, provide that gain on stock acquired after September 27, 2010 and before January 1, 2012, and held for at least five years, is not subject to federal income taxes. The benefits of the small business stock exclusion can be passed by gift or inheritance.

In order to be eligible for this favorable tax treatment, the following qualifications must be met:

1. The stock must have been issued by a domestic C corporation after August 10, 1993.

2. The stock must be acquired at its original issue and held for more than five years.

3. The issuing corporation must be engaged in a "qualified trade or business," which is defined to be *any trade or business other than* those involved in:

    a. the performance of services in the fields of health, law, engineering, architecture, accounting, actuarial science, performing arts, consulting, athletics, financial services, brokerage services, or any trade or business where the principal asset is the reputation or skill of one or more of its employees;
    b. banking, insurance, financing, leasing, investing or similar business;
    c. farming (including the business of raising or harvesting trees);
    d. the production or extraction of products for which a percentage depletion deduction is allowed; or
    e. operating a hotel, motel, restaurant, or similar business.

If all requirements are met the corporation need not be a newly formed business. But stock is not eligible if the corporation, within certain periods of time, purchases stock from the stockholder, or persons related to the stockholder.

There is an active business requirement, meaning that the corporation must use at least 80 percent by value of its assets in the active conduct of one or more qualified trades or businesses. Also, there is a gross asset test requiring that, both before and immediately after the stock's issue date, the corporation's gross assets cannot exceed $50 million. The corporation must also agree to submit periodic reports documenting its status as a qualified small business.

RABBI TRUST

The term "rabbi" trust comes from an early IRS ruling on the subject, which involved a trust established by a religious organization for its rabbi. A rabbi trust is used to accumulate assets to support deferred compensation arrangements and to provide the employee with some measure of assurance that he will actually receive the promised future payments. Because the funds placed in such a trust continue to be subject to claims of the employer's creditors, the security is in large measure "psychological."

However, because the trust is generally made *irrevocable*, it does protect the employee from being denied payment of the funds by a change of management, as might occur under the conditions of a hostile takeover.

The rabbi trust has been a popular device for informally funding deferred compensation. In fact, this popularity caused the Internal Revenue Service to publish a model trust instrument in Revenue Procedure 92-64. The model trust serves as a safe harbor for employers adopting rabbi trusts; used properly, the model trust will not cause current taxation of employees under either the constructive receipt or the economic benefit doctrines.

The law provides two specific prohibitions relative to the funding of deferred compensation plans. The first rule prohibits the setting aside of assets in an off-shore trust for purposes of paying deferred compensation. (This prevents the use of offshore rabbit trusts but should not affect domestic rabbi trusts.) The second rule prohibits the use of triggers designed to protect assets set aside to pay deferred compensation upon a change in the employer's financial health. A properly drafted rabbi trust should not run afoul of this second rule, provided it protects the employee from his employer's refusal to honor the deferred compensation (i.e., offers protection from the *contract* risk, but not the *credit* risk). See also, the discussion of Section 409A on page 517.

Substantial penalties make it important not to violate these prohibitions when drafting, implementing, and funding deferred compensation plans. Violating them can result in an additional 20 percent tax and imposition of interest at a rate that is 1 percent higher than the normal underpayment rate. These rules apply to any amounts deferred after December 31, 2004 and to any plan that is "materially modified" after October 3, 2004.

RECESSIONARY ESTATE PLANNING

In general, investment real estate, publicly traded securities, and closely held business have all undergone major reductions in value over the past few years. Likewise, interest rates have been reduced to historic low levels in an attempt to revive a struggling economy. This combination of depressed asset values and low interest rates has created unique estate planning opportunities. These low interest rates are reflected in the "Section 7520 rate." (Section 7520 of the Internal Revenue Code requires the use of a set of actuarial tables for valuing many popular forms of asset transfers used in estate planning.)

Things To Consider

Specific bequests in wills. Review to make sure the value assumptions underlying them are still valid (i.e., should there be a change in light of falling stock values, etc.).

Trust funding. Review wills to determine whether surviving spouse will continue to have adequate resources with current funding of the family trust (i.e., consider both changing tax laws and falling value of spouse's separate resources).

Sell depreciated assets, then make gifts. Because of the carryover basis, donees are unable to recognize losses that were available to the donor (i.e., when fair market value was less than adjusted basis prior to the gift). Assets with built-in losses should be sold by the owner and the net proceeds used to take advantage of the gift tax laws. See chart on page 47.

Asset valuations. Review current values where assets have been allocated between spouses in order to take maximum advantage of the applicable exclusion amount with bypass trusts. If appropriate, reallocate assets between spouses.

Grantor Retained Annuity Trust (GRAT). Donor creates a trust and retains a right to receive fixed annual annuity payments. Upon trust termination, the remainder interest is paid to trust beneficiaries. The lower Section 7520 rate produces a higher value for the retained annuity interest (i.e., larger retained interest reduces value of gift) and a lower value for the remainder interest (i.e., uses less gift tax unified credit). However, the transfer tax benefits of the GRAT depend upon the transferred property producing a return in excess of the Section 7520 rate. See chart on page 59 and comparison with GRITs and GRUTs on page 419.

Charitable Lead Annuity Trust (CLAT). Donor creates a trust and a charity receives annual annuity payments. Upon trust termination, the principal is paid to individual beneficiaries. The lower Section 7520 rate produces a higher value for the annuity interest to the charity (i.e., higher charitable deduction) and a lower value for the remainder interest to the individual beneficiaries (i.e., uses less gift tax unified credit). Subsequent appreciation of the depressed property held in a CLAT is excluded from the donor's estate.

(continued on next page)

RECESSIONARY ESTATE PLANNING (continued)

<u>Self-Cancelling Installment Note (SCIN).</u> The installment debt obligation involves both a risk premium and market interest. Both of these benefit from a low interest rate environment. See page 520.

<u>Private Annuity.</u> A decrease in the Section 7520 interest rate lowers the payments from child to parent, thereby increasing the efficacy of the private annuity as a wealth transfer technique. See footnote 1 on page 45 and page 479.

<u>Installment Sale To Intentionally Defective Grantor Trust.</u> Grantor creates trust that is defective for income taxes purposes (i.e., grantor will be taxed on all trust income), but irrevocable for gift and estate tax purposes (i.e., growth of trust is excluded from grantor's estate). Once established, the grantor makes a gift to the trust, equal in value to 10 percent or more of the value of the property to be sold to the trust by the grantor in a subsequent installment sale. Property that is currently depressed in value with high appreciation potential is ideally suited for this purpose. For details see the chart on page 67 and discussion of grantor trust rules on page 418.

Things That Might Not Work

<u>Qualified Personal Residence Trust (QPRT)</u> – A depressed housing market reduces the value of the home (good), but low interest rates increases the value of the gift to heirs (not good). An analysis is required to determine whether this technique is viable. See page 490.

<u>Charitable Remainder Annuity Trust (CRAT).</u> The CRAT is the mirror image of the CLAT. Donor creates a trust and retains an annuity for a period of years with a charity as remainder beneficiary. A decrease in the Section 7520 interest rate reduces the charitable deduction. See the chart on page 55 and comparison with other charitable trusts on page 357.

<u>Charitable Gift Annuities.</u> As with the CRAT, the lower Section 7520 rates reduce the value of the remainder interest available for the charity. This results in a lower charitable deduction. Also, in response to the economic downturn the American Council on Gift Annuities has lowered the suggested charitable gift annuity rates, meaning that the purchasers of charitable gift annuities will receive lower payout rates. Despite these negatives, many donors with strong charitable commitments will continue to purchase charitably gift annuities. See page 355

Things That Will Not Work

<u>Gifts of loss property</u> – Generally, if property would result in a loss if it is sold, it should not be given away (i.e., tax basis exceeds potential sales price). A donee receives a carryover basis and would be unable to take the loss. The donor should sell the property, take a income tax deduction for the loss, and give the sales proceeds to the donee.

REDUCED VALUATION

An executor of an estate may elect special methods for valuing real property used in a farm, trade, or business. When available, these methods allow the real property to be valued on the basis of current use, rather than on its fair market value.

To qualify, the following requirements must be met:

1. As of the decedent's death, the real property must have been involved in a "qualified use"; i.e., used as a farm for farming purposes, or in a trade or business.

2. The adjusted value of all business or farm property, *both real and personal*, must be at least 50 percent of the adjusted gross estate.

3. The adjusted value of the business or farm *real property* must be at least 25 percent of the adjusted gross estate.

4. The decedent, or a member of his family, must have owned and been a "material participant" in the operation of the business or farm for at least 5 of the last 8 years preceding the earliest of the decedent's death, disability, or retirement (rental property does not qualify).

5. The business or farm must pass to a "qualified heir," including, among others, his spouse and immediate family.

In determining current use value the following factors apply:

1. The capitalization of the *fair rental value* of the land for farmland or closely held business purposes.

2. The capitalization of *income* that the land can be expected to yield for farming or closely held business purposes.

3. Actual assessed land values if the state provides a use value assessment law for such land.

4. Comparable sales of other farm or closely held business land located in an area where nonagricultural use is not a significant factor in determining the sales price.

5. Any other factors that could be fairly used to determine the farm or closely held business value of the land.

(continued on next page)

REDUCED VALUATION (continued)

Alternatively, when farm land is to be valued, the executor can elect a formula utilizing the average annual Gross Cash Rental for comparable land, less the average annual State and Local Real Estate Taxes for comparable land, divided by the average annual effective Interest Rate For Federal Land Bank Loans in the farm credit bank district in which the property is located. The formula reads:

$$\frac{\text{Gross Cash Rental - State and Local Real Estate Taxes}}{\text{Interest Rate For Federal Land Bank Loans}}$$

Before relying on the reduced valuation provisions, a business owner should give serious consideration to the following qualifications and restrictions that are imposed:

1. The special methods for valuation cannot decrease the estate by more than $1,020,000 (as adjusted in 2011 for inflation, rounded down to the next lowest multiple of $10,000).

2. The business or farm must be continuously operated by a qualified heir for 10 years after the decedent's death (a 2-year grace period immediately following death is available, but it extends the recapture date). It is permissible to make a cash lease to a member of the lineal descendant's family, who then continues to operate the business or farm.

3. If the property is sold or the use is discontinued within 10 years, the taxes must be recomputed based upon the original fair market value (a sale to another qualified heir does not trigger recapture).

4. The qualified heir who receives the property must sign an agreement to be *personally liable* for the additional tax. It is due and payable within 6 months after the date of sale or cessation of the use.

REINSURANCE

In its simplest form, reinsurance is the sharing of a risk by a number of insurance companies so that the mortality and profits of any one company are not greatly impacted by its claims experience. A reinsurance agreement between companies is often referred to as a reinsurance "treaty." The three main elements involved in reinsurance are retention limits, automatic reinsurance and facultative reinsurance.

"Retention" is the face amount of coverage on one life that a company retains. The amount retained is influenced by numerous considerations, including capital, surplus, insurance in force, and average policy size.

Under an **automatic** agreement the primary or ceding company (i.e., the company sending the risk out for reinsurance) must offer – and the reinsurer must accept – all risks that fall within the terms of the reinsurance agreement. The primary company does not provide the reinsurer with underwriting information. For example, the automatic agreement might provide that the reinsurer will accept the lesser of $3,000,000 or four times the primary company's retention limit, provided the total amount of insurance in force and applied for in all companies is $12,000,000 or less. If the total amount of insurance exceeds these limits then the automatic agreement is not effective and the companies resort to facultative reinsurance.

Under a **facultative** agreement the primary carrier submits the application and underwriting information to the reinsurer for review. The reinsurer then makes an independent underwriting decision and communicates its offer to the primary carrier. With larger or special risks the reinsurer may itself have special reinsurance arrangements.

"Best offer" underwriting is often used in substandard cases and typically involves sending the case to a number of reinsurance companies for underwriting. The primary company then issues the case utilizing the best offer obtained.

Reinsurers may refuse to consider a case if they receive notice that multiple applications have been submitted to a number of primary insurance companies. Because of this it is most important not to submit applications on the same insured to multiple companies unless they are fully informed of the submissions.

See also the discussion of financial underwriting on page 414.

REMAINDER INTEREST TRANSACTION (RIT)

Considered an aggressive estate planning technique, the RIT has been used as a means of shifting the future appreciation of an asset from one individual to another. As with GRITs, the RIT falls squarely within the scope of the Chapter 14 special valuation rules (see Estate Freezes, pages 407-408, and **Q 7619**, *Tax Facts on Investments (2011)*). However, a special rule allows for market valuation of RITs involving tangible property with respect to which the non-exercise of rights under the term interest would not have a substantial effect on the valuation of the remainder interest (e.g., non-income producing property such as a painting or undeveloped real estate).

Remainder interest transactions have taken advantage of the fact that property interests can be divided between *life estates* (i.e., the right to the use of property for life) and *remainder interests* (i.e., the right to ownership of property once the life estate of another has terminated). To the extent they are still viable, a RIT for a *term of years,* rather than a life estate, would exclude the property from an estate provided death occurs after the end of the term of years.

Where still viable, it is important that the sales contract for a RIT involving the retention of a life estate require that the purchaser (the remainderperson) pay full and adequate consideration for the remainder interest (there is a split in the courts regarding whether adequate consideration should be measured by the remainder interest or by the value of the entire property). Without payment of full and adequate consideration, the IRS may treat the whole transaction as a gift with a retained life estate, with the result that the full date-of-death value of the property is included in the seller's estate.

RETIRED LIVES RESERVES (RLR)

Retired lives reserves are funds that can be established to continue group term life insurance for retired employees. Contributions to the fund are generally tax deductible to the employer, yet not taxable income to the employee. Upon either retirement or permanent disability, the employee can continue to receive limited amounts of tax-free coverage. In regard to the exclusion of the first $50,000 of coverage, see the discussion on page 202.

If the illustrated interest rate assumptions are not achieved, or if the employees live beyond actuarial life expectancy, the employer must make additional payments to the fund in order to provide the anticipated death benefits for the retired employees.

Much of the attractiveness of RLR rested upon the tax deductibility of corporate contributions to fund large amounts of insurance for key employees. Because of this, the RLR concept lost favor with passage of the Deficit Reduction Act of 1984, which imposed the following restrictions on RLR plans:

1. Generally, no deduction can be taken for RLR funding for insurance in excess of $50,000.

2. A separate account must be established for each covered key employee and benefits paid only from that separate account.

3. The group term rate for excess coverage after retirement must be reported in income (i.e., coverage over $50,000).

4. In a discriminatory plan the higher of the Table I or the actual term cost of the coverage (including the first $50,000) is taxable to retired key employees.

5. There is a 100-percent excise tax on funds returned to the employer to the extent they are attributable to deductible contributions.

Because of these severe restrictions, it may be advisable to consider other alternatives for funding personal insurance for key employees. Executive Equity (chart, page 211), Restrictive Bonus Plan (chart, page 215) and Split-Dollar Insurance (chart, page 219) offer viable alternatives to RLR.

RETIREMENT INCOME PLANNING

Retirees are living longer, healthier, and more active lives. For example, according to the 2000 Annuity Mortality Tables, the life expectancy of a male age 65 is 20.4 years. This means that there is a 50 percent chance that a 65-year-old male will live beyond age 85. Under these same tables the life expectancy of a female age 65 is 23.0 years, meaning that there is a 50 percent chance that a 65-year-old female will live to at least age 88. Further, with a couple who are both age 65, there is a 50 percent chance that one or both of them will live beyond age 92. Such long life expectancies make it essential that adequate retirement income planning take place.

Retirement income planning requires a shift of focus from performance and accumulation to withdrawal and sustainability. The basic objective is to assure that the retiree will receive an *inflation-adjusted stream of income that will not be outlived*. In retirement jargon . . . a "sustainable withdrawal strategy" must be developed.

Determining resources. The first step involves identifying potential sources of retirement income. Sources of income, and assets that can be converted into income, include:

1. Government benefits such as Social Security and veteran benefits.

2. Tax-favored retirement plans including:

   a. Qualified retirement plans, both *defined contribution plans* (pension plans such as money purchase and target benefit plans, and profit sharing plans such as 401(k) plans and savings/thrift plans) and *defined benefit plans* (traditional defined benefit plans, cash balance plans, and 412(i) plans).
   b. Individual retirement arrangements, such as traditional IRAs, Roth IRAs, SIMPLE IRAs, and simplified employee pension plans (SEPs).
   c. 403(b) plans and 457 plans.

3. Cash reserves including checking accounts, money market accounts, regular savings, CDs, and life insurance cash values.

4. Income assets such as bonds, fixed annuities, installment payments, and nonqualified deferred compensation plans.

5. Equity assets including stocks, mutual funds, variable annuities, and business interests.

6. Tangible assets such as real estate investments (primary residence, second home and commercial rental property).

7. Anticipated inheritances and life insurance death benefits.

Establishing a plan. The planning process is significantly different and can be more complex than that needed when accumulating assets. However, having a well thought out plan can

(continued on next page)

RETIREMENT INCOME PLANNING (continued)

bring peace of mind to those who would otherwise be uneasy about beginning the drawdown of a lifetime's savings and investments. There are a lot of variables to be considered and tradeoffs to be made. For example, the process will likely include:

1. Determining *retirement income needs* using realistic inflation assumptions (typically between 2 and 4 percent per year, but increases in healthcare costs have been substantially higher). Life expectancies must be estimated. Lifestyle choices and increases in the years of healthy life during retirement will significantly impact income needs (see table on page 557). The spending lifecycle of persons during their retirement years must be anticipated. For example, in the early retirement years retirees typically spend more on travel and entertainment, whereas the latter years bring increased health care expenditures.

2. Projecting realistic *rates of return on investments*, taking into consideration the retirees' time horizons and tolerance for risk. For example, because investment returns are not linear, Monte Carlo simulations are used to determine the likelihood that a particular withdrawal rate can be sustained (typically between 4 and 6 percent annually). Asset allocation, rebalancing of investments and annual plan review are essential.

3. Determining income, if any, that will come from part-time *employment* (e.g., the trend toward "phased" retirement has led the IRS to issue regulations that permit workers who are near retirement age to reduce their working hours and make up lost wages by taking in-service distributions from defined benefit plans, see 72 FR 28604).

4. Avoiding *penalties* associated with tax-deferred savings (e.g., before age 59½ withdrawals and after age 70½ distributions) and determining the impact of early retirement on Social Security retirement benefits (see page 313).

5. Evaluating and using *techniques* and *products* that are effective in meeting retirement objectives. These include using systematic withdrawal plans with mutual funds and annuities, laddering of bonds, purchasing long-term care insurance, and using reverse mortgages to access home equity. Indexed annuities can mitigate not only the longevity and inflation risks, but can reduce the investment risk by providing a guaranteed minimum income benefit.

6. Determining the tax consequences of distributions, minimizing taxes, and selecting those accounts to be drawn down first.

7. Implementing estate *plans* involving powers of attorney, wills, trusts, gifts, and asset protection.

8. Establishing and monitoring a *retirement budget*.

REVERSE MORTGAGE

A reverse mortgage is a loan against a home that requires no repayment so long as the homeowner lives in the house. With a traditional mortgage, payments *made by* the homeowner increase home equity (rising equity, falling debt); whereas, with a reverse mortgage, payments *received by* the homeowner reduce home equity (falling equity, rising debt).

The qualifications to obtain a reverse mortgage generally include: (1) all of the homeowners must be at least 62 years old; (2) the home cannot be subject to a mortgage (or the mortgage must either be paid off prior to the loan or paid from loan proceeds); and (3) the home must be the homeowner's principal residence (single family house, 2-4 housing unit, federally-approved condominium, or planned unit development). Note that there are no income qualifications. The 2011 lending limit is $625,500 (i.e., the maximum the home value that can be borrowed against, no matter what the appraised value may be).

In addition to the costs found with the typical mortgage (e.g., interest charges, origination fees, and closing costs), the reverse mortgage can include an "equity sharing" or "shared appreciation" fee.

The mortgage is a "nonrecourse" loan, meaning that the amount owed can never be more than the net proceeds received from the eventual sale of the home. For example, assume that upon a homeowner's death the amount owed under the reverse mortgage is $76,000, but the amount realized from the home's sale is only $70,000. The estate is not liable for the $6,000 difference. On the other hand, if the net proceeds from the sale were $100,000, the estate would be entitled to the excess $24,000.

The most widely available reverse mortgage program is the federally-insured "Home Equity Conversion Mortgage" (HECM). The amount obtained from a reverse mortgage *can vary substantially* depending upon the program selected, the interest rate, the homeowner's age, and the home's value. Funds can be paid as an immediate cash advance, a creditline account, a monthly cash advance (payable either for a specific number of years, as long as the homeowner lives in the home, or for life by purchasing a commercial annuity), or any combination of these methods. Creditline accounts can be either flat or increasing each year by a specified rate. A commercial annuity offers the advantage of ongoing income for life whether or not the home is sold, but the disadvantage of a high loan balance in case of early death (i.e., cash advance purchases annuity).

The National Center for Home Equity Conversion, an independent not-for-profit organization, is an excellent source for more information (see www.reverse.org). See also the information provided by the National Reverse Mortgage Lenders Association at www.reversemortgage.org.

Any party participating in the origination of a reverse mortgage insured by the FHA is prohibited from participating in, associating with, or employing any party participating in any other financial or insurance activity, unless certain firewalls are maintained.

RISKS – TYPES OF

There are many categories and types of risks, from physical risks to social risks, and ethical risks to monetary risks. The following risks are associated with risk management in financial and retirement planning.

1. **Market Risk** - the risk that unrelated factors will decrease the value of an investment (i.e., world events or legislation). Market risk can be lessened by diversification of investments and dollar cost averaging (see chart, page 318.

2. **Interest Rate Risk** - the risk that interest rates will rise, decreasing the value of bonds or other fixed interest rate investments (see table of interest rates, page 184).

3. **Concentration Risk** - the risk that concentration of investments in a particular stock, bond, or market segment could result in a large loss of portfolio value (e.g., investing 50 percent of a portfolio in a particular stock). This risk can be reduced by acquiring a combination of fixed and equity investments, including mutual funds.

4. **Economic Risk** - the risk that the economic environment will decrease the value of an investment or other source of income. For example, the increasing costs of the Social Security system might require a change in the amount or timing of benefits (see footnote 2, page 261).

5. **Political Risk** - the risk that the political climate will result in changes in regulations and laws that impact the economy, tax laws, and Social Security benefits.

6. **Tax Risk** - the risk that changes in the tax laws will result in greater taxes. For example, prior to 1984 Social Security benefits were free of income taxes, but under present law up to 85 percent of Social Security benefits may be subject to income taxes (see discussion, page 526).

7. **Inflation Risk** - the risk that goods and services will cost more in future years and that inflation will erode the purchasing power of fixed income or investments (see inflation adjuster, page 88, and consumer price index, page 314).

8. **Longevity Risk** - the risk that a person's longevity will result in outliving his income or suffering a loss of purchasing power (see mortality table, pages 555-556). This risk can be reduced through the purchase of life annuities and equity investments.

9. **Security Risk** - the risk that there could be a failure of a financial institution (e.g., bank or insurance company).

10. **Currency Risk** - the risk that a decrease in the underlying value of a nation's currency will reduce the purchasing power of income or investments paid in that currency.

ROTH 401(k)

The Roth 401(k) feature combines the structure of a 401(k) plan with tax benefits similar to those of a Roth IRA. Under a Roth 401(k) feature employees who make after-tax contributions may take fully tax-free withdrawals in retirement (i.e., to the extent there is a "qualified distribution" the growth is never subject to federal income taxes). This is the reverse of the traditional 401(k) which allows employees to make before-tax contributions, but then fully taxes all retirement withdrawals (see chart, page 263).

Contributions are governed by the 401(k) rules, meaning that up to $16,500 may be contributed in 2010 and 2011, plus an additional $5,500 as a "catch-up" contribution if the participant is at least 50 years old. These maximum elective deferrals apply to *total* contributions to both the pre-tax and Roth accounts. Participants in 401(k) plans that have adopted Roth provisions have three choices: (1) continue to contribute only to the pre-tax account; (2) divert all contributions to the after-tax Roth account; or (3) split contributions between the two. (Note that stand-alone Roth 401(k) plans are not allowed.) Plans must provide separate accounts for the designated Roth contributions and earnings on these contributions. Unlike the Roth IRA, there are no income limits beyond which contributions may not be made (e.g., in 2011 if taxable income exceeds $179,000, a married couple filing jointly cannot make a Roth IRA contribution, see page 308). Likewise, there are no maximum age limits for participants; they need only be working for an employer offering a 401(k) plan with a Roth feature. A similar "qualified Roth contribution program" known as a Roth 403(b) plan may be made available to participants in 403(b) plans. Participants in these programs are able to designate all or a portion of their elective deferrals as Roth contributions (see also the 403(b) Plans chart on page 283).

Distributions from a Roth 401(k) are generally treated very much like distributions from Roth IRAs. Once the participant is age 59½ tax-free "qualified distributions" may be made, provided the account is at least five years old (i.e., five years have passed since the first contribution). Tax-free distributions are also allowed after the participant's disability or death. Although subject to lifetime required minimum distributions, funds in a designated Roth contribution account may be rolled over into a Roth IRA that is not subject to these requirements (see pages 506 and 551). This makes the Roth 401(k) attractive for those wishing to leave their children an income-tax-free inheritance (i.e., no taxable "income in respect of a decedent," see page 425).

The Roth 401(k) feature is likely to be most attractive to younger employees in lower tax brackets who can take advantage of many years of tax-free growth. However, for many other individuals it will not be easy to determine whether the tax-free withdrawals in retirement years will be worth the upfront cost. The decision may be made easier by today's relatively low tax brackets (i.e., future tax rates are more likely to go up, not down).

ROTH IRA

The Roth IRA permits individuals in 2011 to make nondeductible contributions to an IRA of up to the lesser of 100 percent of compensation or $5,000 per year. Husband and wife may each contribute $5,000 per year provided there is sufficient compensation. An additional "catch-up" contribution of $1,000 is allowed for individuals who attain age 50 before the close of the taxable year. Unlike traditional IRAs, contributions may be made after age 70½.

As with the traditional IRA, the Roth IRA accumulates tax-deferred. Provided the account has been held for at least five years, distributions are not subject to income taxes if: (1) the owner is at least age 59½; or (2) the distribution is made after the owner's death (e.g., to a surviving spouse or children); or (3) the distribution is attributable to the owner being disabled; or (4) the distribution is for qualified first-time home buyer expenses (limited to $10,000 for both the owner and specified family members). A 10-percent-penalty tax may apply to the taxable portion of withdrawals that are not qualified (but even if withdrawals are not qualified the owner can withdraw his original nondeductible plan contributions free of both income taxes and the 10-percent-penalty tax, only the earnings are subject to these taxes). Unlike traditional IRAs, there are no requirements that distributions be started or completed by any particular date, unless the owner dies.

The annual contribution limit is reduced (dollar-for-dollar) by all contributions to a traditional IRA. Also, in 2011 the maximum yearly contribution is subject to a pro rata phaseout for taxpayers filing jointly with modified adjusted gross incomes between $169,000 and $179,000 (for single taxpayers and heads of households with modified adjusted gross incomes between $107,000 and $122,000). In contrast, with a traditional IRA if the participant is an active participant in a qualified plan the deductible phaseout limits in 2011 are $90,000 to $110,000 for taxpayers filing jointly and $56,000 to $66,000 for single taxpayers. See also, pages 307-309 and 427.

A Roth IRA may generally accept a conversion from a traditional IRA (but for tax years beginning prior to 2010, modified adjusted gross income cannot exceed $100,000). Distributions in excess of basis from the traditional IRA are included in gross income (but not for purposes of determining modified adjusted gross income).

The following factors might be considered when determining whether for a particular taxpayer the Roth IRA is better than a traditional IRA, or whether to make a taxable rollover to a Roth IRA: (1) the current age of the taxpayer; (2) the taxpayer's current and anticipated future marginal income tax brackets; (3) the taxpayer's need for a current income tax deduction; (4) the availability of other funds to pay the taxes on Roth IRA contributions or rollovers; and (5) anticipated reduction of taxes on Social Security income caused by receiving untaxed IRA income.

See also Roth IRA Conversion on page 507.

ROTH IRA CONVERSION

The process of converting some or all of a traditional IRA into a Roth IRA is known as a "Roth IRA conversion." There is no longer any income limit on those taxpayers who can convert (in tax years beginning on or before December 31, 2009, only individuals or couples with modified adjusted gross income of $100,000 or less could convert).

Conversion to a Roth IRA provides many advantages. While both the traditional IRA and the Roth IRA provide for tax-deferred growth of retirement savings, only the Roth IRA enables the account holder, the account holder's surviving spouse, or even the account's holders surviving children, to receive distributions free of income taxes (but the account must be held at least five years and meet additional requirements, see page 506).

In addition, since Roth IRAs are not subject to the minimum distribution requirements, no distributions are required during the account holder's lifetime (see page 433). Nor will distributions be required during the surviving spouse's lifetime, provided the spouse is the sole designated beneficiary and elects to treat the Roth IRA as his or her own (but upon the spouse's death the account will be subject to the after-death requirements, see pages 434-435). With respect to inherited benefits: (1) a traditional IRA inherited by a spouse may be converted to a Roth IRA (but a nonspouse beneficiary may not convert a traditional IRA to a Roth IRA); and (2) a *qualified* plan benefit inherited by either a spouse or nonspouse beneficiary may be rolled over into an inherited Roth IRA (e.g., the nonspouse beneficiary of a 401(k) plan can either convert to an inherited Roth IRA or transfer the benefit to an inherited traditional IRA). See the types of Qualified Retirement Plans on page 491.

Potentially tax-free income, no minimum distributions, tax-deferred growth, and the flexibility to stretch out distributions years into the future among multiple beneficiaries all combine to offer the account holder a unique opportunity to create a permanent but flexible tax-free savings plan. With all these advantages, it might appear the decision should be relatively easy. But upon conversion, the account holder must pay *ordinary income taxes* on both the tax-deductible contributions previously made to the traditional IRA and the subsequent tax-free growth. The account holder's decision is influenced by two expectations: (1) that on any given amount distributed, less income taxes will be paid currently than in the future (e.g., as a result of higher future tax rates, fewer deductions, or more taxable income); and (2) that there will be adequate time and investment opportunity for growth within the Roth IRA to more than offset the cost of making an early payment of income taxes.

Recognizing that a conversion is a taxable event, it is generally agreed that the best time for converting is before account values appreciate and tax rates increase. Recent heavy market losses and current historic low income tax rates may make a compelling case for conversion. In addition, as an added incentive, taxpayers had a one-time opportunity to defer gain from 2010 conversions and recognize it ratably over 2011 and 2012.

(continued on next page)

ROTH IRA CONVERSION (continued)

A traditional IRA that has been converted into a Roth IRA may be recharacterized as a traditional IRA until the due date (including extensions) of the account holder's return for the year the conversion was made. This means that the account holder has up until October 15th of the following year to decide whether to recharterize. For example, assume that an account holding stock valued at $80,000 was converted to a Roth IRA in January of 2011. Now assume further, that by September of 2012 the stock's value fell to $65,000. By recharacterizing the conversion, the account holder can avoid having to report $80,000 of ordinary income on stock having a value of only $65,000. On the other hand, if the stock's value had increased, the account holder can let the conversion stand, report taxes on the conversion, and enjoy his or her investment returns.

Conversions may also be made from a traditional 401(k), a section 403(a) annuity plan, a section 403(b) tax-sheltered annuity, or an eligible Section 457 governmental plan. See the discussion of the Roth 401(k) on page 505.

There are no easy answers to the question of whether an individual should, or should not, make a Roth IRA conversion. Both tax and non-tax factors should be considered, as well as the account holders individual circumstances. Some of the factors for and against conversion are set forth below.

Factors Favoring Conversion	Factors Against Conversion
Have other sources for paying income taxes due from conversion.	Must use IRA proceeds to pay income taxes (possible early withdrawal penalty).
Will not need funds within the next 5 years.	Might need funds within 5 years (exposed to 10% early distribution penalty).
Expect to be in a *higher* income tax bracket during retirement years (e.g., believe tax rates will likely increase in the future).	Expect to be in a *lower* income tax bracket during retirement years (e.g., expect to have less taxable income in retirement).
Have many years before retirement – opportunity for tax-free buildup of interest, dividends, and capital gains.	Close to or in retirement – limited opportunity for tax-free buildup and distribution of earnings.
Large amount in traditional IRA will be forced out by RMD rules.	Need income from traditional IRA and not concerned about RMD rules.
Desire to leave tax-free income to heirs (i.e., Roth IRA is not taxed as IRD, see page 425).	Not particularly concerned about leaving tax-free income to heirs.
Payment of income taxes will reduce large estate and exposure to estate taxes.	Estate is not large enough to be exposed to federal estate taxes or state death taxes.
Live in state that has extended IRA bankruptcy protection to Roth IRA.	Live in state that has *not* extended IRA bankruptcy protection to Roth IRA.
Estate is large enough to be subject to estate taxes and prepayment of income taxes reduces taxable estate.	Estate is relatively small and assets are needed to provide income in retirement.

RULE AGAINST PERPETUITIES

This is a common law principle that no interest in property is good unless it must vest, if at all, not later than 21 years after some life or lives in being at the time of creation of the interest. The reason for this rule is to prevent an individual from unreasonably attempting to control from the grave the disposition of his estate by creating property interests in succeeding unborn generations. In some states, a wait-and-see rule would permit the trust to function until it became clear the rule was violated, as opposed to an immediate termination of all interests. A few states have eliminated the rule against perpetuities.

EXAMPLE A

Testator leaves Blackacre to "my wife, W, for her lifetime, then to my son, S, for his lifetime, then to S's children who survive him for their lifetimes, and then in equal shares to such of my great grandchildren as are alive when the last of my son S's children dies."

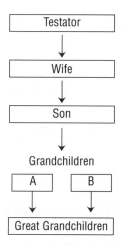

The gift over to great grandchildren fails because it is not possible to know in whom the title ultimately vests until the last of the grandchildren dies, and it is possible that one or more of these great grandchildren would not have been born (in being) within 21 years of the testator's death.

EXAMPLE B

Testator leaves Blackacre to "my wife, W, for her lifetime, then to my son, S, for his lifetime, then in equal shares to such of my grandchildren as are alive when S dies."

This devise is good, since there are no circumstances under which the interest would fail to vest within the required period. The gift over to the grandchildren is good since it is limited to grandchildren who are alive when son dies, son being either a life in being at testator's death or the gift to the grandchildren will vest immediately.

S CORPORATION

This is a corporation that elects to have its income taxed to its stockholders, rather than to the corporation. The manner of taxation is very similar to a partnership, in that it avoids the double taxation that can occur when dividends are paid by a regular C corporation. The following conditions must exist for subchapter S status to be effective:

1. It must be a domestic corporation.

2. It must not have more than 100 stockholders, none of whom is a non-resident alien (a husband and wife are considered one stockholder, and a family can elect to be treated as one stockholder).

3. Only individuals, certain trusts and estates, and certain charitable organizations and qualified retirement plans (but not corporations or partnerships) may own stock.

4. It can have only one class of stock outstanding (but there may be variations in voting rights).

5. A proper election must be made (all stockholders must consent).

S corporations offer the following advantages: (1) they are not subject to the corporate alternative minimum tax adjusted current earnings adjustment (see pages 374-376); (2) provided the S corporation has no earnings and profits, the attribution rules are not a problem (see pages 170-175); (3) there is no double taxation of earnings; (4) under some circumstances they will generate passive income which can offset passive activity losses from tax shelters; and (5) for any given amount of federal taxable income of $379,150 or less in 2011, the individual income tax rates are generally lower than the corporate tax rates (see Federal Income Tax Rates, page 549).

The tax-favored employee benefits that can be received by stockholder-employees are quite restricted. Only those benefits received by stockholder-employees owning *two percent or less* of the S corporation's stock will be deductible as a business expense by the corporation (e.g., amounts paid for certain accident and health plans, and the cost of up to $50,000 group term life insurance). Stockholder-employees owning *more than two percent* of the stock are treated in the same manner as partners in a partnership and the cost of their benefits is generally not deductible to the corporation. However, they can take advantage of the rules covering health insurance premiums and medical expenses (see footnote 1, page 249).

Tracking of basis is very important with S corporations, since a stockholder's basis in his stock shields him from taxation when he receives distributions of income (or sells his stock).

(continued on next page)

S CORPORATION (continued)

The higher the basis is, the higher is the untaxed distribution that can be received. A stockholder's basis increases when the corporation has income, either taxable or tax exempt. A stockholder's basis decreases: (1) when income is distributed; (2) when there is a loss; (3) when there is a nondeductible expenditure (e.g., a life insurance expense); and (4) when there is a capital distribution.

Example 1: How basis works - tax-free distribution of death benefit

A and B form S corporation, with A contributing $14,000 and B contributing $6,000. The corporation purchases a $500,000 term life insurance policy on key employee C. Ignore the Accumulated Adjustments Account (it is explained in Example 3).

Year 1: Corporate income of $35,000 and a $4,700 premium is paid for the $500,000 term insurance policy. Basis is increased for $35,000 of income taxed to stockholders, and reduced for the nondeductible $4,700 life insurance expense.

Year 2: Corporate income of $44,000 and a $5,100 premium is paid. Basis is increased for $44,000 of income taxed to stockholders and reduced for the nondeductible $5,100 life insurance expense.

Year 3: C dies and $500,000 death benefit is paid to corporation. Basis is increased for $37,000 of income taxed to stockholders and the $500,000 death benefit, which is tax-exempt income. Basis is decreased $500,000 for distributions to stockholders.

| | | | Stock Basis | | Accumulated |
		Total	A 70% Owner	B 30% Owner	Adjustments Account (AAA)
Year 1:	Opening Basis	20,000	14,000	6,000	0
	Taxable Income	35,000	24,500	10,500	35,000
	Premium Expense	(4,700)	(3,290)	(1,410)	n/a
	Ending Basis	50,300	35,210	15,090	35,000
Year 2:	Opening Basis	50,300	35,210	15,090	35,000
	Taxable Income	44,000	30,800	13,200	44,000
	Premium Expense	(5,100)	(3,570)	(1,530)	n/a
	Ending Basis	89,200	62,440	26,760	79,000
Year 3:	Opening Basis	89,200	62,440	26,760	79,000
	Taxable Income	37,000	25,900	11,100	37,000
	Tax Exempt Income	500,000	350,000	150,000	n/a
	Total	626,200	438,340	187,860	116,000
	Distributions	(500,000)	(350,000)	(150,000)	
	Ending Basis	126,200	88,340	37,860	

Example 2: A reason to purchase permanent cash value insurance

Stockholder basis is not reduced for any expense "properly chargeable to capital account." The term "capital account" includes policy cash values. Therefore, with permanent insurance the basis reduction should be limited to the amount of the premium less the cash value increase (or cumulative premiums in excess of cumulative cash values). For example, if the $5,100 premium in year 2 of Example 1 was for permanent insurance, a cash value increase of $2,000 in that year would result in basis being reduced by only $3,100. A higher basis allows stockholders to receive increased tax-free distributions from the corporation.

(continued on next page)

S CORPORATION (continued)

Example 3: Dealing with earnings and profits

If an S corporation has earnings and profits (E&P) it maintains an Accumulated Adjustments Account (AAA) in order to prevent double taxation of stockholders, while at the same time assuring that distributed E&P will be taxed as a dividend. This account increases when the corporation earns taxable income and decreases when the income is distributed to stockholders. Referring to Example 1, a distribution of the $500,000 death benefit with prior E&P of $100,000 would be taxed as follows (steps 1 and 3 reduce basis, whereas step 2 does not reduce basis):

		Total	A 70% Owner	B 30% Owner
	Basis At End Of Year 3	626,200	438,340	187,860
1.	Tax-free (up to AAA)	116,000	81,200	34,800
2.	Taxable (up to E&P)	100,000	70,000	30,000
3.	Tax-free (up to basis)	284,000	198,800	85,200
	Total Distribution	500,000	350,000	150,000

Example 4: Avoiding a wasted increase of basis

Now assume that stockholder B was insured by the $500,000 term life policy for the purpose of funding a purchase of B's stock by the corporation. B dies on May 10th of Year 3 and the death proceeds are received by the corporation prior to the sale of B's stock to the corporation on June 11th. Allocating the $500,000 of tax exempt insurance proceeds and the $37,000 of taxable income using the normal "per share, per day" method recognizes that B owns 30 percent of the stock for only 161 days out of 365 days, or 44.11 percent of the year. Therefore, multiplying this 44.11 percent by his 30 percent of ownership results in allocating 13.23 percent of all income to his stock's basis, or a total of $71,045 (.1323 x 37,000 = 4,895; .1323 x 500,000 = 66,150; 4,895 + 66,150 = 71,045). However, allocating the full $71,045 to B's stock is considered a "wasting" of the allocation, because his stock already received a full step-up in basis as a result of his death (page 530).

		Total	A 70% Owner	B 30% Owner
Year 3:	Opening Basis	89,200	62,440	26,760
	Taxable Income	37,000	32,105	4,895
	Tax Exempt Income	500,000	433,850	66,150
	Ending Basis	626,200	528,395	97,805

If the S corporation is a cash basis taxpayer, then an election can be made by *all* stockholders in their stock purchase agreement to terminate the taxable year whenever any stockholder terminates his interest in the corporation (e.g., by sale of all stock after death). This division of the taxable year into two short years is known as a "books and records" election. However, the redemption of stock must take place *prior* to the receipt of the insurance proceeds. Payment for B's stock could be made with a corporate note, which would be paid upon subsequent receipt of the death proceeds. This election would provide A with a basis increase equal to the full $500,000, which could be used to absorb subsequent tax-free distributions to A. The following assumes $20,000 of taxable income *before* the sale of B's stock and $17,000 of taxable income *after* the sale of B's stock:

		Total	A 70% Owner	B 30% Owner
Year 3:	Opening Basis	89,200	62,440	26,760
	Taxable Income	37,000	31,000	6,000
	Tax Exempt Income	500,000	500,000	0
	Ending Basis	626,200	593,440	32,760

SAVINGS/THRIFT PLAN

Savings and thrift plans are defined contribution plans in which employee contributions generally make up a relatively large part of total contributions. Employer contributions typically equal a percentage of at least some part of the employee contributions. Although the Code makes no specific provision for these plans, they may be tax qualified provided they meet the requirements for a pension, profit sharing, or stock bonus plan. Frequently they qualify as profit sharing plans by providing for employer contributions out of current or accumulated profits.

These employer contributions to a profit sharing plan can be entirely discretionary, made according to a formula provision, or a combination of both. If on a discretionary basis, then the employer determines each year whether or not to make contributions to the plan (but a failure to make "recurring and substantial" contributions could result in disqualification of the plan). It is not necessary that the employer actually have current or accumulated profits. If on a formula basis, then contributions are made under a formula typically tied to employer profits (e.g., 5 percent of net profits after taxes, 10 percent of gross profits in excess of $100,000, or some other profit-driven formula). In either case, the employer can deduct up to 25 percent of total payroll of plan participants.

To encourage employee savings, the employer will typically match a portion or all of the employees' contributions. Although employee contributions are not deductible, employer-matching contributions are typically excludable from the employee's taxable income. Earnings on employee and employer contributions are not taxed to the employee until withdrawn.

Convenient payroll deduction of employee contributions, together with income tax deferral on employer contributions and tax deferred growth of both employee and employer contributions made these plans an attractive way to save money. At one time they enjoyed widespread use but have now been largely replaced by 401(k) plans offering the opportunity for before-tax employee contributions (see chart, page 263).

See also, the discussion of qualified retirement plans on page 491.

SECTION 72(t) CALCULATION

In addition to ordinary income taxes, taxable distributions from an IRA prior to age 59½ are generally subject to a 10-percent early distribution penalty tax. (Upon reaching age 59½, an individual can withdraw any amount at any time without being subject to this penalty tax.) A periodic payment exception allows penalty-free distributions prior to age 59½, provided they are part of a series of "substantially equal periodic payments," made at least annually, and lasting a specified duration. Payments made under this exception are referred to as "72(t) payouts."

The **duration requirement** is met if payments are made for the life or life expectancy of the individual or the joint lives or joint life expectancy of the individual and a designated beneficiary. Payments must continue for the longer of five years or until the individual has reached age 59½ (e.g., payments started at age 57½ must continue for five years to age 62½). Payment changes resulting from death or disability do not trigger penalties or interest. Three IRS-approved **calculation methods** are available for calculating penalty-free distributions prior to age 59½:

(1) **Required minimum distribution (RMD) method** is calculated by dividing the account balance by the individual life or joint life expectancy. The annual payment is recalculated each year and varies depending upon the account balance. A one-time change to the RMD method from either of the following methods is allowed.

(2) **Fixed amortization method** is calculated by amortizing the initial account balance over a specified number of years equal to life expectancy (single, uniform, or joint and last survivor) and an interest rate that is not more than 120 percent of the federal mid-term rate. The annual payment remains fixed in subsequent years.

(3) **Fixed annuitization method** is calculated using a mortality table provided by the IRS and an interest rate that is not more than 120 percent of the federal mid-term rate. The annual payment remains fixed in subsequent years.

Comparison of IRA Early Payout Options			
IRA Owner Age 50 – $100,000 Account Balance			
Interest Rate	RMD Method	Fixed Amortization Method	Fixed Annuitization Method
2.5%	$2,151	$4,384	$4,524
3.5%	$2,151	$5,060	$5,255
4.5%	$2,151	$5,784	$6,029
Payouts shown are annual. RMD method shown uses uniform lifetime table. Fixed amortization method and fixed annuitization method shown are based upon a single life. See RMD tables in Appendix F of *Tax Facts On Insurance & Employee Benefits (2011)*.			

SECTION 303 AND THE UNLIMITED MARITAL DEDUCTION

Under Section 303, the partial redemption, or sale, of stock may be made between the corporation and only that party having liability for the federal and state death taxes, funeral, and administrative expenses (see discussion, page 146). Because of this restriction, the utility of a Section 303 redemption to a surviving spouse is limited since no federal estate taxes will be paid if the marital deduction is fully used. For this reason, there may be some *advantage* to incurring a federal estate tax by passing more than the unified credit equivalent in stock to a surviving child, trust, or beneficiary other than the surviving spouse. This would not only allow full advantage to be taken of a redemption under Section 303, but would also avoid subsequent appreciation of the stock in the surviving spouse's estate. For an explanation of the unlimited marital deduction, see the chart entitled Trust Will, on page 25.

In contrast to the chart on page 25, a Marital Plan Will (also referred to as the "Old Marital") divides the estate into two shares, with each share being equal to one-half of the adjusted gross estate. When more than $5,000,000 is placed in the family (or non-marital) trust in 2011 an estate tax is due at the first death, which can often be paid using the provisions of Section 303. Upon the first death, a Marital Plan Will would function as follows:

ESTATE

$11,500,000

UPON THE FIRST DEATH

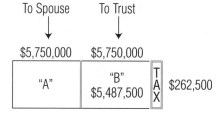

SECTION 306 STOCK

In a recapitalization, preferred stock issued as a dividend on outstanding common stock is generally considered Section 306 stock, to the extent that the issuing corporation has undistributed "earnings and profits." For this purpose, the term "earnings and profits" has a special meaning. Section 306 stock is said to be "tainted," in that a subsequent sale of the stock will produce ordinary income, not capital gain.

Upon the subsequent sale of Section 306 stock, such ordinary income treatment can cause adverse tax consequences beyond the loss of favorable capital gains treatment (see discussion, page 353). If the sale is a capital transaction, the seller can subtract his basis in calculating any gain subject to taxation. If the sale is of Section 306 stock, the amount realized is first treated as a withdrawal of earnings and profits and the seller could be taxed on the full amount received.

Even in a "true" recapitalization (i.e., an exchange of *all* of a stockholder's stock for a different class of stock), the problem of tainted Section 306 stock cannot be avoided if, at the time of the recapitalization, other family members are, and continue to be, stockholders. The family attribution rules (as set forth on pages 170-175) have been extended to apply to such "true" recapitalizations. However, this whole problem can be avoided if the stock is not sold until *after* the death of the stockholder. If the stock is then sold at a price representing the fair market value on the date of death (or on the optional valuation date), the "stepped-up basis" at death will eliminate any taxable gain. In this regard, see the discussion of Stepped-Up Basis on page 530.

SECTION 409A

Section 409A was passed by Congress to eliminate perceived abuses in deferred compensation arrangements (e.g., triggers in Enron's plan provided accelerated payments to senior executives, while lower-level employees were left with 401(k) accounts containing worthless company stock). Virtually every nonqualified deferred compensation plan is covered by the very broad provisions of Section 409A. Included are severance payments, bonus deferral arrangements, supplemental executive retirement plans (page 367), phantom stock plans (page 473), stock appreciation rights (page 473), and nonqualified stock options (page 464). Qualified plans are not covered (see page 491).

Election. Plan participants must elect to defer *before* the beginning of the year in which they earn the compensation. (First time participants may make the election within 30 days after becoming eligible, but only for services performed after the election.) On the deferral date, participants must make a one-time election as to how, and when, they want to be paid (e.g., annual payments for 10 years, beginning at age 60). Provided it is permitted by the plan, participants who desire to further delay receipt of the money for at least an additional five years, may make a re-deferral election no later than 12 months before the payment is due.

Distribution. Participants can receive distributions under only six circumstances: separation from service, death, disability, plan-specified date, unforeseeable emergency, and upon change in ownership or control of the corporation. However, full distributions are not required immediately upon occurrence of these events (e.g., permissible alternatives include "one year after change of control," or "in equal installments over five years after disability"). Certain key employees of publicly traded corporations may not take distributions until six months after separation from service.

Acceleration. Except under circumstances specified by the IRS, a nonqualified deferred compensation plan may not permit the acceleration of payments under the plan. These limited circumstances include distributions made to fulfill a domestic relations orders, and distributions to comply with conflict-of-interest rules (i.e., situations that are unanticipated and nonelective). Triggers may not be used to protect assets from a change in the employer's financial health (e.g., acceleration if profits fall below a certain level).

Funding limitation. In addition to prohibiting triggers, plans may not set aside assets in an off-shore trust for the purposes of paying deferred compensation (but onshore Rabbi Trusts are not affected, see page 496).

Penalties. There are stiff penalties for failing to comply with 409A. Retroactive constructive receipt is imposed, with the money being taxed as of the time of the intended deferral. A 20 percent tax must be paid, in addition to the normal income tax, and interest is charged on the late payment at 1 percent higher than the normal underpayment rate.

SECTION 529 PLANS

Section 529 plans, also called qualified tuition programs (QTPs), are state-sponsored or privately-sponsored programs, authorized by federal law, that allow a taxpayer to: (1) purchase tuition credits or certificates on behalf of a designated beneficiary under a prepaid educational arrangement (PEA); or (2) make contributions to an educational savings account (ESA) established to fund the "qualified higher education expenses" (QHEEs) of a designated beneficiary. However, private colleges and universities may establish PEAs, but not ESAs. QHEEs include tuition, fees, special-needs services, room and board, and the costs of books, supplies, and equipment, required by a designated beneficiary at an eligible educational institution (post secondary education to include graduate school). There is a large difference among individual programs, many of which are more restrictive than required by Section 529. Before selecting a plan, the investor would be well advised to carefully review the individual account agreement and research the past performance of the underlying investment options.

Federal law generally does not place any limits on who may participate as an account owner, contributor, or designated beneficiary (except that the beneficiary must be an individual). In order to avoid excess contributions, they are typically limited to the amount necessary to provide five years of education at more expensive schools (e.g., some programs allow for contributions of up to $250,000). Contributions must be in cash, are not tax deductible, and are treated as completed gifts eligible for the gift tax annual exclusion ($13,000 in 2010 and 2011). This gift tax treatment is unusual, given the owner's power to withdraw funds from the account – subject to penalties and taxes – or to designate a new beneficiary. Gifts in excess of the annual exclusion may be "front-loaded," meaning that a donor may avoid using available unified credit by treating the gift as made over a period of 5 years (for a maximum of $65,000 per spouse, or $130,000 per couple, to each designated beneficiary).

State-sponsored ESAs may permit the owner to choose among different investment strategies offered by the plan: (1) when the account is opened, (2) once every 12 months, and (3) whenever the beneficiary designation is changed. Certain age-based plans automatically move to more conservative investments as the beneficiary ages. Separate accounting must be maintained for each designated beneficiary, with no pledging of the account assets by either the owner or the beneficiary. However, the account can be attached by the creditors of the owner, but not by the creditors of the beneficiary. In contrast, the value of the account is included in the estate of the designated beneficiary.

All account earnings are tax deferred. Distributions used to pay QHEEs are excluded from gross income. Distributions not used for QHEEs are subject to a 10-percent-penalty tax on the taxable portion of the distribution.

SECULAR TRUST

The "secular" trust (as distinguished from a "rabbi" trust) is used to formally fund and secure nonqualified deferred compensation. Funds placed in a secular trust are not subject to the claims of the employer's creditors. So, unlike the rabbi trust (see page 493), the secular trust can protect employees from both an employer's future *unwillingness* to pay promised benefits and an employer's future *inability* to pay promised benefits due to bankruptcy or other financial difficulties.

However, the security offered by the secular trust comes at a price to the executive, because he is generally subject to current taxation. To offset the executive's current tax liability, the employer will sometimes pay a bonus to the executive. Current taxation of the executive is attractive to the employer because it provides the employer with a current tax deduction. Of course, as with any deferred compensation arrangement, all deferrals and bonuses must be reasonable compensation (see page 546).

There are two principal types of secular trusts: the employer-funded trust and the employee-funded trust. Because of its negative tax treatment, the employer-funded trust has lost popularity.

In an *employer*-funded secular trust, it is the Service's position that highly compensated employees will generally be taxed each year, not just on vested contributions to the trust, but also on any vested earnings of the trust. And because the Service further believes that employer-funded trusts cannot be employer-grantor trusts, the trust itself would also be taxed on this same income! Funding the secular trust with life insurance might avoid this double taxation by eliminating trust taxation: the cash value increases should be tax-deferred to the trust. Unfortunately, life insurance funding might not relieve the executive from taxation on trust earnings, because the Service appears to believe that these cash value increases would be currently taxed to highly compensated executives. It has generally been thought that distributions from employer-funded secular trusts will be taxed under the rules relating to annuities. But the Service has questioned the applicability of those rules to distributions to highly compensated employees from most employer-funded secular trusts.

In an *employee*-funded secular trust, either the employee contributes cash to the trust *or* the employer contributes cash to the trust after giving the employee a choice between receiving cash (or some cash equivalent) or a trust contribution. The employee is currently taxed on either the cash he actually receives and contributes to the trust, or on the employer contributions to the trust (he is considered to have constructively received the money). The employee-funded trust is generally considered an employee-grantor trust and its income is taxed to the employee only. Because the employee is fully taxed on both trust contributions and income, distributions from the trust should be free of income taxes.

SELF-CANCELLING INSTALLMENT NOTES (SCINs)

A self-cancelling installment note (SCIN) is an installment debt obligation that by its terms is extinguished at the death of the seller-creditor. SCINs are also referred to as "death-terminating installment sales." Although a hybrid of the installment sale and private annuity, SCINs retain most of the tax advantages of the installment sale. For example, unlike a private annuity, SCINs may be secured without jeopardizing their installment sale status and gain is generally deferred (see chart, page 43).

Under the typical installment sale, deferred gain is eventually recognized by either the seller or the seller's heirs. If the balance of the note is unpaid at death, the present value of future payments is includable in the seller's estate. Cancellation of the installment sale note at death does not avoid inclusion of the fair market value of the note in the seller's estate. When the seller and buyer are related, the fair market of the note is considered to be no less than its full face value (i.e., the unpaid principal of the note).

With a SCIN, nothing will be included in the seller's gross estate (similar to a private annuity). Generally having gain reported in the decedent's tax return offers far more advantages than requiring the estate to report the gain, because the income taxes may then be claimed as a deduction for estate tax purposes. However, the Eighth Circuit has held that gain was to be recognized and reported by the seller's estate (Est. of Frane v. Commissioner, which overruled the Tax Court).

To properly establish a SCIN, the installments should be for a term shorter than the seller's life expectancy (this avoids characterization of the arrangement as a private annuity). In addition, the purchaser must pay a "risk premium" to the seller as consideration for the cancellation of the note at the seller's death. There is no specific statutory or regulatory guidance as to how this risk premium should be calculated. Apparently the premium can be reflected as an increase in the sales price, referred to as a SCIN-PRIN, or as an increase in the interest rate, referred to as a SCIN-INT. Despite these and other unresolved tax issues, the SCIN provides substantial flexibility in allocating income and deductions between seller and purchaser, while freezing the value of an asset through purchase by children or other family members. Under the right circumstances, the SCIN can be an attractive estate and income tax planning tool.

In contrast to a SCIN, a private annuity for a term of years (PATY) is a private annuity for a (fixed) term of years or until the seller's death, whichever comes first. However, the SCIN can be secured and typically offers greater income tax benefits to the seller.

SELF-EMPLOYED RETIREMENT PLANS

There is a great variety of retirement plans available for the self-employed. The following generally lists them in the order of amount of maximum annual contribution, costs to set up, complexity, and difficulty of administration.

1. **Roth IRA.** In 2011 the maximum *nondeductible* contribution is limited to the lesser of 100 percent of compensation or $5,000 ($10,000 for husband and wife), subject to a phaseout for taxpayers filing jointly with adjusted gross incomes between $169,000 and $179,000 (phaseout for single taxpayers is between $107,000 and $122,000). If age 50 or over catch-up provisions allow an additional $1,000 (for a total of $6,000). Husband and wife may each contribute $5,000 per year provided there is sufficient compensation. Early withdrawals of *contributions* are tax-free and penalty-free. Loans are not permitted. Generally low administrative fees and responsibilities. See page 506.

2. **SIMPLE IRA.** SIMPLE stands for Savings Incentive Match Plan for Employees. In 2011 the **maximum** *deductible* contribution is $11,500. If age 50 or over **catch**-up provisions allow an additional $2,500 (for a **total** of $14,000). The employer is required to either contribute 2 percent of the entire payroll or match contributions of up to 3 percent of each employee's salary. Early withdrawals prior to age 59½ are subject to a penalty. Loans are not permitted. Generally low administrative fees and responsibilities. See page 524. There are also SIMPLE 401(k) Plans (see page 305).

3. **SEP-IRA** – Also referred to as a **SEP** or **Simplified Employee Pension**. In 2011 the maximum contribution is limited to the lesser of $49,000 or 25 percent of the first $245,000 of net earned income (with sole **proprietorships** and partnerships, owners are effectively limited to 20 percent). **There** are no catch-up provisions. No minimum funding standards are imposed. Early withdrawals prior to age 59½ are subject to a penalty. Loans are not permitted. Generally easy to set up and administer. See page 525.

4. **Keogh Plan** – Also referred to as a **HR-10 Plan**. The typical Keogh Plan is designed as a defined contribution plan without a fixed contribution formula (in 2011 participants can contribute up to 100 percent of income to a maximum of $49,000). Plans may also be designed as a defined benefit plans (see below). Early withdrawals prior to age 59½ are subject to a penalty but loans are permitted. Administrative responsibilities and fees are high. Used in organizations consisting of ten or fewer highly paid employees.

5. **Individual 401(k) Plan** – Also referred to as a **Solo 401(k) Plan.** In 2011 the maximum contribution is $49,000. If age 50 or over catch-up provisions allow an **additional** $5,500 (for a total of $54,500). No minimum funding standards are imposed. Early withdrawals prior to age 59½ are subject to a penalty but loans are permitted. Administrative responsibilities and fees are potentially high. See page 426.

6. **Defined Benefit Plan.** In 2011, depending upon age and projected income, the annual benefit at age 65 could be as high as $195,000. Nondiscrimination regulations restrict design for ower-employees of closely held businesses. Early withdrawals prior to age 59½ are subject to a penalty but loans are permitted. Administrative responsibilities and fees are high. See page 384.

SELF-SETTLED TRUST

When an individual (the settlor) creates an irrevocable trust for his or her own benefit, it is known as a "self-settled" trust. Generally, the benefit reserved by the settlor is to receive discretionary distributions from the trust. Self-settled trusts provide an independent trustee with full authority to make decisions as to how trust funds will be distributed.

If the trust also contains provisions that prevent creditors from reaching trust assets, the trust is known as a "domestic asset protection trust" (DAPT), "asset protection trust" (APT), or a "self-settled spendthrift trust.". Although spendthrift provisions may have been originally intended to protect spendthrift beneficiaries from themselves, currently such provisions are most often used to protect settlor/beneficiaries from their own creditors (i.e., because the funds are not actually under the control of the beneficiary, the creditors of the beneficiary cannot reach the funds in the trust).

Historically, individuals were not able to create self-settled trusts that protected trust assets from the claims of their creditors. In the 1980's our increasingly litigious society encouraged individuals to turn for help to foreign jurisdictions. In order to attract trust business and capital, some countries had created anti-creditor and specially-drafted trust laws that overrode long-standing rules against self-settled trusts. Sensing an opportunity, in the late 1990s Alaska adopted the first laws in the United States providing for self-settled spendthrift trusts. Delaware soon followed. Missouri, Nevada, New Hampshire, Oklahoma, Rhode Island, South Dakota, Tennessee, Utah, and Wyoming have all adopted some version of DAPT legislation.

However, for public policy reasons, the laws of most states adhere to the long-standing rule that settlors cannot retain beneficiary rights in a trust, while at the same time protecting the trust assets from creditors. Given this environment, it is likely that the courts in these states will continue to issue judgments that provide creditors access to the assets in out-of-state trusts, despite spendthrift clauses (i.e., DAPT states must recognize other state's judgments under the Full Faith and Credit clause of the U.S. Constitution). Unfortunately, while there is a fair amount of state legislation, there is a paucity of case law pertaining to DAPTs. The effectiveness of self-settled trusts continues to be debated among highly respected members of the bar.

Another type of "self-settled" trust is actually a supplemental needs trust used to qualify or maintain a disabled individual's eligibility for Supplemental Security Income (SSI) or Medicaid (i.e., trust funds are not counted for eligibility purposes). These trusts are called "self-settled" because they are funded with the individual's own assets. They are also known as "payback," or "(d)(4)(A)" trusts (referring to the authorizing statute). The disabled individual must be under age 65, and the trust must be created by the disabled individual's parent, grandparent, guardian, or a court (the disabled individual cannot create his or her own trust, even if he or she is otherwise legally competent). At the beneficiary's death, funds remaining in the trust must be repaid to the state for Medicaid costs paid to or on behalf of the trust beneficiary.

See also, the discussion of asset protection on page 348, and trust protector on page 543.

SIMPLE CAFETERIA PLANS

Beginning in 2011, SIMPLE cafeteria plans may be established by employers who employed an average of 100 or fewer employees for either of the prior two years (the concept is similar to the SIMPLE 401(k) and SIMPLE-IRA). [A small employer that establishes a plan and later exceeds the 100-employee limit may continue the plan until the year after a year in which it employs an average of 200 or more employees.] When a plan qualifies as a SIMPLE cafeteria plan for any given year it is treated as meeting any applicable nondiscrimination requirements for that year (i.e., non-discrimination testing is not required). In general, employer contributions are deductible, not subject to Social Security tax, and employee deferrals are not taxable income, so the available benefits can be purchased with pre-tax dollars. A SIMPLE cafeteria plan must satisfy certain eligibility and participation requirements.

Employees with at least 1,000 hours of service during the preceding plan year must be eligible to participate. However, employees that may be excluded include those who: (1) have not attained age 21 before the end of the plan year (the plan may provide a younger age); (2) have less than one year of service as of any day during the plan year; (3) are covered under a collective bargaining agreement; or (4) are nonresident aliens. An employer may have a shorter age and service requirement but only if such shorter service or younger age applies to all employees.

A SIMPLE cafeteria plan must provide for employer nonelective contributions on behalf of every non-highly compensated and non-key employee. This requirement can be meet by contributing: (1) a uniform percentage of at least 2% of each qualified employee's compensation; or (2) at least the lesser of; (a) 6% of the qualified employee's compensation for the plan year; or (b) twice the amount of each employee's contribution. As noted above, these employer contributions are deductible, not subject to Social Security tax, and any employee deferrals are not taxable income. Highly compensated employees (per Code section 414(q)) and key employees (per Code section 416(i)) may participate, so long as they really are "employees" and do not receive disproportionate employer nonelective or matching contributions.

Available benefits may include health and dental insurance, reimbursement for health and dental expenses not covered by insurance, dependent care, group term life insurance, and disability insurance.

SIMPLE IRA PLANS

SIMPLE IRA plans ("SIMPLE" stands for Savings Incentive Match Plan for Employees) are easier to install and administer than a qualified plan. The SIMPLE IRA is considered a replacement for the SAR-SEP IRA and must be established by an employer for employees using either Form 5304-SIMPLE or Form 5305-SIMPLE.

In order to set up a SIMPLE IRA plan, the employer must not maintain another employer-sponsored retirement plan (including qualified plans, tax-sheltered annuities, and SEPs) and in the preceding year must have employed 100 or fewer employees earning at least $5,000. The plan must cover any employee who has earned at least $5,000 in any two preceding years and is reasonably expected to earn at least $5,000 in the current year. However, the employer may establish less restrictive eligibility requirements. Self-employed individuals may establish and participate in a SIMPLE IRA plan.

The employee is allowed to contribute up to $11,500 per year (in 2010 and 2011). Although the deferral amount is expressed as a percentage of compensation, there is no limit on this percentage (e.g., in order to defer the maximum $11,500 per year, an employee earning $11,500 could elect to defer 100 percent of compensation). The $5,000 limit for traditional IRAs does not apply to a SIMPLE IRA. In addition, if the plan so provides, an individual age 50 or over may make catch-up contributions of up to $2,500 in 2010 and 2011.

The employer is required to either contribute 2 percent of the entire payroll (under a nonelective contributions formula) or match contributions of up to 3 percent of each employee's salary (under a matching formula). However, a special rule permits the employer to elect a lower percentage under the matching formula, but not less than 1 percent, and it cannot be used for more than two out of any five years.

A SIMPLE IRA plan is not subject to nondiscrimination testing or top-heavy rules, and the reporting requirements are simplified. All contributions are excludable from the employee's income and must be fully vested. The penalty for early withdrawal prior to age 59½ is 25 percent during the first two years of participation and 10 percent thereafter (unless one of the exceptions applies).

A SIMPLE 401(k) plan is a 401(k) plan that satisfies the non-discrimination requirement by adopting certain SIMPLE 401(k) provisions that are similar to the above requirements. Such a plan is not subject to nondiscrimination tests and the top-heavy rules, but it will be subject to other qualified plan requirements. For details, see **Q 3680**, *Tax Facts on Insurance & Employee Benefits (2011)*.

SIMPLIFIED EMPLOYEE PENSION (SEP)

A simplified employee pension (SEP) is an employee's individual retirement account that may accept an expanded rate of contribution from his employer. Because payments are made into an IRA established for each employee, they are also referred to as SEP-IRAs. SEPs can be established with sole proprietorships, partnerships, or corporations, and are particularly attractive for the self-employed who has no employees or the individual who has additional income from outside employment. Generally, all employees must be included in a SEP except for: (1) employees who have not worked for the employer three out of the last five years; (2) employees who earn less than $550 (as indexed in 2011 for inflation); (3) employees who have not reached age 21; (4) employees covered by a collective bargaining agreement; and (5) non-resident aliens. They are generally easy to set up and require little administration.

SEPs can be established and funded as late as the due date (plus extensions) of the employer's (or self-employed's) tax return. In 2010 and 2011 pre-tax contributions are limited to the lesser of $49,000 or 25 percent of the first $245,000 of net earned income (with sole proprietorships and partnerships the owners are effectively limited to 20 percent). No minimum funding standards are imposed. Contributions are not subject to income tax withholding, FICA or FUTA. Typically these plans are self-directed, in that the individual participant decides how funds will be invested. All earnings within the plan accumulate on a tax-deferred basis. The employer may not prohibit withdrawals from the plan, although they may be subject to a penalty tax if made before age 59½. Essentially, there are four types of SEP plans with varying degrees of complexity:

5305-SEP is very easy to implement, requiring only the completion of five questions on IRS Form 5305-SEP. However, this may not be used by employers who maintain other qualified retirement plans, use leased employees, or have had a defined benefit plan.

SEP prototype plans are provided by financial institutions (with or without a fee). Prototype plans are particularly useful if the employer wants to integrate the SEP contributions with Social Security (i.e., provide increased contributions for highly paid employees).

Individually designed plans are typically drafted by an attorney. They tend to be more expensive and complicated, therefore less often used.

SAR-SEP plans are salary reduction SEPs that allow employees to make pretax contributions to their IRAs. The provisions permitting the establishment of these plans were terminated at the end of 1996. SAR-SEPs already in existence prior to 1997 may continue to operate under preexisting law, receive contributions, and add new employees, but new SAR-SEPs may not be established. In their place, individuals may wish to consider the SIMPLE IRA (see discussion on page 524).

SOCIAL SECURITY - TAXATION OF BENEFITS

Under a two-tier system, up to 85 percent of Social Security benefits may be subject to income taxation. Under the **first tier**, if modified adjusted gross income (adjusted gross income plus tax-exempt income, or MAGI) plus one-half of Social Security income exceeds a base amount, an individual must include in gross income the *lesser* of: (1) 50 percent of the benefit; or (2) 50 percent of such excess over the base amount ($32,000 for married couples filing joint returns, zero for married couples filing separately who lived together during any portion of the year, and $25,000 for all other taxpayers). Under the **second tier**, if a taxpayer's MAGI plus one-half his Social Security benefit exceeds an "adjusted" base amount, he must include the *lesser* of: (1) 85 percent of the Social Security benefit, or (2) the sum of (a) 85 percent of such excess over the adjusted base amount, plus (b) the smaller of the amount includable under the first tier of taxation (see above), or $4,500 (single taxpayers) or $6,000 (married taxpayers filing jointly). The "adjusted" base amount is $44,000 for married couples filing joint returns, zero for married couples filing separately that lived together during any portion of the year, and $34,000 for all other taxpayers.

For example, the taxable benefit would equal $8,550 for a married couple filing jointly who had Social Security benefits of $14,000, adjusted gross income of $37,000 and tax-exempt interest of $3,000:

		The Lesser Of
85% of Social Security benefit (85% x $14,000)		$11,900
		or
Modified adjusted gross income	$40,000	
One-half the Social Security benefit	+ 7,000	
Total	47,000	
Adjusted base amount	(44,000)	
The excess multiplied by 85% ($3,000 x .85)	2,550	
Lesser of amount includable under		
first tier ($7,000) or $6,000	+ 6,000	
Sum of 85% of excess plus smaller of amount		
includable under first tier, or $6,000		$8,550

There is no longer any reduction in benefits once an individual reaches *normal retirement* age (i.e., earnings during and after the month the individual reaches normal retirement age will not reduce benefits). However, *early retirement* benefits will be reduced by: (1) $1.00 for every $2.00 of earnings over $14,160 during the years *before* reaching normal retirement age; and (2) $1.00 for every $3.00 of earnings over $37,680 during the calendar year before the month the individual reaches normal retirement age (e.g., there would be a reduction of $773 if an individual who reaches normal retirement age in April of 2011 had earned $40,000 in January thru March ($40,000 - $37,680 = $2,320 ÷ 3 = $773).

SPECIAL NEEDS PLANNING

Special needs planning involves providing for a physically or mentally disabled member of the family. Most often the disabled individual is a minor or adult child, but special needs planning also involves planning for dependent parents or other relatives. With a disabled adult child such planning should provide for him once his parents (the caregivers) become disabled or die. The ability of the disabled child to function will determine the required level and cost of care. Although caring for a person with a mental illness is generally considered more difficult and complicated than caring for a person with a developmental or physical disability, each situation is unique and must be planned for on an individual basis.

Even when other members of the family, such as siblings, are willing to assume the duties of caregiver, it is still important to provide for the management of assets. Either a testamentary or living trust can be used for these purposes (see chart on page 29). Such a trust, sometimes called a "supplemental needs trust," should: (1) appoint someone to take care of the child's property and money; (2) select a guardian for the child; (3) set out instructions on how the child is to be cared for; (4) ensure, to the extent possible, that the child will not lose payments or benefits from government agencies; and (5) integrate the trust with the remainder of the parent's estate plan (e.g., achieve equity among family members). Survivorship life insurance on both parents would provide a cost-efficient means of funding this trust upon the deaths of both parents (see discussion, page 535). Disability income insurance on a working parent should also be considered.

At one time or another during his lifetime a disabled person could receive benefits from Social Security Disability Income (SSDI), Supplemental Security Income (SSI), Medicare and Medicaid. With a special needs trust the objective is to have the child's inheritance supplement, not replace, these government programs. See also, the discussion of the Self-Settled Trust on page 522.

Eligibility for government assistance can be negatively affected by the *disabled child's assets* (e.g., for purposes of the SSI benefit a single disabled person cannot own more than $2,000 in cash and liquid assets). Even when a trust consists of *third party assets*, if the discretionary powers of the trustee are not carefully limited, state laws may cause trust assets to be "available" to the beneficiary. However, under the federal Medicaid statute a trust established with the assets of a third party, such as a parent, is not considered "available" to the trust beneficiary.

Special needs planning may also affect other estate planning techniques. For example, under federal law a Medicaid recipient cannot refuse a gift. This means that a disabled child should not be given Crummey withdrawal powers, since his failure to make a withdrawal could jeopardize his Medicaid eligibility (see discussion, page 379).

SPLIT-DOLLAR ROLLOUT

This term refers to the termination of a split-dollar agreement when an employer-owned policy is transferred, or "rolled out," to the employee, or the cash values of an employee-owned policy are used to pay off the employer. The rollout can be at any time, but is usually timed to occur once the employee reaches normal retirement age.

As an insured grows older the endorsement and nonequity collateral assignment split-dollar plans taxed under the economic benefit regime can become very costly to maintain (see footnote 3, page 229). Likewise, the nondeductible loan interest due under an equity collateral assignment plan can become burdensome. When there is a permanent need for life insurance, such as to pay estate taxes, it is important to establish some means of maintaining the policy (often described as an "exit strategy").

Under a split-dollar plan taxed under the *loan regime* the employer is generally reimbursed for all cumulative premiums paid under the split-dollar agreement (i.e., employer releases assignment of cash values in employee-owned policy upon repayment of loans). Under a split-dollar plan taxed under the *economic benefit regime* when the employer-owned policy is transferred to the employee, or others (e.g., a trust), either the employer is paid for the policy or the employee is taxed on the value of the policy (as reasonable compensation). This value is determined without regard to surrender charges that would apply if the policy was terminated.

These exit strategies also include transferring the policy as a dividend distribution, distribution of the policy at capital gains rates in liquidation of the company, or funding purchase of the policy by a grantor trust using income from assets transferred into the trust at discounted values (see Intentionally Defective Trust chart, page 67).

Under the split-dollar regulations a "roll out" *without* taxation can occur as part of the transition to the two-regime taxation of split-dollar (see Equity Split-Dollar, pages 399-402). For plans entered into before January 28, 2002 there are two "safe harbor" provisions that protect employee-owned cash values (these safe harbors are further described in Table A on page 296):

1. The employee will not be taxed on cash values in excess of the employer's interest if the plan was terminated before January 1, 2004.

2. The employee will not be taxed on equity if the plan is converted to a loan from the employer to the employee for all periods beginning on or after January 1, 2004 (pre-2004 employer outlays considered beginning loan balance, and subsequent employer premiums added to loan balance).

STEP TRANSACTION DOCTRINE

In construing tax statutes the step transaction doctrine requires that interrelated steps of an integrated transaction be taken as a whole rather then treated separately. The doctrine is used by both the IRS and the courts to link several prearranged steps or contemplated steps, even though there is no contractual obligation or financial compulsion to follow through. The following are examples of circumstances that could attract application of the doctrine:

1. Transfer by the insured of a life insurance policy on his life will cause the death proceeds to be included in the insured's estate if he dies within three years (see pages 409-410). In an attempt to avoid application of this three-year rule, a partner in a limited partnership contributes dollars to the partnership and these funds are subsequently used to purchase the policy from the partnership (a "sale" for adequate consideration is not considered a transfer for estate tax purposes, and is also an exception to the transfer for value rules, see pages 541-542). The step transaction doctrine might be applied to collapse the contribution-to-partnership and sale-to-partnership into one "nonsale" transfer of the insurance contract to the partnership.

2. Parent gives money to a child who then purchases an annuity naming the parent as the annuitant, and the child as both owner and beneficiary. If the child subsequently and consistently gives the annuity proceeds to the parent, the step transaction doctrine might be applied to collapse the parent-to-child and child-to-parent gifts.

3. Borrower places a second mortgage on his house and uses the funds to purchase a single premium annuity. Normally, interest paid on a second mortgage is deductible (within limitations). But no deduction is allowed for loans taken to purchase a single premium annuity. The step transaction doctrine could be applied to collapse the borrowing-on-mortgage and purchase-of-annuity transactions.

In attempting to understand the step transaction doctrine, it is important to recognize that the following overlapping, and sometimes indistinguishable, doctrines can also be applied to any given set of facts: (1) the tax avoidance doctrine (transaction primarily intended to reduce taxes rather than to achieve nontax business or personal objectives); (2) the substance-over-form doctrine (transaction has minimal, if any, nontax consequences); and (3) the business purpose doctrine (transaction has no business purpose). It is suggested that one way of recognizing when a proposed transaction might run afoul of one or more of these doctrines, is to apply the "if it is too good to be true, it probably is" test.

STEPPED-UP BASIS

In Years 2001-2009, 2011 And Later

At death, the income tax basis of appreciated property in an estate is increased, or "stepped-up," to its fair market value as of the date of death. For this reason, when property is subsequently sold, there is no taxable gain if the sales price, or amount realized, is the same as the value on the date of death. However, when property has decreased in value, the basis will be "stepped-down" under the same rules as govern the determination of a step-up in basis.

The step-up in basis applies only to property that is included in the decedent's estate for federal estate tax purposes. This value can sometimes be influenced by the personal representative of the estate by filing an election to have the gross estate, including stock in a closely held corporation, valued on an alternate valuation date, usually six months after death. If this is done, the stepped-up basis equals the fair market value as of the alternate valuation date. Note, however, that use of the alternate valuation date is permitted only if its use would result in a reduction in the value of the gross estate and a reduction in the sum of the estate tax and generation-skipping transfer tax payable.

With property owned jointly between husband and wife, the stepped-up basis applies to only one-half of the property, since only one-half the value of such property is included in the estate of the first to die.

Special rules apply in order to prevent the transfer of property in anticipation of the donee's death. Therefore, there is no step-up in basis when property is acquired by a decedent (the donee) within one year of death and this same property is then at death passed back to the original donor or the donor's spouse.

In Year 2010

The 2010 Tax Relief Act repealed the modified carryover basis provisions of EGTRRA 2001 and restored the stepped-up basis. However, in the case of decedents dying after December 31, 2009, and before January 1, 2011, the executor is given the option of electing back into a modified carryover basis. Electing back means the estate would not be subject to estate taxes, but would receive a limited step-up in basis. This is essentially a *carryover basis*, but modified to allow: (1) an aggregate step-up of $1,300,000; plus (2) a spousal step-up of $3,000,000 for assets passed to a surviving spouse; plus (3) the decedent's unused losses. To be entitled to the $3 million spousal step-up, the property must be "qualified spousal property" (i.e., the interest cannot be a terminable interest). See footnote 1, page 37. Not eligible for a step-up in basis are items considered to be income in respect of a decedent (IRD) and property received by the decedent within three years of death (except for certain gifts from the decedent's spouse). See page 425. In order to comply with this modified carryover basis system, detailed and onerous record keeping must be maintained for virtually all assets.

STOCK BONUS PLAN

A qualified stock bonus plan is similar to a profit sharing plan (see page 484). However, in contrast to a profit sharing plan, the account values are often fully invested in the employer's stock. (A profit sharing plan may not invest more than 10 percent of its holdings in employer stock unless it meets the requirements for an "individual account plan.") Separate accounts are established for each participant and allocation of contributions and distributions of benefits are generally subject to the same requirements as a profit sharing plan.

Contributions are made either in cash (which is then used to purchase the stock of the employer) or in the stock of the employer. If made in stock, the amount of the employer's deduction for the contribution is determined by the fair market value of the stock when it is contributed. Unless the stock is publicly traded, some or all of the voting rights must be passed through to participants. Employer contributions are not fixed or required, may vary from year to year, and may or may not come from employer profits.

Distributions are generally in the form of employer stock, but a stock bonus plan may provide for payment of benefits in cash if certain conditions are met. (If employer securities are not readily tradable on an established market, the participant has a right to require the employer (not the plan) to repurchase employer securities under a fair valuation formula. This is referred to as a "put option.") When stock is received in a lump sum distribution any net unrealized appreciation of the stock while held in the plan is not taxed until it is subsequently sold (i.e., taxation of gain is deferred). For example, assume a stock bonus plan purchased stock for $1,000 and it appreciated in value to $5,000. The stock is then distributed to a participant in a lump sum distribution, at which time the participant pays taxes on $1,000, but would not be currently taxed on the $4,000 of unrealized appreciation.

An employee stock ownership plan (ESOP) must meet the requirements for a stock bonus plan, as well as certain additional requirements (see pages 396-397).

See also, the discussion of qualified retirement plans on page 491.

STRANGER-ORIGINATED LIFE INSURANCE (STOLI)

Stranger-originated life insurance (STOLI), also known as investor-owned, investor-initiated and investor-originated life insurance, includes a variety of plans, or "schemes," to purchase large amounts of life insurance with the present intention of benefiting outside investors. The board of directors of the American Council of Life Insurers has voted to support the creation of a federal excise tax on STOLI contracts settled in less than five years. New York state regulators have issued an opinion that STOLI policies created strictly for resale are contrary to law.

Charitable variation. This is a complex arrangement which seeks to utilize the insurable interests of a charity to provide investment gains to outside investors. A typical arrangement involves the establishment of a trust by a charity. The trust then borrows funds from outside investors with the promise that the investors will be paid a fixed income. These borrowed funds are used to purchase single premium immediate annuities on the lives of a select group of charitable donors (i.e., wealthy and older donors). Life insurance is purchased on these same individual donors – under state laws that give a trust created by a charity an insurable interest in a donor's life. The annuity income is used to pay the life insurance premiums and to make the fixed income payments to the investor group. As the life insurance death benefits are received, the investor group is repaid its investment and the charity receives any remaining proceeds.

Individual variation. These arrangements are more straightforward than those involving charities. Here an individual purchases a life insurance policy on his life using funds from a nonrecourse loan obtained from outside investors. (If a nonrecourse loan is not repaid, the lender has no recourse against the borrower, only a right to seize the policy pledged as security.) Typically, after two years, the insured can choose to repay the loan with interest, sell the policy to a life settlement company, or transfer the policy to the lenders in full satisfaction of the loan. From their inception, these arrangements are structured in anticipation that the outside investors will take over ownership of the policy; it is not intended that the insured will retain the life insurance. In fact, these arrangements are marketed to potential insureds as providing "free insurance" (albeit for only two years), and to "sophisticated" investors as a way of reaping enhanced returns on "portfolios" of life insurance policies.

There is something inherently disturbing about STOLI. These arrangements are suspect for many reasons: (1) the "renting" of an insurable interest to third-party investors is likely to be against public policy (see page 429); (2) investment returns are problematic (i.e., projections are dependent upon the timing of death proceeds from a small group of insureds); (3) participating charities are subjecting themselves to loss of their tax-exempt status; (4) large outstanding policies could negatively effect the insured's ability to obtain future life insurance coverage (see page 414); (5) such "rent-a-life" arrangements may subject "life settlements" initiated by policy owners to regulatory scrutiny (see page 443); and (6) turning life insurance into a commoditized investment could ultimately jeopardize its tax-favored status.

STRUCTURED SETTLEMENT

Structured settlements are used to provide long-term financial security in physical injury cases, by providing the injured party with periodic payments tailored to meet medical expenses and the needs of basic living. Whereas lump sum payments often result in the proceeds being poorly invested or squandered, structured settlements provide a stream of tax-free income from a reliable financial institution.

Situations appropriate for structured settlements involve: (1) wrongful death where a surviving spouse and/or children require ongoing income; (2) worker's compensation; (3) guardianship involving minors or incompetents; and (4) disabled or severely injured individuals.

To initiate a structured settlement, an agreement is reached between the plaintiff and the defendant regarding the benefits due to the injured party. This agreement can be reached before, during, or after a lawsuit. It may be agreed to privately, or it may be by order of the court (e.g., in situations involving the support of a minor child). Calculations on the costs of providing for the injured party's long-term needs are made by a structured settlement specialist, or structured settlement broker. There is great flexibility in designing the terms of a structured settlement. For example, periodic payments can be provided for a specific number of years, or made for the lifetime of the injured party with a guaranteed minimum number of years.

Once a settlement has been reached, the defendant, or its insurer, generally transfers the obligation to a financially secure and experienced life insurance company. This assignment relieves the defendant of any further obligation to make payments to the injured party. The life insurance company will typically use an immediate annuity to make the required payments. To assure that payments are received free of federal income taxes, the injured party, or annuitant, does not own the annuity contract; it is owned by the defendant, or its insurer.

Under Federal law the benefits under a structured settlement may not be assigned as collateral for a loan. However, in recent years there is a growing market involved in the purchase of existing structured settlements. In response, some states have enacted consumer protection statutes strictly regulating these transactions.

SUPPLEMENTAL EXECUTIVE RETIREMENT PLAN (SERP)

A Supplemental Executive Retirement Plan (SERP) is an agreement between an employer and a selected key employee in which the employer agrees to provide a specified benefit at retirement, or upon termination, disability, or death prior to retirement.

SERPs are funded entirely by the employer with no contribution by the employee. In this sense, SERPs are unlike nonqualified deferred compensation plans in which the employee is, at least in theory, *deferring* compensation that otherwise could be taken currently (see chart, page 235). Unfortunately, SERPs are often described as "deferred" compensation agreements. In any case, SERPs are exactly what their name implies, they provide retirement benefits that *supplement* all other retirement plans such as IRAs, 401(k) plans, or qualified defined benefit pension plans.

The retirement benefits to be provided are generally determined using either a defined benefit or a defined contribution approach. A *defined benefit* agreement specifies an exact dollar amount to be paid (in a lump sum or otherwise) upon retirement, or upon termination, disability, or death prior to retirement. In recruiting high level executives, this type of SERP is often used to replace retirement benefits that will be forfeited when leaving another company. Rather than a fixed dollar amount, benefits under a defined benefit approach are more likely to be determined using a formula that considers the employee's years of service and pay (e.g., seventy percent of final 5 years average pay). When a *defined contribution* approach is used, individual accounts are established into which either discretionary or results-tied contributions are made based on company performance (e.g., 20 percent of salary if profitability exceeds a pre-determined target). Vesting schedules are often used to provide for a graded benefit should the employee terminate employment prior to retirement.

Payments under the SERP are taxed as ordinary income to the employee in the year received and are deductible to the employer in the year paid. Should the employee die, payments to the surviving beneficiaries are also taxed as ordinary income (i.e., the life insurance death benefit is paid to the employer, not to the employee's beneficiary).

When life insurance is used to informally fund the employer's obligations under a SERP, the employer purchases cash value life insurance on the employee's life (see notice and consent requirements, page 369). The employer owns the policy, pays the premiums, and is the policy beneficiary (see chart, page 155). If the employee dies prior to retirement, the policy death benefit is payable to the employer. These funds can then be used to provide survivor benefits to the employee's beneficiary under the terms of the agreement. Upon the employee's retirement, the employer can use policy cash values to assist in meeting its obligations under the agreement, maintain the policy until the insured's death, or otherwise sell or dispose of the policy (see Transfer For Value, pages 541-542).

SURVIVORSHIP LIFE INSURANCE

Survivorship life insurance, also known as last-to-die insurance or second-to-die insurance, insures two lives, and pays a death benefit after the death of both insureds. Generally, the premium required is less than that for comparable insurance on either individual life, since the odds of two individuals dying during any given year are substantially less than of one individual dying.

While the many potential uses of survivorship life include charitable gifts (chart, page 55, and discussion, page 356), family income for surviving children (chart, page 15), key person insurance (chart, page 155), and funding installment sales within a family (chart, page 43); survivorship life is most often used to fund the payment of estate taxes, when the marital deduction defers taxes until the death of both spouses (chart, page 25). Survivorship life offers the advantage of simplicity by paying a death benefit exactly when taxes are due – upon the second death. With a rated or uninsurable client, coverage can usually be obtained, provided the spouse is insurable at standard rates.

There are some disadvantages to relying solely upon survivorship life insurance to fund the payment of estate taxes. For example, when the marital deduction is used to defer all estate taxes until the second death, appreciation of assets in the surviving spouse's estate can substantially increase total estate taxes. The flexibility provided by the use of disclaimers may be severely limited when there are no funds for payment of estate taxes at the first spouse's death (see discussion, page 389). After divorce the unlimited marital deduction is no longer available, unless the bulk of the estate is left to a new spouse.

Split-dollar is often used to pay premiums on a survivorship policy funding a life insurance trust (see Split-Dollar Funding Life Insurance Trust chart, page 227). The value of the gift to the trust can be substantially reduced by using the very low joint life rates that measure the probability of *two* deaths in one year. Although Table 38 has been used in the past for this purpose, this particular table may no longer be applicable (see discussion at the bottom of page 553). However measured, use of low joint life rates allows substantial coverage to be purchased within the "present interest" limits (see Gifts & Split-Gifts chart, page 47; and footnote 4, page 53). But it must be recognize that no death benefit will be paid until *both* insureds have died. This means that a survivorship policy must generally be funded for longer periods then a policy insuring just one individual. Also, after the first death, the value of the gift to the trust will be measured using higher single life rates (currently Table 2001, see page 552). This amount could exceed the $13,000 (as indexed in 2010 and 2011) annual exclusion limit for present interest gifts.

TARGET BENEFIT PLAN

Under the target benefit plan, calculation of the employer's contribution takes into consideration not only the participant's compensation but also the participant's age when first entering the plan. By using age as a factor in allocating contributions employers are able to allocate more of their contributions towards older employees. In fact, when compared to a money purchase plan, a target benefit plan can substantially increase the annual contributions for older employees who have higher levels of compensation (see discussion of Money Purchase Pension Plan on page 460).

The target benefit plan is essentially a hybrid plan. Although the target benefit plan is a type of money purchase plan, it initially uses a defined benefit approach to determine a theoretical or "targeted" benefit that is expressed as a defined benefit formula (e.g., 50 percent of average compensation payable at a normal retirement age of 65). Actuarial assumptions involving investment rates of return and mortality are used to develop a table of contribution percentages (called a target benefit table) that is incorporated into the plan. A defined contribution approach is then used and the employer is required to make fixed annual contributions to the separate account of each participant according to the percentages contained in the target benefit table (the table typically sets the annual employer contribution as a percentage of compensation). Because the target benefit plan is a defined contribution plan, the annual additions are limited per participant to the lesser of 100 percent of compensation, or $49,000 (in 2010 and 2011). Any increase in employee compensation will produce an additional benefit under the target benefit table (i.e., the increase in compensation produces a separate benefit that is funded with an additional annual contribution).

The employer does not guarantee the ultimate retirement benefit and the employee/participant bears the entire investment risk. If the earnings are lower than assumed, the actual benefit will be lower than the targeted benefit. Conversely, if the fund's earnings are greater than the actuary has assumed, the participant's actual benefit will be higher than the targeted benefit.

See also, the discussion of qualified retirement plans on page 492.

TAX-FREE EXCHANGE

Tax-free exchanges recognize that when property is exchanged by a taxpayer for "like kind" property, gain or loss need not be recognized and the transaction should not be subject to current taxation, since the taxpayer is in essentially the same position after the transaction as he was before the transaction. Under Section 1031 of the Code real estate transactions are frequently structured as tax-free exchanges.

Life insurance and annuity contracts can also benefit from the provisions for tax-free exchanges. These are often referred to as "Section 1035 exchanges" after the governing Code provision. In an exchange situation, life insurance policies are the most flexible, since they may be exchanged for another life insurance policy, an endowment contract or an annuity. Although an endowment contract cannot be exchanged for a life insurance policy, it can be exchanged for either an annuity or another endowment contract (provided the maturity date of the new contract is not later than the maturity date of the original contract). An annuity contract is the least flexible contract as it can be exchanged only for another annuity contract.

For purposes of a Section 1035 exchange, an endowment contract is considered a contract "which depends in part on the life expectancy of the insured, but which may be payable in full in a single payment during his life." The exchange of an endowment contract must be made *prior* to its maturity date.

In an exchange involving life policies, the policies must be on the life of the *same* insured and the new policy must be issued to the same person owning the old policy. Term insurance appears inappropriate for a tax-free exchange.

Tax-free exchanges can be particularly useful when it is desired to avoid taxation of cash values in excess of the policy owner's basis in the contract (net premiums paid, or generally total premiums paid less dividends, if any), or when it is desired to preserve the old contract's basis (substantial premiums have been paid in excess of available cash values). The old policy need not have been issued by the same company issuing the new policy. Some companies will accept assignment of policies containing an outstanding loan.

If there is a loan against the policy given in exchange, and no loan (or a lower loan) against the policy received in the exchange, the difference is treated as cash received. The lesser of this amount or any gain in the policy given is taxable income. There is gain if total cash values, including loans, exceed total premiums paid, less dividends, if any. If there is no gain, then there is no tax (the amount simply reduces basis).

TAX LAW – SOURCES

Because many sources are cited as tax authority, it is important to understand the differences in the weight given them by the courts and their reliability as precedent. The citation at the end of each paragraph provides an example of how each source is cited.

Legislative and Administrative Sources

Internal Revenue Code. Congressional legislation that is the primary source of our federal tax law. [*IRC Sec. 417(a)(6)*]

Treasury Regulations. Amplify, supplement and interpret the Code. Given substantial weight by the courts and may generally be relied upon by taxpayers. Proposed regulations usually are not considered binding. [*Reg. §1.401(a)-20*]

Revenue Rulings. Issued by the National Office of the IRS. Although not as authoritative as regulations, they are given varying weight by the courts. Can generally be relied upon by taxpayers. Although revenue rulings can be revoked by the IRS, revocation is rarely retroactive. [*Rev. Rul. 72-25*]

Revenue Procedures. Reflect the internal management and state procedures the IRS will follow in specific situations. [*Rev. Proc. 95-3*]

Private Letter Rulings. Issued to a particular taxpayer by the National Office of the IRS. Although letter rulings are only uncertain indications of one line of reasoning by the Service and are not binding precedents, courts have considered them in reaching decisions. [*Let. Rul. 9212024*]

Technical Advice Memoranda. Issued to IRS personnel by the National Office of the IRS to assist with application of the Code, regulations and other precedents. Generally have the same effect as private letter rulings. [*TAM 9050006*]

Field Service Advice. Non-binding opinion written by IRS attorneys for internal use. Provides some insight into the thinking of the IRS at the time written. [*FSA 1998-252*]

Judicial Sources

Supreme Court. All courts follow Supreme Court decisions. The few tax cases it hears are accepted as a matter of discretion (certiorari). [*Gregory v. Helvering*, 293 U.S. 465 (1935)]

U.S. Courts of Appeals. Organized in thirteen circuits. Decisions of a court of appeals bind those lower courts within its appellate jurisdiction. [*Crummey v. Comm.*, 397 F.2d 82 (9th Cir. 1968)]

Tax Court. The majority of tax cases are litigated in this court (it was formerly the Board of Tax Appeals). Taxes need not be paid before initiating a suit and there is no jury. Decisions reviewed by the entire Tax Court take precedence over unreviewed decisions (either regular or memorandum); unreviewed "regular" decisions take precedence over unreviewed "memorandum" decisions. The Tax Court has said that unreviewed memorandum decisions are not precedents, but this policy may be changing. Appeals (where available) are made to the appropriate U.S. court of appeals. Other federal courts and the Service are not bound by Tax Court decisions in future cases. [*Estate of Vandenhoeck*, 4 T.C. 125 (1944)]

Federal District Courts. Taxes must be paid before initiating suit, but a jury may be requested (jury decides facts, judge decides law). A district court is expected to follow its decisions, but its decisions do not bind other federal courts or the Service in future cases. Appeals are made to the appropriate U.S. court of appeals. [*Silberman v. U.S.*, 333 F. Supp. 1120 (W.D. Pa. 1971)]

U.S. Court of Federal Claims. Taxes must be paid before initiating suit and there is no jury. The court (previously, the U.S. Claims Court) is expected to follow its decisions, but does not bind other federal courts or the Service in future cases. Appeals are made to the Court of Appeals for the Federal Circuit. [*Arkla, Inc. v. U.S.*, 27 Fed. Cl. 226 (1992)]

TOTAL RETURN UNITRUST

The total return unitrust is an attempt to reconcile the conflicting interests of the income and remainder beneficiaries by allowing the trustee to invest trust assets for total return (i.e., for capital appreciation as well as income).

The traditional "income and principal" trust directs that the trustee pay all trust income to the income beneficiary, with corpus distributed to the remainder beneficiaries upon the death of the income beneficiary (e.g., "income to my wife for life, then payment of the corpus in equal shares to my children"). In order to provide for the income beneficiary, trust assets were typically invested in fixed *income* investments (e.g., bonds). However, failing to take advantage of strong stock market performance creates disgruntled *remainder beneficiaries* (e.g., the children). To remedy this situation, a majority of states have enacted some form of the prudent investor rule (see discussion, page 485). Under this rule, trustees can utilize modern portfolio theory and invest for capital appreciation in a diversified portfolio of equity and growth stocks. However, foregoing trust income in order to attain greater trust appreciation creates disgruntled *income beneficiaries* (e.g., surviving spouses).

Caught in the middle is the trustee – who has a duty of fairness to both the income and remainder beneficiaries. The "total return unitrust" is an attempt to balance the competing interests of the income and remainder beneficiaries while obtaining greater trust appreciation.

Rather than focusing on income producing investments, under the "total return" approach a trustee, governed by the prudent investor rules, can invest in equities in order to obtain greater long-term growth of trust assets. With a "total return unitrust," the trustee is required to pay out a fixed percentage of the fair market value of the trust assets each year; thereby *enabling the income beneficiary to enjoy the benefits of trust appreciation*. A "smoothing" formula is used to cushion rapid year-to-year changes in trust value (e.g., using a 3-year rolling average to determine fair market value).

The IRS has issued regulations intended to accommodate state law changes to the concepts of income and principal. Under the regulations, allocations between income and principal will be respected by the Service if state law provides for a "reasonable apportionment" between the income and remainder beneficiaries of the total return of the trust, to include ordinary income, capital gains, and unrealized appreciation (e.g., a unitrust amount of three to five percent would be considered reasonable).

Transfers in trust avoid current gift and estate taxes provided a spouse, as income beneficiary, is entitled to all trust income for life (i.e., the trust qualifies for the unlimited marital deduction, as in the "A" trust on page 25). Under the proposed regulations, this "all income to spouse" requirement is met – and the marital deduction is preserved – when a unitrust makes such a "reasonable apportionment" of the total return of the trust.

TRADITIONAL IRA

This is another name for the original (regular) individual retirement arrangement that was first made available in 1974 under the Employee Retirement Income Security Act (ERISA). Under this Act, the primary purpose of the Individual Retirement Account, or IRA, was to give those individuals not covered by an employer's retirement plan the opportunity to save for retirement on their own by establishing tax-deferred accounts with private financial institutions. Additionally, the IRA was also intended to provide a place for transferring, or rolling over, balances from employer-sponsored retirement plans; thus giving both retiring workers and individuals who were changing jobs a way to preserve their employer-sponsored retirement plan assets.

In Publication 590 (Individual Retirement Arrangements (IRAs)), the Internal Revenue Service defines a traditional IRA as "any IRA that is not a Roth IRA or a SIMPLE IRA" (i.e., the term is used to distinguish the original IRA from the Roth IRA and the SIMPLE IRA). See the expanded discussion of the traditional IRA on page 427.

In contrast to the traditional IRA, the SIMPLE IRA must be established for employees by an employer. It is not limited to the traditional IRAs $5,000 per year contribution limit. In 2010 and 2011, with a SIMPLE IRA an employee may contribute up to $11,500 per year, plus age 50 and over catch-up contributions. See the expanded discussion of the SIMPLE IRA on page 524.

Likewise, in contrast to the traditional IRA, the Roth IRA permits an individual to make *nondeductible* contributions to a tax-deferred account up to the same dollar limits. Provided certain requirements are met, distributions from the Roth IRA are not subject to income taxes. See the expanded discussion of the Roth IRA on page 506.

TRANSFER FOR VALUE

The transfer for value of a life insurance contract jeopardizes the income tax-free payment of its proceeds. Under the transfer for value rule, if a policy is transferred for a valuable consideration, the death proceeds will be taxable as ordinary income, except to the extent of the consideration, the net premiums and certain other amounts paid by the transferee.

The transfer for value rules extend far beyond outright sales of policies (see **Q 207**, *Tax Facts on Insurance & Employee Benefits (2011)*). The naming of a beneficiary in exchange for any kind of valuable consideration would constitute a transfer for value. Consideration does not have to be in money, but could be an exchange of policies or a promise to perform some act or service. However, the mere pledging or assignment of a policy as collateral security is not a transfer for value.

Specific *exceptions* to this rule allow a transfer for consideration to be made to the following, without jeopardizing the income tax-free nature of the death benefit:

1. Transfers to the insured.

2. Transfers to a partner of the insured.

3. Transfers to a partnership in which the insured is a partner.

4. Transfers to a corporation in which the insured is a stockholder or officer.

5. Transfers between corporations in a tax-free reorganization if certain conditions exist.

A *bona fide gift* is not considered to be a transfer for value and subsequent payment of the proceeds to the grantee (donee) will be income tax-free.

The transfer for value problem does not exist with a partnership, because a transfer to a partner of the insured is one of the exceptions to the rule. Thus, it is possible to convert from an entity purchase agreement to a cross purchase agreement and use the same policies to fund the new agreement.

With respect to a corporation, once a stock redemption agreement (i.e., entity purchase agreement) has been funded with life insurance, it is *not* possible to change to a cross purchase agreement and use the *same* policies to fund the new agreement. Transfer by the corporation of an existing policy on the life of one stockholder to another stockholder would be a violation of the transfer for value rule (but transfer to a partner or a bona fide partnership of which the stockholder was a partner would fall within exceptions to the transfer for value rule). However, this problem does not exist in changing from a cross purchase agreement to a stock redemption agreement: the transfer to a corporation in which the insured is a stockholder is an exception to the rule (see 4 above).

(continued on next page)

TRANSFER FOR VALUE (continued)

Some planners have suggested the use of a trusteed cross purchase agreement to avoid a problem of multiple policies when there are more than just 2 or 3 stockholders. Under this arrangement, a trustee would be both owner and beneficiary of just one policy on each of the stockholders. However, it is likely that there is a prohibited transfer for value when one of the stockholders dies and the surviving stockholders then receive a greater proportional interest in the outstanding policies that continue to insure the survivors.

For example, assume A, B, C and D are equal stockholders in a corporation with a funded trusteed cross purchase agreement. Under the arrangement each stockholder is the beneficial owner of a one-third interest in the policies insuring the other three stockholders. Now assume D dies. A prohibited transfer for value could occur if D's proportional interests in the outstanding policies insuring A, B and C pass to the surviving stockholders upon D's death. However, the problem can be avoided by having the corporation purchase D's interests in the policies insuring A, B and C, with the intention of funding a combined cross purchase and entity purchase agreement (see chart entitled, "Wait And See" Buy/Sell Agreement, on page 139). Alternatively, the problem could also be avoided by simply using a stock redemption agreement, as shown in Entity Purchase Agreement chart on page 127. See page 134, for an expanded discussion of the Trusteed Cross Purchase Agreement.

The transfer-for-value rule does not apply to the transfer of a life insurance policy to a grantor trust, when the policy insures the life of the grantor of the trust (e.g. the policy is sold to the trust). For tax purposes the trust and the insured grantor are one and the same, and thus the sale is considered a transfer to the insured. See Grantor Trust Rules on page 418.

Transfer for value problems can occur in rather unexpected circumstances. For example, the transfer of existing life insurance policies insuring stockholders to the trustee of a trusteed cross purchase agreement does not fall within one of the exceptions to the transfer for value rule. To avoid this initial ownership problem the trustee should be the original applicant, owner and beneficiary of the policies.

A prohibited transfer for value can also occur when a split-dollar agreement involving a trustee is terminated pursuant to a "rollout" (see page 528). When the agreement is between the employer and the trustee of an irrevocable trust, using endorsement split-dollar with the policy owned by the employer would require a transfer of the policy to a trustee who does not fall within any of the exceptions to the transfer for value rules. However, using collateral assignment split-dollar established under the "loan regime" will avoid this transfer for value problem. See the discussion of Equity Split-Dollar on pages 399-402.

TRUST PROTECTOR

The concept of a "trust protector" owes its origin to the foreign (offshore) asset protection trust (see page 348). In an effort to protect assets from the claims of creditors, the grantor of a foreign asset protection trust will typically transfer substantial amounts of property to a trust that cannot be directly amended or revoked by the grantor. Using a trusted party to act as the trust protector gives the grantor a degree of *influence over*, or even de facto control of, the foreign trust. (Some asset protection trusts name the grantor as the initial trust protector, but the grantor *should not* be named the trust protector of a domestic trust.)

With a domestic trust, such as an irrevocable life insurance trust (chart, page 51), utilization of a trust protector provides a means of *monitoring* the trustee's performance in order to assure that the grantor's original intentions are carried out. Additionally, the trust protector provides *flexibility* in adapting the trust to changing family circumstances and evolving tax laws.

The trust protector *is not* a trustee having fiduciary powers to control trust assets, but rather typically has *limited* authority to: (1) correct any drafting errors in the original trust instrument; (2) modify or amend the trust instrument to achieve favorable tax status, or to adjust to changes in the Internal Revenue Code, state laws, rulings, and regulations; (3) remove or replace the trustee; (4) increase or decrease the interests of trust beneficiaries (e.g., limiting a beneficiary's right of withdrawal or power of appointment); (5) appoint trust assets to another trust created by the same grantor; (6) regulate trust investments; and (7) change the situs of the trust (if possible under state law).

The trust protector is often someone whom the grantor knows and has confidence in, such as a close family friend or a professional advisor. It is important that this person be independent of both the trustee and the beneficiaries. Therefore, the trust protector should not be the grantor, the spouse of the grantor, a person who has either a present or future beneficial interest in either the trust income or principal, a person who has ever made a transfer to the trust, or the spouse of any such person.

With domestic trusts, use of a trust protector is a relatively new practice. Although there is currently little, if any, case law and legislative direction relative to the functioning of a domestic trust protector, the concept appears sound and can be expected to gain in acceptance and usage (e.g., see Idaho statute 15-7-501).

TRUSTS FOR MINORS

In order for a gift to qualify for the annual exclusion, the donee must have the right to immediate use and enjoyment of the property (chart, page 47). As a matter of principle, many donors will object to placing title to property in the name of a minor, and it can create problems in dealing with the property. Fortunately, for those who intend to make substantial gifts over a number of years, the Code authorizes two types of trusts that can be used to obtain the annual exclusion:

Section 2503(c) Trust. Under this trust, both income and principal may be expended by or on behalf of the beneficiary prior to age 21, and the unexpended income and principal *must* be paid to the beneficiary upon attaining age 21 or sooner. If the minor beneficiary dies before age 21, the trust corpus passes to the minor's estate or is subject to a general power of appointment by the minor. It is permissible for the trustee to purchase life insurance on the minor's life and pay premiums from trust income (if the trust authorizes purchase of insurance on the grantor's life, or on the life of the grantor's spouse, there will be a violation of the grantor trust rules, and all income will be taxable to the grantor). Distributed income is taxable to the minor, and accumulated income is taxable to the trust. The donor should not be named trustee, as that will cause the trust assets to be included in his estate if he dies prior to the minor's reaching age 21.

Section 2503(b) Trust. This trust should be considered by the donor who does not want trust corpus and unexpended income to be distributed at age 21 or sooner. The principal can be paid to the beneficiary at whatever dates or times are established by the donor, and need not ever be paid to the beneficiary, but rather paid to another person specified by the donor or the trust beneficiary. However, such a trust must provide for a *mandatory distribution of income* to the beneficiary, at least annually, or more frequently (but could be deposited to a custodial account). Making the gift requires a calculation that involves dividing the gift into an income portion (that which qualifies for the annual exclusion) and a principal or remainder portion (that which is considered a gift of a future interest).

Because establishment of both types of trusts can be expensive and time consuming, many donors may find it more convenient to make gifts under the Uniform Transfers to Minors Act or the Uniform Gifts to Minors Act (page 545).

UNIFORM TRANSFERS/UNIFORM GIFTS TO MINORS ACTS

Gifts can be made to a minor by transferring property to a custodian under the Uniform Transfers to Minors Act (UTMA) or the Uniform Gifts to Minors Act (UGMA). Because the UGMA places restrictions on the types of property that can be the subject of a custodial gift, most states have now adopted the UTMA. It appears that life insurance policies may be the subject of a gift in all states. However, in most states there are restrictions on who may be named insured; there may also be restrictions on who may be named beneficiary (see discussion of Minors and Life Insurance, page 459).

Gifts made under either act can qualify for the annual exclusion (see chart, page 47). All income from the gift will be taxable to the minor (unless it is used to discharge the legal obligation of another person, in which case the income would be taxable to that person). Unlike a minor's trust, the custodian does not file a separate tax return and all income is reported by the minor on his own tax return. The minor has the right to receive possession of the property upon attaining the age specified in the relevant state's statute (age varies from state to state, and may depend upon the instructions of the donor or the nature of the transaction that created the custodianship).

If the donor appoints himself as custodian, the property will be included in his taxable estate if he dies while serving as custodian. There can be only one beneficiary per custodial account, and therefore separate accounts must be established for multiple beneficiaries. Likewise, each account can only have one custodian and successor custodians are usually the minor's guardians.

In 2010 the unearned income of a child that exceeded $1,900 generally was taxed to the child at the *parent's* maximum rate (known as the "kiddie tax"). For this purpose a child is considered an individual who is: (1) under age 18; (2) under age 19 whose earned income does not exceed half of his or her own support; or (3) under age 24, if a full-time student, whose earned income does not exceed half of his or her own support.

However, in 2010 a parent could elect to claim the unearned income of a child on the parent's return if: (1) the child's income is solely from interest and dividends; and (2) the income is more than $950 but less than $9,500; and (3) there has been no backup withholding or estimated tax payments under the child's taxpayer identification number. For this purpose the child must be either: (1) under age 18; (2) under age 19 whose earned income does not exceed half of his or her own support; or (3) under age 24, if a full-time student, whose earned income does not exceed half of his or her own support. If the election was made, the parent includes as income taxable at the parent's rate any gross income of the child in excess of $1,900. With respect to the first $1,900 for each child to whom the election applies, there was a tax of 10 percent of the lesser of (1) $950 or (2) the excess of the gross income of the child over $950.

UNREASONABLE COMPENSATION

The payment of an "excessive" amount to an employee for services rendered is considered to be unreasonable compensation. Whether compensation is excessive, and therefore unreasonable, is often determined by reference to payments by similar corporations to employees performing like services. The problem is most often encountered with regard to employee-stockholders, where a *salary* would be a deductible business expense to the businesses, but a *dividend* would be nondeductible.

Underlying any discussion of employee benefits is the assumption that, if challenged by the Internal Revenue Service, the increased compensation could be shown to be reasonable. Compensation includes not only money, but also payments "in kind." For example, all of the following are considered compensation: the personal use of an automobile, lodging for the employee's family while on vacation, premiums for group term insurance, medical expense reimbursements, premiums paid under an executive equity plan, and the value of life insurance protection under an endorsement split-dollar plan. It should be noted that no deduction is allowed for compensation that is paid to certain highly compensated officers of publicly-held corporations in excess of $1,000,000 (in excess of $500,000 when applied to covered executives of a TARP recipient). See discussion on page 417.

However, it appears to be the experience of many accountants and tax advisors that the threat of a successful challenge by the Service is more imagined than real. This may often be due to a belated recognition by the courts, as well as the Service, that the business owner spent many years being underpaid while the business grew, and now has the "right" to compensation for those earlier services. After all, it was the owner who made the small closely-held business a success, and sooner or later he should be paid for his efforts. However, the determination depends on the circumstances of each situation.

VARIABLE ANNUITIES

With a variable annuity the annuity owner has the opportunity to allocate his premiums among a number of subaccounts. In return for the opportunity to benefit from any appreciation in underlying investments, the owner assumes the risk that his investments may decrease in value, thereby resulting in lower accumulation values or a lower monthly income. The variable annuity is considered a "security" under federal law and anyone selling a variable annuity must have the required securities licenses and the purchaser must be given a prospectus (see footnote 3, page 285). The purchase can be made with either a single premium or a series of premiums (see Annuity Matrix, page 302).

In addition to a fixed or general account, the typical variable annuity might offer the following investment options: (1) growth or common stock fund; (2) balanced fund; (3) index fund; (4) global fund; (5) bond fund; (6) government securities fund; and (7) money market fund. Asset management or investment fees will vary depending upon the type of fund. In addition to an annual administration fee, an annual mortality charge is made for a guaranteed "death benefit" (e.g., provided the owner dies prior to age 80 his beneficiary is guaranteed to receive the greater of his original investment or the policy's value at the time of death, less withdrawals). Some contracts offer "stepped up" death benefits that lock in investment gains at a given point in time.

During the *accumulation* phase premium payments are applied toward the purchase of accumulation units. The value of an accumulation unit is determined by dividing the market value of the underlying investments by the total number of units outstanding. Dividends and capital appreciation or depreciation are reflected in the value of the accumulation units. The owner also has the option to transfer funds between investment subaccounts, subject to certain dollar amounts and timing limitations. Unlike mutual funds, all accumulations are tax deferred and transfers of assets between accounts are free of current income taxes. A decreasing surrender charge is generally applied if the annuity is surrendered within a given period (see chart, page 283).

During the *distribution* phase the annuity owner can cash in the contract, take periodic withdrawals, or annuitize the contract. All gains are taxed as ordinary income when distributed. Annuity payments can be received on a fixed or variable basis, or a combination of both, and can be paid as a single life annuity or joint and survivor annuity. If variable benefits are to be received the accumulation units are first exchanged for annuity units. Unlike accumulation units, the number of annuity units then remains constant. Variable benefit payments will differ from month to month, or from year to year, depending upon the value of the annuity units. A new living benefit feature currently being developed offers a guaranteed minimum account value, or minimum payout amount, regardless of the actual performance of the subaccounts. See also, the discussion of the Guaranteed Lifetime Withdrawal Benefit on page 421.

WELFARE BENEFIT FUND

A welfare benefit fund (WBF) is a fund (which is either taxable or a tax-exempt entity, as with a VEBA trust) into which employer(s) make deposits to provide specific benefits to their employees. Typical benefits include severance pay and preretirement death benefits. A WBF is not a qualified plan, nor is it a plan of deferred compensation (which would result in the employer losing his current tax deduction). To avoid classification as deferred compensation, plans are designed to: (1) include a broad group of employees; (2) cover businesses with more than one employee; (3) base funding on actuarial determinations; and (4) avoid any reversion of assets to employers.

Although strict limits are placed on an employer's deductions for contributions to a WBF, these limits do not apply to contributions made to a "10-or-more employer plan." By requiring the pooling of funds in a 10-or-more employer plan, it was expected that the plan would be "self-policing" (e.g., an employer would not be tempted to make excess contributions beyond that needed to pay promised benefits to its own employees since these contributions might benefit the employees of *another* employer).

Regulations have halted what the IRS considers abusive 10-or-more plans (e.g., plans purporting to guarantee payments based upon contributions for specific employees). Under these regulations a 10-or-more employer plan is a single plan: (1) to which more than one employer contributes; (2) to which no employer normally contributes more than 10 percent of the total contributions by all employers; (3) that does not maintain "experience-rating arrangements" with respect to any individual employer; and (4) that satisfies compliance rules (i.e., written plan document, record keeping, and right of inspection by the IRS and participating employers). A prohibited experience-rating occurs if an *employer's costs* or an *employee's benefits* are based upon the employer's overall experience (e.g., claims or expense experience, investment results, or over or underfunding). Although the regulations do not prohibit the use of cash value life insurance, they do express concern that any pass-through of premiums associated with an employer's employees may result in a prohibited experience-rating arrangement. While not clear, it would seem that benefits provided are included in, or excluded from, income under general tax rules (e.g., fully insured group term life insurance proceeds payable by reason of the death of the employee would be excludable from income).

The single-employer welfare benefit plan to prefund post-retirement medical and life insurance benefits appears to offer an attractive supplemental employee benefit. However, it would be prudent to seek guidance from qualified counsel on plan design and any unresolved tax questions.

FEDERAL INCOME TAX RATES

(Tax Years Beginning in 2011)

MARRIED FILING JOINTLY

Taxable Income Over	To	Tax Equals	Plus %	Of Excess Over
0	17,000	0	10	0
17,000	69,000	1,700.00	15	17,000
69,000	139,350	9,500.00	25	69,000
139,350	212,300	27,087.50	28	139,350
212,300	379,150	47,513.50	33	212,300
379,150		102,574.00	35	379,150

HEAD OF HOUSEHOLD

Taxable Income Over	To	Tax Equals	Plus %	Of Excess Over
0	12,150	0	10	0
12,150	46,250	1,215.00	15	12,150
46,250	119,400	6,330.00	25	46,250
119,400	193,350	24,617.50	28	119,400
193,350	379,150	45,323.50	33	193,350
379,150		106,637.50	35	379,150

SINGLE

Taxable Income Over	To	Tax Equals	Plus %	Of Excess Over
0	8,500	0	10	0
8,500	34,500	850.00	15	8,500
34,500	83,600	4,750.00	25	34,500
83,600	174,400	17,025.00	28	83,600
174,400	379,150	42,449.00	33	174,400
379,150		110,016.50	35	379,150

ESTATES AND TRUSTS

Taxable Income Over	To	Tax Equals	Plus %	Of Excess Over
0	2,300	0	15	0
2,300	5,450	345.00	25	2,300
5,450	8,300	1,132.50	28	5,450
8,300	11,350	1,930.50	33	8,300
11,350		2,937.00	35	11,350

CORPORATIONS

Taxable Income Over	To	Tax Equals	Plus %	Of Excess Over
0	50,000	0	15	0
50,000	75,000	7,500	25	50,000
75,000	100,000	13,750	34	75,000
100,000	335,000	22,250	39	100,000
335,000	10,000,000	113,900	34	335,000
10,000,000	15,000,000	3,400,000	35	10,000,000
15,000,000	18,333,333	5,150,000	38	15,000,000
18,333,333		6,416,667	35	18,333,333

Note: **Personal service corporations** are subject to a flat rate of 35 percent; and include corporations in which substantially all of the activities involve the performance of services in the fields of health, law, engineering, architecture, accounting, actuarial science, performing arts, or consulting, and substantially all of the stock of which is held by employees, retired employees, or their estates. Appendix B, *Tax Facts on Insurance & Employee Benefits (2011)* contains the table for Married Persons Filing Separately.

FEDERAL ESTATE & GIFT TAX RATES

Unified Rate Schedule

TAXABLE ESTATE/GIFT				OF EXCESS
OVER	TO	TAX EQUALS**	PLUS %	OVER
0	10,000	0	18	0
10,000	20,000	1,800	20	10,000
20,000	40,000	3,800	22	20,000
40,000	60,000	8,200	24	40,000
60,000	80,000	13,000	26	60,000
80,000	100,000	18,200	28	80,000
100,000	150,000	23,800	30	100,000
150,000	250,000	38,800	32	150,000
250,000	500,000	70,800	34	250,000

2010 – 2012*

500,000		155,800	35	500,000

2013 and Later**

500,000	750,000	155,800	37	500,000
750,000	1,000,000	248,300	39	750,000
1,000,000	1,250,000	345,800	41	1,000,000
1,250,000	1,500,000	448,300	43	1,250,000
1,500,000	2,000,000	555,800	45	1,500,000
2,000,000	2,500,000	780,800	49	2,000,000
2,500,000	3,000,000	1,025,800	53	2,500,000
3,000,000	10,000,000	1,290,800	55	3,000,000
10,000,000	17,184,000	5,140,800	60	10,000,000
17,184,000		9,451,200	55	17,184,000

* Under the provisions of The 2010 Tax Relief Act the basic exclusion amount for the years 2010 through 2012 is $5,000,000 (after 2011 the basic exclusion is indexed for inflation). The basic exclusion is also referred to as the "tax-free amount." In 2010 through 2012 estates above $500,000 are taxed at a flat rate of 35%. The credit in 2010 and 2011 is $1,730,800.

**Unless Congress changes the tax laws, in 2013 and thereafter estates over $1,000,000 will be subject to the estate tax, the unified credit will be $345,800, and the rate will extend up to 55% on estates over $17,184,000 (under the sunset provisions of EGTRRA 2001).

Gift Tax

In 2010 the gift tax application exclusion limited tax-free gifts to $1,000,000 (except for present interest gifts, see chart on page 47). In 2011 and 2012 the gift and estate tax systems are reunified and the gift tax basic exclusion amount is increased to $5,000,000 (i.e., substantial tax-free gifts can be made in 2011 and 2012). After 2011 the basic exclusion is indexed for inflation. Unless Congress changes the tax laws, in 2013 and thereafter the gift tax credit will revert to $345,800 meaning that the exclusion amount will decrease to $1,000,000.

See page 83 for calculation steps.

LIFETIME REQUIRED MINIMUM DISTRIBUTIONS

(Uniform Lifetime)

Age	Distribution Period	Age	Distribution Period	Age	Distribution Period	Age	Distribution Period	Age	Distribution Period
70	27.4	80	18.7	90	11.4	100	6.3	110	3.1
71	26.5	81	17.9	91	10.8	101	5.9	111	2.9
72	25.6	82	17.1	92	10.2	102	5.5	112	2.6
73	24.7	83	16.3	93	9.6	103	5.2	113	2.4
74	23.8	84	15.5	94	9.1	104	4.9	114	2.1
75	22.9	85	14.8	95	8.6	105	4.5	115 &	
76	22.0	86	14.1	96	8.1	106	4.2	Over	1.9
77	21.2	87	13.4	97	7.6	107	3.9		
78	20.3	88	12.7	98	7.1	108	3.7		
79	19.5	89	12.0	99	6.7	109	3.4		

Application: Used in calculating lifetime required minimum distributions from IRAs, qualified plans, and TSAs. For example, assume an individual turned age 74 in 2011, and on the previous December 31, 2010, his account balance was $325,000. Using this table, his life expectancy is 23.8 years. He must receive a distribution of $13,655 ($325,000 ÷ 23.8 = $13,655) for the 2011 year, no later than December 31, 2011. See the discussion on pages 433-435.

Source: Treasury Reg. §1.40(a)(9)-9, A-2

TABLE I RATES

Value Per $1,000 Of Life Insurance Protection For One Year

Ages	Value	Ages	Value	Ages	Value
Under 25	.60	40 to 44	1.20	60 to 64	7.92
25 to 29	.72	45 to 49	1.80	65 to 69	15.24
30 to 34	.96	50 to 54	2.76	70 & Over	24.72
35 to 39	1.08	55 to 59	5.16		

Application: As a measure of the value of excess group term insurance.

Source: Treas. Reg. §1.79-3(d)(2) – the rates as set forth in the regulation are given in costs per $1,000 of protection for 1-month periods (i.e., the cost at age 42 is 10 cents per $1,000 per month).

TABLE 2001 RATES
&
P.S. No. 58 RATES

One Year Term Premiums For $1,000 Of Life Insurance Protection

Age	Table 2001	P.S. 58	Age	Table 2001	P.S. 58	Age	Table 2001	P.S. 58	Age	Table 2001	P.S. 58
15	.38	1.27	32	.93	2.70	49	2.13	8.53	66	13.51	34.28
16	.52	1.38	33	.96	2.86	50	2.30	9.22	67	15.20	37.31
17	.57	1.48	34	.98	3.02	51	2.52	9.97	68	16.92	40.59
18	.59	1.52	35	.99	3.21	52	2.81	10.79	69	18.70	44.17
19	.61	1.56	36	1.01	3.41	53	3.20	11.69	70	20.62	48.06
20	.62	1.61	37	1.04	3.63	54	3.65	12.67	71	22.72	52.29
21	.62	1.67	38	1.06	3.87	55	4.15	13.74	72	25.07	56.89
22	.64	1.73	39	1.07	4.14	56	4.68	14.91	73	27.57	61.89
23	.66	1.79	40	1.10	4.42	57	5.20	16.18	74	30.18	67.33
24	.68	1.86	41	1.13	4.73	58	5.66	17.56	75	33.05	73.23
25	.71	1.93	42	1.20	5.07	59	6.06	19.08	76	36.33	79.63
26	.73	2.02	43	1.29	5.44	60	6.51	20.73	77	40.17	86.57
27	.76	2.11	44	1.40	5.85	61	7.11	22.53	78	44.33	94.09
28	.80	2.20	45	1.53	6.30	62	7.96	24.50	79	49.23	102.23
29	.83	2.31	46	1.67	6.78	63	9.08	26.63	80	54.56	111.04
30	.87	2.43	47	1.83	7.32	64	10.41	28.98	81	60.51	120.57
31	.90	2.57	48	1.98	7.89	65	11.90	31.51			

Application: As a measure of the value of insurance protection provided under; (1) split-dollar plans, (2) qualified pension and profit sharing plans, and (3) tax sheltered annuities.

Source: Notice 2002-8, 2002-4 CB 398; Revenue Ruling 55-747, 1955-2 CB 228; and Revenue Ruling 66-110, 1966-1 CB 12. Notice 2002-8 provides Table 2001 rates for below age 15 and above age 81 (Appendix C, *Tax Facts on Insurance & Employee Benefits (2011)* contains the full table).

NOTE: For plans entered into *on or after* January 28, 2002, until further IRS guidance is received, only Table 2001, or the insurer's published premium rates, may generally be used; with the qualification that for periods after December 31, 2003, if the insurer's published premium rates are used, the insurer must actually make known and sell term insurance at these rates (see Notice 2002-8 regarding limitations on using an insurer's published premium rates for periods after December 31, 2003). For split-dollar plans entered into *before* January 28, 2002, Table 2001 rates, P.S. 58 rates (if specified by the split-dollar agreement), or the insurer's published premium rates may generally be used.

TABLE 38

Probability Of Dying In Each Year Of Age

Age	Probability (q)	Age	Probability (q)	Age	Probability (q)
20	.00165	49	.00874	78	.09644
21	.00171	50	.00945	79	.10479
22	.00177	51	.01022	80	.11382
23	.00183	52	.01106	81	.12358
24	.00191	53	.01198	82	.13413
25	.00198	54	.01299	83	.14550
26	.00207	55	.01408	84	.15776
27	.00216	56	.01528	85	.17094
28	.00226	57	.01658	86	.18511
29	.00237	58	.01800	87	.20032
30	.00249	59	.01956	88	.21661
31	.00263	60	.02125	89	.23402
32	.00277	61	.02309	90	.25261
33	.00293	62	.02511	91	.27239
34	.00310	63	.02730	92	.29341
35	.00329	64	.02970	93	.31568
36	.00350	65	.03230	94	.33921
37	.00372	66	.03514	95	.36399
38	.00397	67	.03824	96	.39001
39	.00424	68	.04160	97	.41721
40	.00453	69	.04527	98	.44555
41	.00485	70	.04926	99	.47493
42	.00520	71	.05360	100	.50525
43	.00558	72	.05831	101	.53638
44	.00600	73	.06344	102	.56816
45	.00646	74	.06901	103	.60039
46	.00695	75	.07506	104	.63286
47	.00750	76	.08162	105	1.00000
48	.00809	77	.08873		

Explanation of Table. Table 38 has been used as a measure of the value to the employee of insurance protection provided under split-dollar plans involving survivorship life policies. Although based on the underlying actuarial assumptions of the P.S. 58 rates, the only authority for use of the Table 38 rates is an unofficial letter from the General Actuarial Branch of the IRS. In this letter it was suggested that: "it is acceptable to apply the formula for the one year term rate on an insurance of two lives, payable on the second death, as expressed by the symbols v q_x q_y where v is 1/1.025 and q_x q_y are the annual mortality rates for ages x and y computed from values in U.S. Life Table 38." The probability of two individuals dying in the same year can be calculated by multiplying their individual probabilities. For example, the probability of two individuals ages 65 and 70 dying in any one year is .0015911 (.03230 x .04926 = .0015911). The value per year per thousand of death benefit is $1.55 (1/1.025 x .03230 x .04926 x 1,000 = 1.55).

Limitations on Application: In Notice 2002-8 the IRS announced that the P.S. 58 rates can no longer be used for split-dollar plans entered into *on or after* January 28, 2002. Until further guidance is received, an argument could be made for using Table 38 rates in split-dollar plans entered into *before* January 28, 2002. As to plans entered on or after January 28, 2002, it is clear from Notice 2002-8 that the rates used should reflect "appropriate adjustments" to the Table 2001 rates set forth on page 552. Actuarial guidance should be requested from the issuing life insurance company. See also, treatment of Employer/Employee Split-Dollar Plans, on pages 296-298, and the discussion of Survivorship Life Insurance, on page 535.

COMMISSIONERS
1980 STANDARD ORDINARY MORTALITY TABLE

Age	Male deaths per 1,000	Male average future lifetime	Female deaths per 1,000	Female average future lifetime	Age	Male deaths per 1,000	Male average future lifetime	Female deaths per 1,000	Female average future lifetime
0	4.18	70.83	2.89	75.83	50	6.71	25.36	4.96	29.53
1	1.07	70.13	.87	75.04	51	7.30	24.52	5.31	28.67
2	.99	69.20	.81	74.11	52	7.96	23.70	5.70	27.82
3	.98	68.27	.79	73.17	53	8.71	22.89	6.15	26.98
4	.95	67.34	.77	72.23	54	9.56	22.08	6.61	26.14
5	.90	66.40	.76	71.28	55	10.47	21.29	7.09	25.31
6	.85	65.46	.73	70.34	56	11.46	20.51	7.57	24.49
7	.80	64.52	.72	69.39	57	12.49	19.74	8.03	23.67
8	.76	63.57	.70	68.44	58	13.59	18.99	8.47	22.86
9	.74	62.62	.69	67.48	59	14.77	18.24	8.94	22.05
10	.73	61.66	.68	66.53	60	16.08	17.51	9.47	21.25
11	.77	60.71	.69	65.58	61	17.54	16.79	10.13	20.44
12	.85	59.75	.72	64.62	62	19.19	16.08	10.96	19.65
13	.99	58.80	.75	63.67	63	21.06	15.38	12.02	18.86
14	1.15	57.86	.80	62.71	64	23.14	14.70	13.25	18.08
15	1.33	56.93	.85	61.76	65	25.42	14.04	14.59	17.32
16	1.51	56.00	.90	60.82	66	27.85	13.39	16.00	16.57
17	1.67	55.09	.95	59.87	67	30.44	12.76	17.43	15.83
18	1.78	54.18	.98	58.93	68	33.19	12.14	18.84	15.10
19	1.86	53.27	1.02	57.98	69	36.17	11.54	20.36	14.38
20	1.90	52.37	1.05	57.04	70	39.51	10.96	22.11	13.67
21	1.91	51.47	1.07	56.10	71	43.30	10.39	24.23	12.97
22	1.89	50.57	1.09	55.16	72	47.65	9.84	26.87	12.28
23	1.86	49.66	1.11	54.22	73	52.64	9.30	30.11	11.60
24	1.82	48.75	1.14	53.28	74	58.19	8.79	33.93	10.95
25	1.77	47.84	1.16	52.34	75	64.19	8.31	38.24	10.32
26	1.73	46.93	1.19	51.40	76	70.53	7.84	42.97	9.71
27	1.71	46.01	1.22	50.46	77	77.12	7.40	48.04	9.12
28	1.70	45.09	1.26	49.52	78	83.90	6.97	53.45	8.55
29	1.71	44.16	1.30	48.59	79	91.05	6.57	59.35	8.01
30	1.73	43.24	1.35	47.65	80	98.84	6.18	65.99	7.48
31	1.78	42.31	1.40	46.71	81	107.48	5.80	73.60	6.98
32	1.83	41.38	1.45	45.78	82	117.25	5.44	82.40	6.49
33	1.91	40.46	1.50	44.84	83	128.26	5.09	92.53	6.03
34	2.00	39.54	1.58	43.91	84	140.25	4.77	103.81	5.59
35	2.11	38.61	1.65	42.98	85	152.95	4.46	116.10	5.18
36	2.24	37.69	1.76	42.05	86	166.09	4.18	129.29	4.80
37	2.40	36.78	1.89	41.12	87	179.55	3.91	143.32	4.43
38	2.58	35.87	2.04	40.20	88	193.27	3.66	158.18	4.09
39	2.79	34.96	2.22	39.28	89	207.29	3.41	173.94	3.77
40	3.02	34.05	2.42	38.36	90	221.77	3.18	190.75	3.45
41	3.29	33.16	2.64	37.46	91	236.98	2.94	208.87	3.15
42	3.56	32.26	2.87	36.55	92	253.45	2.70	228.81	2.85
43	3.87	31.38	3.09	35.66	93	272.11	2.44	251.51	2.55
44	4.19	30.50	3.32	34.77	94	295.90	2.17	279.31	2.24
45	4.55	29.62	3.56	33.88	95	329.96	1.87	317.32	1.91
46	4.92	28.76	3.80	33.00	96	384.55	1.54	375.74	1.56
47	5.32	27.90	4.05	32.12	97	480.20	1.20	474.97	1.21
48	5.74	27.04	4.33	31.25	98	657.98	.84	655.85	.84
49	6.21	26.20	4.63	30.39	99	1000.00	.50	1000.00	.50

Source: Selected figures from published table. Age is given as nearest birthday.

COMMISSIONERS
2001 STANDARD ORDINARY MORTALITY TABLE

| | Male | | Female | | | Male | | Female | |
Age	deaths per 1,000	average future lifetime	deaths per 1,000	average future lifetime	Age	deaths per 1,000	average future lifetime	deaths per 1,000	average future lifetime
0	.97	76.62	.48	80.84	40	1.65	38.33	1.30	42.00
1	.56	75.69	.35	79.88	41	1.79	37.39	1.38	41.05
2	.39	74.74	.26	78.91	42	1.96	36.46	1.48	40.11
3	.27	73.76	.20	77.93	43	2.15	35.53	1.59	39.17
4	.21	72.78	.19	76.95	44	2.39	34.61	1.72	38.23
5	.21	71.80	.18	75.96	45	2.65	33.69	1.87	37.29
6	.22	70.81	.18	74.97	46	2.90	32.78	2.05	36.36
7	.22	69.83	.21	73.99	47	3.17	31.87	2.27	35.43
8	.22	68.84	.21	73.00	48	3.33	30.97	2.50	34.51
9	.23	67.86	.21	72.02	49	3.52	30.07	2.78	33.60
10	.23	66.88	.22	71.03	50	3.76	29.18	3.08	32.69
11	.27	65.89	.23	70.05	51	4.06	28.28	3.41	31.79
12	.33	64.91	.27	69.07	52	4.47	27.40	3.79	30.90
13	.39	63.93	.30	68.08	53	4.93	26.52	4.20	30.01
14	.47	62.95	.33	67.10	54	5.50	25.65	4.63	29.14
15	.61	61.98	.35	66.13	55	6.17	24.79	5.10	28.27
16	.74	61.02	.39	65.15	56	6.88	23.94	5.63	27.41
17	.87	60.07	.41	64.17	57	7.64	23.10	6.19	26.57
18	.94	59.12	.43	63.20	58	8.27	22.27	6.80	25.73
19	.98	58.17	.46	62.23	59	8.99	21.45	7.39	24.90
20	1.00	57.23	.47	61.26	60	9.86	20.64	8.01	24.08
21	1.00	56.29	.48	60.28	61	10.94	19.85	8.68	23.27
22	1.02	55.34	.50	59.31	62	12.25	19.06	9.39	22.47
23	1.03	54.40	.50	58.34	63	13.71	18.29	10.14	21.68
24	1.05	53.45	.52	57.37	64	15.24	17.54	10.96	20.90
25	1.07	52.51	.54	56.40	65	16.85	16.80	11.85	20.12
26	1.12	51.57	.56	55.43	66	18.47	16.08	12.82	19.36
27	1.17	50.62	.60	54.46	67	20.09	15.37	13.89	18.60
28	1.17	49.68	.63	53.49	68	21.85	14.68	15.07	17.86
29	1.15	48.74	.66	52.53	69	23.64	13.99	16.36	17.12
30	1.14	47.79	.68	51.56	70	25.77	13.32	17.81	16.40
31	1.13	46.85	.73	50.60	71	28.15	12.66	19.47	15.69
32	1.13	45.90	.77	49.63	72	31.32	12.01	21.30	14.99
33	1.15	44.95	.82	48.67	73	34.62	11.39	23.30	14.31
34	1.18	44.00	.88	47.71	74	38.08	10.78	25.50	13.64
35	1.21	43.05	.97	46.75	75	41.91	10.18	27.90	12.98
36	1.28	42.11	1.03	45.80	76	46.08	9.61	30.53	12.34
37	1.34	41.16	1.11	44.84	77	50.92	9.05	33.41	11.71
38	1.44	40.21	1.17	43.89	78	56.56	8.50	36.58	11.10
39	1.54	39.27	1.23	42.94	79	63.06	7.98	40.05	10.50

Source: Composite figures from 2001 CSO published table (ultimate only). Age is given as nearest birthday. Death is assumed to occur at age plus six months. See next page for selected nonsmoker and smoker figures.

COMMISSIONERS
2001 STANDARD ORDINARY MORTALITY TABLE (continued)

	Male		Female			Male		Female	
Age	deaths per 1,000	average future lifetime	deaths per 1,000	average future lifetime	Age	deaths per 1,000	average future lifetime	deaths per 1,000	average future lifetime
80	70.14	7.49	43.86	9.92	100	363.19	2.07	275.73	2.61
81	78.19	7.01	49.11	9.35	101	380.08	1.96	297.84	2.42
82	86.54	6.57	54.95	8.81	102	398.06	1.86	322.21	2.23
83	95.51	6.14	60.81	8.29	103	417.20	1.76	349.06	2.06
84	105.43	5.74	67.27	7.79	104	437.56	1.66	378.61	1.89
85	116.57	5.36	74.45	7.32	105	459.21	1.57	410.57	1.74
86	128.91	5.00	80.99	6.87	106	482.22	1.48	443.33	1.60
87	142.35	4.66	90.79	6.43	107	506.69	1.39	476.89	1.47
88	156.73	4.35	101.07	6.02	108	532.69	1.30	510.65	1.36
89	171.88	4.07	112.02	5.64	109	560.31	1.22	545.81	1.25
90	187.66	3.81	121.92	5.29	110	589.64	1.14	581.77	1.16
91	202.44	3.57	126.85	4.96	111	620.79	1.07	616.33	1.08
92	217.83	3.35	136.88	4.61	112	653.84	.99	649.85	1.00
93	234.04	3.15	151.64	4.26	113	688.94	.92	680.37	.93
94	251.14	2.96	170.31	3.93	114	726.18	.85	723.39	.86
95	269.17	2.78	193.66	3.63	115	765.70	.79	763.41	.79
96	285.64	2.62	215.66	3.38	116	807.61	.72	804.93	.73
97	303.18	2.47	238.48	3.18	117	852.07	.66	850.44	.67
98	321.88	2.32	242.16	3.02	118	899.23	.61	892.44	.61
99	341.85	2.19	255.23	2.82	119	949.22	.55	935.11	.56
					120	1000.00	.50	1000.00	.50

Source: Composite figures from 2001 CSO published table (ultimate only). Age is given as nearest birthday. Death is assumed to occur at age plus six months. See below for selected nonsmoker and smoker figures.

NonSmoker vs. Smoker

	Male					Female			
	Nonsmoker		Smoker			Nonsmoker		Smoker	
Age	deaths per 1,000	average future lifetime	deaths per 1,000	average future lifetime	Age	deaths per 1,000	average future lifetime	deaths per 1,000	average future lifetime
20	.95	57.95	1.27	52.86	20	.45	61.79	.58	56.07
25	.98	53.22	1.63	48.22	25	.50	56.93	.77	51.24
30	1.02	48.48	1.80	43.62	30	.64	52.09	1.03	46.45
35	1.09	43.72	2.00	39.00	35	.89	47.27	1.53	41.72
40	1.46	38.97	2.77	34.42	40	1.20	42.49	2.12	37.07
45	2.33	34.29	4.57	29.96	45	1.71	37.77	3.13	32.49
50	3.32	29.73	6.45	25.70	50	2.81	33.14	5.39	28.08
55	5.50	25.28	10.56	21.62	55	4.68	28.68	9.08	23.96
60	8.92	21.06	16.29	17.88	60	7.40	24.43	13.97	20.16
65	15.47	17.13	26.63	14.51	65	11.05	20.41	20.34	16.67

Source: Selected smoker and nonsmoker figures are calculated from the 2001 CSO published table (ultimate only). Age is given as nearest birthday.

HEALTHY LIFE EXPECTANCY

				Expected Years			
	of life	in excellent health	in good or better health	without any activity limitation	without major activity limitation	without work limitation	without ADL assistance*
Male							
At Birth	72.8	27.1	64.6	60.5	68.5	-	-
20 years	54.0	17.2	46.2	43.0	49.8	47.9	52.9
30 years	44.9	13.0	37.3	34.4	40.8	39.2	43.7
45 years	31.5	7.4	24.6	22.5	27.9	26.9	30.4
65 years	15.9	2.4	11.2	9.9	14.1	14.4	14.9
70 years	12.8	1.7	8.8	8.0	11.8	-	11.8
75 years	10.1	1.2	6.7	5.9	9.1	-	9.1
80 years	7.7	0.8	4.9	4.3	6.8	-	6.8
Female							
At Birth	78.8	25.7	68.4	64.6	74.7	-	-
20 years	59.8	15.8	49.8	46.3	55.7	53.5	58.1
30 years	50.1	12.3	40.6	37.3	46.1	44.3	48.4
45 years	35.9	7.3	27.6	24.6	32.4	31.2	34.3
65 years	18.8	2.8	13.4	11.4	16.8	17.6	17.3
70 years	15.1	2.1	10.6	8.9	13.7	-	13.7
75 years	11.7	1.6	8.0	6.3	10.3	-	10.3
80 years	8.7	1.2	5.7	4.0	7.2	-	7.2

*ADL refers to activities of daily living (see discussion of Qualified Long-Term Care Insurance on page 489).

Source: U.S. Department of Health and Human Services & National Center for Health Statistics, *Healthy People 2010 - Summary Measures of Population Health*, 2003, Tables 3.1- 3.4 (1995 data) on pages 30-33 (http://www.cdc.gov/nchs/healthy_people. htm).

LONGEVITY IN RETIREMENT – Male

Current Age	Chances of Living to Age										
	70	71	72	73	74	75	76	77	78	79	80
60	82.8	80.3	77.7	74.9	72.0	68.9	65.7	62.4	59.0	55.4	51.7
61	83.8	81.3	78.6	75.8	72.8	69.8	66.5	63.2	59.7	56.1	52.3
62	84.9	82.4	79.7	76.8	73.8	70.7	67.4	64.0	60.5	56.8	53.0
63	86.1	83.6	80.8	77.9	74.9	71.7	68.4	65.0	61.4	57.6	53.8
64	87.5	84.9	82.1	79.2	76.1	72.9	69.5	66.0	62.4	58.6	54.7
65	89.1	86.4	83.6	80.6	77.4	74.2	70.7	67.2	63.5	59.6	55.6
66	90.8	88.1	85.2	82.1	78.9	75.6	72.1	68.5	64.7	60.8	56.7
67	92.7	89.9	87.0	83.9	80.6	77.2	73.6	69.9	66.1	62.0	57.9
68	94.9	92.0	89.0	85.8	82.5	79.0	75.4	71.6	67.6	63.5	59.3
69	97.3	94.4	91.3	88.0	84.6	81.0	77.3	73.4	69.3	65.1	60.8
70		97.0	93.8	90.5	87.0	83.3	79.4	75.4	71.3	66.9	62.5
71			96.7	93.3	89.6	85.8	81.9	77.8	73.4	69.0	64.4
72				96.4	92.7	88.8	84.7	80.4	75.9	71.3	66.6
73					96.1	92.0	87.8	83.4	78.8	74.0	69.0
74						95.8	91.4	86.7	81.9	77.0	71.8
75							95.4	90.6	85.6	80.4	75.0
76								95.0	89.7	84.2	78.6
77									94.5	88.7	82.8
78										93.9	87.7
79											93.3

Current Age	Chances of Living to Age										
	81	82	83	84	85	86	87	88	89	90	95
60	47.9	44.0	40.1	36.1	32.2	28.3	24.5	20.9	17.5	14.4	3.9
61	48.5	44.6	40.6	36.6	32.6	28.6	24.8	21.2	17.7	14.6	3.9
62	49.1	45.2	41.1	37.0	33.0	29.0	25.1	21.4	18.0	14.8	4.0
63	49.9	45.8	41.7	37.6	33.5	29.4	25.5	21.8	18.2	15.0	4.0
64	50.7	46.5	42.4	38.2	34.0	29.9	25.9	22.1	18.5	15.3	4.1
65	51.5	47.4	43.1	38.9	34.6	30.4	26.4	22.5	18.9	15.5	4.2
66	52.5	48.3	44.0	39.6	35.3	31.0	26.9	22.9	19.2	15.8	4.2
67	53.7	49.3	44.9	40.5	36.0	31.7	27.5	23.4	19.6	16.2	4.3
68	54.9	50.5	45.9	41.4	36.9	32.4	28.1	24.0	20.1	16.5	4.4
69	56.3	51.7	47.1	42.5	37.8	33.2	28.8	24.6	20.6	17.0	4.5
70	57.9	53.2	48.4	43.6	38.9	34.2	29.6	25.3	21.2	17.4	4.7
71	59.7	54.8	49.9	45.0	40.1	35.2	30.5	26.0	21.8	18.0	4.8
72	61.7	56.7	51.6	46.5	41.4	36.4	31.6	26.9	22.6	18.6	5.0
73	64.0	58.8	53.5	48.2	43.0	37.8	32.7	27.9	23.4	19.3	5.2
74	66.6	61.2	55.7	50.2	44.7	39.3	34.1	29.1	24.4	20.0	5.4
75	69.5	63.9	58.2	52.4	46.7	41.0	35.6	30.3	25.4	20.9	5.6
76	72.9	67.0	61.0	54.9	48.9	43.0	37.3	31.8	26.7	21.9	5.9
77	76.7	70.5	64.2	57.9	51.5	45.3	39.3	33.5	28.1	23.1	6.2
78	81.2	74.6	68.0	61.3	54.6	48.0	41.6	35.5	29.7	24.5	6.6
79	86.5	79.5	72.4	65.2	58.1	51.1	44.2	37.7	31.7	26.1	7.0

Application: Used for estimating years in retirement. For example, a male age 65 stands a 55.6% chance of living to age 80 (i.e., 556 out of 1,000 males age 65 will live to age 80).

Source: Calculations are based upon the longevity data contained in the 2008 Valuation Basic Table developed by the Society of Actuaries.

LONGEVITY IN RETIREMENT – Female

Current Age	Chances of Living to Age										
	70	71	72	73	74	75	76	77	78	79	80
60	88.4	86.7	84.8	82.8	80.7	78.5	76.0	73.5	70.7	67.8	64.7
61	89.1	87.4	85.5	83.5	81.3	79.1	76.6	74.0	71.3	68.3	65.2
62	89.9	88.1	86.2	84.2	82.0	79.7	77.3	74.7	71.9	68.9	65.8
63	90.7	89.0	87.1	85.0	82.8	80.5	78.0	75.4	72.6	69.6	66.4
64	91.7	89.9	88.0	85.9	83.7	81.3	78.8	76.2	73.3	70.3	67.1
65	92.7	90.9	89.0	86.9	84.6	82.3	79.7	77.0	74.2	71.1	67.9
66	93.9	92.0	90.1	87.9	85.7	83.3	80.7	78.0	75.1	72.0	68.7
67	95.2	93.3	91.3	89.2	86.9	84.4	81.8	79.1	76.1	73.0	69.7
68	96.6	94.7	92.7	90.5	88.2	85.7	83.1	80.3	77.3	74.1	70.7
69	98.2	96.3	94.2	92.0	89.6	87.1	84.5	81.6	78.6	75.3	71.9
70		98.0	95.9	93.7	91.3	88.7	86.0	83.1	80.0	76.7	73.2
71			97.9	95.5	93.1	90.5	87.7	84.7	81.6	78.2	74.6
72				97.6	95.1	92.5	89.6	86.6	83.4	79.9	76.3
73					97.4	94.7	91.8	88.7	85.4	81.9	78.1
74						97.2	94.2	91.0	87.6	84.0	80.2
75							96.9	93.7	90.2	86.4	82.5
76								96.6	93.0	89.2	85.1
77									96.3	92.3	88.1
78										95.9	91.5
79											95.4

Current Age	Chances of Living to Age										
	81	82	83	84	85	86	87	88	89	90	95
60	61.4	57.9	54.3	50.5	46.5	42.4	38.3	34.2	30.0	26.0	9.4
61	61.9	58.4	54.7	50.9	46.9	42.8	38.6	34.4	30.3	26.2	9.4
62	62.4	58.9	55.2	51.3	47.3	43.1	38.9	34.7	30.5	26.4	9.5
63	63.0	59.5	55.7	51.8	47.7	43.5	39.3	35.0	30.8	26.7	9.6
64	63.7	60.1	56.3	52.3	48.2	44.0	39.7	35.4	31.1	26.9	9.7
65	64.4	60.8	56.9	52.9	48.8	44.5	40.2	35.8	31.5	27.2	9.8
66	65.2	61.5	57.6	53.6	49.4	45.1	40.7	36.3	31.9	27.6	9.9
67	66.1	62.4	58.4	54.3	50.1	45.7	41.2	36.8	32.3	28.0	10.1
68	67.1	63.3	59.3	55.1	50.8	46.4	41.9	37.3	32.8	28.4	10.2
69	68.2	64.4	60.3	56.0	51.7	47.1	42.6	37.9	33.3	28.8	10.4
70	69.5	65.5	61.4	57.1	52.6	48.0	43.3	38.6	33.9	29.4	10.6
71	70.8	66.8	62.6	58.2	53.6	49.0	44.2	39.4	34.6	30.0	10.8
72	72.4	68.3	64.0	59.5	54.8	50.0	45.2	40.3	35.4	30.6	11.0
73	74.1	69.9	65.5	60.9	56.1	51.2	46.2	41.2	36.2	31.4	11.3
74	76.1	71.8	67.2	62.5	57.6	52.6	47.5	42.3	37.2	32.2	11.6
75	78.3	73.9	69.2	64.3	59.3	54.1	48.8	43.5	38.3	33.1	11.9
76	80.8	76.2	71.4	66.4	61.2	55.8	50.4	44.9	39.5	34.2	12.3
77	83.6	78.9	73.9	68.7	63.3	57.8	52.1	46.5	40.9	35.4	12.7
78	86.8	81.9	76.7	71.3	65.7	60.0	54.2	48.3	42.4	36.7	13.2
79	90.6	85.4	80.0	74.4	68.6	62.6	56.5	50.4	44.3	38.3	13.8

Application: Used for estimating years in retirement. For example, a female age 65 stands a 67.9% chance of living to age 80 (i.e., 679 out of 1,000 females age 65 will live to age 80).

Source: Calculations are based upon the longevity data contained in the 2008 Valuation Basic Table developed by the Society of Actuaries.

COMPOUND INTEREST & FUTURE VALUE OF MONEY

Given the choice of being paid $1.00 today,
or $1.00 four years from now,
you would choose to be paid $1.00 today.

AND

Given the choice of being paid $1.00 today,
or $16.00 four years from now,
you would choose to be paid $16.00 four years from now.

HOWEVER

Given the choice of being paid $1.00 today,
or $1.50 four years from now,
your decision would require you to carefully consider the

FUTURE VALUE OF MONEY

The future value of money is a very important concept in estate and business planning and can be best understood by referring to the Future Value Table on page 562. If you took the $1.00 today and could invest it at 8 percent, you would have $1.36 in four years (read down the 8 percent rate column until year 4). By waiting four years, you could receive $1.50, which is 14 cents more than you would get by taking the money and investing it at 8 percent.

However, if you believed that you could invest your funds at 18 percent, you would expect to have $1.94 in four years ($1.00 × 1.939 = $1.939). In this case you would probably take the $1.00 today rather than the $1.50 in four years.

But what if your choice was as follows:

Being paid $1.00 each year for the next 4 years,
or being paid $5.50 4 years from now.

The Future Value Table on page 563, will help you make the decision, since it shows the sum to which one dollar per year will grow if placed in accounts at varying rates of interest. If you took the $1.00 each year and were able to invest it at 8 percent, you would have $4.87 in four years ($1.00 × 4.867 = $4.867). By waiting four years, you could receive $5.50, which is 63 cents more than you would have by taking the money and investing it at 8 percent.

However, if you believed that you could invest your funds at 15 percent, you would expect to have $5.74 in four years ($1.00 × 5.742 = $5.74). In this case you would probably take the $1.00 each year for the next four years.

COMPOUND INTEREST & PRESENT VALUE OF MONEY

Given the choice of being paid $1.00 three years from now,
or $1.00 four years from now,
you would choose to be paid $1.00 three years from now.

AND

Given the choice of being paid $1.00 three years from now,
or $2.00 four years from now,
you would choose to be paid $2.00 four years from now.

HOWEVER

Given the choice of being paid $1.00 three years from now,
or $1.15 four years from now,
your decision would require you to carefully consider the

PRESENT VALUE OF MONEY

The present value of money can be calculated by referring to the Present Value Table on page 564. If you viewed money as having a time value of 8 percent, the present value of that $1.00 payment due in three years from now is 79 cents ($1.00 × .7938 = $.7938). The present value of a $1.15 payment four years from now is 84 cents ($1.15 × .7350 = $.84525). You would accept payment of $1.15 four years from now.

However, if you viewed money as having a time value of 18 percent, the present value of that $1.00 payment due in three years from now is 61 cents ($1.00 × .6086 = $.6086). The present value of a $1.15 payment four years from now is only 59 cents ($1.15 × .5158 = $.59317). You would not accept the offer to pay $1.15 four years from now, but would rather demand payment of $1.00 three years from now.

But what if your choice was as follows:

Being paid $1.25 at the end of each year for the next 3 years,
or being paid $1.00 at the end of each year for the next 4 years.

The Present Value Table on page 565, will help you make the decision. If you viewed money as having a time value of 8 percent, the present value of that $1.25 payment at the end of each year for the next three years is $3.22 ($1.25 × 2.577 = $3.22125). The present value of a $1.00 payment each year for four years is $3.31 ($1.00 × 3.312 = $3.312). You would accept payment of $1.00 per year for the next four years.

However, if you viewed money as having a time value of 18 percent, the present value of that $1.25 payment at the end of each year for the next three years is $2.72 ($1.25 × 2.174 = $2.7175). The present value of a $1.00 payment each year for four years is $2.69 ($1.00 × 2.690 = $2.690). You would not accept payment of $1.00 per year for four years, but would rather demand payment of $1.25 per year for the next three years.

FUTURE VALUE TABLE

The Sum To Which One Dollar Principal Will Increase

Years	5%	6%	7%	8%	9%	10%	12%	15%	18%
1	1.050	1.060	1.070	1.080	1.090	1.100	1.120	1.150	1.180
2	1.102	1.124	1.145	1.166	1.188	1.210	1.254	1.323	1.392
3	1.158	1.191	1.225	1.260	1.295	1.331	1.405	1.521	1.643
4	1.216	1.262	1.311	1.360	1.412	1.464	1.574	1.749	1.939
5	1.276	1.338	1.403	1.469	1.539	1.611	1.762	2.011	2.288
6	1.340	1.419	1.501	1.587	1.677	1.772	1.974	2.313	2.700
7	1.407	1.504	1.606	1.714	1.828	1.949	2.211	2.660	3.185
8	1.477	1.594	1.718	1.851	1.993	2.144	2.476	3.059	3.759
9	1.551	1.689	1.838	1.999	2.172	2.358	2.773	3.518	4.435
10	1.629	1.791	1.967	2.159	2.367	2.594	3.106	4.046	5.234
11	1.710	1.898	2.105	2.332	2.580	2.853	3.479	4.652	6.176
12	1.796	2.012	2.252	2.518	2.813	3.138	3.896	5.350	7.288
13	1.886	2.133	2.410	2.720	3.066	3.452	4.363	6.153	8.599
14	1.980	2.261	2.579	2.937	3.342	3.797	4.887	7.076	10.147
15	2.079	2.397	2.759	3.172	3.642	4.177	5.474	8.137	11.974
16	2.183	2.540	2.952	3.426	3.970	4.595	6.130	9.358	14.129
17	2.292	2.693	3.159	3.700	4.328	5.054	6.866	10.761	16.672
18	2.407	2.854	3.380	3.996	4.717	5.560	7.690	12.375	19.673
19	2.527	3.026	3.617	4.316	5.142	6.116	8.613	14.232	23.214
20	2.653	3.207	3.870	4.661	5.604	6.727	9.646	16.367	27.393
21	2.786	3.400	4.141	5.034	6.109	7.400	10.804	18.822	32.324
22	2.925	3.604	4.430	5.437	6.659	8.140	12.100	21.645	38.142
23	3.072	3.820	4.741	5.871	7.258	8.954	13.552	24.891	45.008
24	3.225	4.049	5.072	6.341	7.911	9.850	15.179	28.625	53.109
25	3.386	4.292	5.427	6.848	8.623	10.835	17.000	32.919	62.669
26	3.556	4.549	5.807	7.396	9.399	11.918	19.040	37.857	73.949
27	3.733	4.822	6.214	7.988	10.245	13.110	21.325	43.535	87.260
28	3.920	5.112	6.649	8.627	11.167	14.421	23.884	50.066	102.967
29	4.116	5.418	7.114	9.317	12.172	15.863	26.750	57.575	121.501
30	4.322	5.743	7.612	10.063	13.268	17.449	29.960	66.212	143.371
31	4.538	6.088	8.145	10.868	14.462	19.194	33.555	76.144	169.177
32	4.765	6.453	8.715	11.737	15.763	21.114	37.582	87.565	199.629
33	5.003	6.841	9.325	12.676	17.182	23.225	42.092	100.700	235.563
34	5.253	7.251	9.978	13.690	18.728	25.548	47.143	115.805	277.964
35	5.516	7.686	10.677	14.785	20.414	28.102	52.800	133.176	327.997
36	5.792	8.147	11.424	15.968	22.251	30.913	59.136	153.152	387.037
37	6.081	8.636	12.224	17.246	24.254	34.004	66.232	176.125	456.703
38	6.385	9.154	13.079	18.625	26.437	37.404	74.180	202.543	538.910
39	6.705	9.704	13.995	20.115	28.816	41.145	83.081	232.925	635.914
40	7.040	10.286	14.974	21.725	31.409	45.259	93.051	267.864	750.378

Rate

FUTURE VALUE TABLE

The Sum To Which One Dollar Per Annum,
Paid At The *Beginning* Of Each Year, Will Increase

				Rate				
	5%	6%	7%	8%	9%	10%	12%	15%
Years								
1	1.050	1.060	1.070	1.080	1.090	1.100	1.120	1.150
2	2.152	2.184	2.215	2.246	2.278	2.310	2.374	2.472
3	3.310	3.375	3.440	3.506	3.573	3.641	3.779	3.993
4	4.526	4.637	4.751	4.867	4.985	5.105	5.353	5.742
5	5.802	5.975	6.153	6.336	6.523	6.716	7.115	7.754
6	7.142	7.394	7.654	7.923	8.200	8.487	9.089	10.067
7	8.549	8.897	9.260	9.637	10.028	10.436	11.300	12.727
8	10.027	10.491	10.978	11.488	12.021	12.579	13.776	15.786
9	11.578	12.181	12.816	13.487	14.193	14.937	16.549	19.304
10	13.207	13.972	14.784	15.645	16.560	17.531	19.655	23.349
11	14.917	15.870	16.888	17.977	19.141	20.384	23.133	28.002
12	16.713	17.882	19.141	20.495	21.953	23.523	27.029	33.352
13	18.599	20.015	22.550	23.215	25.019	26.975	31.393	39.505
14	20.579	22.276	24.129	26.152	28.361	30.772	36.280	46.580
15	22.657	24.673	26.888	29.324	32.003	34.950	41.753	54.717
16	24.840	27.213	29.840	32.750	35.974	39.545	47.884	64.075
17	27.132	29.906	32.999	36.450	40.301	44.599	54.750	74.836
18	29.539	32.760	36.379	40.446	45.018	50.159	62.440	87.212
19	32.066	35.786	39.995	44.762	50.160	56.275	71.052	101.444
20	34.719	38.993	43.865	49.423	55.765	63.002	80.699	117.810
21	37.505	42.392	48.006	54.457	61.873	70.403	91.503	136.632
22	40.430	45.996	52.436	59.893	68.532	78.543	103.603	158.276
23	43.502	49.816	57.177	65.765	75.790	87.497	117.155	183.168
24	46.727	53.865	62.249	72.106	83.701	97.347	132.334	211.793
25	50.113	58.156	67.676	78.954	92.324	108.182	149.334	244.712
26	53.669	62.706	73.484	86.351	101.723	120.100	168.374	282.569
27	57.403	67.528	79.698	94.339	111.968	133.210	189.699	326.104
28	61.323	72.640	86.347	102.966	123.135	147.631	213.583	376.170
29	65.439	78.058	93.461	112.283	135.308	163.494	240.333	433.745
30	69.761	83.802	101.073	122.346	148.575	180.943	270.293	499.957
31	74.299	89.890	109.218	133.214	163.037	200.138	303.848	576.100
32	79.064	96.343	117.933	144.951	178.800	221.252	341.429	663.666
33	84.067	103.184	127.259	157.627	195.982	244.477	383.521	764.365
34	89.320	110.435	137.237	171.317	214.711	270.024	430.663	880.170
35	94.836	118.121	147.913	186.102	235.125	298.127	483.463	1013.346
36	100.628	126.268	159.337	202.070	257.376	329.039	542.599	1166.498
37	106.710	134.904	171.561	219.316	281.630	363.043	608.831	1342.622
38	113.095	144.058	184.640	237.941	308.066	400.448	683.010	1545.165
39	119.800	153.762	198.635	258.057	336.882	441.593	766.091	1778.090
40	126.840	164.048	213.610	279.781	368.292	486.852	859.142	2045.954

PRESENT VALUE TABLE

The Worth Today of One Dollar Due In The Future

Years	5%	6%	7%	8%	9%	10%	12%	15%	18%
1	.9524	.9434	.9346	.9259	.9174	.9091	.8929	.8696	.8475
2	.9070	.8900	.8734	.8573	.8417	.8264	.7972	.7561	.7182
3	.8638	.8396	.8163	.7938	.7722	.7513	.7118	.6575	.6086
4	.8227	.7921	.7629	.7350	.7084	.6830	.6355	.5718	.5158
5	.7835	.7473	.7130	.6806	.6499	.6209	.5674	.4972	.4371
6	.7462	.7050	.6663	.6302	.5963	.5645	.5066	.4323	.3704
7	.7107	.6651	.6227	.5835	.5470	.5132	.4523	.3759	.3139
8	.6768	.6274	.5820	.5403	.5019	.4665	.4039	.3269	.2660
9	.6446	.5919	.5439	.5002	.4604	.4241	.3606	.2843	.2255
10	.6139	.5584	.5083	.4632	.4224	.3855	.3220	.2472	.1911
11	.5847	.5268	.4751	.4289	.3875	.3505	.2875	.2149	.1619
12	.5568	.4970	.4440	.3971	.3555	.3186	.2567	.1869	.1372
13	.5303	.4688	.4150	.3677	.3262	.2897	.2292	.1625	.1163
14	.5051	.4423	.3878	.3405	.2992	.2633	.2046	.1413	.0985
15	.4810	.4173	.3624	.3152	.2745	.2394	.1827	.1229	.0835
16	.4581	.3936	.3387	.2919	.2519	.2176	.1631	.1069	.0708
17	.4363	.3714	.3166	.2703	.2311	.1978	.1456	.0929	.0600
18	.4155	.3503	.2959	.2502	.2120	.1799	.1300	.0808	.0508
19	.3957	.3305	.2765	.2317	.1945	.1635	.1161	.0703	.0431
20	.3769	.3118	.2584	.2145	.1784	.1486	.1037	.0611	.0365
21	.3589	.2942	.2415	.1987	.1637	.1351	.0926	.0531	.0309
22	.3419	.2775	.2257	.1839	.1502	.1228	.0826	.0462	.0262
23	.3256	.2618	.2109	.1703	.1378	.1117	.0738	.0402	.0222
24	.3101	.2470	.1971	.1577	.1264	.1015	.0659	.0349	.0188
25	.2953	.2330	.1842	.1460	.1160	.0923	.0588	.0304	.0160
26	.2812	.2198	.1722	.1352	.1064	.0839	.0525	.0264	.0135
27	.2678	.2074	.1609	.1252	.0976	.0763	.0469	.0230	.0115
28	.2551	.1956	.1504	.1159	.0895	.0693	.0419	.0200	.0097
29	.2429	.1846	.1406	.1073	.0822	.0630	.0374	.0174	.0082
30	.2314	.1741	.1314	.0994	.0754	.0573	.0334	.0151	.0070
31	.2204	.1643	.1228	.0920	.0691	.0521	.0298	.0131	.0059
32	.2099	.1550	.1147	.0852	.0634	.0474	.0266	.0114	.0050
33	.1999	.1462	.1072	.0789	.0582	.0431	.0238	.0099	.0042
34	.1904	.1379	.1002	.0730	.0534	.0391	.0212	.0086	.0036
35	.1813	.1301	.0937	.0676	.0490	.0356	.0189	.0075	.0030
36	.1727	.1227	.0875	.0626	.0449	.0323	.0169	.0065	.0026
37	.1644	.1158	.0818	.0580	.0412	.0294	.0151	.0057	.0022
38	.1566	.1092	.0765	.0537	.0378	.0267	.0135	.0049	.0019
39	.1491	.1031	.0715	.0497	.0347	.0243	.0120	.0043	.0016
40	.1420	.0972	.0668	.0460	.0318	.0221	.0107	.0037	.0013

PRESENT VALUE TABLE

The Worth Today of One Dollar Per Annum
Paid At The *End* of Each Year

					Rate				
Years	5%	6%	7%	8%	9%	10%	12%	15%	18%
1	.952	.943	.935	.926	.917	.909	.893	.870	.847
2	1.859	1.833	1.808	1.783	1.759	1.736	1.690	1.626	1.566
3	2.723	2.673	2.624	2.577	2.531	2.487	2.402	2.283	2.174
4	3.546	3.465	3.387	3.312	3.240	3.170	3.037	2.855	2.690
5	4.329	4.212	4.100	3.993	3.890	3.791	3.605	3.352	3.127
6	5.076	4.917	4.767	4.623	4.486	4.355	4.111	3.784	3.498
7	5.786	5.582	5.389	5.206	5.033	4.868	4.564	4.160	3.812
8	6.463	6.210	5.971	5.747	5.535	5.335	4.968	4.487	4.078
9	7.108	6.802	6.515	6.247	5.995	5.759	5.328	4.772	4.303
10	7.722	7.360	7.024	6.710	6.418	6.145	5.650	5.019	4.494
11	8.306	7.887	7.499	7.139	6.805	6.495	5.938	5.234	4.656
12	8.863	8.384	7.943	7.536	7.161	6.814	6.194	5.421	4.793
13	9.394	8.853	8.358	7.904	7.487	7.103	6.424	5.583	4.910
14	9.899	9.295	8.745	8.244	7.786	7.367	6.628	5.724	5.008
15	10.380	9.712	9.108	8.559	8.061	7.606	6.811	5.847	5.092
16	10.838	10.106	9.447	8.851	8.313	7.824	6.974	5.954	5.162
17	11.274	10.477	9.763	9.122	8.544	8.022	7.120	6.047	5.222
18	11.690	10.828	10.059	9.372	8.756	8.201	7.250	6.128	5.273
19	12.085	11.158	10.336	9.604	8.950	8.365	7.366	6.198	5.316
20	12.462	11.470	10.594	9.818	9.129	8.514	7.469	6.259	5.353
21	12.821	11.764	10.836	10.017	9.292	8.649	7.562	6.312	5.384
22	13.163	12.042	11.061	10.201	9.442	8.772	7.645	6.359	5.410
23	13.489	12.303	11.272	10.371	9.580	8.883	7.718	6.399	5.432
24	13.799	12.550	11.469	10.529	9.707	8.985	7.784	6.434	5.451
25	14.094	12.783	11.654	10.675	9.823	9.077	7.843	6.464	5.467
26	14.375	13.003	11.826	10.810	9.929	9.161	7.896	6.491	5.480
27	14.643	13.211	11.987	10.935	10.027	9.237	7.943	6.514	5.492
28	14.898	13.406	12.137	11.051	10.116	9.307	7.984	6.534	5.502
29	15.141	13.591	12.278	11.158	10.198	9.370	8.022	6.551	5.510
30	15.372	13.765	12.409	11.258	10.274	9.427	8.055	6.566	5.517
31	15.593	13.929	12.532	11.350	10.343	9.479	8.085	6.579	5.523
32	15.803	14.084	12.647	11.435	10.406	9.526	8.112	6.591	5.528
33	16.003	14.230	12.754	11.514	10.464	9.569	8.135	6.600	5.532
34	16.193	14.368	12.854	11.587	10.518	9.609	8.157	6.609	5.536
35	16.374	14.498	12.948	11.655	10.567	9.644	8.176	6.617	5.539
36	16.547	14.621	13.035	11.717	10.612	9.677	8.192	6.623	5.541
37	16.711	14.737	13.117	11.775	10.653	9.706	8.208	6.629	5.543
38	16.868	14.846	13.193	11.829	10.691	9.733	8.221	6.634	5.545
39	17.017	14.949	13.265	11.879	10.726	9.757	8.233	6.638	5.547
40	17.159	15.046	13.332	11.925	10.757	9.779	8.244	6.642	5.548

AMORTIZATION TABLE

Annual Payment Necessary To Amortize A Loan Of $1,000

				Rate				
Years	5%	6%	7%	8%	9%	10%	12%	15%
2	537.80	545.44	553.10	560.77	568.47	576.20	591.70	615.12
3	367.21	374.11	381.06	388.04	395.06	402.12	416.35	437.98
4	282.01	288.60	295.23	301.93	308.67	315.48	329.24	350.27
5	230.97	237.40	243.90	250.46	257.10	263.80	277.41	298.32
6	197.02	203.37	209.80	216.32	222.92	229.61	243.23	264.24
7	172.82	179.14	185.56	192.08	198.70	205.41	219.12	240.37
8	154.72	161.04	167.47	174.02	180.68	187.45	201.31	222.86
9	140.69	147.03	153.49	160.08	166.80	173.65	187.68	209.58
10	129.50	135.87	142.38	149.03	155.83	162.75	176.99	199.26
11	120.39	126.80	133.36	140.08	146.95	153.97	168.42	191.07
12	112.83	119.28	125.91	132.70	139.66	146.77	161.44	184.49
13	106.46	112.97	119.66	126.53	133.57	140.78	155.68	179.12
14	101.02	107.59	114.35	121.30	128.44	135.75	150.88	174.69
15	96.34	102.97	109.80	116.83	124.06	131.48	146.83	171.02
16	92.27	98.96	105.86	112.98	120.30	127.82	143.40	167.95
17	88.70	95.45	102.43	109.63	117.05	124.67	140.46	165.37
18	85.55	92.36	99.42	106.71	114.22	121.94	137.94	163.19
19	82.75	89.63	96.76	104.13	111.74	119.55	135.77	161.34
20	80.24	87.19	94.40	101.86	109.55	117.46	133.88	159.77
21	78.00	85.01	92.29	99.84	107.62	115.63	132.25	158.42
22	75.97	83.05	90.41	98.04	105.91	114.01	130.82	157.27
23	74.14	81.28	88.72	96.43	104.39	112.58	129.56	156.28
24	72.47	79.68	87.19	94.98	103.03	111.30	128.47	155.43
25	70.95	78.23	85.82	93.68	101.81	110.17	127.50	154.70
26	69.56	76.91	84.57	92.51	100.72	109.16	126.66	154.07
27	68.29	75.70	83.43	91.45	99.74	108.26	125.91	153.53
28	67.12	74.60	82.40	90.49	98.86	107.46	125.25	153.06
29	66.05	73.58	81.45	89.62	98.06	106.73	124.67	152.66
30	65.05	72.65	80.59	88.83	97.34	106.08	124.15	152.31
35	61.07	68.98	77.24	85.81	94.64	103.69	122.32	151.14
40	58.28	66.47	75.01	83.87	92.96	102.26	121.31	150.57

INSURANCE COMPANY RATINGS

Rating Categories[1]	A.M. Best[2]	S&P[3]	Moody's[4]	TheStreet.com[5]	Fitch[6]
Superior	A++ A+	AAA	Aaa		AAA
Excellent	A A-	AA[7]	Aa[8]	A[7]	AA[7] A[7]
Good	B++ B+	A[7]	A[8]	B[7]	
Fair (Adequate)	B B-	BBB[7]	Baa[8]	C[7]	BBB[7]
Marginal	C++ C+	BB[7]	Ba[8]	D[7]	BB[7]
Weak	C C-	B[7]	B[8]	E[7]	B[7]
Poor (Below Standards)	D	CCC CC	Caa[8] Ca C		CCC[7] CC, C
Failed	E[9], F[10]	D[11]		F	

[1] The comparative distribution of rating categories is approximate. Therefore, the ratings definitions of each agency should be consulted. The basic mission of all of these independent agencies is to assess an insurer's financial strength in terms of its ability to meet policyholder and other contractual obligations, and to communicate those findings to the financial and investment communities. Due diligence requires not just a determination of the assigned rating, but an understanding of how each rating agency determines its published ratings.

[2] A.M. Best's Financial Strength Rating provides an independent opinion of an insurer's financial strength and ability to meet its ongoing insurance policy and contract obligations (has rated insurers since 1899).

[3] Standard & Poor's (S&P) publishes Insurer Claims-Paying Ability Ratings (has rated debt issues for over 50 years and insurance companies since 1971).

[4] Moody's Insurance Financial Strength Ratings are opinions of the ability of insurance companies to repay punctually senior policyholder claims and obligations. Moody's Investor's Service publishes Life Insurance Credit Report, which includes the *Life Insurance Handbook* (has rated bond issues since 1904 and insurers since the 1970s).

[5] TheStreet.com was formerly Weiss Research, Inc. which had rated insurers since 1989.

[6] Fitch, Inc. publishes National Insurer Financial Strength Ratings. Ratings below AAA and above CC may be appended with a "+"or "−" to indicate relative position within the rating category.

[7] Includes three levels of ratings (i.e., AA-, AA, AA+; A-, A, A+; BBB-, BBB, BBB+; BB-, BB, BB+; B-, B, B+; CCC-, CCC, CCC+; D-, D, D+; E-, E, E+).

[8] Includes three levels of ratings (i.e., Aa1, Aa2, Aa3; A1, A2, A3; Baa1, Baa2, Baa3; Ba1, Ba2, Ba3; B1, B2, B3; Caa1, Caa2, Caa3).

[9] Under regulatory supervision.

[10] In liquidation.

[11] Payment default on financial commitments.

INDUSTRY ASSOCIATIONS

Conference Dates

Association for Advanced Life Underwriting
11921 Freedom Drive, Suite 1100
Reston, VA 20190
888-275-0092 (www.aalu.org)

AALU Annual Meeting
2011 - Wash., D.C., May 1-4
2012 - Wash., D.C., Apr. 29 - May 2

Financial Planning Association
4100 E. Mississippi Ave., Suite 400
Denver, CO 80246-3053
800-322-4237 (www.fpanet.org)

Annual Conference & Expo
2011 - San Diego, Sep. 15-18
2012 - San Antonio, Sep. 29 - Oct. 2

GAMA International
2901 Telestar Court, Suite 140
Falls Church, VA 22042-1205
800-345-2687 (www.gamaweb.com)

LAMP Annual Meeting
2011 - Wash., D.C., Mar. 20-23
2012 - Orlando, Mar. 18-21

LIMRA International
300 Day Hill Road
Windsor, CT 06095-4761
800-235-4672 (www.limra.com)

LIMRA Annual Meeting
2011 - New York City, Oct. 23-25
2012 - not available as of 12/13/10

Million Dollar Round Table
325 West Touhy Avenue
Park Ridge, IL 60068-4265
847-692-6378 (www.mdrt.org)

MDRT Annual Meeting
2011 - Atlanta, Jun. 5-8
2012 - Anaheim, CA Jun. 10-14

Top of the Table Annual Meeting
2011 - Indian Wells, CA, Sep. 21-24
2012 - not available as of 12/13/10

National Association of Health Underwriters
2000 North 14th Street, Suite 450
Arlington, VA, 22201
703-276-0220 (www.nahu.org)

Annual Convention & Exhibition
2011 - San Antonio, Jun. 26-29
2012 - not available as of 12/13/10

National Association of Independent
Life Brokerage Agencies
11325 Random Hills Road, Suite 110
Fairfax, VA 22030
703-383-3081 (www.nailba.org)

Annual Convention
2011 - Phoenix, Nov. 17-19
2012 - Orlando, Nov. 15-17

National Association of Insurance
and Financial Advisors
2901 Telestar Court
Falls Church, VA 22042-1205
877-866-2432 (www.naifa.org)

NAIFA Career Conference
& Annual Convention
2011 - Wash., D.C., Sep. 10-14
2012 - Las Vegas, Sep. 8-11

National Association of Personal
Financial Advisers
3250 North Arlington Heights Road, Suite 109
Arlington Heights, IL 60004
800-366-2732 (www.napfa.org)

National Conference
2011 - Las Vegas, May 18-20
2012 - Chicago, May 14-19

Society of Financial Service Professionals
19 Campus Boulevard, Suite 100
Newtown Square, PA 19073-3239
610-526-2500 (www.financialpro.org)

Financial Service Forum
2011 - not available as of 12/13/10
2012 - not available as of 12/13/10

COOL WEB SITES

www.benefitslink.com
Internet links to information and services for benefit plans. Check out the Message Boards and Q&A Columns. A lot of "good stuff" but some Authorities material is outdated.

www.fidelity.com
A well designed and easy-to-navigate site, containing concise and helpful information. Check out the Guidance & Retirement tab, it has planning information for individuals with a variety of needs at all stages of life. Lots of helpful calculators everywhere.

www.toolsformoney.com/financial_calculators.htm
This web site contains an absolutely exhaustive listing of "almost every free online financial calculator on the web." If the web site isn't listed here, it probably doesn't exist.

www.iii.org
A very attractive web site maintained by the Insurance Information Institute. Not only does it look good, it is also highly functional and loaded with useful information.

www.allbusiness.com/3470944-1.html
This web site contains a business glossary consisting of eight different dictionaries. The Dictionary of Insurance Terms contains more than 4,200 definitions of key terms used in life, health, property, casualty, and other types of insurance. AllBusiness.com is an online media and e-commerce company that is a subsidiary of Dun & Bradstreet.

www.investorguide.com
There is a lot here. Much of it relates to investment quotes, charts etc. Go to the Personal Finance tab and you will find material on estate planning, educational planning, retirement, and insurance. Also, check out the Investing tab.

www.lifehappens.org
The Life and Health Insurance Foundation for Education (LIFE). Offers a wide range of well-developed insurance topics. Recommend for both advisors and their clients.

www.medicare.gov/LongTermCare/Static
This government web site offers a wealth of information about the types of long-term care services, choosing and paying for care, and a listing of counseling and assistance resources.

www.pgdc.com
Contains sales, marketing and technical resource materials for planned giving. Registration is free and well worth the time. An absolutely first class web site with great resources.

www.smartmoney.com
A very enriched web site. Click on the Tools tab or the Personal Finance tab for easy-to-understand explanations of income tax and retirement planning concepts. Many screens contain "what if" calculators.

www.taxalmanac.org
Billed as "a free online resource for tax professionals," this description does not begin to tell the story behind this website. It is the Wikipedia of the tax world! Most of the content is written and edited collaboratively by the readers. For sure, that is likely to keep the material up-to-date if not a bit unorganized.

http:taxhistory.tax.org
The Tax History Project from the Tax Analysts provides eclectic information pertaining to the history of public finance. Take time to explore the Tax History Museum, the Image Gallery, and the Presidential Tax Returns Gallery. For fun this remains a "very cool" site.

www.taxsites.com
Continues to be an absolutely first class job of how a "link site" should work. No frills, just plain efficiency, well organized, current and incredibly enriched. If you go here, plan to spend more than a little time exploring all the links.

Note: These sites were last accessed on December 12, 2010. Have you discovered a web site that should be included in the next edition of *Field Guide To Estate, Employee, & Business Planning?* If so, please e-mail your nominations to DonaldFCady@gmail.com.

CODE CRIB SHEET

A Listing of Selected Code Provisions

Code Section	Description	2011 Field Guide Page	2011 Tax Facts Question
22	Credits for the permanently disabled.	387	7544
25A	Hope and lifetime learning credit.	310, 362-363	7546
55	Alternative minimum tax (Section 56 provides for ACE adjustment).	374	7548
61	Gross income defined.	210, 299, 323	7505
72	Annuities; living proceeds of endowment and life insurance contracts - income tax treatment.	74, 282, 496	5, 17, 32 , 3501-3510, 3539, 3540
79	Group-term life insurance purchased for employees.	202	171, 175
83	Taxation of property transferred in connection with performance of services - substantial risk of forfeiture.	234, 274, 299, 464, 496, 519, 528	220 3586, 3591, 3603, 3792
101	Certain death benefits - exclusion of life insurance death benefits from income (includes transfer for value rules). Includes the treatment of employer-owned life insurance under Code section 101(j).	70, 89, 343, 367-369, 441, 443-444, 541	26, 27, 30, 32, 36, 38, 98, 205-208, 210-214, 224, 231, 237
102	Gifts and inheritances - exclusion from income.	22, 24, 46	7505
104	Compensation for injuries or sickness.	242, 246, 323, 386	168-170, 288
105	Amounts received under accident and health plans.	242, 246, 321, 387	249-253
106	Contributions by employer to accident and health plans.	242, 246, 323	249, 259
125	Cafeteria plans.	321, 352	3573-3575
127	Educational assistance programs.	310	7930
129	Dependent care assistance programs.	286	3606
135	Income from United States bonds used to pay higher education tuition and fees.	309	7505
162	Trade or business expenses - deductibility.	210, 310, 323, 546	188 190, 197, 203
163	Interest - deductibility.	431, 478	18, 7531, 7533

Note: This table contains selected citations to *Tax Facts on Insurance & Employee Benefits (2011)* and *Tax Facts on Investments (2011)*. A complete listing of citations to IRC Sections is contained in Appendix H of those publications.

Code Section	Description	2011 Field Guide Page	2011 Tax Facts Question
170	Charitable contributions and gifts - deductibility.	54, 356, 357	68-71, 7534, 7958
221	Interest on education loans.	310, 362	7533
222	Qualified tuition and related expenses.	310	7935
223	Health and Medical Savings Accounts.	250	292-305
264	Business life insurance - premiums not deductible but policy loan interest deductible within strict limits.	458	3, 18, 75-76, 188, 190, 199-200, 203
265	Expenses and interest relating to tax-exempt income.	323, 386	286, 288
302	Distributions in redemption of stock.	126, 138, 149	225-226
303	Distributions in redemption of stock to pay death taxes - partial stock redemptions.	146, 150, 515	228, 232
306	Dispositions of certain stock - tax treatment of of stock received as a dividend pursuant to a recapitalization.	166, 516	228
318	Constructive ownership of stock - attribution.	126, 170	225, 228
368	Definitions relating to corporate reorganizations - recapitalizations.	166, 407	215
401	Qualified pension, profit sharing and stock bonus plans - including Section 401(k) plans.	258, 262, 303, 347, 354, 384, 396, 460, 484, 492, 513, 536	86, 3649, 3651, 3654, 3659-3660, 3662-3663, 3670, 3673-3689, 3696, 3703, 3705-3723, 3732-3735, 3737 3753, 3760
402(b)	Taxability of beneficiary of nonexempt trust.	519	3584-3585, 3587
402(e)(4)	Net unrealized appreciation.	461	3763
402A	Elective deferrals as Roth contributions in 401(k) plans.	505	3681
403(b)	Taxation of annuities purchased by Section 501(c)(3) organizations and public schools.	266, 269	3783, 3795, 3797-3802, 3805-3806, 3810, 3818, 3822-3823
408	Individual retirement accounts and annuities.	258, 304, 307 308, 427, 433, 524-525, 540	3611, 3616 3621, 3627-3628 3634, 3640-3642

Note: This table contains selected citations to *Tax Facts on Insurance & Employee Benefits (2011)* and *Tax Facts on Investments (2011)*. A complete listing of citations to IRC Sections is contained in Appendix H of those publications.

Code Section	Description	2011 Field Guide Page	2011 Tax Facts Question
408(q)	Deemed IRA.	382	3611
408A	Roth IRAs.	307-308, 506, 507	3618-3624, 3629, 3634
409A	Nonqualified deferred compensation plans deferral and distribution rules.	370, 493, 517	3589, 3591, 3592, 3595
410-412	Minimum participation, vesting, and funding standards - qualified plans.	258, 262, 270, 303	3652, 3654-3657, 3663-3668, 3674, 3708-3710, 3714, 3736
415	Limitations on benefits and contributions under qualified plans.	258, 303	3620, 3663, 3703, 3714, 3737, 3800
419	Treatment of funded welfare benefit plans.	542	3822-3823
453	Installment method of reporting income.	42, 428, 520	7512
457	Deferred compensation plans of State and local governments and tax-exempt organizations.	274	3597-3600
483	Interest on certain deferred payments.	428	7512, 7584
501	Exemption from tax on corporations, certain trusts, etc. - includes religious, charitable, scientific and educational organizations.	266, 269	3584, 3597, 3796
529	Qualified tuition programs.	310, 361, 518	7517-7518, 7568, 7594
530	Cloverdell Education Savings Accounts.	310, 377	7516
531	Accumulated earnings tax.	346	7559
541	Personal holding company tax.	471	7559
664	Charitable remainder trusts.	54, 357	7950, 7951 7952
671-677	Grantor trust rules.	418	67
691	Income in respect of decedents.	21, 425	3765-3767, 7537
701-761	Partnerships.	162, 465	235 239, 241-243, 7562-7563, 7618
1001	Determination of amount and recognition of gain or loss.	353, 537	288, 3530

Note: This table contains selected citations to *Tax Facts on Insurance & Employee Benefits (2011)* and *Tax Facts on Investments (2011)*. A complete listing of citations to IRC Sections is contained in Appendix H of those publications.

Code Section	Description	2011 Field Guide Page	2011 Tax Facts Question
1014	Basis of property acquired from a decedent (stepped-up).	530	229, 7519
1015	Basis of property acquired by gifts and transfers in trust.	46	7519
1035	Certain exchanges of insurance policies – tax-free exchange of life insurance and annuity contracts.	537	3530
1041	Transfer of property incident to divorce.	390	38, 59, 3544
1202	Gain from small business stock.	353	7505, 7641
1361	S corporation defined.	510	7560
2001	Imposition and rate of estate tax.	18, 550	7570
2002	Executor's liability for payment of estate tax.	383	109
2010	Unified credit against estate tax.	18, 550	7573
2014	Foreign death tax credit	463	7573
2032	Alternate valuation - six months after death.	411, 530	243, 7602
2032A	Valuation of certain farms and other real property.	496	243, 7601
2033	Property in which the decedent had an interest - transfers at death.	18	3562, 7565
2035	Adjustments for gifts made within 3 years of decedent's death - transfers of life insurance.	50, 70, 409	40, 52-53, 166, 7570
2036	Transfers with retained life estate - power to designate possession or enjoyment of property.	410, 477	125, 7565, 7570
2037	Transfers taking effect at death.	410	53, 7565
2038	Revocable transfers - retention of power to revoke interest in property includes value in the estate.	99, 410	120, 7565
2039	Annuities - taxation of surviving beneficiary's interest.	282	54, 3564, 3566, 3571, 3572, 3574, 3645
2040	Joint interests - including co-tenancies with right of survivorship.	10	7565
2041	Powers of appointment - general power of appointment.	450, 477	123, 143, 146-148, 7565

Note: This table contains selected citations to *Tax Facts on Insurance & Employee Benefits (2011)* and *Tax Facts on Investments (2011)*. A complete listing of citations to IRC Sections is contained in Appendix H of those publications.

Code Section	Description	2011 Field Guide Page	2011 Tax Facts Question
2042	Proceeds of life insurance - payable to estate or in which decedent had incidents of ownership.	71, 89, 409	40-41, 44-48 52, 119, 239-242, 245, 7565
2044	Certain property for which marital deduction was previously allowed - qualified terminable interest.	34, 450	123, 144, 7572
2053	Expenses, indebtedness, and taxes - allowable deductions for claims against the estate.	10, 18, 83	7572, 7574
2054	Losses - those deductible from taxable estate.	83	109, 7574
2055	Transfers for public, charitable, and religious uses - estate tax charitable deduction.	53, 356-357	72, 7572
2056	Bequests to surviving spouse - estate tax marital deduction.	22, 24, 450	133-134, 7572
2056A	Qualified domestic trust.	488	7572
2206	Recovery by executor of estate taxes on life insurance proceeds.	21	50
2207A	Recovery by decedent's estate of estate taxes on certain marital deduction property.	21	-
2503	Present interest gifts - including gifts in trust for minors.	46, 99, 379, 544	105, 164, 7584, 7596
2514	Powers of appointment (including lapse of Crummey power).	53, 378	107, 7584
2518	Disclaimers.	389	7586
2522	Charitable and similar gifts.	54, 356-357	73, 7598
2523	Gift tax marital deduction.	450	3536, 7584, 7597
2601-2604	Generation-skipping transfers.	38	7575-7582
2701-2704	Also known as Chapter 14.		
2701	Special valuation rules in case of transfers of certain interests in corporations or partnerships.	122, 166, 407	7618-7619 7621
2702	Special valuation rules in case of transfers of interest in trusts.	61, 407, 419, 490, 499	7619

Note: This table contains selected citations to *Tax Facts on Insurance & Employee Benefits (2011)* and *Tax Facts on Investments (2011)*. A complete listing of citations to IRC Sections is contained in Appendix H of those publications

Code Section	Description	2011 Field Guide Page	2011 Tax Facts Question
2703	Special valuation rules (e.g., with regard to buy/sell agreements certain rights and restrictions disregarded).	407	243, 7620-7621
2704	Treatment of certain lapsing rights and restrictions.	407	7565, 7621
6018	Estate tax returns - generally must be filed if gross estate exceeds applicable exclusion amount.	18	7574
6075	Time for filing estate and gift tax returns.	18	7574, 7600
6166	Extension of time for payment of estate tax where estate consists largely of interest in closely held business (14 2/3 years).	383	7574
6324	Special liens for estate and gift taxes.	18, 383	109, 152
6531	Statute of limitations on criminal prosecutions.	468	-
6651	Failure to file return or pay tax.	468	-
6663	Penalty for fraud.	468	-
7206	Concealment of goods to evade taxes, including false statement, is a felony.	348, 468	-
7520	Valuation tables for valuing life estates, remainder interests, and private annuities.	61, 479	7606
7702	Life insurance contract defined - guideline premium requirements.	442	7-8, 30, 33, 98
7702A	Modified endowment contract defined.	441	7-8, 33, 89
7702B	Long-term care.	254, 489	343-349
7872	Treatment of loans with below-market interest rates.	299, 432	7511, 7584

Note: This table contains selected citations to *Tax Facts on Insurance & Employee Benefits (2011)* and *Tax Facts on Investments (2011)*. A complete listing of citations to IRC Sections is contained in Appendix H of those publications.

INDEX

(References in parentheses are to footnotes – All other references are to page numbers)

(References in parentheses are to footnotes – All other references are to page numbers)

(References in parentheses are to footnotes – All other references are to page numbers)

(References in parentheses are to footnotes – All other references are to page numbers)

(References in parentheses are to footnotes – All other references are to page numbers)

(References in parentheses are to footnotes – All other references are to page numbers)

(References in parentheses are to footnotes – All other references are to page numbers)

(References in parentheses are to footnotes – All other references are to page numbers)

(References in parentheses are to footnotes – All other references are to page numbers)

(References in parentheses are to footnotes – All other references are to page numbers)

(References in parentheses are to footnotes – All other references are to page numbers)

(References in parentheses are to footnotes – All other references are to page numbers)

(References in parentheses are to footnotes — All other references are to page numbers)

(References in parentheses are to footnotes – All other references are to page numbers)

(References in parentheses are to footnotes – All other references are to page numbers)

(References in parentheses are to footnotes – All other references are to page numbers)

(References in parentheses are to footnotes – All other references are to page numbers)

(References in parentheses are to footnotes – All other references are to page numbers)

(References in parentheses are to footnotes – All other references are to page numbers)

(References in parentheses are to footnotes – All other references are to page numbers)

(References in parentheses are to footnotes – All other references are to page numbers)

(References in parentheses are to footnotes – All other references are to page numbers)

(References in parentheses are to footnotes – All other references are to page numbers)

(References in parentheses are to footnotes – All other references are to page numbers)

(References in parentheses are to footnotes – All other references are to page numbers)

(References in parentheses are to footnotes – All other references are to page numbers)

(References in parentheses are to footnotes – All other references are to page numbers)

(References in parentheses are to footnotes – All other references are to page numbers)